Individual Change Through Small Groups

Edited by

**Paul Glasser
Rosemary Sarri
Robert Vinter**

THE FREE PRESS
A Division of Macmillan Publishing Co., Inc.
NEW YORK

Collier Macmillan Publishers
LONDON

The Free Press
A Division of Macmillan Publishing Co., Inc.
866 Third Avenue, New York, N.Y. 10022

Collier Macmillan Canada Ltd.

Library of Congress Catalog Card Number: 73-14113

Printed in the United States of America

Printing number
5 6 7 8 9 10

Library of Congress Cataloging in Publication Data
Main entry under title:

Individual change through small groups.

    Includes six rev. and updated papers published in
1967 under title: Readings in group work practice,
edited by R. D. Vinter.
    Includes bibliographies.
    1. Social groups work--Addresses, essays, lectures.
I. Glasser, Paul H., ed. II. Sarri, Rosemary C., ed.
III. Vinter, Robert D., ed.
HV45.I52   361.4'08   73-14113
ISBN 0-02-911800-X

Contents

Contents

Biographical Notes

PAUL H. GLASSER, Ph.D., is Professor of Social Work at the University of Michigan, where he has been head of the group work program for many years. He has had extensive social work practice experience in child guidance clinics, residential treatment institutions, army hospitals, and family treatment agencies. His research in family functioning and treatment has focused on the single parent family. Dr. Glasser's publications include *Families in Crises,* completed with his wife, Lois N. Glasser. He has served as editor for several social science journals and most recently was senior editor of the *Encyclopedia of Social Work.* He has been a Fulbright scholar in the Philippines and Italy.

ROSEMARY C. SARRI, Ph.D., is Professor of Social Work and Co-Director of the National Assessment of Juvenile Corrections at the University of Michigan. Previously she was a social work practitioner and taught at the University of Minnesota and the University of Connecticut. Co-author of *The School and the Community* and *Pupil Behavior Inventory,* Dr. Sarri has contributed numerous articles in the fields of group work, juvenile delinquency, education, justice systems and human service organizations. She is a member of the Task Force in Corrections of the National Advisory Commission on Correctional Standards and Goals.

ROBERT D. VINTER, M.S.W., Ph.D., is Professor of Social Work and Co-Director of the National Assessment of Juvenile Corrections at the University of Michigan. A former social work practitioner, he was appointed to the Michigan faculty in 1954 to develop the group work curriculum of the School of Social Work. Later he served for some years as Associate Dean. He has written extensively on group work and other areas of professional practice, and was co-author of *Organization for Treatment.* Dr. Vinter's research has focused on social work practice, corrections, and human service organizations. He has served as a consultant to the President's Committee on Juvenile Delinquency and Youth Crime, the President's Commission on Law Enforcement and Criminal Justice, the National Institute of Mental Health, the U.S. Bureau of Prisons, and the Probation Services of the Government of Jamaica.

HARVEY J. BERTCHER received his D.S.W. from the University of Southern California. He is the author and co-author of many articles and reports, and he is Professor at the University of Michigan School of Social Work.

SALLIE R. CHURCHILL received her M.S.W. from the University of Minnesota and her Ph.D. from the University of Chicago. She has several publications in the area of group work with children and youth and is Associate Professor at the University of Michigan.

ALAN N. CONNOR received his M.S.W. from the University of Michigan. He was Director of Community Development with The American Friends Service Committee in Zambia and he is now Assistant Professor at the University of Michigan.

JANE COSTABILE received her M.S.W. from the University of Pittsburgh and is Associate Professor at the University of Michigan.

TOM A. CROXTON received both his D.S.W. and his M.S.W. from the University of Michigan, where he is now an Associate Professor. The author of several articles, he is also a member of the Michigan State Bar.

RICHARD ALLYN ENGLISH received his Ph.D. from the University of Michigan where he is now Assistant Dean and Associate Professor of Social Work in the School of Social Work.

RONALD ARTHUR FELDMAN received his Ph.D. from the University of Michigan. Prior to becoming Acting Dean of the George Warren Brown School of Social Work at Washington University, he was a Fulbright Lecturer in Ankara, Turkey.

MAEDA J. GALINSKY received both her M.S.W. and Ph.D. from the University of Michigan. She is now Associate Professor at the University of North Carolina and is doing research and writing on group work.

CHARLES D. GARVIN received both his A.M. and Ph.D. from the University of Chicago. The author and co-author of many professional articles, he is now Professor at the University of Michigan as well as Research Director for a project "Decision Making in the Work Incentive Program."

YEHESKEL HASENFELD received his Ph.D. from the University of Michigan where he is now Associate Professor.

HARRY LAWRENCE received both his M.S.W. and D.S.W. from the University of California, Berkeley. He is the principal Investigator for N.I.M.H. research on behavior modification with adult groups, as well as Associate Professor at the University of Michigan.

FRANK F. MAPLE, JR., received both his M.A. and his M.S.W. from the University of Michigan where he is now Associate Professor.

ELIZABETH L. NAVARRE received both her M.A. and Ph.D. from the University of Michigan. She is now Associate Professor at Indiana University—Purdue University at Indianapolis.

NORMA RADIN received both her M.S.W. and Ph.D. from the University of Michigan where she is now an Associate Professor. She is currently conducting an observational study of father's behavior with preschool children.

BERYL CARTER RICE received her M.S. from Columbia University. She is currently enrolled as a Doctoral student at the Catholic University of America and is part time Assistant Professor, Department of Psychiatry, Howard University.

SHELDON D. ROSE received his Ph.D. from the University of Rotterdam. He was Deputy Director of the Peace Corps in Nepal and has been Professor at the University of Wisconsin and Visiting Professor at the University of Amsterdam.

JANICE HOUGH SCHOPLER received her M.S.W. from the University of Michigan. She is Assistant Professor at the University of North Carolina.

PAUL VICTOR SOREN received his M.S.W. from the University of Toronto. He is currently Director of the Community Team at the Chedoke-McMaster Centre and Lecturer in Psychiatry at McMaster University.

MARTIN SUNDEL received his Ph.D. from the University of Michigan and was a Postdoctoral Fellow at Harvard University. He is now Adjunct Associate Professor at the Raymond A. Kent School of Social Work at the University of Louisville.

EDWIN J. THOMAS received his Ph.D. from the University of Michigan where he is now Professor. He is a certified consulting psychologist in behavior therapy and the author and editor of many articles and books, including *Behavior Science for Social Workers* (Free Press).

JAMES K. WHITTAKER received his Ph.D. from the University of Minnesota. The author and co-author of many articles and several books, he taught at Boston University and the University of Minnesota before becoming Associate Professor at the University of Washington.

CHARLES WOLFSON received his M.S.W. from Wayne State University. He is Director of Field Instruction and Assistant Professor at the University of Michigan.

Preface

This book aims to provide practitioners in the helping professions with methods of serving individuals within and through small, face-to-face groups, to induce desired changes among the participants. It will have use by a broad range of health, welfare, and educational agencies: antipoverty organizations, child guidance clinics and community mental health centers, school social services, juvenile courts and delinquency control programs, mental hospitals and correctional institutions, public welfare agencies, youth development and recreational programs, and others. The methods are useful for the treatment of individuals defined as "deviant" or "psychologically ill" and for the prevention of the development of their problems.

In this problem-oriented approach, problems must be described in concrete behavioral terms to enable the evaluation of individual changes during or following treatment. The practitioner together with the client must plan specifically and use consciously the interaction among group members to change them. Since the individual is viewed in the context of the intervention group and his social situation in the real world, the methods use much material from all the social and behavioral sciences.

The volume is organized as a text. The first section describes the basic approach; the second, the activities of the professional from the beginning to the end of the intervention process in the group; the third, the activities required by the worker in the client's environment outside the group; and the fourth, the application of this approach to a great variety of fields of practice.

The papers in this publication were authored over several years by faculty members and graduate students at The University of Michigan School of Social Work, primarily for use in the group work curriculum. This School pioneered the development of a problem-oriented approach to group work practice, and teaching materials which were not available in the professional literature needed to be created. These papers are one result of faculty and graduate student efforts to formulate and set forth the major features of group work practice within this general conception.

This is the second such volume; the first, a much smaller and more modest one, appeared in 1967. The six papers from the initial effort also appear in this book, but all have been edited, some completely revised, to bring them up to date. The majority of papers in this volume have not been published before however. This book, much more comprehensive than the first, attempts to provide a great variety of methods and techniques, of the problem-oriented approach developed at the School, for working with groups.

Authors have made considerable effort to integrate theory and findings from the social and behavioral sciences into group work practice. This has been a major orientation of the School since 1955, when the Russell Sage Foundation awarded special funds as part of its attempt to infuse social science into the professions. Some years later the Foundation made a modest but separate grant through Professor Vinter to develop a social science-oriented volume on group work practice. Although the second award supported reviews of literature and curriculum and research development, it did not directly contribute to the present publication. Rather, this volume is a product of the general direction the School has taken as a result of the Foundation's support.

None of this would have been possible without the encouragement and foresight of Fedele F. Fauri former Dean of the School of Social Work and now University of Michigan Vice-President for State Relations and Planning. He made possible the multitude of major developments in the School, through his organizational abilities and also through his personal allegiance and commitment to the scholarly work of each faculty member. His successor, Dean Phillip Fellin, has continued to move the School in this direction.

The authors of these papers are indebted to many graduate students and to agency field instructors for significant assistance in developing, clarifying and modifying the ideas dealt with here. Several of the papers emerged from classroom discourse and teaching notes, and most have been revised earlier in the light of critical response. The authors also acknowledge with appreciation the contributions and suggestions of their faculty colleagues, a number of whom are not listed as authors of the papers here.

Special appreciation is expressed to Kate Grenholm, who did most of the technical editing for the volume, and to Marian Iglesias and Margaret Lemley, who did much of the typing. Finally, thanks must be given to each of our spouses, who not only took on extra responsibilities during periods of intense activity during the book's preparation, but also participated in the editing process. We are hopeful that all of these efforts will be rewarded through better group work service to people in need.

Paul H. Glasser
Rosemary C. Sarri
Robert D. Vinter

I

A Conception of Practice

1.

An Approach to
Group Work Practice

ROBERT D. VINTER

INTRODUCTION

Group procedures are now given specialized use in a broad range of health, welfare and educational agencies, including antipoverty organizations, child guidance clinics, school social services, juvenile courts and delinquency control programs, mental hospitals and correctional institutions, public welfare agencies, and youth development and recreational programs. In group work, individuals are served within and through small, face-to-face groups to induce desired changes among participants. This practice cannot be distinguished adequately from other helping processes, particularly those in the social work profession, by the types of clientele served, the organizational setting, or the goals set for clients. The essential difference lies in the primary, but not exclusive, reliance on the multiperson group session as the basic form of intervention rather than on the two-person interview, which characterizes casework and individual therapies.

Groups are used widely to solve problems or accomplish tasks, although the existence of a group does not assure that group treatment or prevention work is being practiced. There are diverse service procedures and approaches which center on the use of client groups, even within the profession of social work, and each of these may have utility in pursuing distinct service objectives. The professional service agent should have a full repertoire of alternate procedures from which he can select the most appropriate for specific circumstances, resources, and aims (Sarri and Vinter, 1965; Glasser, 1963).

The concern here is to examine social treatment as one major kind of group work practice. The aim in this and in following chapters is to explicate the essential components and the significant dimensions of this particular approach. The objective is to offer a coherent and prescriptive strategy of intervention, which the student or practitioner may adopt or modify as necessary.

A Conception of Practice

GROUP WORK AS SOCIAL TREATMENT

Social treatment through group work practice focuses on ameliorating or preventing the adverse conditions of individuals whose behavior is disapproved or who have been disadvantaged by society (Vinter, 1965). It emphasizes manifest personal and social problems and the rehabilitative potentials of guided group processes to alleviate or avert these problems. Persons most appropriate as clientele for such service include the physically or mentally handicapped, legal offenders, emotionally disturbed, isolated, or alienated persons, and those lacking effective socialization.

Recipients of such group work service are individuals who exhibit or are prone to exhibit problems while performing conventional social roles. The behavioral difficulties and the situations which support them are the specific foci of helping efforts; improved performance is the desired change. Behavioral difficulties may be few and appear in only one of the individual's several social roles, as with some malperformers in the public school; or they may be diffuse and pervade broad areas of social life and careers, as with habitual delinquents, psychotics, and others. Social norms provide general criteria of the nature of the problem behavior and the degree of change actually effected.

An Interactional View of Deviance

For an accurate conception of problem behavior attention must be given to the attributes and capabilities of clients, to the nature of their interactions with others, and to the social contexts within which problems are generated, defined, and manifested. This formulation requires no single conception of the etiology and character of personal deviance or pathology. Assertions that group intervention approaches are effective, however, presuppose an *interactional* conception of the genesis and maintenance of problem behavior. Some of the major features of this view can be outlined as follows. All behavior amenable to change is regarded as socially induced, acquired through learning and related processes; it is exhibited, evoked or constrained within the context of specific social situations. The sources of behavior lie both within the individual (in terms of his enduring attributes and acquired capabilities) and within the social situation (in terms of opportunities, demands, and inducements). Behavior, moreover, is judged, encouraged or sanctioned by others within the person's immediate social situation. These actions between persons constitute a series of interactions which shape and sustain behavioral patterns (Schafer, 1967). The judgments and responses of others must be regarded as crucial features of all behavioral patterns. Social definitions of deviance are necessarily relative, and those who define behavior as problematic often refer to specialized standards of conduct. In this view, therefore, the targets for intervention include not only the individual whose behavior is judged to be inadequate or deviant, but also the judgments and interactional responses of individuals and groups whom he contacts regularly or frequently at the time. This view gives rise to intervention approaches that are centered on the clients' social situations (including relevant others) as well as on clients within and apart from treatment groups.

The interactional view of behavior is hospitable to most schools of thought concerned with client deviance, dependence, or disability. Each of these schools tends to emphasize different sources and facets of problem behavior and, therefore, concentrates on different goals or targets of change. Consequently, the perspective of deviance alters the particular balance of effort under various conditions of professional practice (Rose, 1967). An approach to the treatment group, as a focus of intervention, can be constructed on this general formulation.

The Treatment Group

The treatment group is conceived as a small social system whose influences can be guided in planned ways to modify client behavior. The potency of the social forces generated within small groups is recognized and these forces are marshalled deliberately in pursuing goals for client change. The composition, development, and processes of the group are influenced by the practitioner in accordance with his purposes. The worker attempts to initiate a series of transactions, through the processes of the group and through his own interactions with the clients, which can effect behavioral, attitudinal, and other changes. New behavior or other modifications must be stabilized and transferred beyond the treatment process into the spheres of client life which are regarded as problematic or likely to be so.

The group session is of fundamental importance; *the group is both a means of treatment and a context for treatment.* As a means, it constitutes a vehicle through which peer interactions and influences can be used to affect client participants. As a context, it affords opportunities for direct worker-client interactions which can contribute to change. In order for the group to serve as an effective means of service, the character of the treatment group itself becomes a focus of intervention. The practitioner is concerned with four major dimensions of group development: (1) the social organization of the group, its pattern of participant roles and statuses; (2) the activities, tasks, and operative processes of the group (e.g., modes of decision making); (3) the culture of the group, with its norms, values, and shared purposes; and (4) the group's relations to its external environment, including the agency in which it is served (Sarri and Galinsky, Chapter 5, in this volume). Each of these refers to an area of interpersonal relations which must develop, if the aggregate of client participants is to become a viable group that can generate effective influences upon its members and achieve the purposes set for it. The treatment, or helping, process takes place largely in and through the group, and it is the worker's skill in guiding this process toward desired goals that enables him to serve his clients.

Not all contact with or assistance to clients is pursued within the confines of the treatment group, however. Practitioners confront their clients outside group sessions and engage in many other activities on behalf of group members. Modification of the problematic social situations, in which clients are involved, must also be undertaken if the full potential of this strategy is to be realized. The worker must intervene in these situations, directly or otherwise, in order to ameliorate others' interactions with clients (e.g., teachers or parents), to improve opportunities for clients, or to remove barriers and constraints. The treatment group itself may be helped to change these external patterns that adversely affect its members.

ACTION-ORIENTED INTERVENTION

Our concepts of deviance emphasize patterns of behavior that tend to endure over time, be sustained by social and personal forces, and persist unless these forces are changed. The helping practitioner must, therefore, energetically intervene to modify clients' behaviors and situations. Only by direct, active involvement in the relevant processes can practitioners accomplish desired change. Activity must be planned and focused, with optimal involvement of clients. Efforts must be directed toward obtaining information, making assessments, formulating specific objectives, planning the tactics of intervention, and preparing evaluations. Performance of these tasks is instrumental to service but does not in itself accomplish change. The investment of time and development of skill in such activities must, therefore, be measured against the interventive effort and its outcomes.

These general statements present a rationalistic strategy of service in which group methods and other intervention activities are undertaken in a planned sequence of treatment. Effectiveness is to be assessed in terms of net changes achieved among clients, according to conventional social standards rather than esoteric professional criteria. A treatment strategy must employ known procedures, directed at specified objectives, and must attain objectives at a sufficiently high level to be validated independently outside the helping process. To construct a systematic discipline around such a strategy, codified, decision and action procedures, that rest upon a communicable body of knowledge, must be encompassed by that strategy. Although these are stringent requirements and numerous difficulties in their realization will be encountered, this volume is an attempt to set forth the essentials of such a discipline (Vinter, 1967).

Serious questions about the effectiveness of procedures, the limits of knowledge, and the uncertainty of accomplishments must be acknowledged. These matters can neither be obscured nor ignored. However, group work as social treatment has several advantages. One, it permits a deliberate, open-ended utilization of empirically validated knowledge about individual and group behavior. Thus, for example, knowledge from small group theory and research can be readily assimilated and applied within this framework. Two, it encourages deliberateness in practitioner activity and discrimination in the choice of alternative courses of action. Three, it is receptive to an objective assessment of outcomes and the use of this information in modifying and improving procedures. And four, it provides a basis for systematic teaching and the development of practitioner competence.

This problem-oriented, group work approach lends itself to use in all sectors of the health and welfare fields. Adjustments and modifications are, of course, necessary in keeping with variations in client populations and the program goals of particular agencies. At certain times, group work may be the primary method of service, while at others it may supplement various treatment methods. The major limiting condition in the application of this mode of practice has to do with the appropriateness of *any* individual level method for change, rather than with procedures. Many beneficiaries of social welfare programs are confronted with adverse conditions which must be addressed in the aggregate at community and societal levels. This is especially true when systematic constraints on opportunity or deficiencies in the resources and conditions of life exist. Group work, or any other approach centered on individuals and their behavior, should not be chosen to resolve these broad problems. Nevertheless, even under such adverse conditions, particular individuals may need and benefit from group work service (Vinter, 1959).

REFERENCES

GLASSER, PAUL H.
　　1963—"Group methods in child welfare: Review and preview," *Child Welfare*, 42(June), pp. 312–20.
ROSE, SHELDON D.
　　1967—"A behavioral approach to group treatment of children," in Edwin J. Thomas (Ed.), *The Socio-Behavioral Approach and Applications to Social Work*, New York: Council on Social Work Education.
SARRI, ROSEMARY C. AND ROBERT D. VINTER
　　1965—"Group treatment strategies in juvenile correctional programs," *Crime and Delinquency*, 11(October), pp. 326–40.

SCHAFER, WALTER E.
  1967—"Deviance in the public school: An interactional view," in Edwin J. Thomas (Ed.), *Behavioral Science for Social Workers,* New York: The Free Press, pp. 51–58.

VINTER, ROBERT D.
  1959—"Group work: Perspectives and prospects," *Social Work with Groups,* New York: National Association of Social Workers, pp. 128–48.
  1965—"Social group work," in Harry L. Lurie (Ed.), *Encyclopedia of Social Work,* New York: National Association of Social Workers, pp. 715–24.
  1967—"Problems and processes in developing social work practice principles," in Edwin J. Thomas (Ed.), *Behavioral Science for Social Workers,* New York: The Free Press, pp. 425–32.

2.

The Essential Components
of Social Group Work Practice

ROBERT D. VINTER

INTRODUCTION

This chapter presents the essential elements of social group work practice
and aims to develop the understanding necessary to help individuals through
small, face-to-face groups.[1] As staff members of social agencies, group
workers must engage in many activities: they must participate in staff meetings, make referrals, prepare reports, and interpret their functions to the
public. But these endeavors, however important, are not immediately
necessary to serve people in groups, and the skill and knowledge they require is not distinctive to group workers. The core competencies of group
work practice—the methods and techniques which are directly involved in
serving clients in groups—are addressed here.

Concern for brevity requires that there be no discussion of variations
in practice that occur within different agencies or in work with different
types of clientele. Similarly, in focusing on the essentials of group work,
comparisons with other professional treatment approaches that involve
group methods are ignored.

THE TREATMENT SEQUENCE

Group work service begins when the practitioner first meets the client,
continues through the diagnostic and treatment stages, and ends with
evaluation and termination of contact. This entire process is referred to as

---

[1]This chapter outlines the fundamental modes of intervention for the problem-
oriented approach reflected in this volume. It was the first piece written about the
Michigan approach and provided a seminal framework and foundation for much of
the work that followed. For this reason, while it has been edited by the author, the
decision was made to retain the basic formulation in its original form.

the *treatment sequence*. This sequence consists of several distinct processes and actions; it includes each client's experiences, the group's development as affected by the worker, and the worker's decisions and overt activities. Since the treatment sequence proceeds through time, the identification of significant events, by locating them along this continuum, will be helpful. For this purpose, the several major stages of the treatment sequence can be defined, along with the events and the practitioners' decisions and activities typical of each stage. The recurrent nature of events and activities, more or less distinctive to each period, permits the identification of the segments of the treatment sequence. However, this presentation should not mislead one into supposing that the events and activities are invariant or that one stage is always neatly completed before the next begins.

These stages can be identified only by looking for similarities in a wide variety of actual treatment sequences and by noting the patterns that emerge. Analysis permits a useful, but somewhat arbitrary, codification of the treatment sequence. The practitioner deliberately intervenes in an extended social process which would develop in quite different directions (or not at all) if he acted differently. Helping people requires that practitioners *do* something; therefore, attention will be given to what it is that workers do as they intervene.

The first stage, the process by which a potential client achieves client status, is customarily termed *intake*. For the client this often involves some kind of presentation of himself and his problem or "need," as he experiences it. On the worker's part, this typically involves some assessment of the client and his problem—a preliminary diagnosis—and of the adequacy of resources available to resolve this problem. The intake stage ends in one of two ways: either the worker or the client decides not to proceed, for whatever reasons; or the client commits himself to client status (however tentatively or reluctantly) and the worker commits himself and his agency to provide service (however limited).

The second stage, identified as that of *diagnosis* and *treatment planning* (Sundel, Radin and Churchill, Chapter 7, in this volume), marks a more comprehensive and exacting assessment by the worker of the client's problem(s), his capacities for help and change, and of the various resources that might be useful. This stage involves a preliminary statement of the treatment goal, that is, of the desired changes which can result if the intervention effort is successful. The diagnosis also involves a preliminary plan of the ways the helping process will be undertaken and the direction in which it will be guided. This stage often requires the collection of additional information about the client and his situation and the use of consultation or other resources provided by the agency. At the culmination of the treatment planning stage, a concrete statement should be prepared by the worker to crystallize his assessment of the client and to make explicit the objectives he will pursue and the ways he will seek to implement these objectives.

The third stage is *group composition* and *formation*. During this period, the worker assigns clients to groups, gathering the persons who he believes can be served together. Under some circumstances—as in work with delinquent street groups—the practitioner may exercise relatively little control over this stage. He also sets the purposes for the group, at least within broad limits, in accordance with his treatment goals for its individual members. He begins the establishment of relationships with the group members and helps the group to commence its program. The way he initiates the group's process and the roles he plays initially with the various members have considerable significance for subsequent phases.

The fourth stage is that of *group development* and *treatment*. The worker seeks the emergence of group goals, activities, and relationships which can render this group effective for the treatment of its members (Sarri and Galinsky, Chapter 5 in this volume). The worker guides the group's interaction and structures its experience, to achieve the specific treatment goals he holds for each of its members. The particular nature and degree of group cohesion, client self-determination, and governing procedures, as well as the type of program, are defined by the individual treatment goals, not by any uniform standards workers have about "successful" or "well-organized" groups. His main concern is that each group become the most potent possible to attain the ends he seeks for its members. The worker should not regard the treatment groups as ends in themselves, apart from their contribution to the client members. Since practitioners do not hold the same goals for all groups and because of differences among the members who compose them, no two groups ever appear to have the same experiences or advance along the same developmental path.

The final stage is *evaluation and termination* (Johnson, Chapter 15 in this volume). The treatment sequence may last for short or long periods of time, depending on a variety of circumstances. Obviously, services to clients in groups may be terminated when it is apparent that treatment goals have been substantially achieved. Group services may also be terminated when it appears that maximum benefits for the member clients have been attained or when any anticipated additional gains are insufficient to merit continuation. Groups may also terminate because clients drop out, because pressing commitments arise elsewhere in the agency, or for a variety of other reasons. In any event, the decision to terminate should be made with a view toward the achievement of treatment goals. This decision necessitates a review of the progress made by each of the client members and an estimation of whether continutaion of this group would be worthwhile. The worker is compelled, therefore, to return to his original diagnostic statements and treatment goals, to evaluate the progress made in terms of them.

The presence of several clients requires a more complex termination decision than with a single case since, as expected, group members will show different degrees of achievement. A single termination decision is often inappropriate for all members of the group. Accordingly, the worker may reconstitute the group, keeping those who have not yet shown satisfactory progress (but who may be expected to do so), terminating those for whom maximum benefits have been achieved, and adding new members. Persons also may be transferred to different groups or to other services.

It must be kept in mind that these five stages represent general patterns, not ideal periods that ought to be accomplished neatly. Reality often makes it difficult to determine the end of one stage and the beginning of another. Events and activities, identified in a specific period, also are likely to be evident in others. The worker does not follow a timetable and he must engage in activities that are responsive to the group's process and which advance his treatment goals. Activities that may occur during any stage include the continuing search for diagnostic information to enhance understanding of clients, inclusion of a new group member long after the others have been admitted, and evaluation of change at earlier points in the treatment sequence.

Two crucial distinctions must be made in referring to the treatment sequence. As initially stated, this sequence is inclusive of *all* events that occur during the group work process. The first distinction is between the worker's decisions or mental activities, on the one hand, and his overt behavior or social interactions with clients, on the other. Thus, in the foregoing review reference was made to decisions like diagnosis, evaluation of progress, etc.; workers also talk with clients, participate in group programs, and do many other visible things. Practitioners not only participate in significant interactions with clients, but also they engage in important activities that are not visible to or even in the presence of clients. This leads to the second distinction between the reality of the group's structure and process and the worker's interpretation of and response to its reality.

Although the focus throughout this analysis is on the practitioner, his thinking and his actions, the individuals' subjective experiences, the unfolding of the group process, and the emergence of group structure must each be seen as independent reality. These events are affected by the presence and activity of the worker, but they should not be regarded entirely, or merely, as consequences of practitioner effort. There are other influences on individual and group behavior, only some of which can be known and affected by the worker. Furthermore, the practitioner can neither observe nor assess objectively all the events which occur, even within the group. It is the worker's dual aim to comprehend sensitively and accurately the group's experience and the experiences of its individual members, and to guide these experiences in accordance with treatment goals. But these distinctions can serve as reminders of the complexities of group process and of the constraints on practitioners' perceptions and actions.

TREATMENT GOALS AND GROUP PURPOSES

As stated, specific treatment goals must be established for each member of the client group (Schopler and Galinsky, Chapter 8 in this volume), since individuals never enter the treatment sequence with identical problems and capabilities. Clients are often discussed in terms of certain broad categories (e.g., delinquents) but this tends to obscure the very great differences characterizing individuals within each category. *Treatment goals* are those specific ends the practitioner pursues in the interests of particular clients within particular groups. This emphasis on the unique and idiosyncratic is referred to as *individualization* in social work literature.

A treatment goal is a specification of the state or condition in which the worker would like *this* client to be at the end of a successful treatment sequence. The concept of social dysfunction is sometimes used to denote all the problematic states of social work clientele. Treatment goals, then, embody more desirable states of social functioning. Several considerations must be introduced at this point. *First,* treatment goals must realistically reflect probable outcomes of group work service. It is impractical to think of ideal but unattainable states of well-being. For example, how to "cure" mental deficiency or brain damage through group work is not known. When working with clients having such problems, therefore, the worker should not suggest their resolution in treatment goals. Group work may, however, seek to ameliorate undesirable secondary effects or to achieve optimum functioning within the limits set by these conditions. Given the present development of the helping professions, workers are obligated to think in terms of limited goals. *Second,* treatment goals must relate directly to the presenting problems expressed by individual clients. While diagnosis is discussed in a later chapter (Sundel, Radin and Churchill, Chapter 7 in this volume), it is necessary to assert here that a treatment goal must anticipate improvement in the client's social functioning as defined by individual assessment and diagnosis. The distinct advantages to defining treatment goals in specific, concrete behavioral terms are that the goals can be more readily derived from clearly stated diagnoses and movement toward them can be assessed more definitely. *Third,* the treatment goal must be linked to diagnosis in still another way; it should seek reduction of the stress or difficulty *as experienced by the client.* Treatment goals also must bear a relationship to the capacities of the clients, and to their readiness or motivation to change; in this sense, they include prognoses about the likelihood that clients can and will change.

If two clients manifest identical problems, yet differ in their personality attributes, attitudes, or social circumstances, these differences would have important consequences for treatment outcomes; some would facilitate treatment (e.g., a high level of discomfort); others would hinder this process (e.g., peer support of problematic behavior). Since treatment goals must be realistic, they should reflect such relevant differences.

Fourth, the treatment goal should refer to improved client functioning outside the treatment group itself. Problematic behavior or conditions exist prior to service and pervade major spheres of the clients' lives. Service therefore, should improve these *other* spheres of life. This is referred to as the requirement of *transferability:* gains achieved by clients within the treatment process must be transferable beyond this process. Further, the degree and quality of improvement should be assessed according to conventional standards of the world inhabited by the client. Professional criteria should not subordinate community standards of conduct, achievement, and role performance.

Groups are typically composed of from four to twelve clients and, if unique treatment goals are established for each client, a complex and multiple set of aims must be formulated for every group. The practitioner must seek a composite of treatment goals that can be served simultaneously through a given group's process. Defining and harmonizing goals that serve several clients through the same group's process is obviously no simple task. There are at least two ways that practitioners handle this problem. The worker often has significant leverage in his control over the group's initial composition. He can attempt to compose a group so that the particular treatment goals are compatible and can be balanced. Although group composition involves more than the compatibility of treatment goals, this is one criterion for selecting persons for a given group. The practitioner, also, defines the *purposes* for the group; i.e., the particular collective ends it will pursue. Since the worker often has considerable control over the concrete purposes the group exists for and the activities it will engage in, he can attempt to define group purposes that are consistent with and instrumental to the several treatment goals he has established for the individual members.

Some aims, goals, and purposes pertain to all groups. The agency and the practitioner have certain ends in mind for each group; in most general terms, they seek to develop groups with strong enough influences to change or move clients toward improved social functioning as defined by specific treatment goals. For the worker, then, the group is intended to serve as the best possible means for achieving the composite of treatment goals. For each particular group, the worker must translate these objectives into more concrete purposes, which in turn lead to variations among group programs, plans, experiences, and processes.

Individual client members also have desired aims or objectives even if they are to "have a good time," to accomplish some task, or to achieve something which lies outside the group itself (e.g., prestige in the eyes of nonmembers). Some of these objectives are crystallized in members' thinking and aspirations, while some are only latent. In addition, each group tends to develop its own concrete purposes, which can be thought of as a composite of the members' expectations and motives to be fulfilled by the group. Customarily, these purposes are shared and stated, in various ways, and tend to shift over time.

Thus, four different types of ends can be distinguished analytically: (1) the worker's treatment goals for the group members, (2) the worker's functional purposes for the group, (3) the individual members' goals and objectives for themselves through the group, and (4) the shared purposes of the group. These various ends interpenetrate and are interrelated, as we have indicated. Figure 1 shows typical relations between such aims and expectations:

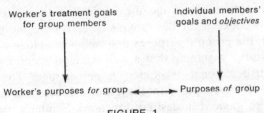

FIGURE 1

The degree of compatibility between these ends always differs among groups and varies through time for the same group. For example, the worker's purposes for a group may differ greatly from the initial expectations and preferences of its individual members. Unless the worker can change these orientations, he may have to make his purposes more congruent with client preferences, in order to achieve greater member involvement and motivation. Practitioners are confronted with increasing difficulties as the degree of compatibility among these ends decreases. The plausible solution of, "Let's do what the members want," is seldom effective.

THE STRATEGY OF INTERVENTION

In addition to the assertions that significant help can be given individuals through experience in groups, and that groups provide both the context and means for treatment, the treatment group can be thought of as a deliberately structured influence system to effect change through social interaction. The kinds of changes sought, as defined by treatment goals, range from acquiring new relationship skills, to changes in self-images and attitudes toward others, to behavioral modifications or integration into conventional social structures. Some tendency exists to regard worker-member interactions not only as having special import, but as being the essential means by which individuals are helped. This view regards the group merely as the context for treatment, as a process carried on primarily and directly between the worker and each client. This limits the concept of the group's potential. Although practitioners do interact directly with clients to implement specific treatment goals, potent influences are also exercised through interactions between members, through the group's activities or program, and through its structure. The skilled practitioner uses all of these to implement his treatment objectives. Frequently, the group implements treatment by directly influencing the individual.

The worker must possess a strategy of intervention to make use of these potential resources. Not only must he know where he wants to go (treatment outcomes) but also he must formulate approaches and techniques, taking maximum advantage of every legitimate way to achieve these ends. Besides his concern for the group's composition, the worker is concerned also with the group's purposes and major activities. Getting groups "off to a good start," assuming that a well-initiated group can move along successfully with occasional assistance, is not enough. The worker must be concerned with every point in the group's movement and must participate actively to guide it in desired directions. Similarly, he is concerned with the group's organization and the governing procedures it develops, as well as the quality of interpersonal relations among all the members.

All of these concerns and the way they are made instrumental is the practitioner's *strategy of intervention*. The formal requirements of this strategy are that the worker act (or not act) to "treat" at any given moment throughout the treatment sequence, and to facilitate the long-term development of the group's structure and process to different treatment effects for the client members. As a corollary, the group can be evaluated at any given moment in terms of its immediate treatment effects *and* its long-run potential for mediating treatment outcomes.

Practitioners may employ several modes of intervention or *means of influence,* to serve these dual objectives.[2] The worker should direct each action at immediate "treating," setting the conditions for treatment via the group, or both. These are viewed as essentially compatible and mutually instrumental, and the approaches are categorized by whether the practitioner is directly or indirectly influencing an individual member. *Direct*

---

[2] Appreciation is expressed to Edwin J. Thomas for his contributions to the initial formulation of these conceptions.

means of influence are interventions to effect change through immediate interaction with a group member. *Indirect means of influence* are interventions that modify group conditions which subsequently affect one or more members. In the former, worker and client join in face-to-face contact (in or apart from the presence of other clients). In the latter, the group mediates the relationship between the worker and the member(s) affected by the intervention. The distinction between direct and indirect provides an analytical reference for the variety of practitioner interventions, and emphasizes the immediate context and effects of interaction, i.e, whether or not a specific client member is directly interacting with the worker, who is being influenced, when and how. While these means of influence refer to actions engaged in by practitioners, they cannot achieve immediate, full treatment outcomes; instead, they are steps toward outcomes, however minute.

Examples are offered to clarify the distinction between the direct and indirect means. When the worker praises a group member while talking with him, perhaps thereby raising his self-esteem, he directly influences the client (i.e., using direct means). Similarly, when he suggests a new solution to a client's dilemma, conducts a marginal interview with him, or visits him at home, he is directly interacting with the client. The effects from any of these actions may not have great consequence, but that is beside the point. The distinction between direct and indirect means of influence does not refer to how potent the worker's actions are, or how subtle his approach is, or even how active he is. Such variations must be characterized in other terms.

In contrast, indirect means are employed to influence the group so that it in turn influences the members. The worker may modify group governing procedures to encourage more voice in affairs for all participants; this may result in greater satisfaction and acceptance for one or two dissident members. Or the worker may introduce new program activities which gratify most members, perhaps raising the status of one who can succeed now but could not in former activities. All members may be influenced by such worker interventions, some more than others.

A third major means of influence is employed by practitioners when they attempt to affect clients apart from both the group and personal contact. *Extragroup means of influence* include activities conducted on behalf of clients outside the group (Vinter and Galinsky, Chapter 17, and Glasser, et al., Chapter 18, in this volume). Targets of these interventions are nongroup persons whose behaviors affect clients and nongroup situations involving clients (i.e., classroom, family). Workers may seek to increase opportunities for their clients in these other situations, to alter attitudes and behaviors of other persons toward their clients, and to restructure elements of clients' social experiences. Parents, employers, classroom teachers, friends, cottage parents (in residential programs), and other agency staff members may be individuals with whom the practitioner interacts on behalf of his clients. Whereas, through the indirect means of influence, the treatment group mediates the relation between worker and client, through the extragroup means these *other* persons and situations mediate the relation. Both working through the group and through "significant others" could be considered indirect approaches, but the distinction between indirect and extragroup is preferred.

These terms largely constitute a codification of what group workers seem to do frequently in actual practice. One advantage of this analysis is to order and categorize what otherwise seem to be a confusing welter of worker activities; however, these categories do not encompass all activities employed by practitioners in groups. Only the direct and indirect means are discussed fully here; additional kinds of actions can be employed to exercise influence.

DIRECT MEANS OF INFLUENCE

The four types of direct means of influence presented all involve direct confrontation and contact between worker and client, in or outside the group session. The specific methods, the areas of client behavior affected, and the techniques employed are stated in each case.

Worker As Central Person—Object of Identifications and Drives

Under most circumstances the worker is preeminent in the treatment group, both with respect to his position in the structure and in terms of his psychological effect on the members. The several sources of this preeminence typically combine and reinforce each other: the worker's activity in initiating the group and in beginning its process; the authority vested in the worker by agency and community, which he can exercise by controlling resources and facilities available to the group and which enhance his prestige; and the personal resources (competencies, skills, and personality attributes) possessed by the worker. The worker's preeminence is particularly marked in newly formed groups; as he may be the only person who knows all the others, he is "mobilized" at the outset and free to participate actively without being cautiously passive, and, typically, he has personal qualities that are valued by the members. These characteristics, coupled with the clients' knowledge that the worker possesses considerable control over the destiny of the group, render the worker highly significant.

For these reasons the worker serves as a "central person," a focal point for group emotions (Redl, 1955; French and Raven, 1959). Emotional responses of members to the worker constitute ties to him; the worker becomes the object of member identifications and drives. The worker serves as the object of identifications when the members want or try to be like him. He serves as the object of drives when the members are emotionally invested in him. Because of the worker's position and his attributes, the potentiality of these psychological relationships with client members might be enhanced for two reasons. First, such worker-client relationships provide the basis for continuing service to individuals, for whom the worker has special psychological meaning. The relationships thus formed are crucial conditions for subsequent interpersonal influence, but the difference between actual relationships and those which are desired or intended by practitioners must be distinguished. Second, such relationships also serve to strengthen member-to-member ties; clients may identify with each other as they experience the similarity of their relationships with the worker. The unity of the group can thus emerge, as common psychological responses among members lead to shared and reciprocated responses between members.

This means of influence focuses on the psychological relationships that are established between the worker and the members. Psychological responses of the members may be manifested in overt behavior (e.g., evidences of liking, affection, compliance with worker requests, or modeling of the worker's behavior), or they may remain at the covert level (changed attitudes toward oneself or others, a shift in values, or resolution of some internal conflict). Covert responses are less readily apparent but may be as significant or real as more obvious behavioral changes.

The specific techniques or actions used by practitioners to exercise this influence are especially difficult to identify. Some of the members' psychological responses are associated with the social or structural position of the worker. Structural sources, that might contribute to the technique, are the worker's status in the agency and his mobilization (i.e., his initiative and freedom of action); however, these represent *potentialities* for influencing members through exercise of power and through active participation in group interaction, respectively. They remain potentialities unless deliberately exercised by the worker; that is, the worker may serve as an insufficient "central person" by abdicating his position vis-à-vis the group or by remaining a passive participant in its processes. As indicated above, the worker's personality attributes, competencies, and skills also generate emotional responses from client members. Such attributes may be either instrumental or socioemotional: an instrumental one is useful in achieving some objective or completing some task (e.g., tutoring or teaching a skill), a socioemotional attribute is one for psychological gratification (e.g., friendly responses to another). Who the worker is as a person, and how he interacts with clients, however minutely or subtly, has consequences for his becoming an object of identification and drives. A wide range of worker attributes and behavior becomes highly relevant in these terms: cordial and interested responses to others, suggestion of good ideas, capacity for responding to nuances of client feeling and interest, ability to do things clients enjoy, and even personal appearance.

Since groups differ in many respects and clients possess different personalities, obviously specific worker characteristics and behavior will have different psychological consequences for different people. A worker's prowess in swimming will be of little salience in a street gang, and his "cool" will not be prized among aged clients. Similarly, a worker's tendency toward repressiveness will have quite different psychological meanings among clients in the same group. The principle of "conscious use of self" directs practitioners to be sensitive to these differences between groups and individuals, and to vary appropriately their presentations of themselves and their specific behaviors. As the worker becomes more skilled, he can achieve these variations to become the kind of "central person" who will advance treatment for a particular group and client. In general, positive identifications are likely to be increased when workers are friendly, manifest warm and cordial relations, and show sensitivity to the needs and interests of individual members. The issue of negative identification is important but will not be developed here.

Worker As Symbol and Spokesman— Agent of Legitimate Norms and Values

Many clients served through social group work manifest difficulties with the values and behavioral norms they have internalized. Indeed, for some clients, these difficulties may be the essence of their social functioning problems. Client diagnoses may indicate no psychological malfunctioning, but an internalization of socially unacceptable values, perhaps through membership in deviant or antilegal groups. Inducing change in these areas is generally termed resocialization. One function of group work service can be socialization, or the acquisition of values and behavioral standards defined by the larger society. Thus, children, immigrants from other societies, or persons moving into new sociocultural situations and strata typically need help to acquire conventional orientations and behaviors. Avoiding the extremes of abject conformity and destructive rebellion, the individual must develop a viable interdependence with others by acquiring the basic values essential to community life, and minimal adherence to the norms of conduct required for effective social functioning.

Without imposing his personal value system and standards or those of any particular stratum on clients, the worker must inculcate the essential values of the larger society. He is obligated not only by his agency but by the community and by his profession to represent both society and the long-run interests of the client. And he must mediate the clients and certain values and norms created informally within the treatment group itself. Thus, values and standards are derived from the larger society environing the group (community, agency, etc.) and are developed within the group. Some are specified as laws, rules, or role prescriptions; others appear less tangibly as orientations, patterns of conduct, and generalized attitudes. The worker's task is to determine which of these are crucial, as treatment goals, to individual clients and to the group. Crucial values and norms are then emphasized in practice.

Values and norms may be transferred by the worker in several ways. They may be *personified* by the worker as they pervade his total behavior and outlook. What the worker does and does not do, the events to which he responds, and his views and attitudes toward persons and issues, all convey to clients basic values and norms. Thus, as the worker continuously responds to client interests and feelings, he "cues" group members to the value of individual dignity and worth and to positive interpersonal norms, without having to state explicitly that he accepts them. Through member-worker identification and modeling, commitments are inculcated or strengthened among members and become the bases for desirable behavior.

The worker may also be a *spokesman* for values and norms; that is, he must frequently give utterance to both. Even when a large degree of permissiveness is necessary in worker-client relations the worker must still set limits and voice expectations. What is important is that practitioners act and speak to exemplify a particular set of values and norms which can become operative for clients, rather than interacting in ways which offer few, ambiguous guides (although a "do what he wants" attitude should be avoided).

Values and norms within the group may also be informally *created* by workers, especially when the group is newly formed. The creation of such norms and values, whether explicit or implicit, may be facilitated by the worker as personifier or spokesman. Worker hesitation or inactivity in the creation of group standards can handicap group development and curtail movement toward treatment goals.

As indicated previously, the behavior of the worker itself serves as a model for clients and the worker may define or strengthen norms by setting limits on the behavior of members, by requesting, requiring, or forbidding certain behaviors. The worker may state precepts and rules of conduct. Or the worker may apply various positive and negative sanctions against members, that is, encourage, reward, or chastise group members for their behavior. Rewards and deprivations may be material or social (e.g., praise). Finally, the worker sometimes must use his power of coercion and physically prevent a client from engaging in certain behavior (e.g., assaulting another person) or must eject him from the group. Generally, positive techniques are more effective than negative techniques, and inducements or rewards more helpful than deprivations. The worker must state precepts to define clearly his expectations for clients, but by itself this has little utility for enduring change.

Although some workers may be hesitant to act in the area of values and norms, in actual practice they often seem to devote considerable energy to this area. The critical problems are determining which values and norms are crucial and what the effective ways are to implement them. Since the group customarily develops its own values and normative system which the members then participate in enforcing, the worker has a potent resource at hand. He can help the group develop a system of norms and values in accord with treatment goals. Since the primary concern here is with direct means of influence, worker-client interactions should modify an individual client's norms and values in accordance with the specific treatment goals for him.

Worker As Motivator and Stimulator— Definer of Individual Goals and Tasks

Throughout the treatment sequence many opportunities occur for practitioners to motivate and stimulate individual members toward specific ends or activities. These opportunities may take the form of encouragement for certain objectives or expectations for individuals, such as undertaking a specific project or acquiring certain skills; or they may enable the stimulation of a member to engage in different behaviors or to act differently in familiar activities or to direct him toward new interests. The worker perceives such opportunities within the developing experience of the group and its larger activities, with reference to the immediate social and material environment of the individual and group or with reference to the larger community and society.

For example, a creative adult may see potentialities in the pebbles and sand of a beach or in the repair of an old car; and the alert practitioner may see many more significant possibilities in the urban community than the adolescent does. Making the most of such opportunities—whether immediately discerned by the client or beyond his horizon—requires that the worker be aware of the potentialities inherent in the social and physical context. Maximizing such opportunities requires that the worker be guided by specific treatment goals.

This means is primarily directed toward individual interests, aims, activities and skills. Essential is the worker's use of his relationship and interaction with members to orient them toward experiences that they might not otherwise engage in and that will facilitate treatment. Regardless of age or problem, clients tend to restrict themselves to conventional and familiar activities, to have limited perspectives, and to be less aware of the full potentialities offered by their social and physical environment. Stimulating clients to use material objects in more creative and satisfying ways is perhaps the most obvious manifestation of this means of influence. But one may also think of motivating clients toward opportunities for the development and different use of their capabilities in social situations (e.g., getting a different job, discovering unknown talents and abilities).

The worker's control over resources permits him to use them as "props" or objects to stimulate clients. Introducing or sharing new and unfamiliar materials or using familiar ones in novel ways are customary approaches. Thus, a worker can show clients new games that can be played with old objects (e.g., cards, dice, boxes), or the worker may call the client's attention to things and events he overlooks in everyday life (e.g., interesting insects or items in the newspaper). Incentives, inducements, and rewards can be employed by the worker to motivate clients. Thus, encouraging, suggesting, proposing, and expressing enthusiasm or excitement are effective interaction techniques. The worker's own interests and responses to objects and situations convey meanings to clients for whom the worker's behavior is especially salient, and the worker may direct or instruct clients in these terms.

Worker As Executive—Controller of Members' Roles

In addition to the discrete and relatively concrete tasks and purposes discussed above, the practitioner is also concerned about clients' more general orientations and roles. These may be thought of as configurations or sets of specific behaviors. Each group develops its own structure of roles, responsibilities, and positions (Sarri and Galinsky, Chapter 5 in this volume). Within the group each member may be characterized as having distinct positions in these structures which may be deliberately modified by the worker with regard to his treatment aims. For example, tasks or projects undertaken by the entire group require some division of responsibilities among the members (Vinter; and Whittaker; Chapters 13 and 14, in this volume). Assignment of these responsibilities may refer to the larger task objective, the abilities of members, and the needs of the individual members. The worker must be concerned not only with what is good for the group, but also with what is desired for individual clients in terms of the treatment goals.

When the worker develops or modifies these group structures (as when he proposes a set of positions or division of labor), he is using indirect means of influence. However, when he directly interacts to modify an individual's particular role or position within these structures, he is using direct means of influence. To continue with the example of task assignments suggested above: when a client is given a specific responsibility, the worker can help him directly in discharging his part of the total task. Such intervention by the worker may have several effects, all different from the effects of allowing the client to "go it alone." Undertaking the task in the way proposed by the worker exposes the client to expectations and experiences he might not have had otherwise. The standards and values implicit in this event may have carry-over effects for the client in subsequent situations; and the response of the group to the client's performance may be quite different than if he had not been helped by the worker (e.g., praise for accomplishment rather than criticism). The worker himself may make the individual assignments, determining the pattern of member tasks as well as helping clients undertake them. The worker may interact directly with clients to affect more general behavior than the mere performance of a specific task. Thus, a worker may assist an individual who holds a particular position in the group's formal structure to perform more effectively or differently in this position. Whether in terms of these positions or of more general roles, the worker can seek to modify the member's behavior with reference to his treatment goals.

As viewed so far, the worker's effort in assigning or modifying membership roles has focused on the behavior and experience of an individual client. Through direct interaction the worker attempts to develop or change a client's personal attributes, thus modifying his role performance. The worker may attempt to increase a member's sensitivity to group norms so that he becomes a less deviant member, perhaps by clarifying the relevant norms for the client or by informing him more precisely of other members' expectations as they apply to him. Or the worker may attempt to change the client member's role behavior by raising his self-esteem, giving him support, or setting limits on his behavior.

The worker can serve as an "executive" by defining new or modified roles for members and by helping the clients to perform differently in their present roles. The emphasis is on interaction with individual clients, in terms of their role behavior, not on the entire role system of the group, which will be discussed later. In the previously discussed means of influence emphasis was on concrete interests and goals. This means of influence can be differentiated by the focus on general patterns of behavior (roles) rather than on specific interests and objectives, and by focus on patterns of client behavior which have particular relevance to other members and to the entire group. All of the techniques previously referred to may also be employed with this means.

These four direct means of influence tend to overlap, particularly with respect to the specific practitioner activities or techniques that may be employed. Distinctions between them mainly have to do with the worker's aims and the consequences for individuals that follow. The range of client experience and behavior which group workers can seek to modify includes attitudes, values, gratifications, tasks, identifications, roles, and so forth. A wide variety of worker-client interactions can be utilized to implement desired change. The similarity of techniques (e.g., praising, encouraging, or setting limits) should not, however, obscure the marked differences in effects for clients when the worker directs activities toward different ends, under varying conditions.

INDIRECT MEANS OF INFLUENCE

Indirect means of influence are those practitioner interventions used to effect modifications in group conditions which, in turn, affect the members. The worker acts on and through the group, its processes, and its program. Some of these approaches closely parallel the direct means of influence, and, conversely, certain direct means might implicate changes in the group.

Group Purposes

Groups that persist over extended periods of time develop distinctive aims. And, for all groups that they serve, social workers have purposes in mind which they make more or less explicit to the client members and which have significance for the nature and development of each group and for the experiences of the members. The kinds of purposes held by a group and the extent to which they are achieved are important determinants of member motivation to belong to the group, and of the satisfactions gained through participation in it. Similarly, the purposes set for the group by the worker are determinant of his own actions and these, in turn, vitally affect the group and its members. Diverse group goals and purposes characterize those served by social group workers: planning groups; groups focused on resolution of members' personal problems; activity groups; groups to orient or prepare members for some event (e.g., new clients entering an institution or patients about to be released); diagnostic groups; socio-education groups for professionals, paraprofessionals, other socialization agents, and adults in role transition; and so on.

The relations between a worker's treatment goals, his purposes for the group, member objectives, and purposes of the group have been discussed above. Here consideration is given only to the worker's purposes

for the group and the purposes *of* the group. Practitioners have considerable control over definition of purposes and goals, although there are wide
variations in actual practice. In some instances, the worker and agency
may set the purposes of the group in advance and select group members
with avowed reference to these. Adherence to these purposes may then be
a condition for continued participation in the group. At the other extreme,
the group may have much autonomy in determining its own purposes (but
this does not imply that the worker lacks treatment goals). In still other
situations, after very broad purposes are set for the group it determines
its own specific plans within these limits. Regardless of the source of initial
purpose determination, the worker has many opportunities during the treatment sequence to modify group purposes and to alter members' objectives.
Thus, even when serving a delinquent street gang which sets its own purposes, the worker can gradually influence the group toward different aims.

Two specific influences on clients that can be indirectly mediated
through group purposes and aims have already been mentioned: selection
of clients for the group can be made explicitly with reference to its established purposes, and a client's attraction to and satisfaction with the group
is partially dependent on its purposes (Cartwright and Zander, 1960). The
purposes of the group also determine the distribution of leadership functions and member roles within it, thereby significantly affecting the experience of each client member. Similarly, group purposes shape the program and the activities developed in pursuit of these aims. And finally,
group purposes will have some implication for the particular kind of
decision-making and governing procedures to be employed (see p. 40). In
these terms a group of adoptive parents contrasts with a play group of
young children. The former may be directed toward consideration of common problems that couples face in adopting children, while the latter is
directed toward pleasurable learning experiences, "having fun" in the
youngsters' terms. Each will involve quite different activities, group
processes, and member roles and will lead to markedly different effects for
their members.

Finally, a word about the relation between purposes of the group and
worker's purposes for the group. Group purposes have been defined as the
composite of members' objectives and motives encompassed in some
definite expression of collective purpose. Worker's purposes for the group,
written in a specific statement, are the aims which a group ought to pursue to achieve treatment goals set for the individual clients. Obviously the
worker seeks compatibility between his and the clients' aims, so that he is
not oriented in one direction while the group is heading in another. Although both sets of aims tend to change over time and there cannot be
perfect identity between them, the worker customarily seeks acceptance of
his purposes as those of the group. Thus, in an institutional context a

worker may attempt to gain members' acceptance of his treatment goals, and to orient them accordingly. Or, with a street gang, the worker may gradually seek acceptance of his prolegal purposes in working with the group. In a very real sense, therefore, client objectives and group purposes are targets, not determinants of worker interventions. However, the distinction between worker purposes and group aims should be kept in mind so that the *intentions* of the practitioner are never confused with the *reality* of member interests and motivations.

Selection of Group Members

Selection of group members and size of group (discussed next) are aspects of group composition. As a basic step in group composition, selection of members is one of the most problematic aspects of group practice. Practitioners cannot always select those who join a particular group; sometimes agency circumstances affect group composition, as when a treatment group consists of all the youngsters in the same orthopedic ward or all the inmates about to be released from an institution. Or the group's membership may be set by a decision to serve an existing or "natural group": friends living in the same housing project or all the members of a street gang. By and large, the greater an agency's general control over the clients, the more probable will be its determination of group membership (e.g., residential settings as contrasted with other community services).

Before considering the various criteria useful in determining membership, some of the consequences of this indirect means of influence will be examined. The experiences of the members, the interpersonal relations and even the particular nature of the activities will differ depending on who and how many others there are in a particular group. Thus, the capacity of the group to meet the desires and objectives of its members, as well as the goals of the worker, is partially dependent on its composition.

The worker's goals and purposes for the group provide a general guide for group composition: the reason the group is established and served, and what it is expected to accomplish, serve as determinants of membership selection. For example, if a group were designed to serve children who manifest serious school conduct problems, it would require the identification of such pupils and their inclusion in the group. Obviously, a group would have different characteristics if its purpose was to serve parents experiencing difficulties in childrearing or home management practices. The statement that purposes for the group should govern selection of its members may seem to be a truism, but in actual practice this is often ignored, usually because the agency and worker's purposes are too general or too unclear to serve as guides. However, group goals and purposes only point to a category of potential clients, and do not indicate specifically which persons within the general category should be selected. Referring to the illustrations cited above, which school children or which parents should be selected for treatment group membership? Or, to state it differently, what particular attributes or characteristics should the clients possess in addition to their belonging to a general category?

More concrete specification of the type of treatment group and its purposes can point toward particular persons within the general categories of potential clients. Regarding the group to serve pupils manifesting conduct problems, the worker might make two other decisions in advance: (1) that the group will include children manifesting classroom conduct problems and will exclude those who exhibit only academic difficulties; and (2) that the group program will include behavioral retraining as well as discussion of members' problems. These two decisions would provide some concrete direction for the worker in selecting clients from among all the pupils belonging to the general category as described.

The conception of the group as the *means* of treatment suggests another set of criteria. Practitioners would seek groups that have maximum impact or change effects for their client members. To accomplish this, treatment groups must be potentially capable of developing appropriate levels of cohesiveness, solidarity and mutuality, viable internal structures, and so forth. These requirements, in turn, direct the selection of members with a view to their similarity of interests, their potentiality of attraction for each other, their adequacy to participate in the general type of activity and group structure planned by the worker, and their capacity to form certain relationships with each other and with the worker. Knowing that the treatment sequence is more likely to be effective if these conditions are met within the group, the worker can attempt to select particular individuals who possess the attributes *with reference to each other* which promise to meet these conditions. Similarity or complementarity is desired with respect to the more important characteristics, however dissimilar the clients may be in other respects (Bertcher and Maple, Chapter 11 in this volume).

Great incompatibilities in age, interest, problems, interaction style, maturation level, and so forth, make it very difficult for group members to form cohesive groups. Reference here is to *compatibility* or complementarity, and not identity. Persons may form effective treatment groups because of the compatibility of their attributes even though they vary in terms of the similarity of attributes. For example, under certain circumstances, age and sex differences among group members may be essentially compatible. Thus, adolescent boys and girls might be placed in the same group on an orthopedic ward, but might not be selected for membership in certain sports activity groups.

A number of guidelines can be summarized. First, the types of primary client attributes for which compatibility and complementarity are desired depend on the nature of the group and its program. Second, complementarity is sought with reference to other members of the same group and not with reference to any absolute standards of personality attributes. Third, clients need not be identical with respect to their characteristics, but should be potentially compatible. Practitioners find that it is impossible to attain homogeneity with respect to many attributes, and must attempt to "match" individuals in terms of primary criteria while expecting considerable difference with respect to secondary criteria.

Size of Group

The size of a group tends to affect members. The worker must determine the appropriate group size for the desired effects for clients as defined by their treatment goals. First, some of the effects associated with differences in size will be examined. *Large* groups (e.g., ten or over) tend toward anonymity of membership, less consensus among the members, lower rates of participation, and higher demands for leadership abilities. Larger groups are able to undertake certain tasks beyond the capacities of smaller groups or to engage in certain types of program (e.g., tasks requiring a complex division of effort). Any of these effects may be desired for individual clients under specific circumstances. More mature and more capable clients are better able to cope with the participation requirements of large groups. Older adolescents and adults are probably more able to participate in larger decision-making units than are younger children.

Small groups, in contrast, tend toward high rates of member participation, greater individual involvement, greater consensus, and increased restraint upon members. Relations among persons in smaller groups tend to be more intensive. Effects such as these are often desired by practitioners for treatment groups. It is also easier for workers to cope with serious problems or acting-out behavior in small groups, when clients present these patterns.

In some agencies clients may participate concurrently in several different groups; this is especially true for most residential programs—camps, institutions, hospitals, etc. Under these conditions it is often desirable to vary the kinds of groups in which clients participate so that they can experience the different effects associated with size, type of program, and so forth. Practitioners must guard against a bias toward small groups so that they are not always established, even when clients might benefit from the anonymity or reduced intensivity provided by larger groups. Although workers are not always able to set the initial size of the group, as members drop out or others are added, there are opportunities to influence the size of the continuing group. Workers may find it desirable to vary the size of the treatment group during the treatment sequence.

Small group effects may be achieved *within* larger groups in many ways. In all larger groups, individuals tend to form smaller subgroups, thereby achieving informally many of the effects of small group participation. Practitioners may deliberately design such opportunities and influence the formation and structure of these subgroupings. Ways of doing this include facilitating interpersonal ties among clusters of members, introducing program activities that provide for smaller participation units, or developing a structure of subgroups (e.g., committees) for task and governing purposes.

Group Operating and Governing Procedures

Group workers have been strongly oriented toward democratic leadership and governing procedures because of their high valuation of client self-determination. Permissiveness in guiding the group, and helpfulness and friendliness in contacts with members, have probably characterized most group workers in actual practice. The very strength of this orientation becomes its weakness, however, as permissiveness by the practitioner and high autonomy for the group are widely sought regardless of differences in treatment goals and group member characteristics. Treatment goals and other specific group characteristics warrant deliberate variations in the degree of autonomy granted each group, in its procedures and formal organization, and in worker control practices. Each of these will be discussed briefly.

The degree of autonomy should vary with the type of group and its purpose, the treatment goals of the worker, and the members' characteristics. With younger, less capable, or more disturbed clients the worker may greatly limit the autonomy of the group, at least initially. The location and situation in which the group exists also affect its autonomy—delinquent groups in their own neighborhoods usually retain high autonomy, while institutional groups composed of clients with similar problems often have limited autonomy. High control by the worker tends to induce dependence upon him, reduces the members' assertiveness, and limits the satisfactions which they may achieve within the group. The practitioner may vary the *areas* within which groups have autonomy, as well as the degree of self-determination. Thus, a group may be granted high autonomy in its program of activities, but little choice in its size and composition.

Democratic relations, generally sought within treatment groups, are associated not only with the quality of worker-member interactions and relationships, but also with the nature of procedures that are used in governing the group. Governing procedures evolved spontaneously within client groups often reflect and enforce inequalities of power, prestige, and gratification. They can also introduce constraints due to members' unquestioned adherence to tradition or sentiment. In contrast, democratic procedures tend to be more rational, permit more flexible change as circumstances dictate, and provide certain guarantees of channels for individual participation. Unfortunately, workers sometimes equate democratic decision-making practices with parliamentary procedures, and often introduce an array of "businesslike" patterns. Parliamentary procedures are essentially formalistic and can easily be subverted, and the same positive effects may be achieved by simple norms as "everyone gets a chance to talk," "the majority rules," and "taking turns." The important concern is to increase group-centered decision making and wide distribution of member gratifications. Group-centered (as contrasted with worker-centered, or clique-controlled) decision-making results in greater member participation, greater consensus, and greater pressures toward uniformity, thus maximizing the impact of the group. The formal organization of a group affects its operating and governing procedures. Along with a predisposition toward parliamentary procedures, practitioners are sometimes inclined to introduce formal systems of officerships within groups. The intent is often to provide members with definite roles within groups and to insure democratic self-determination. Both aims may be achieved by less arbitrary approaches, however, and a system of officerships often achieves neither. The degree and type of formal structure appropriate for groups varies and the worker must sensitively create (or circumscribe) patterns within particular groups according to his treatment goals and client characteristics.

Much that has been stated with respect to group autonomy and governing procedures applies directly to worker control practices. In general, group workers attempt to be friendly, responsive, and permissive to the appropriate degree. They can exercise controls and make crucial decisions without being authoritarian or undemocratic. Particularly with newly formed groups and with less capable clientele, workers must be very active in setting group directions, guiding processes, and exercising controls. The degree and method of worker control should vary among different types of groups and over time within the same group.

Group Development

Group workers typically serve groups that exist for extended periods of time. They are concerned with the entire periods as much as with particular sessions. Their intent is to help the group develop through time as an effective treatment or service vehicle, with cumulative impact on its participants. Groups that maintain themselves through time, whether or not they are served by practitioners, develop definite structures and deal with similar problems. They pass through roughly comparable stages and may develop roughly comparable patterns of organization. The worker's task is to influence the course of a group's development so that it permits maximum attainment of the treatment goals set for clients. Therefore, the worker must act continuously to *effect treatment at any given moment* and to *facilitate the long-run development of a cohesive and viable group*. This dual task requires attention to the immediate events and their treatment potential, and also knowledge of the stages of group development and of the strategic foci for worker intervention. The stages of group development and the implications for practitioner activity as well as additional means of influence will be suggested in subsequent chapters.

REFERENCES

BERTCHER, HARVEY
   1973—"Elements and issues in group composition," in this volume.
CARTWRIGHT, D., AND A. ZANDER
   1960—"Individual motives and group goals," in *Group Dynamics: Research and Theory*, Dorwin P. Cartwright and Alvin F. Zander (Eds.), Evanston, Ill.: Row, Peterson, second edition, pp. 345–69.
FRENCH, JOHN R., III AND BERTRAM H. RAVEN
   1959—"The bases of social power," in *Studies in Social Power*, Dorwin P. Cartwright, (Ed.), Ann Arbor: Institute for Social Research, pp. 150–67.
GLASSER, PAUL, BERYL CARTER, RICHARD ENGLISH, CHARLES GARVIN, AND CHARLES WOLFSON
   1973—"Group work intervention in the social environment," in this volume.
JOHNSON, CAROLE
   1973—"Planning for termination of the group," in this volume.
REDL, FRITZ
   1955—"Group emotion and leadership," in *Small Groups: Studies in Social Interaction*, Paul Hare, Ed Borgotta, and Robert Bales (Eds.), New York: Knopf, pp. 71–86.
SARRI, ROSEMARY AND MAEDA GALINSKY
   1973—"A conceptual framework for group development," in this volume.
SCHOPLER, JANICE AND MAEDA GALINSKY
   1973—"Goals in social group work practice: Formulation, implementation and evaluation," in this volume.
SUNDEL, MARTIN, NORMA RADIN AND SALLIE CHURCHILL
   1973—"Diagnosis in group work," in this volume.

Vinter, Robert and Maeda Galinsky
  1973—"Extragroup relations and approaches," in this volume.
Vinter, Robert
  1973—"Program activities: An analysis of their effects on participant behavior," in this volume.
Whittaker, James
  1973—"Program activities: Their selection and use in a therapeutic milieu," in this volume.

3.

Social Group Work: The Preventive and Rehabilitative Approach

CHARLES D. GARVIN and PAUL H. GLASSER

Groups conducted by social workers for rehabilitative purposes are located in such varied settings as public schools, mental health clinics, correctional institutions, hospitals, child welfare agencies, settlement houses, community centers, and public assistance agencies. Such groups, like all social work groups, are "a mode of serving individuals within and through small face-to-face groups in order to effect desired changes among the client participants." (Vinter, 1965:715) A rehabilitative approach seeks to make changes that will alleviate specific handicaps to the functioning of individuals in their social roles. Recently the group approach has been used to prevent deviant behavior among groups of children or adults who are known to be highly likely to demonstrate social malperformance.

Although groups were used as early as 1928, (Burrow, 1928:198–206) their use for rehabilitative purposes received impetus after World War II, along with similar developments in psychiatry and clinical psychology, through rapid development of programs for the treatment of psychiatrically disabled veterans. In recent years a number of articles and monographs have been devoted to the problems of group work in rehabilitative settings. Among the issues dealt with have been group work with psychiatric patients, the aged, public welfare clients, and delinquents. Work with clients in residential treatment, in the health field, in child welfare, and in the public schools has also been described.

MANPOWER

The highest proportion of group workers has been located in agencies classified as "group services," primarily settlement houses and community

Reprinted with permission of the National Association of Social Workers, from the *Encyclopedia of Social Work* (New York, 1971).

centers. Such agencies have usually been thought of as offering socialization services. The use of this category may be deceptive, however, because a number of community-based agencies offer specialized services such as groups for children referred from public schools for help with classroom management problems, for adults with employment difficulties, or for aged persons coping with retirement stresses.

Throughout the 1950s and 1960s in particular, writers expressed concern with both the proportion of social workers receiving special training for the practice of group work and the proportion of such group workers being employed to serve the high-risk population who suffer from severe emotional, intellectual, physical, and environmental impairments. A statement Vinter (1959:128–148) made is still pertinent to this concern:

> A third major problem confronts group work: namely its retreat from the profession's historic mission of service to those most in need.
>
> In a society inclined to minimize the prevalence of misery, commitment to those most in need is especially crucial. We know that this society directs much of its energy and resources to other purposes than alleviating misery, and we do not assert that such pursuits are improper in themselves. Our question must be: where do we stand and how do we direct our professional energies and resources.

Census statistics support Vinter's assertions. According to the 1960 census, of 105,000 employed social workers in the United States, only 6,300 (6 percent) were employed in direct service positions in group work. An additional 4,600 were employed in supervisory positions. Of this overall total of persons in group work, only 18 percent had completed graduate social work training. Ninety-four percent of these group workers were employed in state or local voluntary agencies, not, therefore, in such agencies as public welfare, mental hospitals, or correctional institutions.

Between 1950 and 1960, the number of group workers employed in rehabilitation settings increased slightly. For example, during this decade trained group workers with MSW degrees increased in psychiatric hospitals from less than .5 percent to 2 percent of social service personnel, in public assistance agencies from 2 percent to 3 percent, and in medical agencies from less than .5 percent to 1 percent. The greatest increase took place in child welfare agencies: in 1950 the proportion was 1 percent and in 1960 it was 4 percent in noninstitutional facilities, 10 percent in institutional facilities, and 5 percent in court services (National Social Welfare Assembly, 1961; Amercan Association of Social Workers, 1952).

Council on Social Work Education statistics for 1964–1969 present a somewhat different and changing picture, however. While social work enrollments have been increasing steadily, the proportion of group work students has remained essentially the same. In 1964–1965 and 1965–1966 group work students constituted 9 percent of the total, while in 1966–1967 a slight rise to 10 percent was reported. This declined to 8.6 percent in 1967–1968, but rose again to almost 10 percent in 1968–1969. However, these percentages are misleading. The 1968–1969 reports lists 156 students in the group work method concentration, 706 students in "generic social work practice," 360 students in "casework plus community organization or group work," and 75 students in "group work plus community organization." (Council on Social Work Education, 1969) If we account for only half of the students in casework plus community organization or group work, more than 30 percent of the graduate schools' student bodies were receiving a substantial but undetermined amount of group work training. This is a considerable increase.

Similar changes are reported concerning fields-of-practice data. The proportion of students in group work receiving training in fields other than group services has been increasing rapidly—28 percent in 1964–1965, 29 percent in 1965–1966, 39 percent in 1966–1967, 45 percent in 1967–1968, and 60 percent in 1968–1969. It can be anticipated that these changes in training patterns will affect future manpower distributions. They represent significant changes in the fields since the 1960 survey.

Major Practice Assumptions

The application of group work methods to rehabilitation and prevention has been accompanied by many developments in practice principles and practice theory. Among the principles on which there has been considerable agreement are the following:

1. *The individual as the focus of change.* This principle stresses the notion that the worker tries to attain specified group conditions only as they help achieve relevant goals for *individuals.* Thus to achieve certain individual goals, a highly organized group with an extensive division of labor and other structures is sought. For other goals, a loosely organized short-term group is chosen. Autonomy from the worker is an issue in some groups more than others. Democratic processes of decision-making, while always important, also may be emphasized in some groups more than others.

Concern with individual goals does not mean that the goals are to be achieved only through changes in the behavior of the individual group member. The group worker may decide, on appropriate consultation with group members, to change conditions within the group, agency, or community, and he may do this with the group members or on their behalf. In any case, the decision to engage in such efforts is always made with reference to individual goals.

2. *Specificity of goals.* Another proposition of this approach to group work is that client rehabilitation goals will more likely be attained when

expressed in precise, operational terms. Goals consist of "a specification of the state or condition in which we would like this client to be at the end of a successful treatment sequence." (Vinter, Chapter 2 in this volume) Any area of human behavior may be chosen for the establishment of goals, and these goals may relate to the individual's cognitive, affective, attitudinal, or instrumental behavioral repertoires. Goals are formulated by client and worker together—a process that frequently occupies the major part of first sessions with the client individually and/or in the group. The worker may also develop explicit goals for a client, as long as these are communicated as clearly as possible to the client and his maximum involvement obtained.

There may be one or more goals, depending on the circumstances. As Vinter has stated in Chapter 2:

> Behavioral difficulties may be few and manifested with respect to only one of an individual's several social roles, as with some malperformance in the public school; or they may be diffuse and pervade several areas of social life and careers, as with habitual delinquents, psychotics, and others.

There may be intermediate as well as terminal goals because individual goal accomplishment and worker planning may be enhanced by specific increments prior to termination. Thus a hospitalized mental patient's ability to dress properly, ask questions clearly, and perform other self-care tasks are intermediate goals related to a terminal goal of being able to meet the expectations of a halfway house.

3. *Contract.* The existence of an individual focus and the specificity of goals lead to the concept of a worker-member contract—a set of agreements between the worker and group members regarding the problems to be dealt with as well as the means to be utilized in this process. In some group work frameworks, particularly that of Vinter, the contract specifically covers the goals to be attained by the members as a result of the group experience. In other models, the emphasis is more on mutual responsibilities for the development of the group process. The group work contract, in contrast to the legal contract, is not a fixed document; rather, it is a process with many subtle components. Modifications in the understanding between members and workers may occur from session to session and even during a given interaction.

The emphasis on contract has both an ethical and a practical rationale. From an ethical point of view, the idea has roots in group work's commitment to the self-determination of the client—that is, the client is not manipulated toward ends he does not seek by means he does not accept. Furthermore, empirical evidence indicates that having a contract increases the likelihood that the goal sought will be reached and that the individual will remain for service (Raven and Rietsema, 1960:395–412).

4. *Group as a means for change.* A distinguishing characteristic of group work as an intervention method directed at individual change, as compared to other group treatment methods, is that the group is used as a means as well as a context for the achievement of goals. Consciously and explicitly, the worker uses peer group pressures, modeling between and among clients, group rules and norms, and the like to obtain and maintain individual change. He tries in every way to put the group and its members to work for each other.

He usually must set instrumental goals concerning such matters as group cohesion, decision-making procedures, or group structures and processes that set the stage for and facilitate the accomplishment of terminal goals. Instrumental goals are never seen as ends in themselves; they vary from group to group and are partially dependent on them. It is through the use of such instrumental group goals that the group becomes a viable means for individual change.

5. *Intervention in the social environment.* Goals achieved in and through the group must be maintained in the client's social environment— his daily living experience. Further, before a decision is made to embark on an intervention method, it must be determined for each client that worker and/or client intervention in the environment alone would be insufficient; and that casework or group work with their emphases on client change would or could be beneficial. Sometimes intervention in the client's life situation must precede small-group interaction. Most often the two approaches must proceed together, because change in one aspect of the client's life is maintained and reinforced in the other until the client is functioning in a socially acceptable and personally comfortable manner.

6. *Empirical basis of practice.* The stress in this approach to group work on specific operational goals is also related to the contention that practice principles are to be derived scientifically. The existence of such goals makes possible the generation of a series of propositions about the effects of practitioner actions on client and client group outcomes. Particularly pertinent are findings from research in clinical and experimental psychology, sociology, and social psychology, which can be tested for applicability to group work situations.

Social Science Bases of Group Work Practice

Significant portions of social science theory and research and group work practice share the view that problematic behavior is generated and maintained through interactions between the client and individuals and/or institutions. Vinter has termed this "an interactional view of deviance." All social science efforts that explain either the individual and institutional effects on problematic behaviors or the small-group processes that can modify the individual's response to such phenomena are important to the group worker. The group worker must know about systems other than the small group because his and his clients' activities are interrelated with those of other systems. The following are some of the major areas of social science investigation pertinent to group work practice.

1. *Role theory*. Role theory seeks to explain how behavior is elicited and maintained in categories of individuals by the responses of other individuals. A detailed exposition of role theory is contained in the 1966 study by Bruce Biddle and Edwin Thomas. Social reactions to such positions as "delinquent," "unwed mother," and "hospital patient" are diagnostically important to the group worker. He is also cognizant of such positions in the small group as "task leader," "social emotional leader," or "scapegoat," and their effects on group members who occupy such positions.

2. *Social systems theory*. Social systems theory deals with how systems are created as well as the processes by which they develop and establish linkages with their environments. In the course of their development, systems evolve structures to deal with such functions as goal determination, energy inputs, communications, and system maintenance. Because the group is really a small social system, the group worker can utilize this type of knowledge to achieve instrumental group goals by encouraging the development of structures that assist members in attaining individual goals. This knowledge is also useful when the worker, alone or with members, wishes to change his own or other community agencies or institutions to maximize benefits to clients. Systems theory applications to group work are discussed by Lawrence Shulman (1968).

3. *Social-behavioral theory*. Learning theories are now making a strong impact on group work. These theories seek to explain behavior in terms of the conditions that elicit behavior and the consequences that the behavior evokes. Such stimuli and responses may make it more or less likely that behavior will reoccur. Applications of this approach can be found in Edwin Thomas' 1967 work and in the 1969 study by Robert Burgess and Don Bushell. In applying this knowledge, group workers help members behave differently in highly specific problematic situations by the manipulation of reinforcing or aversive stimuli in the group sessions. Group members may be taught how to help each other in a similar manner within and outside the group.

4. *Cognitive theories*. Many conceptualizations of group work have emphasized the vital significance for achieving group work goals through group problem-solving and conflict resolution. Theories dealing with these processes, especially as they occur in small groups, have been advanced by Helen Northen (1969), L. Richard Hoffman (1965), and John Spiegel (1960), among others, and are particularly useful to workers. Since there

are important issues regarding the connection between intrapersonal and interpersonal problem-solving and conflict processes, the worker must understand both. The individual's coping mechanisms, as he is confronted with the need to relate himself to group conflict and problem-solving, are also of interest here. Theories of ego psychology, as well as theories specifically dealing with the etiology of social deviance and mental illness, are important in this context.

5. *The social psychology of influence.* Of use to group workers is information about the effects of small-group processes on individual behavior. The attention of behavioral scientists has been called to such phenomena occurring in groups as pressures toward conformity, responses to deviation from group norms, group control mechanisms, socialization processes in groups, and contagion effects in groups. An understanding of these phenomena is essential to the attainment of instrumental group goals.

Group Work Practice Components

Practice approaches in group work deal with (1) the sequential arrangement of the tasks confronting the worker and (2) the appropriate levels of social organization on which the worker seeks to have an effect in order to accomplish these tasks.

The treatment sequence. As the client moves from applicant for service, to recipient of service, to group member status, to the point at which group service is terminated, the worker must take the client's status into consideration. At any phase of this cycle, however, he is concerned with (1) assessing the client's (or applicant's) situation with reference to problems, causal conditions of problems, and goals; (2) planning his own activities in relation to this assessment; (3) executing his plan; and (4) evaluating the outcome and, when necessary, revising his plan based on this evaluation. How the worker engages in these procedures depends on the stage reached in the client's career and the stage reached in the development of the group.

Intake. At the time of intake, the worker's assessment will include information on the nature of the applicant's problem, the circumstances under which the problem occurs, and what responses in the environment are evoked by the applicant's means of coping with the problem. This material should be gathered from the client and relevant others, and the objectivity of each source should be evaluated. The worker should observe the client's interactions with the social systems within the organization itself, as well as in the community.

The worker is interested in obtaining reliable and valid information and helping the client develop trust in the agency and the benign attributes of the worker. (Depending on the agency, the intake worker may or may not be the same as the treatment worker.) The worker evaluates the effectiveness of his actions on the basis of how much and what kind of information is produced and on how willing the applicant is to identify with client status and engage himself with the agency.

During this period the worker must also leave open the question of whether the client will receive individual, group, or family treatment or no service at all from this agency. He should be offered group services only when this is desirable, not just because it is available. To evaluate whether a client can best benefit from group work, the worker must see if he seems ready to engage in group problem-solving, if he is able to accept from or offer to peers information or emotional support, and if he can accept a relationship with a worker in a group rather than in a one-to-one situation. Troubled adolescents, by virtue of their reliance on peers, often make good use of group work, as do psychotics who seek opportunities to relate to others under protected circumstances and parents who wish to find out how other adults are handling behavior problems of children in order to improve their own skills.

Group composition. Following the intake process, and if a decision has been arrived at for group work services, the composition of the group must be determined. The worker obtains information that helps him predict how individuals will behave in the group that he is projecting. Most useful is information on how an individual behaved in a previous group. Even when the worker formulates a sound set of compositional principles, he may not be able to act on them if he is working with a group he did not form, such as an adolescent gang or an institutional ward group, or if there are not enough referrals to the group to permit full choice. The worker acts, however, with the following two questions in mind: (1) What type of group composition will most likely enhance the attainment of individual goals and the establishment of a group purpose consistent with these goals? (2) Given a specific group composition, what types of group purposes can evolve that are consistent with what individual goals?

Several writers have indicated aspects of group composition relevant to these questions. Arnold Goldstein, Kenneth Heller and Leo Sechrest (1966) present information regarding the effects of degree of heterogeneity as well as sources of compatibility. Albert and Bernice Lott (1965:259–309) have reviewed many different sources of interpersonal attraction in groups. Harvey Bertcher and Frank Maple (Chapter 11 in this volume) have developed a framework for considering both behavioral and descriptive attributes in selecting group members. Helen Northen (1969) comments on considerations of stages of psychosocial development of members, coping mechanisms used by members, and group size in determining membership. She also discusses circumstances for working with such natural entities as those found in residential settings. Baruch Levine

(1968) investigated the relationship of social similarity to attraction and indicated implications for group work practice.

Group development and the attainment of individual goals. Once the group is formed, the worker assesses the individuals, the group, and environmental situations and, consistent with individual members' wishes, acts to change these situations and then evaluates their consequences.

In describing the worker's treatment interventions, it is helpful for conceptual purposes to discuss separately his actions with respect to different systems. Allen Pincus and Anne Minahan (1970:34–57) clarify the existence of four systems: (1) change agency system—"The system concept of the worker is utilized to emphasize that the change agent himself normally is not a detached professional worker, but is influenced in his change efforts by the system of which he is part;" (2) client system—who "contracts" with the social worker and is the expected beneficiary of the worker's services; (3) target system—"the person, family, group, organization, or community (or some subpart or combinations of systems) at which the social worker directs his change efforts;" (4) action system— "the system the social worker works with and through in order to influence the target."

Means of Influence

In the rehabilitation and prevention approach to group work, the client system is virtually always the individual who is experiencing or likely to experience the problem in functioning. (An exception is a group made up of married couples.) Under some circumstances the worker may act as if the target, action, and client systems were this individual. Vinter has referred to such interventions as using "direct means of influence." On other occasions the action system is the group, although the target and client systems remain the individual. For Vinter this means using "indirect means of influence." Finally, the worker's action system may be individuals other than group members, his own agency, or other institutions in the community. The target system then can be either the individual client or the group. Vinter and Galinsky (Chapter 17 in this volume) describe such instances as utilizing "extra-groups means of influence."

Direct means of influence. Vinter details four fundamental types of direct means of influence (Chapter 2 in this volume):

1. *The worker as central person—object of identification and drives.* Worker actions appropriate to this category are encouragement, relating to feelings, model presentation, and verbal reward.

2. *The worker as symbol and spokesman—agent of legitimate norms and values.* Some direct actions are clarifying goals of treatment, describing rules and policies, warning, and confronting with long-range consequences of present behavior.

3. *The worker as motivator-stimulator—definer of individual goals and tasks.* Appropriate worker actions include exhorting, interpreting the psychological causes of behavior, exposing client to other organizations, and behavioral assignments.

4. *The worker as executive—controller of membership roles.* Worker interventions in this category are giving responsibility, providing new sociorecreational experiences, subgroupings, and prompting.

Indirect means of influence. It is the indirect means of influence—those means used with the group as the action system—that uniquely characterize group work. When the worker modifies group conditions to help members achieve their goals, he is using indirect means of influence. Group conditions are the group's composition and size, purposes, structures, and processes. Seldom does the composition of a group remain constant. Members drop out and the worker may add members or encourage members to withdraw when this is appropriate for the attainment of individual goals. Group purposes are more clearly identified as member-member and member-worker interactions that occur around the relationships of group goals to individual goals. After the group has come into existence, however, the worker is in a better position to assess the effects of structures and processes on the achievement of goals.

The use of group structures. Patterns develop and maintain themselves over time in interpersonal situations. In group work these regularities can support or hinder the client and worker in attaining their goals. The worker must learn how to develop, maintain, and modify these patterns, usually termed structures, to attain the instrumental and treatment goals of the group. Among the important structures are the communications, sociometric, power, role, and normative structures. The following are some means by which workers modify group structures:

1. *Program.* A task that requires a specified series of steps for its completion—a program—can be used to establish or change group structures. For example, a game that requires one participant to be a leader can change the power structure of the group. An activity that rewards a participant for communicating with others can change the communication structure.

2. *Behavioral modification.* Operant conditioning procedures can be used to modify group structures. Leadership behavior, communication behavior, and task performances, for example, have been modified by these procedures.

3. *Problem-solving, conflict resolution, and logical reasoning approaches.* A group can and often does confront its own structural problems and change such patterns and rules. It may begin with a series of individual behavioral or attitudinal changes, or the group may purposely use programmatic, conditioning, or other interactive methods to change its manner of functioning.

4. *Changes in composition.* Structural changes can also be effected by the addition or subtraction of group members or through a change in the size of the group.

5. *Group development.* When groups exist over time, patterned changes occur in the social organization of the group, the processes of the group, and the group culture. The group worker, by knowing how the group is proceeding with reference to these changes, can enhance the attainment of treatment goals. He can frequently help the members to determine, for example, how far the group must develop for members' objectives to be attained. He can also anticipate changes that are likely to occur in the group and help the members deal with them in a therapeutic manner.

The use of group processes. Group processes—the sequence of behaviors of individuals in interaction with other individuals in groups—may occur within a few minutes, as clients and workers arrive at a quick decision, a subgroup identifies itself, or a behavioral norm is enunciated and clarified. A sequence may also occur over several treatment sessions or the life history of the group, as purposes are clarified, membership is determined, or complex problems are solved. Changes in structures can be identified as processes, although many other group processes have been described.

Propositions can be generated about causes of particular processes and specific social events can be described only if clear categories of analysis are used. The concepts presented here are based upon a series of dimensions detailed by Rosemary Sarri and Maeda Galinsky in Chapter 5 on group development.

1. *Processes related to changes in the social organization of the client-worker system: Sociometric processes*—those having to do with changes in the affectional choices of some participants for others; *processes of role differentiation*—those that occur as either new positions are created or new participants occupy such positions; *communication processes*—those having to do with changes in the patterns of who communicates with whom and about what.

2. *Processes related to activities and tasks: Program task progression*—that sequence of events set in motion in response to performance requirements of the activity; *problem-solving processes*—processes occurring as problems are identified and solutions attempted.

3. *Processes related to the development of group culture:* changes in the structure and content of norms and values held by participants relevant to their behavior in the treatment system and changes in the goals held by clients, individually and collectively, for the treatment system.

Some authors have also considered the emotions as a group process. Theodore Mills (1967), for example, includes in his concept of group emotion (1) the needs and drives that serve in the first place as causes of group formation; (2) feelings of satisfaction or frustration resulting from actual group experience; (3) interpersonal attachments and animosities; and (4) feelings of attachment to or alienation from the group as a whole.

The task of the worker, then, is as follows: The worker, with an awareness of appropriate goals, determines which processes enhance or hinder the attainment of goals. The worker develops a series of propositions regarding forces that are maintaining or could maintain such processes. Depending on the goals of the client-worker system, the worker with or on behalf of the clients seeks to increase the occurrence of specified processes or to decrease them.

Extra-group means of influence.   The use of "extra-group means of influence" refers to "modification of the behavior or attitudes of persons in the client's social environment, or large social systems within which both clients and other individuals occupy statuses, which may in turn lead to positive changes in the group member's own behavior and attitudes." (Glasser, 1968:2–3) Such activities should be integral to all rehabilitative and preventive efforts. The worker, with or without the help of members or the total group, attempts to change specified others in the client's environment (parent, teacher, employer), his own agency's treatment of group members, or other institutions' responses to those whom he serves. Sociological theory has stressed the need for institutional change to diminish the problems of large numbers of people who seek help from social welfare agencies. Behavior modification approaches have emphasized modification of those behaviors of persons in the client's environment which are antecedent to or consequences of the client's own behavior as a means to achieve client change.

Termination and Evaluation

An individual may leave the group while the group continues or the entire group may conclude simultaneously. The decision to discontinue may be made by the worker, the client, or the group; attitudes regarding termination of a given group may differ widely.

Ideally, termination occurs because the treatment goals have been achieved. The worker's task, then, is to reduce the non-functional attachments that the client may have formed to the worker and other members and that may prevent him from realizing his new potential. The worker may also attempt to strengthen the changes that have occurred. Evidence that the termination decision was correct lies in the higher value the client places on leaving the group than on staying, as well as data indicating that he can transfer behavior into contexts other than the treatment group.

When the client's goals have not been achieved, it is the responsibility of the worker to encourage him to seek help from other sources. For example, he may obtain alternative services from the same agency or different services from other community institutions.

At times the entire group is terminated because the group has developed sufficient resources of its own. It is then able to function without the help of a professional, although members may be referred to community institutions, such as community centers, for less intensive service.

It is incumbent upon the worker to evaluate the effectiveness and efficiency of his services periodically throughout the treatment as well as at termination. This allows him to modify his goals and treatment plans and to discard ineffective technologies.

Some Evaluation Studies

A number of studies have been completed on the practice of group work in rehabilitation and prevention using some or all of the methods described above. Elizabeth Navarre and Paul Glasser (1969), reporting on the effectiveness of this method with welfare clients—particularly mothers receiving Aid to Families with Dependent Children grants—found that groups with precise goals and focus were helpful in increasing mothers' responsibilities for their children, especially concerning school-related tasks. Robert Vinter and Rosemary Sarri (1969) have also reported on the effectiveness of this approach for improving school performance of children. The Seattle Atlantic Street Center staff reported that, as a result of intensive social work services, including group work, there were less severe disciplinary problems among acting-out youths. In another sphere, Charles Garvin (1969:127–145) demonstrated that agreement on purposes between workers and members was more associated with group movement in problem-solving than when such agreement was lacking. It is evident, however, that these studies are merely a beginning of research on the effectiveness of group work in rehabilitation and prevention. Work should be done to replicate existing studies as well as to determine the precise interrelationships between client variables, composition characteristics, and alternate group work methods.

Future Developments

Large bodies of research and outcomes of related theory development in the social sciences are now available to the group worker. The major task is the engineering of this knowledge into usable practice theory and the evaluation of these new methods and techniques—particularly in the fields of learning theory, small-group theory, social influence theory, and organizational theory. The application of these theories and findings should help the group worker use his methods with greater precision and have more assurance about his results .

Within practice theory in group work itself, new concepts are helping the worker be more specific regarding his activities. Thus he can inform other practitioners about his techniques and can better engage in evaluative research. Codifying these concepts to facilitate communications among professionals is still a problem, but the situation has begun to improve. Group work practice knowledge should be accumulated more rapidly and efficiently than it has been up to now.

The effectiveness of rehabilitative and preventive group work depends on how well workers can systematically intervene in many social systems. Until now, vital systems (for example, the community system) have either been ignored or workers with different specializations have operated in the same territory without successfully coordinating their efforts. Social work education and the conceptualization of practice appear to be developing resources to cope with this problem.

REFERENCES

AMERICAN ASSOCIATION OF SOCIAL WORKERS
    1952—*Social Workers in 1950*, New York: American Association of Social Workers, Table D-24.

BALES, ROBERT F.
    1958—"Task and social roles in problem-solving groups," in Eleanor E. Maccoby, Theodore M. Newcomb, and Eugene L. Hartle (Eds.), *Readings in Social Psychology*, third edition, New York: Holt, Rinehart and Winston, pp. 437–66.

BIDDLE, BRUCE AND EDWIN J. THOMAS
    1966—*Role Theory: Concepts and Research*, New York: John Wiley & Sons.

BION, W. R.
    1959—*Experiences in Groups*, New York: Basic Books.

BURGESS, ROBERT L. AND DON BUSHELL, JR.
    1969—*Behavioral Sociology: The Experimental Analysis of Social Process*, New York: Columbia University Press.

BURROW, T.
    1928—"The basis of group analysis," *British Journal of Medical Psychology* 8, III(November) pp. 198–206.

CARTWRIGHT, DARWIN AND ALVIN ZANDER (EDS.)
    1960—*Group Dynamics: Research and Theory*, Evanston, Illinois: Row, Peterson.

COUNCIL ON SOCIAL WORK EDUCATION
    1969—*Statistics on Social Work Education*, New York: Council on Social Work Education.

FREY, LOUISE (ED.)
    1966—*Use of Groups in the Health Field*, New York: National Association of Social Workers.

FREY, LOUISE AND MARGUERITE MEYER
    1965—"Exploration and working agreement in two social work methods," in Saul Bernstein (Ed.), *Exploration in Group Work*, Boston: Boston University School of Social Work.

GARVIN, CHARLES

1969—"Complementarity of role expectations in groups: The member-worker contract," in *Social Work Practice: 1969,* New York: Columbia University Press, pp. 127–45.

GLASSER, PAUL, H.

1963—"Group methods in child welfare: Review and preview," *Child Welfare,* 42, 5(May), pp. 213–19.

GLASSER, PAUL, ET AL.

1968—"Group work intervention in the social environment," Ann Arbor: University of Michigan School of Social Work, pp. 2–3. (Mimeographed)

GOLDSTEIN, ARNOLD P., KENNETH HELLER AND LEO B. SECHREST

1966—*Psychotherapy and the Psychology of Behavior Change,* New York: John Wiley & Sons.

HASTORF, ALBERT H.

1966—"The reinforcement of individual actions in a group situation," in Leonard P. Ullman and Leonard Krasner (Eds.), *Research in Behavior Modification: New Developments and Implications,* New York: Holt, Rinehart & Winston, pp. 268–84.

HOFFMAN, L. RICHARD

1965—"Group problem solving," in Leonard Berkowitz (Ed.), *Advances in Experimental Social Psychology,* 2, New York: Academic Press, pp. 99–132.

LEVINE, BARUCH

1968—"Factors related to interpersonal balance in social work treatment groups," University of Chicago. (Unpublished doctoral dissertation)

LOTT, ALBERT J. AND BERNICE E. LOTT

1965—"Group cohesiveness as interpersonal attraction: A review of relationships with antecedent and congruent variables," *Psychological Bulletin,* 64, 4(October), pp. 259–309.

MAIER, HENRY (ED.)

1966—*Group Work as Part of Residential Treatment,* New York: National Association of Social Workers.

MILLS, THEODORE M.

1967—*The Sociology of Small Groups,* Englewood Cliffs, New Jersey: Prentice-Hall.

NATIONAL SOCIAL WELFARE ASSEMBLY

1961—*Salaries and Working Conditions of Social Welfare Manpower in 1960,* New York: National Social Welfare Assembly, Table 28.

NAVARRE, ELIZABETH AND PAUL GLASSER

1969—"Group work practice with AFDC mothers: An evaluation study," (May), New York City: Paper presented at the 96th Annual Forum of the National Conference on Social Welfare.

NORTHEN, HELEN

1969—*Social Work with Groups,* New York: Columbia University Press.

PINCUS, ALLEN AND ANNE MINAHAN

1970—"Toward a model for teaching a basic first-year course in methods of social work practice," in Lillian Ripple (Ed.), *Innovations in Teaching*

Social Work Practice, New York: Council on Social Work Education, pp. 34–57.

RAVEN, BERTRAM H. AND JAN RIETSEMA
1960—"The effects of varied clarity of group goal and group path upon the individual and his relations to the group," in Dorwin Cartwright and Alvin Zander (Eds.), *Group Dynamics: Research and Theory,* second edition, Evanston, Illinois: Row, Peterson, pp. 395–412.

SCHMIDT, JULIANNA T.
1969—"The use of purpose in casework," *Social Work,* 14, 1(January), pp. 77–84.

SEATTLE ATLANTIC STREET CENTER
1965—"Seattle atlantic street center recording system" in *Effectiveness of Social Work with Acting-out Youth, Third Year Progress Report,* September 1964 to August 1965, Seattle, Washington: Seattle Atlantic Street Center. (Mimeographed)

SHAW, MARVIN E.
1964—"Communication networks," in Leonard Berkowitz (Ed.), *Advances in Experimental Social Psychology,* New York: Academic Press, pp. 111–149.

SHULMAN, LAWRENCE
1968—*A Casebook of Social Work with Groups: The Mediating Model,* New York: Council on Social Work Education.

SLATER, PHILIP E.
1965—"Role differentiation in small groups," in A. Paul Hare (Ed.), *Small Groups: Studies in Social Interaction,* revised edition, New York. Alfred A. Knopf.

SLAVSON, S. R. (ED.)
1947—*The Practice of Group Therapy,* New York: International Universities Press.

SPIEGEL, JOHN P.
1960—"The resolution of role conflict within the family," in Norman W. Bell and Ezra F. Vogel (Eds.), *A Modern Introduction to the Family,* Glencoe, Illinois: Free Press, pp. 361–381.

THOMAS, EDWIN J. (ED.)
1967—*The Social Behavioral Approach and Its Application to Social Work,* New York: Council on Social Work Education.
1960—*Use of Groups in the Psychiatric Setting,* New York: National Association of Social Workers.

VINTER, ROBERT D.
1959—"Group work: perspectives and prospects," *Social Work With Groups,* New York: National Association of Social Workers, pp. 128–148.
1965—"Social group work," in *Encyclopedia of Social Work,* New York: National Association of Social Workers, pp. 715–723.

VINTER, ROBERT D. AND ROSEMARY SARRI
1969—"Group work for the control of behavior problems in secondary schools," in David Street (Ed.), *Innovations in Mass Education,* New York: John Wiley & Sons, pp. 91–119.

4.

Behavioral Theory and Group Work

ROSEMARY C. SARRI

All social workers, including group workers, have rapidly increasing interest in the use of behavior modification and sociobehavioral knowledge in social work practice. Just as the period of 1950–1970 witnessed great growth in the research and knowledge of the small group and group behavior, the past decade has seen a very rapid increase in sociobehavioral knowledge of individual change. Many practitioners who wish to use behavior modification in group treatment often encounter difficulty because of prior training in other techniques of interpersonal change.

This chapter will examine some of the areas of behavioral theory which appear most relevant to group treatment. Primary attention will be given to behavior modification that effects interpersonal change through the group, but the approach is eclectic and assumes that each practitioner must tailor his treatment to fit various individuals, organizations providing services, and social environments. Behavior modification has received front-page attention, and the tendency may be to use it without reference to constraints which arise because of these variations. Many of these methods have been empirically tested and are known to be extremely effective when used appropriately. Far too often social workers respond to new technologies as if they were fads or panaceas. It would be most unfortunate if behavior modification in the group were viewed as the panacea for the resolution of the myriad social problems addressed by social workers. Several chapters in this volume (see in particular Chapters 7, 13, 14, 20, 21, 25, 29, and 30) consider use of behavior modification for specific areas of practice. The concern here will include more general exploration of the utility of behavioral theory for group treatment. Some excellent statements of the guidelines for the use of behavioral theory are now available: Gambrill, et al., 1971; Rose, 1972; Bandura, 1969; Franks, 1969; Kolb and Schwitzgebel, 1972; Lazarus, 1971; Patterson and Guillon, 1968; Thomas, 1967; Thorp and Wetzel, 1969; Ullman and Krasner, 1965; Ulrich, et al., 1970.

Theories, research findings and perspectives of the behavioral sciences have a significant impact today upon all the helping professions, including social work. This enhancing resource has only been tapped thus far, but behavioral science knowledge is particularly useful for several elements of social work practice:

1. Interpersonal human relations techniques are the principal means employed to effect change in clients.
2. The tools for change are basically environmental, involving the manipulation of stimuli external rather than internal to the client.
3. Help is planned and intervention is conceived in relation to the problems of the client and the objective of professional service. (Thomas, 1964)

The variables that characterize interpersonal helping are the same as those for other social influence efforts to change environmental and interpersonal relationships. Behavior involved in interpersonal helping also is assumed to be natural, predictable, and lawful and may be investigated and understood the same as social influence in the general context of behavioral control. Thus, a wide range of behavioral science knowledge becomes potentially applicable in group treatment: learning theory and research, experimental psychology, personality theory, social role and small-group theory, mass communication research, knowledge about social organizational behavior, social system theory and theories of social deviancy, to mention only a few areas of study and research.

One consequence of the increased utilization of behavioral science knowledge in social work group treatment is the recognition that group experiences and individual behavior are related. It is generally accepted today that clients have many varied types of group experiences which can be utilized to facilitate social work treatment. Workers in institutions are particularly attentive to the development of treatment methods which will incorporate formal and informal group influence processes and group experiences. In 1935, August Aichorn emphasized the importance of the group environment in an institution and, even as early as 1905, an internist, Pratt, used group treatment methods in a tuberculosis sanitorium. Despite these early beginnings, only within the past two decades has social work, generally, recognized the influence of the group on individual behavior and attempted to apply small-group theory systematically. Hopefully, increased use of behavioral science knowledge will continue rapidly in the future. Systematic application of behavioral theory is relatively new for all the helping professions, but it appears to offer the greatest potential for enhanced social practice where individual and interpersonal behavior change is the goal. Many methods or elements of this theory have been known to skilled therapists for years; what is new is the conceptual framework for predicting and guiding behavior, the use of findings from experimental research, and systematically codified practice knowledge.

The definition by Franks (1969:29) is appropriate: behavior modification is "focused upon the techniques, principles and processes directly relevant to the alteration of deviant or distressing clinical behavior." Thus, it potentially includes a broad range of types of treatment.

A summary of basic behavior modification theory follows so that practitioners unfamiliar with it may picture what this theory offers. Examples and tentative generalizations are given regarding its use in group treatment.

The basic elements of most direct social work service involve interpersonal helping and can be viewed as including the reduction, acquisition, and maintenance of behavior. Sociobehavioral theory asserts that normal and maladaptive behavior is natural, learned and predictable and that environmental conditions control behavior. Social workers have long been concerned with manipulation of the client's environment, and the concept of "social functioning" itself refers to individual behavior in social settings. However, social work has been more concerned with general environmental conditions. Behavioral theory requires that the *specific* conditions controlling behavior be identified and managed. This theory is based on extensive empirical research which has been conducted for many years (Ferster and Perrot, 1968; Eysenck, 1960; Ulrich et al., 1970; Franks, 1969). It seeks to explain and predict overt behavior of persons, groups, organizations and other social systems. The achievement of behavior modification and stabilization has been and is an objective of social work practice at all intervention levels.

The differences between sociobehavior theory and other theories are highlighted when the areas of diagnosis and change goals are considered. No postulation of an internal disease process is given with respect to pathology. Symptoms are viewed as undesirable or maladaptive behavior, but they are not assumed to relate to some underlying internal problem. Behavior is labelled deviant or pathological because of its consequences for the individual, significant others, or society. These consequences are a function of learned maladaptive behavior, behavioral deficits, or of social conflict. In assessment (diagnosis) the worker seeks to specify the behavior which is maladaptive, and the specific environmental conditions which control this behavior. In addition, the worker specifies the desired behavior and the appropriate environmental conditions for its occurrence. Change goals must be explicitly related to diagnosis (Siporin, 1965; Franks, 1969).

Behavior, as viewed, involves a relationship between an individual, a group or other social system and a particular environment. Thus, assessment (diagnosis) must specify the significant behavior of those who judge the behavior as problematic, and the controlling conditions in the environment. Problematic behavior is not viewed as inherently pathological, deviant or maladaptive; instead it is so perceived through the process of social definition. A behavior, or what some authors term a social learning, approach refers to service techniques that focus on behavioral change. Regardless of particular procedures employed, behavior modification focuses on changing behavior, rather than on changing internal states of the person who is the object for intervention. No assumptions are postulated about internal causes of behavior, nor is behavior viewed as only symptomatic of underlying problems. Behavioral theories depict responses as depending on environmental conditions, rather than internal forces. Each person learns different modes of coping with environmental demands and constraints. These learned behaviors may be adaptive or maladaptive, helpful or detrimental, to the individual, but they are not viewed as manifestations of an underlying pathology. Instead, they are ways the person copes with environmental and self-imposed demands. Thus, psychopathology is not a property inherent in the individual, but rather the assessment of behavior by societal agents. Bandura (1969) states that both anti- and prosocial behavior are acquired and maintained through the operation of three distinct regulatory systems: (1) external stimulus control; (2) response feedback processes in the form of reinforcing consequences; and (3) central neural processes where stimuli are coded and organized, propositions tested, and performance initiated. Behavior thus is a consequence of the interaction between environment conditions and the individual actor's learned modes of response.

In the sociobehavioral approach, attention is directed more toward contemporaneous variables which elicit or reinforce behavior rather than toward the past experience and background of an individual. There is considerable evidence to support the assumption that marked behavioral changes can be accomplished without engaging in long-term, intensive study of childhood and without developing "insights" about *"the problem,"* however desirable these might appear to be (Ulrich, 1970; Ullman and Krasner, 1965; Wolpe, 1969).

The concept of inappropriate behavior as learned maladaptive behavior is essential. Maladaptive behavior is acquired through the same processes as adaptive behavior. For example, a complex set of inappropriate behaviors may characterize a schizophrenic, but this behavior is learned in separate sets through direct reinforcement by significant persons in the environment. Another type of maladaptive behavior is phobic behavior. Phobias are viewed as conditioned responses to initially innocuous stimuli. Delinquent behavior, too, can be viewed in terms of reinforcement principles. Many important prolegal social reinforcers are not available to lower-class youth through law-abiding behavior, so they engage in criminal behavior.

Behavior deficits, another class of inappropriate behavior, result because a required adaptive response has not been learned. For example, a person who has been isolated and socially withdrawn as a child is less likely to have practiced, been reinforced for, and learned effective social skills. A number of successful efforts have been reported in using behavior therapy with autistic children. Ferster and De Myer (1962) and Hingsten (1965) have used operant conditioning methods to widen the behavior repertoire of autistic children and to achieve cooperative behavior.

Attention here will be focused on the methods of change employed in behavioral theory and, to accomplish this, some basic concepts must be defined. The concepts considered here are drawn from the work of Skinner (1953), Eysenck (1960), Bandura and Walters (1963), Wolpe (1969), Staats (1964) and others already referred to. It is impossible to be comprehensive in this review of the literature relevant to group work practice, and only a limited number of concepts and behavioral methods are examined. Utility for the practitioner was the primary criterion in this selection.

One of the first distinctions that must be made is between respondent and operant behavior. *Respondent behavior* involves the so-called reflex behavior and consists of "nonvoluntary responses" involving primarily the glands and smooth muscles of the autonomic nervous system. Salivation, eye blinks, and hunger contractions are examples. *Operant behavior* involves "voluntary" movement of the skeletal muscles by the central nervous system. The individual's general behavior is sustained or modified by environmental consequences in the form of reinforcement or punishment.

A broad range of behavior has the characteristic of being influenced by its consequences. Particular consequences tend to bring about rather predictable changes in the rate, frequency, and other characteristics of the behavior. If Mary's whining provokes Mother's attention, this consequence may tend to maintain or even increase the frequency of whining behavior. Unpleasant or negative consequences tend to decrease behavior, whereas pleasant or positive responses increase it. For example, if Mary is punished immediately after whining, that behavior will diminish in time providing the punishment occurs immediately. In other words, the consequences to which behavior is exposed may be reinforcing or aversive. Other things being equal, behavior is as shapeable as the consequences are immediate. The desired effects of a reinforcement may be lost if the elements of timing are not considered.

Because social workers are more likely to be concerned with operant behavior, this will be considered primarily. This does not imply lesser importance for respondent behavior; some social workers will be particularly interested in group desensitization and relaxation techniques to deal with anxiety and other problems (Wolpe, 1969; Paul and Shannon, 1966;

Cohen, 1969). It is impossible, however, to discuss all of the basic concepts important in operant behavior, because there are many and the empirical findings regarding their utilization are extensive. Thus only the concept of *reinforcement* will receive detailed examination, while other concepts directly related to reinforcement will be considered briefly.

The interrelated concepts of stimulus and response are basic to sociobehavioral theory. A response is any measurable change in the activity of the organism as a reaction to a stimulus. Reinforcement, a key response-related concept, refers to specific rewards or supports that affect the strength of the response. Reinforcement must also be understood with reference to the stimulus. A *reinforcer* is a stimulus which changes the probability of occurrence of the response which it follows.

Positive reinforcers increase the frequency of the response, and *negative reinforcers* increase the desired response through removal of negative or aversive stimuli. For example, a mother provides positive reinforcement for Johnny when she praises him for cleaning up his room after she requests him to do so. If Mother has an angry expression on her face until Johnny finishes eating his vegetables, and then it disappears, this would be an example of negative reinforcement of Johnny's eating.

Reinforcers can also be classified as primary and secondary. *Primary reinforcers* are those which are generally effective for all persons, e.g., food, clothing, and shelter. *Secondary reinforcers* are those which come to have reinforcing power through prior pairing with primary reinforcers, e.g., attention, affection, etc. Money is a secondary reinforcer because it has high exchange potential for the holder. Knowledge of social class, cultural, and other differences among persons and groups indicates that secondary reinforcers are highly variable depending upon prior reinforcing history. For example, verbal positive reinforcement or praise for delaying gratification may have little meaning to a lower-class child, because he has not experienced such behavior as positively reinforcing in the past.

Schedules of reinforcement must also be considered briefly. Reinforcement of a behavior may be continuous or variable. Reinforcement is continuous when it occurs each time the desired behavior is emitted. Reinforcement is variable when it occurs periodically, but not each time. The periodicity may be highly routinized as on a "variable ratio schedule" or it may not be regularly patterned. Empirical evidence suggests that behavior which is reinforced on a variable or intermittent schedule is highly resistant to change. This knowledge is important if punishment is used to remove maladaptive behavior or to reinforce new adaptive behavior.

One procedure of operant conditioning applied to modify behavior is *shaping*. This involves a very careful plan where only those responses are reinforced which move in the direction of the goal or successively approximate the goal. All others are not reinforced. Selective reinforcement through shaping is a powerful tool, but it is often difficult to use because of inability to control the environment sufficiently so that only the desired responses are reinforced and no others. A related change procedure, *coaching,* refers to the use of a battery of reinforcement techniques in a planned but less rigorous manner than in shaping. Here the changer monitors the behavior and applies diverse techniques at strategic points to aid in the control process. Learning to swim, to drive or to play a musical instrument often involves coaching procedures. (Chapters 13 and 14 describe coaching procedures in group program activities.)

Extinction is a change procedure whereby reinforcement is withheld each time a previously reinforced but now undesired behavior occurs. Consider the following example. A husband complained to a social worker that his wife's behavior of talking incessantly annoyed him considerably, and the wife complained that she wanted her husband to pay more attention to her. The worker learned that the husband was unconsciously reinforcing the "talking" behavior on an intermittent scale. When he came home in the evening, his wife would start talking immediately, but he ignored her as much as possible and started to read the newspaper. After variable periods of time, he would give in to her request for attention. The worker proposed that the husband spend some time with his wife, complimenting her, and so forth as soon as he came home each evening. Then, he was to read the paper and while doing so, he was not to respond to the "talking" behavior. Gradually, and after a few slips, marked reductions in continuous talking occurred in the wife's behavior. The husband reported that he began to enjoy talking with his wife and also was able to tell her directly when some of her "talking" behavior annoyed him particularly.

Because extinction may be confused with punishment, it is important that the two procedures be distinguished carefully. *Punishment* has a special and limited meaning as a concept in behavioral theory. It involves suppression of an undesired behavior through the presentation of an aversive stimulus following the behavior. Extinction, in contrast, involves the withholding of a reinforcer for a previously reinforced behavior. For example, what a parent views as punishment, scolding, may actually be in some fashion reinforcing to the child, and the behavior will be maintained rather than eliminated. It is, however, important to consider the meaning of the behavior change procedure to the individual whose behavior is being changed. In some cases, it is possible that the withholding of reinforcement could be perceived as punishment and would have harmful effects. Since the effects of punishment are markedly different from those of extinction procedures, the changer must be able to estimate the probable effect.

In deciding how and when to use any of the behavior change techniques identified above, a number of factors must be considered in addition to those already mentioned. The type and amount of reinforcement necessary to effect the desired change must be known. The probability of being able to schedule and deliver reinforcement as required must also be examined before a plan is implemented. The importance of such consideration in treatment planning is apparent when one reviews reports and findings of behavioral treatment. Now a few studies are reviewed in which behavioral theory has been explicitly utilized in treatment.

BEHAVIORAL MODIFICATION AND TREATMENT

The principles and techniques of behavior modification were first developed and validated in laboratory settings and then applied to clinical settings. Therapy based on behavior modification principles has been used to treat neurotic states such as phobias, obsessions and compulsions, and tics. Problems involving bodily functions which have been treated include various types of sexual problems, anorexia nervosa, and eneuresis. It has also been used to treat various types of motor behavior such as tantrums, hyperactivity, hoarding, aggression, physical and emotional withdrawal, and problems of verbal behavior such as stuttering, mutism, delusional speech, and autism. It also is being used widely in the treatment of delinquent and criminal behavior. Use for a wide variety of educational learning problems is also growing (Woody, 1969; Patterson, 1968).

Examination of a few of the clinical experiments will show how behavioral theory is actually utilized in treatment. Illustrations will be limited to cases in which all or part of the effort involved use of the group. Earlier it was emphasized that assessment is a crucial step because the problematic behavior must be delineated as unambiguously as possible. Similarly, the controlling conditions in the environment must be specifically identified to determine the presence of eliciting and reinforcing stimuli so that adaptive behavior can be brought under the control of the reinforcing environment. Why this is so important will become apparent in the following summary of research findings.

Treatment of phobias is a frequently reported type of behavior therapy, reflecting influence and work of Wolpe and his methods of reciprocal inhibition therapy (Wolpe, 1958). For persons interested in group treatment, the following findings from a study conducted by A. A. Lazarus (1965) are relevant. He compared the results in treating claustrophobia and acrophobia by behavior modification only, by group psychotherapy, and by a combination of the two types of treatment. Systematic desensitization was the behavioral technique used in combination with relaxation. Systematic desensitization is a clinical procedure used to reduce anxiety through deep muscle relaxation and counterconditioning procedures, followed by presentation of anxiety-inducing stimuli through imagery in a hierarchical order from least to most disturbing. Far higher rates of success were obtained when systematic desensitization was used than when the other types were used, despite the fact that it required the fewest number of client contact hours. Procedures for the systematic desensitization in groups included: (1) training in muscular relaxation for two sessions, each followed by practice at home; (2) anxiety hierarchies were constructed on the basis of responses of patients to a series of questions; (3) patients in groups were then exposed to the items in the hierarchy from the least severe to the most severe. In the case of the acrophobics, for example, they were shown pictures taken from high buildings and airplanes, and then gradually were directly exposed to increasing heights. The group was not permitted to move from one stage or item in the hierarchy until all were ready to move, measured by each person's ability to tolerate the new situation for a specified period of time.

Therapy in desensitization was terminated when the final item on the hierarchy was tolerated by all patients for at least ten seconds. All patients were reexamined one month later and again in fifteen months to evaluate recovery. Results from the experiment showed 13 recoveries and 5 failures for the desensitization procedures and 2 recoveries and 15 failures for the traditional group therapy. The combined desensitization-group therapy was not as successful as group desensitization only.

In a later experiment, Paul and Shannon (1966) employed group discussion with desensitization and achieved positive results in anxiety reduction. Cohen (1969) was able to show clearly that group interaction plus desensitization methods were more effective than desensitization only in reducing test anxiety. This set of experiments indicates that group methods combined with desensitization are successful in treating various types of phobia and anxiety. The evidence, however, is less conclusive with regard to change in other problems which may be manifested with the phobia or anxiety. This is in accord with Wolpe's (1958) suggestion, that desensitization is "phobic specific," not "person specific." Rose (1972) discusses a variety of desensitization methods for use in group treatment of children and considers how these may be phased with subsequent treatment for other behavioral problems.

Zimmerman and Zimmerman (1965) reported that unproductive classroom behavior of emotionally disturbed children in a special education setting was eliminated through the selective use of extinction and reinforcement. They ignored all undesired behavior and positively reinforced the desired classroom behavior immediately after its occurrence. Among the behaviors eliminated were: severe tantrums, baby talk, irrelevant verbal behavior and bizarre types of spelling.

In a group of twelve male patients diagnosed as schizophrenic, King, et al., (1965) observed pronounced physical and verbal withdrawal. He used an operant conditioning apparatus in which rewards were contingent upon the performance of a variety of behaviors. They paired the machine-delivered reward with reinforcement from the therapist in order to achieve generalization to social reinforcement from the therapist. They reported significant increases in verbal and physical activity by these patients in comparison to groups of equal size treated by verbal therapy, recreation therapy, and no therapy.

Bandura (1969) observed that when children experience the pairing of one adult with positive reinforcers, they will imitate that adult later more than an adult who has not been so paired. Lott and Lott (1964) reported that when child "A" was positively reinforced in the presence of "B," "A" later selected "B" as a companion. These experiments point to the relationship between social power theory and principles of learning, and are directly relevant for social work practice with groups. Polansky and Blum (1961) reported that staff role structure in a residential facility was an important determinant of how children would initiate and respond in interaction situations with staff. Staff were differentially perceived and employed as "reinforcing agents."

Where the problem is one of behavioral deficits, studies of *token economy* procedures provide excellent examples for increasing the performance of desired behavior (Ayllon and Azrin, 1968). Token economy is a system created to effect behavioral control through the use of tokens as reinforcers in groups or organizational settings. Many of the traditional therapeutic approaches view behavior problems in terms of various intra-psychic processes assumed to result in deviant behavior. Little attention is given to those whose social, personal and cultural deprivation is so serious that they never had the opportunity to learn behavior acceptable in the larger society. Many social work clients fall in the latter category; they are deficient in speech and language, manners for approaching employment situations, culturally acceptable means of expressing anger and hostility, and other social skills.

The work of Cohen, et al., (1968) at the National Training School for Boys demonstrated the utility of programmed learning and a token economy to increase the educational achievement of delinquent boys. They utilized a point system which was initially developed to encompass the entire 24-hour day for a cottage of 28 boys. Boys earned points to purchase desired material things and also services such as special tutoring. The total environment was planned to have specific effects on the boys' behavior. Points were earned only by the individual's satisfactory performance in specified activities. A record was kept of the earning and spending of points by each individual. Cohen and his colleagues tried to simulate an actual economy to improve academic, vocational, and social behaviors of delinquent youth. For example, the requirements for parole included attainment of (1) a specific academic grade, (2) a vocational skill at a specified level, and (3) a demonstrated ability to work forty hours per week for six months to earn sufficient funds (in points) to support himself in terms of food, housing, clothing, and so forth. Later, this program was reestablished in a modified form at the Kennedy Youth Center in West Virginia. A report by Vinter and Sarri (1973) explicates the extension of this program and highlights some of the difficulties encountered when a token economy is designed and engineered for a large, complex organization. Among the frequent problems which they observed were inconsistencies among staff in reinforcement patterns, inability to reinforce behavior immediately upon its occurrence, and cultural differences in response to behavioral criteria. Nonetheless, the use of the token economy in this correctional agency resulted in far more humane practices in control and custody than are typically observed in correctional agencies.

Ayllon and Azrin (1965) completed an experiment involving a token economy in one ward of 45 females in a mental hospital. All relevant activities were controlled, to examine the effects of reinforcement by tokens, on patient job performance. Six types of reinforcers such as having a private room, leaves, social interaction with staff were among the reinforcers selected. Tokens were exchanged for the performance of both on- and off-ward jobs.

Cooperative behavior among children has been developed, maintained and even strengthened through the use of reinforcement procedures. Azrin and Lindsley (1964) reported that pairs of children, matched by age and sex, developed and maintained cooperative behavior without specific instruction concerning such behavior. Cooperative responses increased when reinforced and decreased when extinction was applied, but returned to the preextinction rate almost immediately when reinforcement was reapplied.

Hastorf (1965) conducted a number of experiments in which he deliberately attempted to modify the structure of groups by differentially reinforcing the behavior of individuals while they were participating in group problem solving. He stated that the same variables which apply to the individual situation with regard to reinforcement, also apply to the group. These include prior history of reinforcement, the reinforcing stimulus, the schedule and amount of reinforcement, the behavior upon which reinforcement is contingent, and the change in the rate of response. In addition, the ways in which the group has experienced crises, success, and failure are to be considered.

Because many social workers work with lower- and working-class children and youth, the report of a project by Staats and Butterfield (1965) is of particular interest. Using a token system of reinforcement, Butterfield, a probation officer in Tucson, Arizona, taught a culturally deprived

Chicano boy to read. This fourteen-year-old boy had experienced repeated school difficulty because of misbehavior and poor academic achievement. His parents controlled his behavior in the home through the use of physical and verbal abuse. Both admitted that they were unable to assist the boy with homework because of their own lack of education. The authors reported that the school staff described the boy as follows:

> . . . He has been incorrigible since he came here in the second grade. He has no respect for teachers, steals, and lies habitually and uses extremely foul language! He has been promoted to get rid of him! He was described by the principal as mentally retarded even though the tests indicated a score within the normal range. (p. 928)

A special procedure for teaching reading was selected involving the use of word cards. The boy was given a token for a correct response, and when he made an error or failed to respond, the worker gave the correct response, but no token. Only the correct responses were eliminated from the card deck. In four months of training, he advanced from reading at grade 2 level to the 4.3 grade level. In addition, his school grades began to show marked changes. Misbehaviors noted in school were reduced from ten in the first month to none in the fourth month.

In summarizing their study, Staats and Butterfield say,

> The procedures are very specific and relatively simple. The present study suggests that these conditions (cultural deprivation) can be reversed through the application of learning principles and reinforcement variables to the task of repairing the child's behavioral-achievement deficit. There were indications that this treatment resulted in improvement in the reinforcement value of school for this child and, consequently, in the decrease in incidents of misbehavior in school. (p. 939)

Changing environmental conditions which maintain certain behavioral patterns is often extremely difficult, as experienced social workers and other helping professionals are well aware. Marked differences can be observed between change efforts when clients remain throughout treatment in their usual social environment and when they are moved from this environment, as in a closed institution (Thorp and Wetzel, 1969; Gambrill, et al., 1971). Findings from research on behavior modification provide many new insights about change and control of environmental conditions, however. Saslow (1965) has described the actual operation of behavior modification in a mental hospital. He emphasized the importance of training *all* staff in contact with the patient to respond favorably to the help-eliciting cares of the patient. Ayllon and Michael (1964) demonstrated the utility of operant conditioning principles in the treatment of hospitalized patients. They further suggested that much of the inappropriate patient behavior is actually shaped and maintained within the hospital. On the basis of their observations, they designed procedures whereby psychiatric nurses were trained to function as behavioral engineers on the ward. Nurses used techniques of extinction, satiation, and positive and negative reinforcements to modify patient behavior in the ward.

Davison (1965) reported that undergraduate college students were able to employ behavioral techniques successfully in a day care center for severely autistic children. Pickard and Dinoff (1965) reported on similar procedures for training camp counselors working with emotionally disturbed children in group situations. These findings indicate that paraprofessionals can be trained successfully in the use of behavior modification and control techniques and highlight advantages of behavioral techniques over more traditional methods of management of clients in residential settings.

Marked results in client change were observed in a demonstration research project from the application of sociobehavioral theory in the Palo Alto Veteran's Hospital (Fairweather, 1964). This project involved a more thorough effort than those described above, because several aspects of the patient's experience in the hospital were modified, and staff roles of psychiatrists, psychologists, social workers and nurses were significantly changed. A limited form of behavior therapy was attempted, namely, coaching combined with the use of a "buddy system" and patient peer groups which served as a basis for behavioral control. Fairweather and his colleagues were particularly concerned with career structuring of patient roles with respect to role expectations and requirements in the world outside the hospital. They also showed that a program could be developed and engineered within a large hospital.

Another approach to the control of environmental conditions has been the training of parents as behavioral therapists. It is generally acknowledged that parents often play a significant role in the disturbed or deviant behavior of a child. Few have considered how parents could be instrumental in modifying behavior which they may have reinforced in the past (Patterson and Guillon, 1968). Bijou (1965) has done considerable research in use of parents, particularly mothers, as therapists. His efforts have been directed to the social environment of parent-child interactions rather than on the disturbance or deficiencies of the child per se. He and his associates have completed several studies of behavioral treatment of children by parents or auxiliary persons. In one study a six-year-old boy was described by his mother as overdemanding. The behavior of the mother and child were observed and recorded systematically to learn how she was reinforcing commanding behavior and cooperative behavior. She was instructed to reinforce cooperative behavior only, and then to discriminate between the two classes of behavior. These procedures also were employed to control tantrums, isolation and regressed behavior. Some child guidance clinics have reported using similar procedures in group sessions to train mothers in desired parental behaviors for childrearing. In describing various professional roles Bandura suggests, "The primary tasks of the professionally qualified clinics should be to develop effective therapeutic procedures based on social learning principles, to train available persons in the application of these principles and set up programs which these persons may implement under guidance and direction. In this way, more people will receive more help than they do under current professional practice." (Bandura and Walters, 1963:258)

It becomes quite obvious from this brief, cursory review, that behavior modification research has many implications for social work practice, in general, and for group treatment in particular. Regularities in techniques are emerging, particularly consistencies in assessment procedures. Attention is focused on specific problematic behavior only, not the total person. Following that, if the target is to increase the occurrence of a given behavior, operant techniques are likely to be used. If the target is reduction or elimination of maladaptive behavior, some form of reciprocal inhibition is likely to be effective to develop responses which are incompatible with the maladaptive behavior. In the state of reciprocal inhibition the ability of a given stimulus to evoke anxiety is permanently weakened if a response antagonistic to anxiety can be made to occur in the presence of anxiety-invoking stimuli so that it is accompanied by a complete or partial suppression of the anxiety response.

The practice of desensitization and other forms of reciprocal inhibition seem to require that professional personnel be in direct contact with the client. However, cooperation is solicited from significant persons in the client's environment. Operant conditioning procedures appear to offer greater latitude, and a wide variety of paraprofessionals have been successfully instructed in the use of these principles. A competent therapist must design and supervise the program, but detailed procedures can be "engineered" by a variety of persons.

Thus far behavioral therapy literature places no limitations on the types of clients who can be treated with this approach, but this area has not been fully explored. Research now under way in a wide variety of settings should yield results to help formulate more valid statements about the importance of variations in client characteristics.

IMPLICATIONS OF BEHAVIORAL THEORY
FOR GROUP WORK PRACTICE

Now the implications of sociobehavioral theory for group work practice will be considered in a direct, rather than indirect, manner. Social science literature, including sociobehavioral theory, has been and is being utilized to develop the practice principles for this model of group treatment, which is characterized by the use of the group as a *means* and *context* to modify behavior of individuals. One of the obvious implications from this examination is that role behaviors of group workers are likely to differ greatly from one situation to another in behavior treatment. Specification of the task to be done facilitates clarification of the role behaviors required of the worker. A number of models for group treatment can be delineated using behavior modification principles and techniques, but several factors must be considered in deciding which of these may be appropriate in a given situation.

1. The worker must know the recent reinforcing history of the group if the group is already established. Some models are inappropriate for groups that are already in existence and should be eliminated from consideration.
2. The worker must determine if the group is to be primarily a means, target, or context for change, or all three as might occur in family treatment. In most situations, different models are more appropriate for one condition rather than another.
3. The requisites for use of selected techniques must be feasible and operational, and resources and the constraints on the model must be considered.

The following list of potential models is presented tentatively, for illustrative purposes. It is far from complete and additional research and practice will suggest new models, but it incorporates behavioral knowledge with variable worker roles.

Model 1

Problematic behavior to be addressed in the group is essentially the same for all clients, e.g., the Lazarus experiment of group treatment of acrophobias. Treatment involves the same procedures for all clients. Each member moves through the identified stages and the group moves from one stage to another when all members have performed the required behavior for the stage.

Model 2

A group might be composed of pairs specifically selected so that one member within each pair would act as stimulus toward the desired behavior by the other. Through the use of a "buddy system" or a similar device, a series of potential modeling situations would be available.

Model 3

A group composed with worker's roles so structured that he can serve as a model for the members' desired behavior. Bandura (1969) has had much success with children using this approach. He has observed that children in nursery school more frequently imitated models who themselves were positively reinforced in the presence of children than models who were not so reinforced.

Model 4

A group may be composed or programmed so that selective peer leaders serve as models. The worker may deliberately instruct leaders in certain behaviors so that they can serve in specific modeling situations. Bijou (1965) has worked with parents in this general type. The worker also may employ indirect means of influence to change group structures and processes so that peer leaders can serve as effective models.

Model 5

A group can be structured so that the social system itself becomes the effective control agent. The worker must carefully structure tasks and activities and members' roles so that the desired type of social system will emerge. The Essexfield project (Pilnick, 1966), and the Cohen (1966) experiment at the National Training School for Boys in Washington, D.C. represent forms of this model and have been extended now to include an entire institution with several distinct cottages.

Model 6

A group may be structured deliberately in subgroups, each with a specific behavioral curriculum. It appears preferable to have some tasks or activities of the subgroups interrelate. To a degree the Schwitzgebel (1964) experiment with delinquents exemplifies this model, because various activities were planned for different subgroups of delinquents with some common tasks.

Model 7

A different approach would be the physical and/or social relocation of a natural group to a new environment so that the conditions controlling the problematic behavior are markedly changed. Thus it would be posssible to have within the environment modified controlling conditions and new types of social reinforcers.

Model 8

An ideal model would be a group so composed that all members complemented each other in their separate treatment plans. Such a situation could probably not be created very often, although some earlier writers imply that it could be done.

Some of the specific implications of behavior theory are being incorporated in a few agencies, but most are not yet utilized in a systematic manner. The use of sociobehavioral theory continually focuses the worker's attention on the links between means and ends. With such an approach the dangers of goal displacement are far less likely.

REFERENCES

AICHORN, AUGUST
  1935—*Wayward Youth,* New York: Viking Press.
ALDEN, S. E., L. E. PETTIGREW, AND E. A. SHIBA
  1970—"The effect of individual contingent group reinforcement on popularity," *Child Development* 41, pp. 1191–1196.
AYLLON, T. AND N. H. AZRIN
  1965—"The measurement and reinforcement of behavior of psychotics," *Journal of the Experimental Analysis of Behavior* 8(November), pp. 357–385.
  1968—*The Token Economy: A Motivational System for Therapy and Rehabilitation,* New York: Appleton-Century-Crofts.
AYLLON, T. AND J. MICHAEL
  1964—"The psychiatric nurse as a behavioral engineer," in Staats (Ed.), *Human Learning,* New York: Holt, Rinehart and Winston.
AZRIN, N. H. AND O. R. LINDSLEY
  1964—"The reinforcement of cooperation between children," in Staats (Ed.), *Human Learning,* New York: Holt, Rinehart and Winston.
BANDURA, A.
  1969—*Principles of Behavior Modification,* New York: Holt, Rinehart and Winston.
BANDURA, A. AND D. ROSS AND S. ROSS
  1964—"A comparative test of the status envy, social power, and the secondary reinforcement theories," in Staats (Ed.), *Human Learning,* New York: Holt, Rinehart and Winston, pp. 372–383.
BANDURA, A. AND R. WALTERS
  1963—*Social Learning and Personality Development,* New York: Holt, Rinehart and Winston.
BIJOU, S. W.
  1965—"Experimental studies of child behavior, normal and deviant," in L. P. Ullman and L. Krasner (Eds.), *Case Studies in Behavior Modification,* New York: Holt, Rinehart and Winston.

BUEHLER, R. E., G. R. PATTERSON AND J. M. FURNISS
   1966—"The reinforcement of behavior in institutional settings," *Behavior Research and Therapy* 4, pp. 157–167.
CARTWRIGHT, D. AND A. ZANDER
   1968—*Group Dynamics: Research and Theory*, New York: Harper and Row.
COHEN, H., J. A. FILIPSICZAK AND J. S. BIS
   1968—"Contingencies applicable to special education of delinquents: Establishing 24-hour control in an experimental cottage." (Mimeographed) Silver Spring, Maryland: Institute for Behavioral Research, Inc.
COHEN, R.
   1969—"The effects of group interaction and progressive hierarchy and presentation on desensitization of test anxiety," *Behavior Research and Therapy* 7, pp. 15–26.
DAVISON, G. C.
   1965—"The training of undergraduates as social reinforcers for autistic children," in Ullman and Krasner (Eds.), *Case Studies in Behavior Modification*, New York: Holt, Rinehart and Winston, pp. 146–148.
EYSENCK, H. J.
   1960—*Behavior Therapy and Neuroses*, New York: Pergamon Press.
FAIRWEATHER, G.
   1964—*Social Psychology in Treating Mental Illness*, New York: John Wiley & Sons.
FERSTER, C. B. AND M. K. DE MEYER
   1962—"A method for the experimental analysis of the behavior of autistic children," *American Journal of Orthopsychiatry* 32, pp. 88–98.
FERSTER, C. B. AND M. C. PERROT
   1968—*Behavior Principles*, New York: Appleton-Century-Crofts.
FRANKS, C. M. (ED.)
   1969—*Behavior Therapy: Appraisal and Status*, New York: McGraw-Hill.
GAMBRILL, E., E. J. THOMAS AND R. D. CARTER
   1971—"Procedure for sociobehavioral practice in open settings," *Social Work* 16(January), pp. 51–62.
HASTORF, A. H.
   1965—"The 'reinforcement' of individual actions in a group situation," in Krasner, L. and L. P. Ullman (Eds.), *Research in Behavior Modification*, New York: Holt, Rinehart and Winston, pp. 268–284.
HINGSTEN, J. N., B. J. SANDERS AND M. K. DE MEYER
   1965—"Shaping cooperative responses in early childhood schizophrenics," in L. P. Ullman and L. Krasner (Eds.), *Case Studies in Behavior Modification*, New York: Holt, Rinehart and Winston, pp. 130–138.
KING, G. J., S. G. ARMITAGE AND J. R. TILTON
   1965—"A therapeutic approach to schizophrenics of extreme pathology: An operant-interpersonal method," in L. P. Ullman and L. Krasner (Eds.), *Case Studies in Behavior Modification*, New York: Holt, Rinehart and Winston, pp. 99–112.
KITTRIE, N. N.
   1971—*The Right to Be Different*, Baltimore, Maryland: Penguin.

KOLB, D. A. AND R. SCHWITZGEBEL (EDS.)
  1972—*Behavior Change,* New York: McGraw-Hill.
LAZARUS, A.
  1971—*Behavior Therapy and Beyond,* New York: McGraw-Hill.
  1968—"Behavior therapy in groups," in G. M. Gozda (Ed.), *Basic Approaches to Group Psychotherapy and Group Counseling,* Springfield, Illinois: C. C. Thomas, pp. 149–175.
  1965—"Group therapy of phobic disorders by systematic desensitization," in L. Ullman and L. Krasner (Eds.), *Case Studies in Behavior Modification,* New York: Holt, Rinehart and Winston, pp. 208–216.
LOTT, B. E. AND A. J. LOTT
  1964—"The formation of positive attitudes toward group members," in A. Staats (Ed.), *Human Learning,* New York: Holt, Rinehart and Winston, pp. 356–371.
LUNDIN, R. W.
  1969—*Personality: A Behavioral Analysis,* New York: Macmillan.
McMONUS, M.
  1971 "Group desensitization of test anxiety," *Behavior Research and Therapy* 9, pp. 51–56.
PATTERSON, G. R. AND D. ANDERSON
  1964—"Peers as social reinforcers," *Child Development* 35, pp. 951–960.
PATTERSON, G. R. AND M. E. GUILLON
  1968—*Living with Children: New Methods for Parents and Teachers,* Champaign, Illinois: Research Press.
PATTERSON, G. R., S. MCNEAL, N. HAWKINS AND R. PHELPS
  1967—"Reprogramming the social environment," *Journal of Child Psychology and Psychiatry,* pp. 181–195.
PAUL, G. L. AND D. T. SHANNON
  1966—"Treatment of anxiety through systematic desensitization in therapy groups," *Journal of Abnormal Psychology* 71, pp. 124–135.
PHILLIPS, E. L.
  1968—"Achievement plan: Token reinforcement procedures in a home style rehabilitation setting for 'pre-delinquent' boys," *Journal of Applied Behavior Analysis* 1, pp. 213–223.
PICKARD, H. C. AND M. DINOFF
  1965—"Shaping adaptive behavior in a therapeutic summer camp," L. P. Ullman and L. Krasner (Eds.), *Case Studies in Behavior Modification,* New York: Holt, Rinehart and Winston.
PILNICK, S., A. ELIAS AND N. W. CLAPP
  1966—"The Essexfield concept: A new approach to the social treatment of juvenile delinquents," *Journal of Applied Behavioral Science* 2(Winter), pp. 109–124.
POLANSKY, N. AND A. BLUM
  1961—"Effect of staff role on children's verbal accessibility," *Social Work* 6(January), pp. 29–34.
ROSE, S.
  1972—*Treating Children in Groups,* San Francisco, California: Jossey-Bass.

SARASON, I. G. AND V. J. GONZER
1969—"Developing appropriate social behaviors of juvenile delinquents," in
J. D. Krumholtz and C. E. Thoresen (Eds.), *Behavioral Counseling:
Cases and Techniques*, New York: Holt, Rinehart and Winston,
pp. 178–193.

SASLOW, G.
1965—"A case history of attempted behavior manipulation in a psychiatric
ward," in L. Krasner and L. P. Ullman (Eds.), *Case Studies in Behavior Modification*, New York: Holt, Rinehart and Winston, pp.
285–304.

SCHWITZGEBEL, R.
1964—*Street-Corner Research: An Experimental Approach to the Juvenile
Delinquent*, Cambridge, Massachusetts: Harvard University Press.

SIPORIN, M.
1965—"Deviant behavior theory in social work," *Social Work* 19(July),
pp. 59–67.

SKINNER, B. F.
1953—*Science and Human Behavior*, New York: Macmillan.

STAATS, A. W.
1968—*Language, Learning and Cognition*, New York: Holt, Rinehart and
Winston.
1964—*Human Learning*, New York: Holt, Rinehart and Winston.

STAATS, A. W. AND WILLIAM BUTTERFIELD
1965—"Treatment of nonreading in a culturally deprived juvenile delinquent:
An application of reinforcement principles," *Child Development* 36
(December), pp. 925–942.

THOMAS, E. J.
1964—"Selecting knowledge from behavioral science," in National Association of Social Workers (Eds.), *Building Social Work Knowledge*,
New York: National Association of Social Workers, pp. 38–48.

THOMAS, E. J. (ED.)
1967—*The Socio-behavioral Approach and Application to Social Work*,
New York: Council on Social Work Education.

THORP, R. AND R. J. WETZEL
1969—*Behavior Modification in the Natural Environment*, New York:
Academic Press.

ULLMAN, L. AND L. KRASNER (EDS.)
1969—*A Psychological Approach to Abnormal Behavior*, Englewood Cliffs,
New Jersey: Prentice-Hall.
1965—*Case Studies in Behavior Modification*, New York: Holt, Rinehart and
Winston.

ULRICH, R., T. STACHNIK AND J. MABRY (EDS.)
1970—*Control of Human Behavior*, Glenview, Illinois: Scott, Foresman and
Company.

VINTER, R. D. AND R. C. SARRI
1973—*Comparative Study of Federal Correctional Programs for Young
Offenders*, Ann Arbor: University of Michigan.

WOLPE, J.
1958—*Psychotherapy by Reciprocal Inhibition*, Palo Alto, California: Stanford University Press.
1969—*The Practice of Behavior Therapy*, New York: Pergamon Press.
WOODY, R. H.
1969—*Behavioral Problem Children in the Schools: Recognition, Diagnosis and Behavioral Modification*, New York: Appleton-Century-Crofts.
ZIMMERMAN, E. H. AND J. ZIMMERMAN
1965—"The alteration of behavior in a special classroom situation," in L. P. Ullman and L. Krasner (Eds.), *Case Studies in Behavior Modification*, New York: Holt, Rinehart and Winston, pp. 328–330.

5.

A Conceptual Framework for Group Development

ROSEMARY C. SARRI and MAEDA J. GALINSKY

Group development has major relevance in social group work. Practitioners who seek systematic control of and change in group conditions to attain treatment goals need to understand what group development is and how it relates to specific principles of social work practice.

A frame of reference which limits, focuses and directs practitioner's efforts is a prerequisite for the development of systematic practice theory, however modest and limited. In social group work the frame of reference has been largely implicit with the exception of that provided by dynamic psychology, which has affected the perceptions, cognitions, communications, and explanations provided by social workers who focus on the individual level. An orientation specifically addressed to group level efforts is also required. Knowledge from sociology and social psychology, because they deal with precisely such group phenomena, is required for an adequate group work practice theory. Social group work practitioner's goal is to achieve change in individuals who manifest social functioning problems by using the group as the means and context to accomplish desired changes. Because the group provides the primary situation for change, it is viewed as a "context" for treatment. As a "means" for change the practitioner explicitly uses group conditions to change individuals. Group development is one of these conditions.

Individual member characteristics and environment may strongly influence the development of the group. Here, however, focus is on the regularities and consistencies of group development that can be ascertained, rather than on the total complexity of variables which may impinge on any group.

The concept of group development is based on a number of assump-

An earlier version of this statement was included in *A Conceptual Framework for the Teaching of the Social Group Work Methods,* Council on Social Work Education (New York, 1962).

tions, some of which also apply to other areas of concern in social group work. (1) The group, a potent influence system, can be used as an efficient vehicle for individual change. (2) The group is not an end in itself. The aim of social group work is to maximize the potentials of the group for individual change rather than to create an enduring, small social system. (3) Group development can be controlled and influenced by the worker's actions. (4) There is no optimal way in which groups develop. Earlier literature has often asserted that all groups must develop into democratic self-directing entities, embellished with formalized operating and governing procedures. However, in order to attain individual goals for clients, the practitioner must intervene to affect group development in ways which facilitate the pursuit of these goals.

This analysis of developmental phases will refer to all groups, regardless of their objectives, composition, environmental location, and whether or not they are served by a professional or other practitioner. "Worker" will be used to refer to a professionally trained social worker or psychotherapist. "Leader" and "leadership" are reserved to refer to group members and aspects of the group structure. The developmental process discussed in this chapter occurs over a series of meetings, not in one meeting. The assumption is made that the group membership would not change frequently. Where membership is more fluid the group would be expected to recapitulate earlier phases of group development (Hock and Kaufer, 1955).

Group development is defined as changes through time in the internal structures, processes, and culture of the group. Three dimensions of group development can be identified: (1) Social organization of the group—the group structure, patterns of participant roles and statuses (for example, changes in the power structure at different stages of development) (2) Activities, tasks, and operative processes of the group (e.g., changes in decision-making processes over time) (3) The culture of the group; *its* norms (i.e., expectations of members for one another), values, and shared purposes. These include most of the group dimensions that can be observed and manipulated. What distinguishes them as dimensions of group development is that they change over time, and that there are certain regularities which may be noted in their manifestations at different times in the life of the group. It is possible to classify these recurrent patterns into several phases.

Despite extensive research on many aspects of small groups, very few systematic studies of group development have been carried out.[1] Nevertheless, some phase regularities have been identified and reported (Theodorson, 1953; Martin and Hill, 1957). Comparisons between reports are

---

[1] Literature on small groups is voluminous; for an extensive bibliography on small group research, see Hare (1962).

difficult because few observers use the same categories or concepts for describing developmental patterns, and because some studies are the result of relatively rigorous study, while others are less systematic observations of practitioners (Psathas, 1960; Northen, 1958). Furthermore, there are few tools for quantifying degrees of change and only terms such as "increasing," "higher," and "lower" can be relied on. Groups also clearly do not always move through the several phases sequentially—movement backward as well as forward has been observed—and groups spend differing amounts of time in each phase. Despite these and other problems, delineation of the phases of group development and identification of essential elements of each phase are attempted here.

Several authors fail to distinguish group developmental processes from workers' interventions and individual clients' reactions (Weisman, 1953). The range of worker interventions required by each phase of group development will be examined separately in the subsequent discussion of the treatment sequence.

PHASES OF GROUP DEVELOPMENT

Phases of group development and the events which characterize each are presented in the order in which they typically occur.

1. *Origin Phase* refers to composing the group and is distinguished primarily for analytic purposes, because events that occur precondition later development.

2. *Formative Phase* is characterized by the initial activity of group members in seeking similarity and mutuality of interests. Initial commitments to group purpose, emergent interpersonal ties and a quasi-structure are also observable in this phase.

3. *Intermediate Phase* is characterized by a moderate level of group cohesion (i.e., interpersonal bonds among members), clarification of purposes, and an observable involvement of members in goal-directed activities.

4. *Revision Phase*. In this phase, a challenge to the existing group structure can be expected, accompanied by modification of group purposes and operating procedures.

5. *Intermediate Phase II*. Following the revision phase, while many groups gradually progress toward maturation, the characteristics outlined in phase 3 may again appear; however, the group generally manifests a higher level of integration and stability than that of the earlier intermediate phase.

6. *Maturation Phase* is characterized by stabilization of group structure, purposes, operating and governing procedures, expansion of the cul-

ture of the group, and the existence of effective responses to internal and external stresses.

7. *Termination Phase.* The dissolution of the group may result from goal attainment, maladaptation, the lack of integration, or previous planning to terminate the group.

Each of the phases will be examined in greater detail, using the three dimensions of group development—social organization; activities, tasks and operating procedures; and group culture—as a basis for analysis.

Phase 1. Origin

As suggested, this phase preconditions or sets limits for possible later development of the group. Regardless of when the worker comes in contact with a treatment group, he must obtain knowledge about the beginning of the group. Major variables that affect further group development are size of the group, members' characteristics and initial orientations, and environmental location of the group.

Present knowledge indicates that group size has specific effects upon the development of the group's structural properties, upon patterns of individual participation and performance, and upon individual members' satisfaction (Thomas and Fink, 1963).

Member characteristics influence subsequent activities, tasks, and operating procedures, as well as the culture of group. For example, urban lower-class children are not likely to respond to activities which require a high level of verbal skill or to be able to participate readily in a group operated under parliamentary procedures.

The initial orientation of members to the group has a significant impact upon its later social organization. For example, voluntary membership affects participants' initial attitudes or orientations toward the group, and therefore will influence patterns of relationships among members. Where membership in groups is involuntary, dependence upon the professional worker can be expected to last longer and the leadership structure within the group can be expected to develop more slowly.

Environmental location, the community and/or agency setting in which the group exists, is of particular concern because it influences the norms and values of members and it sets limits for activities and tasks of the group (Miller, 1957). Frequently, environmental conditions may allow fluidity in group structure and participation patterns in the early phases of development (for example, an informal hospital ward group).

Phase 2. Formative

The group's social organization during this phase is observable in the emerging interpersonal ties among members and in the appearance of a quasi-structure. As Theodorson observed, this quasi-structure is most often characterized by leadership roles played by the more assertive and aggressive individuals, who give order and direction to the group and who receive some initial deference from other members (Theodorson, 1953). Thus, a partial prestige and status structure can be expected to emerge.

In the formative stage, members seek common and compatible personal values and attitudes, group purposes, and activities and tasks. During this process, norms based on common values and attitudes and relating to ways of behaving in the group are established,[2] frequently through the development of simple operating procedures. Attraction to other members and to the group purposes or tasks is likely to be enhanced, resulting in a basis for group cohesion and for further progressive development of the group (Martin and Hill, 1957; Foulkes and Anthony, 1957; Northen, 1958; Theodorson, 1953).

If these conditions are not satisfactorily attained in this phase, the group will most likely be unable to meet the requirements of subsequent phases and will terminate prematurely. In many groups where membership is voluntary, lack of attendance by members is symptomatic of the failure to establish satisfactory conditions in this phase.

Phase 3. Intermediate

Increasing interpersonal ties with a moderate level of group cohesion characterize this phase. Purposes are clarified, and observable involvement in goal-directed activities and specialized roles gradually emerges; task and socioemotional leaders can be more clearly identified at this time.[3] Cliques and subgroups may begin to form.

Additional norms and values are acquired that specifically relate to group functioning. Social control mechanisms develop, and deviation from norms often tends to be dealt with in a harsh or punitive manner by the

---

[2] See Riecken and Homans (1954) for a review of empirical studies where findings support the generalization that while extensive choice changes occur in newly formed groups, a stable social structure emerges early and a given member's relative status tends to remain the same over time. See also Jennings (1950). The acquisition of norms pertaining to ways of behaving in the earliest phases of group psychotherapy is described by Foulkes and Anthony (1957). Hock and Kaufer (1955) also mention the establishment of group norms in the initial stage, which they term the "climate setting stage."

[3] See Bales and Slater (1955). Martin and Hill (1957) describe the development of subgroups and specialized roles in their Phase IV. Foulkes and Anthony (1957) discuss this occurrence during their intermediate phase. During their second phase, that of approach-avoidance, Hock and Kaufer (1955) note how differential roles are assumed by members and also how in this phase and in other phases social control mechanisms and operating procedures are developed. See also Theodorson (1953).

group. Because norms and values for a number of areas of attitudinal expression and overt behavior are not yet established, member participation may be somewhat restricted in fear of sanctions, or because members do not yet know what is expected of them. Pressures toward uniformity and consensus are clearly apparent (Festinger, 1962). Members have now experienced some events in common and are beginning to build up common traditions, sentiments, and values.

The actual emergence of norms, values and social control mechanisms may be difficult to observe empirically; they are, nevertheless, as necessary to the development of groups as more easily discernible variables such as leadership structure. Considerable evidence shows that crucial norms and values are established during both the formative and intermediate phases.

Phase 4. Revision

Careful scrutiny of the literature suggests that prior to, or following, Phase 3 a revision phase (Theodorson, 1953; Martin and Hill, 1957; Foulkes and Anthony, 1957; Bennis and Shepard, 1962) occurs that involves a challenge to and a revision of the leadership structure of earlier stages; most likely it occurs if the leaders in previous stages are aggressive and attempt to prevent other members from engaging in leadership activities.

Change in group operating procedures is likely to accompany the revision in leadership structure. Increased role differentiation can be expected, with more members assuming leadership functions in their particular areas of competence. A leader who is able to adapt to new group demands for the operation of the group may retain his initial status. As members feel more secure in their specialized roles, as they depend more on one another for satisfaction in the tasks and activities of the group, and as they interact more frequently, group members are likely to have more positive feelings toward each other. An increase in negative reactions can also be expected (Bales, 1950; Psathas, 1960; Foulkes and Anthony, 1957). The norms, values and traditions of the group may change in varying degrees depending upon the extent of the revision. If they do not change, they will at least be strengthened and clarified. Further clarification of group purposes can also be expected both during and following the revision in leadership structure.

Phase 5. Intermediate

Equilibrium following the revision should be restored early in this phase. A significant proportion of groups appear to manifest characteristics which resemble the earlier intermediate phase, but a higher level of group integration, greater stability in goal-directed activity and in group structure is expected. In addition, because participants have been together longer, there are more traditions, clearer norms, and more collective memories, which can be expected to increase group cohesion and the influence of the group upon members. Many of the problems confronting the group earlier are likely to be resolved by this time. Consequently, specific goal-required activities can be given greater attention, with higher levels of interdependence and cooperation among members in these activities.

As mentioned previously, not all groups experience an identifiable revision in group structure; nevertheless, some modification in structure will be apparent with a more complex division of labor. Leadership becomes more diffused among members and roles are differentiated and increased. These changes are likely to precipitate or accompany changes in operating procedures.

Phase 6. Maturation

Movement into this phase is marked by a relatively high level of group functioning. Maturation is clearly distinguishable from earlier phases of group development. Well-developed group structure is characterized by obvious ranking, specialized and interdependent roles, formalized patterns of interaction, subgroups and proliferated interpersonal ties. Customary operating procedures include patterns of participation, problem solving, decision making and implementing of decisions. Relatively stable relationships exist with the physical and social environment, and effective procedures for change have been established. Substantial progress along these lines is likely to be found only in well-integrated groups that have existed over a long period of time.[4]

Changes in the group's environment force internal changes; internal conflicts and shifting needs of members generate crises for which the group must develop adaptive mechanisms.[5] Successful groups enter the maturation phase—and remain there—only when they can respond to both extra-group and intragroup pressures for change. Maturation may be viewed as a state of "dynamic equilibrium," rather than one of static maturity.

Phase 7. Termination

There are four general conditions which result in termination of groups. (1) When goals are attained, the group may have no further reason

[4] Homans' analysis of W. A. Whyte's "Norton Street Gang" suggests that this group possessed many of the necessary characteristics of the maturation phase (1950).

[5] The final phase described by Martin and Hill (1957), the group as an integrative-creative social instrument, resembles the maturation phase described here. However, Martin and Hill believe that this phase is an important one for treatment groups.

for existence. (2) Some groups are planned for definite preiods of time (for example, orientation or diagnostic groups). (3) Also, lack of integration occurs if a group is unable to achieve essential conditions for endurance: basic consensus among members about goals, a high level of interpersonal ties, a role system which permits sufficient personal satisfaction and successful completion of major tasks, or effective operating procedures. (4) Maladaptation is most notable when a group has not developed effective means for responding to external changes and environmental pressures. It may never have developed change mechanisms; on the other hand, it may have developed mechanisms which were effective at one time but became rigid or institutionalized and, consequently, would not allow for adaptation to new conditions.

THE TREATMENT SEQUENCE

These phases of group development have disregarded the presence or absence of a professional worker. When a worker is present, his ability to recognize, understand, and guide phases of group development can facilitate treatment planning and enhance efforts to attain individual treatment goals within the group. Specific strategies for worker intervention can be related to successive phases of group development.

Practice principles, intervention techniques, and workers' actions are generally formulated within the "treatment sequence," which includes intake, diagnosis, formulation of goals, treatment, and evaluation. Throughout the following review of stages of the treatment sequence, a primary concern will be intervention techniques which the worker uses with groups at different phases of development.

Stage I. Intake, Selection, and Diagnosis

This treatment sequence stage corresponds to the origin phase of group development and occurs prior to the first meeting. Worker actions at this point include intake, diagnosis, and the formulation of treatment goals. Although diagnosis will not be discussed here, diagnosis directly implicates treatment planning so the two processes must be considered simultaneously.

The use of the group as the means and context for treatment imposes requirements upon the worker for specific actions in this stage. These include the following:

1. Determination of group purposes from the synthesis of individual treatment goals

2. Establishing a "contract" with individual members concerning the particular type of social work service to be provided
3. Determination of the basic mechanics of the particular type of group treatment: frequency of meetings, time and place for meetings, projected length of service, and necessary resources

Stage II. Group Formation

In this stage, which corresponds to the formative phase of group development, the workers' actions are especially crucial, because the conditions must be set for subsequent group development and treatment. From the first meeting, the worker serves as a central person, or a psychological core of the group, and intervenes to influence group development in the desired direction.

Specific actions required of the worker at this stage include

1. Fostering members' attraction to the group
2. Initiation and/or support of group norms which facilitate treatment
3. Definition of general purposes and of limits within which members may develop their own goals
4. Maintenance of an open, flexible leadership structure

Initial attraction to the group is fostered through worker assistance to members, individually and collectively, in their search for common values and interests. His relationship to each member also serves to increase group attraction potential. Where appropriate, special emphasis is placed on values and experiences related to treatment goals; the worker motivates and stimulates members not only toward activities they enjoy but also toward those which are therapeutically useful. Thus, he facilitates and enhances commonality among members, including shared recognition of their common difficulties (Foulkes and Anthony, 1957).

The worker's influence on the development of appropriate group norms is particularly important during this stage because norms tend to persist and may be difficult to modify later (Merei, 1958; Hock and Kaufer, 1955). He therefore initiates, supports, and stimulates group norms in line with his objectives. Simultaneously, the worker de-emphasizes and may even suppress those norms which may have negative implications for treatment objectives, but this must be done with caution so that he does not jeopardize his relationship with members.

The worker defines general purposes for the group, reinforces the contracts established in initial interviews, and sets limits within which members may develop their own goals. The statement of the general purpose will further serve to direct members' activities and tasks.

Groups may develop initial leadership structures with aggressive members predominating. External statuses may be important in their initial prestige, but the worker can expect a gradual shift to prestige based on intragroup performance. During this stage in the treatment sequence, the worker influences the structure so that initial leadership will be supportive of his norms, values and group purposes. The worker is careful not to give positive sanctions to leaders who hinder the treatment process. Primarily through the use of indirect means of influence, the worker attempts to forestall premature formalization or stabilization of the leadership structure in order to preserve opportunities for other members to assume leadership functions later. If the worker does not maintain an open and flexible structure, the group may never attain the level of integration required for viability (Martin and Hill, 1957). One way the worker can ensure more flexibility is to introduce group operating procedures that foster participation by all members to the highest possible degree. These operating procedures will then serve to initiate norms for effective participation by all members.

Finally, the worker can expect considerable "testing" of himself in this stage. Members will evaluate his acceptance of them, his concern for them, his reliability, and his tolerance of their behavior (Northen, 1958; Miller, 1957).

Stage III. Building a Viable and Cohesive Group

At this stage of the treatment sequence, which corresponds to Intermediate Phase I of group development, a wide range of worker interventions may be required:

1. Fostering interpersonal ties among members
2. Planning program activities
3. Assessment of leadership structure
4. Supporting the maintenance or revision of leadership structure
5. Assisting members to fulfill roles
6. Encouraging efforts to develop effective operating procedures
7. Mediating group sanctions
8. Supporting norms and values which facilitate treatment

A moderate to high level of group cohesion is expected during this stage, and the worker facilitates the growth or interpersonal ties among *all* members of the group. While cohesion is necessary if the group is to become a potent and viable influence system, evidence suggests that a very high level of cohesion induces strong pressures for uniformity which, in turn, may lead to the rejection of any deviant (Schachter, 1951).

One prime way the practitioner can influence norms and encourage the role structure along the lines he desires, is through the planning of program activities. The worker must be aware of how activities influence norms and roles. They are planned both to support present, and to develop additional, legitimate norms. For example, the worker can initiate activities that foster considerable cooperation and teamwork (e.g., volleyball). Program activities must implicitly or explicitly underline the problem-oriented focus of the group. If the worker established a treatment contract with individual participants and with the group, he will likely receive greater receptivity to this problem and change focus, but frequent reinforcement or restatement of the contract is required.

Several observers have noted that a "honeymoon period" occurs in this stage; members may be highly attracted to the worker, to other members, and to the program. Although attraction and satisfaction are required to maintain a viable, potent group, the worker must sense the pitfalls at this time or the group may become static, thus seriously jeopardizing movement toward change goals.

Cliques or subgroups often emerge during this phase; the worker must respond to this process by supporting the structures that have positive consequences for group functioning and treatment. However, if subgroups form factions that pull members in opposite directions, this may lead to dissatisfaction, isolation of members, and disintegration. Depending upon his assessment, the worker can support or seek to revise the leadership structure developed in the formative phase. In any event, he encourages leadership by more and different members. According to knowledge of the developmental processes, during this phase the group is expected to begin to hold different role expectations of members because of their particular skills or other attributes. Direct and indirect means of influence can be employed to place members in positions of therapeutic benefit, so long as such actions do not have negative consequences for other members. Simultaneously, direct means of influence can be used to help selected members meet expectations of particular roles within the groups. Observation of different patterns of behavior provides important information to the worker to support his initial diagnostic impressions or to suggest the need for modification of earlier impressions. Corresponding alterations in treatment goals may then be necessary.

More effective operating procedures are encouraged by the worker at this time, but the group should not be expected to develop highly efficient or effective problem-solving or decision-making processes. Premature efforts to formalize operating or governing procedures might hamper treatment objectives and even result in maladaptation. For example, in discussion treatment groups, the worker should avoid establishing rigid participation requirements that block spontaneity.

Because group efforts to develop social control mechanisms are often apparent during this stage, the worker must realize that peer discipline can be harsh and extreme pressures can be exerted on deviant members through the enforcement of group norms. The worker mediates procedures and sanctions so that members are not isolated or made scapegoats. He encourages the group to develop appropriate control mechanisms thereby enhancing its potential for influence upon individual members. As in the prior stage, norms and values which facilitate treatment are supported by the worker who serves as a spokesman for such norms and also symbolizes them in actions. Special assistance can help members act in accordance with group norms and values.

Stage IV. Maintaining the Group Through Revision

The following worker actions may be required during this stage of the treatment sequence which corresponds to Intermediate Phase II:

1. Revising group's quasi-structure
2. Modifying group norms, operating procedures
3. Maintaining group cohesion

The worker should expect a challenge to and/or a revision of the quasi-structure established in the formative phase and solidified in the first intermediate phase. Only limited modification may achieve increased participation, or there may be need for rather drastic changes. As pointed out, revision of the initial structures may have been guided by the worker's actions, his lack of support for initial leaders and positive responses to other members who attempt to fulfill leadership functions. Thus, revision of the quasi-structure need not occur suddenly and dramatically, but can unfold over a period of time.

If leadership roles are changed significantly, the worker may intervene directly so that former leaders will be retained in the group. He may also modify group participation patterns so that all members will continue to derive satisfaction. Direct activity with new leaders can help them assume leadership roles that enhance treatment for all members.

Since this stage is often quite fluid and dynamic, it offers the worker opportunity to modify group norms which he could not influence earlier. This task, of course, is much easier if the new leaders are oriented toward desired norms and purposes. Changes in operating procedures can be expected to accompany the revision of leadership structure. The worker supports changes that increase participation, democratic processes of decision making, and mature approaches to group and individual problem solving.

During the processes of revision, group cohesion equilibrium is upset so the worker must help reaffirm members' ties to each other and their support for group purposes and tasks. Assisting the group to select a program carefully will be useful at this point. Program activities are directed to provide positive support for the new leaders, to aid role differentiation and specialization so that all members feel like contributing participants, and to provide enjoyable activities so attraction to the group will be enhanced.

Stage V. Guiding Group Processes Toward Treatment Goals

During this advanced stage, corresponding to the beginning of the Maturation Phase, worker's interventions will be supportive and evaluative:

1. Supporting (modified) leadership structure
2. Supporting group's efforts to cope directly with pressures
3. Assessment of progress toward individual treatment goals

If the group has gone through revision, the worker acts to stabilize the modified leadership structure, helps clarify new norms that relate to treatment objectives, and enables the operating procedures that have developed lead to greater self-direction by the group. The problem-focused nature of the group is strongly emphasized since equilibrium should be reestablished.

If the group structure has not been revised substantially, the worker fosters the continuation of the developments noted in Stage III—the formation of appropriate norms and effective social control mechanisms, a group structure that encourages maximum participation, an expanded division of labor, and a differentiated role system with most members having the opportunity to fulfill some leadership functions.

During this stage significant movement toward treatment objectives is expected. Periods of progress, however, are often followed by periods of regression. Although the worker acts to prevent serious disruption during these cyclical changes, he does not prevent their occurrence because of the valuable learning opportunities provided for group members. Members, individually and collectively, learn to cope with increasingly complex problems and tasks, and thus, the group is enhanced as an effective treatment vehicle. Observable increases in the level of integration are expected by this time.

Although the group may experience several "revisions" and appear to revert to earlier stages, different dynamics can be expected in each of these regressions and progressions because of prior experiences. Repeated challenges to the leadership structure often occur, as do attempts to revise norms, purposes, tasks, or operating procedures. If the challenge is negative vis-à-vis treatment objectives, the worker intervenes firmly and directly to constrain the process. Conversely, he will intervene to support challenges which have positive implications.

Prior to this stage the worker may have assumed major responsibility for helping the group cope with internal and external pressures to change. Actions should now make the group itself responsible for coping directly with these pressures. Miller has described the dynamics of group development of delinquent gangs, particularly the changes in the gangs' ability to respond to and alter their environment. He has also identified several worker actions that are required if the group is to be successful in this task (Miller, 1957).

Greater use of indirect rather than direct means of influence will be expected in this stage, because worker's actions in earlier stages should have resulted in the development of norms, social control mechanisms, operating and governing procedures that allow for greater self-direction by the group.[6] The worker's objectives and members' attributes influence the group in establishing norms that support problem-focused actions and lead to treatment goals. Since the danger of reaching a static equilibrium always exists, the worker's interventions should be sufficiently disruptive to maintain that degree of instability required for the group to serve as a continuing vehicle for treatment. In this stage the worker must be especially careful to avoid the danger of perceiving the group as an end in itself. He must remain alert and sensitive to group processes so that he can intervene to influence norms, purposes, operating procedures, control mechanisms and group structures to facilitate the attainment of treatment goals for individual members.

Stage VI. Maintaining the Group

Groups can move fully into the Maturation Phase but never reach this stage in the treatment sequence because individual client goals are likely to be achieved in one of the prior stages, and service is then terminated. This stage is considered briefly because few groups in the Maturation Phase of development are assumed to require the services of a professional group worker.

[6] Frequently noted in the literature on psychotherapy groups is the change from a worker-centered to a group-centered group; see Martin and Hill (1957) and Hock and Kaufer (1955). This phenomenon may reflect the worker's inactivity during later states or his use of more indirect means of influence. Northen (1958) cites the worker's change from an active to a supporting role.

From the previous review, the following characteristics are expected of a group in the Maturation Phase: a high level of integration, stabilized group structures, consensus of and direction toward goals, customary operating and governing procedures, an expanded group culture, and effective mechanisms for change. When these characteristics are observed, it is safe to assume that individual members are relatively mature persons who do not require professional group work service. Groups are often terminated at this stage and members may be referred to agencies for socialization or other services, but generally not for social work treatment. Under special circumstances professional workers might continue to serve such groups for limited periods of time. The role of the worker would be primarily to facilitate continued group functioning and indirect means of influence would definitely predominate. The worker's main assistance to the group would occur when crises arise because of internal or external pressures, or in especially difficult phases of problem solving.

A question can be raised whether groups such as street gangs are in the maturation phase at the time of the worker's initial contact and, therefore, do not need the professional services. Many such groups appear to be in the maturation phase at first contact, but the central problem is that they maintain antisocial values and norms. Interventions by the worker are directed toward a drastic revision of existing group conditions, to modify norms, structures and operating procedures. If the worker's efforts are successful, the group can be expected to move back to and through the earlier revision phase. Accurate assessment of such groups is essential, because superficial observation may suggest that the group is in the maturation phase when, in fact, this is not the case.

Stage VII. Terminating the Group

Four reasons were offered for termination of a group: (1) achievement of goals for individual members; (2) predetermined duration of the group by agency policies and/or objectives; (3) lack of minimal integration, and the worker's decision that a satisfactory level cannot be achieved; (4) maladaptation because the group lacks appropriate mechanisms for coping with internal and external pressures. Briefly, the worker's role in each of these termination situations will be examined.

Termination for achievement of goals or objectives results when the worker evaluates his original treatment goals for each individual and determines that they have been attained satisfactorily. It is highly desirable that members be engaged in parts of the evaluation and they clearly perceive what has been accomplished. In terminating the group, the conditions of the contract, established in the first phase between worker and members, can be evaluated in a similar manner. Since changes were sought that were stabilized and transferable outside the treatment sequence, careful evaluation prior to termination is essential. Indeed, at this point the worker may help the group to devote special attention to extragroup experiences of its members.

Even when groups are established for specific periods of time (for example, orientation or discharge groups), termination must be carefully considered. Such groups can be expected to have wide variations in the types and degrees of change that occur among individual members. Goals may have been reached at a satisfactory level for some individuals, but others will require referral for additional treatment.

To determine which factors contributed to lack of integration, the worker examines the composition of the group, the members' commitments to group purposes and tasks, pressures from the environment, and his own service to the group. Lack of integration results from inadequacies in one or several of these areas. Whatever the reason, if a decision is made to terminate the group, the worker must do so in a manner which is not harmful to any member. For example, if faulty group composition appears to be the problem, the group may be re-composed with different membership. Other situations also may require dissolution of the group and the referral of members for services elsewhere.

Termination because of maladaptation is likely to result because of inappropriate mechanisms for coping with external and internal pressures, or because previously successful mechanisms have become rigid and inflexible. Maladaptation is likely to occur in the later phases of group development. In determining causes and possible solutions, the worker needs to examine factors similar to those for lack of integration. Frequently the worker can intervene to prevent the dissolution of the group.

Termination may take place in any phase for the reasons given or even because of other factors. It is expected, of course, that when termination occurs because of satisfactory goal achievement, the group will be in one of the later stages of development.

REFERENCES

BALES, ROBERT F.
  1950—*Interaction Process Analysis: A Method for the Study of Small Groups,* Cambridge, Massachusetts: Addison-Wesley Press.
BALES, ROBERT F. AND PHILIP E. SLATER
  1955—"Role differentiations in small decision-making groups," in T. Parsons and R. F. Bales, *Family, Socialization and Interaction Process,* Glencoe, Illinois: Free Press, pp. 239–306.

BENNIS, WARREN G. AND HERBERT A. SHEPARD
  1962—"A theory of group development," in W. G. Bennis, K. D. Benne and R. Chin (Eds.), *The Planning of Change*, New York: Holt, pp. 321–340.
FESTINGER, LEON
  1962—"Informal social communication," in Dorwin Cartwright and Alvin Zander, *Group Dynamics*, second edition, Evanston, Illinois: Row, Peterson, pp. 286–299.
FOULKES, S. H. AND E. J. ANTHONY
  1957—*Group Psychotherapy*, London: Wyman and Sons.
HARE, PAUL
  1962—*Handbook of Small Group Research*, Glencoe, Illinois: Free Press.
HOCK, E. AND G. A. KAUFER
  1955—"A process analysis of 'transient' therapy groups," *International Journal of Group Psychotherapy* 5, pp. 415–421.
HOMANS, GEORGE C.
  1950—*The Human Group*, New York: Harcourt, Brace & Co.
JENNINGS, HELEN H.
  1950—*Leadership and Isolation*, New York: Longmanns, Green, pp. 209–217.
MARTIN, ELMORE A., JR. AND WILLIAM F. HILL
  1957—"Toward a theory of group development: Six phases of therapy group development," *International Journal of Group Psychotherapy* 7, pp. 20–30.
MEREI, FERENC
  1958—"Group leadership and institutionalization," in E. E. Maccoby, T. M. Newcomb and E. L. Hartley (Eds.), *Readings in Social Psychology*, New York: Holt, Rinehart and Winston, Inc., pp. 522–532.
MILLER, WALTER B.
  1957—"The impact of a community group work program on delinquent corner groups," *Social Service Review* 31, pp. 390–406.
NORTHEN, HELEN
  1958—"Social group work: A tool for changing behavior of disturbed acting-out adolescents," in *Social Work With Groups*. New York: National Association of Social Workers.
PSATHAS, GEORGE
  1960—"Phase movement and equilibrium tendencies in interaction process in psychotherapy groups," *Sociometry* 23, pp. 177–194.
RIECKEN, HENRY W. AND GEORGE C. HOMANS
  1954—"Psychological aspects of social structure," in G. Lindzey (Ed.), *Handbook of Social Psychology*, Cambridge: Addison-Wesley, pp. 786–833.
SCHACHTER, STANLEY
  1951—"Deviation, rejection, and communication," *Journal of Abnormal and Social Psychology* 46, pp. 190–207.

THEODORSON, GEORGE A.

    1953—"Elements in the progressive development of small groups," *Social Forces* 31, pp. 311–320.

THOMAS, EDWIN J. AND CLINTON F. FINK

    1963—"Effects of group size," *Psychological Bulletin* 60, pp. 371–384.

WEISMAN, CELIA B.

    1953—"Social structure as a determinant of the group worker's role," *Social Work* 8, pp. 87–94.

6.

Socioeducation Groups

NORMA RADIN

Several major trends with important implications for social group workers have emerged in the late 1960s: (1) a burgeoning in the use of paraprofessionals in the helping and educational professions; (2) an increased emphasis on prevention in virtually all the people-serving professions; (3) greater resistance by those with limited incomes and/or minority status to be "treated" by social workers and to the assumption that they are impaired, if not ill, and in need of therapy; (4) rising expectations that all people share in the good life, and (5) the corollary expectations that professionals serve a large number of people rather than a select few. These trends suggest that the time may have come for group workers to examine the ability of their methodology to meet the needs of the coming decade.

Robert Vinter in 1959 took a controversial stand that called for a reordering of priorities of the late 1950s and urged group workers to give prime attention to the poor, the disadvantaged, and those with severe problems in social functioning. In keeping with this, the group work faculty of the University of Michigan School of Social Work developed a methodology focused on group services for these clients and trained hundreds of students in its use. Times and conditions have changed, however, and now there is greater professional commitment to expanding such efforts. The most pressing issue in the profession today is not who should be served first, but which is the most efficient and effective way to deliver service. Today in schools, community mental health centers, public welfare agencies, and residential settings, social workers are being asked to provide in-service training to small groups of paraprofessionals or to offer group consultation to professionals in other fields. Workers are also being asked to help "socializers" (teachers, daycare mothers, ministers, etc.) in their roles to facilitate the development of those for whom they are responsible. Requests are also being made to impart knowledge and skills to youths and adults who function adequately at present but are likely to have difficulties filling important future roles (i.e., as mothers or retirees). Social workers frequently are seen as professionals who can organize and lead these programs. Many accept the assignment reluctantly because the emphasis in their training has not been on what they perceive as education. In some instances, it does not occur to the agency executive or the group worker to take advantage of such opportunities.

Although direct service to the most distressed is still important, group workers must elaborate alternative methods for reaching more people in need; two such strategies are to offer consultation to the "caregivers" (i.e., foster mothers, nurses, parents, teachers) and the "socializers" of those with difficulties, and to provide service to those most in need before problems become severe and affect a network of people around them. These extensions are consistent with the original intent and the purposely open system of the Michigan practice model, as will be shown later.

To prevent the problem of reluctant, unprepared, or unaware social workers, a school can develop an orientation that is distinct from casework, group work, community practice, or administration. Portland State University School of Social Work has developed a program called "Facilitative Services" in which students are prepared for facilitative positions such as teaching, consultation, and supervision positions. (Bontje and Longres, 1971) For interested second year students the program offers courses of study and a practicum experience.

A different strategy is to train people outside the social work profession to serve as consultants, educators or facilitators. The Community Mental Health Consultant, as described by Gerald Caplan (1969), fits this strategy, as does the Crisis Teacher depicted by Morse (1965).

Another path suggested in this chapter would prepare professionals in other fields for social group work with clients (such as teachers or nurses). This extends the Michigan model of group work to train workers at schools of social work to use the basic methodology of the Michigan model with relatively capable individuals, who would in turn work to improve social functioning of troubled or oppressed individuals. When the Michigan model is used with relatively capable individuals the label *socioeducational* (rather than treatment) *groups* will be used as it highlights the importance of member interaction and input of knowledge. (Navarre, Glasser and Costabile, Chapter 24 in this volume; Wittes and Radin, 1971; Bertcher, et al., 1973)

Major changes in the practice model are not required. In work with both treatment and socioeducational groups, the group is perceived as a deliberately structured influence system that effects changes through interaction relationships. In both, the worker attempts to develop a group with maximum potential for influencing its members, and the group becomes both the medium and target for change. The basic principles of social group work that apply to treatment groups apply to socioeducation groups as well. The individual is the focus of change; the goals are specific, capable of being described operationally; a contract is made between worker and group members specifying the focal areas and means to be used. Social forces within the group such as peer pressures, modeling, and group norms are used to obtain and maintain individual change; and extragroup means of influencing are used to facilitate the attainment of individual goals.

Four major types of direct means of influence are the same: The worker as (1) a central person and the object of identification; (2) a symbol and spokesman of desired norms and values; (3) a motivator, stimulator, and definer of individual goals and tasks, and (4) an executive and controller of roles and activities. Relatively competent adults usually are able to share in these roles with the worker earlier than a group composed of members with major social functioning problems. Such participation in the planning and operation of the group facilitates, rather than impedes, goal attainment in all groups.

Further, the indirect means of influence employed are virtually identical. Group, communication, sociometric, power, role, and normative structures are modified to maximize the attainment of individual goals. Group processes such as decision making and group development are also influenced by the worker to achieve individual change.

An evaluation of the attainment of goals is made at the conclusion of the program, and the group is terminated in such a way as to assure maintenance of these goals. It is more likely that some socioeducational groups may go on to become agents of system change, in Cartwright's (1967) terminology, than do treatment groups. However, the desire for social action which developed in a group of low-income mothers (Wittes and Radin, 1971) is not unlike the desire for more patient self-government that develops out of small-group discussions among hospital patients or residents of group homes.

The major variations in emphasis and application of the Michigan model between work and socioeducational and treatment groups lie in five areas: (1) the worker's orientation, (2) the nature of the worker-client relationship, (3) group composition, (4) intake procedure, and (5) content of group discussions.

Work with socioeducational groups must not imply that the group member is inadequate, ill, or that pathology is involved. The use of treatment labels and terms (often considered generic to the profession) with group members is often dysfunctional to the achievement of individual goals in all groups, and particularly in those with a socioeducation orientation. In describing the nature of family life education Lois Glasser (1971) expressed the matter clearly when she differentiated the role of the family life educator from that of the traditional social worker. In family life education groups, she stated, membership is voluntary, the approach is educational, and the worker views himself on an equal basis with the group members, learning from them as he teaches, and "building on strengths by imparting to the student additional knowledge and skills which he is motivated to learn." Many group workers have had a similar orientation but it clearly cannot be considered universal.

This egalitarian relationship is the heart of the worker-member relationship in socioeducational groups. In pragmatic terms, it is the only type of relationship likely to succeed between social workers serving as consultants-educators to caregivers and socializers such as groups of teachers, nurses, aides, or parents and to others not presently experiencing problems but who require or request help in the transition from one set of roles to another. It is certainly true that skilled and sensitive therapists can have egalitarian relationships with their clients, but Maier (1971), in a plea for a more peerlike relationship, suggests that equality does not typify most therapeutic interactions.

Further, many lower-class and middle-class adults do not view probes into their personal problems or inadequacies with equanimity. Those who have worked with low-income adults have found, on the other hand, that they tend to welcome opportunities to learn new skills and knowledge that will help them reach the goals they hold for themselves and their families. Perhaps the essential difference is that learning new skills is seen as education, whereas exploring personal inadequacies is perceived as therapy and tends to evoke client resistance. The scope of the change to be effected may also be relevant. Almost by definition, learning a new skill implies a minor alteration in one's way of life. Therapy sometimes suggests a major reorganization. Along the continuum between education and therapy, it is suggested here that work with socioeducational groups lies closer to the educational end, whereas work with treatment groups lies closer to the therapeutic end.

Differences in group composition involving the intake and the diagnosis phases are also significant to the practitioner. According to the Michigan model, the first phase customarily is that of intake, when the client presents himself or is presented with his problem or need, as he and/or others perceive it. In the second phase, the worker and client together diagnose the client's problem, his capacity for help and change, and then develop a statement of treatment goals, or changes which hopefully can result if the treatment effort is successful. In the third phase the worker assigns clients to groups, composing them of persons whom he believes can be served together. One sentence in Vinter's delineation of the group composition phase suggests that the differences between composing a socioeducational group and a treatment group may not be as great as the following section will imply. "Under certain circumstances—as in work with delinquent street groups—the practitioner may exercise considerably less control over this phase. . . ." (Vinter, in Chapter 2 in this volume p. 11).

Sallie Churchill, in a personal communication in 1970, suggested that lack of control may exist even more frequently in treatment groups than the literature on the Michigan model suggests.

In composing all groups, the first step is the choice by the worker, and others involved in the program, concerning the target group, i.e., the group to be offered a program. This decision involves selecting the nature of the problem to be dealt with and the specific goals to be achieved. The problem may vary from school failure to inability to adjust to widowhood. In reality the type of agency, its location, its resources, and community pressures, tend to highlight the specific problems which are most salient, and thus limit the range of choices.

Another decision for those working with socioeducational groups is whether the program required is for individuals who are likely to have problems in social functioning in the future, or to work with socializers and caregivers of these individuals; for example, daycare mothers, class-room teachers, school aides, ministers, older siblings, etc. Again, this choice is often limited by the prevailing context of practice. If the worker is employed by a welfare agency, it is often simpler to work with the caregivers, for example, the parent receiving aid to Families of Dependent Children, or the foster mother. If the worker is employed in a school, more options are usually available, such as direct work with children in trouble or likely to get in trouble, work with their tutors, their teachers and teacher-aides, their parents, or even their student teachers.

In composing socioeducational groups for preventive programs, one of three factors is usually given major consideration. The first pertains to demographic information such as the potential member's employment status, age, neighborhood of residence, etc. Geismar (1969) used this approach in his primary prevention program. The relevant issue is what data vividly predict future problems. A second variable is that of the potential member's entry into a new role such as that of parent, widow, disabled worker, or caretaker of an aged parent. Difficulties in role performance are likely to occur, according to Duvall (1962), when the role players are unfamiliar with the relevant expectations and knowledge. To gain such proficiencies, socioeducational groups can be very appropriate. The third factor given consideration as a predictor of future problems and an opportunity for prevention is a crisis, such as major surgery or the birth of a handicapped or premature baby. Caplan (1964) has discussed in great depth the opportunities for prevention in such situations. Goode's classic study of divorce (1956) suggests the conditions under which a divorce may also be characterized as a crisis and an ideal opportunity for programs in secondary or tertiary prevention.

In any of the above situations, socioeducational programs should be offered to all who fit the target group description, not merely those who visibly are having difficulties or who ask for help. Through this technique, it is likely that the net tossed out will catch some highly skilled members who have little need for group service. These people are not excluded but welcomed into the group, since they can be highly effective as role models and developers of new norms, both in the group and among peers who are invited but refuse to join. A program is then developed around the persons who join the group.

If the characteristics of the target group have been carefully considered before the program is initiated and efforts to reach out to potential members have been made such as provision of transportation, several reminders, and refreshments, the worker should find a high percentage of potential group members who could benefit from the group work service. At the same time, the danger of a negative effect from a member's having been especially selected because he has a problem is reduced. The group members can feel, justifiably, that they have voluntarily chosen to join a group to improve their knowledge and skills in a specific area.

A different approach can initiate a socioeducational group. An administrator may ask a social worker to conduct a series of in-service training sessions for the staff, professional or paraprofessional. Or the social worker may perceive the need and offer to do such training. Many social workers, for example, conduct in-service training programs for other professionals, such as nurses and teachers and their aides (Churchill and Glasser, 1965; Michigan Department of Education, 1971). Although voluntarism varies widely, membership should be as voluntary as feasible in such groups. It was found in one study (Chesler and Wissman, 1968) that when all teachers were given time off from their classroom duties and required to attend in-service training sessions, considerable resentment developed toward the program because attendance was not self-chosen. Nonvoluntary groups may be effective where other opportunities for participation in groups or helping relationships are scarce, as with inmates of a correctional institution or children in school, but nonvoluntary membership in socioeducational groups tends to be irritating, if not antagonizing, to adults who perceive themselves as free to make decisions about their own life experiences.

Intake procedures of socioeducational groups may also have to be altered from those of treatment groups. While it may be possible to interview each member prior to organizing the first session of the group, in many situations an invitation is extended to a relatively large target population such as workers soon to be retired, and the members are seen for the first time at the initial group meeting when a contract or agreement between members and worker is made. On occasion, if a member asks to see the worker individually or if the worker visits a member who missed a session, lengthy individual discussions can take place. Such interviews are not perceived as essential, however. An assessment of each individual's strengths and weaknesses, relative to the preestablished goals, can be based entirely on observations of member behavior during the group meetings themselves and on the informal discussions before and after the sessions. As the individual assessments gain clarity, goals can be specified for individual members. Some of these may pertain to in-group behavior, and others to out-of-group behavior. For example, in a program established for a group of daycare mothers (Green and Valenstein, 1971; Radin, 1970), the initial goals included an increase in the mothers' skills in managing the children and an increase in their perceptions of themselves as professional childcare workers. After several weeks, more specific goals were delineated for individual members. One mother was to increase her repertoire of discipline techniques to include strategies other than punishment; another was to participate more actively in the group discussions so that her creative child management techniques would become known to more women; for a third mother, the goal was for greater honesty during the group discussions so that difficulties she was having with some children in her care (which consultants visiting the home had observed) could be discussed and group solutions suggested.

Ideally, after several weeks, the worker will be able to determine terminal and intermediate goals for all the members, as well as goals pertaining to group behaviors. The worker must plan carefully to be certain that members who functioned exceedingly well before joining the group play an active part and help support other members in their movement toward the goals. As shown in the Provo study (Empey and Rabow, 1961), such group members are invaluable in creating highly desirable new norms that keep within the worker's goals for the group. Similar procedures have been used extensively with natural groups, such as neighborhood gangs and cottage groups in correctional and psychiatric institutions.

Frequently it has been found that after a series of socioeducational group meetings, members feel an enhanced sense of efficacy and wish to use the new found power to attain new goals for themselves; often the group decides to work as a unit to achieve change in a larger system to meet their needs. (Gray and Klaus, 1970; Wittes and Radin, 1971; Badger, 1971; Navarre, Glasser and Costabile, Chapter 24 in this volume) This phenomenon has been observed with populations as diverse as low-income mothers, aged hospital patients, and parents of retarded children. The role of the worker when that stage is reached depends upon his own preference and organizational factors. If there is another agency or group available for the members to join, they may be helped to become integrated into the new group. Occasionally, the worker may wish to continue working with the group on a reduced basis, decreasing his own contacts as the members develop their own leadership and begin to function independently. Under any circumstances, it would be impractical and unwise to continue the group indefinitely.

Regarding the program of socioeducation group sessions, here the emphasis differs somewhat from that in treatment groups; the focus is not on the problematic behavior of the group member. Rather, it is only the needs of the individual in the care of the socializer, or on the role demands and potential role conflicts of persons likely to be experiencing a new role. The skills and knowledge needed by the caregiver to foster the development of the person being supervised occupies most of the meeting time. In both types of socioeducational groups, specified content serves to guide the worker; for example, the material on childrearing developed by Karnes, Studley, and Wright (1966), Wittes and Radin (1969), Patterson and Guillon (1968), Becker (1971), or the material on behavior modification for use by teachers (Buckley and Walker, 1970), or information about problems likely to be encountered in different life stages (Duvall, 1962). In some cases, workers conducting socioeducation programs may have to create their own "curriculum" through a review of the literature, talks with experts, and use of their own experiences. The content to be imparted to socioeducational group members is a more important element in treatment groups.

It is possible to combine very effectively the treatment approach with the socioeducational approach. The combination has been highly successful in the Cross-Age Program, developed by Peggy Lippitt (Lippitt and Lohman, 1965). In a Cross-Age Program, students with problems in social functioning were asked to become tutors for younger pupils who were experiencing academic and/or social difficulties. Often some very competent students are included in the group of tutors. The tutors were informed that they were selected for the program because they possessed certain skills that were suitable. Once the program got underway the tutors met weekly in a "seminar" with a special teacher or social worker to discuss their programs and problems as tutors. In essence, the seminar was a socioeducational group for paraprofessionals who were caregivers for malfunctioning individuals.

The essential component of the Cross-Age Program was in placing students with academic or behavioral problems in a new role, that of a helper to someone else in need. The net effect was to raise the tutor's self-image, enhance his empathy for other teachers, and stimulate his desire to learn so that he could be a more effective tutor. This strategy began with a treatment focus since the members were selected carefully on the basis of their current difficulties as well as strengths. Beyond that criterion, however, the program functioned like any other socioeducational group for paraprofessionals, with the very act of playing the caregiver role being the essence of the helping process. The principle obviously can be extended to many other groups of malfunctioning individuals.

Several problems and unresolved issues related to work with socio-educational groups are evident. Determining which population is likely to encounter difficulties in social functioning based on demographic data, new role entry, or crisis situation is clearly a matter of judgment. No one can know for certain. All that the worker can do is examine the research literature carefully, and try to obtain the most specific information possible about the characteristics and condition of those who develop problems. In some cases, only correlational data are available from published articles and books. That is, a published report may state that a high correlation was found between characteristic A, such as low income, and behavior B, such as leaving school without a high school diploma. The correlation does not prove causality. It is possible that the behavior in some way caused the characteristic or that a third variable was responsible for both the characteristic and the behavior, for example, racism or the state of the economy. Nevertheless, those who wish to engage in preventive interven-tion must accept responsibility for formulating hypotheses concerning the type of people who are most vulnerable, and then proceed to design a program for those individuals. It is assumed that other social workers (such as community organizers), other change agents (such as community psychologists), and other groups in society (such as the Welfare Rights Organization, the Urban League, or the National Organization of Women) are working on the environmental factors which contribute to the problem (e.g., discriminatory legislation or employment practices). The group worker will attempt to alter the damaging environment where possible, through extragroup means of influence. This may involve efforts to modify school procedures or welfare department regulations. But the group worker, like the caseworker, is involved essentially in modifying interpersonal rela-tions and cannot attempt to effect change on all levels simultaneously. Hopefully, those working on the same problem will be coordinated closely so that the efforts of change agents who are attempting to intervene at the system level, the interpersonal level, and the community level will be coordinated.

Some damage might conceivably result from offering the wrong pro-gram to a group; for example, one that stimulates the curiosity of young potential drug users (Stuart, 1973). A more likely consequence of poor judgment in selecting a target group is that money and effort will have been wasted. There is no avoiding this risk since human behavior cannot be predicted with complete certainty. To reduce disservice to group mem-bers, however, the worker about to embark on a preventive intervention program must review the literature as carefully as possible to be certain that he has the most recent information and is making use of hypotheses that are strongly supported by data.

Specifying goals for socioeducation groups is also difficult. If one wishes to increase the skills of a mother, classroom teacher, or aide in handling young children who are interfering with the activities of others, a wide array of behaviors might be increased. As mentioned by Sundel and Lawrence (Chapter 20 in this volume) concerning goal setting in a preventive approach, when the objective of the worker is for a group member to add behaviors that are not in his current repertoire, it is more difficult to be specific than when the goal is to reduce the frequency of a currently held behavior.

It should be pointed out that group supervisory sessions conducted by leaders empowered to hire, fire, promote, and evaluate group members are not socioeducational groups. The power relationship between members and leaders is too unequal.

An issue that needs exploring is the difference in work techniques of an educator-consultant with individuals likely to experience problems, with paraprofessionals, and with professionals. Thus far, little differentiation has been made among the three groups. In one successful program in Tennessee where low-income mothers were taught to become teachers to their children, it was emphasized that the women were treated as much like professional teachers as possible (Badger, 1971). Some daycare centers have deliberately created groups composed of parents and teachers to reduce the social distance between the two. Possibly, in this era of increasing community control of schools, daycare centers, and poverty programs, social workers cannot establish two distinct modes of functioning, one for vulnerable populations and one for socializers. The question is rather one of matching the program to the abilities and wishes of the group. At this point in the development of this approach it seems useful to perceive all members of socioeducational groups as competent adults wishing to enhance their knowledge and skills.

Perhaps the most debatable portion of this chapter is the assumption that a more educational approach is more acceptable to many people than treatment is. Potential members of socioeducational groups might be as resentful about the notion that they could benefit from more training as they are about the suggestion that they need treatment. Thus far, those who have used this approach have experienced that it does not engender hostility. Perhaps the voluntary nature of the group filters out those who might be resistant. Undoubtedly some people will refuse to become part of any type of group. For these individuals, other programs will have to be developed.

In summary, a pressing need has arisen for those in the helping professions to supplement direct service to malfunctioning individuals with a program of preventive intervention and of consultative service with caregivers and socializers. Social group workers are ideally suited to perform these tasks since they are skilled in using group processes and structures to achieve specified goals for individual group members. Training social work students to use both the treatment approach and the suggested revision, emphasizing work with relatively competent adults, may be an important step in preparing graduates to function more effectively and flexibly in the coming decade.

REFERENCES

BADGER, EARLADEEN
    1971—"A mothers' training program," *Children* 18, 5 (May), pp. 168–173.
BERTCHER, HARVEY, JESSE GORDON, MICHAEL HAYES, MEL LAWSON, AND
        JEROME MUNSAY
    1973—*Group Leadership Techniques: A Self-Instructional Workshop*, Ann
        Arbor: Manpower Science Services, Inc.
BONTJE, AD AND JOHN LONGRES
    1971—"Introducing the social services educator training component within
        the social work master's degree curriculum," Paper read at the Council on Social Work Education, Seattle, Washington.
BECKER, WESLEY
    1971—*Parents are Teachers: A Child Management Program*, Champaign,
        Illinois: Research Press Co.
BUCKLEY, NANCY K. AND M. WALKER HILL
    1970—*Modifying Classroom Behavior: A Manual of Procedures for Classroom Teachers*, Champaign, Illinois: Research Press Co.
CAPLAN, GERALD
    1964—*Principles of Preventive Psychiatry*, New York: Basic Books.
    1969—"Types of mental health consultation," in Warren Bennis, Kenneth
        Benne, and Robert Chin (Eds.), *The Planning of Change*, New York:
        Holt, Rinehart and Winston.
CARTWRIGHT, DORWIN
    1967—"Achieving change in people: Some applications of group dynamics
        theory," in Edwin P. Hollander and Raymond G. Hunt (Eds.),
        Current Perspectives in Social Psychology, second edition, New York:
        Oxford University Press, pp. 520–529.
CHESLER, MARK AND MARGARET WISSMAN
    1968—"Teacher reactions to school desegregation, preparations and processes: A case study," Center for Research on the Utilization of Scientific Knowledge, University of Michigan, Ann Arbor, Michigan.
        (Mimeographed)
CHURCHILL, SALLIE R. AND PAUL H. GLASSER
    1965—"Small groups in the hospital community: lectures and proceedings,"
        Lansing, Michigan: Department of Mental Health, State of Michigan.

DUVALL, EVELYN M.
1962—*Family Development*, New York: J. B. Lippincott Co.

EMPEY, LAMAR AND JEROME RABOW
1961—"The Provo experiment in delinquency rehabilitation," *American Sociological Review*, 26, pp. 678–695.

GEISMAR, LUDWIG L.
1969—*Preventive Intervention in Social Work*, Metuchin, New Jersey: The Scarecrow Press.

GLASSER, LOIS
1971—"Family life and sex education," in Robert Morris, (Ed.), *Encyclopedia of Social Work*, New York: National Association of Social Workers, pp. 386–392.

GOODE, WILLIAM J.
1956—*Women in Divorce*, New York: The Free Press.

GRAY, SUSAN W. AND RUPERT A. KLAUS
1970—"The early training project: A seventh-year report," *Child Development*, 41, 4 (December), pp. 909–924.

GREEN, MELINDA AND THELMA VALENSTEIN
1971—"The educational day care consultation program progress report," Ann Arbor, Michigan: University of Michigan, School of Education. (Mimeographed)

KARNES, MERLE B., WILLIAM M. STUDLEY AND WILLES R. WRIGHT
1966—"An approach for working with parents of disadvantaged children: pilot project," Urbana, Illinois: Institute for Research on Exceptional Children, University of Illinois.

LIPPITT, PEGGY AND JOHN LOHMAN
1965—"Cross-age relationships: An educational resource," *Children*, 12, pp. 113–117.

LIPPITT, RONALD, JEANNE WATSON AND BRUCE WESTLEY
1958—*The Dynamics of Planned Change*, New York: Harcourt, Brace and Co., Inc.

MAIER, HENRY
1971—"A sidewards look at change," *Social Services Review* 45, 2 (June), pp. 132–136.

MICHIGAN DEPARTMENT OF EDUCATION
1971—*Packet: School Social Work Evaluation Study*, Lansing, Michigan: State Department of Education.

MORSE, WILLIAM C.
1965—"The 'crisis teacher': public school provision for the disturbed pupil," in Nicholas J. Long, William C. Morse and Ruth G. Newman (Eds.), *Conflict in The Classroom*, Belmont, California: Wadsworth Publishing Company, pp. 251–254.

PATTERSON, GERALD R. AND ELIZABETH M. GUILLON
1968—*Living with Children*, Champaign, Illinois: Research Press.

RADIN, NORMA
1970—"Evaluation of the daycare consultation program of 1969–70," Ann

Arbor, Michigan: University of Michigan, School of Social Work. (Mimeographed)

STUART, RICHARD B.
1973—"Teaching facts about drugs: Pushing or preventing," *Journal of Educational Psychology,* 65, 2 (October), in press.

WITTES, GLORIANN AND NORMA RADIN
1968—*Helping Your Child to Learn: The Reinforcement Approach,* San Rafael, California: Dimensions Publishers.

WITTES, GLORIANN AND NORMA RADIN
1971—"Two approaches to parent work in a compensatory preschool program," *Social Work,* 16, 1 (January), pp. 42–50.

II

The Treatment Sequence

7.

Diagnosis in Group Work

MARTIN SUNDEL, NORMA RADIN, and
SALLIE R. CHURCHILL

A judgment made by a social worker regarding the condition of his client, based upon information gathered by the worker, and oriented toward achieving specific goals with the client is called *diagnosis* or, at times, *assessment*. Recent changes in theory and practice have been used to update an earlier study that dealt with various factors involved in group work diagnosis according to the Michigan model. (The authors are indebted to Sarri, et al., 1967) The goal-oriented, Michigan group work model posits two objectives of social work service for achieving change at the individual level: (1) to solve explicit problems defined by the client, others of significance, or a referral source; and (2) to reduce problems that might occur when clients lack required skills or knowledge for new roles or for changing demands of old roles. The first objective describes the treatment orientation; the second, the preventive orientation.

An essential step in both treatment and preventive social work is the thoughtful assessment of the client, his present or predicted problems. In making a diagnosis, the social worker seeks to organize systematically his understanding of the client so that he can effectively focus interventions. Having organized his information about the client, the group worker can better use himself, other group members, and the external environment to execute a goal-directed strategy for the client's improved social functioning. Diagnosis and treatment are elements of an overall process which begins with initial contact between the client and the agency and ends when service is terminated.

Although it is useful to distinguish diagnosis from treatment for analytic purposes, in practice neither can be viewed as independent of the other. To determine whether a client will benefit from one specific treatment, the worker must have a clear understanding of the client's problems. The same information that provides specific direction for intervention and treatment, also serves as a basis for evaluation of change or lack of it.

Historically, diagnosis has involved a continuing search aimed at understanding the problem of the individual within his environment. Two contrasting theoretical perspectives have been employed: (1) *the environment* has been viewed as the primary source of problems, with treatment directed at modifying environmental conditions; (2) *the individual* has been seen as the primary target for change, with the environment serving as a constant against which individual problems could be examined. From the latter perspective, treatment has been aimed mainly at changing personality structure. Recent practice and theory emphasize the need to understand the individual in a *specific* environment. The dynamic interaction between an individual and his own environment has been recognized and assessed; his problems are assumed to be a function of this interaction.

Social work practice has been eclectic in developing practice principles about individual behavior and environmental influences. Social workers believe that multiple perspectives are necessary to understand human behavior adequately. No single body of knowledge provides this kind of "total" understanding. Social work principles are derived from the various social, behavioral, and biological sciences, including learning theory, egopsychology, social psychology, sociology, cultural anthropology, economics, political science, anatomy and physiology. Although some theoretical inconsistencies may exist, it is necessary to draw from all of these disciplines, for the social worker assumes that the problematic behavior of clients has multiple causes and influences. Learning theory and the concept of role have been particularly helpful in developing precise diagnoses of clients in ways which lend themselves to relatively effective technologies of change.

An eclectic approach is useful because of the great variety of situations that hinder or block the clients' effective functioning. A client may lack the social, psychological, cognitive or physical resources required to maintain adequate role performance or to assume new roles. Patterns of performance that are effective under one set of conditions may become problematic when circumstances change. Persons who perform satisfactorily for many years, for example, can face severe stresses when they retire from full time employment. Similarly, a serious physical illness may lead to social malfunctioning in one or several roles.

Current or predicted problems may be located at an intrapersonal, interpersonal, or environmental level, and often they exist at more than one of these levels. For example, at the intrapersonal level a husband may feel inadequate about his sexual capacity, at the interpersonal level he may be having conflicts with his wife about childrearing, and at the environmental level he may be unable to provide for his family because of periodic unemployment. Each of the husband's difficulties may be unrelated to the others or the problems may be manifestations of a single problem, the difficulties being interrelated in a complex manner. In developing a treatment strategy, the worker might focus on any one or more of these levels to change the relevant behaviors.

The focus here is on stresses and difficulties that are manifested in observable behaviors and environmental conditions. To be sure, statements reflecting attitudes and feelings should be considered, especially when they are problematic to clients; however, such subjective states are best described in terms of their behavioral manifestations. Specific behavior is the object of diagnostic concern to the worker; explanations of behavior can be sought at the intrapersonal, interpersonal or environmental level, or any combination thereof.

The theoretical orientation of the worker will influence the nature of the data that he consider necessary to collect. However, the large majority of clients who reach social work agencies manifest problems of social deviance or are seen as likely to by themselves and others (Garvin and Glasser, Chapter 3 in this volume). Goals for them must be set in behavioral terms for two reasons. The problems are usually described in behavioral terms, e.g., truanting and fighting; and only with expressed behavioral goals can the community objectively evaluate the professional's effectiveness. Accountability is becoming increasingly important. Whatever the practitioner's orientation, his diagnosis must be related to specific behavior goals.

THE DIAGNOSTIC PHASE IN THE CHANGE SEQUENCE

The concept of diagnosis was introduced into the literature of social work as early as 1917 by Richmond, and since then it has been employed in a variety of ways:

1. As a procedure in which the social worker and the client collect and synthesize information regarding the client's condition.
2. As a statement of the client's condition and the ways in which his environment and personality affect it.
3. As the assignment of a formal typology to an individual and his condition.

In social work the first two meanings are used.

Diagnosis is viewed as a distinct phase in the change sequence in the Michigan model. Specific intervention plans such as planned worker activities are produced directly from diagnostic statements. Prior to intervention, a worker develops a diagnosis of specific problems or situations in order to form the basis for his activities and for subsequent evaluations of his strategy to elicit change. Data-gathering is focused on contemporaneous influences on the client's situation, as opposed to the early historical influences in the individual's life. Past experiences are considered, however, when they exert an influence on the client's current behavior.

A thoughtful diagnosis must precede implementation of an intervention strategy. In some instances, after diagnosing the client's situation, the worker may conclude that intervention is not indicated or that the appropriate service cannot be provided by his agency. This presents the major ethical consideration of determining properly whether a client's situation requires social work services and, if so, by whom is it best offered.

Although diagnosis involves a continuous assessment of the client's situation, the emphasis here is on the *diagnostic phase,* that is, the period from intake to the formulation of the worker's change-directed intervention strategy. The term *diagnostic procedure* will be used to indicate the activities carried out by the worker which result in a written *diagnostic statement*. The diagnostic procedure includes the "how to" aspects of collecting pertinent information for the diagnosis; the diagnosis statement includes the content or the "what" of diagnosis. This presentation will focus primarily on the content of diagnosis and on the information required in a diagnostic statement, but some attention will also be given to the diagnostic procedure.

Diagnosis as Procedure and Statement

The diagnostic procedure includes client and worker activities aimed at collecting and synthesizing information which will enable them to set specifiable intervention goals. The worker sets down these goals in writing as part of the diagnostic statement. Interaction of the client and worker with others may be a necessary part of this procedure. Considering the significance and importance of the collected data is essential. During diagnosis the client and worker determine, by careful examination, the nature of the client's problem(s) in relation to the agency's helping resources.

The diagnostic statement represents the worker's judgment of the client's present or potential problem(s) at a given point in time, including assessment variables which he assumes gave rise to the problem(s), which contribute to the maintenance of the problem(s) or which are likely to be barriers to the client's successful problem solving. The variables are viewed individually as well as collectively to assure that interactive influences are identified. In addition to the known data, the worker may specify what additional data are required to assess adequately the client's problems.

The diagnostic statement guides the worker's intervention effort by providing boundaries, relevance, and direction for him. Essentially, it represents a set of hypotheses about the client's behavior. Necessarily, such a guide is written with an awareness of agency resources, the length of time available for service, and the characteristics and skills of the worker. The importance of the written statement cannot be overemphasized; without it, the social worker is likely to lack direction and to be more subject to the influences of immediate events than is desirable.

Diagnosis is a dynamic and continuing process. At any stage in the helping process worker intervention may serve to effect change in client behavior and to obtain additional data in order to increase diagnostic understanding of the client. While the practitioner seeks to prepare an accurate, differential diagnostic statement for initial planning, new circumstances will continue to arise. The worker must continue the diagnosis with the client and frequently he will need to modify parts of his diagnostic statement. The diagnostic phase is an arbitrary division of the intervention sequence, useful for analytic purposes only.

Following the initial diagnostic phase, diagnostic activity is no longer the primary focus of the worker; however, frequent evaluation of progress takes place between the client and the worker and, in a group, among members. Such mutual evaluations serve as one important source of new data.

Components of the Diagnostic Phase

Three major components of the diagnostic phase are 1) conducting the intake interviews, 2) formulating the initial assessment, and 3) preparing a diagnostic statement. The *intake interview* provides an opportunity for the worker to determine the client's suitability and desire for service from a particular agency and for social group work in general. Factors to be considered are the type of problem presented, agency location, and client attitudes toward the various agencies offering similar service. In addition, the worker evaluates the skills of the client that could be used as a model for appropriate behavior by other members of a group. Group work service tends to be most appropriate when the client's concerns are of an interpersonal nature or are related to peer conflicts.

The *initial assessment* is a tentative diagnosis based upon information obtained from the referral source and from the client during the intake interview. This assessment includes the client's problem, tentative goals, and the worker's rationale for group work service. The initial assessment provides the focal point for obtaining the appropriate information for the more detailed diagnostic statement.

An early requirement in problem assessment is the examination of the client's present situation. In this effort, the *presenting problem*—the verbalized reason given for a client's election or referral for social work service—provides a basis for study of various current role performances. The worker identifies how presenting problems are defined, by whom they are defined, and what aspects of the individual and his environment are involved. Problems may be differentiated by varied perceptions:

1. The client's manifestation of stress or dissatisfaction in role performance
2. Ineffective role performance as viewed by others (e.g., parents, teachers) in the client's environment
3. The practitioner's judgment, based on his own observations of the client's role performance problems

Intake situations greatly test the skills of the social worker. People who seek help often are overwhelmed by the multiplicity, severity or confusion of their problems. People who are sent to social workers often fear, deny and/or are very ashamed of "their problems." Often clients will test the worker's reactions to fantasized problems before trusting him enough to reveal their critical concerns. Some clients may try to guess the acceptable symptoms to present in order to receive agency services. To assess significant aspects of the problem, the social worker should observe sufficient examples of the client's behavior during interviews and in the group, i.e., how he sits, tone of voice, when he changes the subject, smiling, crying, etc. The worker has the very difficult task of corroborating the problem(s) for which the client seeks (or is sent for) assistance. The starting point is the presenting problem, which is the focal point for initial worker-client interaction, but which may or may not be the primary focus of treatment at the conclusion of the diagnostic process.

Before gathering specific information during the diagnostic phase, the worker might have to establish himself as one to be trusted by the client. This is particularly important in open community settings such as lower socioeconomic neighborhoods where workers must reach out to clients in order to provide services. In such situations, the worker's actions, language, mannerisms, and personal qualities should be directed towards establishing a trusting relationship with the client—a prerequisite for any intervention program. These efforts may take hours or months and may take place in groups or one-to-one relationships. They must culminate in a client-worker agreement on the goals and conditions for worker services.

In typical situations, identifying information is obtained directly from the client in the intake interview, and from significant others and/or from referral sources, prior to or shortly following, the first client interview. Pertinent information varies depending on the facts considered critical by the agency. Prior to placement in a formed group, an individual intake interview should be held to formulate an initial assessment and to determine the client's suitability for group or individual service. In the case of natural groups, the worker should observe the group, and also interview clients individually in making the initial assessment.

The essential decision at intake is whether the agency and client are agreed that he will become a client at that agency. Diagnosis then builds on the initial assessment and focuses on goals that are related to the resolution of presenting and other identified problems and to how social work service can proceed.

Problem Identification

Since social work is directed toward specifying behavioral goals, the diagnostic procedure, as outlined, relies heavily on social role and learning theory approaches. Emphasis is on helping clients change their social functioning by identifying their roles and specifying the behavior related to the roles that have led to or are likely to lead to the client's difficulty. This method of analysis is not meant to limit or constrain the practitioner's intervention techniques. Rather, the procedure opens up the possibilities of a greater variety of intervention approaches, which can be evaluated responsibly by the client, the professional and the community.

During the intake interview, the worker should record the problem presented by the client in the client's words; the same rule applies to initial interviews with the referral source. A teenager in a training school might consider his problem as that of failure to get along with friends, whereas the referring authorities might view the youth's problem as that of physically injuring other children. In order to illustrate the stated problem, examples should be obtained that provide concrete representations of the client's and referral source's perceptions of the situation.

When preventive services are provided, the term "presenting problem" can be misleading, since the focus of service is on improving the knowledge and skills of clients. For example, groups may be formed to help parents foster their children's preparation for school. Parents whose educational background is low might wish to learn more effective ways of guiding, teaching and communicating with their children. In these cases, the term "client's service goals" or "predicted problems" might be more appropriate.

Target Roles and Behaviors

After the problem, present or predicted, has been identified, the most relevant client role is determined. Such a role could be that of parent, spouse, employee, friend or student. The identification of this *target role* provides a framework for delineating the client behaviors that must be acquired, maintained, increased, decreased, or eliminated to attain adequate role performance. Early specification of target roles enables the worker to scan, effectively and efficiently, the domain of possible concerns that the client brings to the agency. Considerable time and effort in irrelevant data gathering and investigation can thereby be avoided.

After identifying the target roles, *target behaviors*—the behaviors likely to be the focus of intervention—are selected and then ranked in order of their importance. In determining the priority for service, the worker should consider the following criteria:

1. the most immediate expressed concern of the client
2. the behavior that has most extensive aversive consequences for the client, significant others, or society, if not handled
3. the most immediate concern expressed by the referral source
4. the behavior that can be handled most quickly and/or effectively
5. the behavior that must be dealt with before others can be handled

In considering these criteria, the worker should involve the client, the referral source, and others whenever possible in determining the priorities for service. A checklist including a variety of roles can be used to help the client order his evaluation of the behaviors to be investigated.

Behavioral Specification and Analysis

Analysis of the target behaviors selected for service involves delineation of the client's inappropriate or deficient responses, their antecedents and consequences. The client's behavior should be described in terms that clearly specify the client's verbal and motor responses in affirmative, observable terms. In the treatment model, negatively stated descriptions such as "John is not doing his homework" are insufficient, since they fail to describe what the client is doing other than his homework. Therefore, negative statements should be accompanied by descriptions of what the client is doing in the problematic situation. In the example above, an appropriate description might be, "John is watching television when he should be doing his homework."

In the preventive model, the affirmative behavior might never be exhibited or even considered by the client and, thus, it might be irrelevant to describe affirmative behaviors along with negatively stated descriptions. For example, a mother may not read to her preschool age child; the alternative activities she engages in need not be cited by the worker in his delineation of the target behavior because they are not viewed as competing responses of the mother.

Behavior that is judged by the client or others as problematic usually indicates either a behavioral deficit or surfeit. Behavioral deficits exist when appropriate behaviors are absent or infrequent; behavioral surfeits are inappropriate behaviors. Examples of deficient appropriate responses typically include smiling, talking, attending work regularly or turning in class assignments when-these are performed insufficiently; examples of maladaptive surfeit behavior often include lying, stealing, truanting, fighting or crying. In addition, behavior might be judged as problematic when it occurs under inappropriate conditions; e.g., walking around in one's undershorts might be appropriate in the privacy of one's home, but inappropriate in the lobby of a hotel (Staats and Staats, 1964; Ferster, 1965).

Labels, such as "hostile" or "passive-aggressive," are insufficient to describe accurately a client's behavior or speech with regard to a specific situation. These terms lack sufficient explanatory value and often are unnecessary when observed descriptions of the client's behavior are made. If such labels are used, they should be accompanied by explicit descriptions of the client's performance that justify their use.

Although levels of specificity vary in describing a response, the basic criterion for descrpition should be that of delineating the response in observable terms. For example, if a client complained that his son John was "physically aggressive" with his brother, doubt remains as to how he was "physically aggressive." Where did he hit his brother? Was it with his hand or with a weapon? A more acceptable description might be, "John pushed his brother and knocked him to the ground." Thus a stranger reading this description would be provided with a concrete, observable instance of John's "physical aggression" with his sibling.

Determining Behavioral Magnitude and Severity

A useful way to determine the magnitude of a behavior is to count its frequency of occurrence within a given time period or to measure the duration of its occurrence for each incident. This information is referred to as baseline data. For example, "Harold completed two out of three school assignments this week." "Sally cried at the dinner table for 15 minutes on Tuesday and 25 minutes on Friday." Frequently, when a client, worker, or another records and keeps a chart of a behavior that has been labeled problematic, it is found that the behavior actually occurs less frequently than was originally stated by the client or referral source. Subsequent attention should be given to pursuing other behaviors that in reality give greater cause for concern.

Another recording method called *time sampling* is sometimes necessary "where behaviors occur at extremely high rates, are difficult to observe continuously, or cannot be broken down into small discrete units, i.e., babbling, nail-biting, or nonattending. Time sampling involves recording behavior at certain times during the day, rather than continuously. This method will give an accurate count of behaviors when extended over long periods of time" (Buckley and Walker, 1970). During this sampling, an observer records the occurrence or nonoccurrence of a response during a series of predetermined intervals.

The intensity, force, or severity of behaviors, such as punching, screaming, kicking or crying, are usually difficult or impractical to measure, although instruments that can measure these behaviors in physical units, such as decibels, are available in a laboratory setting. The crucial feature of these behaviors, however, involves the negative consequences or effects these behaviors have for the client, others, or society. Because individuals differ in their tolerance for the behavior of others as well as in their own reactions to stimulation, examining the negative consequences of a client's behavior provides a basis for judging the severity of the behavior. For example, the severity of Sam's "tapping" a classmate is indicated by his victim's bruises or complaints to a teacher. When problems occur infrequently, such as violent arguments between marital partners, the severity of the argument is usually judged by the negative consequences occurring to each person or to others as a result of the argument. Behavior can produce short and/or long term consequences for the client and/or others, and all possibilities should be considered. For example, Sam's use of obscene language in class might produce the short term consequence of approval from his classmates, but it might later lead to suspension from school and failure to obtain desired employment as an adult.

Specification of Antecedents and Consequences

After specifying a client's response(s) in a problematic situation, the worker should investigate the antecedent and consequent conditions related to the behavior needing to be changed. *Antecedent* refers to an event that precedes or triggers a specific behavior, so that the existence or onset of the event is related directly to the occurrence of the behavior. For example, an antecedent for Bob's striking Joe could be Joe's calling him "stupid." A second antecedent might have been two of Bob's friends urging him to strike Joe. As indicated by these examples, antecedents should be described with the same degree of specificity as the responses that they preceded. Traditionally, antecedents have included early historical events that are presumed to influence the client's current behavior. Inferred socio-emotional states such as "low self-image" or "feelings of insecurity" also have been cited as antecedents to problematic behavior. Emphasis is placed on the importance of observable antecedents that are related functionally to the occurrence of specified behavior. If an inferred or hypothetical statement is made, specific behavioral examples are essential. To illustrate, low self-image may be indicated by the client's looking at his feet when others speak to him.

As expected, *consequence* refers to an event which follows a behavior. *Reinforcement* occurs when consequences increase the probability of that behavior recurring. Descriptions of reinforcing consequences require the same level of specificity as descriptions of antecedents and responses. For example, if Judy screams when asked to do the dishes and her mother hugs her and does the dishes herself, the reinforcing consequences of Judy's screaming are her mother's hugging her and doing the dishes for her. These events reinforce Judy's screaming and the likelihood of Judy screaming when asked to do the dishes in the future is increased. Correct assessment of the reinforcing aspects of the mother's behavior could be incorporated in a treatment plan that involved the reduction of Judy's screaming when asked to do the dishes by her mother's withholding hugs and not doing the dishes.

At times certain reinforcing consequences might be discovered to follow a target behavior intermittently. Then it is important that the worker determine the pattern of when the reinforcers follow the behavior, for the schedule of reinforcement can provide information regarding the maintenance of the behavior (e.g., Ferster and Skinner, 1957). If Judy's mother sometimes did the dishes and hugged her when she screamed but ignored her screaming on other occasions, Judy's screaming would be more resistant to extinction because it has been intermittently reinforced (Buckley and Walker, 1970, p. 50).

Unless the worker understands the multiple antecedents and consequences for behavior, he may have an oversimplified explanation for a client's difficulty. Sarah may truant from school only when (1) she has failed a test the previous day, (2) she has had an argument with her mother about her poor school performance after returning from school, (3) she interprets her mother's criticism as rejection of her as a person, (4) she meets friends on the way to school who suggest that they truant together, and (5) there is something attractive to do in the community, like a new movie. Following her absence from school, she may regard the criticism from her mother and school officials as further punishment. As the rewards of truanting increase and the punishment of the school experiences increase, fewer antecedents and consequences may be required to lure Sarah into repeating this behavior.

In the example above, some of the antecedents and consequences of behaviors that are interpreted by others as anti-social involve the client's thinking process. Staats and Staats (1964) refer to these antecedents and consequences as implicit responses, that are typical antecedents of most observable behavior. Sometimes they can be inferred through observation or confirmed through careful interviewing. In addition, this concept highlights the importance of considering the subjective interpretation of any behavior by the client and others. Many practitioners have encountered children who seek punishment through anti-social behavior in order to get the attention such behavior elicits. What the general community interprets as punishment the child interprets as rewarding because he believes that he cannot get attention in any other manner.

Sometimes the client and worker wish the client to acquire, increase, decrease or eliminate certain sequences or chains of responses. Such chains, which occur in learning to talk or to drive, often include both observable and implicit responses in a particular order (Staats and Staats, 1964). In the illustration above, unless each of the five antecedent stimuli and response patterns occurred in the order given, it may have been unlikely that Sarah would have truanted.

Finally, sometimes a client's behavior may have as antecedents a series of behaviors in which the client has not been directly involved at all. The well known example of the father who gets angry at the mother, who gets angry at the oldest child, and so on until the youngest child kicks the dog is illustrative. The practitioner may have to trace the stimuli leading to—or the reinforcers of—client behavior to the behavior of others in the client's social environment, such as the actions of family members for some time before or after the target behavior of the client. For this reason, interaction and/or social systems analysis may be useful in understanding and dealing with the client's behavior.

The practitioner is urged to determine the antecedents and consequences for the client's target behavior, although this is not always an easy process. The determination of antecedents and consequences facilitates accurate diagnosis and the development of the intervention plan.

DIAGNOSIS IN THE GROUP

The social group worker's distinctive contribution in diagnosis and treatment grows out of his observation of the individual within the context of the diagnostic or treatment group. When feasible, target behaviors, their antecedents and consequences, should be verified by observation of spontaneous behavior in the group. The client as a group member not only interacts with the worker but, typically, does so in the presence of his peers. Of equal importance, the client interacts with his peers in the presence of the worker. The group worker is able to observe individual patterns of behavior in a context that closely approximates some of the client's usual social situations. He observes and confirms patterns of behavior which might emerge slowly or not at all through the client-worker interview situation. The group worker's diagnostic statement includes his observations of clients' attitudes and behaviors within and outside the treatment group. In the diagnostic group, the worker also evaluates clients' skills which could be used as models for appropriate behavior by other members of the group.

In order to determine more accurately the controlling conditions of a behavior, the technique of *behavioral reenactment* can be used in the group situation (Lawrence and Sundel, in this volume). Behavioral reenactment is a role–playing technique used to test the adequacy of the description of the response, antecedents, and consequences given by the client before entering the group. It attempts to simulate a client's target behavior in the group. If a client complains that his foreman at work is always "picking" on him, a member of the group is assigned the role of the foreman while the client assumes his own role. In order to simulate what occurs in the client's work situation, other role players are cued and coached to fill in collateral roles where indicated. The worker or other group members assume the role of the client or a significant other directly involved in the target situation. If the role-play is not congruent with the client's verbal description of the situation, he would be assigned to gather further information utilizing the knowledge about antecedents and consequences that emerged from the role–play.

For the most part, current social work practice is to hold individual intake interviews with each prospective client prior to assignment to any social work service. Many practitioners have found that accurate data can be collected in a formed group and that clients may be more willing to provide personal information in a group setting when the knowledge that others share similar problems detoxifies their own attitudes about themselves as people with problems seeking help (Churchill, 1965; Landy, 1965). In fact, group intake procedures are being used extensively with adoptive parent applicants. In the case of natural groups, families, and gang groups, the worker should observe the group or family if possible. He may also interview family or group members individually if he thinks that individuals need privacy to express themselves completely.

The diagnostic group is arranged especially to provide a means and context for the assessment of each individual member, not for assessment of the group itself. The group worker plans a series of meetings with several selected clients so that each member is exposed to selected emotional, cognitive and social tasks and stresses. These experiences simulate situations in which the clients' reported problems occur. The worker can identify the patterns of a group member's behavior, his ability to maintain certain behaviors and his adaptive behaviors. The group worker sometimes finds it useful to measure the functioning of each member against the expected behavior for people of the client's own age, sex and cultural group. The diagnostic statement analyzes behaviors in terms of reactive, provocative and interactive patterns.

In an article describing a diagnostic group of elementary school chil-

dren referred for services because of problems with peers, parents and
school, Churchill (1965, p. 586) lists potential observations:

> For example, in regard to the child's relationship to other children in the
> initial group meeting: (1) Can he show he wants a relationship? (2) Can
> he accept friendly overtures? (3) Does he provoke feelings of protective-
> ness? (4) Under what situations can he relate and to whom? (5) Can he
> maintain relationships when tension is high? Or in his relationship to an
> adult in the presence of other children over the period of four meetings:
> (1) What is his pattern of relating to the group worker? (2) How does
> a child use the proffered relationships? (3) Is this a child whom adults
> like in a one-to-one situation yet who shows gross problems in the
> group when he must compete with other children for the attention of
> the adult? (4) Do his feelings toward the worker shift when the worker
> gives to, compliments or supports another child? (5) Do his dependency
> demands vary with the reality of the situation? In his knowledge of and
> use of social skills in the context of stress: (1) Can he accept appro-
> priate roles in basic games? (2) Does he quit a game if another child
> gets a favorite role? (3) Will he disrupt activity when he doesn't want
> to play? (4) Are his social handicaps caused by lack of knowledge
> which can be remedied? (5) Do conferred moral attitudes cause emo-
> tional reflection of activities?

The social worker plans the activities of a diagnostic group to increase the availability of relevant observations. A craft activity which requires sharing of equipment may be planned to reveal the manner and
extent to which members engage in cooperative behavior.

The group worker's special expertise in understanding individual
behavior in the context of the group can be put to use for diagnostic as
well as treatment purposes through his observation of members in natural
and formed groups, some of the latter developed primarily for client
assessment.

Validation of Assessment Data

In addition to making direct observations and obtaining a self-report
of the client's behavior, the worker should check the accuracy of data
reported by interviewing individuals who were present during manifestations of the client's problem—with the client's permission if at all possible.
A description of the problem as stated by these individuals should be
obtained. Possible sources of validation are parents, relatives, neighbors,
teachers, and peers. Such individuals can be used also as monitors to observe and record occurrences of the target behavior and the conditions
under which it occurs. Frequently this monitoring procedure effectively
points out the monitor's role in stimulating or maintaining the target be-

havior. In general, accurate and reliable assessment of a target behavior can be obtained by comparing the descriptions of specific behaviors made by different individuals and adding the information provided by direct observations of the client in the group.

Goal Setting

A full discussion of the variables to be considered in recommending group work rather than casework intervention would be beyond the scope of this paper. However, some factors to be considered include the sensitivity of the client to peer pressure, the availability of other clients with similar or complementary problems and the possibility that group members will serve as desired models for one another.

After the client's problem has been analyzed and a decision reached that social group work is the appropriate method of intervention, a list of goals is formulated with the client. It is essential that goals be realistic and appropriate to the services offered by the agency. In addition, goals should be directly related to the target behaviors. Whenever possible, goals should be agreed upon by worker and client. As a first step, they would delineate the desired terminal behaviors. Immediate, intermediate, and terminal levels of goal attainment would then be ordered along a single continuum showing progressive changes in the client's behavior. Goal specification at each of these levels involves the same considerations as those in assessment: (1) a precise description of the desired response; (2) its rate or duration of occurrence if this can be determined (it is not always possible in the preventive model); (3) the antecedent conditions under which it should occur; and (4) the consequences of the altered behavior.

The priority of choosing one terminal goal over another involves the same criteria used in selecting one target behavior for consideration over another, as indicated earlier. Priorities among goals might be changed during the course of intervention as some goals are achieved or other problems become more salient.

The following excerpt illustrates the process of assessment and goal setting:

A common problem with which the Hartwig workers had to deal was that of school truancy. One boy, a constant truant from school, attended on the average of once every two weeks. He also had failing grades and conflicts with several of his teachers. From the client's report, the conditions for truancy occurred as he walked to school in the morning with his friends and one peer would suggest that they truant. Consequences maintaining the behavior were the avoidance of academic failure at school and the enjoyment of being "on the streets with his friends." The influence of parents and school officials was insufficient to induce school attendance. The goal chosen for immediate treatment was the reduction of truancy, both because the consequences of truancy would be severe, and because school attendance was a necessary condition for treating the other school problems. The projected terminal goal was attendance at all classes five days a week with intermediate goals such as three days of attendance per week. (Rose, Sundel, DeLang, Corwin, and Palumbo, 1970, p. 222)

Note that the intermediate goal was stated in terms of the same behavioral dimension as the terminal goal, the intermediate behavior of attending school three days per week was an approximation toward the desired terminal behavior of attending school five days per week.

Behaviors which are prerequisites for attaining the intermediate or terminal goal, but which are not in the same behavioral dimension, are labeled *instrumental behaviors. Instrumental goals* refer to the attainment of skills in these areas. An adolescent boy in a training school might have to gain more skill in talking with strangers before he can apply for a clerical job. In determining the instrumental goals, the worker would go through a procedure similar to that followed in determining intermediate and terminal goals. A clear delineation of the desired instrumental behavior would be made along with an analysis of its antecedents and consequences. The desired frequency or duration of the behavior's occurrence would also be determined.

Goal Attainment: Resources and Barriers

In developing the intervention plan, the worker should consider resources and barriers facilitating and impeding achievement of the goals—immediate, intermediate, terminal, and instrumental. This might require the worker's investigation (with the client's permission if possible) of his peers, community, school, and/or work situation. Also of significance are personal, interpersonal and organizational factors. Personal factors might include the client's intellectual ability, personality predispositions, physical handicaps and financial state. Interpersonal factors include power conflicts between the client and others and the trust the client feels toward others. Organizational factors include such variables as administrative structure of the client's place of business or school, the goals of the service agency and the worker's legitimate functions within it.

Preparation of the Intervention Plan

After delineation of conditions influencing the client's target behaviors and the formulation of specific behavioral goals—all of which are summarized in the diagnostic statement—the worker plans an intervention strategy. The worker's intervention strategy usually includes steps to modify the client's behavior as well as to control conditions surrounding that client's situation. Modification of the client's behavior utilizes interventions directed toward acquiring, strengthening, weakening or eliminating specific behaviors. The worker may also make plans to increase intermediate behaviors and/or instrumental behaviors. A wide range of intervention modalities is usually available to the worker, only one of which is group work.

In order to select the appropriate intervention for a particular target behavior, it is vital that the worker diagnose all aspects of the problem. If a child has stolen money to replace old school clothes, the worker's intervention might best be directed toward modifying antecedent conditions, that is, increasing the provisions of adequate school clothing, rather than focusing on the target behavior of stealing. The worker's intervention strategy may involve modification of institutional, agency, community, or outside factors related to the client's life. For example, an in-service program for junior high school teachers may be planned in addition to, or instead of, group work with truanting students. Such strategies are said to employ "extragroup means of influence" (Vinter and Galinsky, Chapter 17 in this volume).

The intervention techniques used by a worker are influenced largely by his theoretical orientation. Whatever techniques are selected, their application must be based on careful consideration of their potential effectiveness in light of client resources and barriers. The worker also should evaluate continuously the effects of his interventions in relation to the target behavior and goals set for the client.

Before an intervention strategy is carried out, the worker should discuss the various procedures to be used with the client as fully as possible, particularly those which involve the client directly. The client should agree to fulfill his obligations and the worker should promise to follow through with the procedures as indicated. This should be done both for ethical reasons and because it serves as an aid in goal attainment. The agreement between the worker and the client prior to implementation of the intervention strategy is referred to as the contract.

Diagnosis and Crisis Intervention

Because intervention strategies should be founded on diagnostic statements, interventions made by the worker prior to development of a diagnostic statement are inappropriate. In some settings, however, much of a worker's activities consist of on-the-spot or crisis-oriented interventions.

In these instances, the worker makes rapid judgments of the client's situation and takes immediate action. (See, for example, Parad, 1965.) The worker might immediately refer clients to agencies that provide special resources such as services for the physically handicapped or mentally retarded, housing information or employment counselling. Such rapid assessments and interventions depart considerably from the more systematic diagnostic procedure considered here. Such actions may be necessary but should be taken cautiously (Rose, et al., 1970) in order to avoid jumping to inappropriate conclusions. Even when adequate information appears to be available, the worker should avoid two pitfalls in diagnosis: that of premature generalization based on limited information and that of positing false assumptions about problem causality.

Procedural Guidelines for Diagnosis in Group Work

Preparing the Initial Assessment
  I. Identifying Information about Client
  II. Nature of Client's Initial Contact with Agency Worker
  III. Problem Presented by Client or Referral Sources
  IV. Description of Tentative Client Goal(s)
  V. Rationale for Acceptance or Rejection of Client for Social Group Work
  VI. Recommendation Regarding Further Work with Client

Preparing a Diagnostic Statement
  I. Identifying Information
    A. State information about individual: age, sex, race, occupation, school grade, length of participation in group, significant others in client's life, etc.
    B. Give information about the group:
      1. Name of agency and group
      2. Member composition
        a. age, sex
        b. voluntary/involuntary; natural/formed
        c. race, ethnicity
        d. occupations
        e. worker goals for individual group members
        f. other
      3. Number of sessions held prior to current diagnosis; frequency and length of meetings.
  II. Problem Identification
    A. State the problem (present or predicted) as given by (1) the client and (2) the referral source. Be as specific as possible.

B. Briefly state the rationale for social group work as appropriate intervention strategy for this client.

C. Specify the client roles which will be the focus for the intervention program, e.g., parent, spouse, employee, friends, student.

D. Specify the target behaviors that are to be the focus of the intervention program in each role.

E. Order these target behaviors according to their importance for investigation, and state the criteria used to determine priorities among them.

III. Preliminary Interventions and Referrals

A. Describe worker interventions that are required prior to further analysis of the selected target behaviors and give the rationale for their use.

B. State worker referrals that have been made to other agencies and community resources and/or those that are required.

C. Describe worker contacts with other individuals that have been and/or must be made.

IV. Behavioral Analysis and Goal Setting

A. Select the target behavior of highest priority.

   1. Give one representative example of the occurence of the target behavior(s) or situation where the desired behavior should occur.

   2. Specify the responses made by the client when the problem occurs. These responses should be described precisely in terms of what the client *says* or *does*.

   3. Describe the antecedent conditions related to these responses.

   4. Describe the consequent conditions that are related to the occurrence of these responses in terms of (1) reinforcing consequences (or potential reinforcers) for the client, (2) negative consequences for the client, others or society.

   5. Give more examples of the problem as observed in the group and/or in a natural environment and as reported by others and/or by the client.

   6. Display graphs or charts completed by the worker, the client, and/or others describing the responses, the antecedents and the consequences.

   7. From the examples describing the occurrence of the client's responses, group the antecedents and consequences so that consistencies are apparent in their relation to the client's responses.

B. Goal Setting

   1. Formulate specific *terminal, intermediate,* and *instrumental*

goals that are directly related to the analyzed target behaviors in terms of:

a. the responses to be observed and their desired frequencies or duration of occurrence;

b. the desired antecedent and consequent conditions to be present during the occurrence of desired responses.

Each of these goals should describe responses to be acquired, increased, maintained, decreased or eliminated. If a response is to be decreased, then a concomitant response should be specified for occurrence in its place. An *instrumental* goal should also include specification of its *intermediate goal(s)*.

2. State the manner and the extent to which the client has been involved and is in agreement with the established goals.

3. Specify environmental barriers that impede attainment of the client's goals, e.g., economic deprivations, lack of transportation.

4. Specify personal factors that impede attainment of the client's goals, e.g., speech impediments, rural background, divorced parents.

5. Specify environmental resources that can be used to facilitate achievement of treatment goals, e.g., interested relatives.

6. Specify personal resources that can facilitate goal achievement, e.g., a dropout has good mechanical skills.

C. Select the target behavior ranked second highest on the list of behaviors requiring service and establish appropriate goals by following the above procedures.

REFERENCES

BUCKLEY, NANCY K. AND HILL M. WALKER
  1970—*Modifying Classroom Behavior: A Manual of Procedures for Classroom Teachers,* Champaign, Illinois: Research Press Company.
CHURCHILL, SALLIE R.
  1965—"Social group work: A diagnostic tool in child guidance," *American Journal of Orthopsychiatry,* 35, 3 (April), pp. 581–588.
FERSTER, C. B.
  1965—"Classification of behavioral pathology," in L. Krasner and L.P. Ullman (Eds.), *Research in Behavior Modification,* New York: Holt, Rinehart and Winston, pp. 6–26.
FERSTER, CHARLES B. AND B. F. SKINNER
  1957—*Schedules of Reinforcement,* New York: Appleton-Century-Crofts.

LANDY, DAVID
  1965—"Problems of the person seeking help in our culture," in Zald Mayer
      (Ed.), *Social Welfare Institutions: A Sociological Reader,* New York:
      John Wiley & Sons, pp. 559–574.
PARAD, HOWARD J. (ED.)
  1965—*Crisis Intervention: Selected Readings,* New York: Family Service
      Association of America.
RICHMOND, MARY
  1917—*Social Diagnosis,* New York: Russell Sage.
ROSE, SHELDON, MARTIN SUNDEL, JANET DELANGE, LINDA CORWIN, AND
      ANTHONY PALUMBO
  1970—"The Hartwig Project: A behavioral approach to the treatment of
      juvenile offenders," in Roger Ulrich, Thomas Stachnik, and John
      Mabry (Eds.), *Control of Human Behavior,* Glenview, Illinois: Scott
      Foresman Co., pp. 220–230.
STAATS, A. A. AND CAROLYN STAATS
  1964—*Complex Human Behavior,* New York: Holt, Rinehart and Winston.
WITTES, GLORIANN AND NORMA RADIN
  1971—"Two approaches to parent work in a compensatory preschool pro-
      gram," *Social Work,* 16, 1 (January), pp. 42–50.

8.

Goals in Social Group Work Practice: Formulation, Implementation and Evaluation

JANICE H. SCHOPLER, and MAEDA J. GALINSKY

Goals are crucial in effective social group work practice; they represent the ends toward which service is aimed, they give direction and meaning to the encounter between social group worker and clients. The way goals are defined can determine the acceptability of group work service to clients, agencies, and society.

Social work literature affirms the need for goal setting by client and worker. Although terminology may differ—ends, goals, objectives, foci, and purposes often are used synonymously—the importance of formulating goals is stressed. There is, however, some disagreement as to whether the worker or clients should set goals.[1] The position adopted here is simply that both parts of the group system, clients and worker, formulate goals, and goals need to be examined from the perspective of each. In addition, through its institutional agents and values, the community determines certain goals or range of goals for the group system (i.e., the collectivity of both worker and members).

Goal formulation begins very early and continues to affect the activities of the group throughout the treatment sequence. Initially, the group's purpose is the single most important factor in group composition (Levine, 1967; Northen, 1969; Spergel, 1965). After making an assessment of

[1] Practice literature indicates a range of opinions regarding who determines goals. In the view of Klein (1970) and Schwartz (1966), goals emerge from the client group and are not set independently by the worker; according to Levine (1967) and Phillips (1957), the worker represents the agency and helps members find a common purpose in accord with agency purpose; others, including Konopka (1963), Lowy (1970), Northen (1969) and Vinter (1967) point to the worker as one of the independent sources of goal formulation.

each client's current role performance problems, the worker formulates goals for individual clients. In addition, he refines and redefines his perspectives on group goals after diagnosis. Each client comes to the diagnostic interview with some notion, however vague and ill-defined, of the individual and group goals he wishes to pursue. These goals are verbalized and reshaped as he explores his situation with the worker. In the early stages of group development, the worker and members arrive at mutually acceptable individual and group goals. Their ability to set such goals will largely determine the success of the group. The goals selected guide the choice of group activities, influence the worker's strategy of intervention, and serve as a standard for measuring the achievements of individual members and of the group.

Even though goal formulation is a complex and difficult process, few guidelines exist to direct the worker's actions (Lowy, 1970). Social work literature presents differing concepts of goal formulation. Social science literature on goals, relatively unexplored by social workers, can be helpful to the worker in deriving principles for action. In this chapter the process of goal formulation and its influence on group activities will be examined by using concepts from both social work and social science literature. First, client and worker perspectives on individual and group goal setting are discussed; then, the steps are given that lead to a commitment by group members and the worker to shared goals; and, finally, the implementation and evaluation of goals are explored.

CLIENT AND WORKER PERSPECTIVES

The client and worker have different perspectives in formulating goals. They enter the group for different reasons, have different roles within the group, and have different bases for formulating goals. However, for success, clients and worker must mutually understand and agree on appropriate goals to pursue during treatment.

The Client's Perspective

The client may come to the agency through self-referral, referral by an organization or concerned person, or the worker may seek him out. In any case, he comes with some idea of what he, personally, would like to gain from this encounter. Goals held by the client at the point of entry may or may not be relevant to reasons for his referral. He will add ideas about what he would like the members to accomplish as a group.

Each client's individual and group goals are derived from his view of himself, his view of the group, and his view of the group's relationship to its surroundings.[2] The many internal and external forces that influence the client's perspectives include his values, his environment, his reference groups, his capabilities, and his experiences. The client's community and his status within it determine much of the content of his values; and his values provide him with a frame of reference for defining his problem. The expectations held by significant others (e.g., husband, mother, teacher) for the client may also influence the client's perception of his problem and his motivation to do something about it. His capabilities provide resources and define limits for work on his problems and his contributions to the group. Further, as he enters the group, each client has some idea, however vague, of what the worker, agency, and group will be like. The client may have gathered his impression of social work services from previous experiences with an agency or from "grapevine" reports of friends whose experiences with social workers may have been successful or unsuccessful. The client's view of groups and their effectiveness is also based on personal experiences from school, work, and friendship groups and from reports from others. Thus, various factors determine what goals the client sees as relevant and what goals he thinks are attainable (Alissi, 1965; Maas, 1964; Zander, Medow, and Efron, 1965).

The initial goals a client holds for himself and the group, whether defined vaguely or specifically, may reflect what he expects in terms of personal gains and outside recognition. His reasons for entering the group do not necessarily relate to his own presenting problems but may encompass a variety of motivations (Cartwright and Zander, 1968, pp. 403–406). He may hope that his involvement with the group will help him meet expectations in systems outside the group; or he may view the group only as a means to escape pressure about solving his problem. A delinquent may have only self-oriented goals for the group, such as, "the group should teach me how to stop fighting with my parents," "the group should keep my parents off my back," or "the group should throw some parties so I can have fun." As inappropriate as the client's goals may be, they define what he wants from the group.

Members are able to formulate group level goals only after each client shares his goals within the group and the similarities are identified.[3] In the process of accepting and rejecting individual goals for the group,

[2] Cartwright and Zander (1968:403–406) conceptualize an individual's choice of goals as deriving from his personal and group-oriented motives, his conception of the group's superordinate goals, and his view of relations between the group and its social surroundings.

[3] Zander (1968) finds the determinants of goals that members choose for a group are similar to those for individual performance; thus, if a member is to develop concern for the group's success, the group goals must reflect individual preferences.

more group-oriented motives develop, and members set priorities about what the group as a whole should and can accomplish. At times, the client's goals may be primarily group-oriented before a group meets with the worker. For instance, in a cohesive natural group, members may have selected group goals prior to the worker's intervention and may be more clear about preferred goals for the group than for themselves. In formed groups, the worker will almost always have some influence on the client's initial formulation of individual and group goals. It is important to remember, however, that in both natural and formed groups the clients' and worker's perspective of appropriate goals may differ.

The Worker's Perspective

The worker begins goal formulation at a very general level; objectives are partially determined for him by his professional orientation, his agency affiliation, and the agency's mandate from the community. Professional values guide the worker toward enhancing an individual's social functioning and contribution to social goals.[4] The agency provides a focus for selecting the specific group of clients to receive assistance, as well as for the methods used to aid them. The agency will also constrain the types of goals that can be formulated. The lay community provides the agency with a mandate that may specify or reject certain goals and methods. (See further, Roberts, 1968)

Profession, agency, and community do not always agree on general goals for the group, and conflicts can and do arise. The community and profession, for example, may present the worker with disparities; depending on the social climate, either a need for social action or an individual focus may be emphasized (Brager, 1960). In addition, the worker's personal and professional values may conflict with community, agency, or current professional objectives, as when an agency emphasizes containment of prisoners and the worker opts for rehabilitation.

Many writers assume that the social worker mediates between agency and client, although they do not say how this mediation is accomplished (Schwartz, 1966; and Phillips, 1957). Since they see the worker and agency as one, they do not account for the worker as an independent source of purpose or goal. In fact, the worker brings his own values and experiences that influence his view and use of agency purpose. The worker may interpret the agency goal in an idiosyncratic manner; he may even

---

[4] That the agency and profession provide the worker with direction in goal setting is generally agreed in social work literature; however, there is disagreement as to how much influence the agency should exert. For a variety of viewpoints, see Klein (1970); Levine (1967); Northen (1969); Phillips (1957); and Schwartz (1966).

disagree with the agency purpose. In a loosely structured setting, the agency may leave formulation of group purpose almost solely to the worker. In any case, the worker interprets the agency purpose to the group. Worker goals must be considered as independent and significant.

The worker's general goals for the group direct his efforts toward a target population with identifiable problems, and provide a range of objectives which can be pursued. For instance, a worker composing a group of AFDC mothers with school age children might have the general goal of helping these mothers find employment. As the worker meets members individually or as a group, he formulates treatment goals for each member based on his social diagnosis of the group member's role performance problems, where such diagnosis is possible (Sarri, et al., 1967; Sundel, Radin and Churchill, Chapter 7 in this volume). Individual goals for one mother in the AFDC group might include increasing her perception of her competence for work and arranging transportation. The worker, considering each member's presenting problems and personal goals, discusses individual goals with the group, and attempts to reach consensus with the members during goal formulation. In particular groups, the worker's purpose may be to help clients formulate their own goals; then the worker may not formulate individual treatment goals and more specific group goals.

Typically, after helping to formulate group and individual treatment goals, the worker presents a more specific set of goals for the group that he would like to see the particular group pursue. He presents them for consideration when the group system is engaged in formulating goals. The worker seeks specific goals capable of steering group action to meet individual needs (Cartwright and Zander, 1968, pp. 409–410). More specific goals for the AFDC group might be to increase competence in job interviewing; to find common child-care arrangements for special situations; to arrange for joint transportation; and to locate sources of current employment. Actually, the worker may formulate these specific goals before diagnoses are completed. As he gains new knowledge about group members, at any time during the group's existence, the worker must modify his group goals.[5]

To summarize, clients and worker enter a group treatment system with different perspectives. Both clients and worker formulate goals at the individual and group level. The clients enter the system with various objectives for themselves and the group and, together with the worker, they formulate goals for the group while retaining some of their own individual goals. The worker enters the system with professional, agency, and

[5] Vinter's concept of treatment goals and group purposes provided the basis for defining the worker's perspectives. See Chapter 2 in this volume.

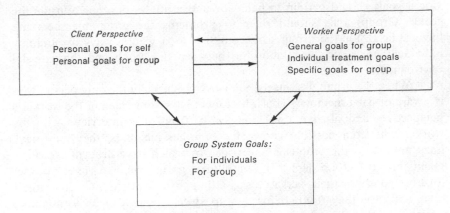

FIGURE 1   Interrelations among Client Perspectives, Worker Perspectives, and Group System Goal

personal sets, and he formulates individual treatment goals and goals for the group using these sets and his acquired knowledge of the clients. Client and worker goals at both levels may change over time as clients and worker gain new knowledge of each other's perspectives.

FORMULATION OF GROUP SYSTEM GOALS

During contract formation, the worker and clients come to a common working agreement about individual and group goals.[6] Client and worker perspectives continue to influence the degree of aceptance of the individual and group goals, but the shared goals guide the group system and represent an initial common ground.

Goal formulation is a process, not an event; goals are constantly evaluated and reevaluated. At any given moment, however, the goals formulated by the group system should meet certain criteria if they are to serve to guide action. (Chin, 1960; Gottlieb, 1967; Krumboltz, 1966; Sarri et al., 1967; Vinter, 1967) To be effective, goals must be formulated in clear, specific, and realistic terms. If these criteria are met, clients and worker can observe and, perhaps, measure changes as they occur using the initial situation of each client and the group as a base line. The goals also must be relevant to the lives of the individuals and the group. Indi-

[6] Definition of goals is one aspect of contract formation. Rose (1967) discusses other elements of the treatment contract such as clarification of roles and means of treatment. See also Croxton, Chapter 10 in this volume.

vidual goals should pertain to behavior and attitudes desirable outside the group. Group goals should refer to problems the group members are having, tasks for the group to accomplish as a whole, ways of attaining individual goals, or the relationship between the group and the external environment.

When the group first meets, the worker is usually the only person who is aware of each member's goals. Members have some idea of the worker's perspectives and of their own goals; also, from their interviews with the worker and from possible knowledge of other members, they may have hazy notions of the problems and concerns which have brought the other clients into the group. Unless it is a natural group, members have not met together to share their perspectives, although individuals may have their own goals for the group. Before group system goals can be formulated, various client and worker perspectives must become a part of the group's shared reality.

Formulating goals involves both cooperative and competitive processes.[7] Although the worker seeks to encourage cooperative aspects of group interaction, he must recognize the competitive feelings involved as members strive to get their own ideas accepted. Goal formulation can be used as a two phase process: first, worker and members explore their common and conflicting interests to establish a basis for mutually acceptable goals; then the group engages in a bargaining process to determine which goals will be accepted and how they will be implemented.[8] During the first, the *exploratory phase,* cooperation is dominant; in the second, the *bargaining phase,* some competition among group members and between worker and group members is expected.

Exploration

In the exploratory phase of goal formulation the worker and members must identify areas of mutual concern, consider different means to pursue these concerns, and discuss the relative values these various alternatives hold for them. An atmosphere of sharing and cooperation is necessary if members are to feel free to state their perspectives, their preferences, and their disagreements. The group must obtain a true and complete picture

[7] The distinction between an exploratory phase, that emphasizes cooperation, and a bargaining phase, with resultant competitive interaction, is derived from the literature on problem-solving. See, especially, Thibaut and Kelley (1959); Kelley and Thibaut (1969) and Walton and McKersie (1966).

[8] Goal formulation, including both exploration and bargaining, should occur during the first part of the treatment sequence, in Stage II, Group Formation. The goals selected at this time may solidify during Stage III, Building a Viable and Cohesive Group, and may be revised at any point. See Sarri and Galinsky, Chapter 5 in this volume.

of common and conflicting interests, concerns, and problems. Only through a sharing of individual perspectives will members be able to sort out their differences and to synthesize their individual interests into common goals which are more group, than individually, oriented.

The group's ability to formulate effective goals—and, ultimately, the group's success—depends on how adequately information about problems and goals is exchanged among members and between members and worker during this exploratory phase. Members must be encouraged to reveal enough about their own personal needs, resources, and interests so that they can establish a basis for commonality—a reason for continuing as a group (Walton and McKersie, 1966). As each member presents his situation, he reflects his values and the expectations of other people and systems that are important to him. As members interact with each other, they learn that they have mutual concerns. Two girls in a school group may find they both have fights with their mothers about dating. Several welfare mothers who hold part-time jobs may find they have similar difficulties in providing supervision for their children. As members recognize their common situations, they can begin to see the possibility of common solutions to their problems and, therefore, common goals. The worker's responsibility is to help group members perceive their similarities and view their differences with respect. (Sarri and Galinsky, Chapter 5 in this volume; Schwartz, 1961)

It is critical to remember that only the worker has knowledge of all members' interests and goals as exploration begins. He has developed goals for individuals and for the group based on his perspectives. Unless the worker recognizes that his goals are formulated from his own perspectives, he may dominate the group and short-cut the exploration phase, thinking that he is representing the interests of all the members. The worker, after all, has the authority of his agency and his expertise backing him. The members, initially, have little authority, little clarity about what the group should do, and little understanding about their relationship to the group. Unless the worker recognizes the importance of member contributions and exercises his skill and prior knowledge to help members define their roles and express their concerns and interests, he may sacrifice member involvement in the group.[9] While the worker generally is aware of which concerns need to be discussed in order to formulate goals and to prevent future dissatisfactions, the members usually need time to go through the process

[9] In a study manipulating different status, different role clarity and different goal clarity, Gerard (1957) concluded that high status individuals perceived themselves as more effective and assumed broader prerogatives in situations where goals and roles were unclear, but low status individuals were impotent in unclear group situations and required a definite set of role expectations and clear goals before they could contribute to the group task.

of getting acquainted and setting goals for themselves as a group.[10] For instance, a worker who composes a group of mental patients who are ready to be released may view preparation and planning for discharge as an essential goal for the group. The members may be ambivalent about leaving the hospital and may resist planning. They may need to learn what each member is like and what his problems and plans are before they are ready to formulate group goals. When goals are openly determined in the group and not imposed by the worker, they will be more likely to influence the group's activities and individual behavior (Krause, Fitzsimmons and Wolf, 1969; Raven and Rietsema, 1960).

While the worker should not impose his goals on members, he does have goals and should communicate them to the group members. Some social workers contend that formulation and transmission of goals by the worker robs the client of his right of self-determination. However the opposite is true. Only with open discussion of worker goals does the client have a choice. The worker, as a professional, has objectives that he would like to see pursued with and for clients. He will formulate goals for clients as he gains information about them, whether or not he admits his role in goal formulation. Clients who come to a worker or who are sought out by him have problems of concern to them or others in their social environment; the worker must have some idea about how these problems might be resolved by the conclusion of treatment. If the worker does not share his perspectives with group members, they do not have the chance to consider the worker's goals and they may wonder why the worker has chosen to meet with them. When the worker states his goals clearly and specifically, clients generally perceive them accurately. When the worker is vague and nonspecific, clients tend to assume the worker has a hidden agenda or no purpose at all. (Schmidt, 1969; Northen, 1969) Further, the worker's explicit statement of his own goals enhances, rather than detracts from, client self-determination. The client has the opportunity to accept, revise, or reject the worker's honestly stated goals.[11] Clients are still free to formulate their own goals.

Giving group members an opportunity to examine and explore worker perspectives does not imply that the worker relinquishes his goals; the worker still tries to gain acceptance of and commitment to the purposes

[10] Kelley and Thibaut (1969) review literature that suggests that the extra time groups require to reach a solution to a problem reflects the time needed to resolve differences between members. This is especially true when the group contains members with strong opinions and may be lessened when members share similar views.

[11] Seymour Halleck (1963) discusses problems created when professionals are dishonest with their clients and points to seven areas in which adolescents are deceived by conscious or unconscious communication from professional workers.

that he feels the group can attain through the group experience. If the worker has based his goals not only on his own and the agency's purposes and values, but also on a knowledge of each client's wants and needs, he is more likely to have his purposes accepted by the group members. It is crucial, however, that the worker be willing to modify his objectives as he gains new information through interaction with group members and as he begins to help members find their common purposes.

The worker must be able to state and restate goals in terms that will be clear to all members of the group. It is not sufficient for the worker merely to enumerate his goals at the outset. In working with a group of mothers at a child guidance clinic, the worker has to do more than speak about the improvement of mental health of the children; he needs to illustrate problems and goals through reference to the day-to-day problems the parents are having with the children. One mother, whose three-and-one-half-year old child is extremely dependent, may be reinforcing her child's problems by her overprotective behavior. Instead of discussing problems in general terms, the worker can encourage the mother to focus on incidents such as mealtime behavior. As the mother describes to the group her exasperation at spending two hours every meal feeding her child, the worker may suggest that an appropriate goal for the mother would be to teach her child to feed himself with a limit of one-half hour each meal. The worker must elicit members' discussion of his objectives to make sure that they are understood. If the worker does not make the goals clear, he is not offering the clients the chance to consider them, and he also loses the opportunity to influence the group's own selection of goals.

The problems of clarity relate to goal specificity. General goals tend to be less clear than specific ones. In the process of searching for commonality among members, the worker and members may be tempted to state goals at a general level, so that agreement of all members to goals will come easily. For example, the goal for a group of school children could be "to act better in the classroom." This level of generality may suffice when, with agency function and professional mandate in mind, the worker is first considering formation of a group or selecting members. Such a goal merely indicates a broad concern, but does not identify problem behaviors that the group must deal with. If the school children are expressing hostility to the teacher through rude and inappropriate behavior, goals should be developed to change the specific problem behaviors. Specific objectives provide direct guidance for the group's actions, since they indicate exactly which problems need to be resolved.[12]

[12] Cartwright and Zander (1968:409–410) discuss a group's inability to act without operational goals; further, Locke and Bryan (1966) in a series of studies lend support to the proposition that specific goals lead to higher performance and more task interest. See also Bryan and Locke (1967); and Locke and Bryan (1967).

Through mutual exploration of goals, the group members and the worker come to an understanding of each other's perspectives. As exploration occurs, the worker must help develop an atmosphere of mutual trust, clearly defined roles, and relevant norms. As members begin to feel comfortable with each other, they can tolerate the pressures of the bargaining phase of goal formulation.

Bargaining

Exploration is a necessary precondition for achieving group consensus about goals. Once members and worker understand each other's perspectives and motivations, they must decide which goals to pursue and how to pursue them. The bargaining phase of goal formulation necessarily involves disagreements among group members and the worker. It would be naive to expect all the goals of members and worker to mesh perfectly and be accepted, even when group members have been selected on the basis of compatibility. Members may differ about the goals to select, the goals that are most important, and the most appropriate means for pursuing goals.

Thus priorities must be determined. Individuals enter the group with preferences about goals for themselves and for the group; however, these initial preferences usually are influenced by group membership (Cartwright and Zander, 1968:405). The group system considers member preferences and decides on goal priorities that will guide the group and that each member will be helped to achieve.[13] The worker helps members set these priorities, taking into account the members' abilities and needs, the environment in which the group is located, and the time the group has to work on problems.

Priority setting may be relatively simple, especially when members have very similar problems. A group of patients who just learned they have arthritis may immediately decide to focus on coping with this physical disability. In other situations, members may have multiple, varied problems; and then, more specific criteria must be used. The group system will need to relate goal preferences to their importance for social functioning, the immediacy of the problem, relationship to the achievement of other goals, accessibility to change, and availability of resources. For example, a group of low-income mothers who have been asked to meet because their children have behavior problems in school may present a range of problems,

---

[13] Although Mencher (1964) indicates that setting priorities is always a value based decision, the worker should attempt to make this a rational process by directing the group to relevant considerations.

including difficulty in communicating with school personnel, lack of money for school supplies, behavior problems with children at home, lack of recreational facilities, and discrimination in the school system. The group may decide to place highest priority on communicating with school personnel, since this problem is most closely related to the reason for forming the group and since success in this area may lead to avenues for approaching discrimination and resolving school supply difficulties. Behavior problems at home may be assigned lower priority because they do not have such immediate social repercussions. The lack of recreational facilities may also be given low priority because the group has insufficient resources and motivation to deal with this problem.

Certain priorities may be established, explicitly or implicitly, during the exploration phase, or even during a member's first interview. Criteria for priorities become crucial when the group enters the bargaining phase and determines the goals that will guide the group. The goals for the group, once selected, provide the guidelines for setting final priorities for the goals individuals will pursue; group goals and individual goals must, of course, be congruent. A husband entering a group of couples who are meeting to resolve marital difficulties may give budgeting problems high priority, although he and his wife also indicate there is much dissension in their home about disciplining their children, recreation, and their sexual relationship. If the group agrees to focus on communication difficulties between spouses, this husband's initial priority may be unacceptable as a major focus of interest to the group as a whole and he will be urged to reconsider his goal preferences.

The high priority individual goal of one member will not necessarily interfere with the specific individual goal setting of another member. In group goal formulation, however, when the goal of one or more members is accepted as a high priority, necessarily another group member's competing goal will assume a lower priority. At times, it may be impossible to meet all of an individual's identified needs within the group system. When possible, the worker should help these clients meet their goals through additional means such as individual or family counseling or membership in another group.

Trust among members can provide one basis for the acceptance of lower priorities. If mutual trust has not been developed among members and between worker and members during the exploratory phase, bargaining is likely to be conducted almost entirely on the basis of power, manipulation, and prestige (Mencher, 1964; Walton and McKersie, 1966). The worker must be aware of potential conflict in this bargaining phase and he must make certain that all members are heard, that consideration is given to all members' views, and that when priorities are set they are fair to all.[14] High status members should be prevented from dominating the group; and, recognizing that the group may go through a revision phase, the worker must be careful not to give his sanction too early to the apparent leaders and the goals they are promoting. In fact, the worker can help foster a revision phase if this seems desirable (Sarri and Galinsky, Chapter 5 in this volume).

Since use of power is a part of bargaining among members and worker, it is important to note that the worker has the most power in a newly formed group system. He has legitimate power by virtue of his assignment by the agency. He has control over material resources and personal qualities with which to exert positive or negative sanctions. He can claim expert power because of his training, and he may have referent power from personal characteristics and interest (French and Raven, 1968). The worker, therefore, is potentially in a position to influence greatly the selection of goals. While the worker can utilize his power in the group for positive ends, he must be cautious not to abuse this power. Unless members are directly involved in selecting goals, they will be less likely to commit themselves to the goals, and the goals will be less likely to influence their behavior (Raven and Rietsma, 1960).

The worker will, of course, vary the degree of autonomy he allows the group in goal selection. The agency may prescribe or proscribe certain goals. A probation group may be required to focus on regulations and rules specified in their court orders. Clients themselves differ in their ability to formulate goals. A group of preschool children in a therapeutic nursery would be allowed less freedom in choosing goals than a group of teenagers in a low-income housing project. In any case, the worker must involve the members to some degree in the goal selection process.

No matter how goals are selected, the worker can expect resistance from members that may come from a variety of sources. If members have vested interests in particular goals they may want group priorities to be set in accordance with these interests. Members may be concerned that group goals will not represent what is most important for them, or they may be unsure about which goals would be good for the group to pursue. A man entering a group for spouses of alcoholics may be overwhelmed with his problems. In addition to having an alcoholic wife, he and his

---

[14] Cartwright and Zander (1968:405–406) discuss "fairness" and "group effectiveness" as two criteria for group decisions. They point out that decisions which reflect the preferences of all members may result in greater group effectiveness; further, only when members are aware that the achievement of group goals will provide benefits to all is the norm to help each other aroused. Thibaut and Kelley's (1959) formulation also emphasizes that an individual is unlikely to become involved unless he believes that his own outcomes are being improved by group actions.

family are facing eviction, his oldest son is appearing in court for car theft, and two younger children are ill. As he hears other members discuss their extensive problems, he is confused about which problems the group should handle and which group goals would benefit him. Members may also avoid particular goals because they feel the group does not have enough consensus or enough power to act on them. For example, a group of delinquent boys, meeting with a court social worker, may resist setting a goal to decrease incidence of street fighting because they doubt that all members will comply. If members lack clarity on any aspect of goal formulation, their concerns may take the form of resistance which may lead to procrastination in goal setting or conflict among group members (Thibaut and Kelley, 1959).

Group discussion with all members and worker participating provides information and reassurance to resistive members and also may lead to goal selection and means that are more acceptable to a larger proportion of group members. Open discussion increases the chance that the most widely shared concerns and values will be incorporated in the selected goals. As members exchange information, they may find new bases for agreement and may even change opinions about the value or attainability of certain goals. Members who question the group's ability to achieve goals may have increased confidence in the group as they view members effectively engaging in the decision-making process. The delinquent members cited above may agree to the group goal of decreased fighting after they have heard all members share their concerns and have adopted a system of monitoring each other's behavior outside the group. A fair hearing of all views and open discussion are the worker's responsibility. Commitment of members to common goals and, therefore, action on these goals will more likely occur when members discuss the pros and cons of these goals (Thibaut and Kelley, 1959; Horowitz, 1959).

Although not all members have to agree on goals, it is necessary for a relatively large number of members, possibly a majority, to reach consensus (Thibaut and Kelley, 1959). Even if members differ in their commitment to group goals, the worker may urge all members to express openly some degree of commitment to work toward these goals.[15] Expressed commitment may provide pressure to convince reluctant members to go along with the majority and may permit more effective use of group pressures. Once all members have stated their intention of working toward goals, whatever their reservations, the group can influence deviant members

[15] Bennett (1955) finds that variables other than group discussion and openly expressed commitment may be equally important in making a successful group decision; although her results emphasize the importance of high perceived consensus, they do not invalidate the use of discussion and commitment in many situations.

to engage in activities that will bring the group closer to achieving its goals. A highly cohesive group is likely to be more successful in exerting these pressures (Cartwright and Zander, 1968).

Goal formulation may appear to be a lengthy, complex process. In some situations, the exploratory and bargaining phases can be very time consuming. Clients who have no previous knowledge of each other, who have trouble in defining their problems, or who are in nonvoluntary settings may have difficulty in selecting appropriate goals and achieving even a minimal degree of consensus about these goals.[16] In other cases, however, members may agree quite readily on goals and be prepared to move quickly toward group action. With all groups, the worker's responsibility is to make certain that goals are formulated clearly and specifically in relation to the group members' problems and that the group reaches some initial consensus on these goals.

Once goals have been selected, they serve as a standard against which members can measure their own and the group's progress. It is important to remember, however, that goal formulation is not a one-time transaction. Goals may be reformulated and additional goals may be established as new information is received, as member interests and satisfactions change, as pressures from the environment shift, and as some goals are achieved. The worker, while helping members to reach the goals they have selected, should be ready to change his own formulation of goals and to help members reevaluate and readjust their goals.

IMPLEMENTATION AND EVALUATION OF GOALS

When initial consensus has been reached, the group system can focus on implementing and evaluating their goals. *Implementation* refers to all activities, worker intervention and group action, which the group system directs toward the achievement of individual and group goals. *Evaluation* comprises all activities aimed as assessing progress toward goals, continued relevance of goals, or achievement of goals. Implementation and evaluation activities may occur within the group system or in related social systems. Although evaluation may frequently be regarded as a terminal activity, evaluation and implementation are concurrent and complementary processes. The group system can use goals continually to evaluate the effectiveness of its implementation activities.

[16] Thibaut and Kelley (1959) point out that individuals who do not assemble voluntarily may resist and obstruct any consensus about group goals and tend to be self-oriented rather than group-oriented. In such groups, special emphasis may need to be placed on creating attraction to the group during the exploratory phase.

The literature on group work intervention and evaluation alerts the practitioner to a multitude of specific practice principles. Some general principles dealing with the relationship of worker intervention and group action to implement and evaluate goals can be identified. Several important factors in facilitating goal achievement are that priorities need to be reconsidered, intermediate goals must be delineated, and programs planned. The worker's strategy of intervention and the members' relationships as well as their commitment to help each other are critical. The internal culture of the group must be conducive to appropriate goal directed activities. In addition, the worker and members interact in and with external systems that are relevant to the achievement of goals. Evaluation of activities and goal attainment occur throughout the treatment process and conclude the treatment sequence.

Reconsidering Priorities

At the conclusion of the bargaining phase, individual and group goals have been selected and priorities have been set. The sequence in which goals will be pursued must be decided. Some individual and group goals can be worked on simultaneously. For instance, students about to be expelled from junior high school for fighting would have the common goal of limiting physical aggression within the school; programs can be planned to work toward possible ways of reaching this goal. Other goals must be worked on serially, so that at certain points one or several individual goals take precedence over others. In a mental hospital predischarge group, some members may be returning to their previous communities, family problems, and job situations; others may be considering foster care in new communities. Activities and discussion planned to deal with the various individual goals would, at times, be difficult and would have to be handled serially. As the group system becomes involved in goal implementation, it may be necessary to reconsider the priorities determined in the goal formulation stage.

Intermediate Goals

It may be most feasible to achieve priority goals by determining intermediate steps that the group can take to achieve long-range goals.[17] Intermediate goals are stated in terms of attitudes or behaviors that are necessary before long-range goals can be reached. An intermediate goal may constitute a lesser quantity of certain behavior than a long-range goal

---

[17] This concept is derived from the literature on programming and sociobehavioral approaches.

(e.g., consistent completion of one assignment a week for a pupil who rarely finishes any assignment) or one aspect of the final desired behavior (e.g., respectful listening to a teacher on the part of a student who interrupts, is rude and disrupts the class). Intermediate goals should be related logically to long-range goals, and the connections should be stressed by the worker. In addition, intermediate goals should be geared to the members' current abilities. Different goal levels may affect client motivation. If goals are too low, clients may become apathetic; and if too high, clients may become frustrated (Gottlieb and Stanley, 1967). Since intermediate goals are more easily attainable than long-range goals, their achievement provides tangible evidence to members of their competence, motivating them to proceed to the next step in goal achievement.[18] Breaking down long-range goals into intermediate goals facilitates program planning from session to session. In fact, most planned program activities represent means to achieve intermediate goals.

Program Planning

Discussions and activities should be planned so that they relate directly to the achievement of goals. Activities that re-create problem situations (e.g., role-playing) allow members to reenact their behavior in a supportive environment, providing them with an opportunity to gain insight into their problems and to discuss new ways of coping. Situations structured to elicit problem behaviors can provide members with an opportunity to develop and practice new behaviors. A competitive game may arouse aggressive behavior that a member has been denying and will make this behavior directly accessible to change efforts. In a group of couples discussing marital problems, a wife's dominance over her husband may be apparent; the group may reinforce her for allowing him to express his opinion. Because such activities could be viewed by members as ends in themselves when performed in other situations, the members should understand that in this particular setting these activities are means to achieve defined goals. The relevance of each activity should be discussed before, during, and after group action. Individuals who are clear about goals and the means to achieve them have a tendency to show more interest in their personal tasks, to express less hostility, and to have a greater feeling of

[18] A study by Zander and Wulff (1966) lends support to the notion that group members will perform more effectively under conditions where they receive feedback indicating they are doing a good job. In groups composed of either high or low anxiety subjects, the individual subjects were given varying reports of their competence. Subjects in the high competence condition were more involved in and approving of the group and more concerned about its success whether they were highly anxious or not.

group belongingness, which is particularly apparent in their involvement with group goals and willingness to accept influence from the group (Raven and Rietsema, 1960). Unless the relationship between means and goals is stressed, members and worker may become so involved in discussions or activities that they lose sight of the goals and concentrate solely on the means (Zinberg and Friedman, 1967).

Worker Intervention and Member Interaction

The foregoing discussions have emphasized the worker's role in goal implementation. The worker's strategy of intervention includes the various means the worker may use to help members achieve goals.[19] Through his direct relationships with members, his attention to group conditions, and his participation in systems external to the group, the worker's role is to help members create a climate in which goal directed action can take place and to facilitate movement toward individual and group goals. The members have contracted to help each other work toward goals. In their roles as group members, they will engage in activities and interaction within the group system and with outside systems in pursuit of goals. The degree of autonomy the worker allows the members in implementing group goals should depend on member abilities.

The conditions which are created within the group system are crucial if the worker and members are to facilitate the mutual accomplishment of goals. Meetings should be planned so that all members can contribute to goal achievement and can receive recognition and support for their goal directed behavior by other group members and the worker.[20] Effective group treatment requires interaction where members exert influence on each other toward goal attainment and sanction each other's behavior. Group cohesiveness, group consensus, group norms, and group structure are important in developing this system of interaction. A continuing emphasis on commonalities of members and attention to group maintenance is required.

The worker needs to remember that, even where consensus on goals has been reached by the group system, individual and worker perspectives

[19] The worker's choice of strategy will be determined by his philosophy, training, experience, and assessment of the group members. Discussion has been based on Vinter's conceptualization of direct, indirect, and extragroup means of influence but other strategies for achieving goals would be equally relevant. See Vinter, Chapter 2 in this volume.

[20] Zander and Medow (1965) support previous findings that members with a large share in the group's task are more concerned about group output and find that members of attractive, well-defined groups have a stronger desire for group success and work harder when success is rewarded.

continue to influence behavior and interpretation of group system goals. The worker may try to change individual and group goals, if he feels they are inappropriate or unrealistic, by seeking to renegotiate the initial group contract. Members may also try to undermine or force changes in goals. The worker should react to these attempts, supportively or negatively, depending on his evaluation of the situation.

Interaction with External Systems

Both workers and members will be involved with external systems as they seek to implement goals. Individual goals always pertain to behavior and activities outside the group system. Group goals may focus on the relationship of the group to its environment. In addition, the environment in which the group system is located influences group effectiveness and member motivations.

The worker enlists the assistance of persons outside the group. He should communicate goals and member progress toward goals to persons significantly involved in the definition of members' problems (e.g., teachers, parents, prison guards). The worker will also seek their opinions of member change; and he may want to gain their cooperation in trying out new ways of handling difficulties or in rewarding indications of individual progress (Vinter and Galinsky, Chapter 17 in this volume). For instance, a worker and housemother, after discussing one member's extensive problems with verbal and physical aggression, may agree that the child should be praised for his progress each time he stops at name-calling and resists becoming involved in a fist fight. Since individual goals are directed toward problematic behavior outside the group situation, changing behavior and perspectives of others in the clients' lives may be essential to goal attainment.

Group members are vitally involved in external systems as they test new behavior. The reactions of persons in the environment help members evaluate their progress toward goals. They may find themselves rejected or rewarded by others for changed behavior. Rewards for new behavior may further motivate members; however, if changes are ignored, members may become discouraged. A child who remains seated during a whole class period for the first time may fail to repeat this behavior unless the teacher comments favorably. Members may find their own perspectives have changed during the group experiences so that their ideas and behavior are no longer compatible with people who are important to them. Delinquent youth who begin to pursue constructive goals may lose face in their neighborhood. In such cases, if the previously relevant external systems cannot be changed, the worker must help the members form new supportive relationships.

Evaluation

When the group is ineffective or having difficulty achieving goals, the worker should help the group reassess their goals.[21] Whether or not problems occur in implementing goals, all groups need periodic evaluations of movement toward individual and group goals. Systematic evaluation should be structured into group activities and into the worker's feedback to clients on their progress.

Information for evaluation must be obtained from the group system itself and from related systems. When assessment of group goals focuses on the effectiveness of the group as a treatment means, the worker and members together can assess the achievements of the group, members' capacity to help each other, and various members' contributions to group performance. Since individual goals always refer to behavior and attitudes outside the group, the worker needs to obtain information about the client's behavior in external situations from his contacts with significant others (Vinter and Galinsky, Chapter 17 in this volume). The group may decide that members should observe each other's behavior in settings outside the group and provide feedback. The individual client should add his own evaluation of his progress.

Final evaluation of the accomplishment of individual and group goals should come with termination of the group. The group may terminate for a variety of reasons; but whether or not the group members have been successful in achieving some or all of their goals, they should participate in the final evaluation process.[22] Only if final assessment is a mutual effort will both worker and members have an understanding of their successes and failures. A review of successful individual and group efforts may reinforce members' achievements; discussion of the reasons for failure may make members more amenable to future treatment. The worker should share his independent assessment of group and individual progress with group members and elicit their opinions in order to achieve a joint evaluation. During this process, the worker is not only able to obtain a more complete understanding of this particular group but may also gain information that will help him improve his own interventive skills. For group members, a final summation of successes and failures in meeting goals is equally important because it clarifies what has been accomplished and what remains to be done when the group no longer exists.

[21] Klein (1970) lists exploitation, apathy, conflict, scapegoating, failure to listen to each other, attacking ideas before they're expressed, and intolerance as some of the indications that members have no interest in goals. A lack of commitment, lack of cohesion, or lack of clear contract may underlie these expressions.

[22] The importance of involving members in evaluation cannot be overstressed. See, for example, Gottlieb and Stanley (1967). For a guide to terminal diagnosis or evaluation, see Sarri, et al. (1967).

REFERENCES

ALISSI, ALBERT S.
1965—"Social influences on group values," *Social Work,* 10 (January), pp. 14–22.

BENNETT, EDITH B.
1955—"Discussion, decision, commitment and consensus in 'group decision'," *Human Relations,* 8 (August), pp. 251–273.

BRAGER, GEORGE
1960—"Goal formation: An organizational perspective," in *Social Work With Groups, 1960,* New York: National Association of Social Workers, pp. 27–36.

BRYAN, JUDITH F. AND EDWIN A. LOCKE
1967—"Goal setting as a means of increasing motivation," *Journal of Applied Psychology,* 51 (June), pp. 274–277.

CARTWRIGHT, DORWIN AND ALVIN ZANDER
1968—"Motivational processes in groups," in Dorwin Cartwright and Alvin Zander (Eds.), *Group Dynamics,* Third Edition, New York: Harper and Row, pp. 403–406 and 409–410.
1968—"Pressures to uniformity in groups," in Dorwin Cartwright and Alvin Zander (Eds.), *Group Dynamics,* Third Edition, New York: Harper and Row, pp. 144–147.

CHIN, ROBERT
1960—"Evaluating group movement and individual change," in *Use of Groups in the Psychiatric Setting,* New York: National Association of Social Workers, pp. 35–45.

FRENCH, JOHN R. P., JR., AND BERTRAM RAVEN
1968—"The bases of social power," in Dorwin Cartwright and Alvin Zander (Eds.), *Group Dynamics,* Third Edition, New York: Harper and Row, pp. 259–269.

GERARD, HAROLD B.
1957—"Some effects of status, role clarity and group goal clarity upon the individual's relation to group process," *Journal of Personality,* 25, pp. 475–488.

GOTTLIEB, WERNER AND JOE STANLEY
1967—"Mutual goals and goal-setting in casework," *Social Casework,* 48 (October), p. 471.

HALLECK, SEYMOUR
1963—"The impact of professional dishonesty on behavior of disturbed adolescents," *Social Work,* 8 (April), pp. 48–56.

HOROWITZ, MURRAY
1968—"The recall of interrupted group tasks: An experimental study of individual motivation in relation to group goals," in Dorwin Cartwright and Alvin Zander (Eds.), *Group Dynamics,* Third Edition, New York: Harper and Row, p. 444.

KELLEY, HAROLD AND JOHN THIBAUT
1969—"Group problem solving," in G. Lindzey and E. Aronson (Eds.), *The*

Handbook of Social Psychology, Second Edition, Volume 4, Reading, Massachusetts: Addison-Wesley Publishing Co., pp. 35–47.

KLEIN, ALAN
1970—*Social Work Through Group Process,* Albany, N.Y.: School of Social Welfare, State University of New York.

KONOPKA, GISELA
1963—*Social Group Work: A Helping Process,* Englewood Cliffs, New Jersey: Prentice-Hall, Inc.

KRAUSE, MERTON, MARGARET FITZSIMMONS AND NORMA WOLF
1969—"Focusing on the client's expectations of treatment: Brief report," *Psychological Reports,* 24 (June), pp. 973–974.

KRUMBOLTZ, JOHN
1966—"Behavioral goals for counseling," *Journal of Counseling Psychology,* 13 (Summer), pp. 153–159.

LEVINE, BARUCH
1967—*Fundamentals of Group Treatment,* Chicago: Whitehall Co.

LOCKE, EDWIN A. AND JUDITH F. BRYAN
1966—"Cognitive aspects of psychomotor performance," *Journal of Applied Psychology,* 50 (August), pp. 286–291.
1967—"Performance goals as determinants of level of performance and boredom," *Journal of Applied Psychology,* 51 (April), pp. 120–130.

LOWY, LOUIS
1970—"Goal formulation in social work with groups," in Saul Bernstein (Ed.), *Further Exploration in Group Work,* Boston, Massachusetts: Boston University School of Social Work, pp. 94–118.

MAAS, HENRY S.
1964—"Group influences on client-worker interaction," *Social Work,* 9 (April), pp. 70–79.

MENCHER, SAMUEL
1964—"Current priority planning," *Social Work,* 9 (July), pp. 27–35.

NORTHEN, HELEN
1969—*Social Work With Groups,* New York: Columbia University Press.

PHILLIPS, HELEN
1957—*Essentials of Social Group Work Skill,* New York: Association Press.

RAVEN, BERTRAM H. AND JAN RIETSEMA
1960—"The effects of varied clarity of group goal and group path upon the individual and his relation to his group," in Dorwin Cartwright and Alvin Zander (Eds.), *Group Dynamics,* Second Edition, Evanston, Illinois: Row, Peterson and Co., pp. 395–413.

ROBERTS, ROBERT W.
1968—"Social work: Methods and/or goals," *Social Service Review,* 42 (September), pp. 360–361.

ROSE, SHELDON
1967—"A programmed course of instruction," Ann Arbor, Michigan: The University of Michigan School of Social Work. (Unpublished paper)

SCHMIDT, JULIANNA T.
1969—"The use of purpose in casework practice," *Social Work,* 14 (January), pp. 77–84.

SCHWARTZ, WILLIAM
   1966—"Some notes on the use of groups in social work practice," address
       delivered to Annual Workshop for Field Instructors and Faculty,
       Columbia University School of Social Work.
   1961—"The social worker in the group," in *New Perspectives on Services
       to Groups,* New York: National Association of Social Workers, pp.
       19–23.
SPERGEL, IRVING
   1965—"Selecting groups for street work service," *Social Work,* 10 (April),
       p. 49.
THIBAUT, JOHN AND HAROLD KELLEY
   1959—*The Social Psychology of Groups,* New York: John Wiley & Sons.
WALTON, RICHARD AND ROBERT MCKERSIE
   1966—"Behavioral dilemmas in mixed-motive decision making," *Behavioral
       Science,* 11 (September), pp. 370–384.
ZANDER, ALVIN
   1968—"Group aspirations," in Dorwin Cartwright and Alvin Zander (Eds.),
       Group Dynamics, Third Edition, New York: Harper and Row, pp.
       418–429.
ZANDER, ALVIN AND HERMAN MEDOW
   1965—"Strength of group and desire for attainable group aspirations," *Jour-
       nal of Personality,* 33 (March), pp. 122–139.
ZANDER, ALVIN, HERMAN MEDOW, AND RONALD EFRON
   1965—"Observers' expectations as determinants of group aspirations,"
       Human Relations, 18 (August), pp. 273–287.
ZANDER, ALVIN AND DAVID WULFF
   1966—"Members' test anxiety and competence: Determinants of a group's
       aspirations," *Journal of Personality,* 34 (March), pp. 55–70.
ZINBERG, NORMAN E. AND LEONARD J. FRIEDMAN
   1967—"Problems in working with dynamic groups," *International Journal
       of Group Psychotherapy,* 17 (October), pp. 447–456.

9.

Modes of Integration and Conformity Behavior: Implications for Social Group Work Intervention

RONALD A. FELDMAN

Social group work is "a way of serving individuals within and through small face-to-face groups in order to bring about desired changes among the client participants" (Vinter, 1965:715). According to this formulation the group is viewed as a "small social system whose influences can be managed to develop client abilities, to modify self-images and perspectives, to resolve conflicts, and to inculcate new patterns of behavior." In contrast with various other treatment approaches utilizing a group setting the small group in social group work is considered as not only the context for treatment but also the means for service (Sarri and Vinter, 1965). It can be presumed, therefore, that social psychological models of small group structure should constitute a central portion of the knowledge base of social group work and should serve as a basic resource for group work interventions directed toward the enhancement of client social functioning. This paper is a report of an experimental study of three modes of integration and their consequences.

Useful alterations of group structure have typically represented a major feature of group work practice. The operating, governing, and developmental patterns of small groups have frequently constituted preferred foci for worker interventions directed toward individual client change. Worker interventions at the individual level, including the active control of membership roles and the definition of goals and tasks for individual members, have been posited as crucial foci for effecting desirable

The original title of this article was "Determinants and Objectives of Social Group Work Intervention." Reprinted with permission of the National Conference on Social Welfare and Columbia University Press, from *Social Work Practice, 1967,* New York: Columbia University Press, 1967.

alterations in group structure. (Churchill, 1959; Vinter, Chapter 3 in this volume.)

Despite the central importance of group structure and of knowledge concerning its effects upon group members, the literature of social group work appears, for the most part, to be barren of group-level conceptualizations that promote either the systematic ordering of knowledge concerning groups or the elaboration of prescriptions for worker intervention designed to produce adaptive changes in group structure and individual functioning. Few theoretical frameworks have been subjected to the rigors of empirical examination, whereas others have been extraordinarily global in nature, thus diminishing their promise for meaningful application to group work practice situations. Silverman (1966), following a review of major social work journals and books published between 1956 and 1964, concluded that 85 percent of the group work publications represented mere descriptions of programs, groups, or areas of practice, appeals for knowledge and direction of service, traditional statements of principles, historical articles, and comparisons of group work with more clinical orientations. Only 15 percent represented the application of social science knowledge, reports of research or surveys, or innovations in practice theory. The proportion of this latter segment, which in turn focuses directly upon group structure, was not ascertained.

The infrequency of references to group structure in the literature seems all the more surprising in view of the considerable effort devoted to delineation of criteria for the development of social work knowledge and for the application of social science knowledge to social work (Greenwood, 1955; Hurwitz, 1956; National Association of Social Workers, 1964; Schwartz, 1963; Thomas, 1962). The dearth can probably be attributed to numerous factors, including the relative immaturity of the social sciences and of modern social group work, the limited manpower and resources devoted to research in both areas, and the distinctive developmental patterns of each. In part, the gradual rate of development may also be related to certain values and attitudes widely shared within the social work profession which, although functional in certain respects, serve to retard systematization, codification, and generalization in social work. Harriett Bartlett (National Association of Social Workers, 1964:11), for instance, in referring to the rate of knowledge development in social casework, suggests that progress "has been slowed by an anti-intellectual attitude, resulting from the emphasis in casework on the uniqueness of the individual and the fear that analyzing and classifying problems will militate against the emotional sensitivity of the social worker." The self-awareness concept, she notes, has been applied to the social worker's feelings but not to his knowledge and value assumptions. Implicit in Bartlett's statement, and explicit as a central assumption of this discussion, is the contention that knowledge concerning small groups and individuals, although derived and categorized in a generalized manner, can serve to individualize service to clients and thus lead to more effective social work.

It also has been difficult for group work practitioners to influence systematically the "integration" or "cohesiveness" of groups and to anticipate accurately the therapeutic outcomes from such interventions.

Terms such as "group integration" and "group cohesiveness," although frequently noted in the literature of sociology, social psychology, and social group work, have rarely been examined at the applied levels. Their global, ill-defined use renders them extraordinarily resistant to operationalization and empirical study.[1]

To enhance the effectiveness of their treatment efforts, workers must be able to identify clearly the various bases of group integration, differentiate them from one another, and then within the ethical purview of social work to influence them predictably and economically.

It might be noted that the basic skills, clarifying and specifying worker activity, are not requisites for social group work alone. Kadushin (1963), for instance, has expressed the need for similar skills in order to prevent the articulation of broad, undifferentiated "Aunt Fanny" diagnoses in social casework. The diagnostic process, he notes, is one of "particularizing our generalizations so that we can differentiate this client from all other clients." Likewise, determination of the structural characteristics of small groups can be meaningful and can contribute to the formulation of specific and attainable treatment goals, only to the extent that the worker can clearly define the features of a group that render it different from most other groups.

In order to enhance the utility of the small group as a treatment vehicle it is posited that social group work research should pursue at least three central objectives:

1. Varying modes, or bases, of group integration ought to be defined clearly both conceptually and operationally. If the structural components of groups are to be the objects of viable group work intervention they must be clearly distinguishable from one another and accessible to the group worker's direct and indirect efforts at intervention.

2. Systematic, empirical investigation should be done to determine the relationship between different modes or bases of group integration and client adaptation. This investigation would help to identify the most important foci for group work intervention.

---

[1] For a discussion of the conceptual and operational inadequacies of the terms "group integration" and "group cohesiveness" see Feldman (1967).

3. Efforts should be made to identify the specific individual positions within various group structures that are most likely to be productive foci for group work intervention.

The above goals are posited upon the following basic assumptions:

1. Various modes of group integration are identifiable, both conceptually and operationally, and are accessible to group work intervention.

2. Worker interventions in certain group structures are more likely to facilitate attainment of desired treatment goals than are worker interventions in other group structures.

3. Individuals who occupy certain positions within given group structures are likely to be more amenable to selected group work change efforts than are individuals who occupy other positions.

To test some of these issues, measures of group and individual structural characteristics were related to members' performance in an experiment involving conforming behavior.

THREE MODES OF INTEGRATION

The notion of group integration generally refers to the regularity and coordination of behavior among the members of a group (Newcomb, Turner and Converse, 1965:369). Such a perspective focuses upon the extent of patterned social interaction among group members. Although numerous bases of group integration can be posited, three of special relevance for social group work have been selected for the present study: normative integration, interpersonal integration, and functional integration.

Normative Integration

Norms have been defined as behavioral rules that are accepted by all or most members of a group (Thibaut and Kelley, 1959:129). Normative integration of a group, therefore, refers to the degree of group members' consensus about norms regarding certain types of group-relevant behavior. An individual's normative integration into a group refers to the extent to which any given person shares the norms of his fellow group members. In the present investigation no value judgments are conferred upon the norms selected for study. Normative integration refers only to the extent of group members' consensus concerning norms and not to whether the norms can be classified as more or less "desirable."

In order to measure both group and individual normative integration, an index was devised based upon group members' responses to a questionnaire consisting of twenty normative items.[2] Groups characterized by

[2] Details of index construction, including a copy of the normative integration questionnaire, are reported in Feldman (1966).

great member consensus were considered to have high normative integration, whereas groups with little consensus were considered low in normative integration. Likewise, individual members who consistently shared the norms of the group were considered to be highly normatively integrated, whereas individuals who rarely shared those norms were considered to be characterized by low normative integration into the group.

Interpersonal Integration

Interpersonal integration refers to that mode of group integration based upon the group members' liking for one another. The present formulation emphasizes the reciprocal nature of interpersonal integration. Depending upon the extent to which an individual likes his fellow group members and, in turn, is liked by them, he can be interpersonally integrated into a group to varying degrees. Although an individual may greatly like his peers, it clearly cannot be presumed that he is highly interpersonally integrated into the group if those peers dislike him. Conversely, a group member could not be considered highly interpersonally integrated into a group if his peers expressed considerable liking for him but he did not reciprocate that liking (Blau, 1960).

Interpersonal integration was determined by asking each subject to rate his fellow group members according to the question, "How much do you like him (her)?" One of five responses, ranging from, "I like him (her) very much," to "I dislike him (her) very much," could be checked and was utilized as the basis for index construction (Feldman, 1967). Interpersonal integration of a group, then, refers to the average of all such ratings for any given group, that is, to the general extent of interpersonal liking within the group.[3] An individual's interpersonal integration into the group refers to the average of the liking scores that a person assigned to all other group members and received from them.

Functional Integration

Functions have been defined as regularly performed, specialized activities that serve one or more requirements of a group (Freedman, et al., 1956). It will be assumed that at least three major functional requirements must be satisfied by most small groups: (1) goal attainment, (2) pattern maintenance, and (3) external relations (Parsons, 1951; Homans, 1950). The goal attainment function refers to the capacity of a group to progress

---

[3] Sociologists and social psychologists have often equated concepts such as interpersonal integration or interpersonal attraction with "group cohesiveness." See for example, Cartwright and Zander (1960); Festinger, Schachter, and Back (1950); Lott and Lott (1965); Weller (1963).

toward whatever goals have been explicitly or implicitly selected by its members. Pattern maintenance refers to the capacity of a group to maintain harmonious and consistent intragroup relations. The external relations function refers to the capacity of a group to maintain viable relationships with other groups.

In order to measure both group and individual functional integration, subjects were asked to rate each member in their group according to his ability to perform the three functions (Feldman, 1967). An individual's functional integration into a group, then, refers to his perceived effectiveness at performing the functions of goal attainment, pattern maintenance, and external relations for the group. Individuals who receive high ratings on the three functions are considered highly functionally integrated into the group and, conversely, individual functional integration into the group is considered low if low ratings are received on the three functions.

Effectiveness is not the sole criterion of group functional integration; the extent to which responsibility for the performance of key functions is distributed among the group's members is also considered. Functional integration of a group refers both to the effectiveness of group members in performing the three foregoing functions and to the extent of complementary specialization among the group members. A group in which all three key functions are effectively performed by only one member would be considered less functionally integrated than a group in which two or more members effectively perform those functions. The notion of complementary specialization refers to the extent of functional interdependence among group members.

In children's residential camping, a cabin group characterized by high functional integration would be one in which some members usually suggest the ideas for group activities and/or the means for successfully accomplishing them (goal attainment function), certain other members effectively prevent and/or resolve conflicts within the group (pattern maintenance function), and several others effectively represent the cabin at intergroup meetings (external relations function). In contrast, a group characterized by low functional integration would be one in which the same individual usually assumes responsibility for performances of all three functions, or one in which none of the members is found to perform the functions effectively. Table 1 schematically indicates the expected functional integration of groups characterized by varying combinations of high or low effectiveness and complementary specialization.

Methodology

Since functional, interpersonal, and, especially, normative integration develop over considerable periods of time, laboratory groups were deemed

TABLE 1.   Expected Functional Integration of Groups Characterized by High or Low Complementary Specialization and Functional Effectiveness

		Complementary Specialization	
		High	Low
Functional effectiveness	High	High Functional Integration	Moderate Functional Integration
	Low	Moderate Functional Integration	Low Functional Integration

undesirable for this study. The subjects selected were members of sixty-one cabin groups at four residential summer camps for children. Two of the camps were conducted by community-sponsored organizations, were co-educational, and served predominantly middle-class Jewish children. The other two camps were conducted under private auspices and served predominantly middle-class and lower-upper-class Jewish children. One private camp was coeducational; the other served boys only.

A total of 538 subjects, ranging in age from nine to sixteen years, constituted the cabin groups. There were 34 boys' groups, comprised of 288 subjects, and 27 girls' groups, comprised of 250 subjects. Group size varied from six to thirteen members. The average number of members per cabin group was 8.8 and the mode was 10. At all four camps cabin members took their meals together and frequently participated in recreational and work activities as a unit. Group members at the two community-sponsored camps had lived together for slightly more than two weeks prior to the experiment, whereas most of those at the two private camps had lived together for more than six weeks.

After the extent of normative, interpersonal, and functional integration had been determined for each group and individual member, subjects were asked to participate in a brief experimental situation designed to measure their tendencies to conform to the perceived expectations of peers. Knowledge received from these groups regarding conformity behavior (that is, behavior reflecting the successful influence of other group members) (Bass, 1961) may be considered pertinent for social group work in at least two respects. Conformity, whether the result of overt or covert change pressures from one's peers, may constitute the first in a series of behavioral modifications leading to the development of internalized adaptive change (Kelman, 1963). Also, the tendency to conform to peer expectations may serve as a rough indicator of an individual's receptiveness to change through group work methods.

Conformity Experiment

The most important features of the conformity experiment are as follows. A trained experimenter met separately with the members of each cabin group and announced that all the cabins in their unit were to compete for a prize. The subjects were shown a drawing of an American Indian symbol and were asked to select, from a list of eleven possible answers, the single object they thought to be represented by the symbol.[4] Each subject was given an answer sheet and was asked to circle his choice. Following selection of their answers the experimenter informed the subjects that he would tabulate their responses, report the two "leading choices," and offer everyone a second opportunity to select an answer. Subjects were informed, furthermore, that they would be expected to report publicly their second answers to the group following completion of the experiment and that the cabin in the unit with the highest proportion of correct answers would be awarded the prize. Following selection of the subjects' initial answers the tabulations were reported by the experimenter in such a manner as to lead each group member to believe that everyone in the group except himself had selected one of the two leading choices. In actuality, however, none of the group members had selected the two answers reported as "leading choices."

Conformity behavior was then measured by determining whether or not the subject, for his second choice, shifted to one of the announced leading choices. In order to assure a more conservative measure of conformity, that is, to increase the likelihood that the conformity measure actually reflected a tendency to conform toward the perceived expectations of peers, the experiment was immediately repeated, utilizing a different symbol and a different list of eleven possible answers. Only those group members who conformed on *both* tests were classified as "conformers." Following termination of the experiment the subjects were informed that it was unnecessary to divulge their answers and that they need not do so. All the cabin groups were then brought together, the true purpose of the experiment was explained, and, if permitted by camp policy, each participant was awarded a prize. Utilizing this design it was possible, therefore, to classify certain group members as "conformers" or "nonconformers" and to determine the proportion of "conformers" and "nonconformers" in each group.

---

[4] The two symbols were utilized for different purposes in a study by Bachrach et al. (1961). In order to control for the effects of expertise the true answers were omitted from the list of eleven choices.

FINDINGS AND THEIR IMPLICATIONS FOR
SOCIAL GROUP WORK INTERVENTION

Relationships Among Modes of Group
Integration

For the groups studied, it was found that functional integration and interpersonal integration are highly correlated in a positive direction. That is, groups characterized by effective goal attainment, pattern maintenance, and external relations, and in which responsibility for performance of those functions is distributed among many members, tend to be characterized by high degrees of reciprocal liking. Conversely, groups that are relatively ineffective in the performance of such functions, or in which responsibility for their performance is monopolized by one or a few members, tend to manifest low levels of interpersonal liking.

Group normative integration is also positively correlated with interpersonal integration, but to a much lesser extent than is functional integration;[5] consensus regarding group-relevant norms appears to be frequently accompanied by high interpersonal liking among group members. Conversely, low consensus regarding norms appears to be frequently accompanied by low interpersonal liking.

In contrast to these findings, group normative integration and functional integration exhibit a very weak correlation. Consensus regarding norms does not necessarily correspond with effective and shared member efforts toward goal attainment, pattern maintenance, and external relations.

For all three modes of group integration girls' groups exhibited greater integration than did boys' groups. Larger groups tended to attain somewhat higher levels of functional integration than did smaller ones.[6] A similar tendency for interpersonal integration was less pronounced, and there was no clear trend in the case of normative integration. Integration scores varied somewhat according to camp; however, only in the case of interpersonal integration was there a marked tendency for groups at the

_____

[5] Using somewhat analogous measures, Gross reported empirical evidence supporting the conclusion that both functional integration and normative integration are positively related to interpersonal integration, but that the former relationship is stronger than the latter. See Gross (1956). Indirect supporting evidence for the observed relationship between group functional integration and interpersonal integration is also provided by a number of other investigations. See, for example, Bovard (1951); McKeachie (1954); Kipnis (1957). Numerous studies also indirectly support the observed relationship between group normative integration and interpersonal integration. See, for example, Lundy (1956); Newcomb (1961); Precker (1952).

[6] In part, this tendency may be an artifact of the functional integration index. For a detailed explanation see Feldman (1967).

private camps to attain scores different from those at the community-sponsored camps.[7] Group members' ages exhibited no systematic relationship to any of the group integration measures.

Implications. If a social group worker's main objective is the enhancement of interpersonal liking among the group's members, these findings suggest the efficacy of interventions directed toward maximization of the group's functional and normative integration. Program activities, designed to facilitate the development of functional interdependencies and to facilitate the elaboration or clarification of shared norms, such as camping trips or other group projects, would probably constitute more effective intervention strategies than ones which deemphasize those features, such as free swimming activities.[8]

Even more important, in view of the data, is the indication that group functional integration rather than normative integration should be a preferred locus for worker intervention. Positive intervention in group functional integration, it appears, would be more likely to result in enhanced interpersonal liking than would similar intervention in group normative integration. Moreover, it seems apparent that programming skills could be more flexibly and effectively utilized toward intervention in the functional structures of groups than in their normative structures since the latter tend to change only very gradually (Merei, 1958). Direct or indirect allocation of certain roles among group members (Vinter, Chapter 13 in this volume), or facilitation of members' efforts toward goal attainment, pattern maintenance, or external relations, would be likely to promote the growth of reciprocal liking.[9] In contrast, if the worker's efforts should be directed toward diminution of interpersonal liking among group members, countervailing intervention strategies would be indicated (Spergel, 1966; Yablonsky, 1966).

These findings also serve to forewarn the group worker against interventions that might otherwise prove to be maladaptive or inefficient. They further question the efficacy of intervention in group normative structures

---

[7] Interpersonal integration scores tended to be higher for groups at the private camps than for groups at the community-sponsored camps. This finding may be related to one or more variables that differentiate groups at the two camps. Thus, for instance, group members at the private camps had lived together for longer periods of time, prior to data collection, than had members at the community camps. Also as noted previously, group members from the private camps generally came from families of high socioeconomic status.

[8] Considerations regarding group work programming have been discussed in detail by a number of writers. See, for example, Gump and Sutton-Smith (1955); Redl (1959); Redl and Wineman (1952); Vinter (Chapter 13 in this volume).

[9] Numerous descriptions of such social work interventions are provided in the literature. See, for example, Konopka (1963); Lott and Lott (1960); Maier (1965); Redl and Wineman (1952); Riessman (1965).

since it appears that alterations in normative integration are unlikely to produce clearly predictable effects upon the key variable of functional integration. They also raise the possibility that worker intervention in the functional integration of groups may, indeed, produce conflicting effects upon group interpersonal and normative integration. Although increments in group functional integration are likely to enhance interpersonal integration, it is possible that, through increased specialization and diversification of role expectations, they could simultaneously lead to decreased member consensus concerning norms. Hence group work interventions, especially if they are likely to stimulate countervailing tendencies, must be directly based upon the worker's treatment goal priorities for individual group members.

Modes of Group Integration and Conformity Behavior

Table 2 reports the percentage of conformers found in groups of varying type and extent of integration. It is seen that larger proportions of members conform in highly integrated groups, for each of the three modes of group integration, than in groups characterized by low integration. Although the results do not attain high levels of statistical significance, they tend to suggest that groups characterized by high normative consensus, great interpersonal liking, and effective shared performance of key functions are likely to produce stronger conformity pressures than groups that are markedly deficient in such qualities.[10]

All the observed relationships between modes of group integration and conformity behavior, however, are not monotonic since it it seen, in the case of interpersonal integration, that the greatest incidence of conforming behavior occurs in groups that are moderately integrated. It appears that high degrees of interpersonal liking among group members provide them with the opportunity occasionally to act contrary to group conformity pressures without incurring undue peer hostility or sanctions.[11]

Following mathematical adjustments for the effects of sex, age, camp, and group size, it was found that slightly larger proportions of group members conformed in girls' groups than in boys' groups. Furthermore, camp milieu was shown to bear a distinct relationship to conformity behavior.

[10] Several other investigators have also concluded that groups characterized by high functional integration, or analogous features, are likely to be characterized by strong conformity pressures. See, for example, Berelson and Steiner (1964); and Blake and Mouton (1961).

[11] This interpretation is similar to Hollander's (1958) notion of "idiosyncracy credits." Hollander, however, refers to task competence rather than to interpersonal integration.

TABLE 2.   Percentage of Conformers in Groups of Varying Normative, Functional, and Interpersonal Integration

Type and Extent[a] of Group Integration	Percent of Conformers	N
Normative integration		
Low	39.8	21
Medium	39.4	20
High	43.1	20
		61
Functional integration		
Low	37.5	12
Medium	39.8	36
High	46.4	13
		61
Interpersonal integration		
Low	34.8	21
Medium	45.3	20
High	42.5	20
		61

[a] Low, medium, and high categories were derived by trichotimization of groups on the basis of index scores. Analysis of difference between low and high categories for normative integration, functional integration, and interpersonal integration (difference of proportions test, one-tailed) results in respective p values of .39, .30, and .26.

Significantly larger proportions of group members conformed at the private camps than at the community-sponsored camps. The reasons for this observation cannot be readily inferred from the data collected. A number of characteristics other than social class could have differentiated subjects at the two types of camps. Subjects at the private camps lived together for longer periods of time prior to experimentation than did subjects at the community camps. Social class, time spent together, and other distinguishing factors (such as differences in staff composition, programming, and so forth) could plausibly serve to mediate additional undetermined factors that influence the conformity behavior of group members.

   Implications.   Pending replicative studies more directly linked to group work practice situations, these findings suggest that in order to maximize peer group conformity pressures and, therefore, to enhance the effectiveness of the group as a treatment vehicle, it would appear advisable for practitioners to work toward the development of high levels of normative and functional, but only moderate levels of interpersonal, integration within their groups. Conversely, if individual members' treatment goals can be most readily attained through the weakening of peer group conformity pressures, the worker's efforts should be directed toward the development of low levels of normative, functional, and interpersonal integration.

Relationships among Modes of Individual Member Integration

Analysis of the data reveals that functional integration and interpersonal integration are strongly correlated at the individual level. That is, the tendency for individuals to perform major group functions effectively appears to correspond with the tendency for them to like, and to be liked by, their peers. In contrast, individuals' normative integration into groups appears to manifest a markedly weaker association with interpersonal integration. Adherence to peer group norms does not necessarily correspond with liking or being liked by the members of a group.

In view of the low correlation between normative integration and functional integration, it appears that the effective performance of key group functions does not necessarily correspond with adherence to the group's norms. Nor is adherence to group norms necessarily a concomitant of effective functional performance.[12] For all three individual integration measures girls were found to be somewhat more highly integrated into their groups than were boys.

Implications. If a group worker wished to increase a given member's interpersonal integration into the group (that is, to increase the individual's liking for the group's members and to increase their liking for him), an effective focus for worker intervention would appear to be the member's capacity to perform necessary functions for the group. The worker might directly attempt to enhance the member's skills in certain activities or to develop recognition of the need for, and skills essential to, group harmony. Or, through the skillful use of programming the worker might indirectly promote group activities that facilitate the exhibition of effective, but rarely displayed, member skills (Gump and Sutton-Smith, 1955; Redl and Wineman, 1952; Vinter, 1974, Chapter 13 in this volume). The efficacy of such prescriptions, however, is not likely to be especially novel to the group worker with a modicum of practice experience.

The data also suggest that worker activity directed toward the clarification and acceptance of group norms for a given member may not be especially likely to facilitate great interpersonal integration into the group

---

[12] Some authors have suggested that effective group leaders must occasionally be able to deviate from group norms or elaborate new norms in order to introduce innovative solutions to problems confronting the group. See, for instance, Fiedler (1960); Hollander (1958); Homans (1961).

for him. Neither would increased member adherence to group norms seem especially likely to result in significantly greater functional integration.

Modes of Individual Member Integration and Conformity Behavior

Table 3 indicates that members who are highly interpersonally integrated into a group tend to be more likely to conform to peer group pressures than those who are less integrated. The greatest proportion of conformers are found among those group members who express considerable liking for their peers and who, in turn, are greatly liked by them.[13]

The opposite trend is noted for the relationship between conformity behavior and an individual's functional integration into the group. Those

TABLE 3.   Average Individual Member Conformity Scores

Type and Extent[a] of Individual Integration	Conformity Score	N
Normative integration		
Low	.36	175
Medium	.44	195
High	.40	168
		538
Functional integration		
Low	.44	179
Medium	.38	179
High	.38	180
		538
Interpersonal integration		
Low	.38	179
Medium	.38	178
High	.43	181
		538

[a] Low, medium, and high categories were derived by trichotimization on the basis of index scores. Analysis of the difference between low and high categories for normative integration, functional integration, and interpersonal integration (difference of proportions test, one-tailed) results in respective p values of .16, .07, and .11.

[13] In general, most investigators have concluded that the relationship between interpersonal integration and conformity behavior is a positive montonic one. See, for instance, Berelson and Steiner (1964); Lott and Lott (1961); Schachter (1960). Exceptions to their conclusions, however, have been raised by a number of other investigators. See, for example, Walker and Heyns (1962).

individuals who are least functionally integrated exhibit the greatest frequency of conforming behavior, whereas those who are moderately or highly functionally integrated conform less frequently. It appears, therefore, that occupation of a marginal position, or of a group position that contributes little or nothing toward the group's functional effectiveness, is associated with heightened susceptibility to peer group conformity pressures. The immediate sources of such heightened susceptibility, however, cannot be readily inferred from the above data. Whether or not such conforming behavior can be traced to the ambiguous role expectations associated with a nonintegrated position or to other sources of role strain in unclear.[14]

In the case of normative integration, the probability of conforming behavior is greatest among those group members who are moderately integrated into the group and lowest among those who are least integrated into it. It would appear that prior adherence to group norms is not an especially effective predictor of conforming behavior but that prior nonadherence suggests a relatively low probability of conforming behavior.

Implications.   Depending upon the group worker's specific treatment goals for individual members, the findings suggest the efficacy of varying group work intervention strategies. To enhance a given member's receptiveness to peer group change pressures, the worker would be advised to promote interpersonal integration for him. Further, the worker's efforts should be directed, through programming and other means, toward decreasing the member's functional integration into the group.

It should be emphasized that the efficacy of such intervention strategies must be considered within the total framework of treatment goals for a given individual. Enhanced member receptiveness to peer group pressures might be gained only at the cost of lowering the member's self-esteem or sense of individual competence. However, if the worker's treatment goals consist of strengthening a given member's resistance to peer group pressures, the appropriate treatment strategies seem clearly indicated: to lessen his adherence to group norms, to decrease his interpersonal integration into the group, and to enhance his ability to perform important functions for the group thus, in effect, decreasing his dependence upon the peer group.

The study described here represents one conceptual and empirical approach designed to investigate the nature of group integration and to determine the relevance of the concept for social group work. It should be considered as only an initial effort leading to research more directly focused upon group work practice settings. Its foremost utility, it is posited, rests

---

[14] Explanations for related observations have been set forth by a number of investigators. See Mannheim (1966); Berkowitz and Lundy (1957); Dittes (1959); Darley (1966); Morse and Wineman (1957).

in the elaboration of one type of conceptual and research model designed to study group level, as well as individual level, variables and their relevance for social group work practice. Additional effort must be devoted to the investigation of group level variables; other conceptual and operational techniques must be created; and, ultimately, treatment-oriented research must be conducted or replicated with appropriate groups of social work clients. Workers should eventually be able to determine whether or not group members who strongly share the norms of their peers (members who are highly normatively integrated into the group) are markedly more or less receptive to group work change efforts than are members who occupy less normatively integrated positions. Workers may wish to determine whether or not occupation of certain positions in the affect structure, or other structures, of a group tends to enhance or diminish given members' receptiveness to group work treatment efforts. The knowledge base of group work should progress toward the delineation of crucial positions within group structures and toward empirical specification of their relative importance for group work change efforts. Further examination of varying modes of group and individual integration is warranted to identify the unique features of small group structure that contribute to the attainment of social group work objectives.

REFERENCES

BACHRACH, ARTHUR J., ET AL.
    1961—"Group reinforcement of individual response experiments in verbal behavior," in Irwin A. Berg and Bernard M. Bass (Eds.), *Conformity and Deviance,* New York: Harper and Brothers, pp. 258–285.
BARTLETT, HARRIETT M.
    1964—*Characteristics of Social Work,* New York: National Association of Social Workers.
BASS, BERNARD M.
    1961—"Conformity, deviation, and a general theory of interpersonal behavior," in Irwin A. Berg and Bernard M. Bass (Eds.), *Conformity and Deviation,* New York: Harper and Brothers, pp. 38–100.
BERELSON, BERNARD AND GARY A. STEINER
    1964—*Human Behavior: An Inventory of Scientific Findings,* New York: Harcourt, Brace and World, pp. 325–61.
BERKOWITZ, LEONARD AND RICHARD M. LUNDY
    1957—"Personality characteristics related to susceptibility to influence by peers or authority figures," *Journal of Personality,* 25, pp. 306–15.
BLAKE, ROBERT R. AND JANE S. MOUTON
    1961—"Conformity, resistance, and conversion," in Irwin A. Berg and Bernard M. Bass (Eds.), *Conformity and Deviance,* New York: Harper and Brothers, pp. 1–37.

BLAU, PETER M.
1960—"A theory of social integration," *American Journal of Sociology*, 65, pp. 545–56.

BOVARD, EVERETT W., JR.
1951—"The experimental production of interpersonal affect," *Journal of Abnormal and Social Psychology*, 46, pp. 521–28.

CARTWRIGHT, DORWIN AND ALVIN ZANDER (EDS.)
1960—*Group Dynamics: Research and Theory*, second edition, Illinois: Row, Peterson.

CHURCHILL, SALLIE R.
1959—"Prestructuring group content," *Social Work*, 4, pp. 52–59.

DARLEY, JOHN M.
1966—"Fear and social comparison as determinants of conformity behavior," *Journal of Personality and Social Psychology*, 4, pp. 73–78.

DITTES, JAMES E.
1959—"Attractiveness of group as function of self-esteem and acceptance by group," *Journal of Abnormal and Social Psychology*, 59, pp. 77–82.

FANSHEL, DAVID
1966—"Sources of strain in practice-oriented research," *Social Casework*, 47, pp. 357–62.

FELDMAN, RONALD A.
1966—"Three types of group integration: Their relationship to power, leadership, and conformity behavior," Ann Arbor: University of Michigan School of Social Work. (Unpublished doctoral dissertation.)
1967—"Interrelationships among three bases of group integration," Berkeley, California: University of California School of Social Welfare. (Dittoed.)

FESTINGER, LEON, STANLEY SCHACHTER, AND KURT W. BACK
1950—*Social Pressures in Informal Groups*, New York: Harper and Brothers.

FIEDLER, FRED E.
1960—"The leader's psychological distance and group effectiveness," in Cartwright and Zander (Eds.), *Group Dynamics: Research and Theory*, second edition, Evanston, Illinois: Row, Peterson and Co., pp. 586–606.

FREEDMAN, RONALD
1966—"Sources of strain in practice-oriented research," *Social Casework*, 47, pp. 357–62.

GREENWOOD, ERNEST
1955—"Social science and social work: A theory of their relationship," *Social Service Review*, 29, pp. 20–33.

GROSS, EDWARD
1956—"Symbiosis and consensus as integrative factors in small groups," *American Sociological Review*, 21, pp. 174–79.

GUMP, PAUL AND BRIAN SUTTON-SMITH
1955—"Therapeutic play techniques," *American Journal of Orthopsychiatry*, 24, pp. 755–60.

HOLLANDER, E. P.

    1958—"Conformity, status, and idiosyncrasy credit," *Psychological Review,* 65, pp. 117–27.

HOMANS, GEORGE C.

    1950—*The Human Group,* New York: Harcourt, Brace, and World.

    1961—*Social Behavior: Its Elementary Forms,* New York: Harcourt, Brace, and World.

HURWITZ, JACOB I.

    1956—"Systematizing social group work practice," *Social Work,* 1, pp. 63–69.

KADUSHIN, ALFRED

    1963—"Diagnosis and evaluation for (almost) all occasions," *Social Work,* 8, pp. 1–18.

KELMAN, HERBERT C.

    1963—"The role of the group in the induction of therapeutic change," *International Journal of Group Psychotherapy,* 13, pp. 399–432.

KIPNIS, DOROTHY MCBRIDE

    1957—"Interaction between members of bomber crews as a determinant of sociometric choice," *Human Relations,* 10, pp. 263–70.

KONOPKA, GISELA

    1963—*Social Group Work: A Helping Process,* Englewood Cliffs, New Jersey: Prentice-Hall.

LOTT, BERNICE E. AND ALBERT J. LOTT

    1960—"The formation of positive attitudes toward group members," *Journal of Abnormal and Social Psychology,* 61, pp. 297–300.

    1961—"Group cohesiveness, communication level, and conformity," *Journal of Abnormal and Social Psychology,* 62, pp. 408–12.

    1965—"Group cohesiveness as interpersonal attraction: A review of relationships with antecedent and consequent variables," *Psychological Bulletin,* 64, pp. 259–309.

LUNDY, RICHARD M.

    1956—"Self perceptions and descriptions of opposite sex sociometric choices," *Sociometry,* 19, pp. 272–77.

MAIER, HENRY W. (ED.)

    1965—*Group Work as Part of Residential Treatment,* New York: National Association of Social Workers.

MANNHEIM, BILKA F.

    1966—"Reference groups, membership groups and the self image," *Sociometry,* 29, pp. 265–79.

MCKEACHIE, WILBERT J.

    1954—"Individual conformity to attitudes of classroom groups," *Journal of Abnormal and Social Psychology,* 49, pp. 282–89.

MEREI, FERENC

    1958—"Group leadership and institutionalization," in Eleanor E. Maccoby, Theodore M. Newcomb, and Eugene L. Hartley (Eds.), *Readings in Social Psychology,* third edition, New York: Holt, Rinehart, and Winston, pp. 522–32.

MORSE, WILLIAM C. AND DAVID WINEMAN
1957—"The therapeutic use of social isolation in a camp for ego-disturbed boys," *Journal of Social Issues,* 13, pp. 32–39.

NATIONAL ASSOCIATION OF SOCIAL WORKERS
1964—*Building Social Work Knowledge,* New York: National Association of Social Workers.

NEWCOMB, THEODORE M.
1961—*The Acquaintance Process,* New York: Holt, Rinehart, and Winston.

NEWCOMB, THEODORE M., RALPH H. TURNER, AND PHILIP E. CONVERSE
1965—*Social Psychology: The Study of Human Interaction,* New York: Holt, Rinehart, and Winston.

PARSONS, TALCOTT
1951—*The Social System,* Glencoe, Illinois: Free Press.

PRECKER, JOSEPH A.
1952—"Similarity of valuings as a factor in selection of peers and near-authority figures," *Journal of Abnormal and Social Psychology,* 47, pp. 406–14.

REDL, FRITZ
1959—"The impact of game ingredients on children's play behavior," in Bertram Schaffner (Ed.), *Group Processes: Transactions of the Fourth Conference,* New York: Josiah Macy, Jr., Foundation, pp. 38–81.

REDL, FRITZ AND DAVID WINEMAN
1952—*Control from Within,* Glencoe, Illinois: Free Press.

RIESSMAN, FRANK
1965—"The 'the helper' therapy principle," *Social Work,* 10, pp. 27–32.

SARRI, ROSEMARY C. AND ROBERT D. VINTER
1963—"Group treatment strategies in juvenile correctional programs," *Crime and Delinquency,* 10, pp. 326–40.

SCHACHTER, STANLEY S.
1960—"Deviation, rejection, and communication," in Dorwin Cartwright and Alvin Zander (Eds.), *Group Dynamics: Research and Theory,* second edition, Evanston, Illinois: Row, Peterson, pp. 260–85.

SCHWARTZ, WILLIAM
1963—"Small group science and group work practice," *Social Work,* 8, pp. 39–46.

SILVERMAN, MARVIN
1966—"Knowledge in social group work: A review of the literature," *Social Work,* 11, pp. 56–62.

SPERGEL, IRVING
1966—*Street Gang Work: Theory and Practice,* Reading, Massachusetts: Addison-Wesley.

THIBAUT, JOHN W., AND HAROLD H. KELLEY
1959—*The Social Psychology of Groups,* New York: John Wiley & Sons.

THOMAS, EDWIN J.
1962—"Behavioral science and the interpersonal helping process," Annual Meeting of the American Sociological Association. (Mimeographed.)

VINTER, ROBERT D.

1965—"Social group work," in Harry L. Lurie (Ed.), *Encyclopedia of Social Work,* New York: National Association of Social Workers.

WALKER, EDWARD L. AND ROGER W. HEYNS

1962—*An Anatomy for Conformity,* Englewood Cliffs, New Jersey: Prentice-Hall.

WELLER, LEONARD

1963—"The effects of anxiety on cohesiveness and rejection," *Human Relations,* 16, pp. 189–97.

YABLONSKY, LEWIS

1966—*The Violent Gang,* Baltimore: Penguin Books.

10.

The Therapeutic Contract in Social Treatment

TOM A. CROXTON

The treatment contract, or working agreement, has been given little attention by the social work profession; however, it deserves a prominent place in a comprehensive discussion of therapeutic processes. From these agreements client-worker relationships are formed and treatment roles are engineered; they provide the platform on which the entire therapeutic process is built. Components and negotiating processes of the treatment contract can be clarified by examining the perspectives of legal history, traditional social work practice, and social science theory and research.

LEGAL/HISTORICAL PERSPECTIVE

Whenever man creates a community, he makes an agreement or covenant to abide by specified and relatively certain norms to obtain a more secure and permanent relationship with his fellow man.[1] The concept of contract is basic to the maintenance and stability of any social system. If the establishment of the monogamous group in man's early history were traced, definite sets of behavioral expectations between the parties, i.e., an implied contract, would probably be found.

Historically, the concept of contract was a primary part of the beginnings of law as a recognized and viable institution. According to Corbin (1963), "That portion of the field of law that is classified and described as the law of contracts attempts the realization of reasonable expectations that have been induced by the making of a promise."

[1] For a novel dramatizing this notion, see Becker (1965). Although this concept may constitute a Lockean myth, the author offers it in idyllic splendor. In *Human Nature and Conduct,* John Dewey writes, "It is easy to criticize the contract theory of the state which states the individual surrenders some, at least, of their natural liberties in order to make secure as civil liberties what they retain. Nevertheless, there is some truth in the idea of surrender and exchange."

In legal terminology, contract has been defined as "a promissory agreement between two or more persons in which there must be subject matter, consideration and mutuality of agreement" (Corbin, 1963). Generally there is an offer, acceptance and consideration; the agreement must not be so vague and uncertain that the terms of the contract are not ascertainable. These same elements are present in the working agreement in the therapeutic situation.

Since contracts necessarily reflect human quality, to look at such instruments in a mechanistic fashion (as is sometimes the case in law) is to overlook the essence of such agreements, for, in effect, the contract *creates or modifies a social relationship*. This function has profound consequences for the parties involved. Ideally, such covenants should be viewed as the dynamic interaction of two or more persons arriving at a point of mutual understanding and agreement which requires a new set of responses and imposes new responsibilities upon the participants.

Consider, for example, the institution of marriage; certainly no other social contract has such dramatic implications for the parties involved. Legally, marriage is seen as a contractual arrangement between two parties, the *offer* being in some romantic form of "Will you marry me?" and the *acceptance* being some form of affirmative response. The *consideration* is the marriage state itself (which *implies* mutual benefit, rather than mutual detriment, to the parties). Although state legislatures have placed other hurdles on the path toward marriage (e.g., license, blood tests, ceremony, and so forth) no such elements were and are recognized by common law (Goldstein and Katz, 1965).

The terms of the marriage contract per se are usually ambiguous, but the parties seldom worry about the more "mundane" aspects of the contract until after the ceremony has been performed. However, society resolves some of those ambiguities, for superimposed upon the agreement is a socially and culturally predetermined set of behaviors. The more gross aspects of such role expectations have legal sanction: one can no longer beat one's wife; one must support one's family. If certain behaviors are not forthcoming, e.g., sexual intercourse, one can annul the contract. Despite the various technicalities within the marriage law, the essential ingredient is the creation of a relationship which has complex social and psychological implications.

The study of role, role conflict, and role discontinuity rests on the basis of contract, expressed or implied (Biddle and Thomas, 1966). A man's relationships with his wife, his children, his parents, and the extended family group are based on various sets of expectations including his own, those of other parties, and of society. In establishing such relationships, the expectations become implied contractual obligations. The role of father demands certain responses; by fathering a child, a man undertakes a new set of expectations. By performing an act, the man agrees by implication that he will henceforth respond to others and to his environment in a different way. Even if he explicitly denies such obligations, society may impose them over his protestations, e.g., through a paternity action. When the terms of such contracts become vague, when a contract contains internal contradiction, or when there is a set of incompatible or conflicting covenants, problems frequently arise.

CONTRACTUAL RELATIONSHIPS IN SOCIAL WORK

Social agencies enter into a variety of contractual relationships. Harry Bredemeir (1964) in his analysis of social agencies, essentially speaks of an implied, if not explicit, tripartite contract between the agency, the community and the clientele. He writes of the vagueness of promises made and of the agency's frequent inability to fulfill its implied promises both to the community and to its clientele. An agency may sell its wares to the community on the promise that it will provide certain services but fail to do so, thereby failing to fulfill its contract. Family service agencies have been criticized for implying promises to the community that they will serve the poor and disadvantaged when, in fact, most of their cases treat middle- and upper middle-class clientele.[2] Settlement houses have been criticized for similar reasons.[3] One justification for juvenile courts is that they provide treatment; yet they have been aptly described primarily as people-processing organizations (Vinter and Sarri, 1965). The adoption agency provides the majority of its services to the unwed mother and the illegitimate child, yet the agency may refuse, as a matter of policy, to accept releases on Negro children. What the agency says it does and what it actually does often follow separate and divergent paths. Although a variety of forces produce these discrepancies, one cannot dismiss the fact that the agency is not fulfilling its covenants. Too often, only pressure from the outside forces the agency to consider its contracts.

Many communities—economic, political, ethnic, professional—are served by an agency. Thus, any one agency has many outstanding contracts with many communities. For the agency to survive, some of these contracts necessarily may be in conflict. However, the agency must recognize this "fact of life" and seek to reduce or eliminate the discord, by making explicit its offers or promises to the various parties, including the consumers of its services. Until this occurs, the ambiguities of the contracts will continue to plague the agency, the community, and the clientele.

[2] Cloward and Epstein (1965:623–644). A rebuttal was made in a Family Service Associations of America Memorandum, August 7, 1964; also see Beck (1962).
[3] Gans (1964:3–12). In rebuttal see *Social Work* (1965).

A client may come to an agency for help of a self-determined nature only to find that the agency insists on a different sort of helping agreement (Overall and Aronson, 1964; Rosenfeld, 1964; Briar, 1966). If out of this conflict a new contract were truly negotiated, one could have little quarrel with it. But, in fact, the agency may not be able to negotiate; its policies, its intake criteria, its therapeutic processes may be set and regarded as being nonnegotiable. Therefore, the client either accepts treatment on the agency's terms or he cannot get served. The bind does not end there; the client must meet a whole set of vague and uncommunicated behavioral expectations. In return he receives only vague and unspecified promises about rewards. He does not know exactly how he is going to be helped, only that he will be better adjusted and more content with himself if he cooperates and conforms to the system. In effect, he must surrender himself to the professional hands of the agency on faith alone.[4]

The primary and crucial relevance of the contract considered here lies in the professional relationship between the social worker and the client. As in the doctor-patient relationship, the contract is either explicit or implied by the verbalizations and/or actions of the parties. However, such contracts are perceived too often in simplistic terms as money-for-service arrangements or as a set of behavioral responses for service. Like the marriage contract, the worker-client contract includes essential terms that are either unperceived, disregarded, or seen as unimportant. Yet it is when these elements are overlooked or misinterpreted that confusion and hostility may result. To see such arrangements as a qualified partnership agreement or as a joint venture would seem to be a preferable perspective. The physician, generally, would be horrified at the thought of such a perspective, since he usually does not see himself as much a servant of his patients as a dispenser of expertise. He may or may not tell his patient the source of the problem or for what purpose the treatment is imposed. He may not keep the patient informed during the medical explorations or the treatment process. The physician becomes the dominant and central person of the relationship; the patient, a necessary adjunct, is simply the raw material.[5]

---

[4] The consequence of this is usually the client's refusal to participate. See Rosenfeld (1964) and Goldstein (1966). It is apparent that the inequity of the parties may demand the employment of a bargaining agent on behalf of the client if a meaningful contract is to be secured, e.g., an attorney in Juvenile Court processing, a lay advocate in welfare proceedings.

[5] Mechanic (1968:90) notes, "It is a fact, however unfortunate, that the more scientific and technically developed aspects of medicine are concentrated on the evaluation of the patient's symptoms as compared to his overall needs, and thus both in the training of doctors and in daily medical activity, the major emphasis tends to be given to medical diagnosis and treatment of acute illness."

All such professional behavior is rationalized on the basis that "the doctor knows best." Much the same, one fears, is the state of affairs within the social work profession which too often has imitated or assumed the medical model. The professsion has paid little heed to defining the terms of the relationship between the worker and the client. The profession has not seen this as essential to the relationship, despite the fact that the worker-client relationship is taught as one of the prime factors in the social work process. One simply does not share with the client the diagnosis, the treatment plan, or the problem focus. The contract thus remains vague, unstructured and nonspecific; it arises through ill-defined, almost magical processes, or it is part of somebody's "hidden agenda." Since the worker is not sharing—and is often hiding from the client—the real purpose of treatment, such vague contracts may lead toward a basic sort of professional dishonesty. The client may expect and feel that he is being treated for a particular problem that is completely outside the intent of the therapist as he formulates and implements treatment goals. The essential terms of the contract remain hidden. Frustration, inefficiency, and defeat are frequently the consequences.

A notable exception to this pattern was the St. Paul Family Centered Project where an approximation of a partnership agreement was achieved. In one of the project reports it is noted, "As we go along, we review what we are doing together and look at the reasons for any gains or losses the family has made. To give the families a sense of 'being in on the deal,' we show them copies of letters we are writing to the court about them and parts of the case record. In a few instances, parents have been invited to participate in interagency conferences about their situation. Also . . . we have asked our working associates to give us their observations on social work method" (Overton, Tinker and Associates, 1959).

SOCIAL SCIENCE AND SOCIAL PRACTICES PERSPECTIVES

A working agreement or contract does not exist in a vacuum; it presupposes interaction between two or more persons operating within a particular milieu. It is a social transaction. While we can, and indeed do, look at such behaviors microscopically, we must be aware that behavior can be neither understood nor meaningfully evaluated without reference to the environment within which that behavior occurs. Bateson (1958) reminds us that "to increase awareness of one's scientific universe is to face unpredictable increases in one's awareness of self . . . . Such increases are always in the very nature of the case unpredictable . . . . No one knows the end of the process which starts from uniting the perceiver and the perceived—the subject and the object—into a single universe." The lack of mathematical certainties should not serve as an excuse for ignoring social transactions or being imprecise in reference to them.

Watts (1961) has suggested, "in a pattern so mobile and volatile as human society, maintaining consistency of action and communication is not easy. It requires the most elaborate agreements as to what the pattern is, or to put it another way, as to what are the consistencies of the system. Without agreement as to the rules of playing together, there is no game. Without agreement as to the use of words, signs, gestures, there is no communication." There must be communication in the typical therapeutic transaction. And consensus about the rules of the game as well.

Social scientists—theorists, researchers and therapeutic strategists— have different perspectives on contractual relationships. But they share the conviction that a voluntary and unambiguous contract between observer and observed, psychoanalyst and patient, worker and client is crucial to the effectiveness of any therapeutic transaction. Erikson notes that one can study the human mind only by engaging the fully motivated partnership of the observed individual and by entering into a sincere contract with him. The dimensions of Freud's discovery are contained in a triad which, in a variety of ways, remains basic to the practice of psychoanalysis. Freud's triad is, one, a therapeutic contract; two, a conceptual design; and three, a systematic self-analysis (Erikson, 1964). Wolberg, in writing of the working therapeutic relationship, states,

> Unless a cooperative contract is established with the patient, the therapeutic process may come to naught. An effective system must maintain this as a prime objective during the first part of therapy. The techniques of achieving a relationship are rarely formalized, but usually they involve a gaining of the patient's confidence, an arousal of his expectations of help, a mobilization in him of the conviction that the therapist wishes to work with him, and is able to do so, a motivating of the patient to accept the conditions of therapy, and a clarifying of misconceptions. Without a working relationship, there can be no movement into the exploratory and working-through phases of therapy; the patient will be unable to handle his anxieties associated with the recognition and facing of unconscious conflict (Wolberg, 1967. Also, Biestek, 1957; Menninger, 1963).

Both Greenson (1965) and Powell (1967) have written of the "working alliance" and have noted the importance of separating the alliance from other transference phenomena. Saul Bernstein writes,

> In several human relations fields, the idea is developing that as service begins, there should be some clarification as to what it involves, mutual expectations, and whether each part wants to enter into the relationship (Bernstein, 1964).

Perlman adds,

> The client, if he is to know what he is undertaking, and if he is to be enabled to organize himself appropriately, must have a true sample and demonstration of what is to be expected. . . . The client takes part from the first using the agency's means; he can anticipate what the ongoing experience is to be like (Perlman, 1957).

It would appear that a rather high degree of transactional explicitness is advocated by Haley (1963), Bateson (1958; and Bateson and Ruesch, 1951), Satir (1964), and to a lesser degree by Berne (1961), and perhaps Rogers (1967 and 1951). Among group workers, one must cite Bertcher (1966), Frey and Meyer (1965), and Konopka (1963) as advocates of clearer and more precise messages throughout the therapeutic process.

Kanfer and Marston (1961) have shown empirically that the effects of ambiguity on learning and transfer in a verbal conditioning situation are that ambiguity may retard learning and that the more ambiguous the messages, the more retardation in learning. Raven and Rietsema (1960) show evidence that the client working toward a clear goal increases his interest in his work; a lack of structure in the situation makes his work less attractive or more threatening and increases group hostility. To a group member, a clear group goal and goal path give meaning to membership in the group, increase his attraction to his fellow worker, make him more group oriented and increase the power of the group over him. Goldstein, Heller, and Sechrest (1966), in an exceptionally fine chapter on message ambiguity, after a review of relevant research, conclude that ". . . reducing ambiguity in therapy will decrease threat and increase the likelihood that the therapist's remarks will be understood and accepted."

Wolpe and Lazarus (1967) seem to suggest a great deal of explicitness in the therapeutic process when they state that the therapist should give the client an explanation of the therapist's theoretical orientation: "The behavior therapist does not moralize with his patient, but on the contrary, goes out of his way to nullify the self blame that social conditioning may have engendered." They illustrate this point with examples in which the theoretical base as well as the process are explained and clarified. In speaking on the contract, Boszormenyi-Nagy (1965) notes that the family therapist must "sell" his approach to the family as a valid treatment approach. It appears that he, too, would have a therapist explain his orientation and, to some extent, the process. Framo (1965) notes that, in the Pennsylvania Project, treatment was enhanced by demanding of the families adherence to certain preconditions to therapy. Each member of the family had to sign an application in which the entire family agreed to participate regularly in therapy and to adjust their individual schedules accordingly, to pay a fee, to demonstrate that they could give more than lip service to the notion that the problems of the designated patient were family problems. Steinzor writes,

> I think it would be a good idea and quite useful for every patient to obtain from the therapist a concrete description—perhaps even in writing —of just what philosophy he is 'selling.' The patient does have the right to know what kind of person he is choosing and what he is 'buying.' And since we therapists prize honesty, we should warn the patient that it does make sense to hesitate before entering psychotherapy. A democratic society is based on the making of choices which grow out of the voter's consideration of as much information as can be obtained. Throwing in one's lot with a therapist is one of the most crucial votes a person can cast (Steinzor, 1967).

A written contract has also been used by Family Service of Ann Arbor, Michigan. Although a written contract is not being advocated, it does have certain advantages in that it allows for greater explicitness, serves as a reinforcer, involves a specific commitment, limits rationalizations, and serves to overcome resistance.

COMPONENTS OF THE TREATMENT CONTRACT

The following definition of the treatment contract (working alliance) is proposed: *The treatment contract is an agreement between two or more persons in which there must be mutuality of understanding concerning treatment goals (product), reciprocal obligations relating to treatment means (specifications) and ultimate expectations (terminal behavior).*

The contract may be seen to consist of several types of interactions: (1) reciprocal obligations relating to mutual expectations, (2) shared experience relating to treatment means and (3) shared goals relating to the purpose of the relationship. Certainly the treatment contract cannot meet the specification of such esoteric outpourings as the Uniform Commercial Code, nor would one hope or want the agreement to contain such inflexibility; but some specification as to the terms of the covenant needs to be stated, negotiated, and reinforced throughout the therapeutic situation.

Bertcher has described requirements for effective contract presentation in group work; contract presentation in individual one-to-one therapy also should meet similar standards:

> Effective presentation of the group work contract requires (1) that the worker is able to state clearly the goals of this group for this client in such a way that each client will understand the worker's intent as shown

by his response, (2) that the goals, as stated, are compatible with the philosophy and nature of the agency and the profession, (3) that if each client will minimally commit himself to these goals, as evidenced by his responses that continue to relate to the worker's goals, he can reach some agreement with the worker on limited goals which are compatible with the agency's philosophy and nature, and the worker's goals for the group (Bertcher, 1966).

PHASES IN THE CONTRACTUAL SEQUENCE

The negotiation of a treatment contract is a gradual and complex process. The stages of this process are not discrete, nor can one specify an exact time sequence. The contract, in whole or part, may have to be renegotiated as new areas of concern develop. Delineation of the process into phases, however, facilitates understanding and analysis of its significant components.

Precontractual Conditions

The set of prior conditions may affect the freedom with which the therapist operates. Within an agency setting, the agency partly defines the contractual limitations. Thus, the agency's definition of function, the purpose of the agency, and its goals will guide and limit the worker in his contractual deliberations.

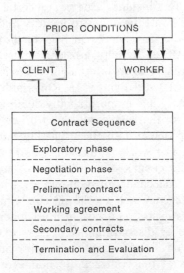

FIGURE 1   The Contract Sequence

For example, a juvenile court worker could not, without agency sanction, contract to help a child who is having problems in school but who is not a ward of the court. Neither can one promise as a term of the contract that communications will remain absolutely confidential if the agency demands records or other styles of intra-agency case communications. So too will the worker and the client be influenced in their deliberations by the organization's capacity to produce clear and unambiguous norms or expectations for performance. Welfare departments, under the AFDC program, often produce ambiguous messages concerning the man in the house rule or other dating behaviors. Since neither the agency, the worker or the client can clearly define the restrictions, ambiguous and conflicting messages result. As another example, the school's failure to communicate clearly its own expectations and reward system for those in the general (noncollege prep) curriculum leaves the students and the teachers in am-·biguous positions. Other factors which impinge upon the contractual negotiations as *a priori* conditions include ethics, legal sanctions, professional training, worker and/or client experience. The worker's own theoretical and methodological predilections will be a strong determinant in negotiations; thus, specifications will vary depending on the therapeutic methods invoked by the therapist, e.g., the behavioral *vis-à-vis* the neofreudian.

Exploratory Phase

During this phase, all parties begin to "test out" other members of the transaction, and they begin to define and specify expected role relationships and behaviors. For instance, there are certain "sell" tactics which the therapist uses. He wants the client to identify him as a problem-solving person, as someone who cares and will help in the solution of problems. Thus, the therapist, at least initially, presents himself as a benign person; he accords the client the usual social amenities. He is nonauthoritarian and he treats the individual with dignity. In Rogerian terms, he presents an image of a genuine, accepting, empathic individual.

During this phase, there is a mutual worker/client concern in defining the presenting problem with the usual information-gathering strategies being applicable. The worker must not be so intent on diagnosis that he is inattentive to the client's own "diagnosis" and problem definition. Both the worker and the client must ultimately decide whether the case is appropriate to the agency and to the process which ultimately may be offered. Both members in the relationship must independently or mutually decide on continuance or discontinuance. The worker, during this phase, explains what the agency is about—its strengths, limitations, and restrictions. If certain terms of the contract are nonnegotiable, they should be made explicit. Time, place, and fee terms may be established through agency policy or norms in rather inflexible, nonnegotiable patterns. The worker may require that significant others must agree to participate in therapy.

During this phase the worker begins to orient the client to the treatment process. Orientation material may be presented in rather generalized terms, but it seems preferable to give the client some case examples of others with similar problems who have been helped and/or to give the client written material that illustrates the process for his study and his critical response. If one is working with ongoing groups, other members may provide orientation information to new members concerning how they have been helped through their present or prior group experiences. The client must have a fair opportunity to know what he is "buying." As well as possible, giving consideration to age, intelligence, and cognitive functioning, the *offer* must be made in clear, precise terms. And the worker must begin to define with the client the elements of the consideration which flow between the participants.

The goal during the exploratory phase is to bring the client to a relatively unambiguous position. Not only does this approach present the therapeutic process on an honest, clear footing; it also helps the client to determine better whether or not he wishes to participate in the process Another secondary, but important, benefit from such an approach is that it allows the client to test the expertness of the therapist and to ascribe to him expert status. Thus a very powerful influence base may be established.

Negotiation Phase

During this phase, it is necessary to become as specific and explicit as the understanding of the client seems to allow. Generally the client's cognitive powers are underrated; workers tend to "talk down" inappropriately and thus alienate clients. If concepts cannot be explained in rather simple, illustrative terms, there exists either a fuzzy grasp of concepts or loss of the ability to communicate. To say merely that the worker is going to "help them with their problems" or that he will "help them to reconceptualize their roles" is so generalized and nonspecific as to be meaningless. Roles in treatment can be clarified by defining and explicating the treatment process. The expectations of both parties must be specified and conflicting expectations explored. At least minimum norms for performance must be defined. There must be dialogue concerning goals and goal path, or the immediate and successive tasks in the treatment process. If time, place, and fee terms are negotiable these must be discussed. Needless to say, many of these terms may be reviewed and possibly renegotiated throughout the treatment process. The traditionalist, using transference phenomena, will refer to the beginning role conceptualizations within the contract; as new role expectations develop during treatment, further clarification and interpretation may be necessary.

Preliminary Contract

The mere proposal of a term does not, of course, guarantee its inclusion in the contract; there must be specific acceptance of the term by the offeree who may be either the worker or the client. A rule of contract law is that generally the written word takes precedence over the spoken word; in the treatment contract, the behavioral agreement should take precedence over the spoken word. That is, if there is verbal agreement, one must seek corroboration in the client's behavior; if that consenting behavior is lacking, then one should assume that there is no agreement. The client may agree to come regularly at appointed times or to pay a specific fee and then not perform the behaviors which indicate that he has agreed to these terms. Agreement may come at once, or with major reservations, or never at all.

The preliminary or beginning contract is often no more than agreement to try out the process. The therapist may make this explicit by saying, "Why don't we try out this process and see how it works with no long-range commitments on either side." Helen Perlman suggests,

> The initial phase ends, as phase, when a kind of pact has been arrived at in the nature of a 'trial engagement' between client and caseworker to go forward together in their problem-solving efforts. This pact may sometimes be reached in a single interview, but sometimes it may take four or five discussions before clarification, mutual understanding, and decision are arrived at. (Perlman, 1957)

The client, at this point, may not have enough information about the therapist or the process. Realizing that he can gain that knowledge only through further experience, he may agree tentatively to participate in the process.

Bertcher gives an example of a worker who religiously attends to the terms of the initial contract with each individual member in his group prior to their first meeting, and then proceeds to open the first meeting by stating, "Well, I guess we know why we are all here?" only to be met with a group of blank or confused expressions (Bertcher, 1966; also see Vinter and Sarri, 1965). The worker's initial statement of contract may reflect only his own state of mind and this initial effort too often becomes a monologue; it is the worker's dictate as to the terms of the agreement.

Even if the matter is thoroughly discussed, the client may often feel he is being coerced or manipulated; he is unsure of his grounds, his ability to negotiate, and his bargaining power. He may only agree passively to participate in the enterprise without having negotiated on any terms.

The Working Agreement

The treatment contract is not a static set of agreements. Terms are added and withdrawn with the mutual consent of the parties. Such alterations are made with specific deliberation regarding relevancies of these modifications to the treatment situation. During this phase, client and worker clearly define their roles and expectations and the treatment process; and both parties verbalize their agreement and present behavioral corroboration of that agreement. At this point consensus is reached concerning the nature of the problem and the goals to be pursued. And goal path, with immediate and successive tasks, will be tentatively defined as well.

Secondary Contracts (Churchill, 1966)

This phase is limited to the group work process or to those transactions involving more than two persons, e.g., family therapy, and will not be elaborated upon here. Secondary contracts refer to those mutual obligations among the group members themselves in pursuit of treatment goals. For example, when member A agrees to help member B seek different solutions to a particular problem, then a secondary set of contracts has been established.

Contract Termination

Within the contract sequence, termination refers to that stage of the treatment process when the parties agree that their goals have been achieved and there is no longer need for the contract. In a sense it is a "letting go." It constitutes, among other things, a review and evaluation by both parties of the goals, the process, and the product. It is not within the purview of this paper to elaborate upon the termination process; however, in addition to currently recommended procedures and techniques, an evaluative process should be undertaken in which the client participates fully with specific reference to and evaluation of each of the contractual terms.

A basic contract must be achieved between client and worker no matter what the negotiation sequence if effective treatment is to result.

Failure to negotiate and reach agreement in clear, precise terms leaves both the worker and the client in ill-defined, ambiguous positions. Failure to resolve such ambiguities in the early stages of treatment results in an inefficient, ineffective, discouraging treatment process, for the therapist and most especially for the client.

REFERENCES

BATESON, GREGORY
1958—"Language and psychotherapy," *Psychiatry,* 21, p. 100.
BATESON, GREGORY AND J. RUESCH
1951—*Communication: The Social Matrix of Psychiatry,* New York: W. W. Norton & Co., Inc.
BECK, DOROTHY FAHS
1962—*Patterns in Use of Family Agency Service,* New York: Family Service Associations of America.
BECKER, STEVEN D.
1965—*Covenant with Death,* New York: Atheneum.
BERNE, ERIC
1961—*Transactional Analysis,* New York: Grove Press, Inc.
BERNSTEIN, SAUL
1964—*Youth in the Streets,* New York: Association Press, p. 84.
BERTCHER, HARVEY
1966—"The influence on field instruction of one approach to the teaching of social group work." Paper delivered before the Council on Social Work Education (January).
BIDDLE, BRUCE J. AND EDWIN J. THOMAS (EDS.)
1966—*Role Theory, Concepts and Research,* New York: John Wiley & Sons, Inc.
BIESTEK, FELIX P.
1957—*The Casework Relationship,* Chicago: Loyola University Press.
BOSZORMENYI-NAGY, IVAN
1965—"Intensive family therapy as process," in Ivan Boszormenyi-Nagy and James L. Framo (Eds.), *Intensive Family Therapy, Theoretical and Practical Aspects,* New York: Harper & Row, pp. 96–98.
BREDEMEIR, HARRY C.
1964—"The socially handicapped and the agencies: A market analysis," in Frank Riessman, Jerome Cohen, and Arthur Pearl (Eds.), *Mental Health of the Poor,* New York: Free Press, pp. 88–109.
BRIAR, SCOTT
1966—"Family services," in Henry S. Maas (Ed.), *Five Fields of Social Service,* New York: National Association of Social Workers, Inc., pp. 9–50.
CHURCHILL, SALLIE R.
1966—"State of second treatment contract," Ann Arbor: The University of Michigan School of Social Work. (Unpublished.)

CLOWARD, RICHARD A. AND IRWIN EPSTEIN
1965—"Private social welfare's disengagement from the poor: The case of family adjustment agencies," in Mayer N. Zald (Ed.), *Social Welfare Institutions,* New York: John Wiley & Sons, pp. 623–644.
CORBIN, ARTHUR LINTON
1963—*Corbin on Contracts,* Volume I, St. Paul: West Publishing Company, p. 2.
ERIKSON, ERIK H.
1964—*Insight and Responsibility,* New York: W. W. Norton & Co., Inc., pp. 28–29 and 42–43.
FRAMO, JAMES L.
1965—"Rationale and techniques of intensive family therapy," in Ivan Boszormenyi-Nagy and James L. Framo (Eds.), *Intensive Family Therapy, Theoretical and Practical Aspects,* New York: Harper and Row, pp. 146–147.
FREY, LOUISE A. AND MARGUERITE MEYER
1965—"Exploration and working agreement in two social work methods," in Saul Bernstein (Ed.), *Exploration in Group Work,* Boston: Boston University School of Social Work, pp. 1–11.
GANS, HERBERT J.
1964—"Redefining the settlement's function for the war on poverty," *Social Work,* 9, 4 (October), pp. 3–12.
GOLDSTEIN, ARNOLD M.
1966—"Patient's expectancies and nonspecific therapy as a basis for (un)-spontaneous remission," in Arnold P. Goldstein and Sanford J. Dean (Eds.), *The Investigation of Psychotherapy,* New York: John Wiley & Sons, Inc., pp. 202–206.
GOLDSTEIN, JOSEPH AND JAY KATZ
1965—*The Family and the Law,* New York: The Free Press, pp. 584–585.
GOLDSTEIN, ARNOLD P., KENNETH HELLER, AND LEE B. SECHREST
1966—*Psychotherapy and the Psychology of Behavior Change,* New York: John Wiley & Sons, Inc., pp. 146–211.
GREENSON, R. R.
1965—"Working alliance and transference neurosis," *Psychoanalytic Quarterly,* 34, 2 (April), pp. 155–179.
HALEY, JAY
1963—*Strategies of Psychotherapy,* New York: Grune & Stratton, Inc.
KANFER, F. H. AND A. R. MARSTON
1961—"Verbal conditioning, ambiguity, and psychotherapy," *Psychological Reports,* 9, pp. 461–475.
KONOPKA, GISELA
1963—*Social Group Work: A Helping Process,* Englewood Cliffs, New Jersey: Prentice-Hall.
MECHANIC, DAVID
1968—*Medical Sociology, A Selective View,* New York: The Free Press.
MENNINGER, KARL
1963—*The Vital Balance, The Life Process in Mental Health and Illness,* New York: The Viking Press, pp. 315–360.

OVERALL, BETTY AND H. ARONSON
    1964—"Expectations of psychotherapy in patients of lower socio-economic
        class," in Frank Riessman, Jerome Cohen, and Arthur Pearl (Eds.),
        Mental Health of the Poor, New York: Free Press, pp. 76–87.
OVERTON, ALICE, KATHERINE H. TINKER, & ASSOCIATES
    1959—*Casework Notebook, Family Centered Project,* Second edition, St.
        Paul: Greater St. Paul United Funds and Councils, Inc.
PERLMAN, HELEN HARRIS
    1957—*Social Casework: A Problem Solving Approach,* Chicago: The Uni-
        versity of Chicago Press.
POWELL, THOMAS
    1967—"Two types of superego impediment to the working alliance," Ann
        Arbor: The University of Michigan School of Social Work. (Un-
        published.)
RAVEN, BERTRAM H. AND JAN RIETSEMA
    1960—"The effects of varied clarity of group goal and group path upon the
        individual and his relationship," in Dorwin Cartwright and Alvin
        Zander (Eds.), *Group Dynamics, Research and Theory,* Second
        edition, Evanston: Row-Peterson, pp. 395–413.
ROGERS, CARL R. (ED.)
    1967—*The Therapeutic Relationship and Its Impact,* Madison: The Univer-
        sity of Wisconsin Press.
ROGERS, CARL R.
    1951—*Client Centered Therapy,* Boston: Houghton Mifflin.
ROSENFELD, JONA MICHAEL
    1964—"Strangeness between helper and client: A possible explanation of
        non-use of available professional help," *Social Service Review,* 38, 1
        (March), pp. 17–25.
SATIR, VIRGINIA M.
    1964—*Conjoint Family Therapy: A Guide to Theory and Technique,* Palo
        Alto: Science and Behavior Books.
SOCIAL WORK
    1965—"Points and viewpoints," *Social Work,* 10, 1 (January), pp. 104–
        107.
STEINZOR, BERNARD
    1967—*The Healing Partnership, The Patient as Colleague in Psychotherapy,*
        New York: Harper & Row, p. viii.
VINTER, ROBERT D. AND ROSEMARY C. SARRI
    1965—"The juvenile: organization and decision making," in *Juvenile Court
        Hearing Officers Training Manual,* Vol. II, Ann Arbor: Institute for
        Continuing Legal Education, The University of Michigan, pp. 173–
        219.
    1965—"Malperformance in the public school: A group work approach."
        Social Work, 10, 1 (January), pp. 3–13.
WATTS, ALAN W.
    1961—*Psychotherapy East and West,* New York: Pantheon Books, p. 100.

WOLBERG, LEWIS R.
 1967—*The Technique of Psychotherapy,* Second edition, New York: Grune
   & Stratton, p. 48.
WOLPE, JOSEPH AND ARNOLD A. LAZARUS
 1967—*Behavior Therapy Techniques,* New York: Pergamon Press.

11.

Elements and Issues in Group Composition[1]

HARVEY J. BERTCHER and
FRANK MAPLE

The effectiveness of any group is determined partially by the particular attributes or characteristics that each individual brings to the group. Deliberate grouping of clients who have certain attributes can yield benefits for all group members. But what is an optimum mix? And how can the composition of a group influence its effectiveness?

The answers presented here are far from being completely satisfying. The prediction of group effectiveness is a complex matter. Many of the studies that have been done in this area pertain to effectiveness in completing some discrete task, rather than focusing on the development of a group that is effective in bringing about change in the problematic social functioning of individual social work clients. Useful material has been drawn from studies in small group theory related to member characteristics which influence group effectiveness as well as from research in group psychotherapy.

Many workers underestimate the powerful effect of a group's composition on the interaction that ensues or they ignore the potential benefits that could accrue from changing the make-up of a group once it has begun to meet. (The exception to this rule is worker willingness to remove a group's most obstreperous member.) A dearth of empirical data on this subject in reports of research with social work groups and unsatisfactory presentations of material on this topic led to the development of the instructional program on which this discussion is based. Hopefully it will facilitate learning about group composition and stimulate some definitive research on composition of effective treatment groups.

---

[1] This chapter is an exposition of concepts and other teaching material presented by Harvey J. Bertcher and Frank F. Maple, with Henry Wallace (1971).

GROUP CREATION AND GROUP MODIFICATION

Social workers use group composition skills and knowledge to create and modify treatment groups. In group creation, members are selected from a collection of people, who are often strangers, for a group that does not yet exist. In group modification, the composition of an existing group is changed by adding new members, either because old members leave or to maintain the size of the group, or by removing present members to enable those who remain in the group to achieve treatment goals more effectively. Both in creating and in modifying a treatment group, the worker's goal is to achieve a situation in which the attributes of each member can have beneficial consequences for every other member or, at least, no serious negative consequences for any other member of the group.

A wide range of individual attributes have potential consequences for group members. They include both *descriptive attributes,* which classify an individual as to age, sex, marital status, occupation, or other "positions" that he can be said to occupy; and *behavioral attributes* which describe the way an individual acts or can be expected to act, based on his past performance. An individual can be characterized by both descriptive and behavioral attributes with regard to any aspects of his life:

Descriptive Attributes	*Behavioral Attributes*
sixteen years old	acts like a two-year old
ward of the court	conforms well to the expectations of
marijuana user	his probation officer
member of high school football team	encourages his peers to use marijuana
	plays football aggressively

Descriptive attributes were once thought to be most useful in selecting group members. However, research has shown that behavioral attributes, which indicate how an individual interacts with others, are much better predictors of an individual's behavior in a treatment group.

Selecting Critical Attributes

Every human being can be characterized in terms of an enormous number of descriptive and behavioral attributes. How is it possible to decide which attributes will be *critical* to the effectiveness of a group?

A group of adolescent unwed mothers is to be created within an institution (population: 120; age range of residents: 13–30, with an average of 15; residents typically enter the home in their sixth month of pregnancy). The problematic behavior leading to the creation of the group is widespread violation of doctor's orders. The girls can be classified according to such descriptive attributes as race, socioeconomic status, educational attainment, number and age of siblings, place of birth, etc., and such behavioral attributes as enjoying long walks, knitting skillfully, being very possessive of friends, participating actively in group singing, etc. Which—if any—of these might be *critical* attributes for *this* group?

Group Objective. The major criterion for the selection of critical attributes is group objective: those activities members should be able to do well as a result of being in the group. Initially, a group's objective may be based on an agency's view of the needs and interests of several clients or potential clients. Once the group begins, the members themselves may negotiate a modification of this objective with the worker. Group objective must be stated in measurable terms, or no one can be sure it has been achieved (Goldstein, Heller and Sechrest, 1966).[2] Helping a group of unemployed men *to secure and hold a job,* or a street corner gang *to avoid antisocial actions,* or a group of classroom malperformers *to improve all of their grades to a passing level* are directed toward *measurable* group objectives.

In the hypothetical home for unwed mothers, the group is to be created for several girls who are not following the doctor's orders, thus presenting a definite health hazard for themselves and their babies. A discussion group could be created with the objective to reduce or eliminate violations of doctor's orders with regard to good prenatal care, e.g., the eating of inappropriate foods, failure to get sufficient rest, etc. Some of the *descriptive* attributes which might be regarded as critical to the achievement of the group's purpose include age, length of time before delivery, and physical condition. Some critical *behavioral* attributes include eating habits, rest habits, and behavior with regard to doctor's orders.

Group development. A secondary consideration in designating attributes as "critical" is group development. Sometimes, particular individuals are selected because they can help a group to grow. Group membership for such individuals, even if it is initially counterindicated, can be appropriate for group development. Behavioral attributes that facilitate the development of an effective group include certain task performance, group maintenance acts, and the ability to model desired behaviors. The task role can help keep the group on target toward its goal or objective. The group maintenance role might keep the group together by effecting compromises, soothing hurt feelings, making members feel important, etc. The inclusion of individuals who have demonstrated good task role performances as well as some who have performed maintenance roles effec-

---

[2] A more thorough examination of group objectives can be found in Robert F. Mager (1962). A shorter (five-page) discussion of objectives is in Robert F. Mager (1968).

tively will help any group to survive and develop. An exception would be if two strong task specialists are likely to clash.

The kind of task role performance or task leadership needed is related both to the task itself and to the situation in which the task is to be addressed. A person who has the behavioral attributes of being well-organized and purposeful might be the best task leader for a time-limited group; but an individual who has many community contacts and knows how to use them might be the best task leader for a group that is meeting in order to improve its members' use of community, rather than agency, resources. On the other hand, the type of group maintenance skill needed is less a function of the task than of the behavioral attributes of most group members. In a group with several verbally aggressive members, a calm, friendly member may be able to help the group navigate troubled waters; but in a group whose members are likely to be reluctant to participate, a person with a good sense of humor could ease the situation, thereby fostering participation.

The other kind of behavioral attribute that can be particularly helpful in enhancing group development is the ability to serve as a good model for others to emulate. An individual may be selected for group membership because of a specific skill or personality trait, appropriate for others in the group to imitate and adapt to their own style of behavior. A person who has developed some talent or interests or who can keep his temper in an argument may be a potential model. In seeking individuals capable of modeling desired behavior, workers often overlook an excellent source: people who have "graduated" from client status. An appropriate model for a group approaching discharge from a psychiatric hospital could be a former patient who is doing well in a new job.

Obtaining Information About Behavior

When critical attributes have been selected with reference to group objectives and development, the worker must find the potential members who have the relevant descriptive attributes and learn as much as he can about the degree to which each individual shows critical behavioral attributes in settings similar to the group treatment setting. Behavioral information may be obtained by developing a list of questions about specific interpersonal behaviors and seeking answers from persons who have seen the potential member function in group situations. Other approaches involve giving the potential member an opportunity to observe an effective group, then eliciting relevant information from the potential member during an individual interview; or placing the potential member in a special diagnostic group (Churchill, 1965).

Obtaining accurate and complete behavioral information is difficult. Someone may tell you that a particular boy is very good at effecting compromises. He sounds like someone who could play a group maintenance role and serve as a model for less patient boys. In your first group meeting, you discover that he effects compromises by beating up everyone who disagrees with him. Such crucial behavioral information often is not contained in diagnostic statements.

Developing Behaviorally Specific Objectives

Since they constitute the bases for deciding which attributes are critical, the first step in selecting members for a treatment group is to specify, however tentatively, the objectives of the group. While initial objectives should be tentative, they should also be specific and explicit, not vague. Behaviorally specific group objectives indicate where, when, how well, how often and/or how much a desired behavior is to be performed. A behaviorally specific objective indicates the conditions under which the desired behavior will occur; it states the desired behavior in terms of observable activity—what people will be able to do, not how they think or feel; and it specifies standards or criteria by which performance of desired behavior is to be measured.

Examples:

GIVEN	In a mental hospital, six patients to be discharged within the next three months
BEHAVIOR	will develop plans for activities regarding family relationships, job, school, etc.,
CRITERIA	which, in the opinion of the group and the worker, should make it unnecessary for any group member to return to the hospital.
GIVEN	When presented with any situation in which he could violate the law, each member of the gang
BEHAVIOR	will act according to the law
CRITERIA	voluntarily, in a majority of cases.

The "given" conditions, the desired behavior, and the criteria for measuring results should be stated specifically.

Example: When confronted with an opportunity to eat forbidden food, girls who are members of a group in a home for unwed mothers will have a good understanding of the dangers to themselves and their babies.

In the above example, while the conditions under which the girls are to act are specific, the desired behavior is not (what will they *do* with their understanding?), nor are the criteria for measuring behavior specific (how well or how often should they be able to do whatever they should be able to do?).

Not only should initial group objectives be behaviorally specific, they should also be clear to potential members. Potential members should believe that the achievement of objectives is possible. Their achievement should include beneficial outcomes for each individual member. And they should be optional with potential members having some power to select, create or modify them.

Client Choice

Should individuals be able to choose whether they or others become members of a particular group? Many social work clients receive service on a quasi-voluntary or involuntary basis. A psychiatric hospital patient is expected to participate in a discharge planning group. A rebellious youngster is brought to a child guidance clinic by his mother. An AFDC mother is strongly encouraged by her caseworker to attend meetings of a group with the purpose of orienting her to seek employment. Can a group be effective if some members don't want to be in it?

There are no pat answers. But when an involuntary client enters a group, he has more chance to like the group if he sees others liking it. On the other hand, an individual who feels that he has some or total choice about becoming a member will more likely accept the group from the start. Since effective groups tend to have members who want to be there, an individual's decision to join or not to join may be regarded as a critical attribute. A group with involuntary members may knit more quickly with voluntary members, and the greater the number of voluntary members the more likely it will become an effective group quickly.

Determining the potential member's attitude toward entering a particular group requires talking with him before the group begins. The degree of choice he feels he has about joining the group will probably be influenced by the amount of choice he has in determining or affecting group objectives. In the same vein, members may feel more positively toward a group if they can exercise some choice about new members who enter the group. Finally, the truly voluntary group member should know who the group worker is going to be, so that he can consider this factor when making his decision about joining the group.

Attributes of the worker. Experience has demonstrated that some workers perfer and/or perform better with certain clientele, e.g., children, senior citizens or hospital patients. Initially, certain clients may experience greater comfort with—and thus be more willing to be influenced by—a worker who has descriptive attributes similar to their own, such as age, sex, race, religion, etc. Although the worker is not a client-member he is a central person in the group, and his behavioral attributes may be crucial to group effectiveness. His ability to perform task, maintenance, and/or modeling roles, as well as his ability to function as an advocate of the interests of each potential group member, need to be considered. The likelihood of group effectiveness will be increased by a high degree of client involvement in group creation, including some decision-making power, particularly regarding the group's purpose but also regarding the choice of other group members and even the worker.

Client Pool

If the worker and the clients are to have a choice in determining group membership, an agency must have a pool of potential clients. The worker should play a major role in nominating and selecting group membership, in order to maximize the utility of group composition as a means of influencing the treatment process. To maintain a reservoir of potential clients, when referral is appropriate, the worker should inform all referring agents of the critical attributes for each prospective group.

Often social workers must rely on others to make referrals, and this can lead to an ineffective referral process. Juvenile court workers may be instructed by their supervisor to refer any of their clients who, in their opinion, might benefit from group services. The psychiatrist at a clinic may list five of his patients who are "having trouble with peer relationships" and ask the social worker to work with them as a group. Even when referrals are the only source of potential group members, the worker can increase the likelihood of group effectiveness by clearly specifying to the referring person a definite set of objectives for the prospective group by identifying critical attributes in some detail, and by striving to develop a reservoir of potential clients.

Reliance on others to make referrals usually leads to no referrals at all unless some supporting administrative procedures are developed.

> *Example:*   A group worker was hired to introduce group work services in a public welfare agency. To acquaint him with the agency's operation, he had been assigned a small caseload.
>
> Seeking to create a group, he had told the caseworkers that the group's purpose would be to assist AFDC mothers in solving problems of raising children when the children's father was not living at home.
>
> In order to avoid administrative hassling, the group worker had discussed the group with several caseworkers, on an individual basis, but had not talked about it with any supervisor. Although caseworkers expressed interest in the group work service for their clients, referrals were not forthcoming.

To reduce the caseworkers' resistance to making referrals, the group worker could have stated what he regarded as critical attributes in greater detail; he could have discussed his intentions and cleared his plans with supervisors, so as to gain greater influence; and he might have developed a demonstration group from his own caseload.

EFFECTIVE GROUPS

Group effectiveness is partially determined by the attributes that each individual client and worker brings to the group. Effective groups tend to have interactive, compatible, and responsive members. Interactive members like each other. Responsive members are interested in helping each other.

Research indicates that a group often is more effective if members have homogeneous descriptive attributes and heterogeneous behavioral attributes (Goldstein, Heller and Sechrest, 1966). Common descriptive attributes help foster interactiveness and compatibility: a young adult in conflict with his parents would probably not be very compatible or interactive in a social club for senior citizens. Heterogeneous behavioral attributes, on the other hand, increase the chances that members will be constructively responsive to one another and have something in their behavioral repertory that will be useful to the group. When all members have similar behavioral attributes, similar descriptive attributes, have faced similar problems, tried the same solutions and experienced the same failures, the group typically holds little promise for those who are seeking new answers for themselves. Members sometimes talk about "the blind leading the blind" in such a group.

In one study, male psychiatric patients in a Veterans' Hospital were observed and scored for their behavioral attributes of "social activity," i.e., the degree to which they talked to others, were chosen by others, spoke in group meetings, and were helpful task group members (Fairweather, 1964). Four groups were then created, as follows:

	High Social Activity	*Low Social Activity*
	Group I	*Group II*
Homogeneous behavior attributes	All above average	All below average
	Group III	*Group IV*
Heterogeneous behavior attributes	⅔ above average ⅓ below average	½ above average ⅔ below average

Groups I and II were homogeneous with respect to the composite of behavioral attributes called "social activity." Groups III and IV were heterogeneous. After making sure that there were no significant differences among the four groups as to the descriptive attributes of age, length of stay in the hospital, and living situation prior to hospitalization, the researchers found Group III—the heterogeneous group with a predominance of members having high "social activity" attributes but several having low "social activity"—to be significantly better than any other group at complex problem solving and general performance.

Barriers to Group Effectiveness

Several compositional factors can hinder the development of effective groups:

1. *Too much compatibility* can enable group members to resist effectively all efforts to modify their behavior.
2. *Too much or too little stress* can result in a surplus of anxiety or a surfeit of apathy.
3. *Negative subgroups* can sabotage group purpose, victimize individual members and control "democratic" decision-making processes.

Balance

Most effective groups are composed of members who differ with respect to behavioral attributes. In addition, the critical behavioral attributes of members of such groups tend to fall along a "linear continuum." Balance—an optimum mix of critical behavioral attributes—is an important characteristic of effective groups.

Locating potential group members along a linear continuum for a particular critical attribute can facilitate selection of a balanced group.[3] In a residential program for adolescent unwed mothers, experience had shown that unless some anger toward doctors could be openly expressed and dealt with, group interaction did not effectively reduce violation of doctors' orders. At the same time, the venting of too much fury had been known to blow such groups apart. The worker decided that the ability to express anger toward authority figures, e.g., doctor, nurse, social workers, etc., was one critical attribute which should be carefully balanced within the group.

---

[3] The authors are indebted to their colleagues, Paul Glasser and Sallie Churchill, for the approach used to describe balance in terms of a linear continuum.

Worker's Assessment of Ability to Express Anger Toward Authority Figures

too little	in between	about right	in between	too much	much too much
−2	−1	0	+1	+2	+3
Bea	Ann	Maude	Sue	June	Cookie
Mabel	Sarah				
Louise					

Although all nine girls were regarded as "eligible" with respect to other critical attributes, the worker decided that a group of six would be more effective. Bea's group maintenance skills were badly needed; Mabel, Louise and Cookie were eliminated from this particular group.

Environment

People continually overlook the effects of a group's immediate environment on the level and quality of interaction among group members. Many variables in the environment or setting of a group meeting can be influential: size of meeting room, arrangement of chairs, place to meet (home, car, agency, ward lounge, etc.), privacy, location of meeting place and ease of reaching it. Basically, choice of setting should be guided by the group's purpose, by evidence of preplanning and atmosphere.

Evidence of preplanning. Most people like to know that some consideration has been given to their comfort. Meeting at a time that is convenient for all, having ash trays for smokers, being able to shut a door to insure privacy, having coffee available when members arrive are all indications to clients that the worker cares enough about them to have made some preparations.

Atmosphere. The situation in which a group of people find themselves has a definite effect on the mood of the group. A small room can provide a feeling of intimacy for one group, a feeling of crowding for another. For some groups, a station wagon can be an exciting, attractive meeting place. Providing an appropriate environment can be a significant contribution to group effectiveness.

Time

Some groups need to meet only once to accomplish their objective effectively; others require a considerable amount of time and many meetings to achieve their goal. Some groups are limited in their time, by prior agreement; others are open in terms of the time that individuals stay in the group and the lifetime of the group itself. There is no optimum lifetime for all groups; on the contrary, the duration for a group should be determined by its objective.

Establishing definite time limits helps groups develop quickly. Recent research in psychotherapy indicates that when a worker expects treatment to take about two years, it usually takes that long; if he expects that treatment goals can be achieved in only three months, three months often prove sufficient (Goldstein, 1962). Optimistic estimates are well-advised.

Groups are more likely to be effective if the worker, perhaps with the group, makes carefully considered decisions about the frequency, length, and time of meetings than if the traditional "fifty-minute hour once a week" is used automatically. Time is viewed differently by different cultural groups. How will the group feel about meeting at the same time, each time?

Number

How large is an effective group? Substantial research has been done on the effects of group size, yielding a plethora of propositions. As groups get larger, participation, satisfaction, consensus, and intimacy among members decrease; subgroups emerge; leadership requirements and the group's ability to tackle more complex tasks increase; opinions are asked of others (Thomas and Fink, 1960).

There is no optimum size for all groups; rather, size depends upon the objectives of the group and the attributes of its members. Many considerations should enter into decision making about the best size for a particular group: How important is group morale? How complex a program is desirable? How capable are members of helping each other? of sharing the attention of the worker?

If clients need to have an opportunity to move gradually into group participation, without having immediate demands placed upon them, a larger group may be preferable. If members need to be convinced from the start that the group is designed to provide maximum benefit for each individual, a smaller group will permit rapid involvement. If group morale is all-important, a larger group will permit some members to be absent or to drop out without having negative consequences for everyone else. A larger group may be good if it requires members to turn to one another for help. A larger group may be disastrous if members are likely to panic without the immediate support of the worker or to be very jealous of attention given by the worker to other members.

Most treatment groups are composed of individuals who are likely to interact in negative ways from time to time. It would appear that some degree of conflict is inevitable and potentially useful. If a tolerable amount of useful stress is to develop, a group should not be too small (e.g., three) or too large (e.g., fifteen); there should be enough people to interact in resolving conflict.

Composition and Effectiveness

No matter how "good" the composition of a group may be, it cannot assure the achievement of treatment goals. But the skillful composition of a group can enhance its effectiveness. By basing his definitions of critical attributes and his decisions about matters of time, place and size upon explicitly stated group objectives, the worker can create a group whose members will be interactive, compatible, and responsive.

GROUP CREATION: A PROBLEM

As a focal point for consideration of issues and difficulties associated with group composition, the following information is offered about a number of boys who are potential members of a group to be sponsored by a juvenile court. Given the following objectives, create the most effective treatment group possible, noting what further information you would like to have and why you need it. When no mention of probation status is made, you should assume that the boy is still on probation.

Group Objectives

Once members have terminated from this group, they will no longer engage in illegal behavior, so that institutional placements will not be necessary for any of them. In addition, they will develop and act on pro-social goals for themselves, e.g., return to and maintain satisfactory performance in school, become involved in training for employment, seeking, securing and holding a job, etc., and will work consistently to achieve their goal(s).

1. *Donald W*. (Age 14) --- 8th Grade - Black. Interests: none known. Lower-lower class. Below average intelligence. Docile, uninvolved in any on-going activity. No previous group or institutional experience. Little interest in socializing; a "lone wolf." *With gang in breaking and entering.*

2. *Robert T*. (Age 16) --- 10th grade - Black. Interests: mechanical work. Lower class. Average intelligence. Spent six months in Boys Training School with group experience. Aggressive, domineering, hostile.

Loud voice, compulsive talker, pushes own ideas on group but doesn't take responsibility for following through on own ideas. *Broke probation. (His mother stated that he was out of her control.)*

3. *Ray D.* (Age 16) --- 10th Grade - White. Now living in detention home. Interests: chemistry, athletics. Low middle-class family. Well above average intelligence. No previous group work or institutional experience. Independent, somewhat aloof from peers and adults. Seems to be afraid of getting too close to anyone. Won't talk in social groups; remains uninvolved when group takes action. *Stealing cars and reckless driving; incorrigible according to parents.*

4. *Gene R.* (Age 15) --- 9th Grade - Black. Interests: does good school work; likes fighting, exciting activities. Lower class. High intelligence. Spent eight months in detention home. No group work experience. Leader of delinquent gang. Effective at controlling group—but not by physical aggression—rather is good at effecting compromises; has a good sense of humor. Has been off probation for several months, doing well in an auto mechanics training school. *Breaking and entering.*

5. *George D.* (Age 16) --- 10th Grade - White. Interests: athletics, cars. Lower-middle class. Above average intelligence. No previous group work or institutional experience. Conforming; a follower. Can become very verbal when cars are discussed; otherwise rarely opens his mouth. *Several drinking violations; drunk and disorderly in public.* Is not now on probation.

6. *John V.* (Age 16) --- 10th Grade - Black. Interests: track, football. Lower class. Average intelligence. Participated in group work program at Community Center—noninstitutional experience. Blows up, falls apart when frustrated. Gene R.'s close friend; Gene plays an important role in helping John to control his temper. *Breaking and entering.*

7. *Jim S.* (Age 15) --- 9th Grade - Black. Interests: biology and track. Lower class. Above average intelligence. No previous group or institutional experience. Subtle leader—skillful manipulator—the "cool" type. Distrustful of adults so that he operates behind the scenes—particularly dislikes social workers but, in their presence, appears to be a conformist. Off probation, doing passing work in school. *Stealing.*

8. *Jerry M.* (Age 15) --- 10th Grade - White. Interests: hunting, fishing. Lower class. Average intelligence. No previous group work or institutional experience. Very aggressive; assaulted father twice with hammer although provoked each time. Uncomfortable in the presence of Blacks. Hot temper; fears he will lose it so avoids group contacts. *Assault with weapon (father).*

9. *George A.* (Age 16) --- Out of school - White. Interests: metal work, welding. Lower class. Below average intelligence. Eliminated from a previous group work experience because of aggressive behavior. Breaks

rules, acts as a "know it all." Backs down when confronted by forceful person. *Chronic truancy.*

10. *Robert B.* (Age 15) --- Out of school - White. Interests: unknown. Lower class. Below average intelligence. Unemployed—deemed "uneducable." Docile, quiet, meek. Will follow any leader. *Stealing.*

11. *Joe F.* (Age 16) --- 11th Grade - Black. Interests: music (drums). Lower class. Above average intelligence. No group work or institutional experience. Follower; small boy, docile. Music teacher indicates he has exceptional talent but Joe is afraid to try for fear he will fail; others like him because of his musical ability and the fact that he poses no threat. *Stealing.*

12. *Pete S.* (Age 16) --- Out of school - Black. Unemployed. Interests and skills unknown. Lower class. Below average intelligence. One year in Boys Training School. No group work experience. Aggressive—huge—takes over. Clumsy; covers his embarrassment at being awkward by a "don't care" manner. *Several breaking and entering and car thefts.*

13. *Ralph O.* (Age 17) --- 9th Grade - Black. Interests: sports, gang activity. Lower class. Average ability. Poor school performance—reading problem. No previous group work or institutional experience. Involved in gang fights. Witty, quick in remarks. Verbally cuts others down. Close friend of Gene R's. *Gang activity—destruction of property.*

14. *William C.* (Age 16) --- 10th Grade - White. Interests: carpentry, woodworking. Lower middle class. Above average ability. In Boys Training School six months. Quiet, a loner; can be angered if teased. Spends most of his time with one girl. Does not want to be in a group. *Two breaking and enterings.*

15. *Stan W.* (Age 16) --- 10th Grade - White. Interests: football, basketball. Middle class. Superior ability; poor school performance. No previous group work experience. Plays it smart, wise, initiates action. Pseudo-sophisticated. Aggressive, tense and nervous. Always on the go; excitement seeker. In previous social contacts has been seen as initiator of antisocial behavior. *Drunk and disorderly.*

A SOLUTION TO THE PROBLEM

Rationale for Group Objective

The purpose of a juvenile court with regard to youth who are adjudicated delinquent is to see to it that those juveniles who violate the law do not continue to do so. We assume that law-abiding behavior is more likely to occur if the individual is "making it" in society in some legally acceptable way. Accordingly, the group purpose must include both restraining aspects (no further law violation) and facilitating aspects (working to achieve prosocial goals).

Time. Ten of the fifteen boys are 16 years of age or older. It was stated that if they break the law once they are 17, they will be placed in an institution. Since it is the purpose of the group to avoid the necessity for such a placement, short duration (three to six months) might be appropriate. On the other hand, it could be useful to make this an "open-ended" group, i.e., one in which new members are added as old members leave, because of the prosocial modeling that the remaining older members could provide for newer members. Accordingly, each boy could be told that he would be expected to "graduate" in three to six months, with the understanding that as members leave, new members would be added. (Graduates could retain a quasi-official membership and be involved as helpers.)

Incidentally, note that the given age for the boys, e.g., "16" is quite non-specific. Are they all just about to turn 17? Did they just become 16? In other words, age might prove to be a critical attribute. If so, you would need to have birth dates for purposes of decision making.

Meeting time is often a question of convenience; i.e., some boys may be in school, others on a job, and so forth. Accordingly, this decision can probably be delayed until some tentative ideas about grouping emerge. For example, if all but one potential member could meet in the late afternoon, that individual might be eliminated from that particular grouping. Again, more specific information is needed—this time with regard to the boy's current situation vis-à-vis school, job, etc.

For this group, a regular once-a-week meeting (always on the same day at the same time) could establish a reliable pattern for adolescents whose world may otherwise be chaotic and unpredictable. Once a week would perhaps be as much contact as the boys would want. However, should the group so decide, frequency of meetings could be altered.

Numbering. While groups of six to eight appear to be preferred by many group workers (small enough to allow for individualization, large enough to remain a group in spite of absent members), such a group automatically eliminates nine (or seven) other individuals. It is possible that two groups could be created. It is also possible that several of the boys would profit more from a one-to-one contact. Again, let's defer this decision for the moment.

Environment. For many juveniles, the setting of a juvenile court is not conducive to the kinds of relaxation that might prove necessary for boys to share concerns comfortably in the group. In their city, there is a Community Center located four blocks away from the County Court. It is centrally located, and thus easily accessible by car or bus. The Center's program is flexible enough for use of the building, e.g., rearrange furniture, serve refreshments, etc. Accordingly, plans are to meet at the Center.

Limiting Conditions

Client Pool. In this case, it is sufficiently large to allow for choice. Since this is to be an open-ended group, some procedure would have to be worked out so that potential new boys could be routinely referred.

Worker Control of Intake. In working out a referral procedure it would be essential to indicate critical attributes, so that boys who would be inappropriate would not be referred for possible inclusion in the group only to be turned away.

Critical Attributes

With regard to group purpose.

1. *Descriptive Attributes:*

While it may be unnecessary to say this, considerable selection has already clearly preceded actions in creating a group; all of the potential members share certain descriptive attributes:

   a. all are males

   b. all are adolescents (although a 14-year-old adolescent may be at a very different level of maturation than a 16-year-old)

   c. all are now (or have been) on probation

   d. all are likely candidates for placement in a correctional institution

These four factors represent critical descriptive attributes for this group. At this time, in the community, racial differences are not as significant as they might be elsewhere so "race" would not be labeled as a critical attribute. Socioeconomic class differences do not appear to be a significant factor for this group.

Nature-of-offense might be of importance, e.g., nine boys have engaged in some kind of theft activity—stealing, breaking and entering, car theft—which may be considerably different from truancy or alcoholism, but not of sufficient importance to make the actual legal offense itself a critical attribute.

2. *Behavioral Attributes:*

In only one instance (William C.), is there any information about client voluntarism with regard to group treatment. Nevertheless, it seems that it would be important to know how each boy views the group purposes of eliminating illegal behavior and at the same time "making it" in a prosocial way. Accordingly, client voluntarism would be established as a critical behavioral attribute, with a goal of achieving some balance in the degree of voluntarism. If this information is not available, it may have to be done without. Some elimination of illegal behavior is a prime purpose of the group, a second critical behavioral attribute could relate to the degree to which the individual has previously been known to initiate illegal acts. Thus, the following continuum based on subjective assessment of available information could be established.

History of Initiating Illegal Acts That Others Follow

None	Little	Average or Unknown	Some	Very Much
-2	-1	0	$+1$	$+2$
1. Donald W.	(No one)	6. John V.	2. Robert T.	4. Gene R.
3. Ray D.		8. Jerry M.	7. Jim S.	15. Stan W.
5. George D.		13. Ralph O.	9. George A.	
10. Robert B.			12. Pete S.	
11. Joe F.				
14. William C.				

One is immediately struck by the number of boys who have been seen as "followers." While it would be premature to select or eliminate any boys at this stage, this continuum should be kept in mind when the attempt eventually is made to achieve a balance of behavioral attributes.

A third critical behavioral attribute for group purpose relates to the interests, experiences and abilities individuals have that might be capitalized on in moving boys toward school or employment opportunities.

Possession of Interests and Skills Related to School and Work

Antisocial Interest and Skills	Neither School- nor Work-oriented Interests or Skills	No Known Interests or Skills	Some Interests	Considerable Interest and/ or Skills
-2	-1	0	$+1$	$+2$
13. Ralph O.	6. John V.	1. Donald W.	2. Robert T.	4. Gene R.
	8. Jerry M.	10. Robert B.	3. Ray D.	14. William C.
	15. Stan W.	12. Pete S.	5. George D.	
			7. Jim S.	
			9. George A.	
			11. Joe F.	

Again, information is inadequate—although typical of the kind of information most workers have to work from—but it does appear that a number of the boys have interests and/or skills that could be useful in work and/or school.

With regard to group development.

1. *Descriptive Attributes:*

It was stated earlier that race is not a major descriptive attribute in terms of the purpose of this group. Obviously, were the purpose different, e.g., fostering "black pride," then race would be critical. On the other hand, if many of the boys have strong negative feelings about associating with members of another race, the group's development would be hindered. While information here is sparse, Jerry M. might be considered for membership only if the group turns out to be composed predominantly of white boys.

    2. *Behavioral Attributes:*

    Task and group maintenance ability, plus the ability to model prosocial behaviors appear to be critical behavioral attributes in this group.

Ability to Perform Task (Leadership) Acts

None	Very Little	Average	Some	Quite a Lot
−2	−1	0	+1	+2
1. Donald W.	5. George D.	4. Gene R.	2. Robert T.	(No one)
3. Ray D.	15. Stan W.	6. John V.	7. Jim S.	
8. Jerry M			12. Pete S.	
9. George A.				
10. Robert B.				
11. Joe F.				
13. Ralph O.				
14. William C.				

Ability to Perform Group Maintenance (Leadership) Acts

None	Very Little	Average	Some	Quite a Lot
−2	−1	0	+1	+2
1. Don W.	(No one)	(No one)	11. Joe F.	4. Gene R.
2. Robert T.				
3. Ray D.				
5. George D.				
6. John V.				
7. Jim S.				
8. Jerry M.				
9. George A.				
10. Robert B.				
12. Pete S.				
13. Ralph O.				
14. William C.				
15. Stan W.				

Selection of appropriate models would be based on those particular attitudes and/or behaviors that would be desirable to be imitated. In a sense, each continuum developed so far provides potential models and modelers, e.g., a boy who has particular interests and/or skills could model this behavior for those who have no such involvement, etc. However, one further critical attribute should be added since it appears to be a serious deficit for some: the ability to control impulsive, antisocial behavior.

Ability to Control Impulsive, Antisocial Behavior

Very Poor Control	Little Control	Average Control	Good Control	Excellent Control
−2	−1	0	+1	+2
6. John V.	2. Robert T.	1. Don W.	3. Ray D.	4. Gene R.
8. Jerry M.	5. George D.	11. Joe F.(?)	7. Jim S.	
9. George A.	10. Robert B.		15. Stan W.	
	12. Pete S.			
	13. Ralph O.			
	14. William C.			

Taken together, these critical attributes could all be classified as being prosocial or antisocial in quality. That is, involvement in some interest or skill could be expected to be associated with prosocial behavior while a lack of such skills, although not necessarily associated with antisocial acts, would be less likely to lead to socially acceptable behavior. (The only exception to this is the "initiation of illegal acts" attribute, in which a "plus" score means that the individual has acted this way frequently; in other words, a plus score is associated with antisocial acts. In the summation that follows, the signs of this particular rating have been reversed to bring it into conformity with our prosocial/antisocial dichotomy.)

Summing the ratings each boy received on the five critical attributes produces the following table:

Names	Initiating Illegal Acts	Interests and Skills	Task Acts	Socio-emotional Acts	Self-Control	Totals
1. Donald W.	+2	0	−2	−2	0	−2
2. Robert T.	−1	+1	+1	−2	−1	−2
3. Ray D.	+2	+1	−2	−2	+1	0
4. Gene R.	−2	+2	0	+2	+2	+4

Names	Initiating Illegal Acts	Interests and Skills	Task Acts	Socio-emotional Acts	Self Control	Totals
5. George D.	+2	+1	−1	−2	−1	−1
6. John V.	0	−1	0	−2	−2	−5
7. Jim S.	−1	+1	+1	−2	+1	0
8. Jerry M.	0	−1	−2	−2	−2	−7
9. George A.	−1	+1	−2	−2	−2	−6
10. Robert B.	+2	0	−2	−2	−1	−3
11. Joe F.	+2	+1	−2	+1	0	+2
12. Pete S.	−1	0	+1	−2	−1	−3
13. Ralph O.	0	−2	−2	−2	−1	−7
14. William C.	+2	+2	−2	−2	−1	−1
15. Stan W.	−2	−1	−1	−2	+1	−5

Recasting the totals, the following clusters of scores emerge:

Total		Names
+4		Gene R.
+3		
+2	A	Joe F.
+1		
0		Ray D., Jim S.
−1	B	George D., William C.
−2		Donald W., Robert T.
−3		Robert B., Pete S.
−4	C	
−5		John V., Stan W.
−6	D	George A .
−7		Jerry M., Ralph O.

In an attempt to create a balanced group of eight boys, the total was arbitrarily divided into clusters of 4 (note broken lines) and the decision was made to select two boys from each cluster. Believing that four factors that could lead to an ineffective group (too much compatibility, too much stress, inadequate alternative models and negative subgroups) an attempt was made to avoid these difficulties in the selection. Also, an effective group consists of members who are interactive, compatible and mutually responsive.

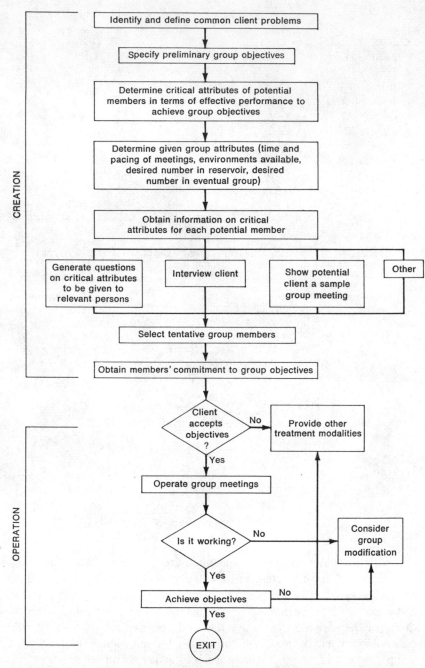

FIGURE 1 Group Composition Sequence

The selection process went something like this:

a. First Gene was seen as a potentially strong, positive group member. In selecting him his two friends were eliminated (danger of negative subgroup), John V. and Ralph O.

b. Since Gene R. had been known to initiate illegal acts, the other "high initiator," Stan W., was eliminated to reduce potential stress.

c. William C. was chosen for his "skills and interests" since this could provide a good model for others.

d. Robert T. and Jim S. were selected because they had demonstrated task ability.

e. The fact that Gene and Jim S. were no longer on probation, and were apparently doing well, was an additional reason for wanting them in the group (as potential models for prosocial behavior).

The group then consisted of:

> A. Gene R.
> Jim S.
> -----------------------
> B. William C.
> Robert T.
> -----------------------
> C. Robert B.
> Pete S.
> -----------------------
> D. George A.
> Jerry M.
> -----------------------

In addition, Jerry M. was known to be uncomfortable with Blacks. Since this was to be a racially mixed group, it was decided to drop him from this group and lower the total to seven boys: Gene R., Jim S., William C., Robert T., Robert B., Pete S., George A.

Alternatives to the group creation problem are entirely possible. Furthermore, the boys not selected for the first group might be formed into a second group. (How effective would you expect such a group to be? Why?) The boys not selected might be seen individually or regarded as a reservoir of potential members should any of the original group members "graduate," fail (get in trouble again) or prove unworkable in the initial grouping.

REFERENCES

BERTCHER, HARVEY J. AND FRANK F. MAPLE (WITH HENRY WALLACE)
1971—"Group composition: An instructional program," Ann Arbor: University of Michigan School of Social Work. (Mimeographed.)

CHURCHILL, SALLIE R.
  1965—"The use of the social group work method as a diagnostic tool in the interdisciplinary evaluation of a disturbed child in the Pittsburgh child guidance center," *American Journal of Orthopsychiatry,* 35 (April), pp. 581–588.
FAIRWEATHER, GEORGE W.
  1964—*Social Psychology in Treating Mental Illness: An Experimental Approach,* New York: John Wiley & Sons.
GOLDSTEIN, ARNOLD P.
  1962—*Therapist-Patient Expectations in Psychotherapy,* New York: Macmillan Publishing Co., Inc.
GOLDSTEIN, ARNOLD P., KENNETH HELLER AND LEO B. SECHREST
  1966—*Psychotherapy and The Psychology of Behavior Change,* New York: John Wiley & Sons.
MAGER, ROBERT F.
  1962—*Developing Instructional Objectives,* Palo Alto: Fearon Publishers.
  1968—*Developing Attitudes Toward Learning,* Palo Alto: Fearon Publishers, pp. 13–17.
THOMAS, EDWIN J. AND CLINTON F. FINK
  1960—"Effects of group size," *Psychological Bulletin,* 60, pp. 371–384.

12.

Group Process: Usage and Uses in Social Work Practice

CHARLES D. GARVIN

One of the most hallowed concepts in social work practice is the term "process." The use of this concept, however, is frequently ambiguous, obscure, or even mystical. It is assumed that the word is so commonplace that any definition will be an insult. At the same time, "process" is used to denote a force which can account for all desirable practice outcomes. The significance of "group processes," however defined, is well stated by Whitaker and Lieberman (1964:3):

> Processes characteristic of the group as a whole are an intrinsic and inevitable aspect of all groups no matter what their size or function. In a therapy group, group processes not only "exist" but are a major factor influencing the nature of each patient's therapeutic experience. The manner in which each patient contributes to, participates in, and is affected by the group processes determines to a considerable degree whether he will profit from his group therapy experience, be untouched by it, or be harmed by it.

The clarification of the "process" concept for the group work practitioner will enable him to understand and, when necessary, modify processes occurring in treatment groups to attain appropriate treatment goals.

DEFINITION OF PROCESS

A review of the social psychological as well as group work literature demonstrates the ambiguity and diversity of the usage of the group process concept. Durkin (1964:96), for example, points out that group process is often used interchangeably with such concepts as "group phenomena" and "group dynamics." She suggests that group process "could . . . be reserved specifically for the functional aspect of group determined phenomena such as the formation of standards, the exercise of pressure toward uniformity, role assignment, subgrouping, and the like."

The group process concept has been described in terms of both overt and covert phenomena. Such writers as Bales (1951:31) have emphasized the overt aspects of communication among group members. Whitaker and Lieberman (1964:246), on the other hand, point out that "Bales' unit is defined in terms of the group's public goal and ours in terms of the covert shared need to achieve some solution to the group focal conflict."

Some writers conceive of group process as a series of events related to interference with and restoration of an equilibrium; others view it as a developmental sequence, involving gradual group movement from one level of social organization to another. Bales (1965:444–476) sees equilibrium occurring during a period of introduction and solution of a specified problem, while Whitaker and Lieberman (1964:19) relate equilibrium to the occurrence of and response to a "disturbing motive." Writers who see group process as a developmental sequence primarily are concerned with the evolution over time of stages or phases in the condition of the group. (Mills, 1967; Sarri and Galinsky, Chapter 5 in this volume; Garland, et al., 1965)

Still another distinction stems from use of group process to describe interactions among two or more individuals in the small group, or to refer to changes in the conditions of the whole group. Newcomb and his colleagues use the former as a unit of analysis when they first state that interactional processes

> refer not just to what goes on within each of the interacting persons but also what goes on *between* them . . . to understand this we must note the relationships between the perceptual content of each of them about the other. (Newcomb, et al., 1965:155)

They then conclude, however, that group processes are:

> The basic interactional processes through which groups effectively achieve their goals—social facilitation and group reinforcement, in particular— tend to enhance a group's cohesive power. (Newcomb, et al., 1965:492)

An alternate conception of group process emphasizes a change in group conditions: specific interactional sequences are seen either as independent variables or as a "part" of a "whole" which can be described. This view is taken by writers who study the nature of changes in groups, for example, changes in goals, control procedures, problem solving, emotional investments, or task accomplishments.

The concept of group process as a group level phenomenon rather than merely interpersonal behavior is illuminated by Etzioni's (1968:45) analysis of variables at a higher level of social organization. He states that:

> the properties added (or removed) by a transition from one level to another are "emergent properties" from the viewpoint of the other level.

The transition from role analysis to group analysis illustrates this point. Assume that we are studying marriage compatibility. We may study the role of wife (or husband) internally. How compatible are various segments of the role? Or externally, what is the degree of articulation between the two marital roles, e.g., how compatible are the expectations the husband has of his wife with her expectations of him? All this, however, still amounts to the study of the properties of roles and inter-role relations; it is not an analysis of the family as a social group or supra-unit. We shift our theoretical focus from a unit to a supra-unit when we view the family not as a mere combination of roles, *but as an entity having a structure and process of its own.*

Another issue that divides authors is whether their primary concern is with cognitive, problem-solving processes in groups or whether changes to be investigated are broader and include emotional, instrumental, or normative dynamics as processes and not merely as independent or mediating variables. Inasmuch as emotional behaviors are sometimes covert, this issue is related to the overt/covert distinction mentioned earlier.

In view of these conceptual alternatives, the proposed definition of *group process* in this paper is *those changes occurring in the activities and interactions of group members that are related to changes in goal attainment and group maintenance.*[1]

A major contrast must be drawn between group process and "group structure." Collins and Raven (1969:103) define group structure as follows:

> the regularity of person-to-person and person-to-task relationships observed in many groups has led social scientists to search for a patterning of interpersonal relationships which can be considered in the abstract, transcending the personalities and idiosyncratic relationships of a given group. With perhaps more optimism than is justified, the concept of "structure" has been borrowed from the physical sciences. *Social structure* may be defined as the relationship among elements of a social unit. The *elements* may be individuals, or positions for which no individuals have yet been designated as in a formal organization chart. The dimensions of structure (the ways in which the elements can be interconnected) include communication, attraction, prestige, role, power, locomotion, and dependence.

As can be seen, then, the major focus in the *structure* is on the existence of a pattern, or on the relationship among units. The major emphasis in *process* is on changes occurring in group conditions. At times process changes might refer to structural changes and here the analyst must be clear as to whether the pattern of relationships is being changed (struc-

---

[1] This definition is closely related to the analysis by John W. Thibaut and Harold H. Kelley (1959).

ture) or whether the quality of the interactions that reflect these relationships is being changed (process).

The following rationale is offered for the working definition of group process; other definitions are compared and contrasted when possible:

1. The definition does not exclude either a concept of shared public goals or shared private goals as subject matter for inquiry. It does, however, place the responsibility upon the investigator or practitioner to produce evidence of (a) the existence of such goals and (b) the relationship of these goals to activities and interactions of group members.

2. This formulation is intended to include processes related to the maintenance of equilibrium in groups as well as developmental processes. Bales' (1965:444–476) definitions of group functions have been incorporated into this definition of group process. Processes relevant to shifts in equilibrium can be described through an analysis of relations between goal attainment and group maintenance. Processes associated with group development can be analyzed by examining changes in goal attainment and group maintenance activities in each developmental phase.

The relationship between task and socioemotional activities is complex. The attainment of intermediate goals may have maintenance functions. Also, socioemotional (maintenance) activities may, in fact, constitute group treatment goals.

3. Through this definition of group process, a definite limitation is placed on the kinds of interactions identified as *group* processes. Only those interactions intrinsic to properties that emerge on a group level of social organization are intended. This issue will be approached later by a categorization of member activities and interactions which are related to the goal attainment and group maintenance.

4. Lastly, the definition of group process used here includes much more than cognitive processes in groups. The research applied to group problem solving has not been given to a sufficient range of sequences in groups such as programmatic progressions (e.g., playing a game, forming a self-government body) or behavioral modification programs (group desensitization, group mediated reinforcements), and has mainly been limited to study of concrete intellectual problems.

AN ORDERING OF GROUP PROCESSES

Group processes include a range of activities and interactions related to goal attainment and group maintenance. Some relate either to goal attainment or to group maintenance functions; others may relate to both, and these will be described first. In characterizing each group process, the following will be examined:

1. The function of the specific process within the small group system.

2. The "states" which are found as the process evolves and which identify the process. *State* is used to describe the sequence in which a specific task is accomplished (Thibaut and Kelley, 1959). These states for some processes may include only the presence or absence of a single condition, or they may include movement among several qualitatively different conditions.

3. Etiological and mediating factors in the evolution of the process. Specifically included here are the forces that determine the initiation of the process, its content, its maintenance, and its termination. At times available knowledge may allow for causal inferences; often all that can be asserted are conditions that vary together.[2]

4. Illustrations of the kinds of phenomena, observable events, or circumstances which characterize the process, particularly in the context of group work.

5. The character of the process in differing phases of group development. The relationship of group process to group development is integral. One important aspect of group development is the nature of the changes in group processes over time. This formulation draws upon a definition of group development offered by Sarri and Galinsky (Chapter 5 in this volume) as "changes through time in the internal structures, processes, and culture of the group."

Activities and Interactions Relevant to Both
Goal Attainment and Group Maintenance

Two group processes occur that relate to changes in both the goal and maintenance functions of the group. They are role differentiation and communication-interaction.[3]

The Process of Role Differentiation. As Guetzkow (1968:512–516) points out, "An important feature in the development of groups is the differentiation of roles into an organizational structure." Differentiation of roles occurs in the emergence and modification of roles necessary for both task and maintenance functions in groups.

States of role differentiation. In a general sense, the process may involve a change from (1) an undifferentiated condition to one in which roles are clearly defined or (2) a state in which one set of roles exists to a state where a different set of roles prevails. For example, a group may embark

---

[2] In examining etiological factors, an important consideration is whether the group is viewed as a closed system, or as an open system engaged in regular exchanges with its environment. In this paper, the analysis will be largely limited to the closed system although, when feasible, environmental exchanges will be identified.

[3] For empirical treatment of this process, see Harold Guetzkow (1968) and Philip E. Slater (1965).

upon a new project requiring skills that were not required previously. Behaviors required for this activity will be defined and roles will be assumed or assigned.

   Etiological factors in role differentiation.   Guetzkow classified etiological factors under two headings: "those *external* environmental factors that induce role formation because of the task components and those *internal* processes involved in the establishment of particular persons in particular roles."

   The external factors considered by Guetzkow include task characteristics such as information exchange (i.e., patterns of information distribution), solution formation (i.e., requirements for satisfactory solutions), and answer exchange (i.e., patterns of communication of possible solutions). Other external factors were seen as communication restrictions and group goals. Internal factors included whether individuals withheld information, how individuals perceived the situation, and what kinds of organizational planning were involved. Personal characteristics of members such as intellectual abilities and social ascendance tendencies were also considered as internal variables (Guetzkow, 1968:515–522).

   Phenomena characteristic of role differentiation.   Observable indications that the process of role differentiation is occurring include the planning for group statuses and the assumption by members of roles associated with such positions. The definition of *role* throughout this discussion follows that offered by Linton (1936) as the "dynamic aspects of a status." Another major indication is the reactions of some members to position planning or role assumption of other members. These reactions may tend to reinforce the behavior of persons who have assumed roles, to ignore such behavior, or to punish it. Such processes have been described in terms of role conflict (Thomas, 1967:27–28), role complementarity (Garvin, 1969:127–145), and role collision (Hare, 1962: 19).

   In group treatment situations, members go through a role differentiation process when they clarify and assume the role of client and when they develop behaviors appropriate to the use of the group as a mutual aid system. This process also occurs when the worker tries to help members assume roles in activities (e.g., playing the role of teacher in a role play) which relates to his treatment planning.

   Group development and role differentiation.   The process of role differentiation assumes different characteristics in each stage of group development. In the orientation stage as described by Northen (1969:116) or the formative phase as described by Sarri and Galinsky (Chapter 5 in this volume), roles are relatively undifferentiated and the process is primarily one of seeking role definitions, including the role of being a member.

Sarri and Galinsky assert that in the next, or intermediate phase, specialized roles gradually emerge; the task and socioemotional leaders can be more clearly identified at this time. They also identify a revision phase in which the existing roles are challenged, particularly the leadership roles. This will lead to an acceleration in role differentiation during this period, again with particular reference to such leadership roles. This process can stimulate divisive reactions among group members; and the resolution of such conflicts will lead to a further differentiation of socioemotional as well as task leadership roles.

When the group moves into later "intermediate" phases and a maturation phase, a continual process of role differentiation can be expected to occur. This process will be affected by changes in goals and other phenomena as the group moves toward a phase which Sarri and Galinsky term "maturity" and Mills (1967:111) calls "growth." In this last phase, according to Mills, a "generative role" emerges that embodies creative experience and is "able to translate it into a communicable form so that it may be either stored for future use or made the basis for the formation of a new group."

The Process of Communication-Interaction

The concept of a communication-interaction process has been adapted from Collins and Guetzkow (1964:166). As used here, the process of *communication-interaction* refers to all interpersonal events as efforts are made to cope with the existing or emerging differentiation of roles in the group. As such, the communication-interaction process refers to a major integrative function in small groups.[4]

States of communication-interaction. The states, present as the process of communication-interaction evolves, encompass the initiation, maintenance and termination of message exchanges that relate to the goal attainment and group maintenance functions of the group. A second dimension is that of changes in the content of communications (Bales, 1951). This dimension, however, will be analyzed later in this paper in terms of whether the content is associated with task or maintenance functions.

---

[4] Actually Collins and Guetzkow (1964) quote Blau and Scott (1962) as stating that processes of communication and interaction "refer to the same processes but to different aspects of them. The concept of social interaction focuses principally upon the formal characteristics of social relations: such terms as frequency, initiative, superordination, and reciprocity indicate its dimensions. The concept . . . conveyed in the encounter, and its characteristics are described by such terms as flow of messages, obstacles, positive and negative reactions and exchanges."

Etiological factors in communication-interaction.   Six factors determine the course of the communication-interaction process.

1. The hierarchical status of group members affects the quantity and
direction of communications. As Collins and Guetzkow (1964:171–173)
have indicated, high status persons initiate more interactions and receive
more communications than low status members do. Persons seeking higher
status are also more likely to direct interactions to lower status persons
than to other high status persons.

2. The likelihood of being rewarded affects the communication-interaction process. Reinforcement may well stem from the power of a group
member to control the use of his expertise, possession of resources, or
ability to inflict harm (French and Raven, 1968).

3. The structure of the group affects the communication-interaction
process. The structural component may include not only interaction patterns among group members but also their physical location (Collins and
Guetzkow, 1964:177–178).

4. Control problems within the group have major effects upon the
communication-interaction process. It has been observed, for example,
that "a high number of communications will be addressed to an *accepted*
group member who expresses deviate opinions" and "rejection of the
deviate and subgroup formation will result in a low number of communications addressed to an unaccepted group member who expresses deviant
opinions." (Collins and Guetzkow, 1964:180) The issue of control processes will be discussed as a major topic later.

5. The characteristics of the message itself will help to determine
communication-interaction process. An important issue here is the relationship of the content of the message to the attitudes of group members
and the normative structure of the group.

6. Forces in the environment may also have effects, particularly as
these interact with or determine the above five factors.

Phenomena characteristic of communication-interaction.   In group
treatment, after the roles of worker and client have been clarified and
assumed, many communications and interactions are initiated in order to
fulfill the task requirements of these roles. Communications may be directed
at the worker to determine his expertise, his attitudes, and his expectations. Communication also takes place among members as they seek to
share relevant experiences. Participants may inform each other about role
expectations and the nature and quality of role performances. The group
worker may describe what he intends to do and what he expects members to do. Members in turn may tell the worker of life areas he may or
may not touch upon or express ideas about the ways they expect the
worker and other members to respond to sensitive material.

In addition, maintenance of the group requires that members test how far they can trust each other in the client/group member roles before they share sensitive information. Thus, this second type of communication-interaction occurs when members and workers express or betray emotions regarding role assignments or attempt to respond to emotional expressions when they form barriers to group maintenance. Members may express fear or anger regarding the role of the worker or the roles assumed by other members.

Group development and communication-interaction process. In the group's formative stage, the communication-interaction process occurs as members "seek common and compatible personal values and attitudes to group purposes and to activities and tasks." In the intermediate phase that processes of communication and interaction among persons in various positions must be occurring. The revision phase, characterized by a chalthere is "observable involvement in goal-directed activities" which implies lenge to the existing leadership structure, must also be accompanied by a change in communications processes in order to effect this challenge. An increase in interactions in general, has also been noted as occurring during this period. (Sarri and Galinsky, Chapter 5 in this volume)

When a group reaches "maturity," changes in communication-interaction processes will occur as "external pressures force internal changes." (Sarri and Galinsky, Chapter 5 in this volume) These changes are accomplished self-consciously and with minimal conflicts among group members.

Activities and Interactions Relevant to Goal Attainment

Two group processes relate to goal attainment, but not to group maintenance. The first is the determination of the goal to be attained. The second is goal pursuit, the sequences of behaviors members engage in so that a goal may be reached.

The Process of Goal Determination

This process takes place as members interact to select the desired end-state to be achieved through actions by members. The end-state might be a specific event like taking a trip, constructing something, or having a party. Or it might constitute an ultimate and often abstractly defined series of goals. Often the aim is toward achieving such group purposes as "improved school performance" or "reduction in antisocial activities."

States of goal determination. As pointed out by Thibaut and Kelley (1959:256), "group goals are social matters and require some degree of *consensus* before they can be processed by enough of their members to warrant their being called group goals." They describe consensus as follows:

> . . . it is probably necessary that this consensus rest largely on the *acceptance* of these goals by a relatively large number, possibly a majority, of the group members. By the acceptance of a group goal it is meant that the individual believes that he will attain good outcomes when the task is put into the state designated by the goal. And for consensus to be based on acceptance, there must be correspondence among the members in this respect: each must believe he will attain good outcomes . . . acceptance of goals implies that the person is dependably ready to enact the behavior thought to put the task in the goal state even in the *absence* of enforcement by the techniques of gaining compliance: surveillance and sanctioning. (Thibaut and Kelley, 1959:257–258)

Generally, the process of goal determination begins when alternative outcomes for the group are posed. The step that follows consists of discussion of these alternatives in which factual information and evaluative criteria may be introduced. Choices are then made and more specific goals derived. This process follows the same sequence as the more general problem-solving paradigm discussed later.

Another way of examining states of goal determination is to inspect, not only the development of consensus around a goal, but also the succession of goals which occurs when one goal is attained or when the group abandons efforts toward attaining a goal. Goal determination occurs either when intermediate goals are developed or when a new episode of consensus seeking takes place.

Etiological factors in goal determination.   The forces affecting the achievement of consensus on a group goal and the progression of group goals may be examined on three levels: (1) the characteristics of individuals, (2) group characteristics, and (3) environmental characteristics. Cartwright and Zander (1968:405) summarize individual level forces when they state:

> The attractiveness for any given member of a particular goal for the group is influenced by the nature of the member's person-oriented and group-oriented motives, by his judgment of the rewards and costs involved for him and the group in activities relevant to the goal, and his subjective probability that the group will attain this goal.

On a group level, a range of variables can have an impact on goal determination process. The following questions suggest possible variables. Do cooperative or competitive conditions prevail in the group? Do members have power to compel nonconforming members to accept specified goals? Is there consensus that the group has the resources to achieve the goal? Is the group cohesive enough to secure behavior consistent with the group goal? (Thibaut and Kelley, 1959:257–261) Structural elements also play a major role: Does the pattern of participation in the group lend itself to securing consensus on goals or not? Existing group norms and patterns of dealing with conflict are important considerations, too.

Finally, influences from the environment affect goal determination processes. Cartwright and Zander (1968:405–406) summarize these environmental variables as the extent to which members need to please persons in the social environment and the extent to which the group is seen as relevant to furthering or obstructing the objectives of those persons.

Phenomena characteristics of goal determination. The process of goal determination may take the form of a discussion of the kinds of member problems to be dealt with in the group. A group of unwed mothers might spend time discussing whether their greater priorities are to relinquish the child, how to handle the putative father, or how later to pursue their own careers.

Another type of goal decision frequently encountered is whether to change some aspect of the clients' environment or to change the clients' responses to that environment. When this decision is made initially, the subsequent goal decision may be to move on to the alternate decision after attaining the first goal or to give up on it.

Group development and goal determination process. The long-term goals of the group are frequently at issue during the formative phase of group development. Members also may seek to select short-term goals to demonstrate that sufficient commonality exists for the group to continue. In the intermediate phase of the group, there is less emphasis on the selection of goals and more upon carrying them out. The revision phase is the time when new goals emerge as new leadership is identified. (Sarri and Galinsky, Chapter 5 in this volume) Either may occur first: new leadership may bring about a reformulating of group goals or a reformulation of goals may initiate the replacement of the existing leadership.

The Process of Goal Pursuit

The ensuing discussion utilizes the definition of goal pursuit provided by Thibaut and Kelley (1959:263), "the processes by which actions are chosen as means of attaining (the) goal." The literature describes two types of actions in this respect. One is primarily cognitive and relates to the process of group problem solving; the other may involve cognitive, motor, and affective elements[5] in order to accomplish a *task*.

The concept of task has been defined by Thibaut and Kelley (1959: 150) as a "problem, assignment, or stimulus-complex to which the indi-

---

[5] Affective elements may occur when the task is consummatory such as appreciating an artistic work.

vidual or group responds by performing various overt or covert operations which lead to various outcomes." This is, of course, a generic definition and for purposes of analysis, the problem component has been identified as a separate process.

States of goal pursuit. The work of Bales and Strodbeck (1968: 389–440) on the phases through which the process of problem solving evolves is quite definitive. These phases are identified as those in which acts of either "orientation," "evaluation," or "control" predominate. Orientation behaviors include a member's "giving or asking for orientation, information, repetition, clarification, or confirmation." Evaluation activities occur when a member "gives or asks for opinion, evaluation, analysis, expression of feeling, or a wish." In control activities, members "give or ask for suggestions, direction and possible ways of action."

When the task relevant to attaining the goal is not primarily a cognitive one, the states have to be described more abstractly. Thibaut and Kelley (1959:151) define such a state at any given point in time "in terms of its yielding a unique repertoire." In his analysis of program activities, Vinter (Chapter 13 in this volume) stresses that activities in pursuit of treatment goals may vary in any one of the following dimensions:

1. prescriptiveness of the pattern of constituent performances
2. institutionalized control governing participant activity
3. provision for physical movement
4. competence required for performance
5. provision for participant interactiveness
6. reward structure

Etiological factors in goal pursuit. An excellent summary of variables that affect group problem solving, provided by Kelley and Thibaut (1969:1–101), points out that problem-solving behavior is initiated with the receipt of outcomes below the "comparison level." (Kelley and Thibaut, 1969:11) By this they mean that outcomes through individual efforts are perceived to be less desirable than alternate outcomes resulting from group efforts. Subsequent problem-solving events will be determined by such group structures as communications structure, affectional structure, reward structure, and power (or status) structure. (Kelley and Thibaut, 1969:19–41)

The leadership structure of the group will also affect the pursuit of goals. Two types of leadership are task and socioemotional and each type fulfills a corresponding group function. Task leadership acts are, of course, the relevant behaviors for the process being discussed here.

Similar variables affect all other problem-solving or task-completion behaviors. Among those which have been described are the individual's power to determine the states the task will take (Thibaut and Kelley, 1959:153), the sources of social definitions of reality (Thibaut and Kelley,

1959:155), and the behaviors which are defined socially as basic and essential to the activity. (Vinter, Chapter 13 in this volume.) The structure of the task itself also affects the pursuit of goals. Some tasks are conjunctive (all participants have to make a response to receive the reward) while others are disjunctive (some subset of the small group system can act so that the reward will be secured).

Phenomena characteristic of goal pursuit. If a group of prisoners discuss how they can overcome the onus of having been in jail when seeking employment, they have begun the process of problem solving. This process, using the propositions described above, has been initiated because the "comparison level" of undertaking employment without having solved this problem is lower than what may be achieved through the group's solution to their common "problem."

The group of prisoners may then role play interviews with prospective employers, using a "script" developed through the problem-solving process. The "script" represents the completion of the first task. A powerful individual may seize a particular role because of outcomes he desires. From the point of view of the group worker, the way the role is played may appear dysfunctional, but the prisoners may not object because of their definitions of reality. However, to the degree that a satisfactory outcome depends on the satisfaction of all participants, the task is conjunctive and will not terminate until such satisfaction is attained. This example illustrates a "program activity" to pursue a goal in which elements of the sequence have been prestructured.

Group development and goal pursuit processes. The major emphasis in the formative period of group development is on goal determination, not problem solving or task completion. Activities, if engaged in, are primarily used for members to discover common goal and activity interests. The intermediate phase is characterized by "observable involvement in goal-directed activities." This involvement continues through the period of revision, with shifts in activities made necessary by changes in purposes and in leadership. A higher commitment to goal-oriented activities is found in later intermediate stages as earlier problems are resolved and as group cohesiveness is stronger. Subsequently, a termination stage may coincide with the completion of the tasks for which the group was organized. (Sarri and Galinsky, Chapter 5 in this volume)

Activities and Interactions Relevant to Group Maintenance

Now changes in member activities and interactions related to maintaining or strengthening the group will be described. These changes have been characterized as taking place in three subsystems:

1. On the level of behavior, the subsystem is the *interaction system*

which is the organization of overt actions among persons over time.

2. On the level of emotion, the subsystem is *group emotion,* the patterns of feelings among members and of their emotional responses to events that occur.

3. On the level of norms, the subsystem is the *normative system* which is the organized, and largely shared, ideas about what members should do and feel, about how these should be regulated, and about what sanctions should be applied when behavior does not coincide with the norms. (Mills, 1967:58)

These three subsystems will serve as the basis for the discussion of maintenance processes.

Maintenance Processes

Behavioral level. At this level conflict resolution and behavioral control occur. These processes are directed at behaviors that can cause the destruction of the group. The first stems from the shortage of resources and other constraints that may exist in a group. Mills (1967:14), while quite critical of a conflict model of groups, describes this process as follows:

> To organize, a group must coordinate one part with another, and in doing so must limit the freedom of some parts. So long as persons value freedom, there is an inevitable conflict between their latitude, and demands upon them for conformity and coordination. Too, some members are more competent, more powerful and more prestigeful than others; and since the interests of those on top are opposed to those on the bottom, positional conflict also is unavoidable. And further, groups accept and reward some members more fully than others. . . .

Although Mills correctly points out that assumptions which give primacy to these processes over others are fallacious, the existence of such processes cannot be denied.

The universal quality of pressures in groups toward behavioral as well as attitudinal uniformity has often been commented upon. As Cartwright and Zander note, "If a cohesive group has developed a standard or a norm, it may exert strong pressures on any member who attempts to deviate." The function of such pressures toward behavioral conformity is to enable group locomotion, group maintenance, and social definitions of reality (Cartwright and Zander, 1968:141–142).

Emotional level. The emotional processes important for group maintenance are the attractions among group members and the attraction toward the group as a whole. This latter attraction includes the development of group cohesiveness and the state of morale among members regarding group tasks. Cognitive components will not be considered at this time. Only the emotional experiences of members as they express likes and dislikes of each other and for the group are considered. The group maintenance process, at the emotional level, concerns changes in such emotions over time; the pattern of member likes and dislikes at any given moment constitutes a group structure.

Normative level. According to Mills (1967), norms "help orient persons to each other, providing guidelines as to how certain universal interpersonal issues are to be managed by the parties in question."[6] Since it is impossible to imagine a group without a system of rules to govern the behavior of members, the emergence of norms is a *sine qua non* of group existence. External conditions change, however, and new tasks require new rules. Norms, as a consequence, may be in flux as the group develops.

States of Maintenance Processes

Behavioral level. Group states related to conflict resolution will vary from the state of severe conflict among members to the termination of such conflict. This continuum can be described further by the nature of subgroups which embody the conflict, the variance in the content of the conflict, and the mechanisms used to resolve the conflict. Behavioral control, to secure uniformity in groups, has states which vary (a) from the observation of the deviant act by another group member to (b) the initiation of behaviors directed at the deviant to (c) a resolution of the issue. The resolution may be to the satisfaction of the deviant, of the group, or of both.

Emotional level. The attractions of group members for each other will change in intensity and direction. The feelings members have for the group will also change over time and may differ among subgroups. Group emotional states, therefore, depend on the intensity of the emotion, the direction of the emotion, and the differences which may exist in the emotions expressed by different members.

Normative level. Mills draws upon Parsons for a series of categories regarding the states in which norms may be found in the group.

Norms in any society or group, he suggests, must provide answers to questions relating to at least four issues: (1) Are relations among members to be based upon the expression of the feelings they have toward one another, or upon the assumption that those feelings are to be supressed

[6] Mills adds that norms are "cognitive and moral statements which screen, evaluate, prescribe and proscribe feelings and action. As statements they are distinct from feelings and from behavior. They exist in symbolic form in the mind, and are elements of group culture."

and controlled. . . ? (2) Is involvement with one another to be total and unbounded (as with parent and child) or is it to be restricted and specific . . . ? (3) Is the significance of the other to be due to the unique relation one has with him . . . or is it to be due to the fact that he represents a type, or a class, or person . . . ? (4) Is the significance of the other to be due to his qualities . . . or is it to be due to how he performs . . . ?[7]

Mills (1967:75) also indicates other classifications. One such approach generates a matrix in which the variables are combinations of the member's rights, duties, demands and privileges. Another paradigm is provided by Thibaut and Kelley (1959:241) who see three stages: (1) stating a rule, (2) maintaining surveillance, and (3) applying sanctions.

Etiological Factors in Maintenance Processes

Behavioral level. The use of conflict resolution and behavioral control techniques may be required by the presence of one or more of the following sources of conflict or deviance (Collins and Guetzkow, 1964: 88–98):

1. Motives of individual members which differ from either the motives of other members or from the stated objectives of the group
2. Personality traits of some members which conflict with the personality traits of other members
3. The desire of several members to occupy the same group position or the existence of several group positions with ambiguous or overlapping functions
4. Role requirements which conflict with the status attributed by the group to a member or by a member to himself

Additional propositions regarding the resolution of conflict or the attainment of uniformity have been developed by Collins and Guetzkow.[8]

1. The expression of many self-oriented or personal needs by the participants is detrimental to the reaching of consensus.
2. A positive affective atmosphere in a meeting is an important condition for bringing groups in conflict toward agreement.

[7] Derived by Mills from Talcott Parsons and Edward A. Shils, Eds., (1951). It should also be noted that for social work groups, these maintenance processes may also be task processes, since changes in norms may be the very purposes for which the group has been developed.

[8] These proportions are quoted with a few minor word changes from Collins and Guetzkow (1964).

3. Meetings in which discussion was orderly in its treatment of topics and without backward references to previously discussed issues, tended to end in more consensus, despite large amounts of . . . conflict.
4. Groups that have more expertise available and that utilize this knowledge are those whose substantive conflict ends in more consensus.
5. Chairmen of groups in high substantive conflict which ended in consensus did three times more seeking for information of an objective factual nature from members of their groups than did chairmen in groups which did not end in consensus.
6. When the members of the group seem to like each other personally, substantive conflict tends to be more easily resolved.

The circumstances related to a definition of deviance and the handling of the deviant will be further explicated when processes in the normative system are described. Such processes regarding deviance depend upon the norms which exist or develop in the group.

Emotional level. Extensive research has been conducted into sources and consequences of attraction in groups (Lott and Lott, 1965: 259–309). Attraction among members is associated with frequency of interaction and similarity among the members on variables relevant to the existence of the group. Dissimilarity can also lead to attraction when members are able to meet complementary needs. Attraction to the group itself, referred to as group cohesiveness, has been found to be associated with the value place upon group outcomes as opposed to possible outcomes from other sources, the probability attached to the meeting of personal needs in the group, and other rewards available from the group experience.

Other possible sources of attraction to a group include the goals of the group and the nature of the group's activities. The size of the group may also be a factor; small groups are attractive when intimacy is desired and larger ones when members wish multiple opportunities to form emotional bonds with others.

Normative level. The following list includes some of the major factors that determine the operation of group norms:

1. "Greater pressure to conform in groups is associated with greater group cohesiveness." (Mills, 1967:77)
2. "When a member in a cohesive group deviates, others will first actively try to convert him to the norms and then, if they fail to do so, will reject him." (Mills, 1967:78)
3. "Outside agents (which may even be thought of as supernatural forces) may be used to support norms if there is consensus in the

group regarding their action and power." (Thibaut and Kelley, 1959:241)

4. "Norms about behavior that are highly important to the life and success of the group will be more thoroughly publicized, more carefully monitored and more strongly enforced than norms about behavior of little importance." (Thibaut and Kelley, 1959:248)

5. "Good communication in the group permits more accurate transmission of the norm." (Thibaut and Kelley, 1959:254)

6. "For surveillance to be effective, the behavior of the member must be open to view and individually identifiable." (Thibaut and Kelley, 1959:254)

Phenomena Characteristic of Maintainance processes

Behavioral level. Two major types of conflict are likely to occur in treatment groups: one related to the purpose of the group and the other to the power of the worker, as such. Conflict over purpose may arise because of the existence of behavior defined as deviant. The group worker may be trying, for example, to help a member with deviant behavior within the group which corresponds to the problem for which help is sought. The entire group, on the other hand, may be defined as deviant by the larger society, in which case the worker often reinforces the behavior of a member whose behavior is "deviant" within the context of the group.

Conflict over the power of the worker is likely to occur in any therapeutic encounter because of the threat to the existing equilibrium which the worker presents. Thus, members will often defy worker's suggestions regarding such relatively innocuous matters as meeting times and places, procedural suggestions, and so forth.

Emotional level. Members often spend time in the first group meetings eliciting information about one another as they search for commonalities. The result of this process then determines subgroup patterns based on interpersonal attraction. Emotional reactions are directed to the group worker as his likeability is assessed. Members may express verbal or nonverbal concerns that the group's activities be attractive. Members also evaluate the group atmosphere and may attribute it to external factors such as agency receptivity, as well as to internal factors such as friendliness among members. Many emotional responses relevant to this last issue will occur.

Normative level. When deviant behavior occurs in a group, deviant norms are likely to be operating. The worker in such groups frequently challenges antisocial norms and reinforces the expression of socially desirable norms. Discussions take place on the desirability or undesirability of specified behaviors, such as stealing, sexual promiscuity, and rule breaking in the institution itself.

The worker who does not desire to impose any normative system, nevertheless, engages a group in examining and analyzing specified norms. Such discussions, in appropriate groups, might deal with abortion, conflict over models of social change, or values in childrearing.

Group Development and Maintenance Processes

Behavioral level. The general trend is for processes of conflict initiation and resolution and behavior control to increase throughout the life of the group, as the group becomes more cohesive and as task progression and decision making occur. Conflict is likely to be intensified in revision phases as leadership is changed and tasks modified. In the stage of maturity, however, the group is characterized as possessing the resources to effectively meet both individual needs and group maintenance requirements in a complementary fashion.

Emotional level. Group development is associated with an increase in attraction among group members and for the group itself. The formative period is when members seek the commonalities upon which attraction depends. An increase in interpersonal ties occurs in the intermediate phase after the testing in the formative phase has been completed. The revision phase, according to Sarri and Galinsky, is one in which "as members feel more secure in their specialized roles, as they depend more upon one another for satisfaction in the tasks and activities of the group, and as they interact more frequently, group members are likely to have more positive feelings toward each other." (Sarri and Galinsky, Chapter 5 in this volume.)

It has also been noted that, in the revision phase, as members become more involved with each other an increase in negative reactions can also be expected." Groups that reach a maturity phase will be well able to resolve tensions among members, thus maintaining the equilibrium which is characteristic of mature groups.

Normative level. The establishment of norms begins during the formative period of the group as members explore each other's personal values. In the intermediate period, "Additional norms and values are acquired that specifically relate to group functioning" (Sarri and Galinsky, Chapter 5 in this volume). Sarri and Galinsky also point out that

> Social control mechanisms develop, and deviation from norms often tends to be dealt with in a harsh or punitive manner by the group. Because norms and values for a number of areas of attitudinal expression and

overt behavior are not yet established, member participation may be somewhat restricted in fear of sanctions, or because members do not yet know what is expected of them. Pressures toward uniformity and consensus are clearly apparent.

In the revision phase, the norms, values, and traditions of the group may change in varying degrees depending upon the extent of the revision. In any case, the revision stage ends with a strengthening and clarification of the group's norms. In later phases of group life, because the group has existed for a longer time, norms can be expected to be more clearly enunciated and deviation more likely to secure a response from other group members. Throughout, the worker is aware of the potential of group norms for the support of prosocial behavior.

INTERVENTIONS IN GROUP PROCESSES

As each process was discussed above, etiological factors associated with the process were described. Inferences can be made, then, as to how group processes may be modified by selecting and manipulating the etiological variable most accessible to influence. To modify a process, this manipulation can be accomplished by the worker or the group members. This decision should not be prejudiced either way. If there is any bias, it is toward the goal of enabling members to become conscious of their own group processes so that they can modify them, when necessary, to accomplish their goals. It is almost a truism to note that when members are fully able to do that, they are not likely to be in need of a group worker and this is, therefore, one of the ultimate goals of work with groups, to be achieved whenever possible.

In examining the etiological factors associated with group processes, it is possible to offer a general framework for worker or member interventions. This framework is based on the fact that there can be three immediate targets for change: The first possible target, to modify a group process, may be the behavior of an individual member, as he interacts with other members. The second target of change may be some group condition bearing upon the process. The third target may be some external system which exercises control over an internal group process. The proposition is that group processes can be initiated or modified, whichever of these targets is chosen.

Modification of Individual Behavior To Affect
Group Process

Modifying individual behavior to influence a group process requires skillful tracing of the connection between the behavior and the process.

The first step, therefore, is to determine the interactions in the actual group situation which characterize the process. Examples of such interactions have been offered for each process described. After the worker has identified a problematic behavior in an on-going process, individual behaviors characteristic of a revised process can be determined. Behaviors may be revised by any of the following means:

1. *Operant conditioning.* A vast array of operant conditioning techniques are now available to the social worker for the modification of individual behavior, including reinforcement, extinction, model presentation, and aversive conditioning. (Thomas, 1968:12–26)

2. *Logical reasoning and problem solving.* The worker can help members examine problems related to the members' contributions to group processes, and they may modify their own behavior as a result of this examination.

3. *Removing emotional blocks.* At times, members' behavior may have undesired effects upon group processes because of fears, anxieties, or other emotional blocks which are elicited by the process. The worker can use catharsis or desensitization techniques to relieve the emotional stress that leads to behavior which has deleterious effects upon the group process.

Modification of Group Conditions To Affect Group Process

In many cases, it is more feasible or expedient for the worker or the members to modify a process by changing some group condition. The group conditions which may be so manipulated are as follows:

1. *Group structure.* As has been indicated, some group structures that have effects upon processes include communications structure, power structure, and affectional structure. In seeking to modify a group process, the worker or members can analyze existing structures related to the process and then modify the crucial structure. Such structural changes can be accomplished by changing the behavior of individual members, by changing the size or composition of the group, or by initiating an activity with norms that call for a more desirable structure.

2. *Group Processes.* Some group processes can be used in order to change other processes. For example, normative processes can be used to modify the process of role differentiation. In an analogous way, roles may be differentiated to enhance the process of problem solving. Therefore, processes that are more accessible to modification can be used to affect those which are less so. The problem-solving process can be used not only to resolve difficulties related to group structure and processes, but to modify conditions external to the group and to change the behavior of individual members of the group as well.

3. *Program.* The group can develop a task with specific performance requirements which may have substantial effects upon group processes. For example, a role play requiring members to behave differently
toward authority may lead to the emergence of a different kind of leadership in the group.

Modification of External Conditions To Affect Group Processes

The forces maintaining group processes may be external to the group
and changes in group process may have to begin with modifying extragroup inputs. Some of these inputs are:

1. Goals imposed on the group
2. Leadership imposed on the group
3. Resources made available to the group
4. Expertise available to the group
5. Demands created by linkages between this group and other groups
   (e.g., external reference groups)

In summary, definitions of group process have been examined and
the usage of this term has been presented for purposes of this analysis.
Group process was seen here as "those changes occurring in the activities
and interactions of group members that are related to changes in goal
attainment and group maintenance." Specific processes, stemming from
this definition, were then ordered and discussed, and a framework for
planning the modification of group processes was described.

Several tasks are now called for to further this conceptualization of
group processes and their modification.

1. The usefulness of the concept must be tested in practice.

2. The forces described here as affecting group processes must be
empirically examined as they occur in social work groups. Social science
propositions noted here must also be tested in group work settings.

3. Additional propositions must be generated and data sought concerning the appropriate occasions for worker intervention into group
processes and the actual effects that workers have upon such processes.

REFERENCES

BALES, ROBERT F.
  1951—*Interaction Process Analysis,* Cambridge: Addison-Wesley Press, Inc.
  1965—"The equilibrium problem in small groups," in A. Paul Hare, Edgar
       F. Borgatta and Robert F. Bales (Eds.), *Small Group Studies in
       Social Interaction,* New York: Alfred A. Knopf.

BALES, ROBERT F. AND FRED L. STRODBECK
1968—"Phases in group problem solving," in Cartwright and Zander (Eds.), *Group Dynamics: Research and Theory*, New York: Harper and Row.

BLAU, PETER M. AND W. R. SCOTT
1962—*Formal Organizations: A Comparative Approach*, San Francisco: Chandler.

CARTWRIGHT, DORWIN
1968—"The nature of group cohesiveness," in Cartwright and Zander (Eds.), *Group Dynamics: Research and Theory*, New York: Harper and Row.

CARTWRIGHT, DORWIN AND ALVIN ZANDER
1968—"Pressures to uniformity in groups: Introduction," in Cartwright and Zander (Eds.), *Group Dynamics: Research and Theory*, New York: Harper and Row.

COLLINS, BARRY E. AND HAROLD GUETZKOW
1964—*A Social Psychology of Group Processes for Decision Making*, New York: John Wiley & Sons.

COLLINS, BARRY E. AND BERTRAM H. RAVEN
1969—"Group structure: Attraction, coalitions, communication and power," in Gardner Lindzey and Elliot Aronson (Eds.), *The Handbook of Social Psychology*, Second edition, Reading, Massachusetts: Addison-Wesley Publishing Co.

DURKIN, HELEN E.
1964—*The Group in Depth*, New York: International Universities Press, Inc.

ETZIONI, AMITAI
1968—*The Active Society: A Theory of Societal and Political Processes*, New York: The Free Press.

FRENCH, JOHN R. P. AND BERTRAM RAVEN
1968—"The Bases of Social Power," in Cartwright and Zander (Eds.), *Group Dynamics: Research and Theory*, New York: Harper and Row.

GARLAND, JAMES A., HUBERT E. JONES AND RALPH L. KOLODNY
1965—"A model for stages of development in social work groups," in Saul Bernstein (Ed.), *Explorations in Group Work*, Boston: Boston University School of Social Work.

GARVIN, CHARLES
1969—"Complementarity of role expectations in groups: The member-worker contract," *Social Work Practice, 1969*, New York: Columbia University Press.

GUETZKOW, HAROLD
1968—"Differentiation of roles in task oriented groups," in Cartwright and Zander (Eds.), *Group Dynamics: Research and Theory*, New York: Harper and Row.

HARE, A. PAUL
1962—*Handbook of Small Group Research*, New York: The Free Press.

KELLEY, HAROLD H. AND JOHN W. THIBAUT
1969—"Group problem solving," in Gardner Lindzey and Elliot Aronson (Eds.), *The Handbook of Social Psychology*, Second edition, Reading, Massachusetts: Addison-Wesley Publishing Co.

LINTON, RALPH
1936—*The Study of Man*, New York: Appleton Century Co.

LOTT, A. J. AND B. E. LOTT
1965—"Group cohesiveness as interpersonal attraction: A review of relationships with antecedent and consequent variables," *Psychological Bulletin*, 64.

MILLS, THEODORE M.
1967—*The Sociology of Small Groups*, Englewood Cliffs, New Jersey: Prentice-Hall.

NEWCOMB, T. M., R. H. TURNER AND P. E. CONVERSE
1965—*Social Psychology: The Study of Human Interaction*, New York: Holt, Rinehart and Winston.

NORTHEN, HELEN
1969—*Social Work With Groups*, New York: Columbia University Press.

PARSONS, TALCOTT AND EDWARD A. SHILS (EDS.)
1951—*Toward A General Theory of Action*, Cambridge: Harvard University Press.

SLATER, PHILIP E.
1965—"Role differentiation in small groups," in A. Paul Hare, Edgar F. Borgatta and Robert F. Bales (Eds.), *Small Group Studies in Social Interaction*, New York: Alfred A. Knopf.

THIBAUT, JOHN W. AND HAROLD H. KELLEY
1959—*The Social Psychology of Groups*, New York: John Wiley & Sons.

THOMAS, EDWIN J.
1968—"Selected socio-behavioral techniques and principles, An approach to interpersonal helping," *Social Work*, 13 (January).
1967—"Concepts of role theory," in Edwin Thomas (Ed.), *Behavioral Science For Social Workers*, New York: The Free Press.

WHITAKER, DOROTHY STOCK AND MORTON A. LIEBERMAN
1964—*Psychotherapy Through The Group Process*, New York: Atherton Press.

13.

Program Activities:
An Analysis of Their Effects
on Participant Behavior

ROBERT D. VINTER

CONCEPTION AND USE OF PROGRAM

Social group workers' long understanding that activities have important meanings and consequences for groups and their members has led to a stress on "program as a tool." Since the practitioner may determine the choice and quality of group activities, he may thereby influence both participants and group processes. In this sense, program affords the worker an indirect means of influencing groups and their members and is deliberately used to achieve desired objectives.

Program is a vague term, seldom defined, that has special uses in the literature of practice. It loses meaning when intended to refer to all the social interactions and processes engaged in by group members. For present purposes, program will denote a general class of group activities, each of which consists of an interconnected series of social behaviors that usually is infused with meanings and guided by performance standards from the larger culture. The social behaviors which constitute any particular activity tend to follow a pattern, unfolding in a rough chronological sequence and sometimes reaching a definite climax or conclusion. A game, an athletic event, and a musical performance are archetypes of program activities, but reference to such clear-cut examples should not result in ignoring other kinds, e.g., group discussions, telling a story or a joke, role playing, or swimming. Use of and interaction with physical objects are included within the concept of program activity detailed here.

Problems arise in selecting specific activities to achieve particular treatment objectives. Even the comparatively inexperienced practitioner can choose from a vast range of activities in accordance with his own skills and the interest and abilities of members in a given group. Experience, intuition, even personal preferences of the practitioner, in combination with expressed interests of participants, are typical bases for making selections from the total range of activities. Conventional perspectives on activities, however, provide few indications of their specific effects for groups. Particular activities may be too indecisive (e.g., boxing calls forth aggression) or may be focused on effects for individuals without reference to group results (e.g., finger painting permits catharsis). Discussions or analyses of activities usually are stated in such unique terms that comparisons cannot be made with a number of alternate activity forms.

The worker's task of selecting activities with maximum impact in the desired direction is made more difficult by the necessity of modifying chosen types of activities. Not only must he know when to engage the group in singing rather than discussion, but he must also be ready to select the particular form of singing most suitable for the group at that time.

The intent here is to present a formulation useful in analyzing program activities, in making choices among them, and modifications within them. The specific criteria for making a particular choice for a given group must be consistent with objectives for that group and its individual members. The given formulation permits application of such criteria and has the advantage of encompassing both group behavior (i.e., social interactions) and individual responses to activity.

The present formulation draws heavily on one intially conceived by Gump and his associates (Gump, Sutton-Smith and Redl, 1953). Subsequent field testing has shown considerable utility for the scheme (Gump and Sutton-Smith, 1955:755–760). Gump's original conception has been revised and extended for the following formulation; an important contribution to this revision has been made by Edwin J. Thomas.

ACTIVITY SETTINGS

All activities are comprised of (1) *a physical field,* (2) *constituent performances,* and (3) *respondent behaviors.* Each of these components can be described generally.

1. *Physical field* refers to the physical space and terrain, and the physical and social objects characteristic of each activity. For example, a relatively flat unobstructed field, a ball and bat, and a given number of players constitute the physical and social objects of a baseball game.

2. *Constituent performances* refer to those behaviors which are basic and essential to the activity and which are required of participants. Throwing the ball, hitting and catching it, and running are some of baseball's constituent performances. The behaviors required of various players may vary, although there is typically some rotation: the batter does not also

catch the ball, and so forth. Constituent performances are of two orders: (a) acquiring the necessities, and (b) executing a method.

Since the physical field and constituent performances are intrinsic to each activity, they may be considered together as the *activity-setting*.

3. *Respondent behaviors* are individual participant actions evoked by, but not essential to, participation in the activity. Many activities require few if any verbal interactions yet they customarily accompany participation. In baseball, "talking it up," cheering, and arguing are behaviors which participants almost inevitably manifest in response to the game. Other nonverbal respondent behaviors are also typical: expressional acting from any position, but particularly by the pitcher and batter; patting the successful player; much short running and jumping which are not directly instrumental to playing.

The basic rationale of this analysis may be stated simply. First, different activities *require* different behavior patterns (as "constituent performances") from their participants. Second, different activities inevitably evoke diverse behavior patterns (as "respondent behaviors") of their participants. Third, both types of behaviors are conditioned or determined by the nature of the activity-setting and are relatively independent of the personality characteristics of the individual participants. Fourth, both constituent performances and respondent behaviors have important consequences for the individuals and for the group that are relevant to treatment or service objectives. And fifth, both constituent performances and respondent behaviors may be deliberately achieved or modified by informed selection or modification of particular activities. Practitioners need to know *which* features of an activity are likely to result in *what* behaviors.

ACTIVITY-SETTING DIMENSIONS

Various forms and combinations of the two basic components of the activity-setting (i.e., physical field and constituent performances) are distinctive to different activities. A scheme for assessing activity-settings must detail the elements of the two components which evoke or generate respondent behaviors. It must also encompass all possible combinations of the components. These requirements are partially met by identifying the basic *dimensions* of activity-settings. Six dimensions can be specified as relevant to all activities.

1. *Prescriptiveness of the pattern of constituent performances.* For a given activity, the extent to which behaviors in which participants must engage do exist and the required order of the behaviors, if any. Prescriptiveness denotes the degree and range of rules or other guides for conduct. The activity-setting of chess is highly prescriptive with limited move-

ments possible for each piece, rules of silence during tournament play, etc. Contract bridge is a more prescriptive card game than Old Maid. Simple children's games have few rules prescribing a limited area of behavior, leaving undefined a great range of permissible behavior. Athletic contests are usually characterized by a greater degree and broader range of prescribed behavior.

2. *Institutionalized controls governing participant activity.* The form and source or agent of controls that are exercised over participants during the activity. Controls may be exercised by another person, sometimes a fellow participant, or impersonally (as with rules and shared norms relevant to the activity). Umpires, referees, and team captains are obvious agents of institutionalized controls. They may determine not only how an activity shall be conducted but also who shall participate at a given moment. Often, such agents interpret or are guided by general rules commonly accepted for a given activity. The individual who is "It" in many children's games exercises control over fellow players, although he is a less obvious agent of control.

Note that the first and second dimensions discussed refer to prescriptions, requirements and controls. There is an important distinction between them, however. The first focuses on the content and degree of activity prescriptions, while the second focuses on the form and source (or agent) of requirements that are imposed in the activity process.

3. *Provision for physical movement.* The extent to which participants are required or permitted to move about in the activity-setting. Movement may be of the whole body (as in swimming or football) or of any specific parts of the body (as in bridge or group discussion). Activity-settings that have broad physical boundaries and performances allowing for much motor movement may be contrasted to those with limited boundaries, constricting physical barriers, and performances limiting body movement.

4. *Competence required for performance.* The minimum level of ability required to participate in the activity, not the competence required to excel or to win. In some activity-settings, constituent performances can be executed by inexperienced persons (as with children playing tag or singing); in others, the setting requires special skill or ability (as with playing most musical instruments or water-skiing). Different forms of the same general activity may be distinguished by different minimum competencies. Playing in a string quartet calls for competence far exceeding that needed to play in a rhythm band, yet both activities are classed as "playing musical instruments." The degree of competence required may be assessed with reference to the entire population; or competence may be assessed relatively, with specific reference to the population segment to which the participants belong (e.g., teen-age boys).

5. *Provision for participant interactiveness.* The way the activity-setting locates and engages participants so that interaction among them is required or provoked. In group discussions that adhere to formal procedures, most statements are directed to the chairman. In bridge, players oppose each other in teams of two, bidding and playing follow a strict order, and "table-talk" is often confined within limits. In many types of team sports, players are allocated certain portions of the area and even opposing players to "cover." Interaction may be verbal and/or nonverbal.

6. *Reward structure.* The types of rewards available, their abundance or scarcity, and the manner in which they are distributed. All activities are capable of producing gratifications. They may be inherent in the activity-setting, as with winning, or they may be personal rewards such as those intrinsic to making music and creating attractive or useful objects. Gratifications may also derive from receiving praise for excelling, releasing tension legitimately, improving skill, and so on. Each activity provides distinctive types of rewards for its participants.

Rewards may be scarce or abundant; for example, a weekend of group camping may offer more rewards than a chess game for many participants. The distribution of rewards can be distinguished from their scarcity or abundance, although these characteristics are related. Obviously, if there are fewer rewards than participants, rewards cannot be equally distributed. Whatever intrinsic gratifications are derived by all players through participation in competitive play, only one side can win. In many activities certain positions or roles provide greater rewards for their occupants than do others. Thus, in orchestral playing, the conductor, first violinist, and solo players gain rewards in addition to those earned by all participants. Similarly, in baseball, the pitcher, catcher, and basemen may gain greater rewards than outfielders.

All activities can be assessed with respect to each of these activity-setting dimensions. To illustrate the application of these dimensions, two contrasting types of activities are evaluated in Table 1. Ratings are given in terms of high, medium, and low, where such a scale is appropriate. "Arts and Crafts" refer to such activities as woodworking; "Swimming" denotes noncompetitive free-play in the water. The two activities are conceived as occurring in a children's camp situation and involve group participation with an adult.

A number of shortcomings in this scheme must be recognized. The dimensions are not entirely mutually exclusive and tend to overlap at some points. And they are perhaps not inclusive of all relevant activity characteristics. Difficulty arises in rating activities along these dimensions without standard scales on which they can be assessed. Despite its limitations, the analysis provides criteria for determining the kinds of constituent per-

TABLE 1.   Analysis of Activity-setting Dimensions for Arts and Crafts and for Swimming

Dimensions	Arts and Crafts	Swimming
1. Prescriptiveness	1. HIGH. Patterned sequence of steps. Delayed gratification.	1. LOW. No behavior required. Within limits, one may do as he wishes.
2. Controls	2. HIGH. Staff typically control availability of materials, tools, technique and assistance. Tools and materials impose own constraints.	2. LOW. Staff typically intervene only when behavior exceeds permissible limits of safety.
3. Movement	3. LOW for whole body. HIGH for hands, etc.	3. HIGH. All degrees of movement for all parts of body.
4. Competence	4. VARIABLE. Depends on specific project being made.	4. LOW. Wading requires only ability to walk. Full swimming, diving, etc., require greater competence.
5. Interactiveness	5. LOW to MEDIUM. Individual task orientations and little attraction to others' behavior limits interaction. Close physical contact in small area induces some interaction. High adult control induces interaction with adult.	5. HIGH. No barriers to maximum interaction by all participants. Many people in confined area interact physically while participating.
6. Rewards	6. Types: Mastery of tools, production of valued article, closeness to assisting adult. Distribution: Wide. Everyone has opportunity to gain rewards (if tools and supplies are ample), and some may excel.	6. Types: Maximum freedom of movement, bodily self-expression, mastery of method. Distribution: Wide. Everyone has equal opportunity for basic rewards; greater competence provides greater rewards.

formances that are required by diverse activities. On this basis, the practitioner can choose activities or modify selective aspects of them, with reference to certain of the particular behavioral experiences he wishes to induce for his client participants. (Consideration of any program activity must, of course, take into account the physical, social, and emotional attributes of the participants.) The dimensions do not immediately lead to predictions about different *respondent* behaviors that may be associated with them, but differences in the dimensions between activities can be noted without one's being able to anticipate which respondent behaviors will vary.

DIMENSIONAL VARIANCE AND RESPONDENT BEHAVIOR

Given specific participants, if the activity-setting of two or more of their activities vary with regard to a single dimension, what differences in respondent behaviors might be expected? A number of predictions are presented below.

1. Prescriptiveness of the pattern of constituent performances.

   a. Highly prescriptive activities are likely to be less attractive than less prescriptive activities.

   b. High prescriptiveness is likely to result in a channeling and constricting of behavior.

   c. High prescriptiveness is likely to result in high fatigue and high satiation.

2. Institutionalized controls governing participant activity.

   a. The greater the exercise of controls and their concentration in one or a few persons, the greater the interaction of others with and dependence upon the one or few.

   b. Emphasis on formal controls is likely to freeze the form of the activity and to reduce innovation in rules, etc.

   c. Emphasis on informal controls by participants is likely to increase their pressures on each other to conform.

3. Provision for physical movement.

   a. If movement is specialized (as in instrument playing), the less the bodily movement, the greater the likelihood of fatigue.

   b. The greater the bodily movement, the greater the likelihood of physical interaction and, perhaps, physical aggressiveness.

4. Competence required for performance.

   a. High minimum competence is likely to result in lower interaction among participants.

b. High minimum competence is likely to shift rewards from inter-personal gratifications to those of task performance.

c. High minimum competence accompanied by high prescriptive-ness is likely to induce a strong task orientation.

5. Provision for participant interactiveness.

a. High interactiveness is likely to result in high involvement and effort.

b. Highly facilitated interaction leads to cooperativeness, high sentiment, and friendly relations.

c. Highly hindered interaction leads to competitiveness, rivalry, and hostility.

6. Reward structure.

a. *Type.* The greater the range and variety in the type of desired and expected rewards, the greater the likelihood of attraction for most participants.

b. *Abundance* or *scarcity.* Scarcity of rewards is likely to result in competitiveness, rivalry, and unequal distribution of power.

c. *Distribution.* (1) The more broadly and evenly distributed the rewards, the greater the likelihood of cohesiveness, trust, co-operation, productivity, and responsibility. (2) The more unevenly distributed the rewards, the greater the likelihood of rivalry, com-petition, conflict, factions, and distrust. (3) The greater the dis-crepancy between expected and actual (earned) rewards, the greater the likelihood of frustration, dissatisfaction, and with-drawal.

The general predictions of respondent behavior provide a tool for differentiating between activities that are similar in most respects. Clearly, the differences between arts and crafts and free swimming are too obvious to require close analysis of their contrasting respondent behaviors. But for a rough test and for illustrative purposes, the predictions may be applied to these activities.

1. Prescriptiveness.

a. Arts and crafts are more prescriptive than swimming and, among children, usually less preferred.

b. Arts and crafts behavior is manifestly constricted compared to the expansiveness of swimming.

c. Satiation is probably greater for arts and crafts with typically shorter periods of involvement than for swimming.

2. Controls.

a. Participant interaction with and dependence upon the arts and crafts instructor is greater than upon the swimming lifeguard.

b. Emphasis on formal controls may be introduced into either activity (e.g., following the craft pattern, instructor directions, etc.; swimming instruction, curtailing of free play, etc.).

3. Movement.

a. Arts and crafts permit movement of fewer body parts and less of the whole body than swimming. Swimming is less specialized and more strenuous, but probably less fatiguing.

b. Swimming involves greater bodily movement and, typically, considerable aggressive play.

4. Competence.

a. The more difficult the arts and crafts project, the greater the individual concentration and the less the interaction. Swimming requires low minimum competence and involves much interaction.

b. Arts and crafts performance, in contrast to swimming, involves greater emphasis on achievement and production. It is also more frequently engaged in alone than is swimming.

c. Certain types of arts and crafts performance involve great concentration on technical procedures.

5. Interactiveness.

a. Swimming is characterized by higher activity than arts and crafts and has potential for greater interactiveness.

b. It seems likely that, by limiting excessive aggression, swimming induces somewhat more liking and friendlier relations than arts and crafts.

c. Competitive swimming (e.g., water polo) leads to considerable rivalry; rivalry may also result in arts and crafts work when participants must take turns with tools and equipment.

6. Rewards.

a. The attractiveness of both swimming and arts and crafts may be increased by extending the facilities and equipment, and the alternatives permitted participants.

b. Rivalry stemming from limited essential resources (tools and supplies, instructor's time) is more likely to occur in arts and crafts than in swimming.

c. 1. rewards may be similarly distributed among participants for both activities.

2. the greater tendency in arts and crafts to shift rewards to achievement probably leads to more competition.

3. discrepancies between the expected rewards of achievement and actual accomplishment are greater in arts and crafts, with frustration and dissatisfaction more commonly observed.

It is apparent on the basis of this analysis that two activities, intuitively known to be different, can be distinguished in terms of specific dimensions and the expected behaviors associated with them. It appears that certain predictions based on these dimensions are roughly supported when tested against common experience with the activities.

Activity-setting dimensions focus attention upon the activities' common features affecting participants. Behavior variations of participants engaged in the same activity may be attributed largely to different positions held in the activity-setting, e.g., when they are on the losing rather than the winning side, or when they play different positions in a softball game. These circumstances subject participants to different conditions and should result in differing responses and experiences. Of course, differences among individuals result in dissimilar behaviors, even within the same activity-setting. Variations in skill, competence, intelligence, and motivation all give rise to differences among participants' behavior patterns. Nevertheless, the behavioral consequences of individual attributes are conditioned or limited by the activity-setting and by the individual's location within it. For example, intelligence is more likely to influence behavior in a game of checkers or chess than in free swimming.

Behavioral differences among individuals participating in the same activity may be identified and assessed in several ways:

1. As variations due to different locations in the same activity (e.g., being on a winning or losing team)
2. As deviations from the required pattern of constituent performances (e.g., ignoring the ball in a baseball game)
3. As permissible elaborations or modifications of the constituent performances (e.g., skipping around the bases after a home run)
4. As specific respondent behaviors manifested while participating in an activity (e.g., high anxiety, passivity, etc.)

This list permits the practitioner to identify more precisely which are the *uniquely individual* behaviors, and to attribute these in part to elements in the activity-setting. However, first a focus on the activity-setting and its consequences is required, rather than on the individual differences among participants.

The primary purpose of this scheme is not merely to provide the practitioner with a framework for observation and analysis. Such a framework is necessary to provide a sound basis for the selection of specific activities that are likely to achieve the particular consequences pertinent to treatment objectives. This scheme also directs the practitioner's attention to concrete features of activity that can be deliberately modified to achieve desired consequences. The dimensions outlined suggest that the practitioner can obtain different effects for participants by increasing the level of competence, by altering the rules, or by decreasing participant interactiveness. No attempt has been made here to consider particular client characteristics and interests. However, the practitioner must refer to these just as he must design a program with regard to specific treatment objectives. This formulation makes it more feasible for practitioners to "prescribe strategically activities for specific children and groups; it becomes possible to make activity-settings congruent with diagnostic knowledge and with therapeutic aims." (Gump and Sutton-Smith, 1955)

Lest the emphasis on concrete activities be misleading, the practitioner must also remember to be concerned about program sequences: the introduction of activities during each group session, and their continuity or variation from one session to the next. The group worker may wish to heighten or offset the particular benefits and limitations of an activity in the next session. Attention must be given to the cumulative effects of several program experiences, to the transition problems of moving from one to another, and to the residual or spill-over effects that persist beyond the group meeting. Over several group sessions, the program must be adjusted to the processes of group development and to increased skills and sophistication among participants.

REFERENCES

GUMP, PAUL V., BRIAN SUTTON-SMITH, AND FRITZ REDL
   1953—"Influence of camp activities upon camper behavior," Detroit: Wayne University School of Social Work. (Dittoed)
GUMP, PAUL V. AND BRIAN SUTTON-SMITH
   1955—"Activity-setting and social interaction: A field study," *American Journal of Orthopsychiatry,* 25.
   1955—"The 'it' role in children's games," *The Group,* 17.
GUMP, PAUL V.
   1955—"The ingredients of games and their impact upon players," Detroit: Wayne University School of Social Work. (Dittoed)

14.

Program Activities:
Their Selection and Use
in a Therapeutic Milieu

JAMES K. WHITTAKER*

> A boy, alone, sits on a fence staring sadly, a tear wending its way down his face, at a group of children playing in a yard. This is the lonely isolate, hurting inside to be able to join in but so threatened by relationships with himself and others that he cannot. (DeNoon, 1965)

Anyone who has worked with disturbed children will recognize the plight of the "empty" child: the child who cannot make friends easily or who considers himself so devoid of marketable skills that nobody would want to be his friend. Any treatment plan for such a youngster would have to include his participation in carefully selected and supervised activity programs, where he could begin to learn new peer relating skills and develop his own embryonic sense of self worth. Skilled clinicians have come to think of activity programs not merely as a pleasant adjunct to psychotherapy, but as a meaningful and necessary part of a child's treatment. Redl and Wineman speak of activity program as a "full-fledged therapeutic tool;" they state quite emphatically that: "Programming can play a specific role in the clinical task on its own, not only a 'time filling' substitute for psychiatric contacts during the rest of the day." (Redl and Wineman, 1957:393)

* The author wishes to acknowledge Kathleen Whittaker, Barbara Riggs, Ruth Ann Smullin, Winslow Meyers, Bob Bruzzese, John Magnani, Dana Eddy and Rick Jessel—counselors at The George Walker Home for Children, Inc., in Needham, Massachusetts—who have helped to prove that activities really constitute "full-fledged" therapeutic treatment. A special debt of gratitude is owed to Thomas Gearhart whose thoughts on the selection of activities provided a partial basis for one of the sections of this paper.

Theorists have shown that activities have a reality and a behavior influencing power in their own right (Gump and Sutton-Smith, 1965:414). Others have pointed out that specific developmental needs of children are met through activities: mastery of skills, release of aggression, mastery of relationships and the art of sublimation (Konopka, 1954:141–146). Play, as described by Bettelheim (1950:218), is that area where the child tests and develops his independence and where he learns to hold his own with his peers. Obviously an important part of the child's world, "play" should not be looked upon as a uniform event or as a totally random activity. Piaget (1950) has given some insight into the complex normative structure governing what at first glance appears to be unplanned activity. Erikson (1950:194–195) gives some insight into the potentialities of child's play as a medium for learning:

> Child's play is not the equivalent of adult play . . . it is not recreation. The adult steps sidewards into another reality; the playing child advances forward to new stages of mastery.

Finally, Redl (1966:87) and others have noted the tremendous impact of the structure of games and activities on those participating in them.

With or without the intervention of helping adults, activities can benefit both the individual child and the group. Activities also provide an opportunity to practice group participation, to experiment with new roles in a small group situation, and to try out newly acquired peer relating skills. Participation in activities may enable individual children to acquire a sense of competency and mastery over their environment.

Activities also may be used as diagnostic tools to assess not only individual children, but also group structure and decision-making processes. Most of the case records accompanying children to residential treatment centers have a surplus of interpsychic evaluative data, but a dearth of material pertaining to how the child functions in a group situation. Often there is awareness of a child's learning deficiencies, but the fact is overlooked that many children simply do not know how to have fun, much less how to compete or how to compromise. The mastery of program activities can provide concrete and marketable peer skills. Finally, if it is truly believed that an activity program is not merely a pleasant addition to psychotherapy but functions as a "full-fledged therapeutic tool," then the activity program must be a guaranteed commodity in the therapeutic milieu and not something held out solely as a reward for "good" behavior.

Many of the presenting problems of the youngsters—poor peer relations, aggressive outbursts and low self images—can be treated better in the context of an activity than in a fifty-minute office interview. It is, therefore, important that the use of this "tool" not be limited to those times when children are in good psychological shape.

HOW TO SELECT AN ACTIVITY

The selection of successful and beneficial activity programs involves evaluating such variables as skill and interests of the children, staff coverage, available materials, and the mood of the group. There are other slightly more distant variables that may be crucial to the success of a particular activity, including weather, time of day and other "atmospheric variables." Nothing can ruin a carefully planned baseball game quicker than an unexpected cloudburst; pity the poor child-care worker who does not have an alternate program available.

One of the questions most frequently asked by child-care workers is, "How do I know which activity to choose?" Every worker knows that he can do certain things even before the start of the activity that will influence the course the activity will follow. Group work practitioners know that manipulation of space, time, props and materials can alter the way in which groups will approach and carry out activities (Churchill, 1959); but the activities themselves also have "built in" dimensions which have a good deal to do with the behavior of the participants and which are less well known to child-care workers than they might be.

Comparison of alternate program activities along the dimensions proposed by Vinter in Chapter 13 will help the child-care worker to identify activities that can best serve his group's purpose. The worker's evaluation of certain individual and group variables should also influence his selection of a specific activity for a particular group.

Individual Variables

1. *Skill.* The level of the child's competence to participate in activities. Skills include physical dexterity and motor coordination, as well as specific athletic, mechanical or crafts skills. Many children come to social workers with relatively few specific skills, though their interest might be keen in specific areas. Basically, a question focused on this variable asks, "What is this child capable of doing right now?"

2. *Motivation.* The child's willingness to participate in activities. The more complex and difficult the activity, the higher the child's motivation will have to be to insure successful completion of the activity. Children with relatively low motivation to join in activities may be lured into participation by activities whose rewards are both immediate and abundant.

3. *On tap control.* The amount of self control available to the child at a given time. One would not recommend a game of chess for a hyperactive child who has been struggling to control his behavior in school all

day. With hyperactive, aggressive children, there is not always time to wait for them to be completely in control before attempting to engage them in an activity. Rather, they may be engaged in an activity for the purpose of controlling their behavior.

Group Variables

In planning a program, one has to keep in mind certain group phenomena that may influence the course of the activity. Some of the more important variables are group solidarity (cohesion), group composition, and group mood. Given a loosely assembled group with little cohesion and solidarity, parallel activities might be more appropriate than those requiring a good deal of interaction and interdependence among the members (e.g., model building, rather than soccer). As for group composition, the more heterogeneous the grouping, the more difficult it will be to find an activity which all members can participate in and enjoy. Finally, the child-care worker must use his own sensitivity to assess the mood of the group. A spontaneous suggestion for an unplanned hike may be just the solution for youngsters during the latency period who have been using massive amounts of control to complete a project in school and seem ready to "bust out."

The typical child-care worker will not go through all of the activity-setting dimensions, individual variables, and group variables every time he plans a program; trying to control all variables before making a program decision would be disastrous. However, careful attention to activity dimensions and individual and group variables can facilitate planning for particularly difficult activity times; and they may be particularly useful as guidelines to dissect and analyze particular successes as well as utter disasters.

The "goodness of fit" between any theoretical model and its "real life" counterpart is at best a tentative union. With this in mind, the application of the Vinter material along with the individual variables should represent to the worker a somewhat incomplete framework to help him answer the question, "How do I select an activity?" There will inevitably be some disagreement as to the "ratings" assigned to different activities, as well as to the eight types of program participants identified below. If the following exercise provides even a rudimentary framework for the analysis of activities and the people who participate in them, its purpose will have been well served.

The eight "participant types" in Table 1 represent all of the possible combinations when one controls individual variables of *Skill, Motivation* and *Control.*

TABLE 1.   Types of Program Participants

Participant Type	Skill	Motivation	Control
Type "A"	High	High	High
Type "B"	High	High	Low
Type "C"	High	Low	Low
Type "D"	Low	Low	Low
Type "E"	Low	Low	High
Type "F"	Low	High	High
Type "G"	Low	High	Low
Type "H"	High	Low	High

The following behavioral descriptions will help to illustrate:

Type A

This child has high skill, motivation and control; he is able to participate in a wide range of individual and group activities. He can perform demanding tasks for moderate reward and is able to postpone gratification. This youngster probably "programs" quite well for himself.

Type B

Highly skilled and motivated, this child is plagued by a poor control structure; any activity for him must substitute external controls for his own lack of internal control. He is easily swayed by others, thus should avoid mass group activities, but he can certainly function well in small group situations.

Type C

This child has an abundance of natural ability, but is unable (or unwilling) to utilize it effectively; rewards for him should be abundant and immediate. Controls must be provided externally, but the fewer rules the better. This child will probably work best in a one-to-one situation.

Type D

This youngster presents a real challenge; he is poorly motivated, relatively "empty" of skills and has extremely poor control over his own impulses. He needs very simple activities that assure almost "instant success;" a good deal of external support is required to supplement his poorly integrated control structure. Finally, a good deal of space should be provided for physical movement and this child should not be expected to stick to any one thing for a very long period of time.

Type E

This child is poorly motivated and unskilled but presents no great control problem. He is probably a shy, withdrawing youngster who feels rebuffed by his peers and has a very low self image. He too needs immediate successes and uncomplicated games and projects. Lots of help and praise will enhance his development; the rest of the group could help in this respect.

Type F

This child has good motivation and control, but a low skill level. He is a clumsy youngster, bad at athletics and group games. He is willing and able to work on mastery experiences and could probably use a plan for skill development so that his ego will not be crushed every time he misses the basket or strikes out.

Type G

This child has low skills, a faulty control structure, but really wants to "do well." He must begin with activities that require a low degree of competence and have plenty of provision for physical movement. Probably the most difficult task with this particular child will be getting him to accept the fact that skill or control take time to develop and that he should not become discouraged in the process.

Type H

This youngster has good ability and control, but is poorly motivated to participate in activities. Immediately the thought comes of the sociologically trained delinquent who stands aloof from the "fun and games" of the residence. The key here is, of course, relationship development and finding the most meaningful reward that will enhance his entry into the group (peer status, friendship, privileges).

"Typing" specific children, according to their level of skill, degree of motivation or willingness to participate, and amount of self-control, is tentative at best; skill, motivation and self-control are difficult to assess. It should be somewhat easier to quantify and compare dimensions of program alternatives according to the extent to which they are *prescriptive*; the degree of *control* to which they subject participants; the extent to which they require or permit physical *movement*; the extent to which they provide *rewards*; the level of *competence* they require; and the degree of *interaction* they require or provoke. In Table 2, numerous familiar program activities are analyzed and compared by quantifying all six dimensions of the Vinter scale.

It now becomes possible to identify certain activities as being especially suitable (or inappropriate) for certain types of participants. Monopoly can be seen to be a good activity for Type A and Type H and possibly for Type C; it is clearly not a good choice for Types D and E.

Furthermore, it is possible to project for each type a particularly appropriate set of activity dimensions, an "ideal activity profile," as in Table 3.

Thus, Type E (poorly skilled and motivated, but presenting no great control problem) would require an activity that has a low degree of prescriptiveness, but provides a goodly amount of external control. In addition, the rewards would have to be fairly abundant, but the competency needed to attain them would have to be minimal. Hence, he might try finger painting or papier mâché, but definitely not origami or copper enamelling. In either case, it would be good to substitute for the lack of internal control by keeping the group small and the counselor close to the child. Outdoor games might include tag or dodge ball, but not Chinese tag or baseball as they require a higher level of beginning competence.

The ultimate value of such an Ideal Activity Profile depends upon:

1. the adequacy of the individual variables on which the definition of participant types is based
2. the manner in which the individual variables are assessed in individual cases
3. the accuracy of Vinter's activity-setting dimensions and of their quantification
4. the manner in which they are applied to specific activities

WHEN TO USE AN ACTIVITY

The maintenance of the rather delicate balance between individual and group psychotherapy, remedial education and program activities is

TABLE 2. Activity-setting Dimensions of Program Activities

Activity	Prescriptiveness	Control	Movement	Rewards	Competence	Interaction
Swimming	Low	Low	High	High	Low	Low
Model Building	High	High	Low	High	High	Low
Clay Molding	Low	Low	Low	High	Low	Low
Finger Painting	Low	Low	Medium	High	Low	Low
Papier Mâché	Low	Medium	Low	High	Low	Low
Origami	High	High	Low	High	High	Low
Copper Enamelling	Medium	High	Low	High	Medium	Low
Lanyard Making	Medium	Medium	Low	High	Low	Low
Baseball	High	High	Medium High	Medium	High	High
Touch Football	Medium	Medium	High	High	Medium	High
Hockey	Medium	High	High	Medium	High	High
Kick Ball	Low Medium	Medium	Medium	Medium	Medium	Medium
Dodge Ball	Low	Low	High	High	Low	High
Red Rover	Medium	Medium	High	Medium	Low	High

251

TABLE 2. Activity-setting Dimensions of Program Activities (Continued)

Activity	Prescriptiveness	Control	Movement	Rewards	Competence	Interaction
Tag	Low	Low	High	High	Low	High
Chinese Tag	Medium	Medium	Medium High	High	Medium High	High
Red Light	High	High	Medium	Medium	Low	Low
Simon Says	High	High	Medium	Medium	High	Medium Low
Hide 'n Seek	Low	Medium	Medium	High Medium	Low	Low
Checkers	High	High	Low	Medium	Medium	Medium
Chess	High	High	Low	High	High	High
Monopoly	High	High	Low	Medium High	High	High
Chutes 'n Ladders	Medium	Medium	Medium	Medium	Medium	Medium

TABLE 3.   Ideal Activity Profile

Participant Types	Prescrip-tiveness	Control	Movement	Rewards	Compe-tence	Interaction
"A"	High	Low-High	Low	Medium	High	High
"B"	Medium	High	High	Medium	High	Medium Low
"C"	Low	High	High	High	High	Low
"D"	Low	Low	High	High	Low	Low
"E"	Low	High	Medium	High	Low	Medium
"F"	High	High	Medium	Medium	Low	High
"G"	Low	Low	High	Medium	Low	Low
"H"	High	High	Low	High	High	High

one of the most crucial issues in any good therapeutic residence. Probing the depths of a child's psyche, helping him to overcome a learning problem, or teaching him an alternative behavior are all laudable goals, but the milieu must provide some respite from the rigors and pains of psychic change. Skillful use of activities can often initiate and foment real therapeutic progress. For many youngsters, activities may constitute the key enhancement of growth and development and may also be immensely useful in managing behavior.

Transition Time Activities

All child-care workers face the problem of moving children through the routines and activities of the day. Children must arise in the morning, go off to school, come to lunch and supper, prepare for bedtime and group activities; indeed, much of the child's day is spent moving toward or away from the routines of the milieu. If the worker depends solely upon his "authority" to move children through the day, he soon finds himself making "issues" over fairly simple rules and getting into power struggles where the only goal of the child seems to be, "Whatever you tell me to do, I'm going to do the opposite!" If, on the other hand, the counselor resorts solely to direct appeals, he soon finds himself laying his relationship on the line for every demand and request. Direct appeal also presupposes that the child is motivated to follow the routine (go to school, come to lunch, etc.).

Certain activities are useful management tools. These activities are by definition short-term, since they end as soon as the child is engaged in the routine. Their primary purpose is diversion; if possible, their focus should be on the counselor as the "central figure." Thus, games like "Follow the Leader" or "Red Light" have been found to be quite useful in guiding children from the school room to the lunch table. It helps if certain games become associated with certain times of the day, as the child sees the game as a "marker" which indicates the proximity of the particular routine. One counselor made very successful use of a "timing game" with a child who had particular difficulties getting dressed in the morning (Whittaker, 1969).

Waiting for an activity or a routine to begin can often be the source of a great deal of frustration for the impulsive youngster. One therapeutic camp keeps a long rope outside the dining hall to be used for group high jumping if the dinner bell is late. One need not think of elaborate materials for these diversions. One's own pockets often provide ample props for successful short-term programs. Thus, the stop watch may be used to "see how fast you can run to school;" the penny may be the object of some sleight of hand or the counter in a game of penny-pitch. A few simple card tricks may be enough to keep a group occupied until a broken projector gets fixed. Finally, since these activities are by nature short-term, the counselor might use a whole sequence of them while moving the youngsters from one part of the program to another.

Individual and Group Activities

Activities may be structured around the needs of a particular child or may be designed for the benefit of the entire group. A newcomer to the group might have a particular skill or interest which could serve as his inroad to the group if included in a carefully prepared activity by the child-care worker. Generally speaking, it is good to think of activities that tax the control of the individual child only slightly at first; here, the depersonalized control of the activity is substituted for the internal control the child is lacking. For example, the counselor might wish to outline the rules for dodge ball, rather than leave each dispute to be arbitrated by the children.

The whole question of when to use program activities carries with it a certain aversion to the whole notion of programming. No one likes to think of himself as being "programmed" and the thought of a rigidly designed activity structure (swimming at 2:00, arts and crafts at 3:00) does not take account of the creative abilities of the child-care worker, much less the needs of the impulsive child. The goal should be to weave activities into the fabric of the milieu, taking into account the needs, interests, and limitations of the children, as well as the abilities of the counselor and the resources available to him.

One way to avoid the problem of rigid programming is through the project method. Here the counselor starts with the kernel of an idea from a child or group of children and builds it into an activity or series of activities that may carry on for days and provide many levels of rewards for the participants. The following group log may help to explain one such program.

> Today Bobby greeted me and told me that the class had just concluded the unit on American Indians. He expressed some interest in making a bow and arrow, but said that "It probably wouldn't work anyway." I approached Vince and Rick on the idea and they seemed to be enthusiastic; the four of us set about gathering sticks for the arrows and discovered a natural "teepee" in some large bushes. Two boys began at once to clear the area while Bobby began work on his bow and arrow. By now, Carol, [counselor] had become involved and began making Indian bracelets and trinkets out of scraps of leather. I spoke with Linda [teacher] after school and she said she would introduce the idea of an Indian exhibit in school . . .

This project which began with one boy's idea to make a bow and arrow culminated in an Indian day about a week later, complete with ceremonial dancing, totem-pole making and a cookout. Within the general framework of the program, there was tremendous room for individual tastes and skills. Thus, one child spent most of his time painting shields, while another was engaged in the rather formidable task of "guarding the campsite."

In short, the richest source of inspiration for program may come from the children themselves and may require the child-care worker to refine, modify, and build upon the idea of the child.

USING ACTIVITIES IN A THERAPEUTIC MILIEU

The final section of this paper deals with specific techniques and program hints culled from the collective experience of many child-care workers. These suggestions and observations reflect the goal of every child-care worker in a therapeutic residence to relate the world of fun and activities to the child whose ability to enjoy success is often overshadowed by his fear that "I can't do anything right."

1. One of the worker's key tools in executing a successful activity

is his own enthusiasm. The counselor, who is actively involved in the game and who is quite obviously enjoying himself, provides a model for the child of how a person relates to an activity. It is no small task to juggle the roles of "helping adult" and "playmate" and counselors should guard against becoming so involved in the activity that they cannot step out from time to time to manage a crisis.

2. Activities should be ended when they are going well and while the children are enjoying themselves. Many counselors have experienced dismay when the activity they have been running all evening crumbles before their eyes when it is left to run out. It is better to leave the child with a positive picture of the activity at its high point, rather than with a negative picture of its demise.

3. The timing and sequence of activities are important variables to control. For example, large group activities first thing in the morning usually are not successful because the individual egos of the youngsters are too fragmented and shaky to be exposed to mass group games. Similarly, body contact sports right before bedtime are likely to involve the group in erotic and aggressive play at a time when children are undressing and taking showers. (By the way, the myth should be exploded for all time that "a few laps around the track" or a "wrestling match" will "tire them out and make them ready for sleep.")

4. Often, the counselor must rejuvenate and alter old activities to make them more attractive to youngsters. One counselor changed the old and familiar game of "ghosts" to "rocketships" and enjoyed a good deal of success with it. Allowance also must be made for the child's inability to delay gratification. A rapid rotation of hitters may be better than a conventional game of baseball.

5. With ego-damaged children whose skill level is often pitifully low, too much emphasis must not be placed on the "finished product." Similarly, the counselor should complement his own skills with those of the child and not be overly concerned over "who did what."

6. Despite the most careful planning of an activity, the counselor may be faced with seeing it turn to dust before his eyes according to the pathologies of the individual youngster or the mood of the group. He must always be ready to switch activities in midstream as the need arises.

7. Many child-care workers ask the question, "How do I start an activity?" The answer is simply, "By doing it!" It is quite easy to fall into the trap of wanting to "get the whole group together" (and quiet) before beginning, when often the lure of the activity itself will do most to interest the youngsters.

8. Generally speaking, with a younger group, it is better to begin with parallel activities, i.e., those which do not require interaction between the members. Thus, it is better to have six individual model ships and not

one giant aircraft carrier for "everyone to work on." Participation and facilitative interaction are goals to be sought as the group develops.

9. Similarly, when beginning to work with a younger group, it is wise for the child-care worker to reserve the greater portion of decision making for himself. This somewhat alleviates the problem of each child having to negotiate with every other child about what the activity is to be.

10. Finally, the child-care worker should not attempt activities in which he is not skilled or does not feel comfortable, just because he feels a need to be the "complete counselor." It is far better to develop skills and interests that are most important to him, for there is usually a wide enough variation among child-care staff members to expose children to a whole range of different activities.

REFERENCES

BETTELHEIM, BRUNO
  1950—*Love Is Not Enough*, Glencoe, Illinois: Free Press.
CHURCHILL, SALLIE R.
  1959—"Prestructuring group content," *Social Work* (July).
DENOON, BARBARA
  1965—"Horses, bait and chocolate cake," in Henry W. Maier (Ed.), *Group Work as Part of Residential Treatment*, New York: National Association of Social Workers.
ERIKSON, ERIK H.
  1950—*Childhood and Society*, New York: W. W. Norton and Co.
GUMP, PAUL AND BRIAN SUTTON-SMITH
  1965—"Therapeutic play techniques," *Conflict in the Classroom*, Belmont, California: Wadsworth Publishing Company.
KONOPKA, GISELA
  1954—*Social Group Work in Children's Institutions*, New York: Association Press.
PIAGET, JEAN
  1950—*Play, Dreams and Imitations in Childhood*, New York: W. W. Norton and Co.
REDL, FRITZ
  1966—*When We Deal With Children*, Glencoe, Illinois: Free Press.
REDL, FRITZ AND DAVID WINEMAN
  1957—*The Aggressive Child*, Glencoe, Illinois: Free Press.
WHITTAKER, JAMES K.
  1969—"Managing wake-up behavior," in Albert Treischman, James Whittaker, and Larry Brendtro, *The Other Twenty Three Hours*, Chicago: Aldine Publishing Company, pp. 120–136.

15.

Planning for Termination
of the Group

CAROLE JOHNSON

Writers in the field of social work have tended to emphasize the early stages of group work or social treatment because of the importance of making diagnoses, setting goals, and initiating client-worker relationships. Much has been said about the anxiety, fears, and expectations of the client as he enters treatment and how such feelings affect treatment. But only a few have chosen to deal with the feelings and needs of the client as termination of treatment approaches. Fox, Nelson and Bolman (1969:63) point to this deficiency in the literature. They attribute it, in part, to the defensiveness of workers in dealing with their own emotional loss in termination. Through the course of treatment, the worker, as well as the client, has formed a relationship that he may not want to give up. The reality of termination may be as difficult to face for the worker as for his client. Social workers have been given little help in facing termination or in planning for it, partly due to an overemphasis on initial diagnoses in social work literature, theory, and practice.

If the needs of individual group members—or the worker—at the time of termination have been neglected, the group level phenomena of termination have been ignored. A particular issue faces the group worker in the initial and middle stages of treatment: the need to build and maintain cohesion among the group members. This concern may so occupy the worker's thoughts that he forgets that cohesion must be diminished as the group ends, or a new form of cohesion created to substitute for the continuation of the group. The termination phase can pose still another difficulty for the worker. At this point, he must evaluate the success or failure of the client in treatment, and hence his own success or failure in providing appropriate and adequate treatment. The fear of measuring one's own success or failure may be another reason for the lack of attention to termination. Whatever the reason for its neglect, the termination process is one of the important stages in the treatment sequence; and it needs to be understood as such.

In their discussion of termination, Whitaker and Lieberman (1964: 132) do not see a need for focusing on the termination process per se. They believe that the emotional issues brought forth by termination should be dealt with during the course of treatment, so that particular attention to them at the end should be minimal. Whitaker and Lieberman's view of the treatment group is substantially different from that of others interested in the use of groups for treatment and rehabilitaion. They pay scant attention to the roles played by the clients outside the group. Instead, they see the life of the group as an end in itself, with little connection to what the clients are doing when they are not in the group. Other group work models do the reverse; the roles of the clients outside the group are seen as the loci where change is desired, and the group is seen as the means by which this change is made. In these models, termination is important because clients are anticipated to continue the changed role behaviors that were begun and reinforced in the group. In most cases the loss of the therapeutic group and the loss of the worker is a new experience, one that the group members have not had before in the course of their group life. Consideration of termination and separation can be brought up, dealt with, or made relevant, prior to the beginning of the termination process. The growth that hopefully has taken place within the group members can help them to deal with separation when the time comes.

REASONS FOR AND GROUP REACTIONS TO TERMINATION

Ideally, a treatment group is terminated at the time when maximum gains have been made by the group members. Sarri and Galinsky (Chapter 5 in this volume) offer four reasons for ending the group. *First,* in the ideal situation, the goals set at the beginning for individual members have been achieved, and they can be expected to function satisfactorily and continue to progress on their own. *Second,* the length of time the group may meet has been predetermined by agency policy. *Third*, the group cannot achieve a sufficient level of integration, perhaps due to lack of commitment by the members to the group's purposes, to pressures from the environment, or to inadequacies in the worker's services. *Fourth* and last, the group may need to terminate because the group's mechanisms for coping with internal or external pressures have been maladaptive. Whatever the reason for termination, Sarri and Galinsky say that the group should be ended in a manner that will not be harmful to the members.

In groups that end because of achievement of the goals set, Sarri and Galinsky suggest that the members be involved in the planning of termination. In their treatment model, members have been involved in goal setting in the early phases of the group's development. Termination planning centers on evaluating whether goals have been met and to what degree. Sarri and Galinsky (1967:94) do not specify how group members are to be included in termination planning when the group is malfunctioning. They imply that, in such cases, the worker makes the decision to terminate. It would seem that, at the very least, the reasons for termination should be explained to the group; the group should be given the opportunity to discuss the reasons and come to some understanding of them. Even in these negative instances, it would seem desirable to identify the accomplishments made and to be aware of the members' feelings.

There are differences between termination of a "closed" group, that is, one in which the members enter and leave the group together, and of an "open" group, whose members enter and leave at different times. Even if only one or a few members are leaving, the group dynamics will change, since the roles of those members leaving will be unfilled, at least momentarily. The group's move to fill these gaps will require a restructuring of the group. Members may expect the group to stay the same in spite of the loss of certain individuals; this may prove to be an unrealistic expectation (Levine, 1967:58–59). The worker must be attuned to the needs of members who are leaving the group no matter how many leave at one time.

SEPARATION AND GOAL ATTAINMENT

The experience of termination has two major components, and the worker should help the group be aware of and deal with them. One is the reality of the group's separation, and the other is goal attainment or achievement. Even if termination has not been discussed, the group may show clues that suggest that the members are ready for termination. The members may talk about the gains they have made, and they may express more confidence in the future. Irregularity in attendance, breaking of interpersonal ties, and finding new ties outside the group indicate a weakening of cohesiveness. The structure of the group may become more flexible, with the discarding of old roles or changes in the time, frequency, and place of meeting. The worker may choose to have shorter or less frequent meetings during the termination stage to help members become independent. The members' norms may be in closer harmony with community norms. Communication within the group may become more free and easy. Finally, there may be a lessening of group controls and a strengthening of members' inner controls (Northen, 1969: 225-226).

The group may maneuver to forestall termination or to cope with it. There are several negative reactions to termination. Often there is a denial that it will happen at all. Group members may forget that the worker has announced it or that the group has discussed it; and they may go on with total disregard for the fact that the group is ending (Northen, 1969:230). Denial may also be expressed by a new super-cohesiveness (Garland, et al., 1965:42). In such cases, the worker or the agency may be perceived as an outside threat against which the group must strengthen their bonds. Earlier patterns of behavior may return, such as an inability to cope with situations or tasks that had been mastered earlier or a reactivation of conflicts between group members. There may be a renewed dependence on the worker. The group may express a desire to begin all over again; or the negative symptoms may recur which serve to say, "We still need the group." This may go along with expressions of uncertainty about being able to function on one's own. Some members may leave precipitiously— "I'll leave you before you leave me." Finally, there may be feelings that the worker is rejecting them, and this may be twisted into a rejection of the worker and of the group by denying the worth of the group and the meaning it has held.

There are also several positive reactions to termination. Group members may reminisce about what the group has done and about relationships that have been formed; they may evaluate progress made by themselves and each other; they may tell about new relationships they are forming outside the group; and they may talk about new activities they are pursuing outside the group (Northen, 1969:231–232).

INDIVIDUAL REACTIONS TO TERMINATION
OF THE GROUP

Group members are likely to have ambivalent feelings about leaving the group. They may be pleased at the goal they have achieved, but they may also have a conflicting feeling of fear at the loss of attention from the worker and the loss of the group's support. Just as there was anxiety at the beginning of the group's development, there now may be anxiety over the need to break the bonds that the group has established (Northen, 1969:228–229). As a group develops it produces a bond between the members, a relationship which allows members to share and interact with one another. When the group is terminating, the intensity of this relationship must diminish. The bond may have been very meaningful; therefore, a skilled worker must guide the group so that termination will not have negative consequences. He may guide the members away from the group by helping them to find pleasure and satisfaction in other relationships and in other groups. Ideally, the group bond may continue to provide support and security and to maintain "road horizons" for members (Konopka, 1963:61–62). The worker should encourage the members to express their feelings about leaving behind their affectional ties with the group. It may be valuable to discuss what has been learned about interpersonal relationships in the group, and how new skills in this area can be or have been carried over to new or old relationships outside the group. Especially in interpersonal relationships, the group lives through its own problems and resolves them, and does not merely reflect on extragroup problems.

Three major types of feelings brought on by termination are cited by Fox, et al. (1969:55). The first includes panic, rage, and a sense of worthlessness, that may stem from equating termination with rejection. The second feeling is that of grief and mourning over the loss of the therapeutic relationships. And the third type of feeling is that of a new sense of maturity and independence, and the need to function on one's own. In order for termination to be a growth experience, the worker should not only permit but elicit the group members' expression of such feelings. He should help clarify what the feelings are and show that they are acceptable feelings. If the worker is experiencing sadness over the ending of the group, he may share it with the group, thereby serving as a model for the honest expression of feelings and demonstrating his "humanness."

Levine (1967:60) says that anger from and within the group is to be expected when members realize that separation is impending. It is often important that this anger be expressed. Sometimes group members will not be able to verbalize the anger directly but will express it by acting to increase interpersonal conflicts within the group. Levine also points out that the group may enter a temporary state of depression, but that this usually will be followed by renewed vigor. There will be some individual and/or collective regression to older, inferior levels of functioning. The worker must not be tempted to "take over" at this time, since this would only prolong the regression and undercut movement toward self-dependence. Sometimes the group may push the worker out while they strive toward self-dependence. In either situation, the worker should do nothing to increase the group's need of him. Instead, he should foster the self-dependence and level of functioning that has been achieved.

INTERVENTION APPROACHES: DIRECT AND INDIRECT

In addition to allowing and encouraging expression of feelings about the coming separation, the worker needs to help the group take stock of the progress it has made. As mentioned before, the group might bring up progress of its own accord; but if it does not, the worker ought to bring it up, particularly when the reason for termination is the achievement of the goals that had been set. The group needs to understand that goal attainment is the reason for termination. Mastering new skills greatly heightens an individual's sense of self-esteem. Often improving members' positive feelings about themselves is an implicit, if not stated, goal of the social work group. Ideally, at the end of each session, each member feels that he has accomplished something individually and collectively with the other members (Wilson and Ryland, 1949:63). At the time of termination, accomplishments need to be reviewed. Throughout treatment and at termination, the worker supports those strengths and ego defenses which serve each client constructively. The worker guides the group interaction in such a way that members may develop new behaviors and new attitudes about themselves in relation to each other (Frey, 1962:38).

The program often serves as the tool by which the purposes for the group are accomplished. The worker organizes the actions of the group by structuring the group experience to achieve the group's purposes, partly by selecting or encouraging activities that permit expression of certain emotions (Frey, 1962:40). The worker needs to anticipate the emotional state of the group, by carefully observing the dynamics of recent group meetings and the stage of development in which the group is functioning. Physical activities for each session should be planned around these anticipated emotional and behavioral states. The items available for use should encourage certain kinds of activities and discourage others. In addition to his planned activities, the worker guides and facilitates the spontaneous discussion that arises (Churchill, 1959:52–59).

Three main kinds of group programs are particularly applicable to the termination stage. These program principles apply to any group, regardless of the ages of the group members. (1) The first is any activity in which the members' success can be assured, since feelings of achievement are especially important at this time. The group and/or the worker may want to repeat activities that have provided pleasure earlier. (2) The second main focus for program activity is the reduction of cohesiveness among group members. The worker wants members to demonstrate to themselves that they can be self-dependent and can achieve on their own. For this reason activities that call for a high degree of interaction or cooperation should not be used. Forms of "parallel" play or activity are more suited to termination. A crafts project, where each member has his own tools and materials and the need for sharing is at a minimum, would be an appropriate termination stage activity. Outdoors, a hike would be better than a softball game since fewer cooperative interactions are called for; a hike offers fewer chances for failure since a softball game requires a number of skills. A hike may also offer an opportunity to explore the environment, which leads to (3) the third focus of termination programming: helping group members reach beyond the group for satisfaction of needs. Activities with a high level of mobility, such as trips to places of interest in the community, are good. A trip should be planned for the beginning of the termination stage, however, and not for the final activity, since trips tend to build cohesion. Places visited should be ones to which group members can return on their own later if they should wish to do so. Activities that permit members to share their outside interests with each other are valuable at this stage. In a group of older adolescents, for example, the group may wish to talk about future educational or career plans (Garland, et al., 1965:49).

A problem of program ennui, due to a simple lack of ideas, may occur by this time. The group and the worker may have exhausted their imaginations during the course of the group's life. The refusal by the group to be interested in any activity may result from their anger at the worker for beginning to withdraw from the group. Program activities may be lagging behind the group's development. The challenge to master activities may be present no longer or the challenge may need to be updated. (The need for challenge at the same time as a need for successful achievement puts a demand on the worker's creativity.) Finally, boredom may exist because the members' separation from each other may have been completed, and group activity may have a "post-mortem" flavor (Garland, et al., 1965:45).

The Vinter-Sarri approach to social treatment permits a maximum of client participation within the context of a gently but firmly guided group. The group worker needs to allow freedom for the group members to try out new modes of behavior. Of course, freedom should be present early in treatment, but greater freedom of action is required in the termination stage. Guidance must be provided so that members' new behaviors will be in harmony with established social norms of the community in which they reside (Vinter and Sarri, 1968).

Before the group disbands, it is important for the worker to help the group plan for follow-up needs. The worker should inform the group about his own availability in case any of the members require further help after the group terminates. He should also help the group identify outside resources for help in dealing with later problems. If the group bond has been strong, the group may suggest a future "reunion." Such a reunion could be used by the worker to check the members' success in their new nonclient roles. If the group does not bring up the idea of a reunion, the worker may suggest it as part of his follow-up plan.

An evaluation of the treatment experience by the clients is also desirable. The worker may want to ask members to evaluate the group experience, to say which things they would keep the same if they were to begin the group over again and which things they would change.

The experience of leaving a treatment group brings with it myriad emotional responses from members and worker. The skilled worker will be aware of the demands termination is likely to make upon group members. He will be sensitive to members' feelings of loss—of him and of the group—and to the fragility of the sense of achievement that membership in the group has brought. He will prestructure the activities of the group to foster self-reliance and self-satisfaction, so that members are able to leave the group feeling that they can make it on their own.

REFERENCES

CHURCHILL, SALLIE R.
  1959—"Prestructuring group content," *Social Work* (July).
FOX, EVELYN F., MARIAN A. NELSON, AND WILLIAM M. BOLMAN
  1969—"The termination process: A neglected dimension in social work," *Social Work* (October).
FREY, LOUISE A.
  1962—"Support and the group: A generic treatment form," *Social Work* (October).
GARLAND, JAMES A., HUBERT E. JONES, AND RALPH KOLODNY
  1965—"A model for stages of development in social work groups," in Saul Bernstein (Ed.), *Explorations in Group Work,* Boston: Boston University School of Social Work.
KONOPKA, GISELA
  1963—*Social Group Work: A Helping Process,* Englewood Cliffs, New Jersey: Prentice-Hall, Inc.
LEVINE, BARUCH
  1967—*Fundamentals of Group Treatment,* Chicago: Whitehall Company.
NORTHEN, HELEN
  1969—*Social Work With Groups,* New York: Columbia University Press.
VINTER, ROBERT D. AND ROSEMARY C. SARRI
  1968—"Prescriptions for individual change," University of Michigan School of Social Work, Ann Arbor, Michigan, (May). (Mimeographed)
WHITAKER, DOROTHY STOCK AND MORTON A. LIEBERMAN
  1964—*Psychotherapy Through the Group Process,* New York: Atherton Press.
WILSON, GERTRUDE AND GLADYS RYLAND
  1949—*Social Group Work Practice,* Cambridge, Massachusetts: The Riverside Press.

16.

A Comparison of Two Models of Social Group Work: The Treatment Model and the Reciprocal Model

SALLIE R. CHURCHILL

During the past decade, several educators have been involved in the development of practice models used in the teaching of social work. Some schools have elected to teach only one model, others use more than one. The apparent assumption underlying the development and use of practice models in teaching is that they will later guide practitioner behavior in specific professional roles (Vinter, 1967:425–426).

Identification of three distinct models by Papell and Rothman (1966: 67–77) stimulated the following question. Since practice models attempt to guide practitioner behavior and since there are three currently identified practice models, are there three different forms of social group work practice?

While there had been extensive study of the influence of different theoretical orientations on the behavior of psychotherapists and counselors, there had been no previous study of the influence of group work practice models on social work practitioner behavior. Therefore, an exploratory study was conducted in 1969 with students of group work in six schools of social work.[1] The purpose of this study was to discover whether the particular practice model taught to students actually influenced their behavior and rationale for activities as group workers. The study was carried out by comparing the behavior and reasons for such behavior of students who attended schools where one of two different models was taught. In addition, investigation was made to see the effects, if any, of the student's age, the student's sex and the client's age upon student behavior or rationale for behavior in a group. The student's field practice experience was the context in which worker behavior was analyzed.

[1] Principal support for this research was provided by a special research fellowship from the United States Public Health Service, National Institute of Mental Health (No. 4-FO3-MR-37868 BEH)

A major finding of the study was that at least two models of social group work—the Reciprocal Model and the Treatment Model—have been developed sufficiently so that users of one model behave differently in group situations from users of the other model. The following will describe, in some detail, the Reciprocal and Treatment Models, will discuss the students who participated in the study, present the major findings and implications of the study, and describe the questionnaire and statistical procedures used.

MODELS

The three social group work practice models identified by Papell and Rothman were (1) the Social Goals Model, (2) the Treatment (Remedial or Preventive) Model, and (3) the Reciprocal (or Mediating) Model. The two models used in the study were selected because (1) they are the most completely developed practice models, (2) they are polar models, (3) both models are appropriate in work with clients who are experiencing social or personal problems, and (4) the role of the social group worker is explicated clearly in both models.

Treatment Model

In the Treatment Model, the group is conceptualized as both the means and the context for the treatment of individuals. The group worker's role is directive, planned and goal-oriented. The sanction for this role emerges from a treatment contract which is established individually between the group worker and each group member. The initial treatment contract is established during the first contact the worker has with a potential group member and the contract may or may not be modified during the course of group work service.

The group worker's interventions in the Treatment Model are chosen after he has assessed both the needs of each group member and of the group in relation to the achievement of specific objectives. While reaching the treatment goals set for and by each member is the terminal objective of group work treatment, the worker also establishes two other types of goals, intermediary goals and instrumental goals. Intermediary goals are subgoals, small steps which lead to the achievement of the various treatment goals. Instrumental goals are related to group processes and structures and are objectives which, when achieved, make the group a viable context for treatment. Assessment is followed both by the worker's interventions and by the mutual evaluation of the outcomes. In making the assessments the group worker utilizes past history and theoretical knowledge as well as current observations.

There are two major sets of theoretical and empirical knowledge incorporated in the Treatment Model. One set includes the conceptualization of group processes and group structures and the other set includes the conceptualization of an individual and of individual behavioral change. Social psychology and small group theory and research together provide the bulk of knowledge on group structure, processes and phases. The most important concepts are group development, communication, leadership, and sociometric conflict and normative structures and processes. Behavior modification theories (which are extensions of B. F. Skinner's learning theory) and ego psychological theory are the major theories regarding the individual and his behavior utilized in this model. Usually only one of the two theoretical frameworks (behavior modification or ego psychology) is used by a practitioner at any one time.

The Treatment Model places priority on two types of social work services: remediation service for individuals who have an identifiable problem in social functioning and preventive service for individuals who are in clear danger of future social dysfunction. Clearly specified goals are necessary in preventive services as well as remediation services.

The philosophy underlying the Treatment Model of social group work is implicitly pragmatic. It includes two or more of the following characteristics: (1) problem-solving focus, (2) scientific orientation, (3) goal specificity, and (4) a future orientation.

Reciprocal Model

In the Reciprocal Model, the group is conceptualized as a social system including all the members and the worker. Each system, or group, is itself an organic whole which can be comprehended only as a single entity. Even though the individuals are unique, each is influenced by relationships among the members and the worker. The theoretical basis for the Reciprocal Model is derived primarily from system theory and field theory.

The group worker's role is to act as mediator between the group members and society. He focuses on the systematic interdependence of the group worker, members and society. This role involves five tasks: (1) to search out the common ground between the member's perception of his own need and the social demands with which he is faced, (2) to detect and challenge obstacles that obscure the common ground, (3) to provide information, ideas, and value concepts which group members do not have, (4) to "lend a vision," and (5) to define the requirements and the limits of the situation in which the group is set (Schwartz, 1961).

No specific goals are set in advance of the group experience. Goal setting is conceived as an intrinsic part of the relationship between the worker and the group member. Therefore, it would be meaningless to speak about the worker's goals for a group member as though worker and member were autonomous, independent entities (Whittaker, 1970). The objective of the Reciprocal Model is the enhancement of the inter-personal engagements.

Since no specific goals are set in advance, neither assessment nor diagnosis is used to predict what might occur in the group meetings. The group worker does use "preparatory insight" based on what has happened in the past to better understand behavior as it emerges.

Philosophically, the Reciprocal Model is based on existential beliefs. One such belief is that values and essences are derived. They are not in-herent; rather, they emerge out of existence itself. The process in the Reciprocal group experience is as important as the outcome of the group experience.

The Reciprocal Model does stress the values of remediation and pre-ventive service. It does not exclude the use of group work service for socialization experiences with individuals who function well in most social interactions.

METHODOLOGY

Sample

Ideally this study would have investigated the group work practice of social group workers who had completed their formal social work educa-tion. However, for reasons of feasibility, the worker behavior of students who had already completed a year of social group work education was studied. The group worker behavior of students who were just starting their first year of social work education provided baseline measurements.

A questionnaire was mailed to all schools of social work in the United States and Canada which had a two-year concentration in social group work in the academic year, 1968–69. The chairman of the group work sequence was asked to designate which model of social group was primarily emphasized in the first-year group work method class. Stu-dents in four schools where the Reciprocal Model was taught and students in two schools where the Treatment Model was taught were asked to take part in the research. Participation was voluntary for each student. Both first- and second-year students were included.

Students who attended schools in which the same model was taught were combined into one sample, a nested sample. Four samples were created, First Year, Treatment (n = 62), Second Year, Treatment (n = 40), First Year, Reciprocal (n = 59) and Second Year, Reciprocal (n = 30). The first- and second-year samples were compared in terms of response rates, personal characteristics, educational experiences, employment, and experiences in working with people, course work, and field instruction in a school of social work; and there were no major differences between the first-year and second-year samples in either model sample. Thus it was assumed that the first-year students' responses were the same as those the second-year students would have given, had they taken the research test when they entered school. This enabled the responses of the first-year students to be considered the "before" responses; the responses of the second-year students were considered "after" responses. Differences in the average scores between the first- and the second-year samples were interpreted as changes that occurred by the time the students completed one year of social work education.

Questionnaire

A questionnaire was used to collect data regarding group worker behavior and rationale for behavior. The questionnaire included a series of six analogues of social group work practice in a young boys' group and in an older men's group. Both simulated groups were composed of five members who were patients in a state mental hospital. The members had been placed in a group to help them prepare to leave the hospital and return to community living.

The three practice situations selected for study, examples of troublesome management in both groups, were (1) a scapegoating incident, (2) a conflict concerning group membership, and (3) a member's breaking an agency rule.

Analogues were used in order to provide all the respondents with identical stimuli for the worker behavior. Troublesome management incidents were selected to maximize the stimuli for worker response and were selected from 36 analogues that were pretested with social work students. On the pretest each student was asked to write what he would do if he were the group worker in each of the incidents and why he would behave that way. The three incidents selected for the study met the following criteria: (1) the students in the pretest had responded to the intended stimuli, (2) they had perceived the incidents in the boys' group and in the men's group as having similar consequences, and (3) their responses clearly reflected two distinct worker roles.

MAJOR FINDINGS AND IMPLICATIONS

Several major findings came from this study. While none of the findings should be considered to be descriptive of all social group work students, each finding deserves further investigation and consideration by social work educators and researchers. Perhaps the most important findings are two that relate to the practice model taught for social group work and one that relates to the age of the student.

Two significant differences were found between the behavior of the students of the Treatment Model and the behavior of students of the Reciprocal Model. The group worker behavior of Treatment and Reciprocal Model students differed significantly in two of the incidents: scapegoating a member and conflict over group membership. In addition, students in the Treatment Model schools tended to use similar worker behaviors in the men's group and in the boys' group to deal with similar troublesome management incidents. However, students in the Reciprocal Model schools did not; there was no apparent relationship between the behavior they selected for the men's and the boys' group. The latter finding suggests that the students had developed a conceptual frame of reference for determining their behavior compatible to what was taught in their schools. The Treatment Model emphasizes that the worker base his professional actions on knowledge drawn from small group theory and role theory; concepts are generalized to all groups without a difference for children and adults. The Reciprocal Model emphasizes the use of the group process in immediate situations. The major base of knowledge is systems theory, and the focus is on the experience of the moment. It is reasonable that the worker would be less consistent in his approach to adults and children.

These findings have important implications for theoreticians who have invested in the development of practice models. By definition, a practice model seeks to guide and direct the practitioner's behavior. The findings suggest that these two practice models can serve this purpose, and that the Reciprocal Model and the Treatment Model do offer different guides to practitioner behavior. It is interesting to note that these findings differ from those reported in studies conducted in the 1950s dealing with practitioner behavior of psychotherapists and counselors. The latter studies indicated that different theoretical orientations did not result in different practitioner behavior. Following a review of the research, Leona Tyler (1969) suggested that the results of these studies were "conclusive;" consequently, there was a moratorium on such research in the 1960s. In the opinion of this researcher, the results of this study show that practice models of social group work now have been sufficiently developed so that this research moratorium should be lifted and further investigations made of the influence of various social group work models on practitioner behaviors.

The third finding was that both the group worker behavior and the reasons for behavior of the youngest one-third of the students were significantly different from those of the oldest one-third of the students. These differences were significant whether the samples were uncontrolled or were controlled for year in school, age of the students, and for the model of social group work. The younger students, both upon entering schools of social work and after one year of social work education, were more mediating in their behavior and reasons than the older students. These particular findings can be safely generalized to social work students because of similar findings in research by McBroom (1966) and Horowitz (1969). McBroom (1966) found that younger caseworkers were more active in their work with clients and tended to accept adult socialization theory rather than psychoanalytic theory. Horowitz (1969) found that younger social group workers intervened more actively and powerfully than the older workers in situations of deviant behavior in a group context.

The differences between the oldest and the youngest students suggest that the educator must give serious attention to the different philosophical and theoretical orientations of the students he teaches. The social work educator must attempt to understand what influences such differences will have on the learning of individual students and of an entire class. He must select teaching methods that will enhance internalization learning, i.e., in which the learner accepts and believes what has a genuine meaning for himself because it fits into his value system. Internalized learning involves not only the intellectual comprehension of specific content, but its acceptance as well. For example, the social work educator must determine how best to teach a philosophical stance that appears to be in opposition to the learner's own philosophy. The more scientifically based Treatment Model may be in opposition to the existential learnings of many young students at present.

Other major findings of the study deal with reasons for worker behavior, certainty about actions and reasons, and differences associated with educational backgrounds. At the time they entered school, students had significant differences in their reasons for worker behavior. More mediation-oriented students were likely to attend Reciprocal Model schools, and more intervention-oriented students to attend Treatment Model schools. Thus it would appear that schools of social work do select students partially on the basis of their theoretical and/or philosophical orientation. Heist, et al., (1961) reported that this was true of undergraduate colleges. He found that colleges are differentially selective in their admissions with respect to scholastic aptitude, underlying values, and intellectual dispositions. However, none of the admission officers at the six schools indicated that they made differential selection of students with regard to their philosophical or theoretical orientation. One must wonder about the influence of the personal statement that each student usually submits with his application, and what part this statement plays in his admission or rejection. Perhaps part of the reason for the difference lies in the type of student who applies. The schools of social work might exert an indirect influence on potential applicants. Schools may influence the curricula of nearby undergraduate colleges, and they may influence the practices and policies of nearby social agencies. Potential applicants may be influenced as undergraduate students, as untrained workers, or as volunteers in an agency. The people who counsel students about graduate schools also tend to be selective about the schools of social work to which they refer students.

Students who attended the Reciprocal Model schools were more consistent with each other in the reasons given for worker behavior than were the students who attended the Treatment Model schools. The variability of the reasons for behavior increased among the Treatment Model students in the second year. The increase of the variability could relate to two factors: (1) the composition of the samples and (2) the content of what was taught. The Reciprocal sample was made up from four quite small schools; the Treatment sample came from one very large and one small school. Perhaps the students of quite small classes would tend to form more similar opinions. Students in large classes may not be subjected to the pressures to conform to the same degree. The Treatment Model is taught with much greater emphasis on the theoretical aspects, while the Reciprocal Model is taught with greater emphasis on the philosophical aspects. Therefore, Treatment Model students may develop individual positions with regard to theoretical content, while Reciprocal Model students may develop positions with similar philosophical content.

Men and women students behaved quite similarly in the group worker role, but they gave significantly different reasons for their behavior. These findings are difficult to explain.

With regard to certainty about their behavior and reasons, the findings show that in both model samples the students became significantly more certain of behavior and reasons for behavior after one year of professional education. Such results suggest that a year of social work education does influence the students and that this influence is not limited to a specific model of social group work. The generalized increase in certainty was not related to the type of incident or to the age of the client.

However, just what the greater certainty actually means in terms of practice is not clear. Greater worker assurance could lead to greater effectiveness of his group work practice. Such a conclusion is based on the research of the effectiveness of psychotherapy by Goldstein (1966) whose work showed that an important variable in the success of psychotherapeutic endeavors was related to the therapist's prognostic expectations. Therefore, one could speculate that the increased certainty developed by a student during a year of professional education would contribute to the student's own expectations that he could be an effective worker, since the student knows better his intentions and reasons for behavior. The student may project an image of assurance in the group worker role in a meeting, and thus his clients would be more clear about the worker's expectations for them.

Additional Research Directions

An attempt was made in the study to explore factors that may influence what a student learns about the social group work method through classroom teaching. Two additional aspects that might exert major influences could not be considered: (1) the teaching techniques used by the classroom method teacher and (2) the contributions of the field instructors. Research in both these areas would seem essential for the educator to improve his understanding of the modes by which students learn group work practice.

The factors found to be associated with the orientation of a student—(1) his age and (2) the school he attended, i.e., tendency to select a school in keeping with his own orientation—would suggest that the social work educator needs to seek from others or to conduct his own research regarding how students learn. The educator cannot depend completely on the possession of sophisticated practice models. Answers must be found to the following and to similar questions. What factors influence how a student learns the four types of content inherent in a practice model, i.e., theoretical concepts, philosophical concepts, social work values and practice principles? How can these factors be handled in a classroom in order to maximize internalized learning?

QUESTIONNAIRE CONSTRUCTION AND SCORING

The questionnaire was constructed as a probalistic test which used confidence scoring procedures in order to quantify the responses to the analogues. The probablistic test is a multiple choice test on which the conventional multiple choice items are adapted to intrinsic items. Intrinsic items do not have uniquely correct responses. Intrinsic items require a distribution of belief over the response options which are provided (Rippey, 1968). The quantification of the answers is achieved through the use of a Euclidean scoring function.[2] Multiple scoring for each item was possible, wherein the criterion response was changed, in order to create

[2] Euclidean scoring function: $S = 1 - \dfrac{2D}{D_{max}} C$

both Treatment and Reciprocal scores.[3] This scoring procedure was selected because the process of response closely paralleled the practice situation in that: (1) the worker had a limited number of acceptable options for which he had to estimate the relative merits, and (2) the worker made his choices among the options with various degrees of certainty.

For each question about the worker behavior and each question about reasons for worker behavior, three options were offered. One option was compatible with the Treatment Model of social group work, one option was compatible with the Reciprocal Model of social group work and the other option was an incomplete, "common sense" response.[4] Each respondent ranked his preference for each of the three options. In addition, the respondent rated the degree of certainty which he felt when he answered each question. Social group work theory and practice literature were used to develop the criteria for selecting each response option. A sample analogue and options for answers follow.

BOYS' GROUP: INCIDENT ONE

Please read the following incident:

All of the members were playing a fairly rough, but controlled game of "King of the Mountain." Barry and Gary seemed to have teamed up to hold off the "attack." Eddie seemed quite surprised when the weaker members held up against him. Suddenly Eddie bit Gary. Gary gave up, fell off the mountain, began screaming, "I quit!" Eddie immediately began tauting, "Baby, baby, where's your bottle? Where is your diapers?" The sing-song chant took hold and all five boys shouted it loudly at Gary, apparently ignoring that he had been bitten.

RATE THE FIRST FOUR SETS OF STATEMENTS IN REFERENCE TO THE ABOVE INCIDENT IN THE BOYS' GROUP.
I. ON THE ANSWER SHEET, IN THE *SELF RATING* COLUMN, INDICATE THE STRENGTH OF *YOUR* PREFERENCE FOR EACH *WORKER ACTION*.
II. IN EACH INCIDENT INDICATE ON LINE *D* HOW CERTAIN YOU ARE.

1. A. The group worker helps the group quiet down and reviews the nature of the group interactions that have just occurred. He encourages the group members to discuss their feelings toward Gary.

---

[3] A computer program for scoring these data was developed by Robert Rippey and made available to the researcher for use in this study.

[4] The third option was introduced primarily for the purpose of creating statistically independent options.

B. The group worker stops the game and gathers the boys together. He tells them that he will not permit the group to tease Gary for crying when he has been bitten, nor will he permit the boys to bite each other.

C. The group worker comforts Gary.

2. A. The group worker sends Eddie out of the group for biting Gary. He discusses with the group that boys usually like to play rough but they must play fair and square.

B. The group worker reminds the group of its contract, pointing out that Gary's crying, as well as Eddie's biting when he is upset, are behaviors which the group might help the boys change.

C. The group worker reminds the group of its contract and encourages the group members to discuss what has taken place and how this may affect the functioning of the group.

If you wish to make any comments about the Worker Actions in response to this incident, write them below. (Optional)

FORM II
BOYS' GROUP: INCIDENT ONE

I. ON THE ANSWER SHEET, IN THE *SELF RATING* COLUMN, INDICATE THE STRENGTH OF YOUR PREFERENCE FOR *EACH REASON* WHICH A GROUP WORKER MIGHT OFFER FOR HIS ACTION.

II. IN EACH INCIDENT, INDICATE ON LINE *D* HOW CERTAIN YOU ARE.

3. A. The extent of aggression and/or hostility expressed in a group should be controlled by the group worker.

B. A group member who is excessively teased or hurt needs comforting and/or support.

C. A group may need help in identifying and dealing with obstacles which prevent the group from progressing towards the group goal.

4. A. A group member who intentionally hurts another member physically or psychologically should be disciplined, regardless of whether the hurt member provoked the aggression or not.

B. The group worker should not attempt to retain control of the interactions between or among the members, except in incidents of possible physical danger to a member.

C. When it appears that group members have lost control of themselves, so that their behavior is neither helpful to themselves nor to the other group members, the worker should act so as to restore control.

If you wish to make any comments about the Reasons for Worker Actions in response to this incident, write them below. (Optional)

Statistical Tests

The analyses of the data regarding worker behavior, reasons for worker behavior, and certainty of responses were carried out by the use of four statistical tests: (1) two-way analysis of variance with interaction, (2) the Student's "t" test, (3) the difference of variance F test, (4) correlation. These statistical tests were used to test hypotheses of no difference beween and/or among samples. A significance level of 0.05 was used.

REFERENCES

GOLDSTEIN, ARNOLD P.
   1966—*Therapist-Patient Expectancies in Psychotherapy*, New York: John Wiley & Sons.
HEIST, P., T. R. McCONNELL, AND P. WILLIAMS
   1961—"Personality and scholarship," *Science*, 133 (August), pp. 362–367.
HOROWITZ, GIDEON
   1969—"Worker interventions in response to deviant behavior in groups," Unpublished Ph.D. dissertation, Ann Arbor: University of Michigan.
McBROOM, ELIZABETH
   1966—"A comparative analysis of social work interventions on two types of AFDC families," Unpublished D.S.W. dissertation, Berkeley: University of California.
PAPELL, CATHERINE, AND BEULAH ROTHMAN
   1966—"Social group work models: Possession and heritage," *Journal of Education for Social Work*, II (Fall), pp. 67–77.
RIPPEY, ROBERT
   1968—"Rationale for confidence-scored multiple choice tests," University of Chicago, (Mimeographed) and "Probablistic Testing," *Journal of Educational Measurement*, V (Fall), pp. 211–215.
SCHWARTZ, WILLIAM
   1961—"The social worker in the group," *The Social Welfare Forum*, Official Proceedings of the National Conference on Social Welfare, New York: Columbia University Press.
TYLER, LEONA
   1969—*The Work of the Counselor*, third edition, New York: Appleton Century Croft.

VINTER, ROBERT D.

1967—"Problems and processes in developing social work practice principles," in Edwin J. Thomas (Ed.), *Behavioral Science for Social Workers,* New York: The Free Press, pp. 425–426.

WHITTAKER, JAMES K.

1970—"Models of group development: implications for social group work practice," *Social Service Review,* 44, 3 (September), pp. 308–322.

III

The Group in the Social Environment

17.

Extragroup Relations
and Approaches

ROBERT D. VINTER with MAEDA J. GALINSKY

Events and processes that occur outside the boundaries of the service group, and even outside the treatment sequence, are significant in the treatment group work model explored here. Four major areas of outside influences, termed "extragroup relations," are social roles and relations prior to client status, "significant others" with whom clients currently maintain association, the social systems of which clients are members, and the social environment of the treatment group. Persons and events at issue in one category are also foci in others, although with somewhat different terms of reference. Following an examination of these four areas, some practitioner approaches will be proposed, and, in conclusion, consideration will be given to ways to facilitate the transfer and stabilization of client change beyond the boundaries of the treatment group.

CLIENTS' PRIOR ROLES AND RELATIONS

In keeping with the interactional view of deviance, we have asserted that an individual's problems are generated, manifested, and defined in and through social interactions. The behaviors and events that evidence personal problems or needs occur within these social relations and necessarily *prior* to the provision of group work treatment. They have been characterized in more general terms as problems in role performance, i.e., the failure or inability of individuals to adhere to conventional behavioral standards in one or more of their social roles. This phrasing is not meant to ignore instances where the person's situation or social condition (e.g., orphans) or even the behavior of others (e.g., the abused child), rather than his own behavior, constitutes the essence of the problem. The concept of role emphasizes patterns of interactions between persons and, more precisely, of social expectations directed at individuals by persons in association with them.

Persons maintain multiple memberships or statuses in a variety of groups and small social systems within which they are subject to role expectations. It can be within any one or several of these interactional networks that behavior is perceived as problematic.[1] And generally others' definitions provide the terms of clients' "presenting problems" in their initial confrontation with service agencies. Clients typically have their own perceptions and evaluations of what (and whose) the problems are (or are not), but the definitions of others are crucial even in most instances of self-referral.

Standards of conduct and criteria of judgment vary widely among families, social groups, and subcultures. Behavior, approved by some, may be merely tolerated by others or strenuously proscribed by still others. Readiness to apply a deviant label to behavior and to invoke the formal responses of the community (whether police or social agency) also varies widely. Apart from subcultural differences, critical variations are due to the *kind* of behavior being judged and to the *social contexts* in which its exhibition assumes special meaning. Thus, certain behaviors permitted within the family (or in a recreation area) would not be condoned in a classroom. Variations are also due to disparities in the distribution of available services by law enforcement agencies, social services, or whatever. For example, persons are less likely to be labeled and handled as emotionally disturbed if there are few means to respond with these particular definitions of problems.

These variations lead to a critical aspect of the deviance-defining and -coping process. *Private* judgments that another's behavior or condition violates social norms typically and generally have little consequence outside the immediate social context (e.g., between family members), although they may have adverse psychological effects. When such judgments are rendered or confirmed by persons acting in their *official* capacities as agents of professions and organizations, however, they assume special meaning and can lead to very serious results. The action of a court intake worker transposes a neighbor's complaint into a delinquency or neglect case. The assessment of a teacher transforms an indifferent pupil into an under-achiever. Such authoritative judgments usually are needed for an individual to acquire formal status as a deviant, indeed, as a certain kind of deviant. Each agent controls access only to particular kinds of deviant statuses; psychiatrists cannot create welfare cases, nor can truant officers create patients. A person cannot become a client of most social agencies,

---

[1] Merton's concepts of role-sets, status-sets, and of sequences of role- and status-sets are particularly relevant. Although Merton's analysis is primarily directed at the sociological implications of deviance, his explication of the processes and mechanisms involved is useful for purposes of the treatment model described. See Merton (1957:357–386); also, Biddle and Thomas (1966).

and thereby receive group work or other services, until some agent has made an authoritative judgment that his behavior and/or social situation violates certain social norms.[2]

These behaviors, these judgments and labels, these agents, and these social norms must be specifically addressed in both diagnostic and treatment processes. Failure to keep them at the center of attention risks defining "problems" and setting treatment goals that are socially irrelevant or inconsequential. Moreover, there is risk in overlooking the extent to which people other than the client must be changed (or merely persuaded) for treatment to be successful.

Implicit in this analysis is the fact that those whose judgment must be reckoned with are not entirely the same as those who were or are involved in the deviance interaction process. The client has had significant interactions with two main sets of actors: those who generated the problematic behavior, and those who observed, evaluated, and officially labeled the behavior. Thus, a boy may fight in school corridors or the playground; to understand the nature and origin of this behavior it is necessary to know which peers he was associating and fighting with. But it is also necessary to know which teachers or other school personnel observed or learned about the incidents, reported them, labeled the youngster as disruptive, and initiated sanctioning procedures or services. In such instances, the "presenting problem" is defined as much by the judgments and responses of the school staff as by the peer conflict events. The two interrelated processes of deviance sequences are the one that generates problematic behavior and the one that recognizes, copes with, or otherwise responds to the behavior.

In actual cases, the practitioner may or may not wish to study or recapitulate these earlier events and relations leading up to the point of service. Retrospective analysis of the onset and etiology of problems may have little use in either diagnosis or treatment. Apart from the difficulties and costs of obtaining reliable information from the past, it may offer few guides for present intervention. The primary concern is with understanding the nature of individuals' *current* problematic behavior, the forces maintaining it, and the responses of significant others to it.

Before proceeding, the stigmatizing effects of deviance-defining processes should be noted. Negative judgments and labels by salient persons tend to have adverse effects independent of the sanctions that may also be applied. The experience of being judged as a deviant and violator of social norms may harm the self-image, sense of self-worth, and moral value,

[2] Merton notes the limited consequences of private responses to perceived deviance. He also emphasizes the significance of responses based on the "moral indignation" and disinterestedness of others who are not directly disadvantaged by the deviant behavior but who may cope with it (Merton, 1957:361–362).

whether the agent of judgment is a parent, a school teacher, a policeman, or any other individual perceived as having moral authority and social power. The defensiveness of clients, the denial of being deviant, and the resistance to service, may all be occasioned by an understandable desire to offset the psychological harm from being stigmatized.

INTERVENTION WITH SIGNIFICANT OTHERS

The two sets of persons having crucial relations with clients—those involved in the maintenance of deviant behavior and those involved in coping with the disapproved behavior—exist, for the most part, beyond the boundaries of the treatment group. Practitioners must become informed diagnostically about both and must often undertake intervention efforts directed at both.

The persons toward whom the worker may direct extragroup means of influence are parents, teachers, prison guards, cottage parents, doctors, employers or anyone else whose influence is important to the client's functioning. The modification of the behavior or attitudes of these persons constitutes a change in the social environment of the client which may in turn lead to positive changes in the group member's own behavior or attitudes.

Work with significant others in the client's environment can serve two purposes. First, such interventions can make it more possible to ensure that client changes noted in the group will also characterize extragroup behavior. Typically, significant individuals are encouraged to become sensitive to the client's new behavior and to demonstrate new behavior and attitudes in response to the client's changed behavior and attitudes. For example, an adolescent who used his fists each time he was frustrated may have learned to verbalize his anger in the group. If his parents are alerted to this new behavior as an improvement, they may reward rather than punish him for venting his anger. A mental hospital patient may have expressed increased interest in returning to his community and seeking employment. Both the attendants on the ward and the relatives of the patient may be stimulated to reinforce and to draw out this interest from the patient. A failing student may express to the worker and other members increased motivation and willingness to perform passing work. The worker may then encourage the teacher to take notice of this effort, even though the academic results remain poor. An important point to be noted here is that changes in clients' behavior or attitudes may be slight but, nonetheless, significant in view of the client's past behavior; unless they are alerted to watch for such changes, persons other than the worker may not notice them. If the client receives no outside reinforcement for new behavior, he may become discouraged and regress to his old patterns of action, or he may display his improved behavior only in the treatment group.

A second aim of intervention directed at the attitudes or behavior of significant others is to produce new client behavior. The nature of the desired new behavior may be such that encouragement can take place only outside the group or that first attempts at encouragement from outside the group are specifically advisable. The aim of the worker's intervention is to enable significant others to draw new behaviors or attitudes from group members through their direct interactions. Most likely worker intervention will be required to enable the significant other to change his behavior or attitude toward the client. For example, parents may have set academic standards for a child that he feels unable to live up to. As a consequence, he may do poorly in school and cause trouble there. The worker may seek a relaxation of the parents' standards to enable the child to take a new approach to school. Of course, it may be advisable for the parents to receive independent treatment. But, when the parents are unwilling to accept treatment or when treatment is not feasible in terms of resources, it is important for the group worker to intervene with them. To help a withdrawn, reticent child become more verbal, a houseparent in a children's institution may be encouraged to listen to the child's attempts to explain why he misbehaved instead of immediately punishing the child. A mental hospital attendant may be requested to give a particular inmate more responsibility for his own care. In a training camp for adolescent offenders, a vocational adviser may be asked to give a reluctant client extra encouragement to help him move toward finding legitimate work possibilities and use of his existing skills.

In employing this means of influence, it is important for the worker to obtain the cooperation and understanding of the "significant others." He needs to explain precisely what he is asking of them and why he is requesting this action. The worker must express his awareness of the extra work and effort involved and recognize the importance of the role these individuals play in the treatment process.

It is necessary at this point to distinguish between extragroup means of influence and collaboration. *Extragroup means of influence* refers only to worker attempts to modify the behavior or attitudes of an individual who has a direct, significant relationship with a client in order to attain treatment goals. *Collaboration* refers to contacts between service personnel where the attempt is not expressly to modify the behavior or attitudes of the other professional but to enlist his cooperation or effort in mutual problem solving. For example, a worker may feel that it is advisable for the wife of one of his clients to change her behavior toward the client. If the wife is in treatment with another practitioner, the worker might then have conferences with that practitioner. Although the worker's objective is to affect the behavior of a "significant other" (the wife) as an aid in reaching treatment goals for his client, this intervention would be considered collaboration between the group worker and the wife's therapist.

At times, the distinction between extragroup means of influence and collaboration becomes blurred. When a practitioner works with a teacher to develop a plan for the teacher's behavior toward a child and also seeks possible modifications in the teacher's interactional behavior, this intervention may be classified as either collaboration (since two professionals are involved together) or it may be classified as extragroup means of influence (since the purpose is also to change the behavior of the teacher). Classification of such activity depends on whether the worker's intent in his interaction with the teacher is to engage in mutual problem solving or to influence the teacher directly.

A distinction should also be made between using extragroup means of influence and information gathering. Where the aim of contacting a significant other is solely to obtain information about the client from that individual (for example, an attendant, a guard, a guidance counselor, a parent) and not to influence his behavior, the activity of the worker would not be regarded as employing extragroup means of influence.

SOCIAL SYSTEM INTERVENTIONS

Clients' associations with significant others are components of large social systems within which both clients and other individuals occupy statuses. Patterns and conditions that prevail within these systems may be viewed as resources or barriers to achievement of treatment goals. For example, the public school constitutes an important social system in the lives of its pupils; it contains the processes of interaction between them and their teachers, classmates, special service personnel, et al. Curriculum structure, grading practices, sanctioning procedures, and instructional resources and methods are among the relevant features of this social system that impinge upon pupil experience. A second type of extragroup intervention involves activities intended to alter such features.

Using this approach the worker attempts to change those parts of the social system that are nonsupportive of or detrimental to the client's change and well-being. He seeks modifications so that positive features are enhanced and supported, and negative and nonsupportive features are changed or replaced by more positive ones. For example, the group worker may determine that the sanctioning policies in a school curtail a failing student's motivation to continue in school. Not only is the student a failure academically but, because of his poor grades, he is not allowed to participate in extracurricular activities. The worker may attempt to have the policies altered so that the marginal student, on the verge of being a drop-out, can find some aspects of school life in which he can participate successfully. In a training school setting, if increased responsibility is important for treatment purposes, a worker may try to change cottage routines and regulations to allow more independence for the members of his group in their study hours and in their recreational pursuits. In a prison setting, practitioners may attempt to develop a work release program for their clients, or, in a mental hospital ward, to increase the degree of decentralization so that treatment effectiveness is enhanced.

In employing this type of extragroup influence, the practitioner interacts with others to modify the social system rather than a specific client's behavior. In order to accomplish changes in the social system it may be necessary to work with a wide variety of persons—administrators, employees, family members, or agency board members. If the worker were to seek changes in the rules concerning extracurricular participation by failing students in a school, he would most likely have contact with guidance counselors, the principal, the superintendent, and perhaps even the school board. In addition, interpretation of proposed modifications to teachers may be considered part of his task. Alteration of cottage routines in a children's institution would necessarily put the worker into communication with the director and the houseparent staff.

Intervention at this level on behalf of particular clients may also affect others, since changes in a social system typically affect all members of that system. Change efforts focused on social systems are both greater in scope and less immediate in their effects than are interventions with significant others. A change in teacher-client relations may have rapid consequences whereas the outcomes of modification in grading practices are not realized at once. Both intervention with significant others and social system intervention require the practitioner to work outside the boundaries of the treatment group but with specific reference to his goals for client individuals.

In considering extragroup means of influence, only those situations have been considered in which the worker acts with others to move toward treatment goals for individual clients. There are other instances in which the practitioner works for the benefit of persons who are not members of his group. He may interpret his program directly to board members to ensure their understanding and support for it, even though he may not be serving particular clients at this point. The worker may seek to change the organizational structure of a prison or a mental hospital ward, although he is aware that the contemplated changes would have no possibility of being enacted in time to affect his current clients. The worker may seek to change policy decisions that affect welfare clients' rights to retain part of their earned income without penalty to their grants even though this could not be put into practice in the immediate future. In such situations the practitioner becomes a kind of "lobbyist" or community intervener, concerned with the welfare of persons like his clients, but not expecting immediate benefits for a particular individual.

SOCIAL ENVIRONMENT OF THE GROUP

To this point practitioner activities have been described that may be undertaken without the participation or even the full knowledge of individual clients. Although it is desirable to inform clients, gain their consent, and even obtain their active assistance before intervening with significant others in their life situations, it is not always possible to do this. However, some extragroup approaches necessarily involve client group members.

The environment of a treatment group has been cited as a source of major influences on the group's development and experience. A group's social environment includes the *separate* social affiliations and personal environments of the group's individual members. Influences stemming from these sources have been the focus of most of the discussion in this chapter. Social environment also includes the objects, persons, and other units *collectively* encountered by the group as a social entity. While customarily these two environments overlap, depending on the group's composition and activities, to a significant extent they are mutually exclusive. Treatment groups often occupy places, confront pressures, and develop affiliations which do not characterize the separate, personal environment of any individual member.

Potent demands and constraints are often imposed upon the group by conditions in its external environment. What the group is allowed or expected to do, and the means it is given with which to do it, are often set by the service agency and the surrounding community. The material and resources for group activities are limited to those provided by (if not extracted from) the local context of the group. Responses from salient external persons and other social units often critically shape the group's public identity and its conception of itself.

At the very least, the group's development depends upon how effectively it can cope with critical pressures from the outside, from its social environment. The treatment group need not merely react to or accommodate external persons and events. Spontaneously or with encouragement from the practitioner, the group may undertake active engagement with features of its environment and seek to change, exploit, or redirect environmental forces playing upon it.

Treatment goals can be implemented in important ways through the worker's guidance of extragroup relations. The group itself may be a highly useful mediating vehicle. To supplement his own efforts, the worker may wish to stimulate the whole group to confront the "social system" conditions that impinge upon the individual members. As part of its planned program, a treatment group in a residential institution may be involved in proposing (or negotiating) improvements in cottage life, the daily cycle, or discharge procedures. Within the public school, a group of under-achievers may be helped to persuade administrative and teaching staff to modify practices that reduce achievement opportunities.

The practitioner may also encourage group attention to focus on the outside experiences of its client members, thus creating opportunities to explore individual behavior, to enhance group problem solving, and to enlarge the group's perspectives. The worker may encourage such processes when they occur spontaneously, or he may deliberately introduce them. In a group for disruptive pupils, the worker may call upon members to describe concurrent classroom episodes, or he may initiate discussion of these events on the basis of his outside knowledge. In a group for mothers with childrearing problems, the worker may help members anticipate problematic situations, create and rehearse ways of handling them, and subsequently review members' success in trying out new behaviors. Such outside experiences may have direct relevance for more than one member.

The practitioner ought to plan for and engage in externally-oriented activities as a deliberate step taken in the interest of group development and treatment goals. Extragroup activities expand the horizons and experiences of the group; they provide the group and its members with significant opportunities for learning and for problem solving. Perhaps most significantly, external activities can assure that the treatment process does not become abstracted and disengaged from the social environment. The practitioner and the group must be cautious not to focus on matters only having relevance within the treatment group. Active confrontation and engagement with the social environment facilitate socially meaningful treatment.

TRANSFERRING AND STABILIZING CHANGE

Changes sought through group work service should represent improvements in the client's behavior and/or situation in the social roles and contexts where his problems have been identified. Further, such changes should be evaluated as real and significant with respect to accepted standards of conduct and well-being.

What are the implications of these requirements for the treatment sequence itself? If the worker has formulated individual treatment goals and plans with specific reference to clients' role performance problems, the ensuing treatment process is less likely to be misdirected. Nevertheless, the task remains of focusing this process directly on the problematic behaviors, and, further, of ensuring that changes are not circumscribed by the boundaries of the treatment group. Several lines of effort may be pursued.

1. *Replication of external problem.* The worker can attempt to replicate inside the group the crucial aspects of the interactional situations that manifest client performance difficulties. The treatment group then enables clients to learn more adequate modes of response through direct experience. Suppose, for example, that affect management is a common problem among boys in a group for delinquents. The worker will have ample opportunities to induce familiar stress situations through which the members can explore reaction alternatives, develop personal controls, and rehearse new modes of conduct. Similarly, the treatment group's activities can offer training experiences for clients who lack sufficient social or technical skills to cope with specific role demands elsewhere. In this approach the treatment group affords a protected social environment, partially insulated from but having significant parallels to clients' other social situations, where intensive learning can occur without the usual risks or constraints.

2. *Group discussion of external problem.* The worker can initiate discussion of clients' problematic behaviors or situations, thus enabling members to explore and assess stressful episodes, to gain understanding of cause-effect relations, and to discover alternative courses of action. The group becomes a vehicle for individual and collective problem solving, and provides special advantages in challenging clients' distorted perceptions, in modifying attitudes that may underlie problem behavior, and in generating an expanded range of feasible alternatives.

3. *Initiation and review of external action.* Group members may be encouraged or required to take action between sessions in order to apply, test, or reinforce learning acquired within the group. Individuals in a group for mothers with childrearing difficulties or for disruptive school pupils, may be expected to engage in new behaviors in designated situations outside the group and then to report back on their experiences. When used this way, the treatment group provides incentives to try different behavior, it serves as a reviewing body to assess results, and it provides support and reinforcement for desired change beyond its boundaries.

Needless to say, these procedures can be employed interchangeably or simultaneously. Moreover, the worker may bring (or induce members to bring) tangible evidences, artifacts, or persons into the group from outside. For a group having difficulties in school, it may be advantageous to introduce members' actual grades, or to administer and discuss a test, or to bring in for confrontation the school official who handles discipline problems. Similarly, taking groups to various locations for sessions can create opportunities for guided learning in handling physical materials, social engagements, and the like. In all of these instances, reference is made to events that have a direct and significant relevance to clients' "presenting problems," and not merely to a regimen of benign experiences.

Worker interventions outside the group with significant others and social systems supplement and reinforce changes induced through the group. Extragroup work should be coordinated with treatment group interventions so both are complementary. Client changes first manifested within the group can be extended beyond its boundaries, while episodes and events occurring outside can be connected with or exploited for intragroup purposes.

Throughout their efforts to bring about the transfer and stabilization of client behavior, workers frequently recognize that widely held prejudicial attitudes toward "deviants" constitute a major obstacle. Authoritative judgments of deviance have stigmatizing effects both during and beyond the treatment process. It is often more difficult to lose a deviant identity than to acquire one. Limited opportunities and secondary sanctions reduce motivation. Too often, small but significant changes in client behavior pass unnoticed outside the treatment group. With few apparent routes back to nondeviant status and with no rewards in sight, "deviants" become "locked in" deviant careers.

Efforts by the worker can block, or at least reduce the adverse impact of, deviance labeling. Client attempts to change any area of role performance need to be acknowledged. The worker must actively seek to facilitate both the transfer of change into major phases of daily life and the recognition of change when it occurs. In part, such interventions on behalf of clients are advocacy efforts. Their purpose is to obtain positive reinforcement for treatment gains.

REFERENCES

BIDDLE, BRUCE J. AND EDWIN J. THOMAS (EDS.)
  1966—*Role Theory: Concepts and Research,* New York: John Wiley & Sons.
MERTON, ROBERT K.
  1957—*Social Theory and Social Structure,* revised edition, Glencoe, Illinois: Free Press.

18.

Group Work Intervention in the Social Environment

PAUL H. GLASSER, BERYL CARTER,
RICHARD ENGLISH, CHARLES D. GARVIN
and CHARLES WOLFSON

The social work profession has acknowledged interest in the client's social environment from the beginning (Richmond, 1917). The social environment often maintains or encourages the client's problematic condition that the practitioner is interested in changing. However, relatively little development of practice theory has been made to provide systematic ways of thinking about intervention strategies to deal with the social environment in a comprehensive way. This is so despite the availability of a large body of social and behavioral science theory and research which is relevant to this issue.

Until recently the caseworker and the group worker overemphasized the reorganization of client personality as a means to behavioral change. Consistent with an individualistic, competitive society, once such reorganization was achieved, the client was expected to adapt adequately to his social environment or to change aspects of his situation to make such an adaptation. Little attention was given to a technique that would enable the client or worker to change the environment more directly.

Now social workers have begun to understand that behavioral change usually cannot be achieved or maintained outside the treatment situation without somehow changing the reinforcing agents or systems in the client's environment. Further, it is sometimes more feasible to make changes in the client's environment which facilitate improved social functioning than to attempt personality change first. In any case, these two efforts usually must go together.

This is not to deny that considerable social work literature on the social environment is available. The child guidance movement and psychiatric social work generally have emphasized the influence that nuclear family members have on the patient. The typical recommendation, however, is treatment of individual parents and spouses rather than intervention in whole family-environment situations (Seder-Jacobson, 1971). New sociobehavioral approaches focus more directly on the client's social environment, but they are addressed primarily to the personal interaction level and not to the system level (Thomas, 1971). Traditional approaches in social group work, which grew out of the settlement house social action movement, continue to emphasize how groups may be used to achieve social change, particularly at the neighborhood level. But no clear strategies of intervention seem available (Briar, 1971), although the recent interest in client advocacy procedures is encouraging. Further, this latter approach seems more related to the growing body of literature on community organization rather than to that on rehabilitation methods. Finally, studies of the social organization of agencies and its effect on practice deal directly with the social environment. Nonetheless, like the other approaches, little connection is made between the individual and his problem and strategies to change the social environment that maintains his dysfunctional behavior.

An exception is the paper by Vinter and Galinsky entitled "Extragroup Relations and Approaches" (Chapter 17 in this volume). This chapter attempts to extend their formulation. Vinter and Galinsky's focus is limited to intervention strategies as part of the treatment plan. A framework for analysis is presened here, and within that methods for changing the client or client group social situation are developed.

Extragroup relations, as defined by Vinter and Galinsky in their chapter, refer to the behavior or attitudes of persons in the client's social environment or to large social systems within which both clients and others occupy statuses. Modification in extragroup relations may be initiated by the individual client or the group as a unit, directly by the worker himself, or by some combination of client, group, and worker efforts. Attention may be directed toward persons and/or social systems within which service is being received and the worker is employed, and/or to other institutions in the community.

TARGETS OF CHANGE EFFORTS

Some means for focusing on the environmental context of the client's problematic condition must be developed if the professional is to be effective in his use of extragroup means of influence. There are those who play a role in the generation of a problem, others who serve to maintain or exacerbate it and still others who respond to it. The worker must be able to determine the nature of these interactions and devise strategies that take them into account when working with the client on treatment goals. There are also various useful ways of classifying the social environment to help the worker make choices in responding to those conditions affecting the client. On a general level, the impact on the client of specific social situations can be located as:

1. Serving to cause or exacerbate the problematic condition
2. Interfering with the proper pursuit of treatment goals
3. Serving to enhance the attainment of treatment goals

When attempting to achieve modification among persons in the client's social environment, a general rule might be that attention first be given to those people with whom the client interacts most frequently for it is likely that deviant or dysfunctional behavior is stimulated or reinforced by them. Further, the type of behavior the worker wishes to modify directs him to particular aspects of the client's social environment. When dealing with a child who misbehaves in the classroom, the worker should focus first upon the child's relationships with his classmates and his teacher. The worker involved with the withdrawn schizophrenic in the hospital ought to give attention to aides, orderlies and nurses to whom the patient is exposed on the ward. Other patients with whom the schizophrenic is required to interact may be problematic for him as well.

Within the service agency two levels of personnel require consideration: (1) those with whom the client has person-to-person interaction and (2) those administrators who have authority over the former. In some situations administrators may require the worker to behave in ways that are dysfunctional for the client. In other instances, the power of the administrator may be required to change the behavior of the worker. In closed institutions, clients must interact with large numbers of caretaker personnel—guards, attendants, aides, nurses, doctors, patient workers, child-care staff, housemothers, etc. In open settings the number may not be so large, but the influence of receptionists, secretaries and others may be subtle and important, especially during the client's initial contact with the agency.

Too often professionals do not give staff in agencies and other organizations in the community sufficient attention. It is particularly important to remember that the institutionalized client will be returning to the outside community, where he will have to deal with school teachers and principals, employment agency staff, the police, etc. If the positive changes achieved within the institution are to be maintained, the worker must deal with these personnel.

More frequent contacts during the typical day include other clients, parents, spouse, children, peers, friends, neighbors, coworkers, etc. It is sometimes possible to pinpoint problematic behavior to particular interaction situations. A child may have temper tantrums only in the presence of an older brother. Or violent arguments may take place between a married couple only when the wife's mother is in the home or shortly after she leaves. Sometimes intervention with the relevant other may be easier than with the client himself.

Once a decision has been made about the person in the client's environment with whom to intervene, the worker must be specific about what changes he wishes to accomplish. In general he is interested in making sufficient change in the others' behavior so that the client's problematic actions will not be stimulated or reinforced, or so that the client's new, more constructive reactions will be maintained. Sometimes specific behaviors can be dealt with. Following each of Johnny's temper tantrums, mother spends a good deal of time holding and loving her son, providing a good deal of secondary gratification. At other times attitudes, feelings, and values must be dealt with, because the stimuli and responses are large in number and broad in scope, reflecting other persons' more generalized predispositions to the client's behavior. The teacher may find every excuse to find fault with and punish Johnny, "for lower-class welfare children do not appreciate an education or the teacher's efforts," as Johnny's previous school record proves. There are also times when the goals of relevant others must be redirected. Despite contrary hospital policy, the ward attendant may believe it is more important to maintain strict discipline and control over the patients assigned to him than to permit the type of positive interactions necessary for their rehabilitation.

Social systems are made up of persons. Therefore the distinction between personal and system levels is for analytic clarification. Focus at this level can provide a different set of insights.

Each of the major organizations in the community is made up of a number of subsystems. The types of subsystems each organization develops vary, but usually are dependent on the goals of the organization and the training, experience and technical competence of its personnel (Vinter, 1965; Hasenfeld, Chapter 19 in this volume). Thus, the elementary school can be conceived as five subsystems: (1) administrators, (2) teachers, (3) students, (4) special service personnel, and (5) school board. Each of these subsystems has regularized ways of dealing with other subsystems and defined patterns for dealing with other organizations in the community. To achieve or stabilize client change it is often necessary to intervene in these patterned ways of handling matters within or between subsystems or between organizations. While clients or worker have to deal with individuals in the organization, the focus of their effort is different from that at the personal level.

Changes in organizational or subsystem goals may be required. Efforts are gradually being made to convert mental hospitals from custodial centers to treatment facilities. Middle-class socialization has become an increasingly important goal for schools located in lower-class neighborhoods. Clark (1956) points out that changes in goals are difficult to achieve when (1) they are inadequately defined, (2) the position of the proponents is not fully legitimized, and (3) the values are unacceptable to the "host" population. Without such goal changes, however, the mental hospital patient may have little chance for recovery, or the lower-class child may have little opportunity for upward mobility through education.

Another type of needed intervention may be in the structural relationships within or between subsystems. Communication may be blocked. Most welfare agencies have appeal procedures, but many clients are not informed of these and know of no way to challenge the decisions of the worker. The distribution of power in an agency may be dysfunctional for the rehabilitation of clients. The small amount of power clients possess often has this effect in many agencies. The sociometric structure of an institution may be problematic. Placing large numbers of paranoid patients together on a ward may reinforce their paranoia; certain client roles may increase their disabilities; and labeling clients as criminals, delinquents, school behavior problems or retarded provides the lay community with sets of expectations for these clients which reinforce their problematic behavior.

A third type of change has to do with the formal and informal rules within and between subsystems and with the procedures used to carry out these rules. As Vinter and Sarri (Chapter 27 in this volume) point out, high school rules that deny problematic students access to athletic activity also lower their motivation to achieve or reform. Or the formal bureaucratic application procedures some clients are required to go through in some social agencies discourage them from seeking or continuing service.

Finally, the distribution of resources within and between organizations may prevent maximum utilization of them by the client. The aide in an institution for the retarded who must spend the majority of her time cleaning, toileting and dressing the residents has little energy left for training them in skills required for community living. Or the provision of expensive athletic equipment in some schools may prevent the hiring of additional teachers needed to decrease class size.

It can be noted that these types of changes in the social system are closely related to each other, and at points overlap. However, the concepts and illustrations should make it evident that the focus of effort must be considerably different from that at the personal level and thus leads to differences in intervention methods and techniques. Benefits from changes at the system level often accrue to others as well as to clients in the group. Nonetheless, the initiation of such change grows out of the treatment requirements of members of the group, and the benefits of such system change should be clear to them and the worker.

CRITERIA FOR CLIENT INVOLVEMENT

One of the major decisions to be made by the worker and by clients is how involved clients should be in obtaining the desired changes within the service agency or other organizations in the community. The position adopted by the authors is that clients should be maximally involved in securing changes in the environments which affect them, so that ultimately they will be able to act on their own behalf without professional help. It is recognized, however, that frequently it is untenable to involve certain clients in extragroup change endeavors and, therefore, the following criteria are developed to aid in worker decisions regarding such involvement.

Client Motivation

In motivation, the client's preferences for his own activity must be considered. The worker must guard against meeting his own needs by developing or limiting the client's participation in the change effort. The client must also wish to act to improve his circumstances. The worker, as always, should help the client make as rational a choice as possible by using problem-solving techniques.

Client Capacity

The client must be able to understand the intent of the change effort, perform the actions required, and withstand the anxiety and stress which may be engendered by the effort. It is unlikely, for these reasons, that young children, psychotics, or the retarded will be able to contribute substantially to extragroup means of influence. On the other hand, public welfare clients, inmates of correctional institutions, and parents of school children may have adequate capacity and motivation for participation in such change.

Strategy Effectiveness

The probability that a particular extragroup means of influence will be the most effective strategy must be considered by clients and worker together. For example, it is unlikely that a teacher will change her negative attitudes toward an adolescent who disrupts her classroom unless there is some evidence that he intends to change his behavior. On the other hand, former addicts can demonstrate to prejudiced members of the community that this problematic condition can be given up if treatment is provided and jobs made available, both of which may be necessary for the rehabilitation of drug users.

Risk of Adverse Consequences to the Client

Many clients have suffered severe social stress through unsuccessful change efforts, which may increase their anxiety, reduce their already very limited power, and reinforce their image of the agency as punishing, prejudiced, and destructive. Great caution should be taken in encouraging client participation in events which may possibly lead to this outcome.

Effects upon Group Conditions

As in any task activity, the effects upon such group conditions as cohesiveness, structure and intragroup processes must be assessed. Successful efforts may add to the attractiveness of the group, may present new structural possibilities for member roles, and may aid in problem-solving activities. The opposite is a likely result of unsuccessful activities in the social environment, unless one includes the attraction to the group created by external threats—a poor basis for long-term treatment planning.

Relationship to Intervention Goals

A major consideration in this type of activity is its relationship to the individual treatment goal and contract with each client in the group. Questions need to be asked as to whether the goal is to further assertiveness or to further self-awareness; to further environmental change or individual change; to add to aggressive behavior directed at particular organizations or to ameliorate it; to add to independence at a given point in the treatment sequence or to stress adaptation to the social situation.

INTERVENTION STRATEGIES

Only recently has there been systematic effort in social work literature to specify change techniques, particularly with reference to modification of the environment. Therefore, the techniques described below, and classified according to Figure 1, must be considered as first approximations.

This set of techniques is suggested by social work literature and by material in the social and behavioral sciences. Interventions concerning work with significant persons in the environment are drawn from interpersonal change theory but applied to nonclients. This includes not only casework and group work but also psychoanalytic theory and methods, behavioral therapy and learning theory, and a variety of interactional approaches, such as the social role framework and the knowledge about cognitive dissonance and attitude change. Interventions concerning work with

AREAS OF THE SOCIAL ENVIRONMENT				
Target of Change				
		Attention within service institution		Attention to other institutions in the community
Level of change				
Change agent		Personal	Social system	Personal	Social system
Client	Individual member	1	2	3	4
Intervention	The group	5	6	7	8
Worker intervention		9	10	11	12

FIGURE 1 Intervention Strategies in the Social Environment

significant social systems are drawn from community organization and administration theory in social work, and analyses of bureaucracies, voluntary associations, and interest groups in the social sciences.

No attempt has been made to provide sets of mutually exclusive intervention techniques. Some overlap may be inevitable and preferable, as long as each is sufficiently different to merit special consideration. It is often necessary to use a number of them together in any particular situation. A repetition of techniques is available to the individual client, the group, and the worker at both the personal and system level. Finally, this is not intended to be an exhaustive list of interventions, but rather suggestive of possibilities that may be used for a large variety of problematic situations.

Individual Member Intervention at the Personal Level (Boxes 1 and 3)

Clients continuously are required to deal with their social environments, and sometimes they make attempts to change it so that it will be less problematic for them. However, this is usually not done consciously or with a strategic sense of direction concerning the desired change. The techniques below suggest ways for the worker to arm the client with means for more effective modification of his environment.

1. *Avoidance.* Some situations in which present stimuli lead to problematic behavior can be avoided by the client. If such situations are

clearly identified, the worker can coach the client in appropriate avoidance behaviors. The delinquent who performs antisocial acts only in the presence of one or two buddies may be taught how to stay away from them, and how to find new friends who are unlikely to get him into trouble. This means of intervention presupposes an intermittent or continuous exposure by the client to the problem situation.

2. *Alternate reactions.*   Much of the therapeutic literature assumes that one type of treatment goal is for clients to learn to react differently in a variety of interpersonal situations. However, these situations are rarely defined in explicit terms, nor is the alternate reaction specified. Clients can be taught alternate reactions in the group in a variety of ways, such as behavioral rehearsal, role playing or model presentation (Frankel and Glasser, 1973). The employee who always responds to his supervisor's criticism by withdrawing can be taught (coached) to be more assertive when he believes such comments are unfair.

3. *Manipulation of the social and/or physical situation.*   A lower-class elementary school child was evaluated negatively by his teacher because of her stereotype of children with his background, confirmed by his usually not answering her questions. It was discovered that he had an auditory problem and could not hear well in his seat in the back of the room. When he asked to be moved up front his diligence and intelligence became apparent, and the teacher's reaction to him changed radically.

4. *Education of others.*   There are many times when the reactions of others to a client are based on incorrect information or lack of knowledge. For example, many employers are reluctant to hire workers diagnosed as having epilepsy. They do not know that both grand mal and petit mal seizures can be controlled well with drugs, and efficient performance expected. Epileptics may need to inform potential employers of these facts.

5. *Interpretation.*   Sometimes relatives, members of the lay community, and even professionals are not aware that their interpersonal reactions to clients may stimulate their problematic behavior. By having clients bring these responses to their attention, they may readily agree to change their behavior. A mother may be completely unaware that joking about her adolescent daughter's relationships with boys not only embarrasses the girl but makes her feel uncomfortable in coeducational situations. The mother may be quite willing to stop such behavior if her daughter talks with her about it.

6. *Evaluation.*   This technique is very similar to interpretation but has a different connotation. The emphasis in evaluation is on helping the relevant other see the negative consequences for himself as well as the client. This then serves as additional motivation to change his responses to the client. Each time Don does not complete the class assignment the

teacher reprimands him. In turn, he gets angry in a way that disrupts the entire class and her personally. On worker's suggestion, Don points this out to her, adding that his previous preparation has been inadequate and this is the reason he does not finish the assignments. From then on, she lowers performance expectations for him and refrains from reprimanding him.

7. *Cooptation.* This involves making the relevant other a colleague or friend to aid in client change, sometimes even without awareness of the change in relationship or behavior. The negative attitudes of a child-care worker toward a resident may be changed by having the resident involve the worker in an activity in which they have a strong mutual interest.

8. *Confrontation.* If some of the other techniques do not work, the client may have to employ confrontation. The client forces the other to face the ways in which his behavior or attitudes are problematic for him and demands some change. The group worker may help the adolescent girl confront her mother about the large number of household tasks she is required to perform, leaving almost no time for homework or recreation. Sometimes compromise solutions can be worked out after confrontation has taken place.

9. *Bargaining or negotiation.* In this technique the client agrees to change or do something for someone in the social environment, and in return, the other person agrees to reciprocate in a way helpful to the client. Mother is constantly nagging Bob about how dirty and disorderly his room is, which gets him angry and starts a family argument. Bob agrees to clean his room thoroughly once a week if mother agrees not to mention the matter any more.

10. *Use of influentials.* The client may try to use the aid of others to convince some important person in his social situation to change. He may attempt to enlist other members of the treatment group, the worker, powerful or expert people in the community. This technique leads logically to the next set of techniques involving the client group.

Group Intervention at the Personal Level (Boxes 5 and 7)

Emphasis in this category is on clients working together as a unit. Some aspect of the social environment requires change for the majority of treatment group members, who are both capable and motivated to cooperate to achieve this end. The worker has to be sure that the actions taken will not harm some individuals within or outside the treatment group at the cost of helping others, although sometimes risks must be taken.

Techniques 3–10 above apply to the total group as well. Often they can be used more effectively when the group works together. This is particularly true when modification of organizational personnel, within either their own service agency or some other agency, is required. In addition, another technique may be useful.

11. *Alliance.*   The group may unite with other groups who are experiencing similar problems in the environment to effect change in some person or situation. While this technique may apply more often to system change, it sometimes is useful at the personal level as well. For example, a psychiatric hospital orderly consistently brings the ward patients to the dining room late. As a result they must eat hurriedly and sometimes do not get a full meal. Treatment group patients may enlist the support of other groups on the ward or organize other patients into a larger group, to put pressure on the attendant to change his pattern.

Worker Intervention at the Personal Level (Boxes 9 and 11)

Techniques 3–11 also can be used effectively by the worker. Since he generally possesses considerably more power than an individual client, especially among colleagues in his own agency, he may be more successful than clients acting alone or together in their own behalf. Further, he may often find it useful to form alliances (technique 11) with other colleagues to achieve specified changes. This power that the worker possesses is employed in the additional techniques described below.

12. *Advocacy.*   The worker stands next to and in partnership with the client(s) relative to the problematic condition in the environment (Purcell and Specht, 1965). In many cases this means that techniques 2–11 are used by worker and client or worker and client group together. For example, it is often not enough for the adolescent to change his behavior in the classroom to achieve the designated treatment goal of improved school performance. For the teacher to change his attitude toward the student and provide rewards for his more positive behavior, the client and worker must often bring these changes to the teacher's attention together.

13. *Supervision.*   In some situations the group worker may be in a supervisory relationship with staff who affect his clients in the treatment group. This is true for some closed institutional settings, where professionals play a dual role of being responsible for the treatment of a specified group of clients and being responsible for supervision of other staff such as child-care workers, custodial personnel, housemothers, aides, etc. Under these circumstances, the supervisory relationship can be used to achieve change in the environment for clients in the treatment group. For example, irrational attitudes toward residents in a training school for the retarded might be handled in this way.

14. *Collaboration and/or joint planning.* When the person to be changed is another professional within the service agency or another organization in the community, the worker may attempt to initiate collegial discussion, providing an opportunity to use other techniques. For example, the school social worker may request a conference with the client's teacher to discuss new developments in the case and to initiate some joint planning.

15. *Consultation.* The group worker's specialized skills may provide him with an opportunity to serve as a consultant to other professionals (Radin, Chapter 6 in this volume). This may allow him to induce changes in the attitudes and behaviors of others who he knows have detrimental effects on the clients with whom he is working. The social worker may be asked to consult with teachers on how to handle certain disruptive aspects of classroom behavior. He may deliberately include material on attitudes toward children whose parents are on the welfare rolls, attempting to change negative perspectives of teachers toward AFDC mothers and their children, some of whom are in groups for which he is directly responsible.

Individual Member Intervention at the System Level (Boxes 2 and 4)

System change by individuals is extremely difficult. This is especially true for the client, for in many agencies he has low status and power. System change involves patterns of performance which include numerous persons in the environment, often requiring that the change agent have considerable power to be effective. While techniques 1–10 are available to the client, these usually are not potent enough to achieve changes in structure, goals, rules and procedures and the distribution of resources in an institution. However, there are exceptions, and the worker should be alert to this possibility in order to maximize individual client effort. No new techniques are proposed.

Group Intervention at the System Level (Boxes 6 and 8)

Client groups, particularly in alliance with other groups, can be a potent force for system change. Activities in the civil rights movement, poverty programs and consumer protection area have demonstrated this well.

This category moves into what has often been considered citizen action and community organization. The distinction made in this chapter is that such group action grows out of and is directly relevant to the attainment of treatment goals for the members of the group. For example, when dealing with the very poor or nonwhites, their social functioning problems cannot easily be divorced from their class and caste status. Not all such groups are ready to attempt system change, however. A wise strategy may be to begin with small environmental changes, often at the personal level, and through successful experience, work up to broader system changes within and between organizations.

All of the techniques proposed for groups at the personal level are relevant here. In addition, three other techniques will be delineated.

16. *Mass communication.* The spread of the rationale for system change through written or verbal reports (newspapers, pamphlets, radio, television, etc.) can be an effective means of putting pressure on those in positions of responsibility. The presentation of constructive alternatives to present policies are useful in convincing others of the need for environmental modification. The literature on propaganda and attitude change should be used in planning such a campaign.

17. *Passive resistance.* A number of passive resistance techniques involving noncooperation with key authorities in the institutional system have been developed. These include refusal to perform required tasks or to be present at mandatory meetings. Many clients are not sufficiently confident to use such techniques, or not in a position to use them advantageously. On the other hand, while they may not be able to begin such actions, they may be able to participate in those initiated by others.

18. *Active resistance.* This means playing an active role against the social system, such as picketing, marching, etc. This also can be difficult for many clients, but they may participate under the leadership of others.

The consequences of using resistance techniques, active and passive, should be evaluated carefully by the worker before he encourages clients to initiate or participate in them. The risk of greater damage than benefits to clients and others in the community may sometimes be too great. The use of violence, even to pursue justifiable goals, is usually considered unethical conduct in the professions. Further, many of the other techniques of change proposed may achieve the same end more easily.

Worker Intervention at the System Level (Boxes 10 and 12)

Intervention in these categories has to do with social action and policy formation, i.e., the practitioner as social reformer. He may attempt change as a staff member working through the agency bureaucracy, as a professional with other professionals through social work organizations, or as an independent citizen with a variety of lay and professional organizations. The focus of this paper points to the practitioner's expert knowledge concerning environmental conditions that are problematic to large numbers of clients, some of whom he works with directly.

All of the worker techniques reviewed at the personal level, plus techniques 16–18, are relevant here too. Three additional ones for the practitioner as social reformer are summarized below.

19. *Authority.* A supervisory relationship carries authority with it. However, sometimes the practitioner has no formal supervisory role with other staff but does have legitimate power over them. He may then use his position in the agency hierarchy to modify goals, values, structural arrangements among personnel, rules and procedures, or the distribution of resources. He should be aware that while this may temporarily change staff behavior, it will not necessarily change individual attitudes and values, unless the persons involved become convinced that the system changes work better than the old ways and are more satisfying to them.

20. *Planned contagion.* Sometimes the professional can demonstrate the superiority of certain types of innovations by means of special projects (Herman and Rosenberg, 1967). It is helpful if outside financing for these ventures can be found. Planning such projects with other agency staff can lead to contagion of the modifications throughout the agency, and to other agencies as well. For example, the demonstration of the use of group work service in a local welfare department led to the continued use of group methods after the project terminated and its spread to other county departments (Navarre, Glasser and Costabile, Chapter 24 in this volume).

21. *Social engineer.* Closely related to the foregoing is the social engineer approach. This technique is particularly usful when one or more aspects of a program seem to be failing and there is a request for help. The practitioner plans in detail some aspect of the institutional program and builds in evaluation procedures to demonstrate its success. This approach has been used effectively in some school systems to initiate behavioral therapy programs in the classroom.

CONCLUSION

This paper reviews many of the variables to be considered in extra-group means of influence and suggests a number of strategies and techniques to achieve this end. While its focus is clearly on modification of the environment to achieve treatment goals, by necessity it implies relationships between social group work practice, community organization, and administration methods.

Successful modification of the environment may provide secondary gains beyond the achievement of treatment goals. When clients, either singly or in a group, participate in the process, it may help them to attain a new sense of autonomy. Their involvement may have the same benefits as other carefully planned programs and, in addition, provide them with new and satisfying roles in the community. For many it may be excellent training in tactful and strategic assertiveness, a requirement for successful management of their environment. For the group, this type of experience may help to clarify goals and norms and lead to greater cohesiveness, which permits more effective use of indirect means of influence.

For too long the concept of "environmental manipulation" has been given lip service only. Hopefully this paper will stimulate the development of effective intervention strategies at both the personal and system levels in the social field surrounding the client and his treatment group. In that way, a more comprehensive and efficacious practice technology may be had.

REFERENCES

BRIAR, SCOTT
   1971—"Social casework and social group work: Historical foundations," in Robert Morris (Ed.), *Encyclopedia of Social Work*, New York: National Association of Social Workers, pp. 1237–1245.
CLARK, BURTON R.
   1956—"Organizational adaptation and precarious values," *American Sociological Review*, 21, pp. 327–336.
FRANKEL, ARTHUR AND PAUL GLASSER
   1973—"Behavioral approaches to group work," *Social Work*, in press.
HERMAN, MELVIN AND BERNARD ROSENBERG
   1967—"Effecting organizational change through a demonstration project: The case of a youth-work program," in George A. Brager and Francis P. Purcell (Eds.), *Community Action Against Poverty*, New Haven, Connecticut: College and University Press, pp. 83–103.
PURCELL, FRANCIS P. AND HARRY SPECHT
   1965—"The house on Sixth Street," *Social Work*, 10, 4(October), pp. 69–76.
RICHMOND, MARY E.
   1971—*Social Diagnosis*, New York: The Free Press.
SEDER-JACOBSON, DORIS
   1971—"Mental health services for children," in Robert Morris (Ed.), *Encyclopedia of Social Work*, New York: National Association of Social Workers, pp. 813–822.
THOMAS, EDWIN J.
   1971—"Social casework and social group work: The behavioral modification approach," in Robert Morris (Ed.), *Encyclopedia of Social Work*, New York: National Association of Social Workers, pp. 1226–1237.
VINTER, ROBERT D.
   1965—"Analysis of treatment organizations," *Social Work*, 8, 3(July), pp. 3–15.

19.

Organizational Factors in Services to Groups

YEHESKEL HASENFELD

Group procedures for bringing about planned change in individuals, groups and institutions are being used currently in a wide range of social service agencies. Like other intervention methods in social work, group work practice nearly always is imbedded in a formal organizational setting as a component of the total service of an agency. Group work can be seen, from an organizational perspective, as one of the means by which an agency attempts to fulfill its goals. Nevertheless, much of the theory and practice of social group work tends to be based on a "clinical practice" model rather than an "organizational practice" model. A *clinical practice* model focuses primarily (and often exclusively) on client-change agent relations and the purposeful use of these relations for change, with minimal attention given to the organization within which such relations exist or to the impact the organization has on the entire change process. The clinical model typically assumes that the organization has a limited effect and that decision-making processes concerning every phase of the treatment or change are strictly based on the therapeutic needs and states of clients. Although references to the influence of the organizational setting on group-work practice can be found, this factor tends to occupy a residual position in the model itself.

The clinical practice model ignores the fundamental fact that any planned change method such as group work, when embedded in a complex organization, becomes subject to the dynamics operating in the organization's various subsystems. Such organizational dynamics include pressures to achieve proficiency in service delivery, to maintain a balance between task demands and personal needs, to procure needed resources, to obtain social support and legitimation, to manage relations with various external groups, and to coordinate and direct the functioning of the various subsystems (Katz and Kahn, 1966). Change techniques, group work included, must adapt to these basic functions of the organization and will reflect the constraints and contingencies imposed by other subsystems in the organization.

Organizational properties play a significant role in shaping every phase of the change or treatment sequence (1) by defining the client input, (2) in prescribing the target of change, (3) by defining and prescribing the role of the worker, and (4) in structuring key elements in the environment of the group itself.

TYPES OF SOCIAL SERVICE AGENCIES
AND GROUP WORK PRACTICE

Degrees and patterns of organizational influence upon group work practice vary from setting to setting. It is essential that types of social service agencies be distinguished along the dimensions that have particular impact in shaping the character and function of the intervention methods used. Social service agencies can be sorted into two types: first, according to the nature of the agency, its goals and internal structure; and second, according to the relations between the agency and its clients (Wheeler, 1966:51–116).

Organizational Goals and Structure

A first question to be asked is whether the function of an agency is socialization or resocialization of client (Vinter, 1963:3–15). The function will determine the overall purpose of group work practice and the type of client to be served. In socialization agencies such as the public school, the youth-serving agency, and the community center, the purpose of group services will be to supplement and complement other socialization methods. Clients will be perceived as "normal" and as motivated to change. However, group work may also perform a control function in such organizations to serve clients judged to be failing or lagging in their socialization process. In resocialization agencies such as the child guidance clinic, welfare department, and the mental hospital, the purpose of group work and other techniques is to achieve major behavioral changes in clients who are defined as deviants.

A second consideration is the degree of complexity and the internal differentiation of the agency. The greater the organizational complexity and differentiation, the greater the constraints placed upon the patterns of group work. In a complex organization, group work will need to be coordinated with the activities and schedules of other departments, to conform to general regulations and procedures despite the idiosyncratic needs

TABLE 1.

		Organizational Goals	
		Socialization	Resocialization
Organizational Complexity	Undifferentiated	Youth Club Day care center	Private group therapy Street gang work
	Differentiated	Public school Community center	Psychiatric hospital Residential treatment center

of the clients, and to compete with other treatment or change methods (Cloward, 1956).

Cross-classification of organizational function and internal complexity can result in four kinds of agencies, as exemplified in Table 1.

Organization-Client Relations

The second type of social service agency is concerned with the nature of relations between the organization and its clients. Its first dimension is the degree of control the agency has over the client. At one extreme are agencies that base their services on the voluntary participation of the client, such as the youth service agency or private family service agency. At the other extreme are agencies that have nearly total control over the client, such as the correctional institution or mental hospital. A major task for group work in the former will be to maintain the client's commitment and attachment to the agency; while in the latter, group work will confront the task of maintaining the client's compliance to the organizational regime.

A second dimension of the organization-client relationship is the degree to which the agency transacts with clients as individuals or as groups (Wheeler, 1966:60–66). In an agency that regularly deals with clients individually (child guidance clinic or a welfare department), the deployment of group procedures runs counter to the basic work structure. Group work practice in such settings tends to be marginal and confronts the problem of formulating a common basis for clients to interact as a group. For example, group work practice with AFDC mothers tends to occupy a marginal position in the total service program of the agency. The group worker and the clients are constantly preoccupied with identifying and maintaining a common basis to justify the existence of the group (Costabile and Glasser, 1963). In an agency where clients often function collectively, group work encounters competition from other organizational units that transact with clients collectively in the pursuit of the unit goals. These patterns of interaction may neutralize or negate the group processes instituted by the worker. In a juvenile correctional setting, an internal conflict

TABLE 2.

		Agency Control Over Client	
		Low	High
Mode of Transaction with Clients	Individual	Child guidance clinic Adoption service	Probation Parole
	Collective	Summer camp Street gang work	Correctional institution Psychiatric hospital

may exist between cottage parents, educators, and social workers vis-à-vis the inmate groups (Street, et al., 1966; Polsky, 1962). Similarly, the relationship of a teacher to his classroom may differ radically from the relationship of a social worker to the same group of pupils.

While in an individual-oriented agency the group worker encounters forces reducing the potential attraction and cohesion of the group, in a group-oriented agency, the worker encounters powerful group forces, such as the inmate subculture, over which he has limited control. The cross-classification in Table 2 highlights the various combinations of organization-client relations that impinge directly on the content of group work practice in different settings.

ORGANIZATION AND THE INTAKE PROCESS

Social service agencies direct their services to fairly well-defined populations. The client population is determined by a number of organizational factors the most important of which are its goals and mission, and the relations of the organization with its environment. Through the definition of its basic mission and goals, the organization attempts to institutionalize itself as a viable and important unit within the larger welfare arena. It does so by specifying the type of human problems it claims to respond to, the population to be served, and the services to be offered. The goals of the organization set key parameters that define the attributes of the clients within its domain and, *ipso facto,* the characteristics of the clients outside its domain. In the process of establishing and maintaining itself as a viable organization, the social service agency must also negotiate exchange relations with critical elements in its environment in order to secure sufficient input, to secure social acceptance and legitimation of its activities, to marshal the necessary service technologies, and to establish supportive relations with the consumers and beneficiaries of its services (Perrow, 1961). In so doing the organization must accommodate a wide range of often conflicting constraints and contingencies that these external groups present. An organization's response to such contingencies is reflected in the policies that define the attributes of clients or client problems that fall within the domain of the organization (Hasenfeld, 1972). For example, competition over resources may lead agencies for the blind to serve blind children exclusively (Scott, 1967); the need to show success may lead some rehabilitation agencies to reject seriously handicapped persons as clients (Levin and White, 1961).

The culminating result is that the clients the group worker is asked to serve have been prescreened and preselected, and their problems and attributes have been partly defined by the organization's intake procedures. That is, the initial status of the client and the preliminary assessment of his problems and attributes are presented to the worker in the first stage of the treatment sequence. In the private family service agency, clients referred to a worker are likely to have been selected by criteria such as the nature of the client's problem, his social class, place of residence, and the like (Cloward and Epstein, 1965). Such criteria become crucial constraints in the decision-making processes of the worker during intake, for they define *a priori* the key variables in the diagnosis process. The organization itself is a very "significant other" whose definition of the client and his problem constitutes a basic building block for the diagnostic process.

Furthermore, client problems presented to the group worker may have been partially induced by the organization itself, particularly in "total institutions." In such organizations the worker may be asked to deal with problems generated by the client's isolation from his natural environment, or with problems of maintaining the compliance and acquiescence of the client to institutional requirements for control and order, or with problems generated from the client's interaction with other inmates. Group services are often called upon to deal with organizationally induced problems in other settings as well. Vinter and Sarri (1965) point out, for example, that instances of educational malperformance need to be viewed "as resultants of the interaction of both pupil characteristics and school conditions." Organizational factors can induce similar problems for welfare recipients, probationers, and unwed mothers, among others. The probability that the diagnosis will find organizationally induced problems increases as the control of the organization over the client increases and/or as the organization interacts more with clients collectively.

Organizational goals further influence the diagnostic process in the sense that they pattern the decision making of the worker (Simon, 1964). They do so by defining the boundaries of the agency's concern and by attaching more or less importance to various problems and attributes presented by the client and significant others. For example, the organizational goals of a child guidance clinic may direct the worker toward a diagnostic exploration of parent-child relations, child-peer relations, child attitudes toward authority, and the like, rather than toward an exploration of the employment or economic problems of the parents, adequacy of housing, and membership in various social groups, even though the latter factors may produce equal stress on the client. The worker is not likely to explore client problems to which the organization does not have resources to respond (Hasenfeld, 1971).

ORGANIZATIONAL GOALS, TREATMENT OBJECTIVES, AND GROUP GOALS

The relationship between the diagnosis and the formulation of treatment objectives is mediated not only by the change or treatment theories adopted by the worker, but also by the operative goals of the organization itself. As defined by Perrow (1961:855) "operative goals designate the ends sought through the actual operating policies of the organization." They are in turn established through complex and critical decision-making processes by members of the organization; ultimately, an operating balance is achieved between competing service ideologies and adaptive needs of the organization. An organization's operating goals reflect five interdependent policy issues.

1. The service ideologies of the executive elite
2. The availability of the technical means to achieve various service objectives
3. The costs involved in pursuing different service alternatives and the availability of resources
4. The needs to maintain a stable internal work and authority structure
5. The constraints placed on the organization by external regulatory groups such as legislature, funding agencies, professional organizations, etc.

Decisions and choices made by an agency in these areas are expressed in its operative goals. They influence the definition of worker treatment objectives in ways similar, although more intense than the manner in which organizational goals influence the intake process. In his choice of treatment objectives the group worker, as a member of the organization, incorporates into his decision making some of the following considerations:

1. The extent to which alternative treatment objectives conform to the predominant service ideologies of the agency. The greater the congruency between a worker's treatment objectives and his agency's operative goals, the greater the likelihood of mutual support. For example, if the

predominant service ideology of the welfare department is to encourage AFDC mothers to get off welfare, the worker's treatment objectives are more likely to include encouraging the mothers to seek employment, enter training programs, and use day care facilities for their children, rather than to increase their welfare grants, to develop self-esteem as welfare recipients, and the like. Similarly, if the predominant treatment ideology of a juvenile correctional program is based on education and training, rather than the development of self-awareness and insight, the treatment objectives of the group worker are more likely to reflect the former, rather than the latter.

2. The degree to which the organization has the necessary resources to pursue alternative treatment objectives and plans. The worker will be constrained to choose those treatment objectives for which he can marshal necessary organizational resources. Needless to say, resources such as the availability of manpower, equipment, and facilities necessary for the treatment plan play an important role in the unfolding of the treatment process. In addition, the very selection of treatment goals is affected by the degree of control the organization has over crucial elements in its environment that potentially or actually influence the functioning of the client. The greater the control or influence the organization has over such elements, the wider the range of treatment goals the worker can pursue. For example, treatment goals for a group of mental patients being prepared for reintegration in the community are likely to reflect the referral options most available to the hospital. A group worker in an employment services agency will be influenced by the jobs available to the agency. Similarly, group work with socially deprived youth to introduce changes in their relations with school personnel, parents and police, as advocated by Empey (1968), is preconditioned by the social service agency's relations with and influence upon parents, police, and school personnel.

3. The degree to which alternative treatment objectives conflict with the tasks of other organizational units. Most likely the group worker will be asked to formulate treatment goals that are congruent with the tasks of other staff members vis-à-vis the clients. Yet to do so may pose various dilemmas to the worker, particularly in settings which relate to clients collectively and maintain a high level of control over them. In a school, for example, the worker will be pressured to formulate treatment goals that complement the needs of the teachers rather than the children. In a youth service center, the group worker may be discouraged from pursuing treatment goals for maladaptive behaviors displayed by the youth, if such goals are perceived to conflict with the agency's recreation functions. In a correctional institution, the worker may be prohibited from formulating treatment plans that raise security problems.

4. The extent to which alternative treatment goals can be legitimated

by the organization. The worker is not likely to obtain the support of an agency if his treatment goals call for activities perceived to undermine the legitimacy of the organization or endanger its relations with important external units. This issue becomes particularly problematical when the group seeks to achieve social change. When the target of change is the organization itself or an external unit essential to the survival of the organization, the worker may face considerable sanctions. Consider, for example, the problem the welfare worker will encounter from his agency when organizing welfare recipients to change department policies.

The above discussion points to specific ways in which organizational factors interact with treatment in the process of formulating goals. Individual treatment goals and the motives of individual clients become the two major considerations in shaping group goals. Yet, even the motives of individual clients are affected by the relations between the client and the agency. The referral and intake processes of the agency pattern the motives the client has in relation to the agency. Through his contacts and experiences with the agency, he develops conceptions as to what he can or cannot expect from it; his motives are shaped accordingly. The lay referral system (Freidson, 1961) in the community also influences the client's motives as he approaches the organization. The youth who joins a group at the recreation center is likely to seek "fun" rather than a change in his behavior toward authority figures. Likewise an inmate may join group counseling as an avenue to obtain early parole (Kassenbaum, et al., 1971). In short, the "reputation" of the organization influences the motives that potential clients develop and that they bring with them to the group. The dynamic process through which group goals develop and the impact of the organization on the process is presented in Figure 1.

ORGANIZATIONAL STRUCTURE
AND THE WORKER'S ROLE

If the agency is seen as a significant component of the group's environment, it follows that the greater the control the worker has over resources in this environment the greater will be his influence over the group (Collins and Guetzkow, 1964). French and Raven (1959) identify five bases of influence or power—reward, coercive, legitimate, referent, and expert—all of which are controlled to various degrees by the agency. The position of the worker in the organizational power structure will determine (1) the sources or bases of his power, (2) the amount of power he can mobilize, and (3) the conditions under which such power can be used. The position of the worker in the organization determines his access to rewarding or coercive resources and defines the basis of his legitimacy and expertise. Although the worker may have a high degree of legitimacy and

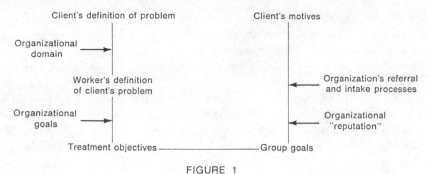

FIGURE 1

expertise in other systems, the agency defines the worker's legitimacy and level of expertise, vis-à-vis the clients, for it controls his range and scope of activities. Zald (1962) found that in correctional institutions which emphasized custodial goals, the power of social workers was significantly lower than the power of cottage parents. Hence the ability of the social worker to influence the behavior of the inmates was significantly lower than that of the cottage parents in such settings. Even referent power, which is based on interpersonal attraction, derives partly from rewarding activities by the worker and is influenced by his organizational position. Other things being equal, the higher the status of the worker in the agency's power structure, the larger his base of power, and consequently, the greater his influence over the group. It is interesting to note that in agencies where group work serves as the predominant intervention technology, the worker occupies a powerful position in the organization, as for example, in the Provo experiment in delinquency rehabilitation (Empey and Rabow, 1961).

The agency influences both the worker's bases of power and the conditions of their use. This factor is of critical importance since each base of power varies significantly in its effectiveness in influencing the client's behavior and in maintaining the altered behavior (French and Raven, 1959). In the Provo experiment, the primary sources of power tended to be coercive, whereas in the youth-serving agency the primary sources of power are likely to be rewards and interpersonal attraction. The goals and resources of the organization are likely to determine the power bases the worker can mobilize, although the worker may be constrained as to the conditions of their use. For example, the worker with AFDC mothers may not be allowed to supply the mothers with additional financial support except under specified conditions. The group worker in the school setting may be constrained from having his clients participate in extracurricular activities without the teacher's consent.

The quality of the relationships the worker develops with his clients is very much affected by the quality of his relations with other staff members in the organization. A process of "isomorphism" occurs in which worker-group relations come to reflect the same structural properties of worker relations with staff members in the agency. Three interrelated dimensions that may characterize the quality of staff relations can be identified:

1. *The use of authority and supervision.* The discharge of authority and patterns of supervision influence the use of authority by the worker himself in the group. The more formalized and rigid the authority relations among staff, the more formalized and rigid the worker's role in the group is likely to be. And the basis of the authority relations—coercive, utilitarian or normative—is also likely to be reflected in the relations between the worker and his clients.

2. *The level of conflict among staff.* The greater the level of conflict between the worker and other staff, the more likely the consequences of this conflict will be reflected in the worker's relations with his clients. The worker, on the one hand, brings into the group the uncertainties of his role definition; and the group, on the other hand, reacts negatively to such uncertainties and the probable precarious position of the worker.

3. When morale among staff is low, when communication channels are broken, and when there is a high rate of change among staff, the worker is likely to function with a low level of motivation and a high degree of uncertainty. The capacity of the worker as a change agent under such circumstances is clearly curtailed. In settings where transactions are with clients collectively, a high degree of structural uncertainty among staff tends to elicit disruptive behavior and disintegration among the clients themselves. This pattern is most evident in mental hospitals and correctional institutions (Denzin, 1969).

The above discussion hints at the problems faced by the professional social worker practicing in a setting in which professional norms may come into conflict with bureaucratic procedures (Billingsley, 1967). The group worker encounters conflicting demands of allegiance from his agency, his profession, the group, and individual clients. The manner in which he resolves these conflicting pressures determines the type of role he assumes in the group.

ORGANIZATIONAL PROCESSES
AND GROUP PROCESS

The uniqueness of group work practice is the planned manipulation of group structure and processes so that the group itself may change its members. Some of the key properties that the worker attempts to influence are group composition and size, group goals, group problem-solving procedures, leadership structure, and group development. The properties of the group reflect both its external and internal systems (Homans, 1950). Here focus is on the external system, and examination is given to the emergence of group properties as a response to the group's external environment, of which the agency is a crucial segment.

Group Composition and Size

The extent of agency control over the composition and size of the group is reflected in the position of the worker. Studies indicate that factors such as conflicting patterns of interpersonal personality traits among members, status incongruency, and heterogeneity of personalities and backgrounds may produce obstacles to the effectiveness of the group (Collins and Guetzkow, 1964:88–119). The less control the worker has over the composition of the group, the greater the probability that such obstacles will arise. Although the agency may not determine who should belong to the group, it usually defines the "pool" from which the worker must draw his clients, thereby limiting the ability of the worker to minimize obstacles to group effectiveness.

Studies on group size point to the fact that with increase in size there is a decrease in group attractiveness, an increase in the tendency toward centralization, and increase in communication difficulties (Thomas and Fink, 1963). The greater the pressure from the agency to include more clients in the group, the less the control of the worker over such group characteristics. In agencies that transact with clients collectively or define fixed career phases for them, the control of the worker over group composition and size is likely to be limited. In such diverse settings as the youth service center and the correctional institution, the worker must either accept every client who wishes to join the group or work with an already well-defined population. If group work is used to deal with problems arising from the adjustment of clients to fixed career phases in the agency such as entry or exit, the worker's choice of clients is limited.

Another dimension of group composition determined by the agency is the degree to which group membership is voluntary or nonvoluntary. In the latter instance, the group is likely to develop apathy, self-aggression, frustration, and inability to adapt to "free situations," which could undermine any treatment objective (Thibaut and Kelley, 1959:169–187).

Ecological Base

Probably the greatest impact the agency has over the group after its initial formation is in determining its ecological base. The *ecological base* of the group refers to its organizational location, the space and time allocated to it, and the resources that are available for carrying its various functions. Unfortunately, the least knowledge has been accumulated about the effects of these variables on the performance of the group. A pioneering study on the effects of the ecological base on group processes was done by Gump, et al., (1957) and Bettelheim (1955:17–41). No doubt, the greater the frequency and duration of interactions among members, the more cohesive the group is likely to become, other things being equal.

Studies on the social organization of inmates in juvenile correctional settings indicate that, when staff discourage and disrupt the interaction among inmates, the latter are likely to form very unstable relations among themselves (Street, et al., 1966:222–254). Likewise, the capacity of the group to develop well-defined boundaries and identity is partly determined by its ability to establish and shape its own "territory" according to its needs. Development of the group requires a space that provides some insulation from the environment and protection from excessive external disturbances. The space must also facilitate rather than hamper interaction and communication among members. Restrictions on the group in the use of time and space are likely to generate problems that must be solved by the group and that divert energies from its major tasks.

Most important are the resources provided by the agency to the group. Basic to group work practice are the resources necessary for program activities. As Vinter (Chapter 13 in this volume) indicates, the activities selected by the worker for the group are a major tool to achieve changes in group processes and the behavior of individual members. The choices of activities and the resources necessary to implement them are organizationally determined in two ways: (1) the resources available to the agency itself will determine the repertoire of activities available to the worker; and (2) the ability of the worker to use these resources in accordance with the needs of the group will be determined by the existence of organizational mechanisms to distribute them.

Finally, the ecological base of the group includes the reaction of other organizational units, including other staff members and other clients, to the group itself. Their attitudes and actions may facilitate or disrupt group processes. In general the group's ecological base as structured by the agency will determine whether the group can develop in a nurturing environment, or whether it must expend most of its energies to protect its survival. It is not surprising that one purpose of street gang work is to move the ecological base of the group from the street to the youth-serving center so that the new base will enable the group to pursue more legitimate goals.

Problem-Solving Procedures

The agency also influences the group's problem-solving procedures, partly through its control over the type and amount of information available to the group for solving its problems. The agency may withhold information about the purpose of the group, information about the attributes of each member, information about treatment decisions, etc. The most extreme example of information control can be noted in the Provo experiment (Empey and Rabow, 1961). The amount and type of information needed varies according to the nature of the problems to be solved. The group's effectiveness therefore depends upon the degree to which the agency provides the proper information when needed. For example, a group of underachievers attempting to develop new learning skills will find the task extremely difficult without knowledge of the evaluative criteria used by teachers. Similarly, inmates preparing for exit from the correctional institution cannot function properly without knowledge of the parole board's decision-making processes.

On the other hand, a group may encounter a great deal of "noise" in its communication network if the agency fails to provide adequate buffers to the group from external stimuli. This situation may occur when the group lacks an appropriate meeting place; when other staff persons interact freely or randomly with the members of the group, and when the group receives conflicting messages about the agency's policies, procedures and regulations, and expectations from the group. Both information deficit and noise can seriously impair a group's problem-solving capabilities.

Leadership Structure

The agency also affects the group's leadership structure through the resources it provides. This aspect of the ecological base of the group is directly related to the division of labor within the group. When the resources are scarce, the group's ability to develop an elaborate division of labor will be limited; and its leadership functions will tend to be concentrated among few. Scarcity of resources also increases competition within the group; strategies to resolve competition and conflict, such as cooperation, domination by a few members, disintegration, etc., have direct consequences for the structure of leadership in the group. The worker's ability to influence the leadership structure depends on the resources available to him. The stability of the emerging leadership also depends on the support it receives from outside the group, from other units in the agency, for example. Again, the presence or absence of such support is more critical in agencies that transact with clients collectively or have control over them. Thus, for example, when the leaders of a treatment group in a mental hospital are not supported by the nurses or psychiatrists, their position in the group is likely to be precarious, and vice versa.

Group Development

The reward structure of the agency needs to be mentioned again in this context. The ability of the group to develop and influence the behavior of its members in accordance with treatment plans is dependent, to a large measure, on the reward structure of the agency vis-à-vis the group. Relations between the two are mediated, by and large, by the worker. The effectiveness of the worker is a function of his ability to reward the group processes that enhance the attainment of the treatment objectives. One important aspect of the reward structure, besides its magnitude, is its internal consistency. The agency's reward structure may simultaneously reward conflicting behaviors or fail to reward appropriate behavior. Such inconsistencies can occur when the structure of an agency is highly differentiated and when various units are likely to transact with the same clients. In this situation the group worker is only *one* of the mediators between the agency's reward structure and the clients, and a continuous source of conflict in such agencies is the application of conflicting reward schedules by various staff members to the same clients. The group worker may discover that while he encourages a certain type of behavior among the members of his group, other staff may discourage such behavior or even punish it. Thus, unless effective patterns of coordination exist in the agency, group development toward treatment goals may be retarded or jeopardized.

CONCLUSION

The common failure of group work theory to recognize the organizational forces that shape the nature of group work practice may help explain the endemic gap between group work theory and practice. An alternative to the clinical model has been adopted through a perspective on group work as a subsystem within a larger organizational system that defines what goes in and comes out of group work practice and also predetermines group work processes.

Analyses of organizational variables that influence group work practice and of the dynamics through which these variables affect the worker and the group imply that the effectiveness of group work is dependent upon certain organizational prerequisites; and that the group worker cannot assume a passive role in the agency but must engage in the analysis of the effects of the setting on the group and himself. As a result, the worker may find that he needs to induce and stimulate changes within the organization itself before he can effectively achieve changes in his clients.

REFERENCES

BETTLEHEIM, BRUNO
1955—*Truants From Life,* Glencoe, Illinois: The Free Press.

BILLINGSLEY, ANDREW
1967—"Bureaucratic and professional orientation patterns in social case-work," *Social Service Review*, 38, pp. 400–407.
COLLINS, BARRY AND HAROLD GUETZKOW
1964—*A Social Psychology of Group Process for Decision Making*, New York: John Wiley & Sons.
COSTABILE, JANE AND PAUL H. GLASSER
1963—"An AFDC mothers' group: Social group work in the bureau of social aid," Unpublished Teaching Record, The University of Michigan.
CLOWARD, RICHARD
1956—"Agency structure as a variable in services to groups," in *Group Work and Community Organization*, Selected Papers, 83rd Annual Forum on Social Welfare, New York: Columbia University Press.
CLOWARD, RICHARD AND IRWIN EPSTEIN
1965—"Private social welfare's disengagement from the poor: The case of family adjustment agencies," in M. Zald (Ed.), *Social Welfare Institutions*, New York: John Wiley & Sons, pp. 623–644.
DENZIN, NORMAN
1969—"Collective behavior in total institutions: The case of the mental hospital and the prison," *Social Problems*, 15, pp. 353–365.
EMPEY, LAMAR
1968—"Sociological perspectives and small-group work with socially deprived youth," *Social Service Review*, 42: 448–463.
EMPEY, LAMAR AND JEROME RABOW
1961—"The Provo experiment in delinquency rehabilitation," *American Sociological Review*, 26: 679–696.
FREIDSON, ELIOT
1961—*The Patient's View of Medical Practice*, New York: Russell Sage.
FRENCH, JOHN J., JR. AND BERTRAM RAVEN
1959—"The bases of social power," in Dorwin Cartwright (Ed.), *Studies in Social Power*, Ann Arbor: The University of Michigan, pp. 150–167.
GUMP, PAUL, P. SCHOGGEN, AND FRITZ REDL
1957—"The camp milieu and its immediate effects," *Journal of Social Issues*, 13, pp. 40–46.
HASENFELD, YEHESKEL
1971—"Organizational dilemmas in innovating social services: The case of the community action centers," *Journal of Health and Social Behavior*, 12, pp. 208–216.
1972—"People-processing organizations: An exchange approach," *American Sociological Review*, 37, pp. 256–263.
HOMANS, GORGE
1950—*The Human Group*, New York: Harcourt, Brace and World.
KASSENBAUM, GENE G., DAVID A. WARD AND DANIEL M. WILNER
1971—*Prison Treatment and Parole Survival*, New York: John Wiley & Sons.
KATZ, DANIEL AND ROBERT KAHN
1966—*The Social Psychology of Organizations*, New York: John Wiley & Sons.

LEVINE, SOL AND PAUL WHITE
1961—"Exchange as a conceptual framework for the study of interorganizational relations," *Administrative Science Quarterly,* 5, pp. 581–601.
PERROW, CHARLES
1961—"The analysis of goals in complex organizations," *American Sociological Review,* 26, pp. 854–866.
POLSKY, HOWARD W.
1962—*Cottage Six: The Social System of Delinquent Boys in Residential Treatment,* New York: Russell Sage.
SCOTT, ROBERT A.
1967—"The selection of clients by social welfare agencies: The case of the blind," *Social Problems,* 14, pp. 248–257.
SIMON, HERBERT A.
1964—"On the concept of organizational goal," *Administrative Science Quarterly,* 9, pp. 1–21.
STREET, DAVID, ROBERT D. VINTER, AND CHARLES PERROW
1966—*Organization for Treatment,* New York: The Free Press.
THIBAUT, JOHN AND HAROLD KELLEY
1959—*The Social Psychology of Groups,* New York: John Wiley & Sons.
THOMAS, EDWIN J., AND CLINTON F. FINK
1963—"Effects of Group Size," *Psychological Bulletin,* 60, pp. 371–384.
VINTER, ROBERT D.
1963—"Analysis of treatment organizations," *Social Work,* 8, pp. 3–15.
VINTER, ROBERT D. AND ROSEMARY C. SARRI
1965—"Malperformance in the public school: A group work approach," *Social Work,* 10, pp. 3–13.
WHEELER, STANTON
1966—"The structure of formally organized socialization settings," in O. G. Brim and S. Wheeler (Eds.), *Socialization After Childhood,* New York: John Wiley & Sons, pp. 51–116.
ZALD, MAYER
1962—"Organizational control structures in five correctional institutions," *American Journal of Sociology,* 68, pp. 335–345.

IV

Group Work in Selected Fields of Practice

20.

Behavioral Group Treatment with Adults in a Family Service Agency

MARTIN SUNDEL and HARRY LAWRENCE

In recent years, there has been an outpouring of new forms of therapy that readily utilize the small group as a means of treatment. Gestalt therapy, existential therapy and transactional analysis, to name but a few, have not only enjoyed public popularity through group approaches but have also influenced social group work practice.

In contrast, behavior modification, though proven to be highly effective in individual treatment, has had a negligible impact to date on group work. The reason may be that behavior modification involves the assessment of the responses of one individual within a specific environmental context. It involves "the application of the results of learning theory and experimental psychology to the problems of altering maladaptive behavior" (e.g., Thomas, 1967; Ullman and Krasner, 1965; Wolpe, 1969). A behavior modifier would not assume that all members of a group have the same problematic behavior or the same environmental conditions that maintain the behavior, even though they may appear to have a common set of problems. Faced with this *apparent* dilemma some practitioners have concluded that there is no advantage to be gained from using behavior modification with groups.

The writers, however, have been successfully experimenting with methods of carrying out individual behavior assessments and problem solving within a group context. Our explorations suggest that a client can often gain greater benefits through behavior modification in a group than in individual treatment.

Behavior modification with groups is a viable approach. To determine its range of effectiveness will require the testing of its procedures under

This article was originally titled "Behavior modification in adult groups." Reprinted with permission of the National Association of Social Workers, from *Social Work*, Vol. 17, No. 2 (March 1972), pp. 34–43.

differing group conditions. This report of its use with adult clients is one probe into what are yet unexplored group applications of behavior modification.

In the treatment model of social group work, a client becomes a member of the group as a means of solving a problem of concern to himself and/or significant others. The goal of treatment, as considered here, is not that the client learn to be a "good group member" or have a "warm group experience." These and other *group functioning* objectives, such as high cohesiveness, democratic leadership and self-revealing communication, are only relevant to the degree that they facilitate the achievement of treatment goals which pertain to desired individual behavior outside the group. Group functioning objectives vary according to the tasks required to solve a problem. They are means to an end, not ends in themselves.

In the treatment approach to group work, goals for the solution of each member's problem are specified early in the group's history. These goals may be revised later or changed, but it is essential that the members and worker have a concrete understanding of each of these treatment goals. The evaluation of success rests on the extent to which a member's specified goal has been reached.

Once the worker and the group have assessed a member's problem with him and delineated a solution or goal, the worker's next task is to find the most *efficient* and *effective* interventions for achieving the outcome desired. These interventions may involve direct, indirect and extragroup means of influence (Vinter, Chapter 3 in this volume). Selection of appropriate interventions is based, in part, on social science knowledge (e.g., small group, social role and behavior theory) of how people acquire, maintain and change their behavior. In this respect, the group worker is like the physician who applies his knowledge of anatomy, physiology and pharmacology to treat an abscess; or like the engineer, who uses physics, metallurgy and geology to construct a bridge.

In contrast to the treatment model of group work, there are other group work approaches that define their goals in terms of the interventions they employ. They are limited in their utilization of social science knowledge because they emphasize one's skill in following uniform methods that have been predetermined by traditional social work practice. Evaluation of a meeting, for example, is often based on how well the worker observed a subtle communication or facilitated a member's participation in a discussion. Skills such as these are certainly important, but if they supersede or become detached from a concern for the goal to be achieved and the tasks to be accomplished, they become stylistic exercises devoid of purpose. A social worker preoccupied with style is like an architect who becomes so carried away by his artistic design that he disregards the function his proposed building is to perform. Science will have relevance to him only if he is concerned with structural-functional outcomes.

THE RELEVANCE OF BEHAVIOR
MODIFICATION TO GROUP WORK

During the past several years, social workers, clinical psychologists and psychiatrists have become increasingly interested in *behavior modification*. Proceeding on the premise that both maladaptive and adaptive behaviors are acquired, maintained or reduced by the same principles of conditioning, therapists have analyzed and treated a variety of problematic behaviors such as phobia, depression, school disruption, and interpersonal hostility and passivity.

The behavior modifier uses four basic procedures:

1. Identifying the problematic situation and specifying the relevant behavior to be changed in that situation
2. Discovering the reinforcers which maintain the problematic behavior and the reinforcers which may be manipulated to change it
3. Programming reinforcement schedules
4. Providing training for behavioral deficits where they exist so that the behavior necessary for problem solution is acquired.

Thus far, the use of behavior modification in group work has been limited but promising. In small group research, Hastorf (1965) used systematic social reinforcement to increase the verbal communication and consequent social status of underparticipating group members. Liberman (1970) successfully employed reinforcement methods to increase group cohesiveness. Rose (1969) reported the successful use of behavior modification with parents' groups (Rose and Sundel, Chapter 25 in this volume), and utilized behavior modification procedures with groups of delinquent adolescents to reduce their antisocial acts. Lawrence (1967) employed behavioral techniques with a group of welfare recipients to significantly improve their marketing and nutrition practices.

This paper describes a model for applying behavior modification principles in time-limited group treatment with adults. The major features of this model include developing pro-treatment group norms; teaching effective problem-solving skills that can be employed during and after group treatment; maximizing the therapeutic effects of social reinforcement by members for each other; developing desired client behavior within the group which the member can then apply in his natural environment.

The treatment described here was conducted at a voluntary family service agency. Most of the clients had been served by the agency for periods of one to five years prior to the beginning of this project. The clients' problems included child management, anxiety, marital discord, depression, and interpersonal difficulties with friends, family and co-workers.

Most of the group members were originally referred by their caseworkers. They were clients who were receiving casework services at the time of referral or were former clients who wished their cases reopened. In these circumstances, the caseworker discussed the possibility of group treatment with the clients. If sufficient interest was indicated, an appointment was made for the client with the group workers to further explore the possibility of his joining a treatment group. In a few instances, new clients were interviewed by the group workers at the point of intake and directly recruited for the group. All casework interviews with clients were terminated during the time they were receiving group services.

Limited attention was given to group composition. Clients were included in groups with minimal regard to age, sex, marital status, social class or type of problem. Educational levels within one group ranged from tenth grade to college graduation and occupations from unskilled to professional.

It was considered advantageous to have at least two members of the same sex in a group. To be eligible for these groups, the client had to have a problem that was primarily concerned with interpersonal difficulties or personal malfunction. Clients with socially deviant behavior problems that would likely lead to their being rejected by the group were not considered eligible.

Three groups were organized in order to achieve concrete, individual goals for a total of 17 participant members. A time limitation of eight weeks was established for the treatment process. Success of treatment was evaluated by the extent to which each member's goals were achieved in relation to the problems he brought to treatment.

In this paper, the treatment sequence of study, diagnosis, treatment and evaluation closely approximates that described in Vinter's "The Essential Components of Social Group Work Practice" (Chapter 2 in this volume).

INTAKE

Intake has been identified as "the process by which a potential client achieves client status." (Vinter, Chapter 2 in this volume) It includes the client's presentation of his problem and the worker's preliminary diagnosis and involves decisions on the part of worker and client as to whether or not treatment should be continued.

An intake interview was held with each client prior to the group's formation. The objectives of the workers for the initial interview were to elicit certain declarations *from each client:* (1) a statement of the problem(s) he wanted to work on in the group in behaviorally specific terms, (2) tentative specification of the goal(s) he wished to achieve from treatment, (3) a statement as to whether or not he wanted to participate in group treatment, (4) verbal agreement to the rules for participation in the group.

The following procedures were used to maximize the achievement of these objectives for the intake interview. They were designed to provide guidelines, rather than a rigid "cookbook" of prescriptions. The worker also considered the idiosyncracies of individuals and any predicaments that became apparent during the interview. Difficulties in achieving interview objectives typically have included worker-client value differences, fear of treatment, denial of the severity of a problem and anxiety in talking to the worker. Each of these circumstances may require alterations of the intake strategy. Despite such difficulties, workers have been successful in reaching the intake objectives in one interview.

Five Intake Procedures

Procedure 1.   The client was oriented to the initial interview before it was conducted. Each prospective group member was given a problem checklist to complete prior to the interview (see Appendix A). The client checked items indicating his areas of role difficulty (e.g., parent, spouse, employer) and double-checked those relationships of major concern to him. He gave written examples of how these relationships were problematic and specified what he desired in the way of change.

By examining the checklist, the workers were cued as to what to focus on in the interview. At the same time, the form had partially structured the way the client presented his problems.

Procedure 2.   The presenting problems were delineated in behaviorally specific terms. Rather than giving explicit descriptions of problems, clients often presented their concerns in one or another of the following forms:

1. Vague statements devoid of interpersonal or situational circumstances, e.g., "What's the point of going on?" or "Everything's going wrong in my life."
2. Assumptions about the causes of their problems, e.g., "Once I discover why I fear my father, I'll be able to handle my boss."
3. Assumptions about the solutions to their problems, e.g., "I've come to the conclusion that the only solution to my marital difficulties is to get a divorce."

Treatment of a problem based on such statements risks the use of interventions that might not alleviate the client's difficulty. Instead, the workers structured the interview to obtain a problem definition with the following components:

1. A statement from the client describing a specific problematic be-

havior of his own or of someone else within the context of the person(s) and circumstances involved, for example, "Whenever I prepare to leave the house in the evening, my mother shouts at me and accuses me of 'sleeping around' with men," or "When the boss asks me to explain my reports, I tremble and answer in monosyllables." Frequently a client described his problems only in terms of another's undesirable behavior, failing to recognize his own contribution to its occurrence. The delineation of a problem did not require the client to obtain this recognition during the intake interview. As the assessment process continued, the client came to describe his own behavior in maintaining the problem.

2. Two or more recent examples of each problem. If the examples were incongruous with the previous statement of the problem, the statement was revised so that it was consistent with the examples provided.

Procedure 3. The client and worker selected the problems to be worked on in the group and determined the priority which each problem would be given. Clients sometimes presented problems which later proved to be less serious or of less concern to them than other unstated problems. To maximize the selection of the appropriate problem, the client's problematic role areas, as indicated on the checklist, were reviewed. These relationships might include family (spouse, children, siblings, parents); work or school (supervisors, colleagues, supervisees); and friends (of the same or opposite sex).

The following criteria for establishing problem priorities were considered:

1. The client's expressed preference for one problem over another
2. The suitability of the problem for time-limited group treatment and its relationship to the problems of other group members
3. The negative consequences to the client or significant others for failure to solve the problem
4. The benefits that might accrue to the client or significant others for successful problem solution
5. The likelihood of success, given the client's existing behavioral repertoire, barriers and available resources
6. The extent to which the problem required handling before other problems could be worked on

In making a decision on the problem to be given highest priority, it has proven best to select the one which meets most or all of these criteria.

Procedure 4. Clients and workers developed tentative treatment goals. A tentative treatment goal is a statement of what the client can reasonably expect to achieve from group treatment. It states a desired alteration in the conditions of the problem as defined by the client. Although an attempt was made during intake to gain high specificity, complete formulation of the goal required the more detailed process of behavioral assessment which took place during the group meetings.

An example of a tentative treatment goal follows:

PROBLEM: Mr. Simpson loudly shouts at his daughter when telling her to do her chores. The daughter subsequently cries, kicks over furniture and avoids social contact with her father.

TENTATIVE GOAL: Without shouting, Mr. Simpson obtains compliance from his daughter in performing reasonable chores.

Procedure 5. An initial treatment contract was established with each client. The initial contract consisted of the worker's statements of the conditions for group participation, the client's agreement to abide by these conditions and the client's decision to enter treatment. During the contract discussion, the workers answered questions and explained the rationale for the procedures to be used. These procedures were discussed again during the first meeting of the whole group for reconfirmation.

GROUP DEVELOPMENT AND TREATMENT

In group treatment, the worker is responsible for guiding the activities and relationships of group members to facilitate the achievement of each individual member's treatment goals. Short-term treatment of problems in interpersonal relationships requires that effective group conditions be developed as rapidly as possible by means of the following activities:

Establishing a set of pro-treatment norms;
Clarifying problem priorities and treatment goals;
Teaching group members to assess each other's behavioral problems;
Teaching group members to develop solutions for each other's problems;
Enabling group members to prescribe and learn new responses;
Increasing the social reinforcement strength of the group.

Establishing Pro-treatment Norms

Five rules were stated by the workers during both the initial contract and group contract discussions. When a member departed from one of these rules, it was easier to point out his digression than it would have been if there had been no prior agreement. The workers initially pointed out deviations when they occurred. They also instructed and cued members to make similar comments when anyone broke a rule. In the beginning the workers assumed most of the responsibility for enforcing these rules. In time, the rules became group norms, with the members intervening where necessary to keep them in operation. The five rules, with the rationale for each, are presented below.

Rule 1. Members are expected to attend every meeting of the group. The meetings were designed according to an orderly progression, involving a systematic sequencing of behavioral concepts, steps in problem solving and tasks to be done. To miss a single meeting was viewed as so seriously hindering a member's subsequent participation that he could no longer keep up with the others. Therefore, it was made clear that a member's absence could lead to his removal from the group.

Rule 2. Members should refrain from socializing outside of the meeting until the series of meetings is concluded. This rule helped to establish that the group was task-oriented and existed as a means for achieving certain problem solutions rather than as an end in itself. Outside socializing may lead to attempts to bypass problem solving through conflicting gratifications gained from alliance with other group members. In one group, a married man was discussing his problem of social isolation. A single female member responded by inviting him to attend a social gathering at her home. A brief reminder by the workers of the contractual rule effectively stopped what could have had negative consequences for both members, as well as for the rest of the group.

Rule 3. Group discussion must be focused on contemporary events that relate to the member's problems. Because of prior therapeutic experiences and exposures to other group therapy approaches shown on television and in movies, members were requested to avoid discussing experiences in their personal histories. Treatment was focused on problems the client agreed to work on in the group; it was not an attempt to understand or change the "total personality."

Rule 4. Members are to refrain from hostile confrontation with each other. Members should comment on behavior observed in another without interpreting unobserved motives for the behavior. In some modes of therapy, members are encouraged to explore their feelings toward each other and to criticize each other's character. In such instances, members frequently impute negative motives for each other's behavior. In contrast, ventilation of hostile feelings was not viewed here as therapeutically useful, since it would have changed the focus of the group from problem solving about members' concerns outside the meeting to exploration of relationships between group members.

Speculation on motives can be counter-productive to problem solving, often stimulating angry interactions and preoccupation with untestable hypotheses. A member asked one group to explore why it was that Mrs.

Main didn't *want* to be assertive with her employer, implying that she was masochistic or enjoyed being abused. The workers explained to the members that this line of inquiry could lead to time-consuming speculations on childhood experiences and prior marital difficulties that had little relevance to the conditions influencing her employment problems.

Rule 5. Members should work on assigned tasks between group meetings. Assignments were formulated for members during each session. These assignments were carried out in the client's environment and the results reported back to the next meeting. By this means, the client learned by observation to discriminate which environmental events were most related to his actions.

It is important to clearly state and enforce the rules from the beginning of the group's history. If the worker waits until the members are behaving inappropriately, he is likely to encounter strong resistance to changing what has become an antitreatment norm. For example, one member may not complete his assignment for the week. If the worker fails to hold him accountable for this, it is likely that in the following sessions other members will also neglect their assignments.

Clarification of Priorities and Goals

In the first group meeting, the workers presented a written statement to each client indicating the previously agreed-upon treatment goals. The clients were offered the option of remaining with the same problem or rearranging their priorities. Such changes may have occurred because of altered life circumstances or previous concealment of major concerns.

Teaching Behavioral Assessment

Group members had had little or no exposure to the behavior modification approach. In order to be effective problem solvers, they had to learn how to assess behavior. The essentials of behavioral assessment were taught by workers, using the following three guidelines:

1. Concepts must be explained with a minimum of jargon and qualifications.
2. Concepts must be taught in the order of their application to concrete tasks required for member problem solving.
3. All members must use one concept correctly before moving on to the consideration of another.

The Components of Behavioral Assessment. Assessment of behavior was focused on the following components: Response, antecedents, consequences, and frequency (to be referred to as RAC-F Assessment).

A *response* is an observable verbal or motor behavior such as laughing, smiling, stealing, fighting, arguing or hitting. Each response must be described in precise terms: "John is aggressive toward his sister" must be restated "John hits his sister." Concepts such as "hostile," "passive-aggressive," or "low motivation" are not responses, since they fail to indicate what a person is doing in observable terms.

Problematic responses indicate either a behavioral deficit or surfeit. Behavioral deficits refer to appropriate behaviors that are absent or occur with low frequency (e.g., a ten-year-old child does not speak in complete sentences; a man rarely compliments his wife's cooking). Behavioral surfeits are inappropriate behaviors occurring with undesirable frequency (e.g., a boy often curses other children in the classroom; a child regularly soils his pants; a man beats his wife).

Antecedents are events that precede a specific response. For example, an antecedent for Bob's striking Joe with his fist was Joe's calling him "stupid." A second antecedent was two of Bob's friends' urging him to strike Joe.

Consequences refer to events that follow a response and which have the effect of increasing or decreasing the frequency of the response. For example, Mr. Smith's shouting at his wife increases if Mrs. Smith complies with all demands made while shouting; Miss Allen decreases her bragging when her boyfriend ridicules her for this.

Frequency refers to the number of times or the length of time a response occurs within a given interval. For example, "Mrs. Smith shouted at her daughter twelve times during the past week"; "Sally cried at the dinner table for ten minutes last Friday."

Teaching the Assessment Procedure. The first step in the assessment procedure was to teach the meaning of response. After explaining this concept, the workers conducted a role play which showed how to identify a response. In one role play, one worker interviewed the other who depicted a client having difficulty in dating. The interview demonstrated how to identify the response the client was complaining about. Following this, one of the workers assumed the role of a husband having marital difficulties. With cueing from the second worker, the members of the group interviewed the "client" and identified his problematic response: the husband was reading the newspaper in the presence of his children who were destroying the furniture.

Following the role plays, each member was interviewed by the group and helped to identify a problematic response in his situation. When sufficient clarity was obtained, he was given a behavioral assignment to observe this response in its natural setting and to record the frequency of its occurrence. RAC-F forms (see Appendix B) were distributed and used for recording this information. The workers checked with each client the following week as they reported on their behavioral assignments to make sure they understood the concept of response before progressing to a discussion of problem antecedents and consequences.

The concepts of antecedents and consequences were explained and diagrammed on an easel board. Role plays similar to those used in demonstrating response were employed to illustrate antecedents and consequences. The members were then given a behavioral assignment in which they were asked not only to observe the problematic response, but also to record the antecedents and consequences of the response.

The following example illustrates how essential data for a behavioral assessment were obtained. The problematic response of concern to Mrs. Dean was her older son George's hitting of his younger sister, Darlene. For the first assignment, Mrs. Dean reported ten instances when George hit his younger sister. The second report revealed twelve occurrences of hitting. Mrs. Dean also identified three antecedents of hitting: the daughter tattled on the brother, teased him, or disrupted the toys that he played with. The consequences of hitting were Mrs. Dean's yelling at the son and threatening physical punishment.

Teaching the Problem-Solving Process

A major advantage of a group over an individual treatment approach is the broader range of observations and experience that can be brought to bear on a client's problem. However, group members usually do not have the basic problem-solving skills that are required by the group treatment approach. These skills must be taught. By progressive steps, as the members demonstrate necessary skills, the workers shift the problem-solving responsibility to the group.

Five requisites for effective problem solving include:

1. A clear definition of the problem, indicating the problematic response, its antecedents and consequences
2. Determination of the frequency of the problematic response
3. Formulation of goals
4. Offering viable alternative solutions for achieving these goals
5. Deciding on the best solution from these alternatives

In order to carry out these problem-solving steps, it was necessary that the members learn to interview each other so as to minimize irrelevant remarks and references to unobservable states. For example, Mrs. Main prefaced her remarks about her boss by saying, "He is always out to get me." The group did not accept this irrelevant comment, but requested that she describe a representative encounter and what she and what the boss did in the interchange. Mr. Jones stated that his wife was "hostile" to him. The group asked him to illustrate exactly what he meant by "hostile" by describing what his wife actually did.

Behavioral Reenactment as a Tool in Assessment

Clients frequently experience difficulty in accurately describing their own actions in a problematic interchange. In such instances, it is advisable to use behavioral reenactment as a way of identifying the member's problematic response. In behavioral reenactment, the member gives a clear description of what occurred in one of the problematic interchanges. He is then asked to reenact the situation with group members performing the roles of significant others. After the reenactment, members indicate to him what they observed about his behavior.

For example, Mr. Jones complained that his wife was constantly criticizing him in a loud voice. He claimed he had done nothing preceding or following her criticism which could be responsible for it. One incident involved Mrs. Jones' accusing her husband of giving inadequate directions for going to a picnic. In the behavioral reenactment of this, Mr. Jones played himself and two members of the group portrayed his wife and daughter.

After the reenactment, the group pointed out to Mr. Jones the discrepancies between how he described his behavior and what they observed him doing during the reenactment. The members noted that during the interchange, Mr. Jones never looked directly at his wife and talked in a monotone. He made frequent irrelevant remarks and rarely answered her questions. In this way, Mr. Jones was told how his behavior served as the antecedents and consequences to his wife's criticisms.

Prescribing and Learning New Responses

After the behavioral assessment for a member is completed, the workers and the group develop an intervention plan with him based on behavior modification principles. Often, the prescription of a procedure which will alter the antecedents and/or consequences is sufficient because the client can perform the actions prescribed. At times, however, a member may not know how to perform the required behavior or may express fear about engaging in the behavior. In such instances, the procedures of behavioral rehearsal and assertive training can be used to develop the required behavioral skills.

Following the behavioral reenactment mentioned in the previous example, Mr. Jones expressed difficulty understanding what the members had described about his behavior. A group member demonstrated Mr. Jones' responses with his wife and daughter so that he could see better what he had done. The group then discussed appropriate ways of responding to his wife. A group member demonstrated the group's recommendations, indicating correct eye-to-eye contact with his wife and making explicit statements in response to her questions. In progressive steps, Mr. Jones imitated the modeled performance until he responded appropriately. This required that portions of the role play be repeated a number of times until he mastered the performance. Group members reinforced his performance through favorable and encouraging comments. He was given an assignment to use these assertive behaviors whenever his wife criticized him.

Increasing the Social Reinforcement
Strength of the Group

An important aspect of group treatment is the social reinforcement group members can provide each other. The group worker must not only maximize these reinforcers but also insure that they are delivered contingent upon desired behavior. Studies have shown that group members tend to value each other highly when they vicariously observe success achieved by another or are rewarded in the presence of other members of the group (Lott and Lott, 1965; Bandura, 1969). Therefore, it is important to arrange individual tasks so that they are likely to be successfully accomplished and so that these tasks be reported on or carried out in the group's presence.

Social reinforcement can be used to increase task-related behavior. The frequency of behaviors such as engaging in problem solving, carrying out prescribed assignments correctly, and reporting back to the group on them, can be increased through expressions of the group's encouragement and approval. During group discussions, workers delivered social reinforcement contingent on desired behaviors. When members made satisfactory comments, carried out their assignments, or engaged in prescribed behaviors outside or inside the group, they received verbal approval from the workers. The members gradually imitated this behavior, when cues were provided by the workers, and were reinforced for this. If someone reported success in carrying out a prescribed intervention, the workers often asked the group to comment with approval. Later, the members reinforced each other without the workers' prompting. In this way, the workers served as models for providing social reinforcement.

Other Concepts Taught

Two important concepts taught to the group were negative and positive reinforcement. One of the behavioral contingencies members most fre-

quently employed in their problematic relationships with others was negative reinforcement. *Negative reinforcement* occurs when an aversive stimulus is presented until the individual makes a response which removes that
stimulus. For example, Mrs. Bronson complained that her husband left
the house immediately after dinner each night and remained away with his
friends until after her bedtime. Assessment revealed that Mrs. Bronson
continuously criticized and nagged her husband during the time he was
present in the house. Thus the aversive stimulus of "nagging" was removed by Mr. Bronson's leaving the house. Unintentionally, Mrs. Bronson
had been employing negative reinforcement to maintain the undesired behavior of her husband.

Prior to group treatment, the group members rarely used positive
reinforcement to increase the frequency of desired behavior. *Positive reinforcement* consists of the presentation of an event following a behavior
that increases the future likelihood of the behavior's recurrence. Mr.
Curren had led a socially isolated life devoid of any interests or friends.
He complained that no one liked him at work. Assessment revealed that
he systematically rejected social invitations and responded with sarcastic
comments to friendly conversation. This resulted in a reduction of conversation initiated by co-workers. Mr. Curren was encouraged to use positive reinforcement procedures with the men at work. He was to watch for
those times when someone approached him and to respond with interest
and approval. As a result, Mr. Curren became engaged in longer, more
pleasant conversations with his co-workers; his new behavior led to new
friendships.

Clients often blame the other party in a problematic relationship
without attempting to change their own behavior in the situation. The
workers explained that changing undesirable behavior in others involves
alteration of the antecedents or consequences of that behavior and that
it is possible to change the undesirable behavior of others through altering
one's own responses. A striking example of a change that involved a person not treated in the group was that of Mr. Curren's wife in the case described above. Mr. Curren had complained that his wife often rejected his
sexual advances. Through his increased use of positive reinforcement and
his reduction of overly aggressive demands, Mrs. Curren became sexually
responsive to him.

TERMINATION AND EVALUATION

The advantage of a time-limited group is that it sets a reasonable
expectation of how long it will take to clear up a problem. When length
of treatment is left open-ended, a client may assume that a problem can be

attacked in a casual manner. To emphasize the reality of time limitation, clients were told that if they followed the treatment procedure they could reasonably expect solutions to their problems within that time limit. A high commitment in terms of work and regularity of attendance was required. Our experience has been that most of the problems dealt with in our therapy groups were adequately resolved during the period of the eight group meetings. The workers were available during two scheduled follow-up sessions to provide further assistance if necessary.

Through systematic data collection and reporting to the group, clients and workers directly evaluated the extent to which treatment goals were achieved. Goals had been formulated as part of the behavioral assessment for each client; the client's desired response had been established, along with the desired supporting conditions. Mrs. Dean had listed her son's hitting of the younger daughter as the problematic response. Her goal was to reduce the frequency of the hitting until it rarely occurred. When the elimination of a particular behavior is the goal, it is important to include a second goal which indicates a positive behavior that should replace the negative one. For example, in addition to Mrs. Dean's goal of sharply decreasing the frequency of her son's hitting the daughter, there was a second goal to increase the amount of time the son engaged in cooperative play with his sister. After completion of treatment, the boy's hitting had been reduced from an average of two times per day to an acceptable level of twice a month. In contrast, the discussion of cooperative play with his sister had increased from less than ten minutes daily to approximately forty-five minutes each day.

Follow-Up Evaluations

One-month and six-month follow-up interviews were held with each of the members in each of the groups. Members were seen separately for research reasons so that follow-up evaluations could closely approximate the pre-group situation. In practice, group follow-up meetings have also been effectively used. The purpose of the following-up interviews was to evaluate the extent to which the goals achieved during group treatment had been maintained. A second purpose was to provide additional interventions, if necessary, for the problem considered during group treatment. The follow-up procedure began with the presentation of a problem checklist. (See Appendix C.) Through this instrument, it was possible to determine the degree to which the client recognized the problem that he had been working on in the group and could evaluate the extent to which his treatment goals had been achieved.

The one-month and six-month follow-ups revealed that in almost all cases the members had either maintained the gains made during the treatment or had substantially gone beyond what had been achieved at termination of the groups. For example, Mr. Curren indicated that sexual relations with his wife had become highly satisfactory. In addition, he had developed satisfactory friendships with several co-workers at his job, where none had existed previously. He had started a hobby of tropical fish collecting, and was also studying for a promotion on his job. Mrs. Bronson reported that her husband, who previously had avoided her, was now spending a considerable amount of time with her at home. He engaged in social activities with her for the first time in years, shared household duties with her and helped in disciplining the children.

In a few cases, additional interventions were suggested to assist in maintaining the clients' gains or to enhance the effectiveness of treatment by showing the client how a newly-arisen problem could be subjected to the same behavioral analysis system that he had learned in the group. One client who needed further help was Mrs. Dean, who reported in the six-month follow-up that her son's fighting had been eliminated. She had become aware, however, that her younger daughter was overly dependent on her and made undue demands on her time and her attention. The workers drew parallels from the problem solving that had been taught in the group, and helped her to see how these principles could be applied in eliminating the attention-demanding behavior of the daughter.

The group treatment approach does not preclude the possibility of additional treatment of other problems following termination of the group. During follow-up sessions, the clients were interviewed to determine whether or not they required further treatment for problems either not touched on during group meetings or because of new events. In the groups conducted to date, there have been no instances where further treatment was indicated.

The procedures described here underwent refinement and change with each of the three groups of clients in the family service agency setting. New knowledge and techniques will be incorporated into this model as it is applied to different client populations, agency settings and types of problems. To confirm its effectiveness, this short-term group treatment approach will have to be compared to other treatment methods under controlled experimental conditions. It is in this spirit of innovation that the practitioner is invited to apply the model, using his critcal judgment to adapt its procedures in order to best meet the circumstances of the particular group with which he is working.

APPENDIX A

Problem Checklist

CHECK WHICH OF THE FOLLOWING RELATIONSHIPS ARE DISSATISFYING TO YOU OR PRESENT PROBLEMS FOR YOU.
USE A *DOUBLE-CHECK* FOR THOSE THAT *MOST* CONCERN YOU.

_____ Parents   _____ Co-workers

_____ Brothers and sisters   _____ Subordinates at work

_____ Husband or wife   _____ Friends of the same sex

_____ Children   _____ Friends of the opposite sex

_____ Other relatives   _____ Neighbors

_____ Work supervisor or employer   _____ Myself

FOR EACH OF THE RELATIONSHIPS YOU *DOUBLE-CHECKED*, WHAT ARE ONE OR TWO PROBLEMS YOU ARE HAVING WITH THAT PERSON OR PERSONS THAT *MOST* CONCERNS YOU?

Examples:

Person or Persons	*Problems*
1. Wife	We are constantly quarreling. She usually sleeps in the children's room instead of with me.
2. Oldest son	When I ask him to do his chores, he doesn't obey me. He often fights with and beats his younger sister.
3. Girls at work	I do not participate in the conversations with the girls during lunch or coffee breaks.

PROBLEMS OF MAJOR CONCERN TO ME

Person or Persons	*Problems*

WHAT WOULD YOU LIKE TO SEE CHANGE AS A RESULT OF TREATMENT HERE?

Examples:

Person or Persons	Change Desired
Wife	That most of our quarreling is eliminated. That she will sleep with me every night. That we will share occasional social activities together without the presence of the children.
Girls at work	To carry my share of speaking during a social conversation without blushing or trembling.

CHANGES DESIRED

Person(s)	Change Desired

IN WHAT WAYS DO YOU THINK YOUR LIFE WOULD BE DIFFERENT IF THESE PROBLEMS WERE CLEARED UP?

IF YOU WERE GRANTED THE FULFILLMENT OF THREE WISHES, NO MATTER HOW PRACTICAL OR FANTASTIC, WHAT WOULD YOU WISH FOR?

1.

2.

3.

APPENDIX B

RAC-F Assessment Form

RESPONSE TO BE OBSERVED: _____

Day and Time	Antecedent (What happened just before?)	Response Frequency (How often? For how long?)	Consequences (What happened just after?)
MONDAY			
Morning			
Afternoon			
Evening			
TUESDAY			
Morning			
Afternoon			
Evening			
WEDNESDAY			
Morning			
Afternoon			
Evening			
THURSDAY			
Morning			
Afternoon			
Evening			
FRIDAY			
Morning			
Afternoon			
Evening			
SATURDAY			
Morning			
Afternoon			
Evening			
SUNDAY			
Morning			
Afternoon			
Evening			

APPENDIX C

Problem Checklist #2

CHECK WHICH OF THE FOLLOWING RELATIONSHIPS, IF ANY, ARE
DISSATISFYING TO YOU OR PRESENT PROBLEMS FOR YOU.
USE A *DOUBLE-CHECK* FOR THOSE THAT *MOST* CONCERN YOU.

_____	Parents	_____	Co-workers
_____	Brothers and sisters	_____	Subordinates at work
_____	Husband or wife	_____	Friends of the same sex
_____	Children	_____	Friends of the opposite sex
_____	Other relatives	_____	Neighbors
_____	Work supervisor or employer	_____	Myself

WHAT DID YOU WANT TO ACCOMPLISH THROUGH YOUR THER-
APY EXPERIENCE?

TO WHAT EXTENT DID YOU ACHIEVE THIS?

THE FOLLOWING ARE THE PROBLEM(S) WHICH YOU WORKED ON
IN THE GROUP AND THE GOALS YOU WISHED TO ACHIEVE
THROUGH THERAPY. PLEASE CORRECT, AMEND OR ADD ANY
PROBLEMS, *IF* YOU HAD A DIFFERENT UNDERSTANDING OF
PROBLEMS OR GOALS THAT YOU WORKED ON.

IF THE STATEMENT(S) ARE CORRECT, PLEASE INITIAL YOUR O.K.

PROBLEMS WORKED ON IN THE GROUP

Problem(s)	*Goal(s)*
#1	#1
#2	#2

TO WHAT EXTENT ARE THE ABOVE LISTED PROBLEMS SOLVED?

	Much Worse	Worse	The Same	Better	Much Better	Completely Solved
Problem #1						
Problem #2						
Problem #3						

TO WHAT EXTENT, IF ANY, HAS THERE BEEN A *CHANGE* IN THESE PROBLEMS *SINCE THE LAST GROUP MEETING?*

	Much Worse	Worse	No Change	Better	Much Better	Completely Solved
Problem #1						
Problem #2						
Problem #3						

TO WHAT EXTENT WERE THE ABOVE LISTED TREATMENT *GOALS* ACHIEVED?

	Not At All Achieved	Small Gain	Moderate Gain	Mostly Achieved	Goal Achieved
Goal #1					
Goal #2					
Goal #3					

IN WHAT WAYS, IF ANY, DO YOU THINK YOUR LIFE SITUATION IS DIFFERENT BECAUSE OF YOUR EXPERIENCE IN THIS THERAPY GROUP?

HAVE YOU CONSULTED WITH OR RECEIVED THERAPY FROM A
SOCIAL WORKER, PSYCHOLOGIST OR PSYCHIATRIST SINCE YOUR
LAST FOLLOW-UP INTERVIEW? _____

IF YOUR ANSWER IS "YES," PLEASE GIVE THE FOLLOWING IN-
FORMATION:

Agency or Therapist	Dates From-To	Nature of the Problem

DO YOU THINK IT WOULD BE HELPFUL FOR YOU TO BE EN-
GAGED IN THERAPY AT THIS TIME? _____

IF "YES," WHAT PROBLEMS WOULD YOU WORK ON?

ARE YOU AWARE OF USING ANY OF THE APPROACHES OR TECH-
NIQUES LEARNED DURING YOUR GROUP THERAPY EXPERIENCE?
_____

IF "YES," PLEASE BRIEFLY INDICATE WHAT THESE TECHNIQUES
ARE.

COMMENTS:

REFERENCES

BANDURA, ALBERT
    1969—*Principles of Behavior Modification,* New York: Holt, Rinehart and
        Winston, pp. 118–216.

HASTORF, ALBERT H.
  1965—"The 'reinforcement' of individual actions in a group situation," in Leonard Krasner and Leonard P. Ullman (Eds.), *Research in Behavior Modification,* New York: Holt, Rinehart and Winston, pp. 268–284.
LAWRENCE, HARRY
  1967—"The effectiveness of a group-directed vs. a worker-directed style of leadership in social group work," Unpublished D.S.W. dissertation, University of California at Berkeley.
LIBERMAN, ROBERT
  1970—"A behavioral approach to group dynamics," *Behavior Therapy,* 1 (May), pp. 141–175.
LOTT, BERNICE B. AND ALBERT V. LOTT
  1965—"The formation of positive attitudes toward group members," *Journal of Abnormal and Social Psychology,* 61 (September), pp. 297–300.
ROSE, SHELDON D.
  1969—"A behavioral approach to the group treatment of parents," *Social Work,* 14 (July), pp. 21–29.
ULLMAN, LEONARD P. AND LEONARD KRASNER
  1965—*Case Studies in Behavior Modification,* New York: Holt, Rinehart and Winston.

21.

A Behavioral Approach to the Group Treatment of Parents

SHELDON D. ROSE

Group work, like casework, has been defined as a method of treatment whose purpose is the improved social functioning of clients (Vinter, 1965). Although the social work literature abounds in descriptive typologies and case studies aimed at facilitating the practitioner's diagnostic skills, few articles have pointed to a specific set of procedures of intervention available to the social worker for the amelioration of the client's problems. In the absence of a theoretical foundation that would aid in specifying the worker's actions, little progress in this direction could be made. With the introduction of learning theory into social work, however, conceptual tools became available for describing in detail a large number of procedures of intervention, many of which have been systematically evaluated and effectively demonstrated in a variety of contexts (Thomas, 1967; Krasner and Ullmann, 1965).

In contrast to the recent introduction of learning theory in social work, the small group has long been used by social workers. Sociopsychological studies have demonstrated the power of the group to modify its members' behavior and attitudes (Collins and Guetzkow, 1964). Many operational hypotheses concerning the group's specific attributes are available to the social worker.

In developing a behavioral approach to the group treatment of parents, the author has taken advantage of the empirical findings derived both from learning theory and from small group theory.[1] Since social workers are more familiar with small group theory, this paper will emphasize the

---

[1] A behavioral approach refers to a treatment approach that focuses on behavioral change and is based, at least in part, on learning theory. The author is by

Reprinted with permission of the National Association of Social Workers, from *Social Work*, Vol. 14, No. 3 (July 1969), pp. 21–29.

procedures and principles derived from learning theory. Examples will be given that have been drawn from the experiences of five second-year students at the University of Michigan School of Social Work who worked with groups of parents and utilized some or all of the procedures reported here. The students worked primarily with parents from the lower socioeconomic strata in a settlement house, child guidance clinic, family service agency, public welfare agency, and school service agency. The groups ranged in size from three to eight members and met once a week for as few as five to as many as sixteen weeks.

ASSESSMENT

One of the major difficulties of parents who come to an agency is the inadequacy or inappropriateness of their child management procedures— the skills necessary to cope with their children's behavior. The purpose of behavioral group treatment for such clients is to increase their repertoire of procedures and to teach them to recognize or create the appropriate conditions under which these techniques should be applied.

Before the parent can be taught these skills, it is necessary to determine the child's presenting behavioral problem.[2] The parent learns to state the problem in terms of observable behaviors that occur or fail to occur in specific situations. He is also shown ways of estimating (or counting) how often they take place, since it is the frequency of behavior that is most often to be changed. Because most parents are not accustomed to speaking in specific terms about behavior and many lack observational skills that are a prerequisite to any description or counting, in most groups considerable time is given to training them to do so.

This training involves observing social situations, counting specific behaviors, charting these behaviors, and reporting the results to the group. In order to increase the probability of success, the parents first observe

---

no means the first to describe a behavioral approach to the treatment of parents. Within the same theoretical framework, the following authors suggest a variety of procedures for parental training, many of which are not included in this article: Walder, Cohen, Breiter, Daston, Hirsch, and Leibowitz (1965); Patterson, McNeal, Hawkins, and Phelps (1967); Russo (1964).

[2] In this paper the author has tried to avoid the technical terminology that assumes the reader has a background in learning theory. An excellent introduction to this material as it applies to behavior is Staats and Staats (1963). These authors review some of the more important research findings on the application to human subjects of behavior modification procedures derived from learning theory. See also the quarterly journal *Behavior Research and Therapy,* from 1963 to 1967, for case examples and recent research findings in this area.

and count behaviors with which they are not especially concerned, e.g., the number of times the child leaves and enters the room, the context and number of situations in which he smiles or laughs. As they gain skill in observation, they note the frequency of the behaviors with which they are concerned, e.g., complaining, temper tantrums, soiling, teasing a sibling, being a truant. At this point a *baseline*—an estimate of the frequency of the problematic behavior prior to any endeavor to change it—is established.

The baseline makes it possible to evaluate the degree or extent of the child's behavioral change as treatment progresses. However, in the experiences described in this paper, several difficulties arose that frequently made it necessary to rely on indefinite estimates or to forego a baseline completely. Some of these problems were the parents' different levels of comprehension, their inadequate training, "forgetting," and a lack of cooperation by one of the spouses.

There is considerable evidence to support the contention that the events that follow a given behavior or the immediate consequences of that behavior have a strong influence on subsequent performances of it (Krasner and Ullmann, 1965; Staats and Staats, 1963). This is one of the basic precepts of learning theory and it forms the foundation for many forms of intervention. For this reason, parents are taught to observe and describe the immediate results of all their child's behaviors with which they are concerned. One set of consequences over which the parents have the most control is their own reactions—emotional, verbal, and motor. Once the parents are able to describe their responses, a major part of the treatment involves assessing them and training the parents in new or more appropriate ones.

In order to determine which behaviors should be modified, the worker also reviews the long-range consequences of each behavioral problem with the parents. In this process, many parents discover that the ultimate effects of one set of behaviors are relatively unimportant or, because of the consequences of previously unconsidered behaviors, they warrant immediate attention.

The following example is an excerpt from a group meeting in which some of the aspects of assessment are demonstrated:

> Mrs. M complained that her 11-year-old daughter had frequent temper tantrums. The members inquired about the conditions that led to them. Mrs. M, after reflecting a moment, indicated that her daughter responded this way whenever the mother said "no" or she became frustrated in any way. When asked what happened when her daughter had these tantrums, Mrs. M said she usually gave her exactly what she wanted in order to quiet her down. Mrs. W asked what might eventually happen if this habit were to persist. Throwing up her hands, Mrs. M replied that it would

drive the whole family out of their minds and probably her teacher and friends, too.

The members then suggested to Mrs. M that she was maintaining the behavior she wanted to eliminate by rewarding her daughter after the temper tantrum. This analysis implied that Mrs. M would have to find some alternative response to the temper tantrum, such as ignoring her, walking away, using calm verbal expression, and/or isolating her until the tantrum wore off.

GOAL-SETTING

After assessing the problem—by analyzing the antecedents and consequences of specific problematic behavior—each set of parents is helped by other parents to establish a goal in terms of the desired frequency or intensity of behavior they would like to see their children achieve. The goals are formulated along the same dimension of behavior previously identified as problematic or in terms of the conditions under which a behavior is appropriate. In stating goals, as in describing initial behavioral problems, the criteria of specificity and accurate description of impinging conditions are essential. Typical goals include increasing the frequency of studying to one hour an evening, eliminating temper tantrums, reducing the frequency of fighting with a sibling to twice a week, learning new ways of responding to external stress or limitations, discriminating between situations in which loud, raucous play is appropriate or inappropriate, and increasing the frequency of coming home on time every evening.

The worker also evolves with each parent or set of parents the goal each parent expects to achieve for himself by the end of treatment. Many parents are initially hesitant to look at ways in which they themselves must change in order to establish the desired changes in their children; they prefer to focus solely on the changes desired in the child. During the first phase of treatment, the worker may postpone encouraging the parent to make explicit the goal of his own behavioral change. However, the need for parental change usually becomes obvious as soon as the children's behaviors are evaluated.

Examples of goals for parental change include ignoring temper tantrums and providing attention for more desirable behaviors, establishing rules and routines and ways of maintaining them, giving rewards in a consistent rather than haphazard manner, and learning and practicing the forms of manifesting interest in the child's school and recreational activities.

The processes of assesment and goal-setting begin in an intake interview and are continued in meetings of the group. Dealing with these tasks in the group provides each parent with an opportunity to help others specify their problems and impinging conditions and to observe on repeated occasions the relation of these conditions to the problem. The group members gradually take over from the worker the responsibility of determining whether the problem and goal are sufficiently specific and the conditions adequately described. By analyzing and dealing with problems other than their own, group members increase their problem-solving skills in general and are better able to cope with new problems that may arise after the group terminates (Goldstein, Heller, and Sechrest, 1966).

MODIFYING CHILDREN'S BEHAVIOR

After each set of parents decides which behavior they will seek to modify first, they begin to learn procedures for altering it. These procedures usually involve modifying antecedent and consequent conditions to improve the performance of desirable behaviors and decrease the performance of less desirable ones.[3]

Some techniques for modifying antecedent conditions are the use of routines (when none existed previously), the introduction of models who have acceptable characteristics that are likely to be imitated, the elimination of seductive parental behaviors that previously triggered off undesirable behavior, and the use of cues to help the children remember the desired behavior. Examples of techniques for modifying consequent conditions are systematically applying limits, rewarding on a frequent and consistent basis, time-out procedures, and withholding attention or other rewards when they seem to be maintaining the undesirable behavior.

Extensive case examples of these techniques are to be found in the literature (Ullmann and Krasner, 1965). For this reason, the remainder of this paper will focus on procedures used by the worker in teaching parents to modify their own—and each other's—behavior.

MODIFYING PARENTS' BEHAVIOR

In order to help parents modify their behavior, the following teaching procedures are utilized by the worker: programmed instruction, model presentation, behavioral rehearsal, and behavioral assignments. These teaching methods should be included in a total group plan in such a way

---

[3] The reader could rightfully raise the question of what is desirable and who determines the desirability of behavior. For purposes of this paper, the author has avoided such a discussion. The behavior modifiers more frequently allude to adaptive and maladaptive behaviors. See Ullmann and Krasner (1965) for a definition of maladaptive behavior from the learning theorist's point of view.

that they enable each client to achieve his stated goals. Each of these procedures involves group members in helping each other work toward the goals of treatment.

Simple techniques are employed at first; gradually, more complex teaching procedures and combinations of different procedures are used to elicit, explore and practice new or modified parental behavior. Although various teaching techniques are usually integrated into a sequential plan, for purposes of analysis each will be discussed separately.

PROGRAMMED INSTRUCTION

When treatment is viewed as a learning process, one can use the same techniques to teach new behavior that have proved effective in teaching academic subjects. One such technique is programmed instruction.[4] In the project, extensive use was made of a programmed instruction book on child management in which the writers attempt to train parents to use a number of basic concepts and principles for working with their children (Smith and Smith, 1966). Some of the principles on which the book focuses are increased consistency in parental behavior, the use of rules to provide increased consistency, and guidelines for selecting and enforcing rules. The book is especially effective for disorganized parents or those who have difficulty in limiting their children. Its contents are less relevant for excessively orderly parents and strict disciplinarians. The following example from the book is a discussion followed by an exercise:

A. *Selecting a Rule*
 1. What Is a Rule?
  Any demand made on a child by a parent is a rule. Any task he must perform is a rule. Any decision regarding what he may have or may not have, what he may do or may not do—any such decision is a rule. Many parents dislike establishing rules. Usually they feel guilty when they require the child to do something which is unpleasant. They are not aware that consistent enforcement of a rule makes the world safer and more comfortable for the child.

  Parents sometimes disguise rules to ease their guilt. They say, "Wouldn't you like to do the dishes?" or "Do you want to take a nap?" If the only acceptable answer to the question is "yes," it is a rule—regardless of the way it is stated. It would be much less confusing to the child if Mother said, "Do the dishes now," or "It's naptime."

---

[4] See Staats and Staats (1963). In this section, the writers discuss the principle of and values underlying programmed instruction as it applies to academic subjects. For a complete bibliography of programs applicable to social work practice, see Thomas and Lind (1967).

Some rules are "long-term." They must be enforced again and again over a long period of time. These rules usually govern the performance of a chore or a family routine. In each item below, choose the long-term rule.

23.—a. Mark must cut the grass every Saturday afternoon.
   —b. Mark can earn 50¢ by weeding the garden.
24.—a. Mother provides Joan with an alarm clock.
   —b. Joan must dress herself without help before she leaves for school.
25.—a. Jeanine has to do the dishes on Monday and Friday.
   —b. Jeanine's brother asks her to substitute for him on Wednesday.
26.—a. Everyone must wash his hands and face before eating dinner.
   —b. It is often necessary to turn on the light in the dining room if the sun has set (Smith and Smith, 1966).

There are several ways in which any such program can be used. A number of principles and exercises may be assigned each week to be completed at home. In the group meeting, the responses can be discussed and applications to the parents' specific situations suggested. Since the Smith and Smith program requires approximately a seventh-grade level of reading, some variation was required for several of the groups with whom the project members worked. In one group, the worker prepared simplified excerpts from the program that were then discussed in the group. He asked the parents to complete the exercises during the meeting and helped them with concepts or words they did not understand. In most groups the entire book was not used. In some groups additional exercises were designed that taught other principles. Programmed instruction was the major vehicle of treatment in one group. In another group the parents thought this particular program was for parents with younger children and preferred discussing their own examples. In the remaining groups, programmed instruction was used to supplement the many other procedures used.

MODEL PRESENTATION

When situations are presented in which some of the parents think a certain principle is difficult or impossible to enforce, the worker may suggest appropriate parental responses and/or may encourage the other members to make suggestions. But such advice, although helpful, is seldom sufficient to add new behaviors to the parent's repertoire or to eliminate inappropriate ones (Lazarus, 1966).

To demonstrate "appropriate" behavior, the worker or a parent who has solved a similar problem plays the role of the parent. Other group members play the significant others in the situation. The parent whose problem is being enacted is the director. In this capacity he instructs the other members in performing their roles and defines the conditions that have led to the problem.[5]

In training the members, the worker may initially play all the roles (Corsini and Cardone, 1966). When the parents begin role playing, the situation is highly structured, i.e., the roles are predetermined in discussion. Anxiety about role playing is usually reduced by giving all participants a set of notes describing each of the roles, by pointing out that dramatic ability is not essential, and by indicating that as soon as the point has been made, the action will be terminated. Another way to reduce initial anxiety is to announce in advance that no situation should be played longer than five minutes; then, after some discussion the role playing may be continued.

The role-play situation may be repeated several times until the parent feels comfortable enough to try it himself. The cast may be modified or various aspects of the situation may be adapted to simulate more nearly the varied conditions of real life.

In evaluating the role play, the entire group is encouraged to discuss the appropriateness of the parent's actions. The worker first discusses with the group what the probable consequences of these actions would be. Then the group discusses alternate actions and examines their probable effects. The members may also discuss the problems of applying any of these actions to their own situations.

There are several additional techniques for model presentation that do not involve role playing and may be used instead of or, preferably, in addition to it. One is to invite parents from previous groups to tell their techniques for handling similar problems. Another is to present the case histories of such parents. Popular films or television programs in which characters have coped with similar problems may also be used.

BEHAVIORAL REHEARSAL

Behavioral rehearsal refers to the client's performance of behavior in the treatment situation that he would like to perform in the real-life situation. Lazarus, in a controlled experiment, has demonstrated the greater effectiveness of behavioral rehearsal in comparison to "advice-giving" or a "reflective-interpretive approach" in the treatment of persons who are unassertive (Lazarus, 1966). Experience suggests that the approach can

---

[5] For an excellent summary of the principles and implications of model presentation for behavioral change, see Bandura (1965).

be used in the treatment of behavioral problems more varied than those for which it was used by Lazarus. It has been used by parents to practice such behaviors as setting limits, establishing new reward procedures, ignoring situations that previously they could not ignore, and even using behavioral rehearsals with their children. Practice in the simulated situation seems to facilitate performance in the real situation by reducing the anxiety associated with it (Goldstein, Heller, and Sechrest, 1966).

Behavioral rehearsal usually follows some form of model presentation. Prior to a person's performance of his own role in a family situation, the worker and the group members review exactly what new behaviors the parent is to perform. After the first rehearsal, the other members evaluate the performance and make additional suggestions for alterations. The situation is repeated at least once. Then the parent is given a behavioral assignment to perform some of the behaviors rehearsed with the group in the real-life situation. It is seldom possible in one session for each person to rehearse his situation. In the course of several meetings, however, it is helpful if everyone who is willing has the opportunity to perform at least once. It is preferable to begin with situations that have implications for several, if not most, of the group members.

BEHAVIORAL ASSIGNMENTS

One of the major problems of group and individual treatment is a lack of concern about generalizing change to situations outside the treatment situation. Although role playing focuses on extra group situations, it is performed within the group context. Role playing demonstrates and behavioral rehearsal provides practice; but neither assures performance of a desired behavior in the real-life situation. For these reasons, at each meeting behavioral assignments are given to group members so that they may try out newly learned behaviors outside the group prior to the next meeting. The following are four requisites for the successful performance of a behavioral assignment:

1. The assignments should be highly specific. The client should know exactly what he must do and the conditions under which given responses should be performed. Furthermore, if certain unexpected conditions arise (e.g., illness), or if the appropriate conditions do not occur, alternate behaviors, such as telephoning the worker, should be developed.
2. The client should be able to handle the assignment, i.e., there should be a high probability of success. If the client succeeds early in treatment, it is more likely that he will continue to try

behavioral assignments.[6] On the other hand, an assignment should not be so easy that no new learning takes place.

3. The client should commit himself, at least verbally, in front of his fellow group members to attempting the performance of his assignment. If the client states exactly what he is going to do, it will be more difficult for him to hedge or explain away his failure.

4. The client should report the details of his attempt to carry out the assignment to the group. Without such monitoring procedures, it seems that assignments are soon neglected. Monitoring by the other group members serves both as a reward for trying the task and a source of information about how it can be done more effectively the next time.

Initially, the assignment may be suggested by the worker on the basis of the previously mentioned criteria. The client, together with the other group members, works out the details. The worker then asks the client if he understands and thinks he can perform the assignment within the allotted time. If not, the assignment is adjusted accordingly. Once he has had some experience in applying the criteria, each client develops his own assignment with assistance from the others.

Each assignment must be viewed as being part of a sequence. As one assignment is completed, a slightly more difficult one should be given. The sequence should ultimately lead to the attainment of the treatment goal. The completion of each assignment is, in a sense, the achievement of a subgoal.

Two examples that point up the interrelationship and typical sequence of the aforementioned teaching techniques are the following:

Mrs. L, Mrs. A, and Mrs. B complained that their children never did chores in the house. After the Smith and Smith program on enforcing rules had been discussed, Mrs. M demonstrated in a role-playing incident (model presentation) how she set and enforced rules. She was followed by Mrs. L who rehearsed behaviors in which she enforced a daily bed-making rule (model presentation *and* behavioral rehearsal). Then Mrs. A played her own role in a situation in which her daughters refused to do the dishes (behavioral rehearsal). Mrs. M prompted Mrs. A about what she should say. Finally, the group gave Mrs. L, Mrs. A, and Mrs. B the assignment of developing and en-

[6] Success in task performance has been shown by Marquis, Guetzkow, and Heyns (1963) to be related to several indications of satisfaction. Success is probably experienced as an intrinsic reward and, therefore, according to learning theory, should function to increase the probability that the behaviors that preceded it would occur with greater frequency or intensity.

forcing a rule with one of their children (behavioral assignment) and reporting to the group at the next weekly meeting.

Mr. and Mrs. N had difficulty limiting the acting-out behavior of their son, aged 11. The group members discussed the antecedent conditions of the child's behavior and the previous ways in which Mr. and Mrs. N responded to it, which included showering him with attention, arguing with each other, and pleading with the child to stop.

The worker suggested several alternative responses, such as immediately removing the child from the scene of the acting out without discussion. Mrs. McA, who had used this procedure effectively, demonstrated how it should be done. The worker played the role of the son (model presentation).

Mr. and Mrs. N were hesitant about role playing but were willing to describe exactly what they would do (behavioral rehearsal). They agreed to try it out during the week (behavioral assignment). The worker pointed out that they could expect an increase in the undesired behavior before the situation got better, and Mrs. McA affirmed this from her experience.

Other group members thought it would be helpful if, after this first attempt, Mr. and Mrs. N called Mr. and Mrs. McA to tell them what had happened so they would not have to wait until the next meeting (monitoring the behavioral assignment).

RELATIONSHIP

Since the worker-client relationship is a core concept in the present-day practice of social work, a description of its place in the behavioral approach seems necessary. Although the worker does not focus on relationship-building as a means of intervention, the low rate of client withdrawal from treatment and the frequent verbal expressions of satisfaction suggest that quite rapidly he becomes a highly attractive individual.

The factors that contribute to relationship-building appear to be the following: (1) The worker provides a highly structured situation in which answers are given to the clients' specific problems. (2) The worker readily recognizes and rewards achievement. (3) Accomplishments are clearly defined in such small steps that everyone achieves something between and during every meeting, which affords the worker ample opportunity to be rewarding. The feeling of success even in small things may be in itself an important internal reward for many parents. (4) Since goals, procedures, and assumptions of treatment are made explicit, the situation is not ambiguous. This reduces anxiety and, in turn, increases the worker's attractiveness.[7]

The group worker does not set aside his natural warmth, understanding, or acceptance of the clients with whom he works. He adds to his skills in relationship the more specific techniques for modifying behavior described in this paper.

VALUE OF THE GROUP

There are many therapeutically facilitating aspects of the group, most of which are common to all group treatment approaches. In a group there is an abundance of models for the client to imitate. Although clients may be undergoing treatment for the absence of behaviors necessary to deal adequately with their children, almost all parents have within their repertoire adaptive behaviors they can demonstrate or teach to other parents in the group. Given this pool of behavioral experience, the worker is able to encourage and structure imitation of those behaviors appropriate to each client in terms of his individual treatment goals. The group also provides a large variety of role-players for model presentation and behavioral rehearsal.

When the cohesiveness of the group is high, approval and disapproval of the group members function as effective controls.[8] Encouraged by the worker, members tend to create a norm of accurate accounting of extra-group activities. Thus the group may be an especially efficient means of monitoring behavioral change outside it. With the worker's help, group members also develop norms for working on their problems, for being specific as opposed to global, and for participating in discussion and role playing. Thus the client, in observing and participating in the treatment of others, develops a range of solutions for a range of problems.

In the groups in which the behavioral approach was used, most parents claimed at termination that they were better able to handle their problems and many felt they would be better able to cope with any new problems their children might have. The workers, too, stated that it was helpful to have prescriptions for what they could do to help the parents. They also indicated that using behavioral assessment, programmed instruction, role playing, behavioral rehearsal, and behavioral assignments made

[7] For a discussion of the relation between ambiguity, message threat, and the therapist's attractiveness, see Goldstein, Heller, and Sechrest (1966).

[8] Compare Bass (1960). On the basis of extensive research experience, Bass points out that the more attractive the group, the greater the rewards that may be earned by its members.

it easier to prepare for meetings and evaluate outcomes than it had been in previous treatment situations.

Although the outcomes reported in this paper are the results of a demonstration project and are anecdotal in nature, they are sufficiently promising to encourage an expansion of this approach and an exploration of the use of additional behavioral procedures to facilitate still further the treatment of parents in groups.

REFERENCES

BANDURA, ALBERT
  1965—"Behavioral modifications through modeling procedures," in Leonard Krasner and Leonard P. Ullmann (Eds.), *Research in Behavior Modification,* New York: Holt, Rinehart and Winston, pp. 310–340.
BASS, BERNARD M.
  1960—*Leadership, Psychology and Organization Behavior,* New York: Harper and Brothers.
COLLINS, BARRY E. AND HAROLD GUETZKOW
  1964—*A Social Psychology of Group Processes for Decision-Making,* New York: John Wiley & Sons.
CORSINI, RAYMOND AND SAMUEL CARDONE
  1966—*Role-playing in Psychotherapy: A Manual,* Chicago: Aldine Publishing Company.
GOLDSTEIN, ARNOLD P., KENNETH HELLER, AND LEE B. SECHREST
  1966—*Psychotherapy and the Psychology of Behavior Change,* New York: John Wiley & Sons.
KRASNER, LEONARD AND LEONARD P. ULLMANN (EDS.)
  1965—*Research in Behavior Modification,* New York: Holt, Rinehart and Winston.
LAZARUS, ARNOLD A.
  1966—"Behaviour rehearsal vs. non-directive therapy vs. advice in effecting behaviour change," *Behaviour Research and Therapy,* 4, 2 (August), pp. 209–212.
MARQUIS, DONALD G., HAROLD GUETZKOW, AND ROGER W. HEYNS
  1963—"A social psychological study of the decision-making conference," in Harold Guetzkow (Ed.), *Groups, Leadership and Men: Research in Human Relations,* New York: Russell Sage Foundation, pp. 55–67.
PATTERSON, B. R., SHIRLEY MCNEAL, NANCY HAWKINS, AND RICHARD PHELPS
  1967—"Re-programming the social environment," *Journal of Child Psychology and Psychiatry,* 8, 3–4 (December), pp. 181–196.
RUSSO, SALVATORE
  1964—"Adaptations in behavioural therapy with children," *Behaviour Research and Therapy,* 2, 1 (February), pp. 43–47.

SMITH, JUDITH M. AND DONALD E. P. SMITH
1966—*Child Management: A Program for Parents,* Ann Arbor, Michigan: Ann Arbor Publishers.

STAATS, ARTHUR W. AND CAROLYN R. STAATS
1963—*Complex Human Behavior,* New York: Holt, Rinehart and Winston.

THOMAS, EDWIN J.
1967—*The Socio-Behavioral Approach and Applications to Social Work,* New York: Council on Social Work Education.

THOMAS, EDWIN J. AND ROGER LIND
1967—"Programmed instruction as potentially useful in social work education: An annotated bibliography," *Social Work Education Reporter,* 15, 1 (March), pp. 22–27, 33.

ULLMANN, LEONARD P. AND LEONARD KRASNER
1965—*Case Studies in Behavior Modification,* New York: Holt, Rinehart and Winston.

VINTER, ROBERT D.
1965—"Social group work," in Harry L. Lurie (Ed.), *Encyclopedia of Social Work,* New York: National Association of Social Workers, pp. 715–724.

WALDER, LEOPOLD O., SHLOMO I. COHEN, DENNIS E. BREITER, PAUL G. DASTON, IRWIN S. HIRSCH, AND J. MICHAEL LEIBOWITZ
1965—"Teaching behavioral principles to parents of disturbed children," College Park: University of Maryland (Unpublished).

22.

Preventive, Short-term Groups for Siblings of Child Mental Hospital Patients

SALLIE R. CHURCHILL

Community Mental Health challenges the practitioner to develop techniques to reduce the incidence of predictable emotional disturbance and disturbed behavior, to identify those people for whom early and brief professional intervention may prevent development of serious difficulties, and to create treatment procedures that can mobilize the healthy aspects of a person as a defense against future dangers. One effort to provide a preventive service, through short-term group treatment, to a potentially vulnerable group—siblings of children who are state mental hospital patients—is described here.[1]

Considerable concern had been expressed by the clinical staff at York Woods Center, Ypsilanti State Hospital (Michigan) as to how best to improve service to child patients. The so-called family approach, typical of child guidance clinics and residential treatment centers, had been adopted. Parents were worked with to help the staff better understand the hospitalized child and to help prepare the parents for the child's return to his home. Whenever clinically advisable, patients maintained contact with their homes through frequent visits; such leaves of absence lasted for a few hours or, in some cases, for as long as a weekend. A survey of case records and discussions with caseworkers revealed that the clinical staff had no specific information on how siblings were getting along or managing to cope with these visits. "Family treatment" was not focused on the family, but on the smaller patient-parent group.

Since the treatment goal for most children was return to their own families, and since frequent leaves of absence reunited the patient and his

[1] The author wishes to express great appreciation to William Kirk, M.D., and Dale Rice, Ph.D., for their cooperation and encouragement in carrying out this project.

family for brief periods, the group work consultant posed several questions: What part do siblings play in the acceptance or rejection of a patient during his leave of absence? What part are siblings likely to play in the reintegration of the patient into the family when he returns? In what way does the hospitalization of the patient affect his siblings? What problems does it introduce?

The consensus was that children suffer when a brother or sister is hospitalized. The problem was defined in terms of role theory. When hospitalization occurs, each child at home acquires the low status or role of being the sibling of a state mental hospital patient. There are common stresses placed upon each occupant of this status; each child experiences some or all of these stresses. Such stresses would interfere with the child's performance of his social roles regardless of his own level of personal adequacy or personal disturbance. How could the hospital staff be used to help siblings of patients deal with these problems? A short-term social group treatment experience was provided for 20 children, who were siblings of state mental hospital patients, as an attempt to modify problems which were specifically related to the role stress which they were experiencing.

THE RATIONALE FOR PREVENTIVE INTERVENTION WITH NONPATIENTS

Why does the sibling of a state hospital patient need help? It is widely assumed that mental illness is a family problem and that siblings of patients are also disturbed. Such assumptions give rise to the role expectations which exert pressure and place stress upon parents and siblings of children admitted to institutions for the mentally ill. The patient's placement in a state hospital requires reorientation of his family's intrafamilial role relationships and of their peer and community relationships.

Frequently, it is theorized that the placement of one child forces the family to reorganize itself and select another child to be the "sick one." Whether we accept this theory or not, and regardless of the amount of illness a child has or the number of problems he demonstrates, the placement of his sibling increases his predicament. Placement is a crisis, a stress which introduces unique difficulties separate and apart from the child's normal functioning.[2]

Those who question the utility of preventive treatment of children

---

[2] Readers are referred to Donald C. Klein and Ann Ross (1965) for a discussion of predicting problems of family role when the "stress" is a common, normal event, e.g., child's start of school.

express the concern that the act of offering service labels the child as a potential problem and that labeling sets up a self-fulfilling prophecy of future difficulty. But these children were labeled when their brothers or their sisters were admitted to a state mental hospital. The social group work intervention was directed at helping such prelabeled children understand and deal with societal reactions to their newly acquired status.

What are some of the problems that patients' siblings inherit along with their new status? Such children experience a wide range of difficulties in coping with their own feelings, their peers, their parents, and school personnel, as well as with their hospital patient-siblings. One child reported he never invited kids over " 'cause I don't want them to see him— maybe he's goofy and maybe not. Either way, how do you explain him?" Another asked "What are you supposed to do with Eddy? I'm always afraid I'll hurt him and he'll have to stay at the hospital longer." Children who attended schools which a patient-sibling had previously attended reported far more serious social problems with school personnel and peers than those children in schools not attended by patient-siblings. In the context of one preventive treatment group, seven children from one family described exactly how their brother became *"spitz-o-phrenic."* The story was told cooperatively by all children, each checking to be sure that all details were included. He became ill on a specific day, because of a specific event. The story told of an event which had occurred before two of the children had been born and when the oldest reporter had been five. It laid the blame for the patient's illness in the lap of the oldest girl who was four at the time. She had been teasing the two older boys (five and six years old) and had accidentally locked them in a closet. The patient, in a fearful effort to get out broke a pane of glass, cut himself badly and became "spitz-o-phrenic." The group had an agreed-upon explanation of which even their parents were unaware.

For our purposes, six sources of stress were hypothesized:

1. *Guilt.* A sibling would experience ambivalent feelings about his part in the hospitalization of the patient. A sibling would be happy to get rid of a problem kid—a trouble maker, an embarrassment. At the same time the sibling would worry about his part in getting rid of his brother and breaking up the family. He would be aware of his part in teasing and making fun of his brother's plight, of increasing his symptomatic behavior, etc.

2. *Fear of Contagion.* A sibling would experience confusion regarding the nature of mental illness. Since the sibling would have observed the mentally ill child's behavior, he might be aware that he had behaved similarly on occasion. When this behavior was not yet defined as mentally ill

he was not concerned. Now he is concerned whether he will become mentally ill because of his similar behavior. A sibling wonders whether mental illness is contagious like mumps and measles. After all, he has been "exposed."

3. *Fear of the "nut house."* A sibling would share in the culturally based fantasy and folklore, regarding the mental hospital, present in peer and adult conversations and highly emphasized in mass media. He would not have access to facts that adults might have gained through experience or from companions who could offer factual clarification. As a child he does not have access to appropriate books that might have information to refute these ideas. The sibling has fear of and anger toward the hospital. He cannot understand it as a place of treatment.

4. *The social stigma.* Hospitalization in a mental hospital continues to carry a social stigma for the patient himself and for all people who are intimately related to the patient. The child will be the recipient of this stigma at school and in the neighborhood. It creates intrapsychic problems as the child is forced to modify his self-image. He needs new social skills to deal with negative social interaction in a self-protective, acceptable manner.

5. *The sibling-patient relationship.* Since many patients are permitted home visits, a sibling cannot use defensive techniques of denying the existence of or forgetting the patient. He cannot "close the family group," but must be able to readmit the patient to the family periodically. He is forced to "account for" the patient's existence in his own social sphere. A sibling experiences confusion about how he is to relate to the patient when the patient is home.

6. *The sibling-parent relationship.* Most children can discuss concerns with parents. Parents of mental hospital patients, for the most part, have difficulty facing the realities of the child's illness and its effect on his siblings. Parents frequently either do not have factual answers for their childrens' questions or are unable to give the answers. They often establish a "rule" of no talking about the problems, and siblings have no resource for discussing these problems. A child who cannot ask important questions frequently creates his own answers. These are often quite frightening and much worse than the truth.

Given these hypotheses and assuming that each sibling was experiencing stress from his status, social group work was used to modify that stress, employing discussion among children who occupied the same status within an environment that legitimized discussion and could provide information necessary for adequate problem solving. The worker's intervention was specifically limited to the problems common to this role stress. No attempt was made to deal with an individual's unique psychological disturbance.[3]

A DESCRIPTION OF THE GROUPS

Three different treatment groups were composed by the group worker after consultation with the clinical staff of the hospital. The caseworker assigned to each family discussed the availability of the group service with the parents. When parents gave permission for their children to participate, the group worker discussed the sibling group with the child patient in the hospital. During this discussion the child patient was informed of the reason for the group, the procedures of the group and invited to participate in one group session. The composition of each group is described below.

1. *Sibling Sets Group* was composed of three boys and four girls ranging in age from nine to fourteen. The group was made up of three sets of siblings: two sisters, two brothers and a sister, and one brother and sister. Two of the girls were approximately ten years old, two girls nearly twelve; one of the boys was nine and the other two were in their early teens.

2. *Family Group* was composed of seven youngsters from one family ranging in age from four and one-half to fourteen. It had not been the worker's intention to include the youngest child beyond the first session, but by request of all the brothers and sisters the most "favorite" member of the Family Group was included.

3. *Boys Group* was made up of five boys, age twelve, unrelated to one another.

THE TREATMENT EXPERIENCE

The Treatment Model of social group work conceptualized by Robert D. Vinter (1967) was used. The group worker defined specifically the goals of the treatment group. All goals were related to the hypotheses stated above. All goals were explained in language which the children would comprehend and in terms that were relevant to their own needs and

---

[3] The social group worker was a skilled clinician who could evaluate the level of each child's emotional health. Interventions were not based on these broad evaluations. The group worker did share her diagnostic impressions with the clinical teams, and on occasion alerted the team to particular problems that the hospital should be aware of or for which it could offer help. For example, with the caseworker, one mother spoke with great pride of her eldest son whom she described as a good, hard working thoughtful boy. The group worker advised the caseworker that

concerns. The goals were limited to changes the worker considered attainable in the short-term group treatment situation. In each group the children were told the reasons why the hospital had initiated this type of group treatment, and that this was a new way of helping children. In addition the children were told that the hospital would want to know whether the group experience was useful to each of them. They were asked in the final session whether they would recommend that other children who had a brother or sister in the state hospital should have a similar group experience. The program activities and interpersonal interactions in group sessions were largely planned and limited by the direct and indirect interventions of the social group worker. The format for each of the four sessions of each group was prestructured (Churchill, 1959).

The worker selected or permitted activities that were thought to contribute directly to achievement of the treatment goals. The major program activities were discussion, confrontation with reality, highly valued physical activity, paper-pencil-crayon "doodling" and eating of refreshments. Discussion was present in all four group sessions and involved the group members in talking about, thinking about, and listening to content related to the above hypotheses. Good discussion requires all three of the above acts; some members participated in listening and thinking while they were unable to participate by talking. The group worker provided a climate where the members could sense that the topics they generally considered taboo could be talked about. In introducing the hospital's rationale for having the siblings' groups, the worker spoke of the strong possibility that there was common concern among the members and of her willingness to try to answer questions and show members places of interest in the hospital. Youngsters were helped by hearing that others lacked important information and that they, too, had "crazy" siblings. All groups seemed to have enough anxiety about common concerns so that discussion got underway relatively rapidly.

Children are quite capable of talking about important concerns. A few examples follow:

> In one group after the worker had suggested that children often are concerned about mental illness when they have a brother who is ill, a ten-year-old blurted out, "Will I?" The group worker, somewhat

---

Johnny was an extremely angry child who had severely limited all expression of anger. In the group meeting he sat quietly while a younger child hit and kicked him so vigorously that the worker had to intervene physically. The group worker was concerned that Johnny would "explode" unless he had help. Another child talked of his confusion about why his stepfather wouldn't adopt him. "Maybe it's 'cause my father doesn't want to adopt a crazy kid and he thinks I may get like my brother." The caseworker was advised of his comments and agreed to discuss it with the stepfather.

taken aback by the intensity of the comment, asked, "Will you what, Susan?" "Will I become mentally ill?"

Ernie stressed that school was "Okay." He didn't think anyone would care that his brother was in the hospital. "Of course, they didn't know it!" He didn't see any reason to tell them but he was sure it would not make any difference. Later when the two fourteen-year-old boys were talking about their mutual girl friends, Ernie's sister asked if the girl friend knew about their brother. He burst out, "I'll knock the hell out of you if you tell her."

Timmy was quiet most of the meetings. He listened and was obviously thinking. At one point he looked up and said, "You know, that's what I've been thinking about. Tommy was always bad, he did the craziest and worst stuff, I could understand it then, he was bad. Then all of a sudden they say he's sick. What's the difference between being sick and being bad?"

All three groups expressed concerns about what mental illness is. What is the difference between badness and craziness? What are the differences between mental illness, brain damage and mental retardation?[4] In each group there was considerable discussion about how mental illness was "caught." All three groups discussed in detail contagion of childhood diseases. All children were aware of who had given them the measles, the mumps, etc., and to whom they had spread the disease. In each group the children, themselves, formulated the question—is mental illness contagious too? Among the other topics discussed were the meaning of commitment; who discharges the patient; does the family have right of appeal of a psychiatrist's decision! what kind of food is served patients; why do patients take medicine; do they get beaten; why is a quiet room used; what do you do when the kids call your mother crazy, etc.

Although latency-age children can talk about their concerns, cognitive activity frequently is not sufficient to enable children to solve these problems. Many children have difficulty transferring conceptual solutions arrived at in treatment situations to their world outside. Generalization often is too undifferentiated or too restricted. Therefore, opportunities

---

[4] All groups showed concern about the differences among these three categories. Of great interest to the group worker was that the dominant concern differed in each group and that the concern reflected the major treatment concerns in their respective siblings' illnesses. The major confused term was talked about only with considerable discomfort and would not be joked about. The two other terms were used quite frequently as insults and "secret childhood jokes." For example, the Sibling Set Group wrote notes accusing each other of being "MRG's," (mentally retarded gorillas) but couldn't tolerate comments regarding "crazy-bad" behavior the source of many "private jokes."

were provided for members to confront the realities of their siblings' treatment situation about which they were concerned particularly. In addition to discussion, reality confrontation within the hospital environment was utilized to detoxify effects of self-answered questions, cultural folklore, and private fantasies about the mental hospital. The groups visited places in the hospital that members wished to see. School classrooms and the dining room were of primary interest. The Family Group wanted to see the occupational therapy room where their teen-age brother worked and the hospital tunnels about which he had talked frequently.

Obviously all requests could not be granted; e.g., for legal reasons, children could not stay overnight. The group worker gave full explanations of why a request could not be granted. As long as some requests were granted, explanations of "why not" seemed as satisfactory to a group as the granting of a request.

Initially, some staff expressed concern about exposing "well children" to sick children and questioned the advisability of siblings' entering the ward or hospital per se. Of course, all of the children had lived with a sick child and had had great prior exposure to his behavior. The children were quite at ease during ward visits and no problems were encountered. In fact, the group visits led to ward personnel allowing other patients selectively to bring siblings to see where "they lived."

Meeting the social group worker, a representative of the hospital treatment staff, was in itself therapeutic. Several of the children discussed quite forcefully what each had expected hospital workers, especially the group worker, to be like. They were relieved that she wasn't "a mean old man." When on tour, children sought out opportunities to speak to other adults, seeming to check out whether others were like the group worker. After a tour of the children's wards, members expressed surprise that hospital personnel liked children. One child summed it up triumphantly, "The nurse even gave *me* a band aid!"

One session was devoted to a highly valued hospital-based activity which included the patients in addition to the sibling group. Two groups had a swimming party and one group had an outdoor picnic. A hospital staff member also joined these activities to provide the patients with a familiar adult and provide the necessary coverage should a patient become upset and need personal attention. This activity placed the patients in a host role. It took place on their "home ground." The patients, for the first time, had something of positive value which they shared with their siblings. The host activity was directed toward reestablising positive relationship potential between siblings and the patients through a pleasurable activity in which the hospital gave overt approval to a relationship between the patient and the sibling.

The brothers and sisters were all excited about "doing something" with the patients. Group members had discussed how they had gotten the idea that either the patient was "bad for" siblings or that the siblings were "bad for" the patient. Therefore, it had been concluded the hospital didn't want them together.

In each group, when the worker proposed such an activity, it was clamored for loudly. Ernie said in surprised tones, "Gee, we didn't think you wanted us around Bill." An unexpected value of this activity was that it provided an opportunity for the siblings to be with friends who readily accepted their patient-brother.[5] As on tour of the ward, the children were remarkably comfortable with patients.

Two other activities were introduced into the group sessions, primarily as backdrops for discussion and as tension releasers. It is difficult for children, as it is for adults, to sit and discuss problems, without something "to do with their hands." They need some outlet for their tension. The provision of activities which allowed them to move their hands in an acceptable way (and to shift around borrowing and grabbing supplies) decreased the need for gross physical activity. In all group sessions, various shapes and textures of paper—tracing paper, index cards, colored paper, typing paper—and a variety of pencils, pens and crayons, were provided so members drew pictures, wrote their name repeatedly, wrote messages, doodled, folded paper, etc. (It was only in the last of the four sessions that the paper activity moved into paper airplanes!) In all group sessions refreshments were served. Refreshments increased the attraction to the group as well as reducing tension. The members of the group decided what refreshments they wanted for the next meeting. In this way the members had opportunities to make decisions and to participate in determining part of what happened and/or was available to the group in each meeting.

The prestructured format for the four sessions of each group was (a) in the first two sessions, primarily discussion with backdrop activities; (b) in the third session, the hosted activity; and (c) in the final session, discussion with emphasis upon evaluation of what the group members thought they had achieved in the meeting. The worker also planned to facilitate the groups' discussion of members' disappointment in the group's discontinuance.

These group meetings were extremely meaningful to the children; so much so the plans for the final sessions had to be modified. The children's desire to attend the group changed remarkably following the first session. Most of the children had initially approached attendance at the group with much anxiety and fear of the unknown. They were all actively positive about returning to subsequent meetings. This change in attitude was

---

[5] The group worker saw each patient on the ward and invited them to join in the host activity. Only one patient refused to attend. This was because the "highly valued activity," swimming, turned out to be an activity he feared greatly.

evident on the part of all children. The degree of group cohesion that developed among the group members in the Sibling Sets Group and the Boys Group was much greater than had been anticipated. The author proposes that these children had been so alienated in their social relationships that the relationships available in these groups provided a much needed social reward. Here they were accepted by age mates. This was well described by a thirteen-year-old boy who stated in the first group session, "School was a place to have acquaintances but not friends." At the time it had seemed a rather mature differentiation. In the fourth session during the evaluation of the group, he stated, "The reason I liked the group was that I was able to make friends."

The author (1965) has had extensive experience with the use of the short-term group as a diagnostic tool in child guidance clinics. The rapid development of group cohesion was not often present in children's groups. Perhaps another explanation lies in the more specific nature of the members' base of commonality, the stress resulting from role expectations of a new status.

The intensity of group cohesion that developed in the two groups made it necessary to modify the original program format for the final group session. Program activity had to be provided that would help to make the group become less cohesive so that the loss of the group would be less difficult for the members.[6] Therefore, in the latter half of the final session in the Sibling Sets and Boys Group the groups took a "walk-run-chase" around the hospital grounds. This activity cut down on the intensity of the interaction supported by close spatial limits in the small meeting room. The children were encouraged to use playground equipment in which individual activity, rather than group or paired activity, was dominant. There were other children (unrelated patients) on the playground. Since the members had to share equipment with them as well as group members, group interaction was further diluted. Care had to be exercised to reduce the group cohesion without removing the pleasurable aspects of the interaction already experienced. Thus, the unexpectedly high level of group cohesion that developed in a short-term group made it necessary to use activities to reduce intensity of interpersonal interactions in the last meeting to facilitate the members' separation from the group.

CONCLUSIONS

The Sibling Sets Group, in which each member had at least one sibling present, began the group experience with less anxiety than the

[6] The author is indebted to Charles Garvin, University of Michigan School of Social Work for his concept of programming to decohesify the group.

other two groups. Communication within the sibling subgroups was high. In contrast, the communication among Sibling Sets and/or between the children and the worker was low. Communication within the Sibling Sets included physical contact, (e.g., children sitting next to one another, poking, tickling and kicking); verbal contact (e.g., using private expressions and "sounds," as well as words); and signaling (e.g., with hand motions and facial expressions). The members limited the "voluntary verbal" communication directed to the worker though they seemed to expect the worker to "listen in" and "get their message."

It seemed as if in coming to a meeting each member had brought his own security—a brother or a sister. By the second meeting the intrafamily subgroup pattern of "private" communication was reduced remarkably. The members sat next to members who were close to their own age and of the same sex. The youngest child, who had no one close to his age in the group, remained physically close to the worker and related to her primarily.

The members of the Family Group were an established group. The first meeting and the first portion of all other meetings were controlled by the use of a "litany technique" which defended the group from the entrance of the worker's influence. The children had worked out a group response to threatening statements regardless of whether the initiator of the threatening comment was a group member or the worker. For example, should a member comment or imply that the patient was retarded, all other children spontaneously recited a response, almost in unison, "Bill's not stupid, remember the record player, he fixed it." The child who initiated a comment which triggered the group litany would participate in any other litany which was started when another member made another threatening comment. It seemed at first that any comments regarding the patient, problems or worries were threatening. The anxiety shown by this group was to the outside intruder, the worker. The group members were aware of the problems their brother's illness had introduced for them and they had developed a method of protecting themselves against outsiders by group action. It was difficult for this group to open ranks for the worker's intervention. However, the members, as individuals, were not so comfortable with the group's solution that they remained closed to the worker's entry entirely. The author felt the family group composition introduced unnecessary complications when compared to the group composed of sibling sets or the group composed of unrelated boys of the same age. These complications could decrease the effectiveness of social group work treatment when time-limited treatment is used.

In the Boys Group, the initial anxiety was more diffuse. None of the members knew the worker or any of the other members. They had no subgroup members to whom they could relate as in the Sibling Sets Group and they were not yet a group like the Family Group. Initially, the members spent time locating safe relationships with each other before they could focus on the task of talking about their concerns. The boys were not sure of each other's involvement with role problems. Children who had other siblings present in the meeting knew that others had similar problems and were, so to speak, "in the same boat." In the initial stage the discussion focused on checking each other's credentials. Early communications between and among members were carried out in an approach-avoidance pattern.

Many of the group members' reactions to worker- or child-initiated statements of concern were defensive. Much use was made of denial and excessive silliness. Comments such as, "Oh, you're nuts" or "We don't care, do we?" were common. Physically, a boy would goof off by darting under the table, tip his chair, always inviting other boys to join him. The worker needed to exert controls and to identify such behaviors and comments as defensive reactions rather than as expressions of the boy's true attitudes. This was necessary to avoid the formation of a norm or pattern of laughing at expressed concerns or running around the room. In the other two groups the siblings had exerted control over one another when physically inappropriate behavior was threatened.

The Boys Group took the longest time to begin to function as a group, free to expose their concerns to other group members for the purpose of discussion. This could be a reflection of how deeply alienated these children feel with their age mates. The author wondered if members of this group may have initially rejected other members because they gave each other the status of siblings of mental hospital patients and reacted to each other in the same negative way others had reacted to them.

Once the initial stage was passed, the similarity of age—and consequently similar interests, e.g., baseball—provided a base of commonality and promoted a rapid increase in group cohesion. The group was composed of children with sixth-grade training in the skill of discussion. The group was able to participate in meaningful problem-solving discussion for a longer period and with greater verbal facility than the other two groups. Yet, when one member was threatened by the content of the discussion neither the worker nor the group could offer as much support to him as was provided in the other groups where a sibling was present. This group would digress more rapidly to safe topics. As a short-term treatment group, the Boys Group was more accessible than the Family Group, but it was less effective in problem solving than the Sibling Sets Group.

Clearly, there were important differences in the rapidity with which the groups approached discussion and accepted the worker in a helping role. These differences seemed to be related primarily to problems involved in the initial reaction to the group treatment situation. On a long-term basis, such difficulties might not prove important. In the use of short-term techniques they appeared to be salient. Although one might anticipate that discussion would be a more useful technique among a group of twelve-year-old boys than in groups which contained much younger children, it was found that the nature of anxieties within the early group experience was such that this apparent advantage was markedly weakened. Sets of siblings would be preferable to a single-age, unrelated group composition. Both the Sibling Sets and Boys Groups were preferable to the Family Group in which the group boundaries were formed against outsiders' intrusion in a private problem.

Proceeding from the assumptions that siblings of state hospital patients are placed under great strain when their brothers or sisters are admitted to the hospital and that regardless of the level of a child's functioning prior to a sibling's hospitalization, a child is made less capable of functioning in his normal social roles and social group work intervention can be used to modify his strain and stress. Group discussion among children experiencing similar role stress and corrective emotional experiences involving reality confrontation of the hospital setting, policies, and personnel can be used to help a child function at least at the level of social adequacy that he had achieved before his sibling was hospitalized and to enable him to participate helpfully in the recovery process of his sibling.

REFERENCES

CHURCHILL, SALLIE R.
  1959—"Prestructuring group content," *Social Work Journal,* (July).
  1965—"Social group work: A diagnostic tool in child guidance," *American Journal of Orthopsychiatry,* 35 (April), pp. 581–88.
KLEIN, DONALD C. AND ANN A. ROSS
  1965—"Kindergarten entry, a study of role transition," in Howard Parad (Ed.), *Crisis Intervention Selected Readings,* New York: Family Service Association of America.
PARAD, HOWARD (ED.)
  1965—*Crisis Intervention Selected Readings,* New York: Family Service Association of America.
THOMAS, EDWIN J.
  1964—*Concepts of Role Theory,* Ann Arbor: Campus Publishers.

23.

Small Groups in the Mental Hospital

SALLIE R. CHURCHILL and PAUL H. GLASSER

Ideally, persons who have severe emotional problems or who are considered mentally ill would be treated on an out-patient basis or as day or night patients in a treatment facility in their own community. If their problems were so severe that they needed the protection of a hospital, they would be admitted to a community hospital for a short time. However, each year thousands of patients are admitted to and reside in large mental hospitals. Can these patients be helped while they are in a large institution to return to the community to live with some degree of acceptance?

The use of group experiences within the mental hospital and the use of groups as a bridge to the community are viable techniques for the modification of the behavior of the mentally ill patient, institutionalized in a large hospital. Group experiences can permit the patient to restore or improve the level of his social functioning so that he can behave in an acceptable manner. The implementation of group techniques requires professional and administrative commitment of institutional staff toward realizable treatment goals, the conceptualization of "improvement" as "behavioral change" rather than "cure," and the acceptance that each hospital stay is temporary.

STRUCTURE OF HOSPITALS

The potential of groups in large mental hospitals can be understood best when the basic characteristics of the hospital structure are understood. Hospital structure is an organized method of achieving goals. It has emerged over the years in an unplanned, utilitarian manner to meet the demands of society and the maintenance needs of the institution. The structure reflects the disparate values of care and custody, on one hand, and treatment, on the other. The structure which has evolved in large hospitals generally is not a structure directed primarily for the treatment of patients. Fragmented treatment programs do exist, but they are frequently subjected to curtailment of funding with each financial crisis. Treatment often is related to student training for professions or the research segments of the hospital.

Hospital structure and the problems inherent in the structure have been the subject of extensive research and subjective evaluation. Perrow (1965) reviewed the literature on hospital structure and with some facetiousness identified six themes in the literature. (1) Communication threads its way through virtually every description; it is always blocked. (2) Attendants and their illegitimate, abused power are the villains of nearly every piece. (3) Psychiatrists are castigated for being poor administrators, for being aloof from nurses, for clinging to the two-person model of treatment. (4) The business staff of hospitals hoard supplies and frustrate change. (5) The hospital structure is characterized as paranoid, granulated and authoritarian. (6) Treatment goals are always displaced by custody. Apparently, the hospital structure cannot be responsive to the treatment-oriented professional's interest in patients as isolated individuals. Such practitioners often are convinced that institutions exist for the benefit of the patient. They believe, in line with the so-called Protestant ethic, that hard, skilled work by the professional on behalf of the institutionalized client can effect a cure. Such beliefs create a dilemma; for they are neither true nor instrumental to patient change in a large institution. Workers need to pay attention to the institution as a social system and to locate where professionals may exert influence and foster changes within that system.

The mental hopital's complex organizational structure has created enduring relationships that use energy in a patterned effort to change conditions of human beings in a predetermined way. The organizational task is the alteration of the behavior of human beings. Three sets of factors interact in the achievement of this organizational task: (1) cultural systems of goals, values and beliefs, (2) treatment techniques employed to bring about change, and (3) arrangements to implement goals.

CHANGES IN VALUES, BELIEFS AND GOALS

During the twentieth century, three aspects of the patient's experience have been the focus of attention in mental hospitals: (1) the social and physical environment of the patient, (2) the internal dynamics or psychological functioning of the patient, and (3) the patient's behavior. Shifts in the attention given to one or another of these foci are related to both the beliefs and values of the general population concerning mental illness and the development of therapeutic efforts among professionals in the mental health field.

At the turn of the century attention was focused on the social and physical environments of the mental hospital patient. The abuse of institutionalized patients by personnel and the deplorable physical conditions of hospitals received much attention. National, state, and local mental health societies and other organizations clamored for reform; and much was done to clean up and repair some of the hospital facilities and to eliminate the physical abuse of patients.

The influence of Freudian psychoanalytic theory began a new era in the 1930s. Various forms of psychosis were seen as illnesses rather than "the work of the devil." Emphasis was placed on changing the internal dynamics or psychic functioning of the patient in order to bring about change in the patient's behavior. Little attention was paid to the social and physical environment of the patient, except to prevent the abuses that had occurred earlier, since therapists thought that patients could handle their environment adequately once certain changes in their personalities had occurred.

The third trend can be seen as a refinement of the second and as one that is predominant in hospitals today. Emphasis is still on modification of the psychic functioning of the patient to enable him to handle his life in a better way, but greater recognition has been given to how the hospital or training school environment itself can hinder the patient's progress in individual psychotherapy. In recent years, the physical and social situation of the patient has been made as neutral as possible so that individualized therapy and training are not hampered by the institutional environment and to permit one-to-one treatment methods to be more effective. The degree of this neutralization varies from one hospital to another; a custodial program is not always consistent with a neutral environment. While patients have had more positive experiences in recent years, negative experiences do continue to occur, although they are often rationalized as being necessary to protect the patient from himself and others and to prevent his escape from the institution.

The final trend, which is just beginning, is characterized by efforts to change the physical and social situation sufficiently to influence each patient's behavior. This approach requires changes in the organizational structure and in the daily living experiences of patients. Most of the changes take place in the context of the small group.

This trend is developing against a background of the relative lack of efficiency and effectiveness of individualized psychological treatment for the large numbers of mental patients in large hospitals. Up to the present, only a small proportion of institutionalized clients have received individualized help. In the foreseeable future, the number of therapists cannot possibly become sufficiently large to treat individually the increasing number of patients. Even when individualized treatment methods have been available, they have not always been successful. A large number of patients can be treated more quickly and successfully in the context of the group, particularly as changes are brought about in their daily living experiences.

A therapeutic milieu approach which makes maximum use of natural and formed groups within the institution can consider and incorporate individual differences among the client population. Some therapists believe that the changes in patient behavior that are produced in groups may be accompanied by changes in their internal dynamics and psychological functioning. In any case, the environment is not neutral, as in the psychoanalytic approach, but it becomes an active and powerful force in the rehabilitation process.

The use of group situations to modify patients' behavior to a socially approved and/or acceptable level of social functioning reflects the acceptance of new beliefs regarding the nature of mental illness and a change in the values and goals of treatment technologies. These new beliefs view mental illness and mental health in terms of a person's behavior. They do not address the question of cure but, rather, the question of restoration of appropriate social functioning. Since "the problem" is viewed as difficulty in behaving in a social milieu, the treatment laboratory logically becomes a social system (or a series of social systems) which simulates the arenas where problems occur and where corrected behavior must be manifest. The treatment locales should be selected group situations.

The goal of better social functioning means that patients must be allowed to become more independent and have increased opportunities for decision making in regard to their own lives. Patients should be permitted to make decisions which they can handle but should not be asked to take responsibilities beyond their capacities. Achieving such a balance is not simple; but efforts at patient government and the increasing patient advocate activities indicate that the danger lies in underestimating and underusing patient capacities rather than the opposite.

The Nature and Technology of Groups Within the Hospital

Cultural systems of goals, values, and beliefs constitute one set of factors relevant to the achievement of the mental hospital's task of altering human behavior. A second set of factors concerns the nature and technology of groups.

Groups can be useful; groups can be very harmful; groups may just be neutral. This is true in any setting: a school, a church, a community center, a mental hospital. Groups may be used as tools. Their value depends on why they are used, how skillfully they are used, and how well they are constructed.

Group experience is an important part of human life, beginning with early family experiences, in the play group, in school, on teams, in church, etc. Through group experiences individuals find acceptance or rejection, develop a self-image, learn and practice reality testing. Through group experiences people become social beings, learning how to deal with other people. For the patient in the institution, groups can be laboratories where the tasks of social living can be reexperienced or relearned.

A great variety of patient groups exist within each hospital at all times. These groups include those organized by the patients themselves, by the staff for specific therapeutic or training objectives, and by staff for administrative purposes. There is practically no time in the patient's hospital stay when he is not in a group. He sleeps, eats, idles, works, plays, walks and waits in groups. Often, much of his group experience has been imposed upon him for hospital convenience without thoughtful utilization of the group as part of a patient's identified treatment opportunities.

Groups in mental hospitals sometimes have had very negative effects on the life of the patient. This has been true when the focus was on the *group* itself, especially as a way to control patients and to force conformity to hospital procedures.

Groups formed by patients often constitute a way for patients to exercise control over one another. These groups can also have antitherapeutic effects. When patients are not permitted to have much responsibility or to participate in making decisions about their own lives, they often find informal means to assert power and authority. One example is a "sitters" group composed of patients, each of whom has a special chair placed in a special position in the day room on the ward. During free time, when they are permitted in the day room, they maintain their positions in specific chairs. Even if patients are nonverbal and passive, they manifest their power in a variety of ways. First, if someone else sits in "their" chair, they will fight for their right to have the occupant removed. Secondly, they exercise power over staff. If the staff attempt to move chairs, the patients will move them back to their original positions. They may fight with someone who attempts to sit in "their" chair. The routine of the ward may be upset, and the staff must intervene. The "sitters" group illustrates that such behavior can affect the therapeutic milieu of the ward and the achievement of treatment goals for individual patients. The staff must evaluate these informal interactions in terms of their potential effects.

Institutionalized clients usually experience social hunger. They are driven to find ways in which to have contact with others. Sometimes the types of relationships patients establish with each other seem bizarre. Even nonverbal interaction can signify a meaningful relationship. Such behavior is the way patients can have meaningful social contact despite their acute illness. It must be recognized that even in such interactions patients can influence each other. Groups can be most valuable when they exist for the needs of the group members; individual needs rather than group needs are the hospital worker's major concern.

In viewing groups as a viable technology in the treatment of hospital patients three assumptions have been made. (1) Informal social processes exist among any in-patient population and these processes affect the treatment and its outcome. (2) Social processes can be molded to enhance a patient's treatment experience and to improve the treatment outcome. (3) A patient's membership in different hospital groups significantly affects his response to treatment and its outcome. These assumptions have found support in a study conducted by Lamberger (1964). She studied four types of formal groups in a Veterans Administration Mental Hospital: occupational therapy groups, group therapy groups, sleeping groups on the ward, and recreation groups. She found that:

1. The more frequently persons interact, the stronger their sentiment of friendship for one another is apt to be.
2. The more frequently persons interact, the higher they will rank each other as having influence on the ward generally.
3. The more frequently persons interact, the more likely they are to have a strong personal influence on each other.

Research and clinical observation leave little doubt that clients and patients have strong influences on each other in a variety of ways in a variety of groups. Some groups are formed by the patients themselves because they are located near each other on a ward or other place in the hospital and have common interests and backgrounds (natural groups). These can be developed for therapeutic purposes. Other groups are specifically formed by professional staff with a therapeutic intent. For both types of groups, these questions must be answered: Who should work with a group? Who should be in a group? What activities should take place? The purpose of the group should largely determine these answers.

Who Should Work With Whom?

The purpose of establishing a group or developing a therapeutic program with a natural group should be specific and clear. The patients selected to compose a group should be determined by the purpose of the group. Additionally, the assignment of a worker, staff member or volunteer, should be related to the purpose of the group. When it is clear what work must be done, then it can be known what skills or expertise a worker will need in order to help the group members successfully work in a group.

A worker who is to help a group become a therapeutic experience for a group member needs to have knowledge of deviant behavior and mental illness, individual needs, and group processes. In addition, a group worker should have some understanding of what constitutes "normal" behavior, a point that is often overlooked, despite the fact that the goal of the group frequently is to have patients achieve more "normal" functioning. He should be aware of the particular nature of deviant behavior of his group and what constitutes a stress situation for each member. He must know what behavior changes are desirable for each member and what barriers need to be surmounted in his efforts to change. Without such knowledge, the worker may err in one of two directions. He may focus on the illness, rather than on the patient's strengths or acceptable behavior and overestimate the limitations imposed on the patient by his illness. Such limitations often appear to be greater than they really are, partly because many workers have difficulty identifying clearly the small gains and partial success that pave the way to major change. Some workers err in the opposite direction; they assume that since the patient behaves adequately in many situations, the patient should behave acceptably most of the time. Neither stance is helpful, for both deny the patient's reality and cloud the areas where he needs help. All who work with groups in a mental hospital must understand that the rehabilitation process is not a straight line process. Improvement involves both forward and backward change. As certain problems are resolved other problems may assume higher priority. Progress also may include periods where no change seems to occur.

"Work with groups" implies that a group itself is being worked with —things are being done for, done to and done with a group. All groups should exist as a means of helping each member, not to be an end in itself. Depending on the purpose of the group, general goals for all group members or specific individual goals can be articulated.

A recurrent problem is that many of the professionals within the mental hospital think that work with patients in groups is restricted to their domain, whatever it may be. Much energy has been expended on experiments and efforts by professionals to try out their methods with groups of patients in an effort to support an elitist view. The old bugaboo "status" plagues even professionals. (Remember George Orwell's *Animal Farm* where "all are equal, but some are more equal"?) One therapeutic group is too often considered "more therapeutic" than another type of "therapeutic" group. Experience shows that professional groups latch on to what is considered high-status work and often drop their own unique professional skills. This simply narrows the treatment opportunities for patients. Mental hospitals, with their broad range of patient needs, must offer a breadth of group services. Currently, psychologists and psychiatrists frequently use groups in order to help patients develop greater insight. Recreational therapists use various types of programs in small group and mass recreation settings to help patients reexperience pleasure in activity and, secondarily, pleasure in activity with others. Remotivation, a technique designed primarily for nursing personnel, uses groups to expand horizons, create group interest, "build a bridge to reality" and promote interaction among people living on the same ward (American Psychiatric Association, 1963). Social group workers use groups as a means and a context for changes in individual behavior.

Paraprofessionals, paid or volunteer, can lead patient groups, particularly where the primary goal is to develop recreational skill or a special interest. Such workers may help patients maintain contact with reality, expand their experiential horizons, continue some contact with the outside community, and simply have fun—a rare commodity in any institution. Volunteers can arrange experiences away from the hospital for patients such as the Project Transition developed at Ypsilanti State Hospital, Michigan. In this program, small groups of community women meet with small groups of patients for a few hours weekly. These meetings are at local churches or other community sites. Two categories of paraprofessionals should be considered more often than they are: ex-patients, who may be useful models to patients, particularly when they are able to share their success and past hospital experiences; and people who are from the same ethnic, racial or social class group. People who are similar to patients' own reference groups can facilitate the patient's resumption of "normal" social intercourse.

Formed groups should be used carefully and selectively. Certain patients may need the specialized services of a highly trained group specialist before they are able to benefit from membership in a group led by a less trained worker. Some patients need a specialized service at the same time that they are part of a group led by a less trained technician. The purposes of the two groups may be quite different. Other patients may need to experience participation in a large group to enable them to invest in and tolerate a group experience before they can make use of a small group.

Size of Group

Small, medium and large groups offer patients different kinds of experiences. No one size is necessarily more beneficial than another size. Actually, many patients need experience in groups of various size. Small groups of four to eight members provide a setting in which patients are forced into greater interaction with one another. In large institutions, where lack of participation in viable decision making is prevalent, small groups can offer opportunities for each patient to be involved in several roles and have part in making decisions.

Large groups allow for anonymity. The roles are more formal. There is some opportunity for interaction among patients, particularly within subgroups in the larger group. In larger groups there is more task role differentiation.

What Can Be Achieved in Groups?

To achieve a reasonable degree of health, all people must be able to find a comfortable balance between being alone and being with others, and a comfortable balance between being like others and being unique. Often there is concern that individuals will get lost in a group. This can be avoided when the worker is aware that the focus in therapeutic groups should be on the individual. Groups are formed to help the clients. Incidentally, while group workers fully acknowledge the value of group experiences, they must be champions of meeting the needs for patient privacy. A group worker must ask "When can the patient have the right to be alone?" In most institutions, the answer is "not very often."

What can be achieved in a group? Towey, et al., (1966) suggest seven major values of groups in an article entitled "Group Activities With Psychiatric In-Patients."

1. *The presentation of ego models.* Despite the occasional gibe that the only difference between the patient and the staff person is that one goes home after eight hours and the other goes to bed, the staff generally is much healthier and more adequate than the patients. The distance between the patients, who are sick, and the staff, who is well, is sometimes too great to allow patients to identify with staff. Patients may feel defeated in attempting such identification before they start. Often, healthier patients are closer to less healthy patients than they are to staff members. Groups can help bridge his gap between degrees of sickness and health.

2. *Social involvement.* Patients can sometimes be characterized as intensely self-centered, dependent and passive. These nonhelpful roles are usually encouraged and sometimes enforced by hospital routines. The identification with other patients in the protected environment of the small, rehabilitation-oriented group helps each member move out of these roles into social interaction and active involvement with others.

3. *Behavioral feedback.* In the security of a group, where the patient has gained the feeling that other members can and do like him and where others also have problems, he can begin to learn how his behavior affects others. This is done without a sense of punishment for misbehavior. It arises from the desire of the individual himself to change in response to the greater acceptance of the people to whom he can relate.

4. *The enhancement of self-esteem.* Through the development of a sense of identification with the group, patients are provided with opportunities for the enhancement of self-esteem. The group provides a sense of belonging, helps to reduce feelings of inferiority and isolation, and en-

courages patients to test reality by reacting to others and perceiving how others react to them. These three characteristics are very important attributes for patients who tend to be perennial isolates or "outsiders" and for the person whose sense of identity is not intact.

5. *Learning new knowledge and skills.* In a group, patients can learn from each other as well as from the worker. Further, they can learn through the observation of others without making a public commitment. They can learn by applying the situations of others to their own circumstances, through analogy rather than confrontation. In this way they can learn that it may be safe to take a chance, to try new ways of handling and solving personal and social problems.

6. *Remedial social education.* Groups can provide patients with opportunities to relearn forgotten social skills. Contacts with the world outside the institution and ways of dealing with it can be reestablished through discussion, role playing, trips to the community, etc.

7. *The support and utilization of social hunger.* Through recognition of the intact portions of a patient's ego, groups can stimulate, nurture, and support social hunger. The normative system established through group relationships can be developed to provide approval for appropriate old and new patterns of behavior as well as to limit deviant behavior. Peer sanction and limits often provide more effective controls for the character disorder than an outside authority affords. On the other hand, peer encouragement and approval often enable the withdrawn patient to take a chance on interacting with others to satisfy his need for social involvement.

A Comprehensive Example of the Group Approach

A rather creative experimental program in the use of groups has been reported by Fairweather (1964). He thinks that the hospital role the patient assumes should be transferable to the community. The patient should not have to face a problem of role discontinuity when he returns to the community. Treatment efforts should be directed toward the patient's learning to perform adequately a role that is appropriate outside the hospital. Such a role would require the patient to make decisions alone and in a group. According to Fairweather, chronic patients often make thoroughly adequate adjustments to the hospital setting. Each finds some kind of niche that enables him to get along in the hospital but not outside it. This role is then stabilized and reinforced within the institutional environment. In order to leave the hospital and make a successful adjustment to community life, the patient must discard this role.

Fairweather reported an extensive research project in a Veterans Administration Hospital in which he demonstrated the validity of his ideas about role continuity. Patients were assigned to task groups that were responsible for many facets of patient routine and government, including orientation of new patients to the program and the formulation of important life decisions regarding each group member, e.g., the money the patient had available to him in the hospital, his passes, and his actual discharge. Patients were placed in groups upon admission. No staff members met with the groups, though the staff did retain some veto power over group decisions. Most patients and staff responded more positively to this program than to the traditional one; in addition, the average length of hospitalization was shortened.

The limits of usefulness of groups are not apparent. Some types of groups, as in Fairweather's experiment, call for extensive modification of hospital structure. Many groups can be utilized within an existing hospital structure, to provide better patient care and treatment and to aid patients to become successful social beings when they are ready to live outside the hospital.

ADMINISTRATIVE SUPPORT

The final factors that must be considered in the achievement of institutional tasks—the change of patient behavior—are the administrative arrangements necessary to implement goals.

While most group programs can be instituted without many structural changes, the operation of a new group program needs the support of administrators. Peal (1965) indicates four ways in which the hospital administration can aid new group programs. (1) Relatively protected meeting times must be arranged and preserved. A social work student went to the ward to meet with his group for the first time. The group had been carefully selected and balanced by the group worker on the basis of referrals from the ward psychiatrist. When he arrived he found one patient had been sent out on a leave of absence, one had gone on a work assignment, and one was at the dentist's. Only two patients were available for the group session. (2) The administration must make provisions for the worker to have time to prepare for and hold the meeting. (3) The administration can support the patient's attendance at meetings when "pro" *status quo* personnel sabotage a worker's efforts to hold meetings by preventing patients' attendance. (4) The administration must allow for failure or mediocre success of a new program and thereby provide protection for the worker who is willing to take a chance with new techniques. Only when failure is acknowledged to be one of the possible and acceptable outcomes of an experiment is a social worker free to try new projects, free to move away from the safety of the tried and true methods. Acceptance of possible failure allows him to experiment to the ultimate benefit of patients.

Perrow (1965) states that the structure of an organization is basically influenced by its technology and, vice-versa, an organization's technology is basically influenced by the structure of the organization. It can be difficult to introduce new technique in an existing structure if the nature of the new concepts implies some organizational change. For example, the concept of the therapeutic milieu probably could not be implemented successfully within an authoritarian structure, since the therapeutic milieu approach demands a nonauthoritarian structure. If, however, the authoritarian structure itself were used to institute a therapeutic milieu, the program once started would introduce a series of changes in the authoritarian structure itself.

According to Perrow, the reasons for the depressing conditions of mental institutions do not lie in their structure, process, or goal commitment but in their technological limitations. He believes there is no valid treatment technology consistent with large mental hospitals.

However, the authors believe that group situations in which the patient can gradually reassume responsibility for decisions regarding himself and in which he gradually increases his obligations for social living—which usually are denied to the mentally ill person—can provide a viable treatment technique for large hospitals. Such treatment depends upon the acceptance of patienthood as a temporary condition in which the patient modifies his dysfunctional behavior and from which he is permitted to reenter his community as a complete citizen.

REFERENCES

FAIRWEATHER, GEORGE W.
    1964—*Social Psychology in Treating Mental Illness,* New York: John Wiley & Sons.
LAMBERGER, LINDA
    1964—"Factors affecting friendship and power relationships among patients on an open psychiatric ward," Master of Social Work Thesis, Ann Arbor, Michigan: University of Michigan.
PEAL, JAMES
    1965—"Responsibility of administration to group therapy programs," State of Michigan, Department of Mental Health, Lansing, (Mimeographed).
PERROW, CHARLES
    1965—"Hospitals, technology, structure and goals," in James G. March (Ed.), *Handbook of Organizations,* Chicago: Rand McNally.
AMERICAN PSYCHIATRIC ASSOCIATION, MENTAL HEALTH SERVICE, AND SMITH, KLINE AND FRENCH LABORATORIES
    1963—*Remotivation Technique,* Remotivation Project.
TOWEY, MARTIN, S. WADE SEARS, JOHN A. WILLIAMS, NATHAN KAUFMAN AND MURRAY CUNNINGHAM
    1966—"Group activities with psychiatric in-patients," *Social Work Journal,* 11(January).

24.

An Evaluation of
Group Work Practice
with AFDC Mothers[1]

ELIZABETH NAVARRE, PAUL H. GLASSER, and
JANE COSTABILE

PROJECT GOALS

Society has begun to return its attention to providing ways for those
trapped in the lowest socioeconomic stratum to be upwardly mobile. Intervention at many levels is directed toward removing barriers to achievement and opening doors to fulfillment. The child in the AFDC family is
particularly prone to school failure, and work with the mothers of such
families is one of many measures needed to break the cycle of poverty and
chronic under-achievement. With many specific efforts under way, attention
must be given to monitoring their effectiveness.

Evaluation studies are relatively new to social work practice. This
chapter summarizes the result of one of the few studies evaluating the
outcome of a group treatment project. Its importance lies not only in its
demonstration of the effectiveness of a particular intervention process, but
also in the fact that it could be done using both objective measures of
change and a control sample.

The project was developed and carried out over a four-year period,
from 1962 to 1966, through the combined interests and cooperative efforts
of The University of Michigan School of Social Work and The Michigan
Department of Social Services.[2] Its focus was upon facilitating the healthy

[1] This chapter is a revised version of the authors' report (April, 1969) based
upon research sponsored by Children's Bureau Grant D-16. The analysis is the
responsibility of the authors, not of the Michigan State Department of Social
Welfare or its staff. The original paper was given at the 96th Annual Forum of the
National Conference in New York City on May 28, 1969.

[2] Department personnel cooperating with the project staff were Tom Cook,
Ora Hinckley, Lynn Kellogg, Roger Lind, Frances McNeil, Winifred Quarton,
Robert Rosema, June Thomas, Jeanne Walters and Fred Wight.

development of children by improving the attitudes and behavior of parents toward their children through the use of group sessions. The setting was the Oakland County Department of Social Services, including the Oakland County Children's Division and the Oakland County Bureau of Social Aid. This county is an urban area which is contiguous to Detroit and has problems similar to Detroit's problems.

Project goals included multiple theory development, the provision of service, and field training of social group work students. This report will confine itself to a summary of the group work methods and techniques used, a review and interpretation of the statistical findings of the evaluation study, and some implications for future research and practice.[3]

DEMONSTRATION AND SERVICE

During the first eighteen months of the project the emphasis was on demonstration and service. The intent was to try out a variety of service patterns in the recruitment, composition, goal orientation and leadership of groups. Toward the end of this period, consistency in service patterns became a requirement as the project moved into the pretesting and evaluation phases. The decision was made to recruit clients for the experimental groups from the Oakland County Bureau of Social Aid because of the much larger number of members available there than in the Children's Division. AFDC mothers who had one or more children who were having learning or behavioral difficulties in public school were recruited to groups which met in a community agency or institution in their neighborhood. Workers focused group attention on parent-child interaction related to these school problems. Three subgoals were identified: (1) the provision of additional resources (clothing, medical care, etc.) related to the children's achievement and attendance in school, (2) changes in mothers' attitudes toward the school system, and (3) changes in mothers' attitudes toward their children's behavior and achievement in school. Throughout the three years there were twenty-one groups of this type, including the twelve groups in the experimental sample. There were other types of groups as well.

AFDC mothers whose children were having difficulty in school were chosen to be clients in the experimental groups only after considerable thought. Since almost all AFDC mothers have this problem, a large supply of potential clients would be available. Furthermore, selection of this goal

[3] Other aspects of the project are summarized in the mimeographed Final Report dated January, 1968. See also Glasser and Navarre (1965 (a), 1965 (b)).

orientation was very much in line with the project's original intent to "center its attention upon the prevention of emotional disturbance and/or delinquency in children through group treatment of parents;"[4] it was related to the prevention of intergenerational financial dependency and the 1962 Social Security Amendments on rehabilitation; and it was an area of great interest to both local and Central Office Department staff.

During the three demonstration years about 500 clients attended group sessions, although a considerably larger number initially had been invited. The number of sessions held for each group in the experimental sample ranged from four to twelve, and the mode was six. Average attendance at each of these sessions was five; the meetings generally lasted about one and one-half hours. The groups were led by both agency-trained workers and a second-year student in the social group work program at The University of Michigan School of Social Work. All group leaders were supervised by a faculty member from the School, and much consultation was provided by the authors.

Members were referred to the groups by regular agency staff. Caseworkers listed names of clients within their caseloads who had relevant problems. They specified which clients had cars or were close to bus lines, and identified children by ages and school grades. They tried to screen out clients known to be unable to attend meetings because of work, illness or some other reason. Following conferences between the group worker and the referring caseworker, home calls to describe the new service and extend invitations to attend were made by the caseworker, the group worker, or both. Clients were told that there were two purposes for the service: to aid them to get and give help in the resolution of problems held in common; and to assist the agency in finding out whether group sessions of this type are useful.

Customarily, arrangements were made for clients to meet at a centrally located neighborhood facility, such as the public school or local recreation agency, so that many clients could walk to the meeting place. A week before the first group meeting clients received reminder letters, which briefly described the group purpose once again, gave specific directions to the site of the group session, and urged attendance. Thereafter, mimeographed notices were mailed weekly. Often, clients who failed to respond to the weekly notices were visited or telephoned. Seemingly, the greater the effort devoted to recruitment, the higher the attendance.

Throughout the history of the project recruitment, diagnostic and group leadership procedures were changed to make them more effective and more efficient. Those described in this report were generally followed in the third and final year of the evaluation study. They reflect careful

[4] Quoted from original project proposal.

thought concerning previous experiences with the integration of social science and practice theory.

Often prior to the first meeting, but always before the second session, the group worker prepared for each client expected in the group a short diagnostic statement, based on record material, home visits and his conferences with the caseworker. Specific behavioral goals related to the purpose of the group and the individual diagnostic evaluation were required as part of this statement. Further, prior to each group meeting, individual goals, group goals and intervention plans were prepared for that session. All of these formulations were in written form, serving as a basis for supervision, but also demanding considerable preparation for the rehabilitation process.

The problem-solving approach, developed out of the Bales material on social interaction, was used as one theoretical basis in all experimental groups (Bales and Strodtbeck, 1960; Bales, 1958). A second emphasis was the group work practice theory formulated at the University of Michigan (Vinter, 1967). Individual difficulties and the concerns verbalized by clients were reinterpreted by the worker into a problem formulation relevant to the majority of group members. The group was then helped to move through the orientation (information gathering), evaluation (proposed alternate solutions), and control (reaching a decision) phases of the process, each member contributing ideas to and learning from others during every session. Each member was able to choose from among the multiple solutions proposed during the third phase and to make use of those most relevant to her situation.

This training in problem solving was repeated a number of times during the history of each group. The women were asked to report the results of their attempts to try out new solutions. After a few successful experiences in the group, the worker explained the process the group had been through in easily understandable terms, and each client was asked to try out the process on a specified problem on her own and report back at the next meeting, at which time reports were discussed and evaluated. At the last group session the problem-solving process was reviewed, and group members were encouraged to continue using this rational approach to the difficulties they were experiencing.

Although the primary activity of all groups was discussion, a variety of other program techniques were used when appropriate. Tape recordings, films, pictures, stories, role play, etc., were attempted to stimulate group members in a variety of ways. In order to orient themselves better to a particular problem, many groups invited outside resource people, particulargly Bureau and school personnel to attend group sessions. Such contacts had intrinsic value in that they often led to more positive client perceptions of these authority figures in their lives.

Following termination of the group, workers prepared reports on each client, summarizing each woman's participation in the project and the degree to which individual goals were achieved. Next, steps for the caseworker were recommended. Once these reports were read by the client's caseworker and/or the casework supervisor, a conference was held between the group worker and one or both of these agency staff members. A group summary report was also written and made available to agency staff.

EVALUATION METHODS

In the first project year, relationships between the local agency and the University were established, concepts of social group work in a public agency setting were developed, and the agency and the project staff explored various means of adapting to the needs of both organizations as well as to the needs of the clients to be served. No research was attempted during that year. In the second year the evaluation study was designed, and instruments developed and pretested. The third year was spent in data collection. During the fourth and final project year the statistical analysis was performed and preliminary drafts written on all project activities.

Four types of populations were used in the research:

1. An initial sample of 158 mothers on AFDC known to be physically able to attend group meetings was selected for twelve experimental groups in Oakland County. Of these 158 mothers, 85 attended two or more meetings whereas 73 attended one or no meeting. The 85 AFDC mothers constituted the *experimental sample*. The time periods when data were collected for this sample will be described during discussion of each measure.
2. Comparisons between the 85 attendees and the 73 mothers who came to one or no meeting was made for social background data to account for selection bias. The group of 73 is called the "no treatment" group; no important differences between it and the experimental sample were found.[5]
3. A *control sample* of 27 mothers on AFDC from Washtenaw County who received no social group work services during the study period was randomly selected. All of the clients were living in either the Ypsilanti or Willow Run school districts, areas similar to Oakland County. A six-month interval elapsed between the collection of before and after evaluation measures.

---

[5] Only one statistically different finding was noted. Twenty-one percent of the experimental grantees were mothers at the time of first marriage, while only 12% of the "no treatment" group reported this.

4. A second type of control sample was attempted in order to hold constant the content, focus and goal orientation of the group. This consisted of 25 parents who attended two groups in the Children's Division. Important differences between these parents and all of the others place great limitations on the meaningfulness of comparative findings, and therefore, they will not be included in the discussion that follows.

POPULATION CHARACTERISTICS

The following description will focus on the experimental population; comparisons with the control group are presented when there is a statistically significant difference between the two groups.[6]

Thirty-four percent of the experimentals were Black and 66% White. The picture reverses itself among the controls, with 63% Black and 37% White. The median number of years experimentals were in school was 8.1. Sixty-five percent reported their normal occupation as unskilled service, and 80% reported no present employment. A larger proportion of controls were employed full-time (15%) than experimentals (1%), because of the selection procedures in the experimental groups.

In the experimental sample 25% of the former heads of the house were employed in unskilled service, 34% in factory work and 25% in skilled service. The occupational status of the family prior to AFDC was lower in the control population, but not statistically significant. However, this difference is reflected in the AFDC grantees' reports of highest income ever earned: Six percent of experimentals reported less than $2,500, 31% as $2,500–$5,000, 32% as $5,000–$7,500 and 4% over $7,500. The controls reported significantly lower "highest incomes."

Median age for experimentals was 37.5 and for controls 40.2. Forty-two percent of the experimental group were 35 or under while only 17% of the control group were within this age category. The health of the controls was significantly poorer than experimentals (37% vs. 14% reporting poor health). More controls than experimentals were never married (11% vs. 3%), but fewer of them reported being married more than once (15% vs. 25%). Seventy-nine percent of the experimentals were divorced.

The average number of children in experimental families was 4.5. About half of these mothers reported no illegitimate children in the family. Few of the children were removed from the home for delinquency or

[6] T Test at .05 level of significance. The initial draft of this material was prepared by Yeheskel Hasenfeld, Lecturer, the University of Michigan School of Social Work, when he served as Research Assistant on the project one summer.

neglect. The majority of mothers were Protestant; 22% more controls than experimentals belonged to fundamentalist sects.

A somewhat smaller percentage of controls than experimentals reported reason for grant as divorce or desertion (44% vs. 59%), but the reverse was true for the report of loss of employment (33% vs. 9%). Among experimental families the median number of children eligible for aid was 3.9; among control families, 3.6. The median number of years since the first AFDC grant was longer for controls than experimentals (5.8 vs. 4.2), and they had had contact with more social agencies (4.3 vs. 2.8).

In general, the population of both groups is typical of AFDC grantees in urban Michigan. However, a difference of some importance between the experimental and control samples was racial composition. In addition, controls were older and had a longer history of deprivation than experimentals. Nonetheless, these differences proved to be unrelated to changes in clients' attitudes and behaviors as measured by our instruments.

FINDINGS

The group worker approaches the complexity of client problems on many levels simultaneously. As a reflection of the practice situation, a number of instruments were used to measure the effectiveness of the service in achieving change in its target population.

Worker Rating Form

The primary objective of the project was to achieve individual change in client attitudes, feelings and behavior related to the purpose of the group. To test this objective a measure of movement that was individualized for each recipient's problems was needed. Also tapping the group leader's personal knowledge of progress within the group that might have been unmeasurable with any of the other testing instruments was desired. Therefore, group leaders were asked to rate each of the members of their groups on progress toward specific goals and on group participation.

The form required the worker to identify three major goals for each client drawn from her formulation of individual goals written earlier on the diagnostic statement. She then had to assess each member's progress toward each of these goals on a scale from 0 to 5. The member's participation was also ranked on a 0 to 5 scale by the group leader. These ratings were completed prior to access to any of the findings on the other evaluation instruments. A mean goal score was derived arithmetically for each group member. In addition, goals were categorized in terms of (1) handling children, (2) school problems, and (3) other. Although tests of coder consistency were performed with the data, awareness existed concerning the limitations of validity and reliability of this type of measure.

Differences in scores between the three categories were not significant. The mean progress score on "school problems" was lowest (2.04), while that on "Other" was highest (2.88), and "handling children" was slightly lower (2.76). Goals falling into the "Other" category tended to be specific and immediate, e.g., arrange a medical examination, so that achievement was likely to be rapid and easily noted by the worker. Mean goal scores were positively and significantly related to attendance (p < .001) and to participation scores (p < .001).[7] Participation scores were also related to attendance but not as strongly (p < .05).

Anxiety

In an exploratory study carried out during the second project year, it was found that one of the major difficulties of AFDC clients was a high level of generalized anxiety, which made it hard for these clients to find and mobilize energy to do something constructive about their problems (Glasser and Navarre, 1965). For this reason the IPAT Anxiety Test was included, to measure initial anxiety level as well as change in this factor over the demonstration period. Respondents were asked to complete this short form at their first group meeting. In administering this and other tests, a literacy problem was anticipated and so questions were read to the respondents while each had a form and a pencil before her; at that time, each was required to check the answers appropriate to her situation.[8] The test was given to each respondent a second time at the last meeting of the group.

The IPAT Anxiety Test had several advantages. It is brief and not stressful. The form has been extensively tested and found to be both reliable and clinically valid. Raw scores have been standardized by sex. The use of standardized scores for women was especially helpful since the sample was relatively small and only the female sex was represented.

The scale is designed to measure free-floating, manifest anxiety level, overt and covert, whether this be situationally determined or relatively independent of the immediate situation. In addition, five dimensions have been isolated by means of factor analysis: (1) defective integration, lack of self-sentiment; (2) ego weakness; (3) suspiciousness, paranoid-type

---

[7] In all cases T Tests were used. Two-tailed tests were used for scores on the IPAT Anxiety and the Day at Home. One-tailed tests were used for all other measures.

[8] For a discussion of the problems in the administration and use of paper and pencil tests with lower-lower class or welfare respondents, see Radin and Glasser (1965).

insecurity; (4) guilt proneness; and (5) frustration tension. The last dimension was particularly important for this study since it includes situational fear.

Scores for the final sten as well as each of the factors were computed for experimental and control groups, and differences in change scores between the two samples were analyzed. In addition, an analysis of the differences between before and after scores for each sample was performed.

As expected, scores on the before tests were high although within normal limits, with the mean of the experimental group somewhat higher than that of the control group. Upon comparing the difference (i.e., change scores) for the before and after tests, an interesting pattern emerged. On most dimensions, the anxiety of the experimental group was lowered. The changes in frustration tension and on the total sten just miss the .05 level of significance (.06 and .07). The change in the control group was more significant, but in the opposite direction, with significantly higher levels of frustration tension, overt anxiety, and total score. The difference in change scores between the two groups on total sten and frustration tension is highly significant (p < .01) because of this move in opposite directions.

These findings are somewhat difficult to interpret, especially since no known particularly stressful situation arose during the study period for the control group that might explain the higher score. General anxiety and frustration tension in particular, may be cumulative for AFDC women, but this process was reversed through the group sessions in at least two ways: (1) the support provided by the worker and mothers for each other reduced anxiety, and (2) the positive changes that took place in their daily living experiences initiated by the problem-solving processes at the group sessions reduced anxiety. In addition, it seems likely that (3) high anxiety serves as both motivation to come to group meetings and motivation to change.

There is evidence for these three hypotheses. Before and after IPAT Anxiety scores were available for nine clients in the no treatment sample, who came to one or no meeting, and for a small number of clients in the second control sample (Children's Division) who also attended very few meetings. In both cases their anxiety scores increased on the total score and the frustration tension subscale. Additional evidence for this point of view will be presented subsequently.

Parental Attitudes

While the group sessions were focused on helping mothers help their children adjust better to school, hopefully one by-product of this experience would be more positive general childrearing attitudes on the part of the mother. Thus a scale that measured both was wanted.

The Parental Attitude Research Instrument (PARI) developed by Schaefer and Bell has been used extensively for tapping general childrearing attitudes. However, studies clearly indicate that its findings lead to theoretically meaningful results primarily when the samples involve homogeneous upper-middle class families (Becker and Krug, 1965). Thus, by means of a variety of pretests it was adapted (Radin and Glasser, 1965).

By means of an item analysis three subscales were developed.

A. Fourteen items which are most class sensitive. Client movement was expected to be toward the middle class.
B. Ten items with which 45% or more of the disadvantaged mothers disagreed in pretests were added, to test for acquiescence response set. The hope was that there would be no change on these items by the AFDC clients.
C. Eight items which showed the least class sensitivity were selected to provide a check on the first fourteen.

Finally, four other scales of five items each were added to test more directly the school adjustment attitudes of the mother: (a) Importance of School; (b) Fate Control; (c) Comfort with School; and (d) Mother's Responsibility.

This test was completed by respondents at the same time that the IPAT Anxiety was given, and in the same manner. Tests in differences between change scores for experimental and control groups, and between before and after scores were performed for each of the seven subscales.

The findings for the three subscales related to social class attitudes in childrearing practices provide little meaning for purposes of the evaluation of the group work method. Clients in the experimental groups significantly reduced the number of positive responses on all three subscales. Clients in the control sample significantly reduced their responses on the class sensitive and least class sensitive items. These scales did not provide the differentiated responses expected from their use in other studies.

Of the four school-related subscales, difference scores for Importance of School, Fate Control, and Comfort with School were not significant. The mothers of the experimental group changed toward taking greater responsibility for their children's achievement in school although the change did not quite reach a .05 level of significance. Once again the control group changed in the opposite direction, leading to a significant difference (p < .05) between the change scores of the two groups.

Day at Home

Measures of change in behavioral interaction within the family are difficult to develop, and some of them, like observation schedules, are costly for samples of the size in this evaluation, and have many technical problems. For this reason it was decided to adapt a scale which requires mothers to subjectively report family behavior in the home.

The Day at Home Test was originally designed by P. G. Herbst (1952) for Australian families. Specific questions are asked concerning who performs tasks and who decides how tasks are to be performed in four family areas: (a) household maintenance, (b) child care, (c) economic activities, and (d) social activities. These questions were adapted to urban American lower-class culture. In addition, a fifth subscale was added that was concerned with school-related tasks. The simplicity of the tasks involved (for example, "Who turns on the radio?" or "Who decides when homework is to be done?") and the specificity of the questions provides partial solutions to several of the problems noted in the discussion of other instruments.

The ten subscales (five on task performance and five on decision) are scored by percentages of actions for each family member. The scoring techniques are rather complicated since they provide a map of family interaction, but they were adapted for IBM coding. The same types of statistical tests were carried out for each of these subscales and the total instrument as is discussed for the preceding measures. The procedure was administered individually to experimental respondents almost always prior to the first group session. Again, it was done orally by the group worker, usually in a home visit. The second phase was not repeated until approximately three months after the termination of the group. The purpose of the extra time period was to evaluate delayed reactions to the group experience. The second test was administered by the group worker, the regular agency worker, a former agency worker, or one of the members of the project staff.

Mothers, of course, bear the largest portion of task performance and decision within the family. Their total scores averaged two to three times the sum of all children's and others' in the household. In the experimental group, girls were second to the mother in both task performance and decision. In the control group, girls and boys were more equal on task performance though girls scored higher. Boys in the control group scored higher than girls in decision. The difference was found in school decisions and social decisions and may reflect a larger degree of autonomy in these areas accorded to teen-age boys. Seventy percent of the mothers in the control group had boys 13 or older while only 32% of the mothers in the experimental group had boys in this age group. The proportion of mothers in each group with girls 13 or over was less disparate.

A comparison of the before and after tests indicates that the mothers in the experimental group scored significantly higher on both task performance and decision while the scores of both boys and girls were lower than in the initial measure. The scores of girls dropped significantly on child-care tasks, school-related tasks, and social decisions ($p < .05$). Boys' scores, already low, dropped significantly on child-care decisions ($p < .05$) and on social decisions ($p < .01$). The differences in mothers' scores were significantly higher in the same areas: child-care tasks, child-care decisions, school tasks, school decisions, and social decisions. There was only one significant change in the scores of the control group but it should be noted that this change, as well as the majority of other changes, were consistently in the opposite direction from that found in the experimental group.

Participation in the group seems to have increased both the mother's task performance and decision making in the home. Since a large majority of the children (77%) were under the age of 13, this finding should be interpreted positively.

Pupil Behavior Inventory

Since behavioral change is an important measure of successful intervention, three measures of the behavior of the children whose mothers attended the rehabilitation groups were included in the study. The Pupil Behavior Inventory (PBI) is one of these.

The PBI was developed as a means of evaluating and classifying the behavior of pupils in the classroom situation. It was standardized for males on the junior and senior high school level and has proven valid and reliable for this group (Vinter, et al., 1966). Essentially, it measures the extent of the pupils' conformity to the behavioral standards of the school. The ratings are made by the pupils' teachers on a standardized form of 34 short items. The teacher indicates the frequency of the indicated behavior for each item. Items are graded in such a way that the higher score always indicates the more conforming behavior or attitude although the items are variously phrased in positive or negative fashion. Obviously the relationship between the pupil and the teacher is reflected in the ratings. However, it is also apparent that the relationship between the pupil and the teacher is a powerful factor in the student's success in school.

Previous research revealed five dimensions through factor analysis: (a) Classroom Conduct; (b) Academic Motivation; (c) Socioeconomic State; (d) Teacher Dependence; and (e) Personal Behavior. Statistical tests were performed for each of the factors and the total scale.

The tests were completed by teachers just prior to or during the week of the first group session. They were completed again by the same teachers at the end of the academic year. A number of problems developed in administration however. Not all teachers of children whose mothers were in experimental or control groups could be located. Some teachers refused to fill out the form, and some filled it out incorrectly. In some cases there was a change in teachers. The sample of children is, therefore, very uneven. However, there is no reason to suspect a strong difference between those children who were included and those who were not, except for the group that dropped out of school.

Significant improvement between before and after scores was found only for the experimental group on the Classroom Conduct factor (p < .01). No significant changes were found in other factors nor was there any significant change for the control group. It is interesting that the improvement was in that factor which is, perhaps, the most directly observable by the teacher.

School Grades and School Attendance

Information on grades and attendance was gathered from school records for the semester just preceding the beginning of the group meetings and at the end of the semester in which the meetings took place. Control sample school information was taken for two consecutive semesters during the year the experimental groups met. In addition to the sampling problems mentioned earlier, there were serious difficulties in comparing the records of the various school districts. Schools use different grading systems, different policies about giving grades in the early years of school, and different patterns in recording attendance. While efforts are made to compensate for these differences, results of this portion of the analysis have to be regarded as merely suggestive.

Grades in the various systems were coded numerically. The subjects were divided into academic (English, Arithmetic, etc.) and nonacademic (Shop, Domestic Arts, Physical Education, etc.) and a mean grade computed for each category. Statistical differences within and between experimental and control groups were computed for the two categories. There were no significant changes in attendance or in grades for children of the experimental sample or those of the control sample.

Cross Comparisons

When appropriate, cross comparisons among the many variables were made for the following purposes: (1) to evaluate the effects of social background factors on client change and attendance patterns; (2) to discern consistency in patterns of change for particular clients among the many measures used; (3) to evaluate which types of changes may be most closely related to other types of changes in clients' attitudes and behavior.

It will be recalled that there were statistically significant differences between the experimental and control groups on a number of social background variables, and that change scores on each of the instruments proved unrelated to these variables.

It was desirable to see the extent to which the IPAT Anxiety, the PARI and the Day at Home tap similar or different problem areas. Little consistency was expected because groups were planned and conducted to aid each member in reaching goals appropriate to her. While women shared many general problems, such as low income and children having difficulty in school, the details of these problems and the extent of difficulty experienced varied considerably among individuals. Only one correlation was found, this not easily explained, and may be accounted for by chance alone.[9] In addition, among the experimentals it was found that only eight of the fifty-six women who completed all sections of all three instruments changed in a negative direction on at least two of the three instruments; only seventeen had consistency on two of the three instruments in the directions predicted by our hypotheses. Among the control group the findings were similar: six of twenty-two had positive consistency and four had negative consistency.

This inconsistency probably is an indication that the worker was successful in individualizing the group process sufficiently for each member to change somewhat differentially. Also this probably highlights the statistical significance of some of the change scores, for despite individualization the demonstration of change was achieved.

Returning to the hypothesis that anxiety may serve as a motivating factor in change, change scores were correlated on the PARI and Day at Home with initial (before) scores on the IPAT Anxiety. No significant correlations were found in the control group, or with the PARI in the experimental group. However, change scores on the Day at Home have high correlation with initial anxiety scores. Both Mother's Task Performance and Mother's Decision scores are positively correlated with IPAT Anxiety Total Sten ($p < .01$). The higher the initial level of anxiety, the greater the change score for the mother. Since anxiety is a bilateral factor, the question still remains: At what range does anxiety serve as motivation for change, and at what ranges does it prevent change because the client is either too comfortable or too anxious to take steps to work on her problems?

SOME CONCLUSIONS

The findings are impressive. Only a small number of all social work evaluation studies include control samples and use objective measures of change rather than worker rating forms or continuance in treatment alone as criteria for success (Briar, 1966). Studies of group work practice constitute a small minority of the total number of outcome or method studies

[9] In the experimental group there is a negative correlation between attendance and Mother's Decisions on the Day at Home ($p < .05$).

in the profession (Schwartz, 1966). And as Scott Briar points out, the findings of the more, as well as the less, rigorous studies are indeterminate.

The typical number of sessions held for each group was only six. The clients' goals were particular, while necessity required the measuring instruments to be more general. Despite these apparent limitations, the findings are not indeterminate. As expected, workers believed that their clients reached goals. But these beliefs were confirmed by many objective measures. Total sten and the subscale related to reality demands (frustration tension) on the IPAT Anxiety showed statistically significant decreases. The PARI revealed that mothers significantly increased their attitudes of responsibility toward their children's adjustment in school. The data from the Day at Home reinforce this conclusion. Mothers scored significantly higher in total task performance and decision making in the home, and in the specific areas of child-care tasks, child-care decisions, school tasks, school decisions and social decisions. Finally, the PBI shows significant improvement in the Classroom Conduct factor.

Note that those measures most closely related to individual and group goals tended to reveal significant changes in the directions predicted. The practice implication seems clear: specificity and clarity of individual and group goals and the means to achieve them are requirements for effective group work practice.[10] Specificity is one reason why the establishment of the contract is so important in practice (Croxton, Chapter 10 in this volume; and Frey and Meyer, 1968). In addition, this supports the emphasis of learning theory on specificity of methods and techniques, particularly when used in conjunction with other social science theory and practice wisdom (Thomas, 1967 and 1968; and Sarri, Chapter 4 in this volume).

The demonstrable importance of clear and specific goals poses dilemmas for both practice and research, however. Most of the clients that social workers see have multiple, interrelated problems. How can priorities be set concerning which behaviors ought to be handled first, second, last or not at all? Or if the point of view is taken that one or more problems underlie many maladaptive behaviors, as was taken in this study (knowledge and ability to solve problems rationally), how can there be certainty that abstractions are correct—that is, directly related to the maladaptive behaviors? Further, researchers are often forced to use generalized measures while the worker-client contract often specifies particular changes. Measured changes, even when positive—in the directions predicted—often do not tell which specific techniques were most or least effective, although they do give some suggestions and provide a framework for further study.

Why didn't more of the data show changes in the predicted directions? Already mentioned are the short-term nature of the groups and the

---

[10] For a summary of the social psychological theory on this issue see Cartwright and Zander (1960) and Raven and Rietsema (1960).

problems of generalized measures and particular client goals. One must add that the PBI, and reports of school grades and attendance, were not directly related to the client population but to their children, that is, clients once removed from the target population. No direct intervention was attempted with the children of the AFDC mothers. For this reason the researchers were pleasantly surprised with the positive finding on the Classroom Conduct factor on the PBI.

The most positive findings were on the Day at Home, the test which asked the most specific behavioral questions of the population being treated. Data for the after measure were collected about three months after termination in order to evaluate delayed reactions to the group experience. There is considerable evidence that therapeutic intervention reverses a downward spiral of behavioral maladaptation and maladjustment (Frank, 1961; and Goldstein, 1962). Since data for all of the other measures were collected immediately after the rehabilitation process ended, it is possible that the full effect of the social group work experience was not tested. A follow-up study might have revealed more improvement.

FINIS

Evaluation studies are relatively new to social work practice. This report summarized the results of one of the few studies evaluating the outcome of a rehabilitation service using the social group work method. Its importance lies not only in its demonstration of the effectiveness of the intervention process, but also in that it could be done using both objective measures of change and a control sample. Hopefully it will serve as a stimulant to others so that the quality of practice may be refined as a means toward helping more people more quickly.

REFERENCES

BALES, ROBERT F.
  1958—"Task roles and social roles in problem-solving groups," in Eleanor E. Maccoby, Theodore M. Newcomb and Eugene L. Hartley (Eds.), *Readings in Social Psychology,* third edition, New York: Holt, Rinehart, and Winston, pp. 437–447.
BALES, ROBERT F. AND FRED L. STRODTBECK
  1960—"Phases in group problem solving," in Dorwin Cartwright and Alvin Zander (Eds.), *Group Dynamics, Research and Theory,* Evanston, Illinois: Row, Peterson and Company, pp. 624–640.
BECKER, WESLEY C. AND RONALD S. KRUG
  1965—"The parent attitude research instrument—A research review," *Child Development,* 36, 2 (June).
BRIAR, SCOTT

1966—"Family services," in Henry S. Maas (Ed.), *Five Fields of Social Service,* New York: National Association of Social Workers, Inc., pp. 16–33.

CARTWRIGHT, DORWIN AND ALVIN ZANDER
1960—"Individual motives and group goals: Introduction," in Dorwin Cartwright and Alvin Zander (Eds.), *Group Dynamics: Research and Theory,* second edition, Evanston, Illinois: Row, Peterson and Company.

FRANK, JEROME D.
1961—*Persuasion and Healing: A Comparative Study of Psychotherapy,* Baltimore: The Johns Hopkins Press, pp. 207–214.

FREY, LOUISE AND MARGUERITE MEYER
1965—"Exploration and working agreement in two social work methods," in Saul Bernstein (Ed.), *Exploration in Group Work,* Boston: Boston University School of Social Work.

GLASSER, PAUL H. AND ELIZABETH L. NAVARRE
1965—"The problems of families in the AFDC program," *Children,* 12, 4 (July–August), pp. 151–157.

1965—"Structural problems of the one-parent family," *Journal of Social Issues* 21, 1 (Jan.), pp. 98–109.

GOLDSTEIN, ARNOLD P.
1962—*Therapist-Patient Expectancies in Psychotherapy,* New York: The Macmillan Company.

HERBST, P. G.
1952—"The measurement of family relations," *Human Relations* 5, 1 (Jan.), pp. 3–30.

RADIN, NORMA AND PAUL H. GLASSER
1965—"The use of parental attitude questionnaires with culturally disadvantaged families," *Marriage and the Family* 27, 1 (Aug.), pp. 373–382.

RAVEN, BERTRAM H. AND JAN RIETSEMA
1960—"The effects of varied clarity of group goal and group path upon the individual and his relation to his group," in Cartwright and Zander (Eds.), *Group Dynamics: Research and Theory,* second edition, Evanston, Illinois: Row, Peterson and Company.

SCHWARTZ, WILLIAM
1966—"Neighborhood centers," in Henry S. Maas (Ed.), *Five Fields of Social Service,* New York: National Association of Social Workers, Inc., pp. 174–182.

THOMAS, EDWIN J.
1968—"Selected socio-behavioral techniques and principles: An approach to interpersonal helping," *Social Work* 13, 1 (January) pp. 12–26.

THOMAS, EDWIN J., (ED.)
1967—*The Socio-Behavioral Approach and Applications to Social Work,* New York: Council on Social Work Education.

VINTER, R. D., ROSEMARY SARRI, D. VORWALLER, AND WALTER SCHAEFER
1966—*Pupil Behavior Inventory: A Manual for Administration and Scoring,* Ann Arbor: Campus Publishers.

25.

The Hartwig Project: A Behavioral Approach to the Treatment of Juvenile Offenders

SHELDON D. ROSE and MARTIN SUNDEL

From December 1965, to April 1968, the Neighborhood Service Organization (NSO) of Detroit sponsored the Hartwig Project, a Demonstration Service Project for the treatment of juvenile offenders in a community setting. NSO was established in 1955 to provide social services within the most seriously disadvantaged areas of Detroit. Services were offered on a decentralized basis through the deployment of workers who provide services for clients in their own neighborhoods (Bernard, et al., 1968). A primary objective of NSO was to develop and demonstrate new patterns of service. The Hartwig Project was one such attempt to demonstrate the use of specific intervention techniques with juvenile offenders and their families in their immediate environment.

SETTING

The target area of the Hartwig Project was the Fifth Police Precinct of the City of Detroit. The area was in the process of rapid social and racial change, and was characterized by a high juvenile crime rate, along with extensive economic and social breakdown. Evidence of deterioration and deprivation was reflected in such demographic data as the low median income, unemployment, housing complaints, and high youth crime rate in the area (Youth Bureau, 1965–67; Woman's Division, 1965–67). The Hartwig Project focused on the treatment of juvenile offenders; its goal was to decrease the frequency of socially-defined maladaptive behaviors.

An earlier version of this chapter appeared in Roger Ulrich, Thomas Stachnik and J. Mabry (Eds.), *Control of Human Behavior,* Glencoe, Illinois: Scott, Foresman and Co., 1970, Vol. II, pp. 220–230.

SUBJECTS

The clients, boys and girls from eight to sixteen years old, were referred by the Youth Bureau and by the Woman's Division of the Detroit Police Department. They presented a wide range of problems, including chronic school truancy, runaway, petty larceny, assault and destruction of property. Several hundred clients were treated by three full-time social workers and five University of Michigan graduate students over a two-and-a-half year period.

METHOD

Behavior modification techniques were employed through a detached worker model. The application of these techniques was experimental in nature, in that the literature did not indicate their use with clients in an open community setting. Implementation of many of the techniques required adaptation to unstable situational variables in the community, such as racial tensions and deficiencies in social, legal, and educational institutions. Techniques were often modified and further developed as information accrued from experiences of the social workers in the field.

Clients were treated either individually or in family or peer groups. Interviews with the children were held at school, in their homes, or in a variety of informal community settings, e.g., the agency vehicle, neighborhood parks, or local restaurants. Parents were usually interviewed in their homes. Group treatment sessions with parents and with children were held in local public and private facilities offered by neighborhood churches, schools, and recreation centers.

In addition to providing a setting for interviews, the agency station wagons were utilized to transport clients to group meetings and to appointments held at other agencies. The vehicles also enabled the staff to be mobile and visible within the community, and to be immediately accessible to clients.

Other individuals in the community who were often involved in the assessment and treatment of clients included neighbors, teachers, probation officers, and other agency personnel. These persons were seen by the worker in their own settings. Cooperative relationships were also established with schools, police, public and private agencies.

When a juvenile offense had been committed, one means of disposition available to the police officer was referral of the case to the Hartwig Project. If the officer chose this alternative, he advised the juvenile and his family regarding the desirability of social work services. If the family verbally consented to meet with a worker, the juvenile was referred immediately to the Hartwig Project.

TREATMENT SEQUENCE

The treatment sequence began with the worker's initial contact with the client and proceeded through four identifiable phases: (1) intake period and initial assessment, (2) formulation of treatment plan, (3) implementation of the treatment plan, and (4) termination of treatment and evaluation.

Intake Period and Initial Assessment

During the intake period, the worker visited the juvenile and his family and provided information regarding available services. The worker obtained the client's permission to explore such areas of his life as school, home and community situations. Subsequently the worker gathered information from these various sources to determine the kind of services that could be beneficial for the client. He also considered factors relevant to facilitating or hindering such services. In this initial assessment, the worker identified the client's problematic areas and determined the appropriateness of the Hartwig Project's services for the client. If the resources of other agencies were necessary, or if no service was indicated, suitable recommendations were made to the family.

Formulation of Treatment Plan

Formulation of the treatment plan involved a detailed and specific assessment of the problems that the worker selected for treatment; a careful consideration of treatment goals appropriate for the client; and a selection of treatment techniques directed to the achievement of these goals.

Assessment in this stage of the treatment process consisted of a specific behavioral analysis of the client's problems. Behaviors of the client were considered adaptive or maladaptive and were differentiated into three behavioral types. The first type included behaviors judged to be maladaptive, such as stealing and school truancy, that required decrease in frequency or elimination. The second type consisted of specific adaptive behaviors which were absent or infrequent; such behaviors needed to be introduced into a client's repertoire or increased in frequency of occurrence. An example of deficient adaptive behavior is that of a child who never or infrequently speaks in the classroom. The third type of problematic behavior comprised those behaviors which were viewed as maladaptive only under certain conditions. For example, fighting behaviors which were inappropriate in interaction with a teacher could have been necessary in defending one's self with peers.

In assessing a specific behavior, the worker attempted to determine the antecedent conditions which provided the occasion for the behavior, as well as the consequences which sustained it. The worker was particularly concerned with environmental shortages which often provided antecedent conditions for maladaptive behavior. For example, some children who did not have adequate clothing truanted from school. Consequences maintaining the truant behavior were playing in the streets (positive reinforcement) and avoiding the derision of classmates (negative reinforcement).

Multiple problems were often presented by a client. In such situations the worker and client constructed a hierarchical arrangement of problems, giving priority to that problem behavior which had most immediate and serious consequences for the client. If talking back to a teacher placed a client in imminent danger of expulsion, modifying this behavior was given higher priority than increasing his frequency of cooperatve interactions with peers.

Following the selection of a specific behavior which the worker and client wanted to modify, a baseline indicating the frequency of the behavior was obtained through observation by the worker, by relevant others, or by the client himself. It was often necessary to train the client, parents, teachers and other relevant persons in observation skills, in order to obtain a more nearly accurate and reliable baseline.

After assessment of the client's problems, the worker established treatment goals describing the desired changes in the client's behaviors. The worker also considered factors related to the hindering and attainment of these goals, such as the availability of necessary resources in the community. In formulating treatment goals, the worker and the client together delineated the desired terminal behaviors. Immediate, intermediate, and terminal levels of goal attainment were ordered along a continuum showing progressive changes in the client's behavior. Goal specification at each of these levels required the same considerations involved in assessment: (1) a precise description of the desired response, (2) its frequency of occurrence, (3) the antecedent conditions under which it should occur, and (4) the consequences of the altered behavior. The priority of choosing one goal over another was determined by the same criteria used in selecting one problematic behavior for treatment before another. These priorities and the goals themselves were often changed several times during the course of treatment as certain goals were accomplished or additional relevant factors became apparent.

An example might serve to illustrate this process of assessment and goal setting. A common problem with which the Hartwig workers had to deal was that of school truancy. One boy, a constant truant from school, attended on the average of once every two weeks. He also had failing grades and conflicts with several of his teachers. From the client's report, the conditions for truancy occurred as he walked to school in the morning with his friends, one of whom would suggest that they truant. Consequences maintaining the behavior were the avoidance of academic failure at school and the enjoyment of being "on the streets" with his friends. The influence of parents and school officials was insufficient to induce school attendance. The goal given priority was the elimination of truancy, both because the consequences of truancy would be severe and because school attendance was a necessary condition for treating the other school problems. The projected terminal goal was attendance at all classes five days a week; with intermediate goals established, beginning with one day of attendance per week. The antecedent conditions for school attendance were considered in terms of peer influence during the walk to school. Consequences of increased school attendance would include social reinforcement from parents and teachers, improvement in grades, and removal of the threat of detention.

Implementation of Treatment Plan

After formulation of the treatment plan, it became necessary for the worker to establish a treatment contract with the client. The treatment contract consisted of a set of agreements between the worker and client system i.e., client and/or significant others) as to goals, procedures, and mutual responsibilities. The client was an active participant in delineating the conditions supporting his behavioral problems and in formulating his treatment goals. The worker wrote out a series of tasks for the client to undertake, and the client signed his name to indicate his willingness to attempt to perform these tasks. Such agreements could be changed throughout treatment as new tasks were indicated or problems of higher priority emerged.

Prior to establishment of the treatment contract, the client agreed to speak with the worker about his perception of the problem, though he might not have agreed to work on it. This gave the client time to "find out" what the worker could and would do for him, and provided a positive image of the worker for the client whose past experiences with welfare workers, probation officers, or other persons in authority were unsuccessful or aversive.

In order for the client to enter into a treatment contract with the worker, it was necessary for the worker to become attractive to the client as a positive reinforcing agent. Because client treatment was voluntary, the worker needed to have sufficient attraction for the client to maintain their relationship. The worker developed such attractive qualities first by offering the client concrete and useful services on a noncontingent basis. For example, the worker directed the client to resources in the community, such as a free clinic for dental care or employment resources, and helped to provide transportation to these resources, since clients often did not reach them on their own. Tangible reinforcers were also provided: clients were given candy, games, and educational supplies or were taken to recreational facilities. While spending time with the worker, the client could also experience the enjoyment of riding in the agency vehicle and having the attention of an interested adult. Initially such rewards were contingent on merely coming to treatment. Later the rewards became contingent on problem-focused discussion. Eventually, rewards were distributed only if the client completed the tasks required to modify his behavior in the direction of the treatment goal. A powerful reward for the client was the worker's availability to him at times of crisis outside of normal working hours. One runaway girl called the worker from a drug store at midnight; the worker picked her up and helped her decide on the most reasonable solution to her immediate problem.

Throughout treatment, measurements of the frequency of occurrence of the client's problematic behaviors were compared with their baseline frequency and desired frequency. Measures were obtained by monitoring procedures in which observations were systematically recorded. Some forms of monitoring occurred every week in relation to the specific home or school behavioral assignments that were given to the client. Behaviors were monitored at termination and at selected intervals after termination.

Monitoring was done by the worker, teachers, parents, other persons in the community, or by the client himself. Charts were kept on which the frequency of the behaviors to be changed was indicated at various stages of treatment. The client or other monitors checked occurrences of the desired behavior on the chart, so that indicators of the client's progress were readily available to the worker. In addition, the client received immediate reinforcement from those who monitored his performance, or from the worker on completion of his behavioral assignments.

The monitoring procedure provided the client and significant others with a precise description of the problematic behavior; and it increased their sensitivity to identifying the conditions under which it occurred. The monitoring procedures had "therapeutic value" for significant others, in that their own contributions to the client's problematic behavior became evident. As a result of such findings, significant others could be trained to modify their own responses to the client in order to modify the problematic behavior.

With some clients, it was necessary to increase their concern about their behavior before a treatment contract could be established. For example, some clients were not concerned about problematic behaviors such as stealing from a local store, which the worker interpreted as having ultimate serious consequences for them. With these clients the worker attempted to increase the client's fear of the ultimate consequences of his behavior. For example, a boy's group was taken to a delinquents' training school and interviewed the inmates.

Termination of Treatment and Evaluation

Termination of treatment for clients was based on the achievement of treatment goals. Monitoring the changes in the client's behavior made it possible to determine how closely his current behavior approximated the desired treatment goal. The client and significant others were involved in evaluating to what extent treatment goals were achieved, and whether or not further assistance from the worker was necessary. If a decision was made to terminate the client's case, the police department and family were told to notify the worker if the client committed another offense or if further help was desired.

There were occasions when treatment was terminated prior to attainment of the treatment goals. These situations arose when the client was unwilling to be engaged in a treatment contract with the worker because of the following reasons: (1) the client's behavior was not aversive enough to him or to significant others, (2) community resources for treatment did not exist, and (3) the inclusion of significant others in the treatment plan was not feasible. In some cases, the family terminated treatment with the worker because they considered that sufficient changes in the client's behavior had been achieved, although the worker believed that further changes were desirable. Occasionally additional information indicated the need for other services; for example, foster home placement of a child, rather than trying to improve his home situation. In other instances, juveniles committed additional offenses which resulted in direct court action that removed them from open society. Finally, early terminations occurred because a few families moved from the area.

Transfer of Change

The Hartwig Project emphasized the direct treatment of clients in the community, so that difficulties of transferring the effects of behavior change could be minimized. If a child engaged in frequent arguing with the teacher, the child's verbal behavior was first role played in the treatment group where the client learned alternate ways of responding to the teacher. The client was then assigned to use these new behaviors in the classroom and to report their effects to the treatment group. If the client's argumentation occurred in other situations, he could practice his new behaviors in those situations as well.

In order to facilitate the transfer of change from the treatment setting to the original real-life situation, each set of new behaviors was practiced in a variety of situations and under a variety of conditions. The practice training during the treatment sessions was structured to simulate as nearly as possible the situation into which the behavior was to be transferred. Reinforcement for the desired behavior usually began with a continuous schedule that was gradually changed to an interval or ratio schedule. Primary reinforcers—candy, notions, articles of clothing—were paired with verbal indications of approval and praise until these social reinforcers were sufficient to maintain desired behaviors. The reinforcing agents were also expanded from the worker to include those significant others who were involved in the context of problematic behaviors.

TREATMENT TECHNIQUES

Specific treatment techniques were directed toward the goals of introducing, strengthening, weakening, or eliminating client behaviors. In practice, workers often found that a variety of techniques could be brought to bear on a single behavioral problem. Since the project was exploratory in nature, workers experimented with a number of techniques in various situations. The choice of treatment, therefore, depended a great deal upon factors such as a worker's personal experience with a particular technique or a client's initial response.

The most frequently used procedures were reinforcement, extinction, model presentation, prompting, programming significant others, behavioral rehearsal and behavioral assignments. In addition, aversive imagery, covert sensitization, confrontation with ultimate aversive consequences, and systematic desensitization (e.g., Wolpe and Lazarus, 1966) were used.

Reinforcement Procedures

Selective positive reinforcement was the most frequently used treatment technique. During the initial phases of treatment, the major means of reinforcement were tangible rewards, including toys, cosmetics, sports equipment and food. These items helped to establish the attractiveness of the worker, and to increase the client's desire to enter into a treatment contract. After the client became involved in treatment, the receipt of these rewards was made contingent upon his performance of desired behaviors. Rewards could be tokens such as poker chips, painted blocks, play money, clicks on a counter, tally marks on a tabulation sheet, stars or any other concrete indicator of response performance.

The disbursement of tokens as rewards for appropriate behaviors is referred to as a token economy system (e.g., Atthowe and Krasner, 1968).

In the Hartwig Project, tokens could be used as money to purchase attractive items from a "store" that was made available by the worker. Immediately following the desired behaviors, tokens were administered according to a preconceived schedule of reinforcement. Different behaviors had different numbers of tokens attached to them. Because most of the clients suffered from economic deprivation, the tokens served as credits for purchase at a local snack bar. The purchase of higher-priced items required members to save their tokens over several meetings. When it was deemed desirable to provide immediate and frequent reinforcement to clients, or to prevent hoarding of tokens, a requirement was established that a portion of tokens earned at a given meeting be spent at the end of that session.

The worker did not move directly from concrete or token reinforcement to nonreinforcement. Praise, attention and other forms of recognition were also used as social reinforcers. In order to make desired behavior more resistant to extinction, the various reinforcers employed were shifted from continuous schedules of reinforcement to intermittent schedules.

In group treatment, the worker disbursed group rewards as well as individual rewards. The use of group rewards created group pressure on members to perform desired tasks appropriately and within a time schedule. Group rewards included activities such as swimming, basketball, ice skating, horseback riding, and bowling. These activities proved to be reinforcing primarily because the juvenile clients were unable to obtain such experiences through delinquent activities.

Model Presentation

In order to facilitate the learning of new behaviors, real or symbolic models were presented to clients under conditions which facilitated social imitation (e.g., Bandura and Walters, 1963). One type of model was the worker or a peer who played the role of the client under conditions which simulated those in which the client was to perform his new behavior. A second type of model included guests who were particularly attractive to group members: athletes, disc jockeys, and popular teachers. Prestigious models were selected whose race and background were similar to those of the clients. A Negro ex-convict, who was a well-known and respected boxer, spoke to a group of Negro youths regarding the aversive consequences of their delinquent acts. During a later meeting, when members spoke about the attractiveness of various delinquent acts, the worker referred to the model's comments on the consequences of those acts.

Behavioral Rehearsal

In behavioral rehearsal, the client practiced behaviors in the treatment setting which were desirable for him to perform in the real-life situation. The desired behavior consisted of either an entirely new sequence of performances or behaviors that had been rarely displayed in the problematic situation. Behavioral rehearsal was frequently preceded by a model's demonstration of the behaviors to be performed or by the worker's precise description of how the client should act in a given situation. If a client did not know how to act during a job interview, a model demonstrated the appropriate behaviors to the client. The client then rehearsed the appropriate behaviors in the presence of another individual, who played the role of the employer.

Lazarus (1966) compared behavioral rehearsal with nondirective therapy and advice-giving and found that behavioral rehearsal was the most effective means of resolving interpersonal problems. In their discussion of the effectiveness of psychotherapy, Goldstein, et al. (1966, p. 236) emphasized the importance of the clients practicing desired behaviors during therapy sessions in order for these behaviors to be performed outside the treatment situation.

In the Hartwig Project, behavioral rehearsals were characteristically brief during the first few times, so that they could be practiced more frequently. Behavioral rehearsal proved to be an especially relevant technique in group treatment. The group situation provided a variety of role players who could demonstrate how they had acted or would act in similar situations. In addition, the group members provided an audience who permitted the client to practice behaviors without the drastic consequences that might ensue if he performed those behaviors inappropriately outside the group.

Behavioral rehearsal was usually employed in combination with other treatment procedures. The first step frequently consisted of model presentation and discussion regarding the behavior to be performed. The second step consisted of rehearsal of that behavior in the treatment situation. In the third step, a behavioral assignment was given to the client to perform outside the treatment situation, along with a procedure for monitoring his performance. Arrangements were also made for reinforcement to be given to the client for appropriately carrying out his behavioral assignments. For example, in a group of adolescent girls, approach responses to a prospective employer were selected for rehearsal. The worker told the girls step by step exactly what would occur in the interviewing process, and a group member who had successfully completed a job interview demonstrated the appropriate behaviors for that situation. The group members first reviewed aloud what they were going to say in the situation. If a member had difficulty verbalizing with regard to a specific question, other members prompted her. After the client performed the prescribed behavior, the members discussed the conditions under which her responses were appropriate or inappropriate, as well as the possible consequences of the client's actions. Finally, the group members were given behavioral assignments related to these newly learned behaviors.

Behavioral Assignments

A behavioral assignment consisted of a specific performance that was required of the client outside the treatment situation. The assigned behavior was to be completed within a given time period, usually prior to the following group meeting or individual conference with the worker. Behavioral assignments provided a viable means of extending treatment into the extratherapeutic situation in which the problematic behavior occurred. The following are examples of behavioral assignments:

> Gwen, who seldom asserts herself in situations outside the group, has recently begun to do so in the group. The group members assign her the task of responding to her sister, who constantly criticizes her clothes. Gwen must say, "It's my clothing and my taste, and I'll wear what I want."
>
> Robert is assigned by the group to keep a record of the time he arrives home and his completed homework assignments. His mother must sign his assignment card, which he is to bring to the next meeting.

Initially, the behavioral assignments were given solely by the worker. As the group members learned the criteria for the establishment of an assignment, they participated not only in formulating their own assignments, but also in making assignments for other members in the group. The group members also participated in determining whether or not a given assignment had been completed.

The behavioral assignment was stated in highly specific terms, that is, the client was told not only what he must do, but also the conditions under which he should do it. If certain unanticipated conditions for the behavior occurred, alternative behaviors, such as telephoning the worker, were specified.

Another requisite was that the assigned behavior should have a relatively high probability of being carried out. For example, if the assignment to the client were: "If someone fights with you, walk away," he would be unable to perform the assignment in the course of the week unless someone initiated a fight with him. Similarly, if a shy girl were given a first assignment of standing up to her older brother who bullies her, the demands of the assignment would probably be too great for her to achieve success. Making an assignment involved considering the probability of occurrence of stimulus conditions for the prescribed behavior, as well as estimating the difficulty of the response required for the client in that situation.

The completion of a given assignment was determined by significant others, the self-report of the client, or by the worker's direct observation. As one behavioral assignment was completed, the same performance was subsequently increased in frequency by further assignments or by the assignment of its occurrence under slightly altered conditions. The difficulty of the assignment was structured so that the client was required to make some effort to accomplish it even though his probability of success was high. When clients expressed reluctance to perform a given assignment, the worker utilized group discussion in which individuals who had already performed the behavior were involved. The assigned behavior was demonstrated by the worker or a peer and was followed by structured rehearsals of the behavior by the client. If conditions did not permit practice of the behavior, the worker and peers described and explained to the client the specific steps he should take in carrying out the assignment.

> One child had the assignment of being home by 9:00 P.M. and remaining there until morning. Although he usually arrived home on time, other children outside his home would taunt him until he went out again. The worker asked the group how they thought the client should handle this situation. The group members suggested that the client move to another part of the house and become involved in a different activity that he enjoyed. After various alternatives were offered, one of the members played the role of the client, and the worker and other members played the roles of the children on the street. Finally, the client played his own role and was assigned to try out the alternative behavior that evening at home.

Clients were required to report back to the worker or group the details of their attempts to carry out behavioral assignments. The client was reinforced for completion of his assignment by the worker or by others who monitored his performance.

Each behavioral assignment was reviewed as a part of a sequence. As one assignment was completed, a slightly more difficult one was given. The sequence of assignments ultimately led to the attainment of a specified treatment goal; the completion of each assignment constituted the attainment of a subgoal.

Extinction

Extinction consists of withholding a positive reinforcer which previously has followed a given response in order to decrease the frequency of that response. An extinction procedure was frequently employed to eliminate undesirable behaviors manifested by clients, such as temper tantrums, argumentative responses, and inappropriate attention-seeking behaviors.

> Juanita's mother told the worker that almost every time Juanita screamed about doing her chores, the mother would attempt to placate her by promising to buy her new clothes. The mother was instructed not to make promises to Juanita when her screaming behavior occurred and to walk away from Juanita under these circumstances. The mother was warned that Juanita's screaming would probably increase in severity and frequency at first, but if the mother held firm, it would gradually decrease and disappear. Following these instructions, Juanita's screaming decreased and soon was eliminated. The worker had also instructed the mother to praise and provide concrete rewards to Juanita when she did household chores. Consequently, Juanita's performance of chores increased.

Programming Significant Others

A crucial aspect of the treatment program involved the training of significant others in the application of treatment procedures so that conditions for sustaining desired client behaviors were created. Significant others included individuals who controlled the delivery of reinforcers to the clients: teachers, parents and peers.

In some cases, modifying the reactions of significant others to the client could be more productive than working directly with the client himself. In such instances, individuals were trained in behavioral observation, so that they could identify the impact of their behaviors on the client's problems. They could then be trained to modify their behaviors to the client in much the same way as the worker directly modified the behavior of clients. In order to enlist the cooperation of significant others, the worker concentrated on selecting for treatment those client behaviors which had the greatest nuisance value for the significant others.

In working with parents, major emphasis was given to training them in child management skills. In many instances, parents were inconsistent in meting out rewards and punishments and in setting and maintaining rules. Such inappropriate practices resulted in the parents' ineffective control of the client's behaviors. A series of steps were involved in training the parents to gain more effective control of the client's behaviors. The worker instructed the parents in monitoring and observational procedures related to the client's annoying behaviors and the conditions which led to those behaviors. After the parents recorded the frequency of a problematic behavior, the worker provided specific training in behavioral techniques such as rule setting, reinforcement procedures, and extinction. In teaching parents how to establish and maintain rules, the worker also used *Child Management,* a programmed instruction booklet (Smith and Smith, 1966). The following example indicates the use of programming with significant others.

PROBLEM: Mrs. B. indicated to the worker that she had difficulty in effectively controlling her daughter. Nancy refused to obey direct orders and nagged her mother incessantly to get her own way. Mrs. B. was inconsistent in disciplining her children; she often gave in after a display of temper by one of them. Mrs. B. was especially upset that Nancy refused to obey Mrs. B.'s boyfriend, who was living in the home. Mrs. B., however, reinforced disobedient behavior by confiding in Nancy about her boyfriend when Mrs. B. was angry at him, viewing Nancy's criticisms of him as "standing up for her mother." At other times, Nancy was punished when she spoke against Mrs. B.'s boyfriend.

TREATMENT: The worker used Smith and Smith's (1966) *Child Management* to teach Mrs. B. consistency in rule-making procedures for handling Nancy. Mrs. B. was first taught to observe the conditions under which Nancy's undesirable behavior occurred and the consequences that followed it. Mrs. B. was also taught to manipulate these consequences by her own responses to Nancy's behavior. For example, Mrs. B. ignored undesirable behaviors, such as tantrums and whining, and reinforced desirable behaviors such as pleasant statements to Mrs. B. and her boyfriend.

As a result of consistently applying these procedures, much of Nancy's demanding, disruptive behavior decreased within two months. Mrs. B. initiated "chore rules" for the children on her own. Mrs. B. decreased her frequency of confiding responses to Nancy, and Mrs. B. was encouraged to talk to friends her own age, thus recognizing the availability of reinforcements from her own peer group. Mrs. B. also became interested in outside activities, such as a job training program which offered an opportunity to increase her earnings, as well as to expand her circle of acquaintances.

The worker also programmed teachers in the use of appropriate treatment techniques. It was frequently difficult to enlist the teacher's cooperation in monitoring the frequency of the client's problematic behavior because of the pressures of overloaded classrooms and lack of time. In exchange for the teacher's agreement to monitor behavior, the worker provided the teacher assurance that the client would be less of a nuisance in the class and would improve his academic performance. The teachers were instructed primarily in the use of selective positive reinforcement and extinction. The teacher was taught how to increase the frequency of behaviors that she considered desirable by providing appropriate reinforcers for them and how to ignore inappropriate classroom behaviors so that they would decrease in frequency. For example, one teacher was particularly disturbed by the frequency with which two boys pouted in the classroom. Her typical response to the pouting was to mimic the boys by making faces at them. This response operated as a reinforcement for the boys' pouting, so that it increased in frequency of occurrence. The teacher was instructed to ignore the boys' pouting, but to reinforce them for appropriate classroom conduct such as working quietly in their seats. Teachers were also trained to distribute points or tokens for the completion of specific assignments given to children who had difficulty in adjusting to the classroom setting.

Workers pointed out to teachers how they were already using rewards, verbal praise, and drawing on the blackboard to increase the frequency of desired behavior. The teachers were praised by the worker for utilizing these techniques and encouraged to increased their usage of them.

LIMITATIONS ON THE BEHAVIORAL APPROACH

It should be emphasized that this program was a demonstration project, in which the various treatment procedures used were not fully developed. Data were not collected systematically in all cases; adequate controls were not available for comparison. Serious problems related to this setting still remain, such as the difficulty in gaining access to the groups and institutions which exert a major influence on the clients and make it difficult to alter the systems of reward and punishment which govern the clients' behavior.

Many parents were unable or unwilling to cooperate with the therapeutic programs for their children because of the overwhelming financial and emotional pressures in their lives which were prevalent in this deteriorating neighborhood. A large number of families contacted were struggling simultaneously with a lack of essential material resources, poor quality housing, large numbers of children in the family, marital conflict and one-parent family situations.

Problems of controlling environmental conditions became even more complex in relation to the larger institutions involved in the lives of the clients. Many of the inner-city schools, for example, were tied to strict regulations which were often incompatible with the individualized, step-by-step treatment required to modify clients' behaviors. It was often difficult for the worker to arrange a transfer for the client to another class or to change his class schedule to accommodate a job or special home problem. In addition, many ghetto schools offered few reward systems even for the motivated student, because the school had to devote so much time and attention to handling numerous discipline problems. Some principals, counselors, and teachers did not make themselves accessible to the Hartwig staff, nor did they assist the worker in making the school experience more rewarding for the client.

In spite of these limitations, there is sufficient support from the results of many of the cases to encourage us to develop our treatment procedures further and to carry out a more systematic evaluation of their effects. A behavioral approach to the treatment of juvenile offenders within a ghetto community can have beneficial outcomes despite the constraints and limitations placed upon it by the complex demands of a tense and unstable environment.

REFERENCES

ATTHOWE, JAMES AND LEONARD KRASNER
  1968—"Preliminary report on the application of contingent reinforcement procedures (token economy) on a 'chronic' psychiatric ward," *Journal of Abnormal Psychology,* 73, pp. 37–43.
BANDURA, ALBERT AND RICHARD WALTERS
  1963—*Social Learning and Personality Development,* New York: Holt, Rinehart and Winston, Inc.
BERNARD, SYDNEY E., EMERIC KURTAGH, AND HAROLD R. JOHNSON
  1968—"The neighborhood service organization: Specialists in social welfare innovation," *Social Work,* 13, pp. 76–84.
DETROIT POLICE DEPARTMENT
  1965–67—Woman's Division Annual Reports, and Youth Bureau Annual Reports.
GOLDSTEIN, A., K. HELLER, AND LEE SECHREST
  1966—*Psychotherapy and the Psychology of Behavior Change,* New York: John Wiley & Sons.
LAZARUS, A. A.
  1966—"Behavior rehearsal vs. non-directive therapy vs. advice in affecting behavioral change," *Behavior Research and Therapy,* 4, pp. 209–212.
SMITH, JUDITH ANN AND O. SMITH
  1966—*Child Management: A Program for Parents,* Ann Arbor: Ann Arbor Publishers.
WOLPE, JOSEPH AND A. LAZARUS
  1966—*Behavior Therapy Techniques,* New York: Pergamon Press.

26.

Integrating Divergent Theories in a Compensatory Preschool Program

NORMA RADIN and GLORIANNE WITTES

From its inception, the program to be described employed the theories of two men, Jean Piaget and B. F. Skinner, whose views are not often integrated. Possibly neither man would feel comfortable about the juxtaposition of their names. Nevertheless, the Ypsilanti Early Education Program,[1] whose objective was to help lower-class children succeed in school, found the combination to be highly effective and practical. Piaget's theory provided the foundation for the preschool curriculum which had as its major goal the cognitive development of the children. Skinner's work formed the basis of the parent education program which focused on teaching mothers child-management skills which would produce greater internal control in children. The program would have been incomplete without either theoretical component.

School success was chosen as the goal of the Early Education Program because it was felt that the educational system is still the most important ladder of upward mobility in our society. It is clear that schools must be restructured if they are to be effective in educating the nation's impoverished children. However, it is also true that youngsters who enter kindergarten with skills, abilities and attitudes that are conducive to learning will be more responsive to virtually any curriculum, as Coleman's (1966) research has indicated. The Early Education Program emphasized the child's preparation for school; it was hoped that other programs were directing simultaneous efforts toward modifying the public school system per se.

In the 1967–1968 school year, the project involved 100 four-year-old children who came from disadvantaged homes. One-half of the young-

[1] The Ypsilanti Early Education Program was partially funded under Project Number 67-042490 of the Elementary and Secondary Education Act of 1965, Title III, and the Public School System of Ypsilanti, Michigan.

sters were black and one-half white; one-half were boys and the other half girls. The children attended class half a day, four days per week from October through June. There were ten children, one teacher, and one aide in each classroom. In addition, each child was visited in his home every other week by his teacher, who conducted a tutorial session while his mother was present. The goal of the home visit was twofold: to involve the mother in the educative process so that she could incorproate the role of teacher in her everyday activities; and to meet the child's individual cognitive needs which could not be dealt with adequately in the group setting. When other children were present, an aide accompanied the teacher and conducted an enriched play program for the younger siblings to insure the maintenance of a tutorial relationship with mother and child.

The project had three major goals, two of which are relevant to this discussion:

1. To develop a preschool curriculum, based primarily on Piaget's theory of the sequential development of intelligence, for use in a classroom and in a home tutorial setting.
2. To develop a group parent education program, focused primarily on teaching mothers how to foster the development of self-discipline in their children, through the use of behavior modification principles.

THE PRESCHOOL PROGRAM

A full description of the classroom and tutorial curriculum would be beyond the scope of this chapter. Part of the curriculum has been described elsewhere (Kamii and Radin, 1967; Sonquist and Kamii, 1967). Fundamentally, the program was based on Piaget's concept that intelligence develops by qualitatively distinct periods, the sensory-motor period, the preoperational period, the period of concrete operation, and the period of formal operations. Attainment of a later stage is not possible without solid attainment of the earlier stages. Although the age at which children enter any of the periods may vary, the sequence is invariant. Passage through the stages grows out of the coordination of actions, at first physical, and then mental, rather than by the manipulation of symbols such as words.

The curriculum employed two aspects of knowledge delineated by Piaget: the operative aspect which pertains to logical-mathematical operations such as classification, seriation, mathematics, etc.; and the figurative aspect which pertains to symbolization which may vary from the most concrete level of manipulating objects to the most abstract level of employing words and mathematical signs. One of the major curriculum objectives was to facilitate the movement of the children from the sensory-motor stage at which they entered the preschool, to the preoperational period. Specifically, movement from the sensory-motor stage required a semistructured setting in which the children could learn to classify objects into an increasing number of categories; to seriate (order on a single dimension) three, four and eventually eight items; and to comprehend the meaning of numbers so that they would be recognized whether a specific number of objects was spaced far apart or massed together. The curriculum objectives pertaining to the figurative aspect of knowledge consisted of helping the children move from the concrete level to the use of increasingly abstract symbols so that the same mental operations could be performed with symbols that had been performed with the objects they represented.

Sociodramatic play, a sensory-motor activity, proved to be a priceless vehicle for achieving both curriculum goals. For example, in playing mother, the children were soon able to use blocks for food, and straws for candles after starting with the objects themselves. Further, as "mother" set out one cup and one saucer for each "child" of her "family," she was gaining experience in one-to-one correspondence which is fundamental to an understanding of mathematical concepts. Other sensory-motor activities, such as climbing over and under objects, were also used to help the children learn spatial and temporal concepts. Although language was seen as important in storing and retrieving concepts that had been learned, action on objects was deemed essential for signifying the attainment of concepts. Physical action was considered critical as these youngsters were not as yet at the stage of concrete operations typically reached at seven or eight years of age, when mental images and symbols can be manipulated with facility.

THE PARENT EDUCATION PROGRAM

The parent program which focused on the child's self-reinforcement of behaviors conducive to school success, the S-R theory of learning, was perceived as the most relevant. Here parental behaviors were to be shaped; cognitive growth was not involved. The short-term goal was to teach mothers how to use reinforcement frequently and effectively so that they would become powerful reinforcing agents. The long-term objective was for their children to reinforce themselves for behaviors previously rewarded by their mothers. Parents were also taught that self-discipline consists of regulating one's own behaviors so that one knows when to stop and when to go, for example, when to move out aggressively to tackle new learning, as well as when to control aggression in interaction with others. A secondary goal of the parent program was helping mothers learn to foster their children's cognitive growth as part of daily life. For this goal, a

Piagetian approach was again emphasized. Mothers were told of the importance of their children's learning by doing, with stress placed on encouraging youngsters to manipulate objects and explore the environment.

A research design was built into the parent program to test the effectiveness of the program per se, and the relative effectiveness of two models for presenting the same content. A pedagogical technique was chosen as an experimental variable because of the scarcity of research in this critical area (Brim, 1959). The two methodologies tested were the lecture-discussion approach and the activity approach. The former focused on learning through verbal communication. The major input came from the leader, although time for discussion was allowed near the end of the meeting. In the latter, the presentation was structured to involve the active participation of members through role playing, behavior rehearsals, home assignments, art activities, etc. In both methods, the group leader made ample use of social reinforcement to strengthen the desired behaviors of the mothers.

The activity approach was predicted to be more effective because it offered more opportunities for reinforcement of specific maternal behaviors. In addition it was hypothesized that the disadvantaged mothers would not be at ease performing mental operations with symbols (i.e., words) in a group setting, in spite of their having attained the level of concrete operations many years before. It was felt their limited exposure to discussions with strangers would create some tension and hence limit their facility with language. Thus it was predicted that the activity method employed to teach concepts to the children would also be the more effective technique of altering the childrearing practices of their mothers.

The parent program was offered to the 93 mothers with children in the preschool program. Seven homes had no mother, seventeen mothers with fulltime jobs were not available, and 11 mothers refused to participate, offering minor excuses. The remaining 65 women were matched on critical, independent variables such as race and education, and placed into three groups: a control group and the two experimental groups. The control group was offered no group parent program; the two experimental groups were offered the same content, via different methodologies. Babysitting and transportation were provided, and incentives for attending the meetings were offered in the form of inexpensive educational gifts for their children. Mothers who attended a specific number of meetings were presented with an additional, more personal gift, such as a certificate, three times during the year.

To test the impact of the program on the participants' childrearing attitudes and practices, two pencil and paper questionnaires were administered to mothers at the beginning and end of the school year. A revision of Schaefer and Bell's (1958) Parental Attitude Research Instrument (PARI) developed by Radin and Glasser (1965) was used to measure attitudes; the Cognitive Home Environment Scale (CHES) (Radin and Sonquist, 1968) was employed to evaluate the stimulation offered in the home. In addition, the weekly reports the teachers made for the curriculum supervisors concerning home visits were analyzed to assess observed maternal influence techniques. The teachers were not informed about the group status of the mothers in order to insure unbiased reporting.

The effect of the parent program on the child's intellectual growth was assessed by examining the scores the children attained on the Stanford-Binet Intelligence Scale administered in the fall when the preschool opened and in the spring when it closed.

The content of the parent program was described in detail in *Helping Your Child to Learn,* a set of three parent handbooks written for the mothers (Wittes and Radin, 1969), and will be reviewed only briefly here. The curriculum was divided into three units of approximately six weeks each, with a break of approximately three weeks between units. Unit I focused on principles of behavior modification as they applied to the child-management problems suggested by the mothers. Lessons dealt with topics such as contingencies that increase, decrease, and maintain the frequency of specific responses; techniques for shaping new behaviors; the consequences of punishment; alternate techniques for reducing the frequency of undesirable behaviors, etc.

Unit II dealt with simple activities that parents could engage in to stimulate their children's intellectual growth. For example, parents were taught how they might engage in sociodramatic play at home while unloading groceries to facilitate the development of firm mental images and the handling of symbols. Singing and clapping were discussed as a means of strengthening temporal concepts and of offering an opportunity for role playing through enacting the words of songs. Throughout the unit, the principles of behavior modification included in the first unit were employed. Thus, for example, the parent was encouraged to praise successful approximations when role-playing behaviors were to be shaped that did not exist in the child's repertoire. The entire unit was introduced by a visit to the classroom when the mothers were given a brief review of the classroom curriculum so that they might understand the relationship between the teachers' efforts and their own.

Unit III focused on essential, student self-reinforcement of behaviors, such as realistic standard-setting which is critical for high achievement motivation. Other school-related behaviors that were emphasized were anticipating the consequences of behavior and evaluating one's own efforts. The importance of parental role modeling and of maintaining two-way communication with youngsters were also stressed. Again, the principles of behavior modification were applied to each of the concepts discussed.

FINDINGS

An evaluation of the total 1967–1968 Early Education Program[2] revealed that the children gained significantly on both the Stanford Binet Intelligence Scale and the Peabody Picture Vocabulary Test. The mean gains were 8.21 and 13.9 IQ points, respectively. In addition, the revised PARI indicated a significant increase in equalitarian attitudes toward child-rearing and a significant decrease in authoritarianism among mothers in the program. An analysis by race and sex indicated that children of both races and sexes gained significantly on both tests.

An evaluation of the parent program revealed that participation in the program produced significant changes in childrearing attitudes in the desired direction. A significant difference was found between the experimental and control groups: the experimental group's changed responses on the questionnaires showed further movement in the desired direction.[3] These women were found to be moving toward practices more supportive of school-relevant behaviors; for example, mothers in the experimental group showed a greater increase in respect for the views of the child.

Although the teachers' reports showed no significant differences between experimental and control groups, a trend developed that suggested that mothers in the experimental group were using punishment less frequently as a disciplinary measure. In 19% of the home visits, experimental group mothers were observed using aversive stimuli to control their children. The figure was 32% for the mothers in the control group. The experimental group mothers also appeared to be more highly motivated to help their children. These women were present for 94% of the home visits. The control mothers were present for only 88%.

No group difference appeared in intellectual growth of the children. The mean Binet IQ gain for the youngsters of both experimental and control mothers was 9 points. The one group significantly different were the children of the 11 mothers who refused to participate. These youngsters lost a mean of .2 IQ points during the year.[4]

When the experimental groups were compared, no differences were found in holding power of the two groups as measured by attendance at

---

[2] The data for the 1967–1968 school year appear in a report entitled, "Analysis of Changes During the Year" (Radin, 1969).

[3] There were 15 items from the PARI and CHES showing significant differences in change scores between experimental and control groups. In 12 of the 15, the experimental group moved further in the desired direction. This difference is significant at the .05 probability level using the sign test. The specific items appear in a paper entitled, "Two Approaches to Work with Parents in a Compensatory Preschool Program" (Wittes and Radin, 1969).

[4] The mean change of −.2 on the Binet IQ was significantly different from the change in IQ of the other children at the .05 probability level.

meetings. In each group, approximately 50% of those who came once went on to attend at least 8 more of the 18 meetings held. The mean attendance per meeting for both groups was 8 members. The revised PARI showed a decrease of 10% in both groups in agreement with items highly supported by a lower-class population, such as approval of an authoritarian stance by parents. The change in total score on the CHES was also similar for both groups. The mean gain in Binet IQ was identical for the children of both experimental groups, 9 points.

To test the effect of maximum exposure to both methods, a comparison was made of the strong group members in the two groups, that is, women who attended at least half of the 18 meetings. Prior comparisons between experimental groups deliberately overlooked the fact that some mothers had attended few or no meetings to be certain that a selectivity factor did not contaminate the findings. This rigorous approach, however, diluted the effect of the treatment. The weak members (i.e., those who attended at least one meeting but less than 9) of both groups were also compared.

The teacher ratings of the strong members of the lecture-discussion group were significantly better than the ratings given strong members in the activity group.[5] For example, strong members of the activity group were observed by teachers to use punishment in 16% of the home visits, vs. 7% for the strong members of the discussion group. There was also a greater trend away from agreement with authoritarian items on the PARI among strong members of the lecture-discussion group than among the strong members of the activity group. No significant differences in IQ changes were found; however, the mean gain of children of the strong members in the activity group was 10 points; the figure was 11 points for the children of the strong members in the lecture-discussion group.

A comparison of the weak members of the two experimental groups revealed a reverse trend. More maternal attitude change and more reinforcing behaviors occurred in the weak members of the activity group than in their lecture group counterparts. For example, during 10% of the home visits the weak members of the activity group were observed punishing their children. The figure was 30% for the weak members of the lecture-discussion group. There were also greater changes on the PARI and the CHES in the desired direction among weak members of the activity group.[6]

[5] The strong members of the discussion group were rated higher in all eight areas assessed, such as mother's use of space, mother's availability, etc. The difference is significant at the .01 probability level using the sign test.

[6] The total score on the CHES increased 1 point in the activity group and decreased 11 points in the discussion group. On the PARI, there was a reduction of 17% in support for authoritarian class-sensitive items in the activity group. The figure was 3% for the discussion group.

As with children of the strong members of both groups, no significant differences in IQ gains were found among children of the weak members of both groups: there was a 9-point gain in the case of children of the activity group and an 8-point gain for children of the lecture-discussion group.

The explanation for these divergent trends may be related to the nature of the actual member-leader interaction in the two groups. Although the lecture-discussion group was started with the leader doing most of the instructing, it soon evolved into a group in which members brought up their own specific concerns and assumed the leadership themselves. They became deeply involved in the discussions and became a very cohesive group with strong liking for one another. Strong group norms developed for utilization of their learning at home with their children. The members of the activity group, on the other hand, participated in the role playing and assignments, but continued to play a passive role. The leader remained the teacher, structuring the program essentially according to her initial plans.

The group cohesion which developed in the lecture-discussion group was powerful in enforcing the new norms; however, this cohesion required time to evolve and those who attended infrequently did not become caught up in the group feeling. On the other hand, the activity approach, which structured the learning situations and involved the total person, appeared to have immediate effects; but such an approach may have been unattractive to more independent women. Thus, strong members of the activity group—possibly the least independent in nature—were least likely to generalize the new learnings to situations at home. The net effect was for the strong members of the lecture-discussion group to show more change than the strong members of the activity approach, but for the reverse situation to hold for the weak members of both groups. In sum, there appeared to be an interaction between length of exposure and pedagogical approach with limited exposure yielding superior results with an activity approach, and with lengthier exposure yielding superior results with a lecture-discussion orientation.

REPERCUSSIONS

In the leader's opinion, the major impact of the program was evident in the mothers' perceptions of their own improved competencies in handling their children. Such perceptions were not evaluated objectively, but the following is an example of similar comments made by many mothers:

> I guess I'm really learning to use new ways of managing our children that you've been teaching us, and it's not just my preschooler who's benefiting.

It's my older boy, too. I've been doing these things with him, too. Instead of yelling at him and spanking him all the time, I've been using some of those other ways we've talked about to handle him. Do you know, he's raised every single one of his grades on his last report card! He seems much more relaxed and happy since I've been less cranky with him.

As the mothers' sense of competence in child management grew, self-confidence appeared to diffuse to other areas. Many women expressed a desire to secure an improved education for their children beyond preschool. It was not long before a plan of action developed to obtain an enriched kindergarten program. The mothers of both groups drew up a petition which was signed by almost all 93 mothers in the program and presented it to the superintendent and school board. A letter was written to the editor of the local paper protesting a feature article which had offended them. A large number of mothers began to take jobs and investigate courses offered by the local community college and high school adult education program. Many working mothers indicated a desire to improve their skills to secure better jobs.

Although the mothers' new childrearing practices were successful in achieveing desired behaviors, the new approach often became a source of friction with their husbands. Mothers reported that their husbands felt they were "too soft" when they gave explanations with their requests. The husbands did not believe in reinforcing a child for his good behaviors which "should be happening anyhow." Rather, they believed in punishment for bad behaviors. The mothers also objected to the men's resistance to playing an active role with the children, spending time with them, reading to them, etc. Their need to educate their husbands concerning improved childrearing practices became the impetus for a husband-wife social evening planned by the mothers. The program consisted primarily of skits on childrearing issues written and produced by the mothers themselves; it was highly successful.

IMPLICATIONS

The absence of evidence of superior intellectual growth by the children of mothers in the experimental groups suggests that in a compound intervention such as the Early Education Program, parent education in effective childrearing practices may be more valuable for long-term growth of the child than for short-term change. In this program, both control group and experimental children received an enriched classroom experience and home tutorials in their mothers' presence. These experiences alone may have produced the maximum short-term intellectual growth. However, it is possible that feelings of competence in the parents foster a feeling of efficacy in the child. If a mother feels incompetent, she is likely to model these feelings for her child and nurture similar feelings in the youngster. If, on the other hand, she has a sense of efficacy or fate control, she is likely not only to model this positive feeling for her child, but possibly also strive for its development in her youngsters. In view of the fact that Coleman (1966) found feelings of internal control to be associated with academic proficiency in youngsters, a sense of efficacy in the parent may be an intervening variable of long-term intellectual growth in the child. This suggests that many indices of growth in feelings of competence should be used to evaluate parent education programs, e.g., greater participation in school and community affairs, enrollment in courses or job training, participation in self-help activities such as reciprocal babysitting, etc.

The finding pertaining to the interaction of methodology and length of exposure to the group offers another suggestion for future parent programs. If a group is to have a long-term existence, it may be most productive to start off with an activity orientation which lends itself to maximum participation and to new learning in a restricted setting. This activity orientation should be transformed, in time, into a member-directed discussion group to enhance the development of group cohesion and formation of group norms, particularly those that support the generalization of learning to home problems.

The findings of the parent program were best interpreted by employing social psychological theories that had not been incorporated into the original hypotheses. Not only learning theories, but also small group theory and efficacy concepts were essential for understanding and evaluating the Early Education Program. Effective action research, certainly in multifaceted compensatory preschool programs, appears to require the integration of divergent theories. While an integrated perspective may be difficult to manage conceptually and equally difficult to implement, it can be the most exciting and fruitful approach in the long run.

REFERENCES

BRIM, ORVILLE
  1959—*Education for Childrearing,* New York: Russell Sage Foundation.
COLEMAN, J. S.
  1966—*Equality of Educational Opportunity,* U.S. Department of Health, Education and Welfare, Washington, D.C.: U.S. Government Printing Office.
KAMII, CONSTANCE K. AND NORMA RADIN
  1967—"A framework for a preschool curriculum based on some Piagetian concepts," *Journal of Creative Behavior,* 1, pp. 314–324.

RADIN, NORMA
  1969—*Early Education Program: Analysis of Changes During the Year,* Ypsilanti, Michigan: Ypsilanti Public Schools.
RADIN, NORMA AND PAUL GLASSER
  1965—"The use of attitude questionnaires with culturally disadvantaged families," *Journal of Marriage and the Family,* 27 (August), pp. 373–382.
RADIN, NORMA AND HONNI SONQUIST
  1968—*Gale Preschool Program Final Report,* Ypsilanti, Michigan: Ypsilanti Public Schools.
SCHAEFER, E. S. AND R. Q. BELL
  1958—"Development of a parental attitude research instrument," *Child Development,* 29 (September), pp. 33–361.
SONQUIST, HONNI D. AND CONSTANCE K. KAMII
  1967—"Applying some Piagetian concepts in the classroom for the disadvantaged," *Young Children,* 22, pp. 231–245.
WITTES, GLORIANNE AND NORMA RADIN
  1969—"Two approaches to parent work in a compensatory preschool program," Paper read at National Conference on Family Relations, Washington, D. C., October 1969. (a)
  1969—*Helping your Child to Learn: The Reinforcement Approach,* San Rafael, California: Dimensions Publishing Company. (b)
  1969—*Helping your Child to Learn: The Learning Through Play Approach,* San Rafael, California: Dimensions Publishing Company. (c)
  1969—*Helping your Child to Learn: The Nurturance Approach,* San Rafael, California: Dimensions Publishing Company. (d)

27.

Beyond Group Work: Organizational Determinants of Malperformance in Secondary Schools

ROSEMARY C. SARRI and ROBERT D. VINTER

The public school today is required to educate every youth without regard to ability, interest, or prior preparation. There is general agreement that the school's primary goal is to prepare individuals to meet the knowledge and skill requirements for adult occupational roles. The public school is also expected to further its pupils' character development and preparation for responsible citizenship; and it is increasingly held responsible for aiding those who have been educationally disadvantaged by cultural, family, or community conditions. The emphasis on enhancing educational opportunities for all pupils has brought into sharp focus some familiar problems within elementary and secondary schools: underachievement and academic failure among those believed to be intellectually capable; pupil misconduct that disrupts classroom procedures and school discipline; and the tendency of youths to drop out before high school graduation.

A variety of approaches are being developed and tested to resolve these problems. A research and demonstration project, employing the use of group service methods to reduce malperforming behavior among junior and senior high school pupils, is reported here. The initial objectives of the project were to modify pupil behavior that curtailed effective learning and/or disrupted classroom procedures; to strengthen pupils' commitments

This chapter is a revised version of an article, "Group Work for the Control of Behavior Problems in Secondary Schools," published in *Innovation in Mass Education*, David Street (Ed.), New York: John Wiley & Sons, 1969, pp. 91–110. Principal support for the project reported here was provided by a curriculum development grant from the Office of Juvenile Delinquency and Youth Development, U.S. Department of Health, Education, and Welfare, in cooperation with the President's Committee on Juvenile Delinquency and Youth Development, and by a research grant from the National Institute of Mental Health, U.S. Public Health Service. The authors gratefully acknowledge the contributions in this project of their faculty colleagues, Maeda Galinsky, Frank Maple, and Walter Schaefer.

to educational objectives and school completion; and to change or to propose modifications in school practices that hampered effective education for malperforming pupils. As the project progressed over a three-year period, it became apparent that school organization, curriculum design, and staff behavior were even more important for pupil malperformance than initially expected. Such discoveries led to some modifications in the intervention approach.

THE PROBLEM IN PERSPECTIVE

Within limits, schools are seeking to increase pupils' motivation to achieve academically, to ameliorate personal and social stresses that circumscribe student learning, and to cope with behavior that jeopardizes classroom processes. In order to perform its new roles, the school must develop special procedures for pupils who are inadequately prepared, insufficiently motivated, or unresponsive to classroom behavior standards. Some efforts center on changing curriculum or teaching procedures or introducing special services for pupils with particular problems, needs, or disabilities. But many defects still exist within the educational system for which adequate solutions have not been devised. As a consequence some pupils, particularly lower-class youth, are especially handicapped by prevailing educational conditions and practices. Because of its strategic role in the lives of all children, the school plays a less than optimal part in helping some children move into legitimate adult roles.

Increased demands upon many public school systems have produced problems, even crises, particularly in large cities: poor physical plants, pressures toward standardization, overcrowding, racial segregation, the lack of special or compensatory education for those most in need, and stable or decreasing economic resources in a period of increasing demand.[1] Students and parents are exerting pressures on schools to provide improved educational opportunities and to allow participation in decision making about curriculum, personnel, and practices. Demonstrations, boycotts, and other forms of protest that have existed for several years at the college level, have increased in junior and senior high schools. Responses to such protests by boards of education and school personnel have often been piecemeal and inadequate.

---

[1] Elder (1966) presents data from a study of a "continuation school" on the West Coast that is particularly relevant for this demonstration effort. He points to the problem of links between the school's curriculum and meaningful adult vocational roles for its graduates and also to the importance of the school's public reputation.

If the new demands are to be met, even at a minimal level, the changes required are substantial. In view of past stalemates and the inadequacy of change efforts, innovation strategies must attend to interrelated parts of the system that form the school and must include plans for phasing each specific change into the on-going operations of the school. To achieve lasting, successful change, the strategy of "phasing in" may be as important as the substantive content of specific changes.

CONCEPTIONS OF MALPERFORMANCE

Standards for academic achievement and criteria of desirable conduct vary among schools and, to some extent, even within the same school. Types of malperformance such as underachievement, poor classroom conduct, and failure to adjust are not defined identically; and the pupil personality, performance, or ability that are at issue in one situation are not the same as those in another.

Second, curriculum, resources, teacher competency, student body, and organization vary widely among schools. Such variations create great differences in learning environments, in opportunities for achievement or adjustment, and in conditions that shape the meaning of the school experience.

Third, schools differ significantly in their procedures for identifying and coping with pupil malperformance. In one school, students who manifest difficulty may become the targets for a full complement of remedial services. In another, pupils who exhibit similar behavior may encounter relative indifference or find that, when attention is given, the result is a loss of status or privileges, perhaps leading eventually to exclusion from classes and even suspension from school.

The theoretical framework for the study of deviant behavior used here is similar to that of Cohen (1966), Lemert (1967), Freidson (1966) and Erickson (1964). *Malperformance* refers to behavior that violates valued norms in the school and/or community to the degree that, if it persists, it will lead to assignment to a status having negative consequences for the person whose behavior is so defined. As Erickson suggests, the consequences of such labeling may have both a long- and a short-run nature.

Deviance is not a property inherent in certain forms of behavior but a property conferred upon these forms by the audiences that directly witness them. The critical variable in the study of deviants, then, is the audience rather than the individual actor, since the audience eventually determines whether or not any episode of behavior or any class of episodes is labeled deviant (Erickson, 1964). Given this concept of deviance, pupil malperformance may be viewed as social or interactional, in that it results from adverse interactions between characteristics of a particular student and conditions within a particular school.

Any type of malperformance must not be considered a unitary phenomenon or one inhering primarily in the attributes of the pupils, but rather as a result of the interaction between the school and the pupil. Pupil difficulties are social since they are manifested through interaction with other pupils, teachers, and the academic tasks of the curriculum. Their problems assume relevance only as they are assessed in terms of the social objectives and values of school personnel. "Deviant" behaviors originate in and are shaped by the pupils' social relations and their experiences in the school and elsewhere. Once the pupil has been identified as a deviant, this social recognition may affect his identity and self-image in a variety of situations. It may induce him to seek compensatory approval through informal associations that support further deviancy. Finally, such identification has important implications for the manner in which the pupil is subsequently dealt with by the school, for the way in which his career is shaped, and ultimately for his life chances (Cicourel and Kitsuse, 1963).

Both the process by which malperformance is identified and the ways in which malperforming pupils are managed within the school are concerns in this chapter.

THE DESIGN FOR RESEARCH AND DEMONSTRATION

Preliminary investigations revealed that the reduction of malperformance is complex and that effective strategies for intervention would require close observation of many facets of organizational behavior. Four main areas for research were delineated. The first was pupil characteristics, behaviors, and perspectives, assessed with particular reference to how these related to both educational achievement and malperformance. Second, in order to understand school organization and behavior, curriculum design, the behavior and perspectives of teachers and other staff members, and organizational mechanisms for defining and coping with malperformance and for processing pupils into different curricular tracks were studied. Third, study of the performance patterns of pupils over the three-year high school career provided opportunities to examine certain interactions between pupil characteristics and school practices. Last, the processes and outcomes of group service methods were evaluated.

Seven schools in five different communities were included in the major phases of the project. Contrasting communities were selected: a rural community with a kindergarten through high school program housed on a single campus; a middle-class college town; a small industrial community; a residential suburb of a large metropolitan area; and an industrial community adjacent to a metropolitan area. Some of the school systems had initiated contact with The University of Michigan School of Social Work because of concerns about behavioral misconduct and underachievement.

Information from the U.S. Census and from local school censuses was used to ensure variation in school district and community characteristics. Although three elementary schools were included in parts of the study, greater attention was directed toward the junior and senior high schools. The intervention strategy was designed primarily for male pupils. Only two of the experimental groups were composed of girls; consequently, generalizations for this population are very tentative.

Before a school was selected for inclusion, it was necessary that school officials agree to maintain the experimental service program, as it was designed, for a minimum of one academic year. In no case was this requirement difficult to meet. Arrangements were made for each school to employ one or more social workers to provide the group service as a part of its social work or special education program. The service program was conducted in each of the schools for more than two years. Since the termination of the project, four of the five school systems have continued and expanded the effort.

In line with the interest in organizational change, it was believed essential that each school contribute to the development and support of the new program from the beginning. Far too often, innovations developed in demonstration projects are not adopted after a project ends, partly because special external resources are used to support the demonstration effort; little attention, if any, is given to assisting the organization to provide for the financial and other support of the endeavor.

Pupil Characteristics and Behavior

In all schools pupils were being identified and referred to receive special attention for underachievement and disruptive behavior; the introduction of group services apparently did not alter the schools' criteria for referral. Detailed information, collected about each pupil referred, included grades, intelligence and performance test scores, family background, and school behavior reports. Thus it was possible to gain some understanding of the different kinds of pupils and behaviors "produced" by each school's distinctive organization and patterns. Later an attempt was made to systematize the selection of pupils who received group service by using standardized referral procedures for teachers, examination of school records, and observation of pupil behavior within the school setting by the research staff. Many more pupils were referred than could be served in the groups. Pupils were screened out whom the research staff judged to be retarded, in need of intensive psychological or psychiatric treatment, or so handicapped that they could not participate in activities with their peers. Systematic screening procedures also helped in identifying problematic conditions that were similar for many students. Although variations existed within and among the schools with respect to the types of students referred for services, certain similarities emerged. Most students fell within the "average" range of intellectual ability, but nearly all were "underachievers" in relation to their capabilities. Most also manifested serious behavior problems, including disruptive conduct in the classroom or in other school areas; poor interpersonal relations with adults and peers; violation of school conduct norms, including frequent truancy and suspension; or withdrawn and isolative behaviors.

Control groups were established in each school system. Referred pupils were matched in pairs; one of each pair was then randomly assigned to a service group, and the other became a control who received whatever attention was customary within each school *except* the group service. A second type of control group was selected randomly from the total population, excluding the referred malperformers, in appropriate grade levels. Matching procedures were slightly modified in one school because of service requirements during one year of the study. In the latter situation, experimental and control groups were "matched" after selection, because two natural peer groups were referred; it was decided to provide service to these groups and then to select their controls.

The design of the study called for the use of a series of before-and-after measures in addition to comparisons between experimental groups and both matched and random control groups. These measures permitted the identification of outcomes that could be attributed directly to group work service rather than to pupil maturation or factors of chance. At the same time, the design allowed attitudinal and behavioral comparisons at a single point in time between malperforming pupils and a sample of the rest of the school population. During the second year of the project, data were collected on approximately 400 pupils in the service, matched control, and random groups, all of whom were closely observed in the five school systems. Data were obtained on a slightly smaller number who were observed in the first year of the project. The demonstration phase took place between 1962 and 1965, with most of the data collection completed by 1964.

Three major sets of before-and-after measures were used to evaluate change. First, an instrument was developed to inventory teachers' assessments of pupil behavior in five areas: classroom conduct, academic motivation and performance, socioemotional state, teacher dependence, and personal behavior (Vinter, Sarri, Schaefer and Vorwaller, 1966). A second set of measures was composed of objective indices of school performance: grades, attendance records, and performance scores normally collected by the schools. The third set was derived from pupils' self-reports of behavior and attitudes obtained in interviews and written questionnaires. Dimensions studied included educational goals and expectations, academic and social skills, attitudes toward teachers, peers, and parents, and reports of school experiences. All of these data were collected on all pupils in the experimental, matched control, and random control groups at the beginning and the termination of service. Matched pairs were used to develop change score differences for the evaluation.

The narrative records prepared by group workers were also used to evaluate change and to see what practitioner behaviors were associated with pupil change. These records were analyzed with reference to targets of change, means of influence, and modes of interaction.

The before-and-after measures of pupil change served as the primary means for evaluating the modifications effected by group services. Means for assessing the processes of change included systematic review of the practitioners' service records, independent interviewing of treatment groups in special group sessions, and direct consultation with service personnel. Practitioners were requested to obtain and record specific information about pupils during the period of treatment. With such information it was possible to assess elements of group processes and to identify some of the key factors in change. This particular phase of the design was important to gain somewhat greater knowledge about processes of change. Far too often evaluative studies of treatment programs have measured only outcomes, with processes of change remaining unknown or unidentified.

Some members of the research staff served as consultants to school personnel actually working with the groups. Planning and problem-solving conferences were held every six weeks with the practitioners to explore service procedures and examine preliminary study findings. Practitioners also undertook study and validation of project materials such as the practitioners' manual.

School Organization and Practices

This area of study comprised school conditions and practices, including school size, staffing, and resources; school goals; curriculum design; grading criteria; means of identifying, labeling, and handling misconduct and malperformance; classroom practices; and teachers' orientations and perspectives. These dimensions were assessed through several procedures: directly observing classroom and other activities in the school; reviewing documentary and file materials; interviewing school administrators, teachers, and special service personnel; and administering question-naires to all professional personnel in the sample schools. In addition, ex-tended observations were made of the daily cycle of school activities, of board, faculty, and committee meetings, and of informal activities among pupils and teachers.

Data feedback sessions were held periodically with school administra-tors during the latter phase of the study. These sessions provided addi-tional information about school practices and, in particular, about executive behavior. Continued observation of the several schools permitted some knowledge of planned organizational changes as attempts were made to implement some of the recommendations from the study. Unfortunately, the project ended before many of these changes were developed to the point where they could be assessed adequately.

Pupil Careers

Study of pupil careers over a three-year period was completed in two of the senior high schools. Interest here was in identifying factors asso-ciated with curriculum placement, performance patterns including grades and test scores, and length of career. Grading practices were systematically analyzed. Other reward systems were also examined, although less sys-tematically.

To accomplish the study of career patterns, all pupils were identified who entered the tenth grade in the fall of 1961 in the two schools. They were followed through the spring of 1964, when the majority completed the twelfth grade. Data abstracted from official files included grades, semester of and reason for leaving for those who did not continue, cur-riculum and changes in curriculum for each pupil, intelligence and per-formance test scores, sex, race, father's occupation, and extracurricular participation.

Group Services

In accordance with the initial intervention strategy, group services for malperforming pupils were provided in seven of the sample schools. Prospective group members were interviewed by the school social workers to review school difficulties, to explain why each had been selected for service and what would happen in the group, and to establish an initial "contract" for working together on specific problems. Workers frequently encountered resistance and skepticism in these interviews. Pupils often had had negative experiences in the school and frequently were doubtful that the school was really interested in helping them or in altering conditions that affected them adversely. The example of Bob White, a fifteen-year-old entering the tenth grade, is illustrative of initial contacts. The social worker reported:

> Bob was referred by his ninth-grade counselor for underachievement, rule breaking, and disruptive classroom behavior. He was on probation in the juvenile court for auto theft and stealing from a bowling alley. The counselor described him as one who elicited both adult and peer rejection. In the initial interview Bob expressed a desire to work on some of his problems. He was negative about his probation experience but did reveal some understanding about his situation and school achievement. He agreed to give the group experience a try but wasn't optimistic about his future.

Groups typically were composed of five to eight members, identical in sex and grade level. Sessions were held one or more times a week during school hours and in the school buildings. Additional after-school-hour sessions were arranged according to workers' plans and group members' requests. The group sessions were the primary means of attempting changes, although individual services were provided, as necessary and whenever possible, by the same worker who conducted the group sessions.

Within the groups, explicit recognition was given publicly to each pupil's difficulties and to the need for mutual assistance in resolving them. Emphasis was placed on mobilizing pupils' motivations for change and directing them toward improved academic achievement and appropriate school conduct. Workers deliberately sought to increase members' attraction to the group and to school, and they sought to help the students develop new skills and alternatives for coping more effectively with stressful school situations. One of the special advantages of working with such pupils in groups was assumed to be that powerful social forces can develop to support the desired changes rather than to encourage continued, covert deviance.

The researchers noted, as have many others, that pupils identified as underachieving and disruptive tended to seek each other out and to form associations that reinforce deviancy. A boy in one of the groups explained this tendency in these words:

> It depends on who you hang around with. Some guys' idea of fun is to see who gets the lowest grades, skipping school and classes, smoking in the bathroom. I started hanging around with guys like that. . . . The only reason me or anyone else did things like skip school was to make an impression on your friends. They'd think you're chicken otherwise. I feel if you can't get good grades, then brag about getting away with it.

The sessions clearly demonstrated the importance of identifying certain primary targets of change, i.e., specific academic skills and abilities;

skills of social interaction with teacher and peers; and pupils' values, goals, and motivations. The means and opportunities for successful performance were insufficiently or inaccurately perceived by malperformers; some of their deficiency in academic skills could be improved within the group (e.g., study habits, efficient use of time, or test preparation), and their readiness for successful interaction with teachers and other school personnel could be improved. Social skills particularly were amenable to influence in the group sessions. Pupils' values, goals, and motivations often contradicted those supported by the school and frequently were the outcome of prior failures that resulted in pessimism and negativism toward school.

The workers often observed that legitimate opportunities for malperforming students were more limited than for other students. In some cases, workers intervened on behalf of the pupils with other school personnel. One tenth-grader's views were typical of malperformers' perceptions of their situation:

> If Mr. Owen [the principal] had believed I was not the one who provoked fights, he would not have kicked me out for three days. Maybe kids like me won't get too far because of our actions in school, and we don't get good grades. He didn't seem interested in helping—kicks kids out real easy. Seems like he's looking for some of us kids to be doing something.
>
>   Should lower standards about getting on teams—lots of times you can't get high enough grades even if you try hard. Am not doing as good as I wanted to regarding grades—wanted to get into wrestling, but in the first marking period grades dropped, came up second period but not high enough and I had been trying real hard. I don't think it's fair—if you try hard enough should be able to get a good enough grade to do what you want to do. Don't know why got those grades—studied harder for tests but still dropped down. . . .
>
>   [Regarding same chances as other kids of getting good grades] No, long ago I might have. At Carr School I don't think they taught kids half as much as other schools did because when us Carr kids got to junior high other kids were twice as smart as us—due to bad teaching at Carr.

Activities of the groups were largely determined by the goals set by workers and members together. Problem-focused discussion predominated, but all groups engaged in other activities as well. Groups with younger members tended to engage in discussion less frequently. In teaching new academic and social skills, the workers employed simulation techniques and other procedures designed to improve study habits and test preparation and to increase their ability for requesting assistance from teachers and classmates, and for completing assignments. Pupils were coached or coached each other in test taking, report writing, and the like. The workers recognized that each of these acts was a complex behavior that subsumed several specific skills. When possible, attempts were made to define these skills so that generalizations could be made to other situations in and out of school.

Workers also became aware that the pupils' opinions about school materials and procedures had to be considered. Pupils often commented that required textbooks were dull and failed to "turn them on." A twelve-year-old boy asked, "Who wants to read *Elmer the Worm*—about a worm who talks to a boy?" To encourage malperformers to join the mainstream of school life and associate with others, workers attempted to encourage and facilitate their participation in extracurricular activities.

The social workers deliberately attempted to create cohesive and viable groups but explicitly pointed out to the members that these groups were instruments to individual change. In a few cases, where the groups were most cohesive, problems were aggravated and few change goals were achieved. An effective solution, however, usually was changing the memberships of the groups.

The workers were able to guide the groups to create desirable change conditions. Similar demonstration projects have reported that workers relied almost exclusively on the peer group and de-emphasized their own roles (McCorkle, 1958). This did not work successfully in this project. Observations and evaluations indicate that the workers tended to be more effective when they carefully structured the program of the group, using a variety of direct and indirect means of influence. The adult exemplified the roles he wished to have the members adopt even though he indicated his acceptance of the problematic situations of the pupils. It appeared that a climate was created in which members felt free to discuss and explore problems without fear of ridicule or rejection. They then were encouraged to try out new patterns of behavior in the group before displaying them outside.

Although most pupils seemed to perceive the groups as rewarding and satisfying, they were continuously aware of the serious purposes of this experience and its relevance to school performance. This was accomplished partly by encouraging pupils to report incidents and difficulties that they were currently experiencing in the school—and for most students there was no lack of such reports. The worker then involved the group jointly in exploring the situation, in considering cause-and-effect sequences, and in discovering more appropriate responses that pupils might have made. Because all pupils had witnessed or participated in similar incidents, they were very effective in curbing each other's tendencies toward denial or projection and in proposing alternative ways for coping with situations.

Despite the positive findings about the intervention strategy, critical limitations were also exposed. The school social workers soon discovered that many problems could not be resolved successfully by changing the pupil's behavior or attributes. School conditions hampered the attainment of desired change goals, such as improved grades, increased participation in extracurricular activities, and reduced dropping out. Malperforming pupils could not be helped when they were isolated from school events. The practitioners needed to have knowledge of curriculum, of teachers and their practices, of classroom climates, and of general school conditions in order to understand the particular circumstances that contributed to each pupil's problems. In addition to providing direct services to group and individuals, the school social workers had to function as mediators and as consultants to teachers and other school personnel about the experiences and difficulties of particular pupils and of the malperformers in general. They also served as lobbyists in and out of school on behalf of malperformers, and they negotiated with families and agencies in the community.[2]

STUDY FINDINGS

Effects of the Demonstration Project

The results of the intervention were partially disappointing. Findings from the effort were evaluated at the end of each of the two years that it ran. The results after the first year indicated that there were no significant changes for either the experimental or control groups in grades received, absences, truancies, suspensions, or leaving school. Similarly, minimal change was observed among the random groups selected from the total population. One change-measuring instrument, the Pupil Behavior Inventory, showed some positive results for the experimental group. This instrument, described later, was designed to obtain teachers' ratings of pupil behaviors before and after the service program.

To understand what happened, it became apparent that more systematic and detailed information was needed about school practices and conditions. Procedures were then developed to study pupil career patterns, curricular design, teachers' perceptions and behaviors, and mechanisms for identifying and coping with various forms of deviancy in the school. The findings of these studies and how they were used to modify the strategy for reducing pupil malperformance will now be discussed.

[2] A set of principles for school practitioners who wish to employ this method of intervention was prepared in conjunction with the project by Sarri, Vinter, and Goodman (1965). Most of the social workers affiliated with the demonstration project engaged in each of these activities at one time or another, but among the different schools variations in emphasis were apparent. Apart from the direct work with service groups, no attempt was made by the project staff to achieve uniformity in role patterns among the school social workers.

Characteristics, Perspectives, and Behavior of Malperformers and Randoms

Intensive study of the pupils referred in each school provided new insights. Data in this section are presented for the sample of malperformers who were identified in their schools as pupils who needed additional attention. These data are compared with similar findings for the random sample of pupils (referred to hereafter as "randoms") selected from the total population (excluding malperformers) of each school.

Table 1 shows the marked differences in overall grade point average and in numbers of absences between the two groups. No difference in mean IQ test score was noted, however. Below-average academic performance therefore must stem from factors other than deficiency in intellectual ability. The important findings can be summarized in five generalizations.

1. *Malperformers placed as great an importance as randoms on achievement and success in school, as well as on long-term goals relating to employment and success in future life.* Frequently school personnel assert that malperformers are not committed to educational goals and are not interested in school. Contrary to these beliefs, the data in Table 2 indicate that malperformers continue to maintain a basic commitment to succeeding in school and that they value educational goals even when experiencing personal failure. Because none of the differences between malperformers and randoms was statistically significant at the .02 level, it can be inferred that the two groups are essentially alike in these basic attitudes.

TABLE 1. Achievement, IQ, and Attendance Records of Malperformers and Randoms

Grade point average, first semester, of tenth grade			
Malperformers		1.84	
Randoms		2.63	
Mean IQ			
Malperformers		107	
Randoms		107	
Average number of single-period absences for year			
	Excused	*Unexcused*	*Total*
Malperformers	3.9	2.4	6.3
Randoms	1.5	0.9	2.4
Average number of whole-day absences for year			
Malperformers	11.5	1.3	12.8
Randoms	4.9	0.2	5.1

TABLE 2.   Pupil's Attitudes Toward Educational Goals and Community Norms

Percentage Saying Item Is Important:	Malperformers	Randoms
Passing courses	76%	89%
Getting the most from school	57	68
Getting along with teachers	40	47
Going to college	67	70
Having a well-paying job when you are an adult	76	70
Having a steady job when you are an adult	92	94

Although data were not obtained directly from parents about their attitudes and values, boys were asked what their parents thought about school and their school performance. Parents of both groups were reported as being strongly opposed to their sons dropping out of school (Table 3). Furthermore, malperformers reported much more often that their parents viewed their school performance as falling below parental expectations. Thus, the academic problems experienced by these pupils were not the simple outcome of a lack of interest in school, intellectual ability, or parental concern.

2. *Malperformers engaged in a number of unacceptable activities more often than randoms. These were truancy, tardiness, leaving class, fighting, and being sent to the office.* Although malperformers were interested in and committed to educational goals, they reported that they did not put the same effort into school work as did the randoms. The findings in Table 4 reveal significant differences between malperformers and randoms regarding the violation of school norms. The former reported that they frequently engaged in a number of unacceptable activities, such as truancy, tardiness, fighting, and skipping school, and they often created

TABLE 3.   Reported Attitudes of Parents Toward School

Percentage Reporting That:	Malperformers	Randoms	Level of Significance
Parents are against dropping out[a]	90%	98%	N.S.
School performance is below parents' expectations[b]	84	28	< .001

[a] "What do parents think about kids dropping out of school?"
[b] "How are you doing in your school work as compared with what your parents expect?"

TABLE 4. Pupils' Behaviors in School[a]

Percentage Reporting:	Malper-formers	Randoms	Level of Significance
Staying home when you could have come to school	57%	28%	< .02
Being late for class	80	54	< .01
Leaving class without a good reason	38	13	< .01
Getting into a fight	35	9	< .01
Being sent to the office	37	11	< .01

[a] "In the past two months how many times have you done each of the following things?" Figures are percentages of each group responding "one or more times."

trouble for teachers in their classrooms. Over a period of time, they increasingly failed to conform to school standards of conduct.[3]

Whatever the psychological mechanisms involved, malperformers seemed to devalue many school norms and standards of conduct. This pattern may represent the gradual development of a general negative orientation toward the school as a crucial source of frustration and disenchantment. Of course, deviant behavior itself decreases the likelihood of achieving a high level because of negative teacher reactions and falling further behind in class work as suspensions and other sanctions are imposed. In turn, low achievers may "try less hard" and thus get into further trouble. They also are likely to turn toward other boys in similar difficulty as referents in support of antischool attitudes and behavior.

3. *Marked differences between malperformers and randoms were noted in "acquired capabilities" such as study habits, classroom conduct, and perceptions of relationships with teachers.*

Malperformers more frequently stated that they did not try as hard, lacked study skills, failed to complete assignments, and found it difficult to ask teachers for help. Table 5 reveals consistent and large differences between the two groups of pupils in reports of their own behavior. Perceptions of teachers as unfriendly and not helpful seemed to be the result of repeated failure or continued difficulty in handling relationships with teachers. The findings in Table 6 illustrate malperformers' reports of their views of teachers. Malperformers also were likely to report lower degrees of self-confidence and self-control in their transactions with teachers. Often

[3] The candor and truthfulness of the malperformers' self-reports, as measured in these and other areas and validated by school records, lent credence to their statements about their own and parental attitudes.

TABLE 5.   Pupils' Reports of Study and Classroom Habits

Percentage Reporting That:	Malper-formers	Randoms	Level of Significance
I try as hard as most other students in my class to do well in school work.	40%	77%	< .001
I can't seem to read as well as most other kids in my class.	34	42	N.S.
I don't seem to get very much done when I study.	56	28	< .01
I find it hard to keep my mind on school work.	78	57	< .05
I can't seem to remember much of what I have studied.	60	30	< .01
It's hard for me to sit still for very long in classes	55	34	< .05
I fail to complete homework assignments once a week or more.	72	49	< .01
When schoolwork is hard, I ask teachers for help.	31	58	< .01
I ask friends for help when school is hard.	27	55	< .01
The way I do in school isn't much to be proud of.	59	32	<0.1
I try as hard as most other students to do well in my schoolwork.	40	76	< .01

TABLE 6.   Pupils' Perception of Teachers

Percentage Agreeing That:	Malper-formers	Randoms	Level of Significance
Most of the teachers at this school are friendly.	69%	91%	< .01
The teachers here don't deserve the respect they demand.	53	23	< .01
I have a fair or poor reputation regarding schoolwork.[a]	77	37	< .01
I have a fair or poor reputation regarding behavior.	37	19	< .05

[a] "What kind of a reputation do you have among teachers as far as your schoolwork (or behavior) is concerned?"

they responded impulsively and aggressively to requests and to difficult situations.

4. *Malperformers were often isolated from the mainstream of life in the school, but they were not isolated from peers.* Contrary to some observations, the findings indicate that malperformers were integrated into cohesive peer groups that supported behavior and attitudes largely inconsistent with conventional and acceptable norms. These peer groups exhibited much antisocial behavior in and out of school and provided encouragement for others to do likewise.

The findings in Table 7 reveal that malperformers often reported having as many friends as other pupils, but that they spent somewhat more time with these friends. They also generally reported that their friends were experiencing difficulties similar to their own and that they were not part of the dominant social system. These friendships were highly valued, perhaps for compensatory reasons. In interviews with both groups of pupils, each group indicated little contact with the other; randoms, in fact, reported that they deliberately avoided associating with malperformers. The latter reported similar behavior, and it is not surprising that pupils experiencing similar difficulties and situations turn to each other and collectively adopt standards of conduct. The lack of support for positive achievement in school is demonstrated by the fact that malperformers asked their friends for help with school work less often than did randoms. These findings are similar to those of Polk and Richmond in a study of Oregon pupils. They suggest that students who fail are progressively shunned by achieving students, teachers, and the "system as a whole" (Polk and Richmond, 1966).

TABLE 7. Pupils' Perceptions of Peers

Percentage Reporting That:	*Malper-formers*	*Randoms*	*Level of Significance*
I have five or more friends.	66%	73%	N.S.
Friends hang around together a lot.	57	19	< .001
Friends take part in a lot of school activities.	29	55	< .01
Friends study a lot.	29	47	< .02
Friends are concerned about grades.	69	87	< .05
Friends look for a good time.	67	34	< .01
Friends have a reputation with teachers as good students.	37	60	< .05
Friends are concerned about behaving as teachers think they should.	20	51	< .01

5. *Malperformers perceived that they had far worse reputations than randoms and that, at least in part, as a consequence of their school experience, they had few chances for success in school or adulthood.* Interviews with pupils, social workers, and counselors all pointed to the conclusion that malperformers were very pessimistic about the future as a consequence of their continued failure and lack of any positive reinforcement from the school. Table 8 clearly indicates their pessimism about success in school. When these findings are compared with those in Table 2, it is possible to see marked differences between goals and the perceived reality of their situations. It is not surprising, therefore, that malperformers turn away from desirable goals which they believe they have little likelihood of ever achieving and accept alternative standards that may violate school or community norms. They are caught in a spiraling situation of diminishing rewards and increasing frustration and negative reactions. A tenth-grade student expressed his pessimism in these terms:

> I wanted a job out of school, but I wanted to get a good job. I dropped out in the fall. . . . I just didn't care. I wasn't getting good grades in the ninth grade. I figured out since I wasn't getting good grades then, it wouldn't change so I just didn't care.

It is reasonable, therefore, that these pupils will view the classroom as confining and classroom tasks as uninteresting. Thus any effort for successful change must be directed not only toward developing the necessary capabilities in the pupils but also toward providing sufficient positive rewards and opportunities in the system. As the findings became known to the practitioners, the group service project was increasingly focused toward the latter ends. The workers emphasized the need to narrow the gap between measured capability and performance; to stress the persistence of pupils' commitments to conventional values, including achievement and success; and to honor the students' desire to reduce the adverse consequences of being regarded and handled as deviants. Experiences within

TABLE 8. Pupils' Attitudes Toward Future

Percentage of Pupils Who:	*Malper-formers*	*Randoms*	*Level of Significance*
Expect to pass courses	24%	62%	< .001
Expect to finish high school	51	70	< .05
Expect friends to finish high school	42	64	< .05
Expect to have a good record when leaving school	16	53	< .001
Expect to have a steady job as an adult	28	60	< .01

the group sessions offered some opportunity for success and for developing additional skills for classroom accomplishment. However, the crucial condition was the extent to which these pupils could find new opportunities for positive achievement and could be rewarded for improved performance in the classrooms. In this regard, teachers apparently noted changes in pupils' behavior, but rewards such as grades showed little if any change.

Teachers' Perspectives and Ratings of Pupil Behavior

Information obtained from teachers indicated that at least two foci were neded for the group work services. Unfortunately, much of this information was not obtained until the demonstration effort was under way and therefore could not be used fully. Teachers regarded adequate pupil motivation as crucial to success. Three-fifths or more of the teachers in the schools reported that the single most important source of difficulty for most or all malperformers was their lack of motivation and interest in school. Motivation was thought to be an attribute that the pupil brought to school, and few teachers seemed aware that educational practices in school can contribute to it.

Because of their perceptions school personnel had difficulty accepting the study findings that revealed relatively high levels of commitment and aspiration among malperformers. Many (but not all) malperforming pupils were perceived as challenging the teachers' authority, and in some schools teachers were especially concerned about this problem. The findings about teacher perspectives indicate that greater emphasis should also have been placed on developing social skills relevant to the classroom and to pupil-teacher interactions.

That the work with the pupils had some positive effects, despite the weaknesses in the design of the intervention, is shown in the findings on the Pupil Behavior Inventory. Teachers' ratings of pupils before and after group work services indicated that impressive gains were achieved. Those in the service groups, as compared to matched controls, showed improvement in many areas of performance.

Statistical analysis of the ratings given the students led to the identification of five major dimensions of student behavior (Vinter, et al., 1966): (1) *classroom conduct:* twelve items; for example, disrupts classroom procedures, teases, provokes other students; (2) *academic motivation and performance:* nine items; for example, is motivated toward academic performance, is alert, is interested in school work; (3) *socioemotional state:* five items; for example, appears generally happy, seems isolated, has few or no friends; (4) *teacher dependence:* two items; for example, seeks constant reassurance, is possessive of teacher; and (5) *general socializa-*

tion: six items; for example, swears or uses obscene words, has inappropriate personal appearance. These dimensions indicate significant facets of pupil-teacher interaction patterns and can be regarded as sets of behavior about which teachers maintain expectations and toward which they focus judgments of pupils' conduct. Within these areas, malperforming pupils apparently lacked sufficient skills and needed assistance in order to gain positive evaluation from teachers.

In Table 9, change scores are presented by dimension for the experimental and matched control groups in seven schools. The scores represent differences in ratings before and after the group services. A positive score means that the treatment groups showed more positive change than their matched controls. Comparison of difference scores across horizontal rows in the table shows variations among schools. The final columns on the right indicate that experimental groups, considered together, made progress during the time they received service on all dimensions except "teacher dependence." The negative scores obtained in several schools on this dimension require clarification. It was reported earlier that many malperforming pupils had considerable difficulty in soliciting help from teachers. One objective of the group service was to increase pupils' skills in relating to teachers and in seeking and using their help within the classroom. The negative change scores indicate that pupils in the experimental groups were perceived as becoming more dependent on teachers at the end of the year. In view of the objective, these particular scores should be considered differently from the other negative change scores.

School Conditions and Practices

It has been asserted that interaction between certain aspects of the school and characteristics of the pupils accounts for malperforming behavior. To clarify this relationship, three aspects of the school will be considered: grading practices, sanctioning procedures, and patterns of dropping out.

Grading Practices. Because so little change was observed in the grades received by pupils in the experimental, matched control, and random control groups over the period of a year, grading practices were examined more systematically. In two senior high schools—hereafter referred to as Industrial Heights and Academic Heights—the grades received by all pupils entering the tenth grade were studied over a three-year period until the pupils either graduated, transferred, or dropped out of school. Important, relevant findings emerged (Schafer and Olexa, 1971). First, grades were observed to be important determinants of location in the curriculum independent of factors such as IQ and reading scores. Second, when grades were analyzed with controls for curriculum location, it was found that at

TABLE 9. Change Scores Expressed as Differences between Treatment and Control Group Scores, by School and Dimension, 1963–1964

	School[a]							Total Negative Values	Total Positive Values
Dimension	A T–C[b]	B T–C	C T–C	D T–C	E T–C	F T–C	G T–C		
Classroom conduct	−0.135	0.528	0.224	−0.259	0.542	0.243	−0.250	3	4
Academic motivation and performance	0.136	0.095	0.200	−0.568	−0.404	0.262	0.850	2	5
Socioemotional state	0.170	0.260	0.292	0.498	0.600	0.340	1.310	0	7
Teacher dependence	−0.127	−0.085	−0.100	0.770	−0.028	0.214	1.260	5	2
Personal habits	0.055	0.105	−0.067	−0.256	0.230	0.033	0.820	2	5

[a] School key: A = senior high school, B = senior high school, C = junior high school, D = junior high school, E = elementary school, F = junior high school, G = elementary school.

[b] T–C = Treatment group score minus control group score.

both schools the distribution of course marks differed notably between college-preparatory and non-college-preparatory tracks (Table 10). Although the performance of pupils could not be measured apart from the grading practices of teachers, the data clearly suggest that differences in course marks are to some degree a result of different grading standards. In other words, if two pupils performed at the same level when measured objectively, their chances of receiving good grades would be different in the two tracks. Some of the differences in scholastic rewards might be thought to reflect underlying differences in reading skill. If this were the case, differences in achievement between curricula should decline similarly across reading skill levels—but, in fact, every comparison revealed that pupils in the non-college-preparatory curriculum fared less well than those with comparable reading skills in the college-preparatory curriculum.

It appears that there may be a universal grading scale in the high schools with an arbitrary devaluation of performance within the non-college-preparatory track. Since a large proportion of the malperformers were enrolled in the latter curriculum, the lack of any increase in their grades over time becomes more understandable. Pupils were aware of the differential opportunity patterns, and it is not unlikely that this knowledge affected their motivation to perform.

TABLE 10.   Distributions of Course Marks by School, IQ, and Curriculum

School, IQ,[a] and Curriculum	Course Marks						Number of Cases
	A	B	C	D	E	Total	
Industrial Heights							
High							
College-preparatory	20%	35	30	11	3	99%	(2102)
Non-college-preparatory	5	25	37	23	9	99	(363)
Low							
College-preparatory	3	19	39	29	10	100	(65)
Non-college-preparatory	2	13	34	40	10	99	(119)
Academic Heights							
High							
College-preparatory	27	35	28	8	2	100	(3553)
Non-college-preparatory	4	44	40	11	2	101	(166)
Low							
College-preparatory	7	25	43	19	5	99	(1946)
Non-college-preparatory	2	18	41	28	10	99	(1652)

[a] IQ cutting points are as follows: Industrial Heights, high, 109 and above, and low, 108 and below; Academic Heights, high, 109 and above, low, 108 and below.

Sanctioning Procedures. In addition to offering rewards and recognition to pupils for acceptable conduct or achievement, teaching personnel used a variety of negative sanctions to curb malperformance. Grades were, of course, the chief means for both reward and punishment. In the short run, poor grades serve as negative judgments, and in the long run they curtail pupils' future opportunities. Sanctions often went beyond grades. Pupils were frequently exposed to a kind of double (or even triple) penalty. Those who performed below a certain standard received adverse grades and, as a direct consequence, might also be denied a wide variety of privileges and opportunities in the school. Also, in several schools policies explicitly provided for the arbitrary reduction of grades for smoking violations, suspensions, and other forms of behavioral misconduct not directly associated with academic performance. Pupils incurring these sanctions lost esteem among most of their classmates, were seldom chosen for minor but prestigious classroom or school assignments, and were excluded from participation in certain extracurricular activities. This process, in turn, often subjected pupils to negative parental responses, representing a third penalty.

The linking of secondary rewards and sanctions to grades may result in far more than reinforcement of academic criteria, since it denies the poor performer legitimate alternative opportunities for recognition and success. His motivation to continue trying and his commitment to educational objectives are thereby jeopardized at the very time when additional supports may be needed to stimulate effort. In these situations the underachieving pupil receives little support for his efforts to improve, as continued failure subjects him to new deprivations. School personnel seldom indicated an awareness of the negative consequences that could result when grading practices and sanctions for behavioral misconduct were interrelated.

Patterns of Dropping Out. Perhaps the greatest determinant of adult role placement is whether or not a person graduates from high school; occupational and income ceilings are much lower for those who lack a high school diploma (Clark, 1962; Miller, 1960; Folger and Nam, 1964). Successful completion of high school is increasingly essential because of technological and bureaucratic demands in this society. Unfortunately many youths still leave school before they have completed the twelfth grade. And in this project the efforts of the social workers did not prevent several members of the target population from dropping out before graduation.

In both senior high schools dropouts tended to be disproportionately represented in the following categories: boys, Negroes, those from working-class families, pupils with lower IQ scores, those lower on reading test scores and in overall achievement, those with lower grade averages, and those in the general curriculum. The data in Table 11 report the percentage

TABLE 11.   Percentages Who Were Dropouts Among Various Categories
of Students

	Dropouts	
Category	Academic Heights	Industrial Heights
Sex		
Boys	17%	24%
Girls	9	22
Race		
Whites	13	19
Negroes	38	27
Social class (based on father's occupation)		
Upper-middle	5	7
Lower-middle	11	11
Upper-working	20	15
Lower-working	32	31
IQ (quartiles)		
1 (high)	3	5
2	3	10
3	13	21
4 (low)	26	43
Reading score (quartiles)		
1, 2 (high)	3	13
3	8	26
4 (low)	25	24
Overall grade point average (quartiles)		
1 (high)	0	5
2	3	6
3	5	24
4 (low)	41	63
Curriculum		
College-preparatory	4	5
General	35	47

of all pupils who were dropouts in each of these categories in the two
schools studied. Grade point average was the single factor most important
in predicting who would drop out and who would not. Forty-one percent
of the students at Academic Heights within the fourth quartile of the grade
point average dropped out, as did 63 percent in the same quartile at Indus-

trial Heights. Dropouts also tended to show greater decline and less improvement in grades than did graduates.

Several other studies have shown achievement to be associated positively with remaining in school until graduation. As one writer suggests, this is not difficult to understand: "It seems entirely reasonable that any normal person would seek to escape as soon as possible from any situation in which he persistently found himself branded as incompetent" (Hand, 1956).

SUMMARY AND CONCLUSIONS

The findings from this study and demonstration effort provide substantial support for the proposition that pupil malperformance is most usefully viewed as a consequence of adverse school-pupil interactions. Both intraschool and interschool variations were noted in teachers' perspectives, in group services, in curriculum placement patterns and outcomes, in grading practices, and in pupil careers. The findings further indicated that pupil careers are shaped in part by motivations, capabilities, and skills that are influenced by the opportunities and responses of the school through which class groups and particular individuals pass. The school itself may maintain and even generate the very malperformance it seeks to eliminate by offering limited opportunity for educational attainment for some pupils, by judging pupils adversely because of attributes that are independent from their actions, by undermining existing motivation through unwise use of control practices, and by making it exceedingly difficult for the pupil "to find his way back" once he has been labeled as a malperformer.

Many of the findings about organizational conditions and behavior were made subsequent to the intervention effort and, therefore, not available for use in it. Had they been available, much greater effort would have been directed toward modification of school policies and practices. As it was, the social workers tended to focus their major effort on providing group services to specified individuals. Limited positive results were thereby achieved. It is of interest, however, that since the formal conclusion of the project four of the five school systems have attempted to make organizational changes on the basis of the study findings.

As was indicated earlier, the design for this research and demonstration project provided for two series of conferences to be held periodically over a two-year period. One series was conducted with practitioners to review study procedures and to systematize their interventions as far as possible. In general, the response of the practitioners was extremely positive, and they participated actively in reviewing preliminary findings and in using this knowledge to modify existing procedures.

A second series of conferences was held with school administrators —principals, superintendents, directors of special education, and so forth. The object of this series was also to review the study findings with reference to their implications for school policy and program design. These sessions were far less successful. Many administrators were reluctant to accept the findings as valid and reliable and maintained strong ideological perspectives about the causes of pupil malperformance. These views inhibited acceptance of the notions that school conditions contributed to malperformance and that basic policies and conditions needed reexamination.

The use of these conferences as a strategy for inducing organizational change proved to be less potent and far more time-consuming than anticipated. However, after the conferences concluded, administrators in three of the five systems reinstituted contact with project staff members, who then provided some consultation about changes in school policies and procedures. In one community a new senior high school was designed with a primary concern that conditions for the pupil in the general curriculum be improved. Modifications have also been made in grading practices and policies governing the application of negative sanctions. Changes in staff assignments have resulted, with some of the more effective teachers being assigned to develop and teach courses in the general curriculum.

In a second community, utilization of the findings led to a demonstration project directed toward modifying the policies, rules, procedures, and practices that serve to identify and label pupils adversely or to reduce opportunities for certain pupils to participate successfully in the academic and social life of the school. A second objective was to provide an opportunity for pupils to participate in educational decision making, and a third was to redesign existing curricula in light of study findings. The third school system has modified explicit policies and procedures that adversely affect malperformers.

It is now apparent that effecting innovation and change in today's public school is a complex and difficult task requiring attention not only to attributes of individuals in the system but also, and perhaps more importantly, to the behavior of the school itself. Findings indicate that planned change can be effected, but that no single technique is likely to succeed unless it is addressed to the complexity of the total situation.

REFERENCES

CICOUREL, AARON AND JOHN I. KITSUSE
  1963—*The Educational Decision-Makers,* Indianapolis: Bobbs-Merrill.
CLARK, BURTON
  1962—*Educating the Expert Society,* San Francisco: Chandler Publishing Company.

COHEN, ALBERT H.
1966—*Deviance and Control*, Englewood Cliffs, New Jersey: Prentice-Hall.
ELDER, GLEN H.
1966—"The schooling of outsiders," *Sociology of Education*, 39 (Fall), pp. 324–343.
ERICKSON, KAI T.
1964—"Notes on the sociology of deviance," in Howard Becker (Ed.), *The Other Side*, New York: Free Press, pp. 9–22.
FOLGER, J. K. AND C. B. NAM
1964—"Trends in education to the occupational structure," *Sociology of Education*, 38 (Fall), pp. 19–33.
FREIDSON, ELIOT
1966—"Disability as social deviance," in Marvin Sussman (Ed.), *Sociology and Rehabilitation*, Washington: American Sociological Association, pp. 71–79.
HAND, H. H.
1956—"Who drops out of school?" in W. O. Stanley, et al. (Eds.), *Social Foundations of Education*, New York: Holt-Dryden, p. 236.
LEMERT, EDWIN
1967—"Legal commitment and social control," in *Human Deviance, Social Problems and Social Control*, Englewood Cliffs, New Jersey: Prentice-Hall, pp. 67–71.
MCCORKLE, LLOYD
1958—*The Highfields Story*, New York: Henry Holt.
MILLER, HERMAN P.
1960—"Annual income and life-time income in relation to education: 1939–1959," *American Economic Review*, 50 (December), pp. 962–986.
POLK, KENNETH AND LYNN RICHMOND
1966—"Those who fail," Eugene, Oregon: Lane County Youth Project. (Unpublished)
SARRI, ROSEMARY C., ROBERT D. VINTER, AND ESTHER GOODMAN
1965—"Group work in the schools: A practitioner's manual," Ann Arbor: The University of Michigan. (Unpublished)
SCHAFER, WALTER AND CAROL OLEXA
1971—*Tracking and Opportunity*, San Francisco: Chandler Publishing Company.
VINTER, ROBERT D., ROSEMARY C. SARRI, WALTER SCHAFER, AND DARREL VORWALLER
1966—*The Pupil Behavior Inventory: A Manual for Administration and Scoring*, Ann Arbor: Campus Publishers.

28.

Reinforcement and Estimation Procedures in a Child Development Program

ALAN N. CONNOR

Many lower-class children, black and white, fail in our school system, drop out, or if they complete high school do not attain sufficient educational qualifications to partake of the affluence of their community or contribute to its growth. Many of these youths fail to approach their intellectual and social potential partly because they do not exhibit the language or behaviors considered appropriate for the classroom by teachers and school administrators (Vinter and Sarri, 1966).

In recent years the terms "educationally disadvantaged" and "culturally deprived" have been used to categorize children and youth who have not been able to adapt academically and behaviorally to the classroom. Children who are supported by Aid to Families with Dependent Children (AFDC) grants are often so categorized. A number of preschool education programs have been established in many communities to compensate for the educational disadvantage to which poor children tend to be subject. Project Headstart has received nationwide attention and a substantial amount of criticism.

The Headstart program with which the author worked appeared to have considerable success in developing language, conceptual, and learning skills in children enrolled in the program. The criticism heard most often is that gains children have made in Headstart often are lost in kindergarten through fourth grade. This seems to be as much a criticism of the elementary school system as it is of Headstart.

No one has yet been able to explain satisfactorily why educational gains made by children in Headstart programs are lost in the early elementary grades. My hypothesis is that children in many Headstart programs benefit intellectually from the program, but do not learn to use social behaviors which are considered appropriate in a classroom setting. Nor do they cease to use certain acquired behaviors in the classroom which are appropriate elsewhere. Consequently these children are not accorded the opportunities given other children to use their acquired knowledge and skills. Interaction between child and teacher tends to be nonrewarding for both (Vinter and Sarri, 1966; Cohen, 1966:341–344). The teacher, frustrated by the pupil's behavior, lowers his grade, scolds him before the class, sends him to the principal's office, etc. The pupil perceives that he is being punished and humiliated for educational effort; motivation to achieve is diminished and perhaps eliminated altogether. To be sure, "inappropriate" classroom behavior probably is not the only factor involved in the failure or underachievement of some of these children. They may not receive much incentive from home, their refusal to perform in school may be reinforced by their peers, etc.

CHILD DEVELOPMENT PROGRAM

Under the aegis of the Michigan Department of Social Services in Genesee County, an exploratory child development program was established in 1968. The program was situated in the Atherton East Public Housing Project because most of the families in residence were clients of the Department; many of their children were categorized as "educationally" or "culturally disadvantaged."

A Headstart program was also established at Atherton East. The child development program, concerned with social learning, was intended to supplement or complement Headstart, which was primarily concerned with intellectual learning. It was hoped that the development of classroom adaptive behaviors would prevent or reduce the loss of gains made by children in Headstart, reduce the probability of failure or underachievement later in their school careers, and break the welfare career cycle of some of the families, thus reducing "welfare rolls" in the distant future. There was no interest in teaching these children to conform to classroom norms merely to avoid trouble. Primary interest was in their learning to discriminate between situations and occasions and to determine when particular behaviors were appropriate and useful and when they were not. Fighting in response to being called an uncomplimentary name may be adaptive in the street; but in the classroom fighting in response to any stimulus is maladaptive. Calling others uncomplimentary names in the classroom is maladaptive, if one gets caught. By learning to make such determinations and perform behaviors in the classroom which are approved by teachers and administrators, these children would be more likely to be accorded the opportunity to use the knowledge and learning skills acquired in Headstart throughout their educational careers.

The child development program was staffed by two graduate students in Social Group Work at The University of Michigan School of Social Work. Each worked one day per week with the same group of eight to ten children. They were assigned to the child development program as part of field instruction and were supervised by a member of the faculty of the School of Social Work.

Method

Before selecting specific children for the program, the group workers and the field instructor discussed children's classroom behaviors with the Headstart teachers. They also observed the children in the Headstart classroom, for a total of eight classroom sessions. After each observed classroom session, the teachers, the workers and, on two occasions, the field instructor identified and defined behaviors that were—or might become—inappropriate or maladaptive in a school classroom. In this way all behaviors were defined in the same terms so that teachers and workers would deal with the same behaviors and the same children in consistent and nearly identical ways.

The next step was home visits. The worker explained the purpose of the child development group to the mothers of the children who were thought to need it most, and the mothers' approval was sought for including their children in the group. The worker explained that the group was a supplement to the Headstart program and another way to help their children get a good start in school and discussed the methods to be used in the group. Each mother was asked what she thought about her child's behavior and often she described difficulties she had in disciplining and controlling her child or children at home. Some mothers asked the workers for advice about how to change behaviors of their children and eventually used the behavioral modification techniques described by the workers. All those visited wanted their children included in the group.

The fourth step in the process consisted of diagnostic groups in which interaction between the children was observed. The workers intervened only to prevent a child from getting hurt in these sessions. They made no attempt to change behavioral repertoires.

Behavioral Sets

For each child a maladaptive and an adaptive set of behaviors was defined. In the Headstart classroom observations and the diagnostic group sessions, the worker also attempted to determine the stimulus which preceded, or triggered, a particular behavior and the reinforcer which followed it. Sometimes the situation itself was the stimulus. It was not possible in every instance to identify the antecedent stimulus. Behavioral acts are not always triggered by stimuli that immediately precede them. Reinforcements or rewards were easier to identify, since they usually follow the act immediately and are contingent upon it.

An example observed in a group session follows:

Mark was surrounded by a number of toy cars and trucks. Steven had none. Mark was not, at the moment, playing with all the toys around him. Steven, without staying anything, started pushing one of the trucks around the floor. Mark grabbed it, put it down, and returned to the two he had been playing with. Steven grabbed the same truck he had pushed around before and another one, and started to go to another part of the room. Mark went after Steven, tried to take the two toys back, but Steven would not give them up. Mark began to shout at Steven and hit him. Steven hit back with a truck.

This incident can be analyzed from two perspectives: first the appropriateness of the behavior for the classroom and, second, the stimulus-response sequence.

Appropriateness. The behaviors observed are not unusual for four- to five-year-old boys irrespective of socioeconomic class. Nevertheless, they are not considered appropriate to the classroom. In Headstart such behaviors are more tolerable than in subsequent grades, especially if they occur during the scheduled free play period.

Mark was monopolizing the toys, whether he was actually playing with them or not. Sharing is the norm society tries to imbue in children and is a norm valued by teachers and school administrators.

Steven took toys from Mark without asking. Such behavior would not be considered appropriate in the classroom and is generally inconsistent with societal norms and values.

Fighting or hitting others is definitely considered inappropriate in the classroom, although protecting one's possessions—even temporary possessions—and retaliating when attacked are behaviors valued by our society. Mark's hitting behavior could be construed as protecting possessions and Steven's hitting back as self-defense or retaliation. However, these behaviors are not tolerated in the classroom irrespective of their acceptance elsewhere.

Stimulus-response sequence. To some extent, speculation must be made about what stimulated Steven's initial behavior. Tentative inference might be made that Steven perceived, correctly, that Mark had many toys while he had none, and that Steven wanted a toy, thus the taking-without-asking response. Further speculation is unnecessary.

Steven's taking without asking stimulated Mark to take back without asking, which in turn triggered Steven to take two toys without asking. The chain continued until the fight resulted.

What triggered Mark's hoarding or monopolizing toys is not known, and speculation about social and environmental influence at home is not profitable at this point. Mark was larger and stronger than most of his peers and usually successful in protecting his possessions by fighting; thus it can be inferred that previous successes had reinforced his monopolizing. As a consequences of such behavior, he was able to play with toys he desired and obtained deference from his peers.

Listed below are the sets of behavior defined for Steven and Mark.

Maladaptive Behaviors to be Decreased	*Adaptive Behaviors to be Increased and Developed*
Steven:	
1. Takes toys from peers without asking.	1. Ask, or negotiate with peers for toys.
2. Hits peers.	2. Reinforce peers who share with him (say "thank you" or exchange objects, etc.)
3. Destroys toys.	3. Put away toy or show it to adult.
Mark:	
1. Monopolizes toys, crayons, clay, etc.	1. Share toys, crayons, clay, etc.
2. Hits peers.	2. Show cooperative verbal behavior with peers.
3. Calls peers insulting names.	

Negotiation and cooperation require a set or series of behaviors which could be highly complex or relatively simple. Labor-management negotiating is quite complex; no attempt should be made to teach such complexity to four- to five-year-old children. However, certain negotiating behaviors are not beyond their capacities—i.e., asking for something, offering to trade off, proposing a simple compromise, etc.

Below is an example of a program one group worker, Mark and Steven used to change the behaviors described in the incident above:

Step 1

   A. Stop the fight by separating the boys. Worker takes the toys they are fighting about.
   B. Tell Mark to return to the other toys he was playing with.
   C. Ask Steven to come with her to her office. Worker and Steven go to office with the two toys.

Step 2

A. Explain to Steven what is expected of him in the future when such situations occur during group sessions and in school.
   1. Ask for a toy.
   2. If Mark or other person shares, smile and tell him "thank you."
   3. If he refuses to share, suggest:
      a. "Let me play with it until you need it," if he is not actually playing with it at the time.
      b. "Let's play together with all the toys."
      c. "Let me have it in five minutes because you will be through with it by then."
B. Tell Steven she will give him an animal cracker the first time he behaves as expected with Mark.

Step 3

Demonstrate Step 2 with worker playing Steven's role and Steven playing Mark's role.

Step 4

A. Have Steven rehearse his own role with worker playing Mark's role.
B. Reinforce role performances in rehearsal as they more closely approximate expected performances, with smiles, pats on the back, and verbal approval. Final rehearsed performance is reinforced with animal cracker because it has satisfactorily approximated expectations.

Step 5

A. Behavioral assignment: Perform with Mark as rehearsed after worker finishes talking to Steven.
B. Remind Steven he will receive animal cracker if he performs assignment as expected.

Step 6

A. Worker explains expectations to Mark.
   1. "When toys are around you and you are not actually playing with them you are expected to let another child play with one or two of them if he asks."
   2. "If you have been playing with a toy a long time, 15–20 minutes or more, and someone else has been asking for it, you are to let them have it after five more minutes and you can do something else."

    B. Tell Mark that next time he does either of the above you will give him some M&M's (he does not like animal crackers).

Step 7

    A. Rehearse Step 6 as was done in Step 4 with Steven.

    B. Reinforce rehearsed performances as was done in Step 4 with Steven.

Step 8

    A. Behavioral assignment: Perform as rehearsed next time Steven asks for a toy.

    B. Remind Mark that he will be given some more M&M's if he performs the assignment as expected.

After four weeks' planned intervention the worker reported consistent and measurable reduction in maladaptive behavior. Increases in adaptive behavior occurred more slowly and required active support by the worker. The developmental level of the boys was one reason for slower manifestation of adaptive behavior without adult inducement. These boys had not developed the ability to function interdependently in a group, and the latter was necessary for consistency in some of the desired adaptive behaviors.

One of the group workers used behavioral modification techniques with Mona, Phyllis, and Thelma. His objective was to increase the rate that each used behaviors which would be useful to them.

In the particular activity described below, increase in listening behavior was not a specified goal, although it might have been incidentally approached. For Phyllis and Thelma, increased asking, negotiating, and sharing were specified goals. For Mona, increased playing with peers was a specified goal. Playing, like negotiating, could include a variety of behaviors and performances. The worker was not concerned with defining specific playing behaviors. The children themselves would do this implicitly. Neither was the worker's goal for Mona that of converting her to a highly gregarious person. Rather his goal was to give her the opportunity to develop social skills that permit her to perform with a degree of competence in a group situation. The stimulus or set of stimuli which set the conditions for Mona's need to withdraw from peer interaction and which depressed performance frequency in a peer group situation could not be isolated. Her teacher and workers observed that such a group situation had become a condition in which behavior was depressed. In fact nonbehavior was Mona's norm under such conditions. The teacher thought such nonbehavior in the classroom could result in underrating Mona's academic capability in the future.

Maladaptive Behaviors to be Decreased	Adaptive Behaviors to be Increased and Developed
Phyllis:	
1. Takes objects from peers without asking.	1. Ask, or negotiate with peers for objects.
2. Monopolizes toys, chairs, etc.	2. Share objects with peers.
3. Calls peers derogatory names.	3. Reinforce peers for sharing.
4. Interrupts peers when they are talking.	4. Listen to peers.
Mona:	
1. Withdraws from peers.	1. Play with peers.
2. Remains mute when adult addresses group she is in.	2. Answer questions addressed to group.
Thelma:	
1. Commands peers.	1. Ask peers to cooperate or to give objects, or negotiate for cooperation and objects.
2. Takes objects from peers.	2. Share objects.
3. Monopolizes objects.	3. Reinforce cooperation and sharing by peers.
4. Calls peers derogatory names.	
5. Defies adult requests.	

In group sessions the worker observed that Phyllis and Thelma enjoyed playing house. They would set the small wrestling mats (30 by 60 inches) on edge making various rooms. Verbal interaction between the two girls ensued. However, this interaction primarily consisted of Thelma giving commands and Phyllis rejecting or acceding to them, with verbal rejection increasing. Mona would sometimes play with a doll in the house, but did not interact with either of the other two girls and they ignored her. Usually Mona watched from a distance or stared off into space and sucked her thumb.

At one group meeting, the worker made dolls available to the three girls but did not make the mats available. He explained that he expected the three of them to play together for 15 minutes without taking things from each other or telling one another what to do and what not to do. Rather they were to ask for things from each other and share with one another. These expectations were explained to each girl individually and to all three as a group. No behavioral demonstration or rehearsal was used. They were told that after meeting these expectations they could play house with the mats.

Each girl took a doll and played with it independently. Phyllis and Thelma played in close proximity to each other but did not interact. Mona withdrew from them in physical distance so that interaction for her was not possible.

Thelma soon asked (five minutes) if they could play house. The worker explained that they had not played together yet and would have to do that first. He suggested that Thelma and Phyllis go over to Mona and ask her to play with them. They went over, but were too embarrassed to ask her to play with them. The worker asked Mona to play with the other girls, but she shook her head negatively. Phyllis and Thelma played alongside Mona and occasionally spoke to her. She responded verbally, but did not join them in play. After five minutes, the worker joined the girls and encouraged Mona to enter into some joint activities with Phyllis and Thelma. After three minutes of minimal interaction he reinforced each girl with a small piece of candy and helped them set up the mats to play house. The worker was coaching Mona and trying to shape playing together behavior.

In scheduling playing house after playing together in some other activity or set of activities, the worker was adapting Premack's Principles to this group situation. According to Dr. David Premack if there is a differential probability that a person will perform a pair of responses, the more probable response will reinforce the less probable. Thus, the worker made the more probable response, playing house, contingent upon the less probable, playing together.

The following two group meetings were programmed similarly to the one described before. Playing together behavior of the three girls increased in frequency (i.e., number of occasions and length of time periods). However, there were still times when Mona preferred to be alone. This desire was respected and accepted. No further overt encouragement was given to her to play together with the other children, except that she was intermittently reinforced socially, i.e., verbal approval, compliments, pat on shoulder, and attention from adult, when she participated with a group. The other children also intermittently reinforced participating behavior by showing pleasure when she joined them in some activity. She received no reinforcement from them or the worker when she withdrew from participation. Neither was she presented with any aversive stimulus at such times.

CONCLUSIONS

A number of tentative conclusions were reached which are more appropriately considered hypotheses and all of which need further empirical testing.

1. Systematic reinforcement and extinction procedures can modify

behavior of four- to five-year-old children and teach them to discriminate between situations and stimuli so that they can appropriately use different behaviors in different environments.

2. Most children aged four or older can understand verbalized behavioral expectations if time is taken to explicate them in simple terms and if they are not overwhelmed with a multitude of expectations at once. It may be useful not only to test this but also to know how best to explicate behavioral expectations to young children, what degree of complexity they can usually understand, and what quantity of explanations they are likely to take before being overwhelmed and confused.

A corollary might be that unless behavioral expectations are explicitly defined for children, the probability is low that they will behave as adults expect. This too needs to be tested, although literature alludes to this likelihood (Bayley and Schaefer, 1960:155–173; Kamii and Radin, 1967: 302–310; Radin and Kamii, 1965:138–146).

3. A group situation is an effective means and context for reinforcement and extinction procedures, because members learn to use them with each other and make them part of their behavioral repertoires, i.e., they form a "reinforcing and extinction community." These procedures also can be used by members in their environment beyond the group and thus become useful social skills.

4. Effective use of "social reinforcers" increases interpersonal attraction between the reinforced and the reinforcing person(s) so that interpersonal interaction itself becomes intrinsically reinforcing to both parties. If the above is true, and experience bore it out, the common contention (Bruck, 1968) that behavioral modification techniques are necessarily "impersonal pushbutton therapy" is only a contention.

Further research is necessary to trace the progress of children who have participated in programs such as the one described here. It is still not determined whether the behaviors and social skills developed for use in the classroom will persist throughout their educational careers and can be useful in reducing academic failure, underachievement and dropping out. Precise behavioral stimulus and reinforcement baselines need to be developed so that measurement of change can be more accurate and subject to statistical tests.

One program objective was to involve parents in the group process so they could learn to apply reinforcement and extinction procedures in a planned way with their children at home. Very limited progress was made in involving them. Ways to stimulate parental involvement need to be developed. Devices for reinforcing and shaping such parental behavior need research (e.g., Radin and Wittes, Chapter 26 in this volume). When parents can be involved, the persistence and effectiveness of their use of reinforcement and extinction techniques need to be measured.

REFERENCES

BAYLEY, NANCY AND EARL S. SCHAEFER
1964—*Correlations of Maternal and Child Behavior with the Development of Mental Abilities,* Berkeley Growth Study, 29, 6 (Serial 97), Berkeley: Society for Research in Child Development (Mimeographed).

COHEN, ALBERT K.
1966—"School and settlement house," in Herman Stein and Richard Cloward (Eds.), *Social Perspectives of Behavior,* New York: Free Press, pp. 341–344.

KAMII, CONSTANCE K. AND NORMA RADIN
1967—"Class differences in the socialization practices of the negro mother," *Journal of Marriage and the Family,* 29, 2 (May), pp. 302–310.

MAX, BRUCK
1968—"Behavior modification, theory and practice: A critical review," *Social Work,* Volume 13, 2 (April), pp. 43–55.

RADIN, NORMA AND CONSTANCE K. KAMII
1965—"The child-rearing attitude of disadvantaged negro mothers and some educational implications," *Journal of Negro Education,* Spring, pp. 138–146.

VINTER, ROBERT D. AND ROSEMARY C. SARRI
1966—*Research Report to the Ann Arbor Board of Education,* Ann Arbor: The University of Michigan School of Social Work (Mimeographed).

29.

Group Treatment of Alcoholics

EDWIN J. THOMAS and PAUL V. SOREN

An experimental group after-care service for alcoholics was established provisionally in 1967 as an adjunct to an ongoing treatment program of a psychiatric hospital: Scalebor Park Hospital, Yorkshire, England. Data were collected to provide the basis for a limited description and evaluation of the service for the benefit of practitioners who desired more knowledge about group methods, professionals in psychiatric hospitals who were considering the establishment of an after-care service using group methods, and researchers who sought to understand the effectiveness of this type of social group work.

THE AFTER-CARE SERVICE

Background and Context

At the time of the study, Scalebor Park Hospital had an eleven-bed Alcoholic Unit that had been functioning for over four years. The unit was staffed by a consultant psychiatrist, a social group worker and two nurses. The unit's central treatment was through insight-oriented group therapy, combined with drugs, such as antabuse. The average length of stay on the unit was from six to eight weeks.

This chapter is a revised version of an article previously published: Paul V. Soren and Edwin J. Thomas, "An Experiment in Group After-care for Alcoholics," *The Journal of Alcoholism,* V (Summer 1970), 48–58. Soren was the social group worker primarily responsible for the design, planning and conduct of the program. Thomas served mainly as a consultant in research and social psychological processes, during his tenure as Visiting Professor of Applied Social Studies and Senior Fulbright Lecturer, Schools of Applied Social Studies, Bradford University, 1967–1968.

The authors are indebted to Dr. P. M. J. O'Brien and the staff associated with the alcoholic unit for valuable support, advice and encouragement and to Mrs. Jean Nursten, Senior Lecturer in the Schools of Applied Social Studies of Bradford University, for her help in making the study possible.

After-care included a monthly "reunion" led by the consultant psychiatrist and periodic follow-up visits by mental welfare officers from nearby cities. As an adjunct to the existing service, in the autumn of 1967, the staff of the Alcoholic Unit established the group after-care program to be conducted and guided by the social group worker. The group was started with former patients from the unit and meetings were held each week, except when the monthly reunion was held. The reunion was in a large hall away from the hospital in Leeds, where discussions could take place, food and refreshments be prepared, and interviews held in adjoining rooms.

Objectives

The therapeutic objectives of the group were essentially extensions of those held for the members when they were patients: the group was intended to help members remain sober and group sessions were oriented primarily toward developing insight into the drinking behavior of participants. A portion of each session was devoted to a social objective. All members understood that the group program was part of an exploratory study and that the program itself was provisional.

Treatment Background

The study sample was composed of thirty clients.[1] At the beginning of the study period, the after-care group was composed of nine outpatients. The remaining twenty-one clients were discharged from the Alcoholic Unit at various intervals following the inception of the program. Sixteen of the clients had been admitted to the Alcoholic Unit on only one occasion, nine had been admitted twice, and five had been admitted more than twice. Slightly over half of the sample had received some other assistance for alcoholism, such as medication or psychotherapy, or were members of Alcoholics Anonymous.

Personal Background Characteristics

Twenty-eight clients were male and two were female. Their ages ranged from 23 to 56, with fourteen clients over 40 years. Twenty-four clients were married and of these, sixteen had spouses who attended the group. Of those not married, four were separated, one widowed, and one

---

[1] This thirty did not include spouses of alcoholics or an additional 15 expatients who joined the group after the termination of the study period.

single. The majority of the married clients lived with their wives and families. The socioeconomic background of those clients in the sample included six in Class II, sixteen in Class III, and three in Classes IV and V respectively.[2]

Program

The major portion of each meeting was spent in a structured discussion, usually lasting one hour. The clients filled out a weekly monitoring questionnaire during the short silent interval which immediately preceded the discussion. Informal conversation took place before and after the discussion. Tea and biscuits were served by spouses who were present. Meetings lasted one hour and a half.

The topic and content of a typical discussion for one session are illustrated in the following example.

Consistent with the theme of working toward insight, the worker asked each group member to report on the conditions that tempted him to drink. The purpose was to prepare and display a list of situations associated with drinking.

The following points were enumerated:

a. *Familial.* Spouse gives alcoholic partner an inadequate allowance; alcoholic's spouse unable to understand that alcoholism is a relapsing illness; family members suspicious and lack trust; interference by relatives; spouse compares the alcoholic with other family members; alcoholic ostracized by family, psychological impotence; arguments with spouse; and lack of social skills.

b. *Social.* Too much or too little money; loneliness, no ideological base, such as that of A.A.; stigma of being an alcoholic; desire to visit friends and play games at pubs; company of women; seasonal festivities; occupation, e.g., building trade, shipping; cultural expectations; and need to uphold former reputation as a heavy drinker.

c. *Personal.* Feeling aggressive or hostile; lack of rewarding nondrinking behavior; depression; elation; loss of confidence; and incipient inebriation.

During the course of the meeting the worker found it necessary to structure only the first half of the meeting, after which the discussion proceeded freely. By expressing and enumerating temptations to

[2] General Register Office, "Classification of Occupations 1966," London: Her Majesty's Stationery Office (1966), pp. 130–137. Information was not available to classify two clients.

drink, many group members were able to learn more about the conditions that could cause them to relapse.

Topics considered by the group during the study period included coping with seasonal drinking, reasons for admission to the Alcoholic Unit, goal setting on a daily basis, the role of insight, handling of employment interviews, effects of sobriety, the use of free time, the meaning of treatment for alcoholism, the results of social drinking, the effects of a slip, and the importance of maintaining continuity in treatment.

Two sessions, one after the seventh week and one after the fifteenth week, were set aside for social evenings during which the clients were responsible for the evening's program. Most of the activities were structured and food was provided by representatives of the group with funds that had accumulated from a collection made at the end of each meeting.

Role of Worker

Each session was begun by the worker who first asked each member to tell the other group members his name. Then the worker asked the group whether anyone had any problems he might like to share with the others. After this the worker presented a topic, such as that given in the example, for the group's consideration.

By adopting the role of a permissive discussion leader, the worker was able to guide the conversation and draw out the more reticent members. The provision of support in general and of approval for appropriate nondrinking behavior was significant throughout. Disapproval was rarely used. In keeping with the focus of the development of insight, the worker would engage in interpretation when this seemed appropriate. Some individual work was also engaged in and is reviewed below.

One of the charge nurses attended most of the sessions and sometimes the local mental welfare officer joined as well.[3]

Role of Client

Expectations of participants were implicit, not explicit and formal. For example, it was expected that members were to attend meetings, support fellow group members, cooperate in the activities of the group, assume the role as a former patient, and stay sober.

The role of the spouse was largely to be a passive observer during discussions and to assist in preparing tea and in serving tea and biscuits.

[3] A local mental welfare officer in England corresponds to a community psychiatric social worker in the United States.

Services to Individuals

Intensive individual services were not planned as part of the program, although some individual attention was necessarily given to many of the members. This generally took the form of individual interviews prior to and after meetings, telephone calls, letters, and occasional home contacts. In addition, intensive individual treatment was planned for one client as part of the study to learn more about combining group care with individual treatment.[4]

GROUP PROCESS AND STRUCTURE

Participation and Communication

When the group was new and in the early stages of discussion at each session, the influence of leader-guided interaction was most apparent, i.e., the communication of most members was directed to the worker and member-to-member interaction was not vigorous. In the later phases of most sessions, especially after the group had been established for a while, clients contributed more actively and addressed one another more freely. In general, approximately one-quarter of the sample participated actively in discussions; the remaining members were moderate or low contributors. Although the discussion content involved various matters of general interest, the subject of alcoholism and the ideology of alcoholism was central.

The Status Structure

Active contributors tended to have higher status in the group and it also appeared that individuals with high socioeconomic status were the most active contributors to the discussions. Participants who had remained abstinent the longest tended to have more prestige than the others but were not always the most active participants.

---

[4] A contract was established to work with one of the group members who had been drinking heavily after his release from the hospital and who had attended a few of the group meetings. The objective was to help the client pay off outstanding debts and to learn to drink moderately. Visits and behavioral assignments were made by the worker on a weekly basis for a period of eight weeks. Each meeting with the client included his spouse and the client was encouraged by the worker to attend the group meetings on a regular basis. The client managed to pay off his debts and to drink moderately on weekends; but, finally, the treatment contract was broken and the patient resumed his former drinking patterns and failed to pay his debts as arranged. The modest, temporary progress was achieved with the investment of approximately 20 hours of worker time.

Selected Roles

The role of observer was perhaps most prevalent; most of the time most members were looking at and listening to others. The role of participant was important also and tended to be specialized. For example, many clients took the role of therapist's helper and gave advice and support to less experienced alcoholics; others took such roles as confessor, notorious drinker, friend, and joker.

The Ideology of Alcoholism

A common base of experience for all members was, of course, being an alcoholic. In addition, their prior tenure on the Alcoholic Unit had exposed the patients to a therapeutic philosophy that was partly indigenous to the therapeutic culture of the Unit and partly sustained by outside influences, such as the dogma of Alcoholics Anonymous. This philosophy was identified as the "ideology of alcoholism"; it was the central norm system for the group. Among the tenets of this ideology are the belief that alcoholism is a disease, that once one is an alcoholic one is always an alcoholic, that total abstinence (not moderation) is the ideal state to achieve, that alcoholics have suffered, that they must reach their own "rock bottom" before improving, that they must avoid all temptations to drink, that alcoholics cannot stop after having had the first drink, that there is no problem that drink won't make worse, and that drinking represents an escape from responsibility. The themes were repeatedly reiterated and affirmed; and rarely if ever did anyone disagree. It would seem that if all members had actually accepted these principles there would have been little reason for such repeated emphasis.

Attendance

Over the thirteen sessions of the study period, one-third of the sample attended from eight to thirteen sessions, one-third from four to seven sessions, and one-third from one to three sessions.

The Visible Progress Chart and Social Comparisons

Group members maintained a visible progress chart, a graph which recorded the progress of each member. The chart was updated at each meeting. The mere fact of attending the meeting tended to signify sobriety; virtually all members were sober at meetings and continued absence from the meetings was generally indicative of relapse. Such apparent progress in remaining sober was confirmed or disproved by the demeanor, participation and testimony of each member. For example, some confessed to having slipped recently, the appearance of others betrayed their drinking habits, those who had been conspicuously successful in maintaining abstinence very often made this a basis of expertise. In such ways, attendance seemed to celebrate sobriety, if indeed there was abstinence, or to mark publicly one's progress toward sobriety.

The effects of such modeling of abstinence or the lack of it were most certainly an important influence upon group members. However, predicting the consequences of modeling can be difficult. The sobriety of a respected or idealized member may be sanguine for many members; retrogression of such a member may have a negative modeling effect. But the processes of comparison can be subtle too. Thus the backsliding of a low-status member may serve as an incentive to the alcoholic, as can the retrogression of the high-status member who is heartily disliked by the observer. These are but a few of the many, complex comparisons that may occur at each meeting. Comparison processes are largely covert and not visible to the worker. Furthermore, neither the visible progress of members, as reflected in the "chart" referred to above, nor the comparison processes and the associated subjective reactions are readily accessible to the worker's control. To the extent that such comparisons mediate powerful modeling and identification, an important locus of beneficial and adverse effects remains variable and indeterminate.

QUESTIONNAIRE FINDINGS

Descriptive and evaluative information was collected by two different questionnaires. The first inventory was administered to each participant when he attended his first session. The questions covered basic background information (e.g., age, sex, marital status), current and past drinking patterns, and areas of problem (e.g., nervousness, marital, employment).[5] The second questionnaire, given each member at the beginning of all meetings after the first one, dealt with daily drinking behavior for the past week and areas in which present problems could be acknowledged. This latter questionnaire was intended to provide information by which the worker could more accurately monitor the progress of each client.

Initial Problems of Participants

Tabulation of the problems indicated on the first questionnaire provided a rough indication of the spectrum of problems the clients had fol-

[5] Copies of both questionnaires may be obtained by writing P. Soren, Department of Psychiatry, McMaster University, Hamilton, Ontario, Canada.

lowing hospital treatment for alcoholism. Twenty-five individuals indicated that they were bothered by nervousness; over half reported domestic difficulties; and slightly over half reported financial difficulties; one-third reported sexual problems (primarily psychological impotence); eleven reported difficulties with their spouse; twelve indicated that they had difficulties with their in-laws (primarily the mother-in-law); and about three-fifths indicated that they were unemployed at the commencement of the study period.

Drinking Patterns

The majority of the clients (20) attending the group did not have occasion to relapse, six reported at least five or more relapses, and the remaining four clients relapsed, but no more than five times.

Changes in Problems

During the course of the study period, a number of group members got jobs. A comparison of the proportion of clients employed at the beginning and end of the study yielded a statistically significant difference.[6] There were no other changes in problems acknowledged on the initial questionnaires.

Continuance

For any means of help that presupposes client-worker contact, continuance is a necessary but not sufficient condition for improvement. Maintenance of contact is particularly challenging in an open setting, especially for alcoholics. Special attention in the analysis was therefore given to an appraisal of correlates of client continuance. An attendance index was constructed on the basis of the number and proportion of sessions attended by each client.[7] Scores on this index were then related to a number of other variables, first by inspection of relationships and, if appropriate, by statistical test.

---

[6] The difference between the two proportions yielded a z score of 3.32 ($p < .005$).

[7] The categories of the distribution of the number of sessions attended was 1–3 (Low), 4–7 (Medium) and 8–13 (High); the categories of the percentage of meetings attended was 0–50% (Low), 51–84% (Medium), and 85–100% (High). The nine categories, going from the highest to the lowest along with the number of clients for each, were Hh(6), Hm(4), Mh(1), Mm(6), Hl(0), Lh(3), Ml(3), Lm(0), and Ll(7). The numerical values assigned to the order of categories were 9 for Hh to 1 for Ll, and each individual received as his score on the attendance index the value of the category into which he was thus classified.

The most noteworthy outcome was the near absence of correlates. There was no relationship found between the attendance index and sex, age, marital status, residency pattern, socioeconomic status, attendance at group meetings by spouse, kinds of problems acknowledged, periodicity of slips, kinds of assistance received other than hospital treatment, expectations of the group after-care service, and conditions acknowledged as affecting temptations to drink. Although there appeared to be an indication that high attenders had had more admissions to the Alcoholic Unit than low attenders and that high attenders were inclined to participate in nonsedentary free-time activities to a greater extent than low attenders, neither of these relationships was statistically significant. One statistically reliable relationship was found between attendance and the number of problems acknowledged at the beginning of the study. Long-term attenders tended to have more problems than did low attenders upon initial contact with the group (Spearman's rho = .87, $p < .0001$).

Readmissions

Over a period of eight months, three members of the original sample required readmission to the hospital for further treatment of alcoholism.

EVALUATION

As a provisional service offered in connection with a limited study of its feasibility and effectiveness, the project can be considered a success. Clients and unit staff valued the after-care service and it was continued under the guidance of others following the termination of the study. The weekly questionnaire to monitor the status of drinking and current problems was a useful adjunct to practice, but the data were probably less valid than ideally desirable. The limited qualitative and quantitative results do not establish the effectiveness of the program because of the lack of control groups and of adequate norms for comparison. (Reviews of literature have indicated that after-care programs for alcoholics are uncommon, that group after-care programs are rare indeed, and that there are no data on outcome of programs, such as the one described here, to which valid comparisons may be made.)

All information obtained here was at least encouraging, since no adverse effects were observed. Attendance was sufficient to maintain the program, friendships were established, social objectives were met and, although it is difficult to be certain, many of the participants seemingly were helped to remain abstinent and to cope more effectively with other problems.

Several constraints and limitations inherent in the experimental service from its inception have become apparent. At the same time, the therapeutic potentialities of such a program have become even more evident. Some of the difficulties encountered are not peculiar to group methods. Lack of continuance, for example, is characteristic of voluntary service in most open settings. Attendance was far from perfect and, in many cases, sporadic or exceedingly low. It is clear that if attendance is to be improved, special inducements, such as increasing the attractiveness of the social portion of the program or more powerful incentives, may have to be provided.

Still other difficulties were associated with the relatively limited resources and time that were devoted to providing social services to the clients, most of whom had acknowledged a relatively large number of problems. Although it is difficult to estimate the time and manpower required to provide the intensive and prompt work needed in such cases, it is clear that the need greatly exceeded the service capability in this project.

The Inadequacy of Norms

Other problems were related specifically to alcoholism itself and its relative intractability. In this treatment context, the ideology of alcoholism was to some extent a constraining factor. Some of the tenets of the ideology of alcoholism are ill-founded, misleading, or irrelevant to the principal norms that a group leader might wish to establish for such an after-care service. For example, the idea that alcoholism is a disease calls to mind the medical model and suggests that conditions which are in fact potentially subject to client and environmental control may be disavowed or abrogated. The idea that total abstinence is a necessity for alcoholics—while indeed a laudable ideal—is an extremely difficult behavioral objective. Without special training procedures and more effective treatment programs, the standard of complete abstinence is unrealistic; for many alcoholics it is too difficult to attain. Controlled drinking does occur with alcoholics. There is every reason to believe that if programs to reduce drinking behavior were so oriented, many individuals could be trained to drink moderately just as most of the population has been trained to do (Gerard and Saenger, 1966). The ideology of alcoholism is more dysfunctional than useful to facilitate abstinence or moderate drinking.

For group programs, a preferable alternative normative system could be evolved by the worker to correspond with his treatment objectives. There are many alternative sets of treatment norms that could serve the worker's particular ends; although no one is necessarily the best. However, the definition of alternative norms should be based upon a behavioral and social model of problem behavior, rather than on a medical and disease conception; the objective of moderation in addition to or instead of complete abstinence and the importance of self- and environmental control techniques in achieving the moderation of drinking should be adopted.

The Group as Means and Context of Treatment

Problems were observed that seemed to be directly related to the group medium itself. As long as there is a turnover of membership and less than perfect attendance, there is a consequent lack of continuity in the group's program which clearly prohibits the use of long-term, sequentially ordered treatment activities.

In the particular program employed here, the group was subject to additional difficulties. The participants were very heterogeneous; aside from their former status as alcoholic patients, they had little in common. Because the discussion was leader-centered, this group program did not exploit as fully as might be desirable the therapeutic potential of fellow group members. The abilities of group members to reinforce, punish and cue the behavior of their fellows was harnessed more in behalf of developing adherence to the various tenets of the ideology of alcoholism than to addressing particular drinking difficulties of individuals or other problems that they may have had.

The group, as a potentially powerful means and context for altering behavior, was in no way fully exploited. The therapeutic orientation was predominantly directed toward achieving insight for the participants. The desired behavior to be displayed by members was primarily that of uttering the right words, not displaying appropriate behavior outside the group; action did not take precedence over talking. Even when insight was achieved, little or nothing was done about assuring that demonstrating insight in fact resulted in other desirable behaviors. Refraining from drinking may or may be not facilitated by what is called insight; like other behavioral problems, drinking is very much influenced by other conditions as well.

A group may be employed to display, through exemplars or bad examples, a much greater variety of models than were employed. The actual desired behaviors, aside from being sober for an hour and a half each week, may be easily rehearsed in a group setting through role playing; the group as well as the worker has powerful reinforcers and punishers that may be dispensed strategically on behalf of therapeutic objectives. Through instructions and behavioral assignments individuals may be prompted to engage in numerous behaviors outside of the group setting.

Implications of Statistical Findings

Although most of the statistical findings in this study do not sustain strong inferences, at least one finding definitely merits additional inquiry. The fact that so few correlates of attendance were found is not consistent with other findings concerning the correlates of continuance in individual and group treatment. For example, there is evidence that the more the client sees his problem as internal rather than external, the more likely he is to continue in treatment; that persons with high anxiety are more likely to stay in treatment than those with low anxiety; and that middle-class persons are more likely to continue than are lower-class persons (Levinger, 1960:40–50). In all cases, using the appropriate indicators, none of the relationships was confirmed. In two instances, however, the results were consistent with prior work. Continuers were found to acknowledge having more problems than discontinuers; this is congruent with the findings that continuers tend to be more insightful, less defensive in reporting their problems, more sensitive, more aware of their inadequacy, and better able to appraise themselves. It was also found that continuers were more able to cooperate and identify with the helper whereas discontinuers were more likely to be resistive. The latter finding was established only by clinical impression because other data were not available. The failure to find more correlates of continuance consistent with the findings of prior research raises questions for further study. Among these are whether a group draws a selective and different clientele, whether the correlates of continuance for alcoholics are different from those of other types of client,[8] or whether the disparities are attributable to the national contexts in which the research was completed.

REFERENCES

GERARD, D. L. AND G. SAENGER
    1966—*Outpatient Treatment of Alcoholism: A Study of Outcome and Its Determinants,* Toronto: University of Toronto Press.
LEVINGER, GEORGE
    1960—"Continuance in casework and other helping relationships: A review of current research," *Social Work* (July), pp. 40–50.

---

[8] For example, this may be the case for social class. Gerard and Saenger (1966:88) also found no relationship between socioeconomic status and the length of contact alcoholics had with clinics.

V

Conclusion

30.

The Bases of Social Treatment

CHARLES D. GARVIN and PAUL H. GLASSER

The "generic" versus the "specific" has been an issue in social work since the profession begain. At various periods it took different forms: policy versus practice; particularization of differences in practice by setting or "field"; characterization of differences by method (casework, group work, community organization, administration and research), and so on (Bartlett, 1961). Once again this issue is in the forefront of current thinking, both in the agencies and in the development of curricula in schools of social work.

Since the end of the Second World War many developments have taken place in the social welfare field and in the social work profession, requiring changes in practitioner approaches. Most of these alterations have been piecemeal and relatively independent of each other. But together they point to the need for a shift in social work practice.

SOCIAL AND BEHAVIORAL SCIENCES

The direct-practice methods, particularly social casework, went through an era in the 1930s and the 1940s when psychoanalytic theory had a dominant influence on the rationale for worker interventions. One can understand why this occurred. In a newly emerging profession the practitioner needed a theory to demonstrate his competence to himself, his colleagues, his clients, and the lay public. Freudian theory seemed to fit the requirements well. It had an aura of scientific validity, seemed applicable to a great variety of personal situations, and was increasingly used by psychiatrists. Further, the other social and behavioral sciences were underdeveloped, and their disciples showed little interest in applying what was known to human problems.

By the late 1940s, however, social workers began to realize that they had a theory without a method. Freud, who began his career as a neurologist, believed that personality developed out of the interaction of the physiological system with experiences in the first years of life. The strength of such characteristics (core or basic personality) could only be changed through psychoanalytic methods, which took many years of intensive therapy and seemed to be most widely used with, and applicable to, middle-class neurotics. It became apparent that social workers saw persons who had specifiable problems and who often did not fit the definition of neurotics; and they were required to help people do something about their problems in a relatively short period of time. Much professional energy went into attempting to resolve these issues.[1]

The first step taken out of this dilemma, with practitioners in other professions, was toward ego psychology, which emphasized the individual's use of reality in the here and now. This development made it possible to introduce role theory, small-group and social psychological theory more broadly defined, and finally learning theory and its application in behavior modification techniques (Taber and Shapiro, 1965; and Silverman, 1966). Distinctions between one-to-one and small-group intervention processes became less clear as some of the common psychological and social psychological processes involved were noted.

New Methods of Practice

Simultaneously, new means to achieve client change were emerging. Some but not all of them were related to theory development. The Second World War, primarily because of quantitative demands placed upon the therapist, led to the increasing use of small-group intervention methods and short-term crisis treatment. Other approaches to which the social worker has been exposed in recent years include marital and family therapy, guided group interaction, T groups and sensitivity training, reality therapy, group psychotherapy, group counseling, and a variety of behavior modification techniques aimed at changing the antecedent or consequent conditions of client problems.[2] This array obscures the traditional distinctions between casework and group work practice.

[1] These issues took many forms: Who had the right to practice insight therapy, and what type of training was required? How long must the practitioner with the master's degree in social work be supervised after he receives his degree? How can traditional theory be used with nonneurotic (psychotic and character) disorders? The literature of the thirties and forties is replete with articles on these subjects.

[2] Only one among many publications on each method is cited here (a) marital and family therapy: Nathan W. Ackerman (1966); (b) guided group interaction:

New Types of Clients

Despite the depression in the thirties and the war in the forties, professionals were predominantly oriented to private agency practice. Providing psychological help was more prestigeous than alleviating environmental conditions; long-term insight therapy was the practice ideal. Such approaches, whether or not they worked at all, were used primarily with the middle-class.[3] But although the white-collar population grew rapidly during the forties and early fifties, the demand for services by blue-collar workers became apparent; and with the war on poverty, demands for services to the public assistance client, the migrant worker, and the inner-city black man could no longer be easily ignored.

In the postwar years, even the middle-class client seemed different. The classical syndrome of hysteria was hardly ever seen. The more typical cases of clients with anxiety neuroses reaching out for help were becoming fewer. They were being replaced by persons who acted out against the community and its institutions (delinquents, school behavior problems, criminals) or who withdrew from participation in the "establishment" (alcoholics, drug addicts). Since the number of such clients seemed to be increasing so rapidly that there was little possibility that all could be treated, the profession became interested in preventive intervention at the interpersonal as well as community and societal levels. Since the older approaches were not being effective, some of the newer ones had to be tried; and professional specialization as a caseworker or a group worker became more and more irrelevant.

New Sources of Funds

These trends were reinforced through the availability and use of tax-supported funds for professional positions, particularly through the Department of Health, Education, and Welfare and the Office of Economic Opportunity. Some of the money went directly to established tax-supported agencies to upgrade practice and increase the number of professionals in administration, supervision, and practice. Some of the money went to private agencies on a contractual basis, which required them to agree to provide additional or new services to low-income and other high-risk and/or deviant groups. Some of the money went to establish new agencies

---

Frank R. Scarpitti and Richard M. Stephenson (1966); (c) T groups and sensitivity training: C. G. Gifford (1968); (d) reality therapy: William Glasser (1965); (e) group counseling: Rosemary C. Sarri and Robert D. Vinter (1965); (f) group psychotherapy: Nathan W. Ackerman (1963); (g) behavior modification: Edwin J. Thomas (1968).

[3] These ideas are reflected in the issues briefly mentioned in footnote 1. For documentation of the class issue, see Richard A. Cloward and Irwin Epstein (1965).

to serve such clients; and the new agencies attempted to employ social work professionals. Some of the money went to schools of social work to train larger numbers of professionals—irrespective of method—to serve these clients. Some of the money went to research efforts to evaluate old and new methods of serving this relatively different type of person.[4] The cumulative effect has been to erode earlier distinctions among methods of practice.

Group Work as a Habilitation Method

Although social group work had been taught for some years, its full acceptance into the profession can be dated to the formation of the National Association of Social Workers in the early fifties. While it had its early growth during the settlement house movement at the turn of the century, during the thirties and forties it tended to be divorced from clients with problems, concentrating its efforts on middle-class education and socialization agencies. Partly in an attempt to identify with the large majority of professionals who were caseworkers and partly because of a new sense of social priorities, more and more social group workers began once again to work with people who were likely to have or already had well-defined, specific, social functioning problems (Vinter, 1959). This trend took two forms. Some of the group service agencies reorganized their programs to serve individual clients with idiosyncratic problems in addition to, or in place of, their former clients. And some of the more traditional casework agencies added group workers to their staffs (Vinter, 1961). For these reasons the designations "casework agency" and "group service agency" have little meaning today.

Many social group workers now work with the same types of clients as do all other direct-practice personnel. The major difference in their orientation is that they see the group as a means for the diagnosis, treatment, or prevention of problems of individuals.

Social Agency Adaptations

Social agencies attempted to meet the new demands by testing the newly emerging methods and techniques, and by employing workers trained in methods other than casework. The revision of agency programs and the inclusion of new agencies in the health and welfare field forced new forms of cooperation, and led caseworkers in many agencies to work with groups and group workers to work with individuals. Some of the new approaches, like family treatment, seemed to fall between the realm of

---

[4] Budget increases for the National Institute of Mental Health reflect heightened public awareness and concern: The original budget in 1948 was $4 million; in 1967 the budget request was for $303 million.

competence of the caseworker and that of the group worker. For many reasons, those who had specialized in one method were exposed to the methods of others, and professionals found themselves learning from each other.

Curriculum Development

If group work is seen as a method for achieving change in individuals through the use of the group for the diagnosis, treatment, and prevention of problems of its members, then the curricula in casework and group work must overlap. Many but not all aspects of the processes of intake, diagnosis, worker-client contract, evaluation and termination are similar. The worker's use of direct influence upon individuals in the group—as distinguished from his efforts to change individuals through the use of the group or indirect means of influence—and his efforts to change the client's environment outside the intervention situation[5] have many elements in common with casework. Increasingly, the organizational settings for practice are similar. In the classroom it has often seemed practical to combine students of the two methods, simply for reasons of expediency and efficiency. More important, the diverse new helping processes and theoretical orientations no longer fit neatly into the old packages taught in casework and group work.

By the late nineteen-fifties, the University of Michigan School of Social Work had begun to combine beginning students of casework and group work in a small number of methods classes.[6] In about 1965, the first course in individual and small-group work was integrated on an experimental basis. In the fall of 1967, under a new curriculum, a new program which seeks to integrate the two methods as well as to develop a framework of its own was instituted. The casework and group work programs were retained while new developments in theory and practice were emerging and being put to the test.

A COMPREHENSIVE APPROACH TO INTERPERSONAL HELPING

Basic Assumptions

The practitioner is now in a position where he can make knowledgeable decisions about his intervention efforts based upon the requests and

[5] This framework is explicated in the present volume.

[6] For an early article on the commonalities in the two methods, which grew out of classroom teaching cooperative efforts, see Mary H. Burns and Paul H. Glasser (1963).

needs of the client and the community without being limited by constraints of the approaches practiced in the past. The helping process can and must fit the client; the client should not be expected to fit a method.

Second, there seems to be more variance as to what is taught and practiced within either of the traditional casework and group work methods than there is between them. The distinction based upon the composition of the intervention situation—worker/one client versus worker/multiple clients—is only one of many that can be made and may be of relatively minor importance.

Finally, knowledge does not belong to any one profession or discipline. All that is known and seems useful from all of the social and behavioral sciences must be utilized in the intervention process.

Professional Identity

If social work help is to encompass what is known from all useful sources, how is it to be distinguished from the other helping professions? In the long run, the lay public will make the distinction on the basis of who is helped and how effectively and efficiently. This has already begun to happen.

Increasingly, persons referred to or seeking help from social workers are those who are defined as deviant; those who are nonvoluntary clients; and those for whom the goal is behavioral and/or situational change. Social workers are becoming caretakers of the deviant.

Society—the lay public—is intensely concerned about departures from the norm in many areas of social life. The pressures of a complex world and a wide range of community dynamics have heightened the importance of taking care of the "misfits." This seems to be emerging as the social worker's function, perhaps because social workers are relatively numerous compared to other helping professionals. While societal expectations and community reliance have provided greater legitimacy for social workers' activities, such expectations and reliance have placed the social worker in the vulnerable position of broker between the norm-defining institution and the person he is trying to help. Note that a functional trend is being characterized, a stance is not being taken on the proper function of the profession.

Since most clients are brought to the social agency by concerns developed in social institutions, most of them are there nonvoluntarily. The prefix "non" is purposely used rather than "in." Many clients seek help because of the forces of environmental pressure (the welfare clients) or of informal social pressure (the unhappy spouses who come for marital counseling). While such persons have sought help—and are thus not "involuntary" clients—the social forces motivating them to do so have been strong behavioral determinants. Of course, there are many truly involuntary clients who are given absolutely no choice (delinquents, psychotics). Few of those who receive help from social workers today are there because they have psychological discomfort but no social functioning problems.

Social workers are expected to change the behavior of the nonvoluntary client and/or his environment so that the functioning of individuals and their institutions will be enhanced. The changes sought by and for such clients are modifications in behavior and/or their social situation, not insight—understanding emotional or intellectual problems—or comfort.[7] Increased insight or comfort may be a means to a change in social functioning or personal effectiveness, but need not be so.

A few examples may be useful. The child who is disruptive in the classroom is often forced into treatment by the threat of suspension from school; the worker's goal is to enable him to manage the class environment without getting into trouble. To accomplish this the social worker may have to work with the child, the teacher, the parents, the school administrator, or all of them. Increasing the child's insight cannot be expected to suffice. The physically handicapped client seeks help because he and others believe that he cannot perform "normal" activities. The goal for him is to find a way to allow him to function as closely as possible to the norm of a productive member of society, not merely to give him comfort or insight into his situation.

Among the identifying characteristics of any profession are its ethics and values; they include means as well as ends. Social work's concern about voluntary change must be separated from the reasons for which the person finds himself in the social worker's office. "Voluntary" in this sense refers to the involvement of the client in the helping process, part of which includes his right to an explicit understanding of the goals sought and the means used to achieve them. This has been referred to as the "contract" and permits the client to reject what is offered (Frey and Meyer, 1965; Croxton, Chapter 10 in this volume). It grows out of the democratic and humanitarian base of social work and reflects a pragmatic knowledge of what is effective (Raven and Rietsema, 1960). The voluntary contract illegitimizes some forms of influence, like brainwashing. Dislike for coercion, however, must not lead to the opposite extreme of allowing the client to make choices on issues of which he has little or no knowledge and, because of his situation, about which he cannot make an objective

---

[7] The relatively small statistical relationship that exists among these three in studies of psychotherapy is spelled out in Herbert C. Kelman and Morris B. Parloff (1957).

decision. On many occasions, the client can learn more about his options and should participate fully in making a choice.

THE INTERVENTION SEQUENCE

No matter what the mehods used and the theoretical approach taken, the helping process must be dealt with in a systematic way. A conceptual framework for the activities of a social worker using a comprehensive approach to interpersonal helping may be expressed in outline form:[8]

1. Study and diagnosis
   a. Preliminary diagnosis and intake
   b. Working diagnosis
   c. Intervention goals
   d. Intervention plan
   e. The helping contract
2. Intervention
   a. Direct means of influence
   b. Indirect means of influence
   c. Extragroup means of influence
3. Evaluation and termination

This outline does not imply that these diagnostic and treatment processes occur as clearly separate and definable episodes in the course of treatment. Any aspect of worker activity may have the potential of both eliciting new information and providing the occasion for client change. The worker should be alert to this responsibility to relate change activities to an analysis of determining conditions and to plan means of assessing effectiveness as a constant corrective to ineffective or even harmful treatment.

Diagnosis and Goal Determination

As outlined above, this approach to social treatment, whether carried on in a one-to-one, group, or family context stresses the importance of goal determination (Gottlieb and Stanley, 1967; Hollis, 1964; Schmidt, 1969). This emphasis comes from two considerations, one ethical and the other empirical. The ethical component stems from a concept of the member-worker contract as including mutual agreement on the ends to be sought through treatment. The empirical element begins with the conviction that the only way in which any specific treatment plan, as well as a treatment technology, can be evaluated is by the achievement of goals; this conviction is supported by a mounting volume of research which indicates the

[8] See also Chapter 7 in this volume.

relationship of goal clarity to goal achievement (Raven and Rietsema, 1960).

The choice of goals, as well as the selection of a treatment plan, must rest upon an adequate diagnosis, which requires assessment of the following elements: (1) how the client and significant others perceive the problem; (2) the conditions under which the problem occurs; (3) the consequences, immediate and long-range, of the client's behavior pertaining to the problem; (4) the client's goals for change; (5) the feasible subgoals related to the ultimate goals; and (6) forces both within the client and in his environment that either facilitate or hinder treatment.

Problem Assessment

Confronted with the wide variety of methods and techniques available to those who would help people in trouble—or likely to be in trouble—how does the practitioner make initial decisions about his approach to the client? This is not an easy question to answer. Combinations of approaches are often required. A clearer understanding of the relationship between means and ends is often useful in the achievement of goals. Some distinctions can be made on the basis of the client's problems as he and others see them. The following categories are not meant to be mutually exclusive but rather to reflect relative emphasis.

The client as social victim. The physical and/or social environment sometimes makes unreasonable demands upon a person and his family which he cannot fulfill, and this leads to malfunctioning. Now that the era of attributing all problems to the intraphysic processes of the person has passed and increasingly dealings are with those defined as different because they are poor, have a different skin color from that of the majority, or a distinctive socialization history, this category takes on special significance. Everyone is familiar with the welfare client who must manage on a budget that the most intelligent of us would find impossible or the child who enters a school system unable to understand its language or procedures despite his willingness to learn. In these situations the client's goals are not discrepant with those of the community or society; rather the person does not possess the means to achieve them and/or the institutions are not geared to help him sufficiently to enable him to succeed. Under such circumstances, knowledge of organizational and interorganizational theory could enable a worker to help the institution become more responsive to the client. In addition, programs of education and training to teach the client to deal more adequately with the organization or institution may be useful.

Seeking environmental changes for the benefit of one or more clients involves a variety of client advocacy procedures, often with the clients' help and involvement (Glasser, et al., Chapter 18 in this volume). Helping a client learn to cope with his environment requires socialization approaches, which include many aspects of preventive intervention (Wittes and Radin, 1971). Often the two approaches must go together. The welfare client must petition for more money, but perhaps he must also learn to budget better. The school must change its curriculum, but the child can also be better prepared to enter school through preschool programs that involve four- and five-year-olds and their parents.

Interpersonal malfunctioning. A second type of problem is interpersonal malfunctioning in one or a few areas of life and/or with one or a few persons. Many forms of marital difficulty or delinquent behavior fall within this category. Most of the newer forms of treatment emphasize manipulating the physical or social environment or helping the client give up dysfunctional patterns of behavior for more constructive and more rewarding patterns. Some would call this a resocialization approach. Social-psychological or behavior modification approaches, separately or together, are most useful here. Family therapy, which attempts to change such characteristics of the group as its patterns of communication, affection, power and influence, or its processes of problem solving or its modes of conflict and conflict-resolution are also relevant. So are some behavior modification approaches, such as trying to reduce a child's disruptive classroom behavior by altering the teacher's or peers' behavior which sets him off, or rewarding him after he has reacted appropriately.

The client as sick individual. Some clients evidence malperformance in many areas of social life or withdraw from reality almost totally. These persons often require the kind of help that makes it possible for them to deal more objectively with their own thinking processes and their derivatives. The neurotic who constantly finds ways to fail in everything he does and the psychotic who interacts minimally with his social and physical environment are illustrations. Effective treatment may require that these people review the development of their approach to life as a means to changing it. More traditional psychoanalytic and ego-psychological methods may be useful here. Certain newer techniques which grow out of learning theory may also be helpful, such as some desensitization procedures or shaping processes. Sometimes the latter procedures are necessary in order to make the client accessible to psychoanalytic, ego-psychological or other specific methods.[9]

Means of Influence

The conceptualization of worker treatment intervention utilized here follows the "Means of Influence" concept developed by Vinter (Vinter,

---

[9] The reader is referred to footnote 2 for reviews of most of these approaches, methods, and techniques. There is an abundant and growing literature in each area.

Chapter 2 in this volume), which places all worker activity into one of three modes:

1. Direct means of influence: the worker's efforts to modify individual behavior as a consequence of worker activity within or outside the intervention system.
2. Indirect means of influence: the worker's efforts to modify client behavior as a result of a change in the structures or the processes of the client-worker or small-group system in which client and worker participate.
3. Extragroup treatment means of influence: the worker's efforts to modify client behavior as a consequence of change in the social environment outside the treatment interaction.

Direct means of influence are obviously applicable to all forms of interpersonal helping. The worker's techniques fall into this category whenever his intent is to use his own actions to modify or maintain client behaviors, regardless of whether he is working with individual clients, families, or groups. Indirect means of influence are used when the worker seeks to modify some conditions of the treatment situation in order to affect client behavior.

A major problem for the social treatment worker is the determination of when to use direct, as opposed to indirect, means. Research is necessary to answer this question, but the following propositions are offered.

Direct means should be used when the group is not yet able or willing to assume the responsibility to help a member.
> EXAMPLE: This might be the case if the member were a scapegoat in the group. Group conditions might be such that group members would reject any implication that they should help the individual recognize and deal with his contribution to the solution of a problem.

Direct means should be used when involvement of the group would help one member but would harm other members.
> EXAMPLE: The group is composed of patients in a mental hospital. The member wishes to discuss a problem related to sexual behavior. The worker has reason to believe that a discussion of sexual problems at this time would cause such severe anxiety that many members would seek to avoid involvement in that group.

Direct means should be used when the rights of an individual demand that he be helped directly.
> EXAMPLE: The client has a problem and because of legitimate concerns over confidentiality he wishes to discuss the problem privately with the worker.

Indirect means should be used when the group is prepared and has contracted to help a member.

> EXAMPLE: A member has indicated that he is seeking alternative ways of looking for employment. Other group members have said that they have similar concerns and that by helping him, they might also help themselves.

Indirect means should be used when present group conditions are more powerful forces for change than direct means of influence.

> EXAMPLE: A group of delinquent boys have begun to set rules of behavior which members are expected to obey. Previous efforts of the worker to modify the delinquent behavior of individuals have failed.

Indirect means should be used when they will increase the potency of the group as a change mechanism by increasing cohesiveness, mutual facilitation, or normative integration, and when the criteria for use of direct means are not applicable.

> EXAMPLE: At the first meeting of a prison group, the members begin to discuss how the group might be helpful to them in their transition to life outside. While the worker sees many areas in which he could help individuals, he recognizes that the members wish to explore to the fullest extent how the group might help them before they seek out any other resources.

This concept may also be applied in an individual treatment context, where the worker and client constitute the "group." Desired changes in client behavior can be effected by indirect means of influence: by manipulating such group characteristics as role definitions, processes, and programs (play therapy, for example).

Another difficult matter is the determination of when to utilize extragroup means of influence instead of, or in addition to, treatment approaches aimed at only modifying the behavior of the client (Glasser, et al., Chapter 18 in this volume). Again, empirical information on treatment outcomes needs to be attained. The following set of propositions is suggested as a basis for such investigation.

Extragroup means lead to the achievement of treatment goals when the client's problem can be identified as reactive to some problematic environmental conditions.

Extragroup means should be used when the client's problem rests in his inability to be assertive in relation to some deleterious social condition.

Extragroup means should be used when the client's perception is that the change ought to take place in the social situation and the worker has no basis for contradicting this objective. When changes are needed in both client behavior and social situation and the client has set his own priorities of change in the social situation, the principle of self-determination leads to respect for the client's decision.

Extragroup means should be used when a set of criteria supporting the use of family treatment can be seen as applicable.

In a broad sense, all problems (excluding some organic conditions) have a counterpart in an institutional response. This suggests that ultimately client change will be associated with some environmental change, either as cause or effect. Institutional change prior to individual change is specifically called for when such responses serve to maintain the problem and are amenable to change.

THE MODIFICATION OF CONDITIONS IN THE TREATMENT SITUATION

It is necessary for practitioners to be able to identify the most important indirect means of influence—particularly, the worker's activity to maintain or modify the conditions of the treatment situation. Conditions which should be examined by the social treatment worker are the composition of the client-worker system; the structure of the client-worker system; and processes occurring in the client-worker system.

Composition of the Client–Worker System

Selection of the worker. Several dimensions can be considered in selecting a worker for an individual client, a family or a group. Attributes and personal characteristics of the worker can be considered, such as race, sex, and social class background. Traits of the worker, such as communication style, assertiveness, or personality needs can be considered also (Goldstein, Heller, and Sechrest, 1966). When necessary the worker can seek to modify his own behavior or he can secure another worker whose characteristic behavior is different.

Decisions regarding selection of a worker can be based on a number of pragmatic considerations:

1. What is the likelihood that actions of the worker will function to reinforce client responses? "Reinforcement" is here defined as any stimulus which, when presented following a response, leads to an increased probability that this response will recur (Bandura, 1969). Such variables as similarity in background and social class of client and worker and the frequency of interaction between them are associated with the likeability of the worker and, therefore, with the proposition that his responses will be reinforcing to clients (Lott and Lott, 1965).

Composing the client-worker system so that it will be conducive to attracting the client to the worker is probably essential where the worker interacts directly with the client, if only to maintain him in treatment. An exception may be when the costs of avoiding treatment are so great that they overshadow the issue of the likeability of the worker. The "liking" factor is, obviously, also important when the worker through praise, encouragement, or other verbal means seeks to maintain or increase desirable client behavior.

2. To what extent will the worker be able to model desirable client behavior? (Bandura, 1969) In a number of situations it is desirable for the worker to offer himself as a model: when the client totally lacks a given response in his repertoire, when modeling is expected to have a disinhibiting effect, and when the worker is attempting to help the client rehearse behavior appropriate to particular situations. It has been hypothesized that imitation of the behavior of another is most likely to occur when some of the responses already exist in the subject's repertoire, when the subject views the model as receiving reinforcement for the behavior, when the subject is rewarded for attending to the model, when the subject is lacking in self-esteem, and when the subject views himself in some manner as similar to the model. The worker in these cases can be chosen so that the modeling opportunities will be based on one or more of these considerations.

3. What expertise possessed by the worker is specifically related to the requirements of the treatment plan? Pertinent here are the worker's skills in individual versus family or group treatment, his skills in specific task performances essential to treatment (for example, ability to use non-verbal means of communication with deaf clients), and language skills for dealing with clients from subcultures were argot is an important treatment consideration.

4. What variables of the worker's personality would be likely to enhance or inhibit the achievement of treatment goals? Literature is available giving empirical information, for example, on the relevance of the following variables:

   a. Countertransference effects (Cutler, 1966).
   b. Overall personality configurations (McNair, Callahan and Lorr, 1966).
   c. Similarity of therapist personality to patient personality (Carson & Heine, 1966).

Determination of the nature of the client-worker system. Five major systems are considered within the social treatment framework:

   1. The worker and a single client.
   2. The worker, the client, and one or more members of his family.

3. The worker and a group composed of several subgroups, each subgroup composed of members of the same family.
4. The worker and a group which existed "naturally" prior to treatment but one whose members are not from the same family (an exception might be siblings in the same group).
5. The worker and a group of unrelated individuals composed by the worker.

It is beyond the scope of this discussion to consider the criteria which are believed to be useful in selecting from among these five systems. In order to predict the outcome of treatment under varying conditions and ultimately to enable the worker and client to select that system which promises to be most effective, the following dimensions of alternative client-worker systems need to be analyzed:

1. The kinds of group structures which emerge from each system.
2. The theoretical framework available for analysis of practice approaches for each system: psychoanalysis or behaviorism for individual treatment; small-group theory for all groups; role theory for analysis of family groups.
3. The nature of norms which exist or are likely to come into existence within each system.
4. The roles which are likely to be assumed by the worker in each system.
5. The roles which are likely to be assumed by the client(s) in each system.
6. The possibility, in each system, of affecting individuals, families, subcultures, organizations, and communities as primary or secondary targets.

Such variables can be used to predict whether indicated types of treatment might be likely to lead to the attainment of goals desired by the client and/or by the worker. For example, given a treatment goal of changing the delinquent norms of a client, consideration of the nature of norms which exist or are likely to exist within alternative systems (dimension 3) might suggest that a formed group would be more effective than a natural group. For the same reason, a group composed of subgroups of spouses might be more effective than other forms of family treatment in changing norms of family behavior.

Considering the kinds of group structures which emerge from alternative systems (dimension 1), family treatment might afford the best approach to a problem of disordered communications among family members. In view of the roles which are likely to be assumed by the worker in alternative client-worker systems (dimension 4), the desire of an individual to emancipate himself from his family might be best achieved in individual treatment.

What is necessary, of course, is a multivariate typology which is empirically tested and which enables the worker and client to make decisions by giving consideration to all the relevant dimensions of alternative client-worker systems. Needless to say, the practice of social treatment is far from this goal.

Composition of treatment groups. A growing literature presents guidelines for determining the composition of treatment groups (Goldstein, Heller, and Sechrest, 1966). An examination of this material suggests two alternatives to the worker. He can compose groups based upon the probability that a particular treatment objective will be achieved. On the other hand, given an existing client system whose composition has been determined, a worker can predict that the given system will be more likely to enhance the attainment of certain types of treatment objectives than others. A corollary of the latter proposition is that the worker can predict that in a particular kind of client-worker system, one treatment technology is more likely to be effective than another.

In the composition of groups, one of the major issues to be considered is the desirability for homogeneity or heterogeneity of the clients in relation to a particular variable or set of variables, e.g., one or more of the following: age, sex, presenting problem, degree of aggressiveness, level of maturity, IQ, race, social class, typical defenses, and educational level. The following issues should be considered in making decisions along the homogeneity-heterogeneity dimension:

1. Should selected clients be able to offer alternative models of desired behavior to each other?
2. Should the behavior and attitudes of clients be more or less dissonant with the behavior and attitudes of other clients within the system?
3. Should client selection encourage or discourage the formation of particular structures such as dyads, triads, subgroups or isolates within the client-worker system?
4. What kinds of reinforcement are homogeneous/heterogeneous clients likely to offer one another?
5. What information is available among homogeneous/heterogeneous clients which can contribute to effective problem solving?

Another variable which should be considered in composing a group is the kind of role that the client may be expected to enact in relationship to the group-maintenance and task-achievement needs of the treatment system. Inasmuch as all systems require these roles to be performed in order to continue (and since there may be valid reasons why the worker cannot or should not perform such roles), their consideration is relevant here. Other roles of members which might be considered necessary to systemic functions are the possession of expertise, previous role fulfillment (as mother, employee), and socialization or resocialization experiences (an adolescent who has been in a training school or who has had a therapeutic group experience).

When the composition of a group has been predetermined, some types of goals may be more feasible than others; and some treatment technologies may be more effective than others. Some goals may not be possible to attain because too much support is available for one type of behavior or not enough for another type; other goals may not be possible because the given group composition is not likely to produce the kind of cohesiveness that will permit the system to exist for the necessary length of time.

Finally, different technologies require alternative kinds of composition. For maximum effectiveness, insight-oriented approaches may require members who are verbal; behavioral approaches may require homogeneity of problems; the use of cognitive dissonance theory may require a degree of heterogeneity.

With an awareness of treatment goals—even within the confines of a predetermined group—the social treatment worker attempts to select with or on behalf of the client the best set of conditions for maximum progress in goal attainment.

The Structure of the Client–Worker System

Social-psychologists have indicated that certain regularities develop over time in the kinds of interactions which exist in interpersonal situations (Cartwright and Zander, 1960:485–502). From the social treatment perspective, these regularities support or hinder the client and worker in attaining the goals which they have mutually agreed upon. The conceptual task of the social treatment worker is to learn how to employ knowledge about the nature of social structures in order to understand the sources of structural problems perceived in the treatment situation as well as their solution. The following discussion largely makes use of small-group concepts. Without implying that the approach exploits all that exists in social work practice theory, *one* approach to a theoretical linkage between casework and group work will be explored in some depth.

Five structural concepts are particularly useful; communications structure (Shaw, 1964); sociometric structure (Moreno, 1934); power structure (French, 1960); role structure (Slater, 1965); and normative structure (Jackson, 1966).

Problems in Communication Structure. Communications structure encompasses who interacts with whom about what. This interaction may take verbal and/or nonverbal forms. Workers deal with problems in communications structure when they are concerned about clients who dominate discussions, individuals who withdraw from participation in discussion, individuals who change the content of discussions inappropriately, individuals who communicate contradictory messages, individuals whose omission from the communications networks gives rise to rumor, and individuals who control the form and content of communications as a means of achieving or maintaining power in the treatment system. It can be seen that all of these phenomena can occur in individual, family, and group treatment systems.

Problems in Sociometric Structure. Sociometric structure describes who accepts or rejects whom and under what circumstances. When individuals reject a relationship with a worker, a problem exists in the sociometric structure of the client-worker system. Within a multiple-client situation, the following are examples of problems in sociometric structure: members of dyads who reinforce undesirable behavior in each other, subgroups antagonistic to the purposes of the group who antagonize other subgroups, the presence of isolates, and lack of cohesiveness in a treatment system.

Problems in Power Structure. Power structure comprises the patterns of influence existing in interpersonal situations. French and Raven (1960) indicate that the sources of power may be reward, expertise, legitimacy, coercion, or identification. In individual treatment, manifestations of problems in power structure include destructive influence from worker to client or client to worker, the client's lack of trust in the expertise of the worker, inappropriate use of reinforcement or punishment, and dysfunctional identifications of the client with the worker.

In the family group, problems often involve the powerlessness of parental figures or, at the other end of the continuum, overly controlling behavior on the part of parental figures. In the group treatment situation, problems related to power structure include the domination of group processes by a deviant member of the group, deviant group members who attempt to coerce nondeviant members into deviant activity, the inability of the social treatment worker to effect appropriate control procedures in the group, the existence of powerful individuals or systems external to the group which interfere with therapeutic group processes, and a deficit of task skills present in the group.

Problems in Role Structure. Role structure involves the kinds of positions which are created in interpersonal situations and the expectations of incumbents of these positions in relation to the expectations held by occupants of other positions. Another issue, particularly related to the concept of leadership, is whether the interpersonal situation encompasses individuals who are equipped to occupy positions that are necessary to the maintenance of the system and to task accomplishment within the system (Bales, 1958).

In dyadic treatment, heavy emphasis is placed upon system maintenance in socioemotional terms, in view of the ease with which the system may be terminated by the withdrawal of one member. This function is frequently, but not always, incumbent upon the worker. Even in the group situation, a major function of the worker is to ascertain the degree to which socioemotional group maintenance functions are being fulfilled.

Roles requiring specialized knowledge must be fulfilled as well as those associated with the division of labor required for specific tasks. The presence or absence of other kinds of roles may be problematic in treatment situations.

Problems in Normative Structure. Normative structure consists of attitudes toward desirable or undesirable behavior which are held by specified group members and the intensity with which they are held. The content of these norms, whether the treatment be one-to-one, family, or group, deals frequently with the same kinds of issues. Such issues are attitudes regarding deviance, the responsibilities of system members toward each other, the goals and purposes of the system, and the means which are legitimate to achieve purposes.

Structural Modification of the Client–Worker System

The social treatment worker can employ any of the following action frameworks in order to deal with structural issues.

Program. A task or a specified series of steps to complete the task can be used to establish a particular role or communications or power structure which offers the possibility of generalization into other social contexts. For example, a game that requires leadership on the part of a participant might teach him how to occupy leadership positions in other situations. An activity which rewards a participant for communicating with others might enable him to occupy other positions requiring ability to verbalize.

Behavior modification. Literature has been developing which indicates that operative conditioning procedures can be used to modify social structures (Hastorf, 1966). Leadership behavior, communication behavior, and task performances, for example, have been modified by these procedures.

Problem-solving and logical reasoning approaches. A group can be confronted with its own structural problems and can employ cognitive procedures to change such structures either through a series of individual behavioral or attitudinal changes or through the group's rational, purposive employment of programmatic or conditioning procedures as outlined above.

Changes in composition.   Structural changes can be effected by altering the size of the client-worker system; such changes occur in addition to other effects brought about by the addition, replacement, or removal of particular individuals.

Processes of the Client–Worker System

Intrinsic to the concept of process is change. The changes of particular interest to social workers are changes in human behavior. These changes may be analyzed in terms of the behavioral predispositions of an individual or in terms of an individual's behavior in interaction with other individuals. The behavioral predispositions of an individual, frequently analyzed through the use of constructs regarding what is presumed to occur in the psyche of the individual, are the domain of various personality theories.

The concern here is with the sequence of behaviors of the individual in interaction with other individuals. Such sequences may occur in a matter of a few minutes as clients and workers arrive at a quick decision, as a subgroup identifies itself, or as a behavioral norm is enunciated and clarified. A sequence may also occur over several treatment sessions as purposes are clarified, membership is changed, or complex problems are solved.

Given a systematic classification of processes, propositions about causes of particular processes can be generated and specific social events can be described. The following categorization is based upon a series of dimensions used by Sarri and Galinsky in their work on group development (Chapter 5 in this volume).

1. Processes related to changes in the social organization of the client-worker system
   a. Sociometric processes: those having to do with changes in the affectional preferences of some participants for others
   b. Processes of role differentiation: those which occur as either new positions are created or new participants occupy such positions
   c. Communication processes: those having to do with changes in the patterns of who communicates with whom and about what
   d. Power processes: those related to control, reactions to deviance, and scapegoating
2. Processes related to activities and tasks

    a. Program task progression: that sequence of events set in motion in response to performance requirements of the activity and related to attaining the goals of the group

    b. Problem-solving processes: processes occurring as problems are identified and solutions attempted; a related process is that of conflict resolution

3. Processes related to the development of group culture

    a. Changes in the structure and content of norms and values held by participants relevant to their behavior in the client-worker system

    b. Changes in the goals held by clients, individually and collectively, for the client-worker system

4. Processes related to the emotional climate of the client-worker system

    a. Morale

    b. Cohesion

Some authors consider emotions as a group process. Mills, for example, includes in his concept of group emotion the needs and drives which serve in the first place as causes of group formation; feelings of satisfaction or frustration resulting from actual group experience; interpersonal attachments and animosities; and feelings of attachment to, or alienation from, the group as a whole (Mills, 1967:67).

When the operative processes in a specific treatment situation are carefully observed and accurately analyzed, they can be manipulated to facilitate the achievement of goals.

EXAMPLE: A group of unwed mothers was formed for the purpose of discussing suitable plans for themselves for the time when they would leave the institution in which they had been living. Much to the annoyance of other members, several members changed the subject each time the issue of leaving the institution was raised.

    The worker analyzed the problem in terms of the sociometric, task, emotional, and communications processes of the group. On the basis of his knowledge of the background and characteristics of the group, the worker hypothesized that several circumstances were maintaining the dysfunctional processes. These circumstances had to do with the desire of the disruptive girls for power, the rewards they were receiving for challenging the worker's purposes for the group, and their lack of skill in participation in discussion.

    This analysis led the worker to include the disruptive girls in a planning committee in the agency, thus meeting their desire for more influence as well as providing the entire group with an opportunity to listen to a tape of group discussion held in a similar group (the planning committee). Furthermore, the entire group agreed to be involved in a problem-solving discussion regarding what kinds of encouragement (reinforcement) the girls had been giving each other for leaving and what some of their feelings and reasons were for resistance to this issue.

The task of the worker, vis-à-vis processes of the client-worker system, can be described as follows:

1. The worker, with an awareness of appropriate goals, determines which processes enhance and which hinder the attainment of goals.
2. The worker develops a series of propositions regarding forces which are maintaining or could maintain such processes.
3. Depending on the goals of the client-worker system, the worker with, or on behalf of, the clients seeks to increase the occurrence of specified processes or to decrease them.

By defining the basic assumptions of a comprehensive approach to interpersonal helping and by describing its integral parts, the authors have attempted to distinguish social treatment from earlier modes and theories of social work practice. They have offered propositions, applicable to a wide range of client-worker systems, concerning the assessment of clients' problems, the choice of goals, and the use of alternative means of influence. They have reviewed ways in which the composition of the client-worker system, its structures and processes can aid or inhibit the achievement of treatment goals. And they have discussed the relevance of the social treatment approach to the current concern of the profession for the deviant nonvoluntary client for whom the goal is voluntary behavioral or situational change.

Further development and testing of propositions related to this approach are clearly required. The concepts and models of treatment developed here have, hopefully, set the stage for such endeavors.

REFERENCES

ACKERMAN, NATHAN W.
  1963—"Psychoanalysis and group psychotherapy," in Max Rosenbaum and Milton Berger (Eds.), *Group Psychotherapy and Group Function*, New York: Basic Books, Inc., pp. 250–260.
  1966—"Family therapy," in Silvano Arieti (Ed.), *American Handbook of Psychiatry* (III), New York: Basic Books, pp. 201–213.
BALES, ROBERT F.
  1958—"Task roles and social roles in problem-solving groups," in Eleanor E. Maccoby, Theodore M. Newcomb, and Eugene L. Hartley (Eds.),

Readings in Social Psychology, third edition, New York: Holt, Rinehart, and Winston, pp. 427–446.

BANDURA, ALBERT
1969—*Principles of Behavior Modification,* New York: Holt, Rinehart, and Winston, pp. 217–292 and 118–216.

BARTLETT, HARRIETT M.
1961—*Analyzing Social Work Practice by Fields,* New York: National Association of Social Workers.

BURNS, MARY H. AND PAUL H. GLASSER
1963—"Similarities and differences in casework and group work practice," *Social Service Review,* 37, pp. 416–428.

CARSON, ROBERT C. AND RALPH W. HEINE
1966—"Similarity and success in therapeutic dyads," in Arnold P. Goldstein and Sanford J. Dean (Eds.), *The Investigation of Psychotherapy,* New York: John Wiley & Sons, Inc., pp. 348–352.

CARTWRIGHT, DORWIN AND ALVIN ZANDER
1960—*Group Dynamics, Research and Theory,* Evanston, Illinois: Row, Peterson and Company.

CLOWARD, RICHARD A. AND IRWIN EPSTEIN
1965—"Private social welfare's disengagement from the poor: The case of family adjustment agencies," in Mayer N. Zald (Ed.), *Social Welfare Institutions,* New York: John Wiley & Sons, Inc., pp. 623–644.

CUTLER, RICHARD L.
1966—"Countertransference effects in psychotherapy," in Arnold P. Goldstein and Sanford J. Dean (Eds.), *The Investigation of Psychotherapy,* New York: John Wiley & Sons, Inc., pp. 263–270.

FRANK, JEROME D.
1961—*Persuasion and Healing: A Comparative Study of Psychotherapy,* Baltimore: Johns Hopkins Press.

FRENCH, JOHN R. P.
1960—"A formal theory of social power," in Dorwin Cartwright and Alvin Zander (Eds.), *Group Dynamics, Research and Theory,* Evanston, Illinois: Row, Peterson and Company, pp. 557–568.

FRENCH, JOHN R. P. AND BERTRAM H. RAVEN
1960—"The bases of social power," in Dorwin Cartwright and Alvin Zander (Eds.), *Group Dynamics, Research and Theory,* Evanston, Illinois: Row, Peterson and Company, pp. 259–269.

FREY, LOUISE A. AND MARGUERITE MEYER
1965—"Exploration and working agreement in two social work methods," in Saul Bernstein (Ed.), *Explorations in Group Work,* Boston: Boston University School of Social Work, pp. 1–11.

GIFFORD, C. G.
1968—"Sensitivity training and social work," *Social Work,* 13, pp. 78–86.

GLASSER, WILLIAM
1965—*Reality Therapy,* New York: Harper & Row.

GOLDSTEIN, ARNOLD P., KENNETH HELLER, AND LEO H. SECHREST
1966—*Psychotherapy and the Psychology of Behavior Change,* New York: John Wiley & Sons, Inc.

GOTTLIEB, WERNER AND JOE H. STANLEY
1967—"Mutual goals and goal-setting in casework," *Social Casework,* 68, pp. 471–477.
HASTORF, ALBERT H.
1966—"The reinforcement of individual actions in a group situation," in Leonard P. Ullman and Leonard Krasner (Eds.), *Research in Behavior Modification: New Developments and Implications,* New York: Holt, Rinehart, and Winston, pp. 268–284.
HOLLIS, FLORENCE
1964—*Casework: A Psycho-social Therapy,* New York: Random House.
JACKSON, JAY M.
1966—"Structural characteristics of norms," in Bruce J. Biddle and Edwin J. Thomas (Eds.), *Role Theory: Concepts and Research,* New York: John Wiley & Sons, Inc., pp. 113–125.
KELMAN, HERBERT C. AND MORRIS B. PARLOFF
1957—"Interrelationships among three criteria of improvement in group therapy: Comfort, effectiveness and self-awareness," *Journal of Abnormal and Social Psychology,* 54, pp. 287–298.
LOTT, ALBERT J. AND BERNICE E. LOTT
1965—"Group cohesiveness as interpersonal attraction: A review of relationships with antecedent and consequent variables," *Psychological Bulletin,* 64, pp. 259–309.
MCNAIR, DOUGLAS M., DANIEL M. CALLAHAN, AND MAURICE LORR
1966—"Therapist 'type' and patient response to psychotherapy," in Arnold P. Goldstein and Sanford J. Dean (Eds.), *The Investigation of Psychotherapy,* New York: John Wiley & Sons, Inc., pp. 279–282.
MILLS, THEODORE M.
1967—*The Sociology of Small Groups,* Englewood Cliffs, New Jersey: Prentice-Hall.
MORENO, J. L.
1934—*Who Shall Survive?* Washington, D.C.: Nervous and Mental Disease Publishing Co.
PERLMAN, HELEN
1957—*Social Casework: A Problem-solving Process,* Chicago, Illinois: University of Chicago Press.
RAVEN, BERTRAM H. AND JAN RIETSEMA
1960—"The effects of varied clarity of group goal and group path upon the individual and his relationship to his group," in Dorwin Cartwright and Alvin Zander (Eds.), *Group Dynamics, Research and Theory,* Evanston, Illinois: Row, Peterson and Company, pp. 395–413.
SARRI, ROSEMARY C. AND ROBERT D. VINTER
1965—"Group treatment strategies in juvenile correctional programs," *Crime and Delinquency,* 11, pp. 326–340.
SCARPITTI, FRANK R. AND RICHARD M. STEPHENSON
1966—"The use of the small group in the rehabilitation of delinquents," *Federal Probation,* 30, pp. 45–50.

SCHMIDT, JULIANNA
1969—"The use of purpose in casework practice," *Social Work*, 14, pp. 77–84.
SHAW, MARVIN E.
1964—"Communication networks," in Leonard Berkowitz (Ed.), *Advances in Experimental Social Psychology*, New York: Academic Press, pp. 111–149.
SILVERMAN, MARVIN
1966—"Knowledge in social group work: A review of the literature," *Social Work*, 11, pp. 56–62.
SLATER, PHILIP E.
1965—"Role differentiation in small groups," in Paul Hare, Edgar F. Borgatta, and Robert F. Bales (Eds.), *Small Groups: Studies in Social Interaction*, revised edition, New York: Alfred A. Knopf, pp. 610–627.
TABER, MERLIN AND IRIS SHAPIRO
1965—"Social work and its knowledge base: A content analysis of the periodical literature," *Social Work*, 10, pp. 100–106.
THOMAS, EDWIN J.
1968—"Selected sociobehavioral techniques and principles: An approach to interpersonal helping," *Social Work*, 13, pp. 12–26.
VINTER, ROBERT D.
1959—"Group work: Perspectives and prospects," *Social Work with Groups*, New York: National Association of Social Workers, pp. 128–148.
1961—"New evidence for restructuring group services," in *New Perspectives on Services to Groups*, New York: National Association of Social Workers, pp. 48–69.
WITTES, GLORIANNE AND NORMA RADIN
1971—"Two approaches to group work with parents in a compensatory pre-school program," *Social Work*, 16, 1, pp. 42–50.
ZALD, MAYER N.
1965—*Social Welfare Institutions*, New York: John Wiley & Sons, Inc.

Index